Lecture Notes in Computer Science

Lecture Notes in Artificial Intelligence   14775

Founding Editor

Jörg Siekmann

Series Editors

Randy Goebel, *University of Alberta, Edmonton, Canada*
Wolfgang Wahlster, *DFKI, Berlin, Germany*
Zhi-Hua Zhou, *Nanjing University, Nanjing, China*

The series Lecture Notes in Artificial Intelligence (LNAI) was established in 1988 as a topical subseries of LNCS devoted to artificial intelligence.

The series publishes state-of-the-art research results at a high level. As with the LNCS mother series, the mission of the series is to serve the international R & D community by providing an invaluable service, mainly focused on the publication of conference and workshop proceedings and postproceedings.

Juan A. Recio-Garcia ·
Mauricio G. Orozco-del-Castillo · Derek Bridge
Editors

Case-Based Reasoning Research and Development

32nd International Conference, ICCBR 2024
Merida, Mexico, July 1–4, 2024
Proceedings

Springer

Editors
Juan A. Recio-Garcia ⓘ
Universidad Complutense de Madrid
Madrid, Spain

Mauricio G. Orozco-del-Castillo ⓘ
Tecnológico Nacional de México/IT de
Mérida
Merida, Mexico

Derek Bridge ⓘ
University College Cork
Cork, Ireland

ISSN 0302-9743 ISSN 1611-3349 (electronic)
Lecture Notes in Artificial Intelligence
ISBN 978-3-031-63645-5 ISBN 978-3-031-63646-2 (eBook)
https://doi.org/10.1007/978-3-031-63646-2

LNCS Sublibrary: SL7 – Artificial Intelligence

This Springer imprint is published by the registered company Springer Nature Switzerland AG
The registered company address is: Gewerbestrasse 11, 6330 Cham, Switzerland

If disposing of this product, please recycle the paper.

Preface

The International Conference on Case-Based Reasoning (ICCBR) is the preeminent international meeting on case-based reasoning (CBR). ICCBR 2024 (http://www.iccbr2 024.org/) was the thirty-fourth edition of this international conference highlighting the most significant contributions to the field of CBR. The conference took place from July 1 through July 4, 2024 in Mérida, Mexico. This was the first time that the conference was organized in this country, with the goal of attracting Mexican researchers to the CBR field. To this end, the conference featured a Special Track on Artificial Intelligence for local researchers not specifically focused on CBR, to introduce them to this AI paradigm. To foster the interest of researchers, the topic of the conference and the special track was "AI for socio-ecological welfare", thus directing the community's attention to the need to highlight the role AI, and CBR in particular, can play in solving current social and ecological problems.

This special track was included as part of the workshops organized during the first day of the conference. During this edition, we had two further workshops dedicated to cutting-edge research topics: XCBR, devoted to the explainability of intelligent systems through CBR, and CBR-LLM, aimed at exploring opportunities for combining Case-Based Reasoning (CBR) and Large Language Models (LLMs), fostering a deeper understanding of their synergistic potential. As in previous editions, the conference also held a Doctoral Consortium (DC) designed to provide opportunities for PhD students to share and obtain feedback on their research and career objectives with senior CBR researchers and peers. The remaining days of the conference comprised presentations and posters on theoretical and applied CBR research and deployed CBR applications, as well as invited talks. The presentations and posters covered a wide range of CBR topics of interest to both practitioners and researchers, including: improvements to the CBR methodology itself: case representation, similarity, retrieval, adaptation, etc.; synergies with other AI topics, such as Explainable AI and Large Language Models; and finally a whole catalog of applications to different domains such as healthcare, education, and legislation.

This volume comprises papers for all of the presentations and posters. These 29 papers underwent a rigorous peer review process, with each receiving three single-blind reviews. Of a total of 91 submissions, the Program Committee selected 18 papers for oral presentation and 11 papers for poster presentation.

Numerous individuals contributed to the success of ICCBR 2024. Juan A. Recio-Garcia (Universidad Complutense de Madrid), Mauricio G. Orozco-del-Castillo (Tecnológico Nacional de México/IT de Mérida) and Derek Bridge (University College Cork) served as Program Chairs. We would especially like to thank Lukas Malburg (Trier University) for serving as Workshop Coordinator, Juan Carlos Valdiviezo-Navarro (CentroGeo) for organizing the Special Track, and Kerstin Bach (Norwegian University of Science and Technology) & David Leake (Indiana University) for the organization of the Doctoral Consortium. We would also like to thank all of the Program Committee for their thoughtful and timely participation in the paper selection process.

The members of the Local Organizing Committee, Nora Cuevas, Carlos Bermejo, Pedro Ortiz, Ana Martin, and Yoldi Piste, together with Carlos Ceron from Jarkol Technologies for the economical management of the conference, and several volunteers of the AAAIMX Student Chapter, were warmly appreciated and acknowledged for their exceptional contribution to organizing the conference.

Finally, we gratefully acknowledge the generous support of the sponsors of ICCBR 2024 and Springer-Verlag for its continuing support in publishing the proceedings of ICCBR.

July 2024

Juan A. Recio-Garcia
Mauricio G. Orozco-del-Castillo
Derek Bridge

Organization

Program Committee Chairs

Juan A. Recio-Garcia   Universidad Complutense de Madrid, Spain
Mauricio G. Orozco-del-Castillo   Tecnológico Nacional de México/IT de Mérida, Mexico
Derek Bridge   University College Cork, Ireland

Workshops Chair

Lukas Malburg   Trier University, Germany

AI-Track Chair

Juan Carlos Valdiviezo-Navarro   CentroGeo, México

Doctoral Consortium Chairs

Kerstin Bach   Norwegian University of Science and Technology, Norway
David Leake   Indiana University, USA

Local Chairs

Nora Cuevas-Cuevas   Tecnológico Nacional de México/IT de Mérida, Mexico
Carlos Bermejo-Sabbagh   Tecnológico Nacional de México/IT de Mérida, Mexico
Pedro Ortiz-Sanchez   Tecnológico Nacional de México/IT de Mérida, Mexico
Ana Martin-Casado   International University of La Rioja (UNIR), Spain

Program Committee

David Aha	US Naval Research Laboratory, USA
Kerstin Bach	Norwegian University of Science and Technology, Norway
Ralph Bergmann	University of Trier, Germany
Isabelle Bichindaritz	State University of New York at Oswego, USA
Hayley Borck	University of Minnesota, USA
Marta Caro-Martínez	Universidad Complutense de Madrid, Spain
Sutanu Chakraborti	Indian Institute of Technology Madras, India
Sarah Jane Delany	Technological University Dublin, Ireland
Belen Diaz-Agudo	Universidad Complutense de Madrid, Spain
Viktor Eisenstadt	University of Hildesheim, Germany
Michael Floyd	Knexus Research, USA
Mehmet H. Goker	OwnBackup, USA
Odd Erik Gundersen	Aneo, NTNU, Norway
Stelios Kapetanakis	Distributed Analytics, UK
Mark Keane	University College Dublin, Ireland
David Leake	Indiana University, USA
Jean Lieber	LORIA - Inria Lorraine, France
Lukas Malburg	Trier University, Germany
Kyle Martin	Robert Gordon University, UK
Stewart Massie	Robert Gordon University, UK
Mirjam Minor Goethe	University Frankfurt, Germany
Stefania Montani	University of Piemonte Orientale, Italy
Emmanuel Nauer	LORIA - Inria Lorraine, France
Enric Plaza	IIIA-CSIC, Spain
Luigi Portinale	Università del Piemonte Orientale "A. Avogadro", Italy
Pascal Reuss	University of Hildesheim, Germany
Jakob Michael Schönborn	DGC AG, Germany
Barry Smyth	University College Dublin, Ireland
Antonio A. Sánchez-Ruiz	Universidad Complutense de Madrid, Spain
Ian Watson	University of Auckland, New Zealand
Rosina Weber	Drexel University, USA
Anjana Wijekoon	Robert Gordon University, UK
David Wilson	UNC Charlotte, USA
Nirmalie Wiratunga	Robert Gordon University, UK

Additional Reviewers

Maximilian Hoffmann
Giorgio Leonardi
Christian Zeyen
Florian Brand
Sophia Sylvester
Lisa Grumbach

Sponsoring Institutions

Jarkol Technologies
AAAI-MX Student Chapter Mexico
Maikron
Instituto Tecnológico de Mérida - Tecnológico Nacional de México
Anahuac-Mayab University
Instituto de Tecnología del Conocimiento - Universidad Complutense de Madrid
Honorary Chair BOSCH-UCM on Artificial Intelligence
Centro Geo, México
Yucatan Meetings Convention and Visitors Bureau
Science Foundation Ireland Insight Centre for Data Analytics
Ozelot Technologies
Brain House

Contents

Integrating kNN Retrieval with Inference on Graphical Models in Case-Based Reasoning

Luigi Portinale[1,2]([envelope]) [iD]

[1] Computer Science Institute, DISIT, Università del Piemonte Orientale, Alessandria, Italy
[2] Interdepartmental Research Center on AI (AI@UPO), Alessandria, Italy
luigi.portinale@uniupo.it

Abstract. In Case-Based Reasoning, when the similarity assumption does not hold, knowledge about the adaptability of solutions has to be exploited, in order to retrieve cases with adaptable solutions. We propose a novel approach to address this issue, where kNN retrieval is integrated with inference on a metric Markov Random Field (MRF). Nodes of the MRF represent cases and edges connect nodes whose solutions are close in the solution space. States of the nodes represent different adaptation levels with respect to the potential query. Metric-based potentials enforce connected nodes to share the same state, since cases having similar solutions should share the same adaptability effort with respect to the query. The goal is to enlarge the set of potentially adaptable cases that are retrieved, by controlling precision and accuracy of retrieval. We experiment on a retrieval architecture where a simple kNN retrieval (on the problem description) is followed by a further retrieval step based on MRF inference, and we discuss the promising results we have obtained in two different setting: using manually-engineered adaptation rules and adopting an automatic learning strategies for such rules.

Keywords: similarity assumption · undirected graphical models · k-NN retrieval

1 Introduction

In Case-Based Reasoning (CBR), the *similarity assumption* states that similar problems have similar solution(s). The similarity defined on the case description is called *problem similarity*, in contrast to the *solution similarity* defined over the solution space. The more valid the similarity assumption, the more efficient the CBR process is, since the retrieved solutions are more similar to the (unknown) solution to the query.

The most common retrieval strategy is based on *k-Nearest Neighbor* (kNN) algorithms, returning the solutions of the k cases stored in the library that are

J. A. Recio-Garcia et al. (Eds.): ICCBR 2024, LNAI 14775, pp. 1–16, 2024.
https://doi.org/10.1007/978-3-031-63646-2_1

most similar (from the problem description point of view) to the query. However, the similarity assumption has been questioned several times [3,21,22], and adaptation guided retrieval can be exploited when it is not possible to rely only on problem similarity. Different solutions have been devised in this context: the most common one is the introduction of specific or task dependent adaptation knowledge into the retrieval step (and thus in the problem similarity measure) [6,18,21]; other approaches include the modeling of solution preferences in preference-based CBR [3] or the learning of a utility-oriented similarity measure minimizing the discrepancies between the similarity values and the desired utility scores [24]. In particular, as noticed by Smith and Keane [21], when there is no link between the problem specification space and the solution space, a possible approach is to complicate enough the similarity measure used for retrieval in order to establish such a link.

In this paper, we extend the work we presented in [16] and we describe and experiment with an alternative and novel technique where standard kNN retrieval is complemented through an adaptation guided inference process; we propose to model knowledge about the adaptability of solutions through the construction of a particular type of undirected graphical model, a metric Markov Random Field (MRF) [14], and to exploit MRF inference to enhance the retrieval step in terms of more adaptable cases.

2   Markov Random Fields

A *Markov Random Field* (MRF) is a pair $\langle \mathcal{G}, \mathcal{P} \rangle$, where $\mathcal{G}$ is an undirected graph whose nodes represent discrete random variables and edges represent dependency relations among connected variables (i.e. an edge between X_i and X_j means that X_i and X_j are dependent variables); $\mathcal{P}$ is a probabilistic distribution over the variables represented in $\mathcal{G}$. We restrict our attention to *pairwise MRFs*: each edge $(X_i - X_j)$ is associated with a *potential* $\Phi_{i,j} : D(X_i) \times D(X_j) \to \mathbb{R}^+ \cup \{0\}$; here $D(X)$ is the domain (i.e. the set of states or values) of the variable X. In an MRF, the distribution $\mathcal{P}$ factorizes over $\mathcal{G}$:

$$\mathcal{P}(X_1 \ldots X_n) = \frac{1}{Z} \prod_{i,j} \Phi_{i,j}(X_i, X_j)$$

where $Z = \sum_{X_1 \ldots X_n} \prod_{i,j} \Phi_{i,j}(X_i, X_j)$ is a normalization factor called the *partition function*.

We consider a special case of pairwise MRF called *metric MRF*. In a metric MRF, all nodes take values in the same label space V, and a distance function $d : V \times V \to \mathbb{R}^+ \cup \{0\}$ is defined over V; the edge potentials are defined as

$$\Phi_{i,j}(x_i, x_j) = \exp(-w_{ij} d(x_i, x_j))$$

given that x_i is a value or state of variable X_i, and $w_{ij} > 0$ is a suitable weight stressing the importance of the distance function in determining the potential. The idea is that adjacent variables are more likely to have values that are close in distance. MRF inference consists in the computation of the posterior probability distribution of each single unobserved variable, given the evidence (the observed ones).

3 Case Solutions and Adaptation Knowledge

The standard CBR process requires the definition of a suitable distance metric over the case description and it employs a kNN algorithm, in order to get the k most structurally similar cases. Given the similarity assumption, we expect that the solutions of similar cases are also similar. If this assumption is not valid, kNN retrieval can result is a set of useless cases, since no adaptation mechanism can be either devised or adopted with a reasonable effort. An abstract notion of adaptation space should be defined, and adaptation knowledge has to be exploited during retrieval [5, 11]. A common approach is to consider the solution space equipped with a similarity or a distance metric [3, 22]. This metric can then be used to measure how close two potential solutions are: the closer the solutions, the more similar the adaptation effort needed to revise them for a specific query. When adapting a solution with respect to a query, we need to use the available adaptation knowledge; depending on the "complexity" of the inference process executed during adaptation, we can devise different adaptation levels corresponding to the effort (or cost) needed to perform this phase. For example, if no adaptation is needed (i.e., the query case is solved through the "Reuse" step [2]) we can map this situation to the minimum level of adaptation effort. On the contrary, suppose that the adaptation knowledge is provided through adaptation rules: the type and the number of applied rules can define a measure of the effort needed to revise the solution, and such a measure can be mapped into different adaptation levels (see below).

Example 1. Suppose we have a case library containing the description of some holiday packages (this corresponds to the case study `Travel` described in Sect. 6). A customer requires a package by specifying some features which are: *Duration* and *#Persons* (numeric), *Accommodation* and *Season* (ordinal), *HolidayType*, *Destination* and *Transport* (categorical). The returned solution consists in a specific package characterized by such features, and completed with a particular hotel and the package final price. Let each hotel be described by an object h with properties h.Name (the hotel name), h.Location (the hotel place) and h.Category (the hotel classification in number of stars). Consider now a customer with a given budget b and with some specific criteria $A(h)$ for accepting a proposed hotel h: if $A(h) =$ `true` then the hotel is accepted by the customer, otherwise it is rejected. Given a query (specification of some of the features), suppose we have the following adaptation rules (where r refers to the retrieved case, q to the query, a to the adapted case and h to a particular hotel) to be applied in sequence.

Init: $a \leftarrow r$ (*retrieved case as basis for the adaptation*)

Price_per_person $\leftarrow r.$Price$/r.$#Persons (*determine the cost for each participant*)

(R1) (*a package can be used for fewer people*)
if $(r.$#Persons $> q.$#Persons) **then**
    $a.$#Persons $\leftarrow q.$#Persons
end if

(R2) (*substitute coach with train with a 10% increase of the price per person*)

if $r.$Transport$=$train $\wedge$ $q.$Transport$=$coach **then**
    $a.$Transport $\leftarrow$ train
    Price_per_person $\leftarrow$ Price_per_person $* 1.1$
end if

(R3) (*substitute train with coach with a 10% decrease of the price per person*)

if $r.$Transport$=$coach $\wedge$ $q.$Transport$=$train **then**
    $a.$Transport $\leftarrow$ coach
    Price_per_person $\leftarrow$ Price_per_person$/1.1$
end if

$a.$Price$\leftarrow$Price_per_person $* a.$#Persons

(*if price is over budget adaptation fails*)
if $a.$Price $> b$ **then**
    flag r as not adaptable and **exit**
end if

(R4) (*if hotel is not accepted, find an alternative hotel of the same category in the same place*)
if $\neg A(r.$Hotel$) \wedge \exists h(h.$Category $=$ $q.$Accommodation $\wedge$ $h.$Location $=$ $q.$Destination $\wedge$ $h.$Name $\neq r.$Hotel$)$ **then**
    $a.$Accommodation $\leftarrow h.$Category
    $a.$Destination $\leftarrow h.$Location
else
    flag r as not adaptable
end if

Given the above adaptation rules, we can in principle define different adaptation levels by considering the type and the number of rules applied during the adaptation process. By way of example, we could devise the following levels:

- Level 1: if no rule is applied
- Level 2: if only rule R1 is applied
- Level 3: if one or more rules R2, R3, R4 are applied with success
- Level 4: if case is flagged as not adaptable

For instance, we can consider a solution with level 1 to be reusable, a solution with level 2 to be revisable with a small cost, a solution with level 3 revisable with a larger cost and a solution with level 4 to be unadaptable. In general, the cost of adaptation can be estimated and a corresponding adaptation level suitably defined. Notice that the approach can be applied to any kind of adaptation rules, both when they are manually defined (as in the case described above) and when they are automatically derived through some form of adaptation rule learning (see Sect. 6). In the following, we propose to characterize the principle "similar inter-case solutions imply similar adaptation levels" by means of a metric MRF built on a given case library; Sect. 4 will discuss how MRF inference can be exploited to provide an adaptation based retrieval approach.

4   MRF Inference for Retrieval of Adaptable Cases

Given a case library of stored cases with solutions, we first construct a metric MRF. Let #adapt_levels be the number of different adaptation levels, sim_s be the similarity metric defined over the solution space and st be a threshold of minimal similarity for solutions. Algorithm 1 shows the pseudo-code for the construction of the MRF. Nodes have the possible case adaptation levels as states, and are connected only if the corresponding cases have a sufficiently large solution similarity (greater than the threshold st); indeed, cases with very low solution similarity typically do not share the same adaptability level with respect to a given query (and then the computed edge potentials would have a low impact on the value of the probability distribution). Edge potentials $\Phi_{n,m}(i,j)$ are determined as in metric MRFs: the smaller the distance between the states

---

Algorithm 1. MRF construction.

Require: #adapt_levels; $st > 0$
Ensure: a metric MRF
   MRF ← empty graph
   for each case c **do**
     add node c to MRF
   end for
   for each node n **do**
     $n.num\_states \leftarrow$ #adapt_levels
   end for
   for each pair of nodes $(n,m)(n \neq m)$ **do**
     if $sim\_s(n,m) > st$ **then**
       add edge $e = (n,m)$ to MRF
     end if
   end for
   for each edge $e = (n,m)$ **do**
     $s \leftarrow sim\_s(n,m)$
     for $i = 1\ldots$#adapt_levels **do**
       for $j = 1\ldots$#adapt_levels **do**
         $\Phi_{n,m}(i,j) \leftarrow \exp(-s\,|i-j|)$
       end for
     end for
   end for

---

i and j of nodes n and m respectively, the larger the related potential entry. When a given node assumes a specific state, connected nodes tend to assume close state values with a high probability (i.e., if a case has a given adaptation level with respect to a query, we expect the cases having similar solution to have a very close adaptation level with respect to the same query). Moreover, the more similar the solutions of the cases, the stronger this effect should be; this is the reason why we use solution similarity $s = sim\_s(n, m)$ as a weight for the metric potential. Once we know the adaptation level of some of the stored cases, MRF inference can be used to propagate this information in the case library; this allows the identification of other cases as good candidates for solution reuse or revision, as well as the rejection of some cases because they are likely to be useless for adaptation or reuse.

The idea is then to start from a standard kNN retrieval, followed by the usual "Reuse" and "Revise" steps [2]; the results of the latter are used as input for MRF inference, in order to find more adaptable cases. Algorithm 2 details this process. Let $al(i)$ be the adaptation level of the i-th retrieved case (through kNN retrieval); for each retrieved case, its adaptation level is set as evidence in the corresponding node of the MRF. Inference is then performed and the posterior probability of each MRF node is computed into the multidimensional vector $Bel[]$. $Bel[i]$ is the posterior distribution or *node belief* of node i; $Bel[i]$ is an l-dimensional vector (where l is the number of adaptation levels) such that $Bel[i][j]$ is the probability of node i being in state j given the evidence. Input parameter $cond()$ is a function testing a condition on the node belief; if this condition is not satisfied, it returns `false`, otherwise it returns the state of the node (i.e., the adaptation level) for which the condition is satisfied. Algorithm 2 finally outputs a set of cases with their adaptability level.

Algorithm 2. MRF inference for adaptable cases retrieval.

Require: $al(1) \ldots al(k); cond()$
Ensure: a set of (cases, adaptation levels) pairs
  for $i = 1 : k$ **do**
    $set\_evidence(i, al(i))$
  end for
  $Bel[\,] = MRF\_Inference$
  for each not retrieved case i **do**
    if $cond(Bel[i])$ **then**
      output $(i, cond(Bel[i]))$
    end if
  end for

Example 2. Suppose we want to determine for each (non retrieved) case the most probable adaptation level, then we will set $cond(Bel[i]) = \arg\max_j Bel[i][j]$. In this situation every case has a potential adaptation level and we can consider it for the next actions: for instance, we could be interested only in the most easily adaptable cases, and if 1 is the minimum adaptation level, we will select only those nodes i for which $cond(Bel[i]) = 1$.

As another example, consider now a more complex condition: suppose we consider as interesting any adaptation level from 1 to a, and suppose that we want to be pretty sure about the adaptability of the case. We could set a probability threshold pt and require that

if $Bel[i,1] + \ldots Bel[i,a] > pt$ **then**
    $cond(Bel[i]) \leftarrow a$
else
    $cond(Bel[i]) \leftarrow$ `false`
end if

In this case we are collapsing all the adaptability levels from 1 to a into a unique level (the choice of a is completely arbitrary here, and any other label would be fine as we no longer need to distinguish them); in case the required confidence on adaptability is not reached, we will simply ignore the case. Of course, several other implementations of the $cond()$ function can be devised.

5   An Architecture for Adaptation Based Retrieval

The problem of retrieving "useful" cases with respect to a given query is characterized by two different aspects: the problem similarity between the query and the retrieved case (addressed by kNN retrieval), and the adaptability to the query of the retrieved solution (addressed by MRF inference); this means that the cases of interest are those which are sufficiently similar to the query, while having an adaptable solution. We call them *positive cases*. We would like the retrieval to return only positive cases, possibly with a large problem similarity and with a low adaptability cost (i.e., a low adaptability level).

While cases retrieved through kNN do not have the guarantee of being adaptable, cases retrieved through MRF inference are more likely to be adaptable, but they do not have any guarantee of being sufficiently similar to the query. Moreover, the reason why retrieval is often restricted to a set of k cases, is because it is in general unfeasible to take into consideration all the positive cases: similarly, considering all the cases returned by MRF inference may lead to an unreasonably large number of cases.

The proposed retrieval architecture starts with standard kNN retrieval; if all the k retrieved cases are actually adaptable, then the process terminates with such k cases as a result. On the contrary, let $0 \leq k' < k$ be the number of adaptable cases retrieved by kNN. Since there is still room for finding positive cases, MRF inference is performed as shown in Algorithm 2, then the top $k - k'$ cases in descending order of problem similarity are returned, from the output of Algorithm 2. The main idea underlying this architecture is that k is the desired output size. In case kNN retrieval tangles with the solution similarity problem, we complement the retrieval set with some cases that are likely to be adaptable. Since they are selected by considering their problem similarity with respect to the query, we also maximize the probability of such cases being positive.

6 Experimental Testbed: The Travel Dataset

As a main testbed for the approach, we consider a dataset called Travel[1] containing instances of about 1500 holiday packages[2]. In addition to the features described in Example 1, stored cases also contain the price of the package and the characterization of a hotel. Local distances for features are defined as follows: for numeric features and for the ordinal attribute Accommodation (mapped into integers from 0 to 5) we adopted the *standardized Euclidean distance* (Euclidean distance normalized by feature's standard deviation); for categorical features we adopted the *overlap distance* (0 if two values are equal and 1 if they are different); finally for the ordinal attribute Season we adopted a *cyclic distance*, since the values are mapped into the ordinal numbers of the months. The cyclic distance on a feature f is defined by the following formula: $d_f(x, y) = \min(|x - y|, R_f - |x - y|)$ where x, y are the values (from 1 to 12 in such a case) and $R_f = \text{range}(f) + 1$ (12 in this case). In all the above cases, when there is a missing value, the maximum distance value for the feature is considered. We also have defined a vector of feature weights and the aggregation function producing the global distance $d(i, j)$ between two cases i and j is the weighted average.

The solution of a case is actually a complete description of a package (including a specific hotel and the computed price). Since adaptation knowledge considers the price and the hotel characteristics, in order to revise a potential solution, the characterization of the similarity of solutions only requires information about the price, the destination and the hotel category. Distance between two solutions is again computed as a weighted average of the three local distances on Price, Accommodation and Destination. Similarity measure for both case descriptions and solutions is computed as $s(i, j) = \frac{1}{1+d(i,j)}$ where $d()$ is the global distance $(0 < s(i, j) \leq 1)$.

To perform the evaluation we consider two different kinds of adaptations: manually defined adaptation rules (in particular, the adaptation rules illustrated in Sect. 3) and a method of Case Difference Heuristic (CDH) adaptation [10], able to learn a set of adaptation rules directly from the content of the case base. Parameters of the experiments are as follows: a budget b on price equal to the average price of the packages in the case base; a hotel random acceptance with probability of 80%; without loss of generality, we consider a binary characterization of the adaptability levels: 1 = adaptable, 2 = not adaptable. We set the thresholds $pt = 0.9$, i.e., MRF inference considers a case as adaptable if the probability of the corresponding MRF node of assuming state 1 greater than 90% (see Example 2 in Sect. 4). We connect cases in the MRF only if their solutions are very similar, by also setting threshold $st = 0.9$ (see Algorithm 1); we finally

---

[1] This dataset is a small extension of the one obtained from the github repository of the JCOLIBRI2 framework [19] at the following URL: https://tinyurl.com/travel-casebase.

[2] We also tested the approach on another dataset for the prediction of the price of used cars, by obtaining similar results that cannot be reported here for the lack of space.

vary the similarity threshold *thr* on the problem similarity between a retrieved case and a query as shown in the following.

A "positive" case is a case having a problem similarity with the query greater than or equal to *thr*, and such that its adaptability level is 1. With the above characterization of positive cases, given a particular retrieval set, we consider the usual notions of *accuracy, precision, recall* (more precisely precision and recall at k since we focus on retrieving k cases) and *F1-score*. Given a problem, if there are features that are predictive of the solution, then we expect that similar values of such features will correspond to similar values of the solution. In order to stress the "similarity assumption" and to bring out problems related to it, we have considered queries with missing values for such "solution-correlated" features. We decided to evaluate the performance of the proposed architecture by selecting as potential missing features the attributes Duration, Accommodation and HolidayType; taken together they have a correlation coefficient with the Price (the most relevant part of the solution) of 0.77, thus it can be expected that, missing values on such features will reduce the validity of the similarity assumption.

For a given query, we set the probabilities of a missing value as follows: $p_A = 0.15$ for Accommodation, $p_D = 0.3$ for Duration and $p_H = 0.6$ for HolidayType. The construction of the metric MRF (Algorithm 1) and the MRF inference (Algorithm 2) have been implemented in MATLAB by exploiting the UGM toolbox [20]. In particular, we resorted to *mean field inference*, a variational approach where the target distribution is approximated by a completely factorized distribution that well behaves in practice [23]. We finally consider two other evaluation parameters, the problem similarity threshold *thr* and the number of retrieved cases k, and we perform different runs by varying such parameters. In particular, we set $thr = \alpha\mu_c$ where μ_c is the average problem similarity among the cases in the case library, and α is a scale factor. Variation on *thr* influences the set of positive cases,[3] while variation on k models different retrieval capabilities.

7 Experimental Results

To perform the experimental analysis we consider two different situations: using a set of manually defined adaptation rules (when the problem allows one to formalize specific adaptation knowledge domain-oriented), and using a set of adaptation rules automatically learned from the available cases. For the latter situation, several approaches can be adopted such as the exploitation of both positive cases (those having a correct solution) and negative cases (those having an incorrect solution) [12], the exploitation of analogical proportion [13], the determination of an association *description-solution* minimizing a given complexity measure [4]. In this paper we consider a more general strategy based on the Case Difference Heuristic (CDH) approach. Originally proposed in [7], a CDH

---

[3] Others parameters that can be used to vary the set of positive cases are those influencing adaptation, namely the customer budget b and the hotel acceptability criterion $A(h)$; for the sake of brevity we do not consider them here.

strategy automatically learns case adaptation rules directly from the case base. Given a pair of cases, CDH generates an adaptation rule relating differences in the solutions to differences in the problem descriptions. Section 7.1 reports results considering manual defined rules, while Sect. 7.2 focuses on the results obtained using a CDH strategy.

7.1 Manually Defined Adaptation Rules

We consider the adaptation rules discussed in Sect. 3. We set values of k from 1 to 15 with step of 1, and then from 20 to 100 with step of 10. The greater is the threshold thr, the smaller is the set of positive cases and vice-versa; we set α to different values in order to scale the threshold thr with respect to average problem similarity μ_c ($thr = \alpha\mu_c$), with $\alpha = 0.95$ representing the median of case similarities in this experiment. In particular, given a case base of 1470 cases, the average number of positive cases resulted as follows: 559 for $\alpha = 0.75$, 400 for $\alpha = 0.95$, 320 for $\alpha = 1$, 86 for $\alpha = 1.25$, 11 for $\alpha = 1.5$. A few words are needed to explain the choice of the considered k values: small values are reasonable when the query should not return too many results to the user (as in the case of recommending holiday packages). However, our aim here is to use the Travel dataset as an evaluation framework, not tied to the specific application task of recommending travels; in situations where the scale factor $\alpha \leq 1$, the number of relevant cases (i.e., positive cases) is rather large, producing a very low recall for small values of k. For this reason we considered large values of the k parameter (from 20 to 100) as well[4]. We have performed a 10-fold cross validation for every considered value of k, by measuring every time the mean values for accuracy, precision, recall and F1-score, for both simple kNN retrieval (label kNN in the figures) and kNN+MRF inference (label MRF in the figures). If a retrieval does not produce any result, then the corresponding query is not taken into consideration for the statistics. Figure 1 shows the Precision/Recall (PR) curves obtained for the different values of the scale factor α, by varying the value of k: increasing the value of k will increase recall, by decreasing precision. The curves are actually an approximation of the real PR curves, since in the experiments we almost never reached a situation with a recall close to 1[5]. As usual in these cases, we set the last point of the PR curve with the pessimistic estimate for precision corresponding to $\frac{P}{N}$, where P is the number of positive cases, and N the total number of cases. An exception to this situation is the case $\alpha = 1.5$, where with $k = 90$ we get an average recall very close to 1, producing the PR curve shown in the bottom right of Fig. 1. We also computed the Area Under the Curve (AUC); for the reasons outlined above, the computed value is a pessimistic estimate (smaller than the actual one), but in the case of $\alpha = 1.5$

---

[4] Actually, the situations where dozens of cases are retrieved is also reasonable in case of B2B travel recommendation applications.

[5] To obtain this result we should have considered a very large value for parameter k; indeed, when the set of positive cases is large ($\alpha \leq 1$ in our experiments), recall is necessarily low, and can be increased only with large values of k.

where it has been possible to compute it exactly. The graphics of Fig. 1 with $\alpha \leq 1$ only show a part of the PR curve, since the estimated last point $(1, \frac{P}{N})$ would result really far from the last measured point (the reported values for AUC are however computed by taking into account the whole curve).

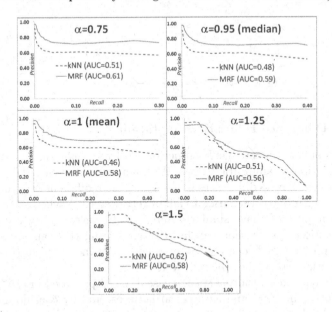

Fig. 1. PR Curves for different scale factors.

Figure 2 shows the behavior of accuracy and F1 measure, in dependence of k, for different values of α. Values for the accuracy are plotted on the right axis, values for F1 on the left axis. Accuracy and F1 measure for the specific case of $\alpha = 1.5$ are reported in Fig. 3 (again, values for the accuracy are plotted on the right axis, values for F1 on the left one). In particular, we report the whole plot ($k = 1 \ldots 90$) on the left part of the figure, and we "magnify" the plot for $k = 1 \ldots 10$ on the right part.

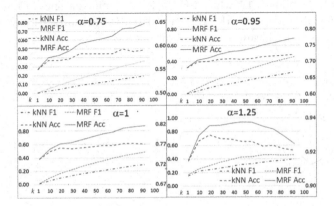

Fig. 2. Accuracy and F1-score vs k for different scale factors.

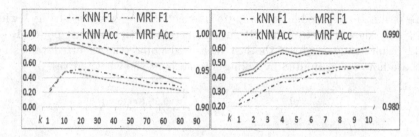

Fig. 3. Accuracy and F1-score for $\alpha = 1.5$.

7.2 Case Difference Heuristic Adaptation

A second set of experiments has been performed by considering a CDH method for the generation of adaptation rules. As already mentioned, CDH generates adaptation rules relating differences in the solutions to differences in the problem descriptions. Each rule is then used to adapt retrieved cases when their problems and the input problem have similar differences. However, given a rule R, the proposed solution modification can fail (in our setting this can occur because of a budget problem or because of hotel rejection by the user), in this case the retrieved solution cannot be adapted by R.

In our analysis we consider a special case of CDH proposed in [9,10], able to deal with both numerical and categorical features, and by considering a *Local cases-Local neighbors* strategy, where the set of adaptation rules is learned by comparing cases in the neighborhood of each query. Following usual CDH, rules generated from a specific case C are ranked and the top n rules are then selected (in the experiments we consider $n = 3$). When a query is performed, for each retrieved case C, the n selected rules generated from C are tested; if at least one of the rules succeeds in providing an acceptable solution modification, then the C's solution is flagged as adaptable and vice-versa.

In the CDH setting we performed the same set of experiments conducted in the case of manually built adaptation rules. We report here the results for the setting $\alpha = 1.25$ and $\alpha = 1.5$ which are the most significant ones.. Figure 4 shows the PR curve obtained, and the accuracy/F1 plots (again accuracy values are on the left axis and F1 values on the right one).

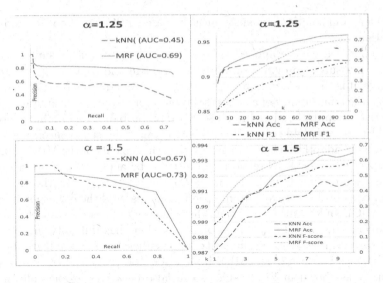

Fig. 4. CDH method: PR (left) and Accuracy/F1 score (right)

8   Related Works and Discussion

The integration of CBR and graphical models for retrieval has been usually investigated by focusing on directed models like Bayesian Networks (BN). In [1,15], a BN model is coupled with a semantic network to address case indexing and retrieval, and a Bayesian analysis aimed at increasing the accuracy of the similarity assessment is adopted. These approaches focus only on problem similarity (even if in complex domains requiring specific knowledge) and there is no attempt to address the problem of retrieval based on adaptation. Our approach can then be seen as the first attempt to exploit probabilistic inference on a graphical model to enhance retrieval through adaptation knowledge.

The importance of retrieving adaptable cases has been pointed out since the seminal work of Smith and Keane in the DÉJÀ VU system [21] questioning the similarity assumption. Different approaches have been proposed, usually focusing on specific tasks. In DÉJÀ VU specific adaptation knowledge is devised in the domain of plant control software design; cases that need specific "capabilities" requiring "specialists" or "strategies" that are not shared with the target, cannot be adapted and thus are not retrieved. In the ADAPTER system (a multimodal diagnostic system) [17] a supervisor module is responsible for retrieving adaptable cases through an approach called Pivoting-based retrieval [18]: the idea is to exploit a heuristic function, estimating the cost of adapting a diagnostic solution, as a guide for retrieval. In [8] similarity profiles are proposed as a way of dealing with situations in which a strict similarity between case descriptions does not necessarily implies a strict similarity between corresponding solutions. In the context of transformational adaptation the idea is only sketched, and consists in searching for a set of promising cases whose predictions depend on how ideal the problem and solution similarity measures are, with respect to the similarity assumption.

Our approach can be applied to any task or domain, just assuming that a similarity measure is provided on both the problem and solution space. To our knowledge, it is the first attempt to provide both a sound probabilistic character-ization of the adaptability of a stored solution with respect to a target case, and an effective computational architecture based on probabilistic graphical models, to get the most adaptable cases. From the experimental results concerning manu-ally generated adaptation rules, we notice that the benefits of the MRF approach with respect to simple kNN retrieval (in terms of balance between precision and recall) depend on how large is the size of the set of positive cases (i.e., for small values of α). This is noticeable from both PR curves (and the corresponding val-ues for AUC), and F1 measure. When there are a lot of cases sufficiently similar to the query and potentially adaptable, kNN alone has difficulty in retrieving positive cases: simple problem similarity is not sufficient and the integration with MRF inference is fruitful. The MRF integration also provides benefits in terms of accuracy as shown in Fig. 2, since some false negatives are actually moved into true positives with respect to simple kNN. In general, accuracy (for both kNN and MRF) turns out to be negatively correlated with the size of the set of positive cases. Moreover, when the number of retrieved cases k is too large with respect to the number of positives, accuracy shows a decreasing pattern as we can expect, since too many false positives can be potentially retrieved (this is evident in the plots relative to $\alpha = 1.25, 1.5$). A better behavior of kNN is apparent in case of $\alpha = 1.5$, but it is worth noting that in this situation we have very few positive cases (11 on average in each run), making not very significant the results for large values of k. This is the reason why in Fig. 3 we considered also the situation restricted to $1 \leq k \leq 10$; by considering reasonable values for k, even in the case of $\alpha = 1.5$, both accuracy and F1 measure show a small advantage in adopting the MRF integration to kNN retrieval.

Comparable results have been obtained by considering adaptation rules gen-erated with a CDH method. We reported results for $\alpha = 1.25$ and $\alpha = 1.5$ (Fig. 4), where a slightly different pattern can be noticed with respect to the manually constructed adaptation rules. Indeed, the benefits of the MRF app-roach are even more clear, as evidenced by the AUC measure; moreover, in case of $\alpha = 1.25$, even the analysis for $1 \leq k \leq 100$ is not sufficient to highlight the decreasing pattern of accuracy shown in the corresponding Fig. 2. This can be explained by the fact that in this situation, the increase of false positives is offset by a major increase in true positive (as usually occurs with smaller val-ues of the scale factor α). In case of $\alpha = 1.5$ the results are reported only for $1 \leq k \leq 10$ since with $k = 10$ we are close to a perfect recall; also in this case a slight advantage of the MRF approach can be noticed.

In conclusions, the evaluation in terms of accuracy, precision and recall sug-gests that the proposed integrated architecture can provide advantages, when simple problem similarity is not able to suitably capture the actual effort in adapting the retrieved solutions to the current query.

References

1. Aamodt, A., Langseth, H.: Integrating Bayesian networks into knowledge-intensive CBR. In: AAAI Workshop on Case-Based Reasoning Integrations, pp. 1–6 (1998)
2. Aamodt, A., Plaza, E.: Case-based reasoning: foundational issues, methodological variations and system approaches. AI Commun. **7**(1), 39–59 (1994)
3. Abdel-Aziz, A., Strickert, M., Hüllermeier, E.: Learning solution similarity in preference-based CBR. In: Lamontagne, L., Plaza, E. (eds.) ICCBR 2014. LNCS (LNAI), vol. 8765, pp. 17–31. Springer, Cham (2014). https://doi.org/10.1007/978-3-319-11209-1_3
4. Badra, F., Lesot, M., Barakat, A., Marsala, C.: Theoretical and experimental study of a complexity measure for analogical transfer. In: Keane, M.T., Wiratunga, N. (eds.) ICCBR 2022. LNCS, vol. 13405, pp. 175–189. Springer, Cham (2022). https://doi.org/10.1007/978-3-031-14923-8_12
5. Bergmann, R., Muller, G., Zeyen, C., Manderscheid, J.: Retrieving adaptable cases in process-oriented case-based reasoning. In: Proceedings of the 29th FLAIRS 2016, pp. 419–424. AAAI Press (2016)
6. Díaz-Agudo, B., Gervás, P., González-Calero, P.A.: Adaptation guided retrieval based on formal concept analysis. In: Ashley, K.D., Bridge, D.G. (eds.) ICCBR 2003. LNCS (LNAI), vol. 2689, pp. 131–145. Springer, Heidelberg (2003). https://doi.org/10.1007/3-540-45006-8_13
7. Hanney, K., Keane, M.T.: Learning adaptation rules from a case-base. In: Smith, I., Faltings, B. (eds.) EWCBR 1996. LNCS, vol. 1168, pp. 179–192. Springer, Heidelberg (1996). https://doi.org/10.1007/BFb0020610
8. Hullermeier, E.: Credible case-based inference using similarity profiles. IEEE Trans. Knowl. Data Eng. **19**(6), 847–858 (2007)
9. Jalali, V., Leake, D.: Enhancing case-based regression with automatically-generated ensembles of adaptations. J. Intell. Inf. Syst. **46**, 237–258 (2016)
10. Jalali, V., Leake, D., Forouzandehmehr, N.: Learning and applying case adaptation rules for classification: an ensemble approach. In: Proceedings of the 26th International Joint Conference on Artificial Intelligence (IJCAI 2017), Melbourne, Australia, pp. 4874–4878 (2017)
11. Leake, D., Kinley, A., Wilson, D.: Case-based similarity assessment: estimating adaptability from experience. In: Proceedings of the 14th AAAI 1997, pp. 674–679. AAAI Press (1997)
12. Lieber, J., Nauer, E.: Adaptation knowledge discovery using positive and negative cases. In: Sánchez-Ruiz, A.A., Floyd, M.W. (eds.) ICCBR 2021. LNCS (LNAI), vol. 12877, pp. 140–155. Springer, Cham (2021). https://doi.org/10.1007/978-3-030-86957-1_10
13. Lieber, J., Nauer, E., Prade, H.: When revision-based case adaptation meets analogical extrapolation. In: Sánchez-Ruiz, A.A., Floyd, M.W. (eds.) ICCBR 2021. LNCS (LNAI), vol. 12877, pp. 156–170. Springer, Cham (2021). https://doi.org/10.1007/978-3-030-86957-1_11
14. Murphy, K.: Undirected graphical models (Markov random fields). In: Probabilistic Machine Learning: Advanced Topics, pp. 164–184. MIT Press (2023). http://probml.github.io/book2
15. Nikpour, H., Aamodt, A., Bach, K.: Bayesian-supported retrieval in BNCreek: a knowledge-intensive case-based reasoning system. In: Cox, M.T., Funk, P., Begum, S. (eds.) ICCBR 2018. LNCS (LNAI), vol. 11156, pp. 323–338. Springer, Cham (2018). https://doi.org/10.1007/978-3-030-01081-2_22

16. Portinale, L.: Exploiting Markov random fields to enhance retrieval in case-based reasoning. In: Proceedings of the 32nd International Florida Artificial Intelligence Research Society Conference (FLAIRS-32), pp. 347–352. AAAI Press, Sarasota (2019)

17. Portinale, L., Magro, D., Torasso, P.: Multi-modal diagnosis combining case-based and model-based reasoning: a formal and experimental analysis. Artif. Intell. **158**, 109–153 (2004)

18. Portinale, L., Torasso, P., Magro, D.: Selecting most adaptable diagnostic solutions through Pivoting-Based Retrieval. In: Leake, D.B., Plaza, E. (eds.) ICCBR 1997. LNCS, vol. 1266, pp. 393–402. Springer, Heidelberg (1997). https://doi.org/10.1007/3-540-63233-6_509

19. Recio-Garcia, J., Gonzales-Calero, P., Diaz-Agudo, B.: jCOLIBRI2: a framework for building case-based reasoning systems. Sci. Comput. Program. **79**, 126–145 (2014)

20. Schmidt, M.: UGM: a Matlab toolbox for probabilistic undirected graphical models (2007). http://www.cs.ubc.ca/~schmidtm/Software/UGM.html

21. Smyth, B., Keane, M.: Adaptation-guided retrieval: questioning the similarity assumption in reasoning. Artif. Intell. **102**(2), 249–293 (1998)

22. Stahl, A., Schmitt, S.: Optimizing retrieval in CBR by introducing solution similarity. In: Proceedings of the IC-AI 2002. CSREA Press (2002)

23. Weiss, Y.: Comparing the mean field belief propagation for approximate inference in MRF. In: Advanced Mean Field Methods: Theory and Practice, pp. 229–240. MIT Press (2000)

24. Xiong, N., Funk, P.: Building similarity metrics reflecting utility in case-based reasoning. J. Intell. Fuzzy Syst. **17**(4), 407–416 (2006)

Automatic Adjusting Global Similarity Measures in Learning CBR Systems

Stuart G. Ottersen[✉] and Kerstin Bach

Department of Computer Science, Norwegian University of Science and Technology
(NTNU), Trondheim, Norway
stuart.gallina.ottersen@ntnu.no
http://www.ntnu.no/idi

Abstract. This paper explores how learning case-based reasoning
(CBR) systems are affected by updating similarity measures. We create CBR systems using the local-global principle and we investigate (1)
how adding new cases changes the CBR system's performance and (2)
how this drift can be mitigated through updating the similarity measure,
especially adapting feature weights for weighted sums. We aim to provide transparent measures to show when the knowledge containers drift
apart to indicate when an update is necessary. We, therefore, explore the
effect feature weight has on predictive performance and the knowledge
containers in online learning CBR systems. Following this, we present a
method to minimize updating feature weights while the case base grows
while maintaining performance. The performance is compared to two
baselines: never updating and always updating. Our experiments with
public datasets show that a smart updating strategy catches the drifting
of case base content and similarity measures well.

Keywords: XCBR · Similarity Learning · Global Weights ·
Explainable AI

1 Introduction

Case-based reasoning (CBR) uses previous experience and its adaptations to
solve new, similar problems [1]. The previous experience is captured in cases
containing the problem description and its solution. The solutions are retrieved
by comparing the new and old problems using similarity measures. CBR systems
are frequently used in decision support for more complex scenarios. This often
warrants using domain experts when developing the knowledge representations
used in the systems, such as similarity measures, case representations, or adaptation knowledge. Recently, data-driven methods have been introduced to create
similarity measures from existing datasets [11,17,21]. Traditionally, CBR systems are built initially, and only a few have active learning phases. In scenarios
where the system should learn, it is crucial to ensure that the knowledge representations represent the content of the case base well. If learned cases introduce

J. A. Recio-Garcia et al. (Eds.): ICCBR 2024, LNAI 14775, pp. 17–32, 2024.
https://doi.org/10.1007/978-3-031-63646-2_2

novel information, the system's vocabulary, similarity measures, and adaptation knowledge might need to be updated. This paper addresses the identification of drifts between a growing case base and similarity measures focusing on data-driven CBR systems. We explore data-driven approaches to detect change and then update existing similarity measures to avoid the high cost of having domain experts update the similarity measures manually. Similarity measures are often limited to the scope of the data present when they are built, possibly causing a more narrow domain than an expert would have modeled. The creation of data-driven similarity measures relies on: *Problem-solution regularity* and the *representativeness assumption*, which can be informally stated as "Similar problems have similar solutions" and "The case base is a representative sample of the target problem space" respectively [14]. A CBR system's case base can grow dynamically while learning, so the size and content can shift considerably, causing these core assumptions to be broken. Concept-drift causes the breach of said assumptions [22]. This can happen in multiple ways as described in [14] where our work will focus on how the distribution of the problems can cause concept-drift. This drift can then be reflected in a degradation in performance as the similarity measures no longer cover the problem space and/or have a poor representation of its distribution.

This paper explores the effect of updating similarity measures when a system learns. The tested system is built on the local-global principle [5], focusing mainly on updating the global similarity measure. Our main focus here lies on adapting the feature weights for weighted sums. Secondly, we aim to provide transparent measures that show when the knowledge containers drift apart to indicate that an update is necessary.

Therefore, we explore the effect of feature weights on predictive performance and the knowledge containers in online learning CBR systems. We then present a method to minimize updating these feature weights as the case base grows while maintaining performance. The performance is then compared to two baselines. This paper is structured as follows: in Sect. 2 we discuss relevant work, followed by Sect. 3 where the CBR system implementation is explained in detail. We then elaborate on the experimental setup and results in Sect. 4 before discussing these results in Sect. 5 and then concluding in Sect. 6.

2   Related Work

Aamodt and Plaza [1] describe the four phases of case-based reasoning: First, a set of most similar cases are *retrieved*, then they can be *reused* to suit the problem description better. In the learning phase of a CBR system, cases are *revised* before they are *retained* and hence made available for future retrievals. The retrieval phase of CBR systems relies highly on similarity measures that work well, meaning they must represent the information in the case base well to reach the most relevant cases as described by Smyth and Keane [19]. This becomes a challenge as the case base grows due to concept drift or, in other words, a change in the data distribution. As presented by Lu et al. in [15], there are three main types of approaches when detecting drift. These are error rate-based, data distribution-based, and multiple hypothesis test-based. Our work is error rate-based, where Gata et al.'s [12] is probably conceptually the most similar as it uses a warning system to detect a distribution change window on which the induction of a new model is performed. This window is set dynamically to capture as much of the "new distribution" as possible. Bifet and Gavaldà [6] again work on dynamic windows, which are now based on the stationarity of the data. Rather than training new models, it uses incremental models that update as the detection triggers it. More closely related to CBR, we have Leake and Schack [14] that focuses on *predictive case discovery*, meaning predicting what cases will be important for future problems as the distribution drifts. It functions more as a preemptive tool that tries to anticipate the drift rather than being reactive. Other relevant work in CBR includes applying CBR systems themselves for concept drift tracking such as Cunningham et al. [7] and Delany et al. [8]. The former of these uses the user to label spam and then periodically retrains to avoid concept shift, while the latter reselect features periodically and dynamically updates the case base tp reduce the error rate. As for the implementation of the system itself, there are similarities to Bayrak and Bach [4] where a black-box model is used as a twin to set global similarity measure weights by using SHAP-values. There is also considerable work done on concept drift outside of CBR, especially in streaming data in Lu et al. [15], but also more generally in statistics in Pollak [18].

3   Rolling Window Updates to Global Similarity (RUGS)

The process used to build CBR systems in our scenario can be seen in Fig. 1. An initial set of cases is used to construct the vocabulary and to create the similarity measures, this set is subsequently inserted into the case base. When this system is in use and new cases are introduced, the system will be updated

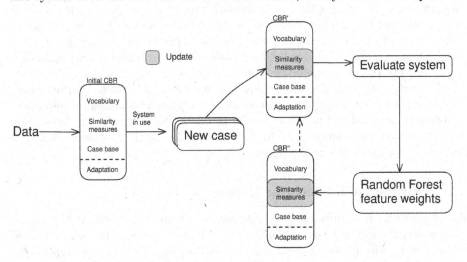

Fig. 1. Process of how an initial CBR system is created, cases are learned over time, and new global weights are determined.

and evaluated. The update consists of directly setting the feature attributions from a random forest classifier as the feature weights of the CBR system's global similarity measure. This process is then repeated each time new cases are added to the case base, giving us a CBR system that is iteratively becoming larger and with a similarity measure that is continuously updated to best represent the population in the case base.

3.1   Vocabulary

The vocabulary for numeric features is defined by calculating the minimum and maximum value for each feature over the entire dataset. For symbolic features, the full list of possible values is required to define the value range in the case representation. In this work, we will focus on the global similarity measures, so updating the value ranges is not considered part of the updating strategy. Setting the value ranges is considered trivial and can often be done automatically or by human experts up-front.

3.2   CBR System Learning

In this work, we explore how the case base grows during the retention phase as cases are added, (1) how this affects the performance, (2) in what way we can detect and mitigate performance loss, and (3) how to adjust the global similarity weights. The case base is initially empty or has a relatively small number of initial cases and will then grow as new cases are introduced. As new cases are added, the information contained in the case base will grow and might shift with time as the data distribution changes. As the CBR system is learning, this shift can cause a misalignment between the data present in the case base and the feature weights. This can cause a change in predictive behavior and possibly a decrease in performance. Updating the global similarity measures as new data is added is a good strategy but can be resource-demanding both computationally and cause delays in scenarios where models need to be approved before being set into production. Finding a balance between maintaining performance and updating the weights is, therefore, important. This can be seen in Fig. 2, where one can see that continuously updating the feature weights will lead to better performance at a high cost, while not updating at all will allow the global similarity measures to become outdated and poorly represent the data. A system that updates only when necessary can maintain performance while reducing the number of updates, as seen in the green line in the figure.

3.3   Defining Local Similarity Measure

Local similarity measures are frequently created by domain experts in the application domain of the CBR system being built, but this can be expensive, so there are a series of data-driven approaches that do this. The one applied in the presented system uses polynomial functions, distance functions, and the

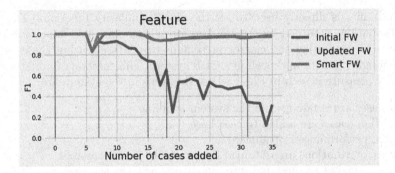

Fig. 2. Showing the difference between naive approaches and intelligent feature weight updating. The red line represents when the global similarity weights are updated. This is just an example, so the axes units are arbitrary, and the figure is meant only to show the concept of a smart updater. (Color figure online)

interquartile range to set the steepness of the similarity decline in said function. This is seen in Fig. 3 where the $IQR = 4$ is aligned to that the polynomial function approximately returns 0.3 and the *range* $= 8$ such that it approximately returns 0. In other words, the interquartile range is used to set the degree of the polynomial function to ensure that the entire similarity range $[0, 1]$ is used [16, 21].

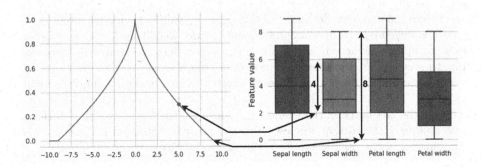

Fig. 3. Example showing how IQR is used to set polynomial function.

3.4   Defining Global Similarity Measure

The global similarity measure can be seen as a weighted average of the similarity values received from the local similarity measures. In the presented work, these are calculated using the feature attributions of a random forest classifier on the data present in the case base. The feature attribution from the random forest classifier is directly used to set the global similarity functions. The feature attributions returned by the random forest represent how important each feature is in separating the classes present in the dataset, using these as the feature weights should work well in a CBR system. This method of updating the similarity measure is seen in Fig. 1 where the steps in the system are:

1. New cases are created while the system is online
2. Retention: cases are added to case base
3. System performance is evaluated
4. Feature attributions are obtained from random forest classifier
5. Feature weights are updated into global similarity measures

3.5   The RUGS Approach

The main contribution of this work is the RUGS method for updating the feature weights using a rolling window of the performance of the CBR system. The aim of RUGS is to avoid unnecessary updates to the CBR system, as each update can in practice, lead to extensive test and validation work. With RUGS we are identifying when the drift between the case base and similarity measures is large enough to suggest an update.

The predictive performance of a CBR system is measured applying a leave-one-out cross-validation measuring the F1-micro score. A rolling window calculates the average score over the last five batches added to the case base as seen in Algorithm 1. If the performance over the last five rolling windows has decreased monotonically and the difference between the first and last of these five values is larger than the standard deviation of the same five values, then a feature weight update is triggered. To discourage frequent feature weight updates, the system does not update if there is no improvement larger than the standard deviation from the last update to the most recent value. In other words, if the last update was quite recent and it did not have an effect, then updating now probably will not either. The *LastUpdate* in Algorithm 1 is a function that fetches the performance of the last batch in the window that updated the feature weights. If there is no update in the current window, then the entire if-statement is ignored (this is not shown in the pseudocode to maintain readability).

Algorithm 1. RUGS

1: **function** UPDATEFEATUREWEIGHTS
2:     $rollingwindow \leftarrow$ F1 scores for 5 past values
3:     **if** $LastUpdate(rollingwindow) + Std(rollingwindow) < rollingwindow[-1]$
4:         **return** false
5:     **if** $MonotonicallyDecreasing(rollingwindow)$ **and**
6:         $rollingwindow[0] > rollingwindow[-1] + Std(rollingwindow)$
7:         **return** true
8:     **return** false

---

4   Experiments and Results

4.1   Experimental Setup

The experiment aims to measure the change in predictive behavior as cases are introduced to the system with how frequently feature weights are updated. This is done through batching. Cases are introduced to the case base in batches of size 3% of the dataset with a minimum threshold of 5. After each batch, a leave-one-out cross-validation on the data in the case base is carried out, and the F1-micro and accuracy scores are calculated. Following the addition of the first batch, the global similarity is set by directly using the feature attributions from a random forest classifier. Consequently, after adding each batch, the system chooses whether to update the global similarity measures. The weights defining the global similarity measures are updated using feature attribution obtained from a random forest classifier trained on cases already added to the case base. Three strategies are tested: no update after the first batch, updates after every batch, or using *RUGS*.

In real-world applications, various case learning strategies can be implemented: either all cases are added, only cases with a certain difference, or manually reviewed cases. In this experiment, we want to create different batches to show how the RUGS method picks up a change. Therefore we simulate the concept drift so that learned cases vary from those existing in the case base. In our simulation, we imitate case learning by creating batches as follows: a single feature is selected and sorted in ascending order on its feature values. This simulates a drift in the data introduced to the case base. The batch size is set to 3% of the original dataset with a minimum threshold of five, which are then added to the case base. This is repeated in separate experiments for each feature individually, as represented in Fig. 4. Sorting on a single feature at a time

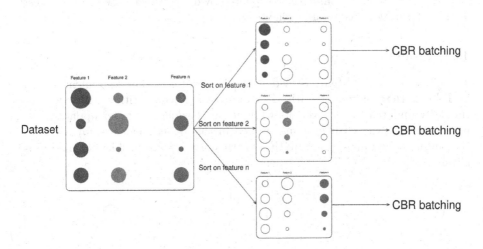

Fig. 4. Batch creation for the experiments: First, data is sorted by feature value, then batches are created that are then incrementally added to the CBR system.

creates an artificial and unnatural distribution for the data to be introduced, but is performed to showcase an extreme and how this can affect performance. Performance is captured using the F1-score, this allows us to indirectly measure the skew in the solution space relative to the problem space that is actually being shifted artificially.

4.2   Data

The experiment is performed on seven datasets which are presented in Table 1. The selected datasets offer a good baseline to show that the effect generalizes over multiple scenarios. The chosen open datasets allow for reproducibility and understandability while capturing a breadth of domains and data types in the features.

Table 1. Overview of the open datasets used in the experiment

Name	# classes	# cases	# of features (cat./bin./num.)	Class ratio
Banking [13]	2	1000	0:0:24	1:0.42
Glioma [20]	2	839	22:0:1	1:0.72
Iris [9]	3	150	0:0:4	1:1:1
Tictactoe [3]	2	958	9:0:0	1:0.53
Wdbc [23]	2	569	1:0:29	1:0.59
Wine [2]	3	178	0:0:13	1:0.83:0.67
Zoo [10]	7	101	15:1:0	1:0.48:0.31:0.24:0.20:0.12:0.10

A CBR system is built for each dataset by setting the vocabulary given the entire dataset and defining the local similarity measures using the approach presented in [16,21]. Following this, the batching is performed as described in Sect. 4.1, and the global similarity is updated by directly using the random forest feature attributions as feature weights.

4.3   Results

The effectiveness of *RUGS* is evident in the results of the experiment shown in Table 2. Here we see that the F1-score remains competitive with the continuously updated feature weights while using considerably fewer updates. The performance of the CBR systems created in this experiment is comparable to the performance ranges given by UCI for the datasets where this information is given.

Table 2. Showing results calculated on all features and all batches. Zoo has fewer updates due to the minimum size of 5 for the batch size.

Strategy	Initial		Updated		RUGS	
Dataset	F1-score	Number of updates	F1-score	Average number of updates	F1-score	Number of updates
Banking	0.69 ± 0.05	1	0.71 ± 0.05	34	0.7 ± 0.05	2.08
Glioma	0.87 ± 0.06	1	0.88 ± 0.05	34	0.88 ± 0.05	5.04
Iris	0.7 ± 0.25	1	0.95 ± 0.07	30	0.94 ± 0.08	3.75
Tictactoe	0.7 ± 0.17	1	0.81 ± 0.07	34	0.78 ± 0.11	4.11
Wdbc	0.87 ± 0.14	1	0.96 ± 0.02	34	0.96 ± 0.04	3.63
Wine	0.7 ± 0.27	1	0.97 ± 0.03	36	0.95 ± 0.08	3.46
Zoo	0.73 ± 0.28	1	0.91 ± 0.09	21	0.84 ± 0.2	1.88

A more in-depth analysis is performed using a boxplot, Fig. 5, where we see that, in general, RUGS can perform similarly to always updating the feature weights. The variance is also very comparable, while for the initial feature weight update, the performance tends to be considerably worse and has a higher variance. For some of the datasets, one can also see that the three methods have similar performance overall, probably caused by very equal distributions of the data, so there is very little drift when adding the batches.

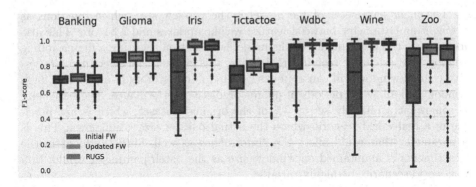

Fig. 5. Showing boxplot of results for each dataset and each feature weight updating strategy. Calculated over all features and batches.

In Fig. 6 we take a closer look at the iris dataset. Each plot represents one experiment where the data was introduced in the order of the named feature. The F1-score is then plotted over the batch number, and one can notice that the RUGS efficiently detects a drop in performance and ensures that the performance of the model rebounds.

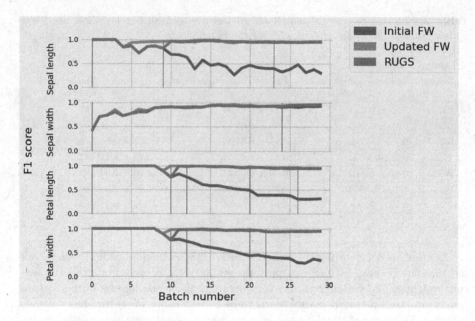

Fig. 6. Showing change in F1 score for each feature over batch number, the red lines represent feature weight updates performed . (Color figure online)

The main parameter of the model is the window size, which functions as a weighting parameter between feature weight updates and F1-score. This also means that the performance of the model is reliant on selecting a fitting rolling window size, as can be seen in Fig. 7, where it is evident that selecting an excessively small window will cause an exaggerated number of updates, while a large window will allow for periods of poorer predictive performance. The batch size is somewhat arbitrarily set to 3% of the original dataset, which is not possible in a real-world scenario where the actual dataset size is unknown. This is a parameter that could affect the performance as well. Still, the focus in the experiments is maintained on window size as the batch parameter would, in a real-world scenario, be highly variable.

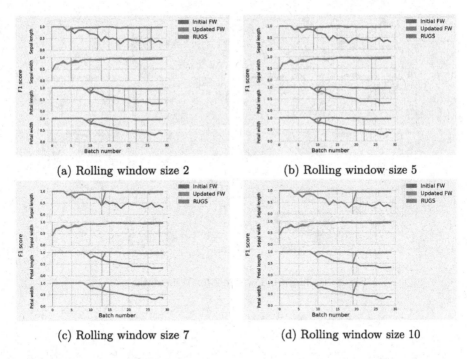

(a) Rolling window size 2

(b) Rolling window size 5

(c) Rolling window size 7

(d) Rolling window size 10

Fig. 7. Showing the effect of rolling window size on predictive performance for iris dataset.

The trends seen in Fig. 6 and Fig. 7 generalize over the other datasets, where smaller windows will prevent longer drops in performance.

Figure 8 and Fig. 9 show the results for the Wine and Tic Tac Toe datasets, which are two examples that show that some features do not require feature updates and will maintain performance. This is especially evident in the Tic Tac Toe dataset where multiple plots have all three lines overlapping. While for the Wine dataset the update of the feature weights has less impact. This indicates that the window size can be varied considerably depending on the scenario. Looking at the overall feature importance at the end of the experiments we see that the features with a low feature importance are the ones that tend to have little effect from updating the feature importance. An example of this is the feature *Mrs* in Fig. 9.

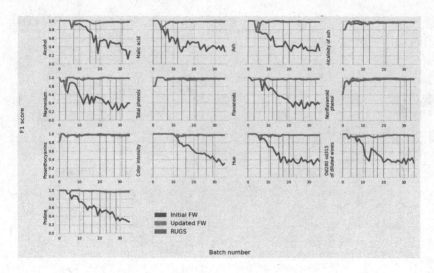

Fig. 8. Rolling window size 2 for Wine dataset

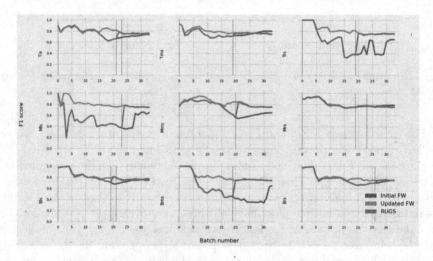

Fig. 9. Rolling window size 10 for Tic Tac Toe dataset

To further emphasize the value RUGS brings we compare the computational cost of updating the feature weights compared to the cost of running RUGS. One can see in Table 3 that RUGS takes about one tenth the time to run, making the trade off worth it in all of the tested scenarios.

Table 3. Showing the running time in seconds for the time random forest uses to calculate the feature attributions and average running time for RUGS

Dataset	Feature weight calculation	RUGS	Calculation/RUGS
Banking	0.35 ± 0.0	0.04 ± 0.01	0.13 ± 0.02
Glioma	0.36 ± 0.0	0.04 ± 0.01	0.11 ± 0.01
Iris	0.34 ± 0.01	0.02 ± 0.0	0.05 ± 0.01
Tictactoe	0.36 ± 0.0	0.03 ± 0.0	0.09 ± 0.01
Wdbc	0.32 ± 0.01	0.05 ± 0.01	0.14 ± 0.02
Wine	0.34 ± 0.01	0.03 ± 0.0	0.08 ± 0.01
Zoo	0.35 ± 0.0	0.02 ± 0.0	0.05 ± 0.01
Mean	0.34 ± 0.0	0.03 ± 0.01	0.09 ± 0.01

5   Discussion

The results show that $RUGS$ can identify drops in performance and improve the predictive performance by updating the global similarity measure. $RUGS$ relies on selecting an adequate window size for the scenario, which simultaneously allows the system to be adaptable for various scenarios depending on the update cost and how critical slight performance loss is to the system.

Sorting features with an overall low feature importance, meaning feature weights calculated over the entire dataset, seems to have little effect on performance. The difference in performance between the system with updated and old feature weights is quite negligible. This is, for example, seen with the feature "sepal width" in the iris dataset in Fig. 6. This trend is noticed in most of the datasets. A converse effect is seen in features with high feature importance, where they separate the classes so well that the initial feature attributions are all 1, as only one class is represented in the initial batch. This is slightly unrealistic as training a prediction system with only one class is pointless but may give some information about the behavior of systems with highly imbalanced datasets. Some datasets with many features seem to have less performance increase from frequent updating, as noticed in Table 2. This might be caused by how the random forest classifier distributes weight early in the batching process, as randomly spreading the weight is a functioning strategy. This works as the feature importance seems to be more evenly spread amongst the features(this is at least the case with the banking and glioma datasets) than with the other datasets, where some features are considerably more important than others. The experimental setup might also create some bias here as single features that separate the classes well will cause a larger performance variance as the data is introduced and sorted on a single feature.

The order in which cases are introduced is somewhat artificial and does not necessarily represent a realistic scenario. Other scenarios were also considered, such as clustering and assuming a cluster represents a case to then introduce outliers first or introducing points close to the cluster centers first. Random batching was also attempted, but due to the simplicity of the data, the system was very quickly able to represent the entire dataspace in its case base, making any feature weight updates unnecessary. The chosen scenario is somewhat extreme, but the others are equally arbitrary, as it is hard to know in what order the data will be introduced. It was also chosen to test on open and known datasets and stay general without focusing on specific scenarios. At the same time, the simplicity and clean nature of the data does potentially introduce some effect on the result, potentially offering more stable results than more complex real-world datasets. The average performance over all batches, as well as the standard deviation for the three updating strategies, can be seen in Table 2.

The datasets used are all classification problems, as adapting the system for regression would require the use of a random forest regressor as well as a different performance measure. The system itself is adaptable as these should be relatively simple changes to make but have not been included for understandability's sake.

Looking back at the research questions, these can briefly be summarized as follows: **(1) How adding cases affects the performance:** The performance change varies depending on the order in which data is introduced. If the distribution changes significantly and the feature in which the distribution change is done is important to separate the classes, this will significantly affect the performance. **(2) in what way can we detect and mitigate performance loss:** By using rolling windows and detecting a decrease in performance over multiple batches, we can effectively detect when to update the weights while maintaining performance. **(3) how to adjust the global similarity weights:** Using the feature attributions of a random forest classifier and updating these when an update is deemed necessary seems to be an effective way of maintaining aligned knowledge containers.

6   Conclusion

In this paper, we present a novel method to detect and update feature weights in learning online CBR systems, allowing for less frequent feature weight updates while maintaining performance. The approach is compared to two baselines on seven datasets and can score comparably to the method updating feature weights after every case addition.

Future work should explore more specific scenarios to see if the method is applicable in a more complex context. Exploring the effect the window size has on performance in more detail could also be interesting, as this parameter could function as a proxy for the sensitivity of the feature weight updates. Comparing the work to more complex baselines would also be a valuable addition.

References

1. Aamodt, A., Plaza, E.: Case-based reasoning: foundational issues, methodological variations, and system approaches. AI Commun. **7**(1), 39–59 (1994). https://www.medra.org/servlet/aliasResolver?alias=iospress&doi=10.3233/AIC-1994-7104

2. Aeberhard, S., Forina, M.: Wine. UCI Machine Learning Repository (1991). https://doi.org/10.24432/C5PC7J
3. Aha, D.: Tic-Tac-Toe endgame. UCI Machine Learning Repository (1991). https://doi.org/10.24432/C5688J
4. Bayrak, B., Bach, K.: A twin XCBR system using supportive and contrastive explanations. In: Workshop on Case-Based Reasoning for the Explanation of Intelligent Systems at ICCBR2023 (2023)
5. Bergmann, R.: Experience Management: Foundations, Development Methodology, and Internet-Based Applications. Lecture Notes in Computer Science, vol. 2432. Springer, Berlin (2002). https://doi.org/10.1007/3-540-45759-3
6. Bifet, A., Gavaldà, R.: Learning from time-changing data with adaptive windowing. In: Proceedings of the 2007 SIAM International Conference on Data Mining, pp. 443–448. Society for Industrial and Applied Mathematics (2007). https://epubs.siam.org/doi/10.1137/1.9781611972771.42
7. Cunningham, P., Nowlan, N., Delany, S.J., Haahr, M.: A case-based approach to spam filtering that can track concept drift (2003)
8. Delany, S.J., Cunningham, P., Tsymbal, A., Coyle, L.: A case-based technique for tracking concept drift in spam filtering. Knowl.-Based Syst. **18**(4-5), 187–195 (2005). https://linkinghub.elsevier.com/retrieve/pii/S0950705105000316
9. Fisher, R.A.: Iris. UCI Machine Learning Repository (1988). https://doi.org/10.24432/C56C76
10. Forsyth, R.: Zoo. UCI Machine Learning Repository (1990). https://doi.org/10.24432/C5R59V
11. Gabel, T., Godehardt, E.: Top-down induction of similarity measures using similarity clouds. In: Hüllermeier, E., Minor, M. (eds.) ICCBR 2015. LNCS (LNAI), vol. 9343, pp. 149–164. Springer, Cham (2015). https://doi.org/10.1007/978-3-319-24586-7_11
12. Gama, J., Medas, P., Castillo, G., Rodrigues, P.: Learning with drift detection. In: Bazzan, A.L.C., Labidi, S. (eds.) SBIA 2004. LNCS (LNAI), vol. 3171, pp. 286–295. Springer, Heidelberg (2004). https://doi.org/10.1007/978-3-540-28645-5_29
13. Hofmann, H.: Statlog (German credit data). UCI Machine Learning Repository (1994). https://doi.org/10.24432/C5NC77
14. Leake, D., Schack, B.: Towards addressing problem-distribution drift with case discovery. In: Massie, S., Chakraborti, S. (eds.) ICCBR 2023. LNCS, vol. 14141, pp. 244–259. Springer, Cham (2023). https://doi.org/10.1007/978-3-031-40177-0_16
15. Lu, J., Liu, A., Dong, F., Gu, F., Gama, J., Zhang, G.: Learning under concept drift: a review. IEEE Trans. Knowl. Data Eng. 1 (2018). https://ieeexplore.ieee.org/document/8496795/
16. Marín-Veites, P., Bach, K.: Explaining CBR systems through retrieval and similarity measure visualizations: a case study. In: Keane, M.T., Wiratunga, N. (eds.) ICCBR 2022. LNCS, vol. 13405, pp. 111–124. Springer, Cham (2022). https://doi.org/10.1007/978-3-031-14923-8_8
17. Mathisen, B.M., Aamodt, A., Bach, K., Langseth, H.: Learning similarity measures from data. Progr. Artif. Intell. **9**(2), 129–143 (2020). arXiv:2001.05312 [cs, stat]
18. Pollak, M.: Optimal detection of a change in distribution. Ann. Stat. **13**(1) (1985). https://projecteuclid.org/journals/annals-of-statistics/volume-13/issue-1/Optimal-Detection-of-a-Change-in-Distribution/10.1214/aos/1176346587.full

19. Smyth, B., Keane, M.T.: Remembering to forget: a competence-preserving case deletion policy for case-based reasoning systems. In: Proceedings of the 14th International Joint Conference on Artificial Intelligence, IJCAI 1995, Montreal, Quebec, Canada, vol. 1, pp. 377–382. Morgan Kaufmann Publishers Inc., San Francisco (1995)
20. Tasci, E., Camphausen, K., Krauze, A.V., Zhuge, Y.: Glioma grading clinical and mutation features. UCI Machine Learning Repository (2022). https://doi.org/10.24432/C5R62J
21. Verma, D., Bach, K., Mork, P.J.: Similarity measure development for case-based reasoning–a data-driven approach. In: Bach, K., Ruocco, M. (eds.) NAIS 2019. CCIS, vol. 1056, pp. 143–148. Springer, Cham (2019). https://doi.org/10.1007/978-3-030-35664-4_14
22. Widmer, G., Kubat, M.: Learning in the presence of concept drift and hidden contexts. Mach. Learn. **23**(1), 69–101 (1996). https://doi.org/10.1007/BF00116900
23. Wolberg, W., Mangasarian, O., Street, N., Street, W.: Breast cancer Wisconsin (diagnostic). UCI Machine Learning Repository (1995). https://doi.org/10.24432/C5DW2B

Even-Ifs from If-Onlys: Are the Best Semi-factual Explanations Found Using Counterfactuals as Guides?

Saugat Aryal[1,2] and Mark T. Keane[1,2(✉)]

[1] School of Computer Science, University College Dublin, Dublin, Ireland
saugat.aryal@ucdconnect.ie, mark.keane@ucd.ie
[2] Insight Centre for Data Analytics, Dublin, Ireland

Abstract. Recently, counterfactuals using *"if-only"* explanations have become very popular in eXplainable AI (XAI), as they describe which changes to feature-inputs of a black-box AI system result in changes to a (usually negative) decision-outcome. Even more recently, semi-factuals using *"even-if"* explanations have gained more attention. They elucidate the feature-input changes that do *not* change the decision-outcome of the AI system, with a potential to suggest more beneficial recourses. Some semi-factual methods use counterfactuals to the query-instance to guide semi-factual production (so-called *counterfactual-guided methods*), whereas others do not (so-called *counterfactual-free methods*). In this work, we perform comprehensive tests of 8 semi-factual methods on 7 datasets using 5 key metrics, to determine whether counterfactual guidance is necessary to find the best semi-factuals. The results of these tests suggests not, but rather that computing other aspects of the decision space lead to better semi-factual XAI.

Keywords: XAI · semi-factual · counterfactual · explanation

1 Introduction

The increasing deployment of black-box AI systems in many application domains has increased the need for an eXplainable Artificial Intelligence (XAI). XAI methods aim to surface the inner workings of such models to improve their interpretability, to foster trust, and to audit for responsible use. Recently, counterfactuals have become very popular in XAI; using "if-only" explanations they tell end-users about how decision-outcomes can be *altered* when key feature-inputs change [12,14,21,32]. For instance, if a customer wants a loan refusal explained, they could be told "if you had only asked for a lower loan, you would have been successful". "Even-if" explanations – so-called *semi-factuals* – are closely related to counterfactuals, but differ in that they inform users about how a decision-outcome *stays the same* when key feature-inputs change [3,16,17]. For instance, if someone is successful in their loan application, they could be told "Even if

© The Author(s), under exclusive license to Springer Nature Switzerland AG 2024
J. A. Recio-Garcia et al. (Eds.): ICCBR 2024, LNAI 14775, pp. 33–49, 2024.
https://doi.org/10.1007/978-3-031-63646-2_3

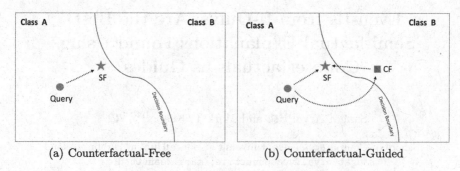

Fig. 1. Visualisation of (a) Counterfactual-Free and (b) Counterfactual-Guided Semi-factual Methods. The semi-factual, *SF*, is found by some computation (a) to be within the query-class at some distance from the query, *Q*, or (b) that is guided by the location of a counterfactual, *CF*, for the query, *Q*. (Color figure online)

you asked for a longer term on the loan, you would still be successful". So, like counterfactuals, semi-factuals give people options for algorithmic recourse in automated decision-making [13]. In this paper, we consider a key question that divides the semi-factual literature; namely, whether the best semi-factuals are to be found by using counterfactuals as guides?

Semi-factual explanations for XAI have received a lot less research attention than countefactual explanations. Although both methods have strong and long-standing roots in explanatory case-based reasoning (XCBR) [6,23,24], research on counterfactuals exploded around 2019 (for reviews see [12,14,21,32]), whereas semi-factuals were largely passed over (for reviews see [3,17,25]). Hence, there are now possibly >150 distinct XAI methods that compute counterfactual explanations using either optimisation techniques [13,22,33], instance-based approaches [5,15,28], genetic algorithms [9,27], deep neural networks [10,30] and so on. In contrast, there are perhaps <10 distinct methods that compute semi-factuals, many of which were proposed almost 20 years ago in CBR [6,23,24]. However, there are reasons to believe that semi-factuals have the potential to be as useful as counterfactuals (c.f., recent work [2,16–18,20,31]).

Interestingly, the motivation for early semi-factual work was to find "better" nearest neighbors for case-based explanations, instances that were not *actually* the closest to the query-case but, nevertheless, ones that provided better explanations. For example, if Mary was refused a loan and Belinda was her nearest neighbor (both are the same age, have same income, same credit score and asked for the same loan), rather than using Belinda to explain the decision we might use Sally (who differs from Mary in having a much higher credit score); here, the semi-factual explanation is saying "Even if Mary had a very high credit score like Sally, she would still have been refused the loan", providing a stronger or *a fortiori* argument for why Mary was turned down [23,24]. Accordingly, semi-factuals fundamentally owe their existence in XAI to decades of CBR research.

One of the key computational steps in computing semi-factuals appears to be identifying the key feature(s) to change to provide a more convincing explanation. Some methods try to achieve this aim heuristically, by finding instances that are as far as possible from the query while still being in the query-class. Figure 1(a) shows this situation graphically with a semi-factual (blue star) that is far from the query (green circle) but still within the query-class (Class-A) and close to the decision boundary with the counterfactual-class (Class-B). Other methods try to find instances that are still in the query-class but which bear some relationship to a counterfactual for the query (e.g., using a nearest unlike neighbour or NUN). For instance, in Fig. 1(b), the semi-factual (blue star) is found between the query (green circle) and its counterfactual (red box), using the latter to guide the search.

This opposition reveals two groups of methods, where one is *counterfactual-free* (i.e., they find semi-factuals without explicitly considering counterfactuals) and the other is *counterfactual-guided* (i.e., they find semi-factuals using counterfactuals as guides). Using counterfactuals makes intuitive sense as they identify key features that flip class-membership, features that might also work well in a semi-factual. However, we do not know whether this counterfactual guidance necessarily or always produces the best semi-factuals. Hence, in this paper, we consider the key question "Are the best semi-factuals found by using counterfactuals as guides?".

Outline of Paper and Contributions. In the remainder of this paper, we first outline the related work on semi-factual methods for XAI, detailing the various methods that have been proposed (see Sect. 2) before presenting our comparison of the performance of 8 different semi-factual methods (4 counterfactual-free and 4 counterfactual-guided methods) across 7 representative datasets on 5 key evaluation metrics (see Sect. 3). We finish with a discussion of the implications and limitations of our findings (see Sect. 4). As such, the work makes several novel contributions to this literature, including:

- A comprehensive analysis of different semi-factual explanation methods divided into counterfactual-free and counterfactual-guided groups.
- The most comprehensive set of tests in the literature using key evaluation measures for determining the best semi-factual explanations
- The discovery of a set of key findings about the dynamics of different semi-factual methods, using/not-using counterfactuals, thus providing baselines and targets for future development in this important area.

2   Semi-factuals: Counterfactual-Free or -Guided

Technically speaking, semi-factuals are a special case of the counterfactual, in that they assert facts that are "counter" to the reality of what actually happened, albeit facts that do not change outcomes, as opposed to facts that change outcomes (as in counterfactuals *proper*). However, in philosophy it has been argued that semi-factuals are fundamentally different to counterfactuals [4] and, psychologically, they cognitively impact people differently [19]; McCloy & Byrne [19] found that people judge an antecedent event to be more causally-related to the outcome when given counterfactuals, but judge antecedents to be less causally-related to the outcomes when given semi-factuals. Aryal & Keane [3] reviewed the history of semi-factual XAI research from the 2000s to 2023, but failed to note that groups of methods differed in their reliance on counterfactuals (i.e., counterfactual-guided v counterfactual-free). Interestingly, these different approaches are not historically-correlated, older and newer methods are equally likely in both groups. So, some researchers consider counterfactuals to be essential in computing semi-factuals whereas others do not. Here we explore these two approaches, to ascertain whether counterfactual guidance is required to compute the best semi-factuals. Hence, in the following sub-sections we quickly profile eight semi-factual methods (4 counterfactual-free and 4 counterfactual-guided methods) tested here.

2.1   Counterfactual-Free Methods

Counterfactual-free methods tend to work within the query-class exploring the relationship between candidate semi-factuals and the query (e.g., using distance) but are all quite distinct in how they work. Historically ordered they are the (i) Local-Region Model [24], (ii) DSER [2], (iii) MDN [3], and (iv) S-GEN [16].

Local-Region Model. Nugent et al. [2009] proposed the Local-Region model, which analyses the local region around the query, using a surrogate model (akin to way LIME works [26]), to select the nearest neighbor in the query class with the most marginal probability, as the semi-factual instance; as follows:

$$Local\text{-}Region(q, C) = \arg\min_{x \epsilon C} LR(x) \tag{1}$$

where, C is the set of candidate neighbors and $LR()$ is the local logistic regression model providing the probability score. Even though this method considers instances from non-query classes (e.g., the counterfactual class) to plot the decision boundary, we consider it to be counterfactual-free as it does not single out specific counterfactual-instances to guide the process of semi-factual selection.

Diverse Semifactual Explanations of Reject (DSER). Artelt & Hammer [2022] proposed a semi-factual method to explain reject decisions in machine learning; that is, to explain why a model should *not* make a prediction. Conceptually, DSER is patterned on the optimisation methods proposed for counterfactuals, though obviously uses somewhat different constraints (see e.g., [7, 22, 33]); it applies its loss function to candidate-instances in the query-class, using four constraints for good semi-factuals (i.e., feasibility, sparsity, similarity, diversity):

$$DSER(q) = \arg\min_{q_{sf} \epsilon \mathbb{R}^d} \ell(q_{sf}) \tag{2}$$

where, q_{sf} is the semi-factual of query q and $\ell()$ represents the combined loss function such that,

$$\ell(q_{sf}) = \ell_{feasibile}(q_{sf}) + \ell_{sparse}(q_{sf}) + \ell_{similar}(q_{sf}) + \ell_{diverse}(q_{sf}) \quad (3)$$

where feasibility is cast as,

$$\ell_{\text{feasible}}(q_{sf}) = C_{\text{feasible}} \cdot \max\left(r\left(q_{sf}\right) - \theta, 0\right) + C_{sf} \cdot \max\left(r(q) - r\left(q_{sf}\right), 0\right) \quad (4)$$

which ensures that the semi-factual is also predictively uncertain but more certain than the original query, q (to be convincing). Here, C represents the regularization parameters for each component, $r()$ is the reject function based on the certainty of predictive function and θ is the reject threshold.

$$\ell_{\text{sparse}}(q_{sf}) = C_{\text{sparse}} \cdot \max\left(\sum_{i=1}^{d} \mathbb{1}\left((q_{sf} - q)_i \neq 0\right) - \mu, 0\right) \quad (5)$$

covers *sparsity* promoting candidates with fewer feature differences between the semi-factual and the query. Here d is the number of feature dimensions and $\mu \geq 1$ is a hyperparameter that controls the number of feature-differences.

$$\ell_{\text{similar}}(q_{sf}) = -C_{\text{similar}} \cdot \|q_{sf} - q\|_2 \quad (6)$$

deals with *similarity* promoting greater distance between the query and the semi-factual in Euclidean space, and finally,

$$\ell_{\text{diverse}}(q_{sf}) = C_{\text{diverse}} \cdot \sum_{j \in \mathcal{F}} \mathbb{1}\left((q_{sf} - q) \neq 0\right) \quad (7)$$

handles *diversity* ensuring that several featurally-distinct semi-factuals are generated. Here, $\mathcal{F}$ represents the set of features that have already been used to generate semi-factuals, feature-sets that should be avoided:

$$\mathcal{F} = \left\{ j \mid \exists i : \left(q_{sf}^i - q\right)_j \neq 0 \right\} \quad (8)$$

Most Distant Neighbor (MDN). Aryal & Keane [2023] proposed and tested this method as a naïve, benchmark algorithm to find query-class instances that are most distant from the query. MDN scores all the query-class's instances on the extremity of their feature-values, determining whether they are much higher or lower than the feature-values of the query, q, to find its most distant neighbor. Its custom distance function, *Semi-Factual Scoring (sfs)*, prioritises instances that are sparse relative to the query (i.e., fewer feature differences), but have the highest value-differences in their non-matching features, as follows:

$$sfs(q, S, F) = \frac{same(q, x)}{F} + \frac{diff(q_f, x_f)}{diff_{max}(q_f, S_f)} \quad (9)$$

where S is Higher/Lower Set and $x \in S$, *same()* counts the number of features that are equal between q and x, F is the total number of features, *diff()* gives the difference-value of key-feature, f, and $diff_{max}()$ is the maximum difference-value for that key-feature in the Higher/Lower Set. The best-feature-MDN is selected as the instance with the highest *sfs* score from the Higher/Lower set for each feature, independently. Finally, the best of the best-feature-MDNs across all dimensions is chosen as the overall semi-factual for the query,

$$MDN(q, S) = \arg \max_{x \in S} sfs(x) \tag{10}$$

MDN finds the query-class instance that is furthest away from query on some dimension(s), one that also shares many common features with the query. As such, MDN never considers instances from other classes (such as, a counterfactual class) when it processes candidate semi-factuals. In the current tests, we use an improved version of MDN based on a new scoring function, sfs_{v2}, that assigns a greater weight to the sparsity component, as follows:

$$sfs_{v2}(q, S, F) = \frac{1}{F - same(q, x)} * \left(\frac{same(q, x)}{F} + \frac{diff(q_f, x_f)}{diff_{max}(q_f, S_f)} \right) \tag{11}$$

as the scoring function in Eq. (9) performs poorly on sparsity (see [3] for tests).

Explanations for Positive Outcomes (S-GEN). In 2023, Kenny & Huang [16] proposed the novel concept of "gain" (akin to "cost" in counterfactuals [29]) as a new constraint for semi-factual methods. They argue that semi-factuals best explain positive outcomes, whereas counterfactuals work best for negative outcomes. For example, if I am granted a loan at a 5% interest-rate, a comparison-shopping semi-factual might suggest that I could be granted the loan at a 2% interest-rate (from another bank). This semi-factual explanation has a quantifiable gain for end users, that can also be used to select explanations. Therefore, S-GEN uses *gain*, along with traditional constraints (such as plausibility, robustness and diversity) to compute semi-factuals that tell users about better, positive recourses that could be used. S-GEN's objective function is:

$$S\text{-}GEN(\mathbf{q}) = \max_{\mathbf{a}_1, \ldots, \mathbf{a}_m} \frac{1}{m} \sum_{i=1}^{m} f\left(P\left(\mathbf{q}, \mathbf{a}_i\right), G\left(\mathbf{q}, \mathbf{a}_i\right)\right) + \gamma R\left(\{\mathbf{q}'_1, \ldots, \mathbf{q}'_m\}\right) \tag{12}$$

$$\text{s.t. } \forall i, j : \mathbf{q}'_i = S_{\mathcal{M}}\left(\mathbf{q}, \mathbf{a}_i\right), H_j\left(\mathbf{q}'_i\right) \geq 0(\text{ or } >)$$

where, $\mathbf{a}_i$ represents an action taken on i^{th} feature-dimension, m is the desired number of semi-factuals to be generated. $P(\mathbf{q}, \mathbf{a}_i) = \Pr\left(S_{\mathcal{M}}(\mathbf{q}, \mathbf{a}_i)\right)$ denotes the plausibility of explanation for $\mathbf{q}$ by taking action $\mathbf{a}_i$ where Pr is the distribution density. S-GEN uses a Structural Causal Model (SCM), $S_{\mathcal{M}}$ to better capture the causal dependencies between the features and hence obtain feasible explanations.

$$G(\mathbf{q}, \mathbf{a}_i) = \mathcal{P}_{SF} \circ \delta\left(\mathbf{q}, S_{\mathcal{M}}(\mathbf{q}, \mathbf{a}_i)\right) \tag{13}$$

represents the gain function for $\mathbf{q}$ by taking action $\mathbf{a}_i$ where $\delta()$ is the distance function. Intuitively, it measures the difference between original state $\mathbf{q}$ and the new state obtained by the transition from $\mathbf{q}$ by taking action $\mathbf{a}_i$ through an SCM, $S_{\mathcal{M}}(\mathbf{q}, \mathbf{a}_i)$. Greater differences indicate higher "gains" (i.e., better explanations).

$$R\left(\{\mathbf{q}_i\}_{i=1}^{m}\right) = \frac{2}{m(m-1)} \sum_{i=1}^{m} \sum_{j>i}^{m} L_p \circ \delta\left(\mathbf{q}_i, \mathbf{q}_j\right) \tag{14}$$

shows the diversity function which is regularized by γ in Eq. (12). L_p is the L_p-norm and $\delta()$ is the distance function used, so as many distinct explanations as possible are generated that are also far from each other. Finally, robustness is achieved in a post-hoc manner as a hard constraint defined by:

$$H(\mathbf{q}, \mathbf{a}) = \min_{\mathbf{q}' \in \mathbb{B}_s(\mathbf{q}, \mathbf{a})} h\left(\mathbf{q}'\right) - \psi \tag{15}$$

where $H(\mathbf{q}, \mathbf{a})$ denotes the post-robustness of an action $\mathbf{a}$ for a test instance $\mathbf{q}$. The intuition is that any instances lying in the neighborhood $\mathbb{B}_s$ of the generated semi-factual $\mathbf{q}' = S_{\mathcal{M}}(\mathbf{q}, \mathbf{a})$ after taking the action $\mathbf{a}$ also have a positive outcome. This function ensures that the output of a predictive model h for $\mathbf{q}'$ is higher than a threshold $\psi = 0.5$ (in case of binary classes).

2.2   Counterfactual-Guided Methods

Both counterfactual-free and counterfactual-guided methods try to find instances that are distant from the query to use as semi-factuals. However, counterfactual-guided methods differ in their use of counterfactuals to the query as indicators/guides to good semi-factuals. The four methods examined are (i) KLEOR [6], (ii) PIECE [17], (iii) C2C-VAE [36], and (iv) DiCE [22].

Knowledge-Light Explanation-Oriented Retrieval (KLEOR). Cummins & Bridge [2006] were the first to use counterfactuals to guide the selection of a semi-factual. They proposed several methods, using different distance measures, that identify query-class instances as semi-factuals, when they lie between the query and its counterfactual (aka its NUN); viewing the best semi-factual as that one closest to the NUN and furthest from the query. Their *Sim-Miss* method:

$$Sim\text{-}Miss(q, nun, G) = \arg\max_{x \in G} Sim(x, nun) \tag{16}$$

where q is the query, x is a candidate instance, G is the set of query-class instances, and nun is the NUN, and Sim is Euclidean Distance. *Global-Sim*, has the semi-factual lie between q and the nun in the overall feature space:

$$Global\text{-}Sim(q, nun, G) = \arg\max_{x \in G} Sim(x, nun) + Sim(q, x) > Sim(q, nun) \tag{17}$$

whereas the third, *Attr-Sim*, enforces similarity across a majority of features:

$$Attr\text{-}Sim(q, nun, G) = \arg\max_{x \in G} Sim(x, nun)$$
$$+ \max_{a \in F} count[Sim(q_a, x_a) > Sim(q_a, nun_a)] \qquad (18)$$

PlausIble Exceptionality-Based Contrastive Explanations (PIECE).
Kenny & Keane's [17] PIECE method computes semi-factuals "on the way to"
computing counterfactuals using statistical techniques and a Generative Adverse-
rial Network (GAN) model, that can work with both image and tabular data.
PIECE identifies "exceptional" features in a query with respect to its counterfactual class (i.e., probabilistically-low in that class) and, then, iteratively modifies
these features in the query until they are "normal" (i.e., probabilistically-high).
As these exceptional features are incrementally altered, the generated instances
gradually move away from the query towards the counterfactual class, with the
last instance just before the decision boundary being deemed to be the semi-
factual. So, the semi-factual is like a point on the trajectory from the query to
the counterfactual.

Exceptional features are identified using the statistical probabilities in the
training distribution of the counterfactual class c'. Specifically, a two-part hurdle
process is used to model the latent features of the query (when it is an image) in
the feature-extracted layer ($\mathbf{X}$) of a Convolutional Neural Network (CNN) with
an ReLU activation function. The first hurdle process is modelled as a Bernoulli
distribution and the second as a probability density function (PDF) as:

$$p(x_i) = (1 - \theta_i)\,\delta_{(x_i)(0)} + \theta_i f_i(x_i), \quad \text{s.t.} \quad x_i \geq 0 \qquad (19)$$

where $p(x_i)$ is the probability of the latent feature value x_i for c', θ_i is the
probability of the neuron in $\mathbf{X}$ activating for c' (initial hurdle process), and f_i
is the subsequent PDF modelled (the second hurdle process). The constraint of
$x_i \geq 0$ refers to the ReLU activations, and $\delta_{(x_i)(0)}$ is the Kronecker delta function,
returning 0 for $x_i > 0$, and 1 for $x_i = 0$. After modelling the distribution, a
feature value x_i is regarded as an exceptional feature for the query image in
situations where,

$$x_i = 0 \mid p(1 - \theta_i) < \alpha \qquad (20)$$

if the neuron $\mathbf{X}_i$ does not activate, given the probability of it not activating
being less than α for c', and,

$$x_i > 0 \mid p(\theta_i) < \alpha \qquad (21)$$

if a neuron activates, given that the probability of it activating being less than
α for c', where α is a threshold.

Once the exceptional features are identified, the query's features are adjusted
to their expected values (x') with generated instances being checked by the CNN
to be in the query or counterfactual-class. The semi-factual is the last generated
instance in the query-class before crossing into the counterfactual-class. Finally,

a GAN is used to visualize the explanations by identifying a latent vector (z') such that loss between x' and $C(G(z'))$ is minimized as,

$$z' = \arg\min_{z} \| C(G(z)) - x' \|_2^2 \qquad (22)$$

$$PIECE(q) = G(z') \qquad (23)$$

where C is a CNN classifier and G is the GAN generator.

Class-to-Class Variational Autoencoder (C2C-VAE). Ye and colleagues [34–36] have proposed several models based on autoencoders that efficiently compute counterfactuals and semi-factuals. Their C2C-VAE model [36] learns an embedding space representing the differences between feature patterns in two classes using a standard variational autoencoder (VAE), with an encoder (f) and a decoder (f'). In the initial learning phase, given a pair of cases s and t from two classes, C2C-VAE encodes the feature difference, f_Δ, where $f_\Delta(s,t) = f(s) - f(t)$ using an encoder g, as $g(<f_\Delta, C_s, C_t>)$ and decodes the embedding using a decoder g' as $f'_\Delta = g'(g(<f_\Delta, C_s, C_t>))$

To derive an explanation for a query, q in class C_q, the method first generates a guide t in the counterfactual class C_t. This guide selection leverages the feature difference embedding space g. Specifically, the method randomly samples vectors from g, decodes them back to the original feature space, and selects the one with the least mean squared error compared to q. Finally, it interpolates between the extracted features of $f(q)$ and $f(t)$ in the VAE's latent space to obtain counterfactuals and semi-factuals as,

$$C2C\text{-}VAE(q) = f'((1 - \lambda) * f(q) + \lambda * f(t)), 0 \le \lambda \le 1 \qquad (24)$$

where λ is a hyperparameter which determines the weight of interpolation between q and t and controls whether the output is more similar to q (for a semi-factual) or t (for a counterfactual).

Diverse Counterfactual Explanations (DiCE). Mothilal et. al's [22] DiCE is a popular optimisation-based counterfactual method that can produce semi-factuals with adjustments to its loss function. They pioneered constraints for *diversity* (using determinantal point processes) and *feasibility* (using causal information from users) optimizing explanations with the loss function:

$$DiCE(q) = \arg\min_{c_1,\dots,c_k} \frac{1}{k} \sum_{i=1}^{k} \text{yloss}(f(c_i), y) + \frac{\lambda_1}{k} \sum_{i=1}^{k} \text{dist}(c_i, q)$$
$$- \lambda_2 \text{dpp\_diversity}(c_1, \dots, c_k) \qquad (25)$$

where q is the query input, c_i is a counterfactual explanation, k is the total number of diverse counterfactuals to be generated, $f()$ is the black box ML model, $yloss()$ is the metric that minimizes the distance between $f()$'s prediction for c_i and the desired outcome y, $dist()$ is the distance measure between c_i and q, and dpp_diversity() is the diversity metric. λ_1 and λ_2 are hyperparameters that balance the three components of the loss function.

3   Experimental Evaluations: To Guide or Not to Guide?

Taking these 8 semi-factual methods we performed a series of evaluations using 7 commonly-used datasets to determine whether the best semi-factuals are found by using counterfactuals as guides. We pitted the counterfactual-free methods against the counterfactual-guided ones, assessing them on 5 key metrics: distance, plausibility, confusability, robustness and sparsity. These tests are the most comprehensive experiments to date in the semi-factual XAI literature, in the number of methods/datasets tested and the metrics used.

3.1   Method: Metrics

Our computational evaluations of semi-factual methods used the key metrics that capture aspects of the desiderata for "good" semi-factuals (see [3]):

Distance. It is commonly-held that good semi-factuals are further from the query; here, measured as L_2-norm distance, where higher is better.

Plausibility. The semi-factual should be plausible; that is, within-distribution; here, measured as the L_2 distance to the nearest training instance, where lower values are better (see also [16]).

Confusability. The semi-factual should not be so far from the query so as to be confusable with a counterfactual. That is, the classifier should have higher confidence in classifying in the query class rather than in the counterfactual class; here, measured as ratio of its distance to the core of the counterfactual and query classes (adapted from Jiang et al.'s [11] Trust Score). This score is reversed (using $1 - score$) so lower values are better (i.e., less confusable).

$$Confusability(x) = \frac{d(x, CF)}{d(x, Q)} \qquad (26)$$

where x is the semi-factual, CF is the counterfactual-class, Q is the query-class and $d()$ measures the distance.

Robustness. The semi-factual method should be robust, small perturbations of the query should not radically change the semi-factuals found; here, measured using local Lipschitz continuity (see [1]). Specifically, we calculate,

$$Robustness(x) = \underset{x_i \in B_\epsilon(x)}{argmax} \frac{\|f(x) - f(x_i)\|_2}{\|x - x_i\|_2} \qquad (27)$$

where x is the input query, $B_\epsilon(x)$ is the ball of radius ϵ centered at x, x_i is a perturbed instance of x and $f()$ is the explanation method. Again this score was reversed so higher values are better (i.e., more robust).

Sparsity. There should be few feature differences between the query and semi-factual to be easily comprehended [15]; here, measured using,

$$Sparsity = \frac{ideal_{f\_diff}}{observed_{f\_diff}} \qquad (28)$$

where $ideal_{diff}$ is the desired number of feature differences (we use 1) and $observed_{diff}$ is the number of differences present, a higher value being better.

3.2   Method: Datasets and Setup

The eight methods were assessed with respect to each evaluation measure across seven benchmark tabular datasets commonly used in the XAI; namely, Adult Income (D1), Blood Alcohol (D2), Default Credit Card (D3), Diabetes (D4), German Credit (D5), HELOC (D6) and Lending Club (D7). For a thorough examination, 5-fold cross-validation was used to evaluate each method on each dataset. We set $\epsilon = 0.1$ in Eq. (27) and obtain 100 perturbations within that radius. In case of PIECE, DiCE, and S-GEN, feasibility constraints were added for the datasets allowing only certain features to mutate (see GitHub repository for details).

The Attr-Sim variant was implemented for KLEOR as it is the most sophisticated variant of this method and used a 3-NN model to build it. PIECE was adapted to accept tabular data by fitting the training data using a gamma distribution and calculating the probability of expected value through cumulative distribution function (CDF). We used feed-forward layers to train the VAE and C2C-VAE models in the PyTorch framework (see details about the architecture and hyperparameters in GitHub). The value of λ was set to 0.2 during interpolation to obtain semi-factuals. For DiCE, we used the publicly available library[1] and customized the objective function to obtain semi-factuals. The classifier model was trained using a Random Forest (RF) Classifier[2] and 3 diverse explanations were retrieved using the randomized search method. In the Local Region method, the surrogate model was trained with a minimum of 200 instances from each class. We followed the original implementation of DSER[3] where we used a k-NN classifier to fit the conformal predictor. The hyperparameters including rejection threshold θ was identified using grid search cross-validation. For MDN method, we used the modified scoring function, $sfs_{v2}()$. For continuous features, we selected the threshold of $\pm 20\%$ of standard deviation to determine if they

---

[1] https://github.com/interpretml/DiCE.

[2] We used default parameters to train RF across the datasets. The classifier's key role is mostly to validate the class-membership of the generated semi-factuals.

[3] https://github.com/HammerLabML/DiverseSemifactualsReject.

are same in the $sfs_{v2}()$ function. Finally, for S-GEN we used the default implementation available[4] for causal and non-causal setting and retrieve 3 diverse semi-factual explanations (see GitHub for causal and non-causal datasets).

All the experiments were conducted in Python 3.9 environment on a Ubuntu 23.10 server with AMD EPYC 7443 24-Core Processor. The source code, data and results is available at https://github.com/itsaugat/sf_methods/.

3.3   Results and Discussion

Table 1 shows the normalized raw scores for the 8 methods across the 7 datasets on the 5 metrics. Figure 2 summarises the results as mean ranks for each method (collapsing over datasets and metrics). This graph immediately allows us to answer our main question, "Are the best semi-factuals found by using counterfactuals as guides?". The short answer is "NO". If counterfactual guidance were critical then the counterfacual-guide methods (the grey bars) should be the top-ranked methods to the left, with the counterfactual-free methods (the black bars) to the right. However, instead, the rank order alternates between the two groups of methods. Indeed, a counterfactual-free method, MDN appears to be the best. Furthermore, the top scores for each metric are distributed over methods of both groups (see bold-text scores in Table 1). Hence, using counterfactuals as guides in semi-factual generation does not determine success on key metrics. So, what is it then that makes one method better than another in these tests?

Figure 3 shows the ranks for each method by metric (collapsing over dataset) with a separate radar chart for each group. In these charts it is clear that no method dominates coming first across most metrics. Indeed, the top-3 methods – MDN, C2C-VAE, Local-Region – are really not that good on further analysis of their performance; many do well on one or two metrics but then poorly on others.

MDN does very well on Confusability (1st) and Plausibility (2nd) but is mediocre on Sparsity (4th), Distance (4th) and Robustness (5th). As MDN selects known instances in the query-class it is not surprising that its semi-factuals are plausible and in the class but they then tend not to be very distant from the query, to be less sparse and (sometimes) unstable outliers.

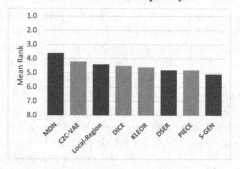

Fig. 2. Mean Ranks of Counterfactual-Free (black) and Counterfactual-Guided (grey) Semi-Factual Methods

In contrast, C2C-VAE does much better on Robustness (1st) and Distance (2nd) and but then is less good on Plausibility (5th) and poor on Confusability (7th) and Sparsity (8th). C2C-VAE analyses the differences between instances with respect to classes, information that clearly enables

---

[4] https://github.com/EoinKenny/Semifactual_Recourse_Generation.

the identification of stable semi-factuals distant from the query; but, these semi-factuals go too far, becoming confusable with counterfactuals and rely on too many feature-differences.

Ironically, the older, third-placed Local-Region method could be said to be the best, if we were adopting a balanced-scorecard approach; arguably, it is moderately good across most metrics showing Distance (3rd), Plausibility (4th), Confusability (4th), Robustness (5th) and Sparsity (7th).

Other key insights can also be gained from these results. Semi-factuals obtained from the methods that select existing instances (MDN, KLEOR and Local-Region) are more plausible as compared to those produced by generative methods (DiCE, PIECE, S-GEN and C2C-VAE). Similarly, on a group-level, the counterfactual-guided methods (C2C-VAE, PIECE and DiCE) produces more robust semi-factuals than counterfactual-free methods.

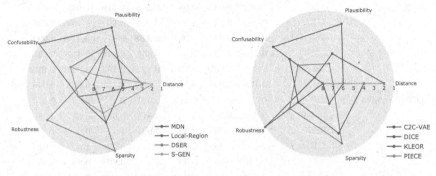

(a) Counterfactual-Free Methods   (b) Counterfactual-Guided Methods

Fig. 3. Median Ranks (across datasets) of Counterfactual-Free (left) and Counterfactual-Guided (right) methods for each measure. Points away from the center of graphs represent higher rank (better performance).

Table 1. Scores for each method on the five metrics across different datasets (values are normalized between 0 and 1). The best score for a given dataset is shown in bold, with arrows after metrics showing direction of best scores.

Metrics	Method	D1	D2	D3	D4	D5	D6	D7
Distance (↑)	MDN	0.255	0.205	0.172	0.471	0.628	0.476	0.285
	Local-Region	0.364	0.305	0.217	**0.65**	**0.984**	0.506	0.152
	DSER	0.024	0.027	0.04	0.026	0.042	0.038	0.035
	S-GEN	**0.518**	0.313	0.488	0.5	0.463	**0.95**	0.23
	C2C_VAE	0.488	**0.352**	0.36	0.451	0.762	0.586	0.361
	DiCE	0.427	0.304	**0.492**	0.399	0.354	0.494	**0.498**
	KLEOR	0.176	0.143	0.245	0.363	0.714	0.446	0.151
	PIECE	0.124	0.2	0.459	0.141	0.076	0.194	0.135
Plausibility (↓)	MDN	**0.046**	0.041	0.035	0.223	**0.285**	0.205	0.023
	Local-Region	0.069	0.047	0.049	0.258	0.302	0.219	0.037
	DSER	0.062	0.052	0.085	0.267	0.319	0.263	0.045
	S-GEN	0.126	0.104	0.209	0.261	0.39	0.489	0.038
	C2C_VAE	0.078	0.064	0.091	**0.158**	0.377	**0.169**	0.024
	DiCE	0.201	0.099	0.352	0.351	0.428	0.473	0.228
	KLEOR	0.048	**0.031**	**0.032**	0.193	0.294	0.203	**0.022**
	PIECE	0.108	0.095	0.123	0.254	0.359	0.313	0.046
Confusability (↓)	MDN	0	0	0.419	0.321	0	0.134	0
	Local-Region	0.888	0.988	0.344	0.913	0.66	0.567	0.688
	DSER	1	0.99	0.925	0.991	1	0.9	1
	S-GEN	0.9	0.88	0.95	0	0.226	1	0.91
	C2C_VAE	0.975	0.99	0.957	1	0.901	0.867	0.869
	DiCE	0.844	0.614	0.913	0.758	0.595	0.634	0.915
	KLEOR	0.227	0.318	0	0.525	0.033	0	0.014
	PIECE	0.796	1	1	0.719	0.611	0.867	0.978
Robustness (↑)	MDN	0.996	0.866	0.9994	0.548	0.991	0.748	0.905
	Local-Region	0.967	0.908	0.983	**1**	0.889	0.873	0.942
	DSER	0.999	**0.99**	1	0.984	0.998	0.998	0.995
	S-GEN	0.991	0.982	0	0.785	0.214	0.985	0.626
	C2C_VAE	1	0.975	1	1	1	1	1
	DiCE	0.975	0.894	0.997	0.896	0.983	0.991	0.922
	KLEOR	0	0	0.753	0	0	0	0
	PIECE	0.949	0.988	0.967	0.953	0.983	0.991	0.939
Sparsity (↑)	MDN	0.53	0.43	0.08	0.14	0.17	0.09	0.35
	Local-Region	0.19	0.29	0.06	0.13	0.08	0.06	0.17
	DSER	**0.99**	**0.95**	**0.98**	**0.95**	**0.9**	**0.94**	0.85
	S-GEN	0.33	0.52	0.06	0.16	0.15	0.07	0.21
	C2C_VAE	0.1	0.25	0.05	0.125	0.07	0.05	0.13
	DiCE	0.7	0.81	0.74	0.38	0.65	0.74	0.7
	KLEOR	0.42	0.37	0.06	0.12	0.13	0.06	0.26
	PIECE	0.783	0.81	0.98	0.93	0.608	0.84	**0.96**

4   Conclusions

In XAI literature, semi-factual explanation methods have been studied from two perspectives: counterfactual-free and counterfactual-guided approaches. This paper addressed the question of whether relying on counterfactuals as guides necessarily and always produces the best semi-factuals. We find that methods from both approaches show good results on some evaluation metrics, while performing poorly on others. As such, the use of counterfactual guides does not appear to be a major determining factor in finding the best semi-factuals. Indeed, it is hard to escape the conclusion that other factors better guide the process; for instance, relying on known data-points (as in MDN and KLEOR) rather than on perturbed instances or using the difference-space (as in C2C-VAE). Hence, the most promising direction for future research may be to extract what is best from the current methods and somehow combine them in one.

The current work has a number of limitations that should be mentioned. This work primarily focuses on tabular data; so, it would be interesting to determine whether the results extend to other data-types (e.g., images and time series). We also badly need more user studies. In many respects, we do not know whether people find the semi-factuals produced by any of these methods are psychologically valid. Unfortunately, the few users studies that have been done suffer from design flaws (see [8, 16, 24]). However, what is clear, is that there is a lot more to do on the computation of semi-factual explanations before we can be confident about using them in deployed systems.

Acknowledgements. This research was supported by Science Foundation Ireland via the Insight SFI Research Centre for Data Analytics (12/RC/2289-P2). For the purpose of Open Access, the author has applied a CC BY copyright to any Author Accepted Manuscript version arising from this submission.

References

1. Alvarez-Melis, D., Jaakkola, T.S.: On the robustness of interpretability methods. arXiv preprint arXiv:1806.08049 (2018)
2. Artelt, A., Hammer, B.: "Even if..."–diverse semifactual explanations of reject. arXiv preprint arXiv:2207.01898 (2022)
3. Aryal, S., Keane, M.T.: Even if explanations: prior work, desiderata & benchmarks for semi-factual XAI. In: IJCAI-23, pp. 6526–6535 (2023). https://doi.org/10.24963/ijcai.2023/732
4. Bennett, J.: A philosophical Guide to Conditionals. Clarendon Press (2003)
5. Brughmans, D., Leyman, P., Martens, D.: NICE: an algorithm for nearest instance counterfactual explanations. Data Min. Knowl. Discov. 1–39 (2023)
6. Cummins, L., Bridge, D.: KLEOR: a knowledge lite approach to explanation oriented retrieval. Comput. Inform. **25**(2–3), 173–193 (2006)
7. Dandl, S., Molnar, C., Binder, M., Bischl, B.: Multi-objective counterfactual explanations. In: Bäck, T., Preuss, M., Deutz, A., Wang, H., Doerr, C., Emmerich, M., Trautmann, H. (eds.) PPSN 2020. LNCS, vol. 12269, pp. 448–469. Springer, Cham (2020). https://doi.org/10.1007/978-3-030-58112-1_31

8. Doyle, D., Cunningham, P., Bridge, D., Rahman, Y.: Explanation oriented retrieval. In: Funk, P., González Calero, P.A. (eds.) ECCBR 2004. LNCS (LNAI), vol. 3155, pp. 157–168. Springer, Heidelberg (2004). https://doi.org/10.1007/978-3-540-28631-8_13

9. Guidotti, R., Monreale, A., Giannotti, F., Pedreschi, D., Ruggieri, S., Turini, F.: Factual and counterfactual explanations for black box decision making. IEEE Intell. Syst. **34**(6), 14–23 (2019)

10. Hamman, F., Noorani, E., Mishra, S., Magazzeni, D., Dutta, S.: Robust counterfactual explanations for neural networks with probabilistic guarantees. arXiv preprint arXiv:2305.11997 (2023)

11. Jiang, H., Kim, B., Guan, M., Gupta, M.: To trust or not to trust a classifier. In: Advances in Neural Information Processing Systems, vol. 31 (2018)

12. Karimi, A.H., Barthe, G., Schölkopf, B., Valera, I.: A survey of algorithmic recourse: contrastive explanations and consequential recommendations. ACM Comput. Surv. **55**(5), 1–29 (2022)

13. Karimi, A.H., Schölkopf, B., Valera, I.: Algorithmic recourse: from counterfactual explanations to interventions. In: Proceedings of the 2021 ACM Conference on Fairness, Accountability, and Transparency, pp. 353–362 (2021)

14. Keane, M.T., Kenny, E.M., Delaney, E., Smyth, B.: If only we had better counterfactual explanations. In: Proceedings of the 30th International Joint Conference on Artificial Intelligence (IJCAI-21) (2021)

15. Keane, M.T., Smyth, B.: Good counterfactuals and where to find them: a case-based technique for generating counterfactuals for explainable AI (XAI). In: Watson, I., Weber, R. (eds.) ICCBR 2020. LNCS (LNAI), vol. 12311, pp. 163–178. Springer, Cham (2020). https://doi.org/10.1007/978-3-030-58342-2_11

16. Kenny, E.M., Huang, W.: The utility of "even if" semi-factual explanation to optimize positive outcomes. In: NeurIPs-23 (2023)

17. Kenny, E.M., Keane, M.T.: On generating plausible counterfactual and semi-factual explanations for deep learning. In: Proceedings of the 35th AAAI Conference on Artificial Intelligence (AAAI-21), pp. 11575–11585 (2021)

18. Lu, J., Yang, L., Mac Namee, B., Zhang, Y.: A rationale-centric framework for human-in-the-loop machine learning. arXiv preprint arXiv:2203.12918 (2022)

19. McCloy, R., Byrne, R.M.: Semifactual "even if" thinking. Thinking Reason. **8**(1), 41–67 (2002)

20. Mertes, S., Karle, C., Huber, T., Weitz, K., Schlagowski, R., André, E.: Alterfactual explanations–the relevance of irrelevance for explaining AI systems. arXiv preprint arXiv:2207.09374 (2022)

21. Miller, T.: Explanation in artificial intelligence: insights from the social sciences. Artif. Intell. **267**, 1–38 (2019)

22. Mothilal, R.K., Sharma, A., Tan, C.: Explaining machine learning classifiers through diverse counterfactual explanations. In: Proceedings of the Facct-2020, pp. 607–617 (2020)

23. Nugent, C., Cunningham, P., Doyle, D.: The best way to instil confidence is by being right. In: Muñoz-Ávila, H., Ricci, F. (eds.) ICCBR 2005. LNCS (LNAI), vol. 3620, pp. 368–381. Springer, Heidelberg (2005). https://doi.org/10.1007/11536406_29

24. Nugent, C., Doyle, D., Cunningham, P.: Gaining insight through case-based explanation. J. Intell. Info Syst. **32**, 267–295 (2009)

25. Poché, A., Hervier, L., Bakkay, M.C.: Natural example-based explainability: a survey. arXiv preprint arXiv:19 (2023)

26. Ribeiro, M.T., Singh, S., Guestrin, C.: "Why should i trust you?" explaining the predictions of any classifier. In: Proceedings of the 22nd ACM SIGKDD-16, pp. 1135–1144 (2016)

27. Schleich, M., Geng, Z., Zhang, Y., Suciu, D.: GeCo: quality counterfactual explanations in real time. arXiv preprint arXiv:2101.01292 (2021)

28. Smyth, B., Keane, M.T.: A few good counterfactuals: generating interpretable, plausible and diverse counterfactual explanations. In: Keane, M.T., Wiratunga, N. (eds.) ICCBR 2022. LNCS, vol. 13405, pp. 18–32. Springer, Cham (2022). https://doi.org/10.1007/978-3-031-14923-8_2

29. Ustun, B., Spangher, A., Liu, Y.: Actionable recourse in linear classification. In: Proceedings of the Facct-19, pp. 10–19 (2019)

30. Van Looveren, A., Klaise, J., Vacanti, G., Cobb, O.: Conditional generative models for counterfactual explanations. arXiv preprint arXiv:2101.10123 (2021)

31. Vats, A., Mohammed, A., Pedersen, M., Wiratunga, N.: This changes to that: combining causal and non-causal explanations to generate disease progression in capsule endoscopy. arXiv preprint arXiv:2212.02506 (2022)

32. Verma, S., Boonsanong, V., Hoang, M., Hines, K.E., Dickerson, J.P., Shah, C.: Counterfactual explanations and algorithmic recourses for machine learning: a review. arXiv preprint arXiv:2010.10596 (2020)

33. Wachter, S., Mittelstadt, B., Russell, C.: Counterfactual explanations without opening the black box. Harv. JL Tech. **31**, 841 (2017)

34. Ye, X., Leake, D., Huibregtse, W., Dalkilic, M.: Applying class-to-class Siamese networks to explain classifications with supportive and contrastive cases. In: Watson, I., Weber, R. (eds.) ICCBR 2020. LNCS (LNAI), vol. 12311, pp. 245–260. Springer, Cham (2020). https://doi.org/10.1007/978-3-030-58342-2_16

35. Ye, X., Leake, D., Jalali, V., Crandall, D.J.: Learning adaptations for case-based classification: a neural network approach. In: Sánchez-Ruiz, A.A., Floyd, M.W. (eds.) ICCBR 2021. LNCS (LNAI), vol. 12877, pp. 279–293. Springer, Cham (2021). https://doi.org/10.1007/978-3-030-86957-1_19

36. Zhao, Z., Leake, D., Ye, X., Crandall, D.: Generating counterfactual images: towards a C2C-VAE approach. In: 4th Workshop on XCBR: Case-Based Reasoning for the Explanation of Intelligent Systems (2022)

Improving Complex Adaptations in Process-Oriented Case-Based Reasoning by Applying Rule-Based Adaptation

Lukas Malburg[1,2(✉)] [iD], Maxim Hotz[1,2] [iD], and Ralph Bergmann[1,2] [iD]

[1] Artificial Intelligence and Intelligent Information Systems, University of Trier, 54296 Trier, Germany
{malburgl,s4mahotz,bergmann}@uni-trier.de
[2] German Research Center for Artificial Intelligence (DFKI), Branch University of Trier, Behringstraße 21, 54296 Trier, Germany
{lukas.malburg,maxim.hotz,ralph.bergmann}@dfki.de
https://www.wi2.uni-trier.de

Abstract. Adaptation is a complex and error-prone task in Case-Based Reasoning (CBR), including the adaptation knowledge acquisition and modeling efforts required for performing adaptations. This is also evident for the subfield of Process-Oriented Case-Based Reasoning (POCBR) in which cases represent procedural experiential knowledge, making creation and maintaining adaptation knowledge even for domain experts exceedingly challenging. Current adaptation methods in POCBR address the adaptation knowledge bottleneck by learning adaptation knowledge based on cases in the case base. However, these approaches are based on proprietary representation formats, resulting in low usability and maintainability. Therefore, we present an approach of using adaptation rules and rule engines for complex adaptations in POCBR in this paper. The results of an experimental evaluation indicate that the rule-based adaptation approach leads to significantly better results during runtime than an already available POCBR adaptation method.

Keywords: Process-Oriented Case-Based Reasoning · Adaptive Workflow Management · Rule-Based Adaptation · Drools Rule Engine · Adaptation Operators

1 Introduction

Although Case-Based Reasoning (CBR) [1] systems have been well explored in past research [4], the acquisition of adaptation knowledge still imposes a primary challenge in CBR [12,16,34,35], also known as *Adaptation Knowledge Bottleneck* [17]. For this reason, performing adaptations often requires in-depth domain knowledge by experts [12,18,24,25]. This is particularly evident for synthetic tasks in Process-Oriented Case-Based Reasoning (POCBR) [5,26], wherein cases represent procedural experiential knowledge in the form

J. A. Recio-Garcia et al. (Eds.): ICCBR 2024, LNAI 14775, pp. 50–66, 2024.
https://doi.org/10.1007/978-3-031-63646-2_4

of semantic workflow graphs. Consequently, adaptations performed during the *Reuse* phase in POCBR require profound and detailed knowledge about possible and valid structural graph modifications. For example, adaptation knowledge in POCBR is represented by complex graph fragments that are inserted in or deleted from a retrieved workflow. Creating such comprehensive adaptation knowledge is potentially laborious and error-prone for domain experts [24,25]. In previous work, adaptation methods in POCBR [24,25,28–30] have been developed that learn this needed adaptation knowledge automatically. However, most adaptation methods in CBR and POCBR rely on inherent and proprietary formats, without making the adaptation knowledge intuitively accessible to domain experts. In addition, CBR and POCBR frameworks often do not provide an easy mean for engineering adaptation knowledge, resulting in difficulties for verification and maintaining the learned knowledge or for manually creating new adaptation knowledge [32].

In this paper, we present an approach based on a previously developed adaptation method, in which the state-of-the-art rule engine *Drools*[1] [3] is used for performing workflow graph adaptations in POCBR. For this purpose, we utilize the learning step of the operator-based adaptation [30] and encode the adaptation knowledge directly as corresponding rules. Consequently, instead of encoding adaptations as workflow graph fragments in POCBR, they are encoded as adaptation rules, hiding the complexity of adaptations in suitable predicates in the rules. For adaptation, the rules in the rule base are applied to the retrieved workflow case to increase the similarity to the given query. In an experimental evaluation, we assess the suitability of the rule-based adaptation compared to the operator-based adaptation [30]. By the proposed approach, the adaptation knowledge is more intuitively encoded for domain experts and, thus, enables verification and maintenance of it more easily. Moreover, the approach is domain-independent and also usable for other case representations [4,7] in acCBR or for other process-oriented domains that go beyond the cooking domain used in the evaluation. Finally, by using a state-of-the-art rule engine, the rule-based adaptation approach benefits from new functionalities implemented in the future. For example, advanced search and optimization techniques (e. g., OptaPlanner[2]) can be utilized that are especially tailored for the representation of adaptation rules.

The paper is structured as follows: Sect. 2 describes the basics covering adaptation in CBR and POCBR and discusses related approaches using rule engines in CBR. In Sect. 3, the concept of encoding and applying adaptation rules is introduced. Section 4 describes the experimental evaluation of the proposed approach. Finally, Sect. 5 concludes the paper and discusses future work.

2   Foundations and Related Work

The foundations for this work consist of the *NEST* graph representation and similarity computation introduced by Bergmann and Gil [5] which are necessary

---

[1] https://www.drools.org.
[2] https://www.optaplanner.org/.

to represent and assess cases in POCBR. Further, knowledge representations and adaptation approaches in transformational adaptation, i.e., adaptation rules and operators, constitute a basis for this work. Hence, we introduce the relevant concepts in the following.

2.1   Semantic Workflow Representation and Similarity Assessment

In POCBR, cases represent procedural experiential knowledge [5,26]. In this work, we use semantically annotated graphs, named *NEST* graphs [5], to represent cases. A *NEST* graph is a directed graph and represented by the quadruple $W = (N, E, S, T)$: N is a set of nodes and $E \subseteq N \times N$ a set of edges. $T : N \cup E \rightarrow \Omega$ assigns a concrete type to each node and each edge. Furthermore, $S : N \cup E \rightarrow \Sigma$ specifies a semantic description from a semantic metadata language Σ to each node and edge. These semantic descriptions can be used to describe a node or edge in more detail by semantic knowledge. A case base consists of several such *NEST* graphs that can be utilized in a POCBR system. In Fig. 1, an exemplary *NEST* graph is shown that represents a simple cooking recipe with different node and edge types and exemplary semantic descriptions.

In this context, task nodes describe the cooking steps performed, and data

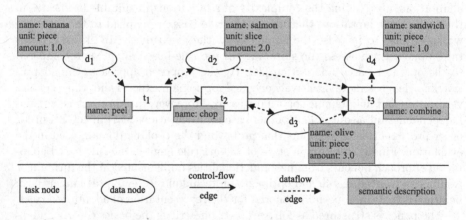

Fig. 1. *NEST* Graph with Semantic Descriptions.

nodes the corresponding ingredients used during preparation of the dish. The semantic descriptions used specify the performed task in more detail, i.e., which task should be executed. For data nodes, the semantic descriptions can be used to specify the type of ingredient, the amount, and unit of it. Task nodes are connected by control-flow nodes that define the execution order of the cooking procedure. Dataflow edges are used to define which task node consumes and produces which concrete data node, i.e., which task node needs a certain ingredient for performing the cooking step and what is the result afterwards.

To calculate the similarity between two *NEST* graphs, suitable similarity measures are required. Bergmann and Gil [5] have developed a semantic similarity measure that computes this similarity based on the local-global principle [4]. During this procedure, the global similarity is composed of the local similarities computed between the individual graph elements, based on corresponding local semantic similarity measures [5]. If the types of the graph elements to be compared are not identical, i.e., a data node compared with a task node, the local similarity is always 0.0. Otherwise, the similarity is calculated based on the similarity of the semantic descriptions attached to the graph elements. A graph mapping is initiated in which the best possible mapping, i.e., the mapping that results in the highest global similarity, between the query workflow elements and the case workflow elements is determined.

2.2 Adaptation Methods

Based on the semantic similarity assessment between a given query workflow and a workflow graph from the case base, the most similar case is used as the basis for adaptation. Adaptation is often required for synthetic tasks in Process-Oriented Case-Based Reasoning (POCBR) to better fit the retrieved solution to the needs of the user. In general, adaptation methods can be divided into two main categories: Generative adaptation and transformational adaptation [4]. Generative adaptation is aiming to solve a problem from scratch, even without using a case with experiential knowledge from the case base [4,34]. Typically, a knowledge-based problem solver is needed that can solve the problem from scratch. CBR can be used to accelerate the adaptation process by reusing already available solutions from the case base. In contrast, transformational adaptation aims to modify a retrieved case from the case base to better fulfill the requirements that a user specifies in a given query. Therefore, adaptation operators or adaptation rules are used that specify the context in which a case can be modified. Depending on the degree of modification, a distinction is made between substitutional adaptation for modifying values at the attribute level and structural adaptation for larger and more complex, structural changes of the retrieved case [4]. In the following, the application of transformational adaptation with adaptation operators and adaptation rules is described in more detail.

Adaptation Operators: Adaptation operators sequentially transform a retrieved case into a successor case if the successor case remains valid, i.e., they describe generally applicable transformations of a retrieved solution. By chaining several adaptation operators together, a retrieved case can be transformed into an adapted case that better fits the user's requirements. The sequence in which operators are applied to a case is determined by search techniques, such as local or global search algorithms. Müller and Bergmann [30] present an approach in previous work in which they learn adaptation operators based on a case base in POCBR. The proposed adaptation operators are inspired by *STRIPS* operators from AI planning [14] and, thus, consist of an add part and a delete part. In the terminology of workflows used in POCBR this means that the add part is handled as an *insertion* into the graph and the delete part as a *deletion*. Both, insertion and deletion part, are comprehensive workflow graph fragments called *streamlets* that are inserted or deleted in a retrieved workflow that should be adapted. Based on these definitions, three kinds of adaptation operators can be created: 1) an *insert operator* only consisting of an insertion part, 2) a *delete operator* only consisting of a deletion part, and 3) an *exchange operator* with both an insertion and a deletion part. During learning of the adaptation operators, workflow pairs from the case base are considered. In this context, one of the workflows is transformed into the other one by deleting and adding parts in the workflow or by exchanging workflow fragments. Since creating, verifying, and maintaining complex workflow graph fragments such as used for adaptation operators are demanding and challenging tasks, domain experts are required to have in-depth knowledge about possible graph adaptations. In addition, state-of-the-art CBR and POCBR frameworks lack the ability to adequately represent such adaptation knowledge for domain experts and knowledge modelers [32].

Figure 2 depicts the *NEST* graph from Fig. 1 with a marked streamlet (dashed line). According to the definition provided by Müller [27], a streamlet consists of a partial workflow that is constructed based on a particular data node. This data node is referred to as the head data node of the streamlet. Starting from this head data node, a streamlet also includes all tasks that are directly connected to the head data node by a dataflow edge. Based on the essential concept of a head data node, the task node that only consumes the head data node is called the anchor task. The anchor task determines the position of modification in the graph. Every other node, e. g., t_2, is a normal part of the streamlet. Looking at the example from Fig. 2, the head data node d_3, the anchor task t_3, and the task node t_2 are part of the streamlet created during learning. Assuming that this learned streamlet represents a delete streamlet means that 1) the head data node is deleted from the workflow and 2) each unproductive task, i.e., task nodes that do not have any incoming or outgoing dataflow edge, are deleted. t_2 is after the deletion of d_3 such an unproductive task that must be deleted. In the example, d_3 and also t_2 are deleted. If there exists an insert streamlet in the learned adaptation knowledge (see left side of Fig. 2), it can subsequently

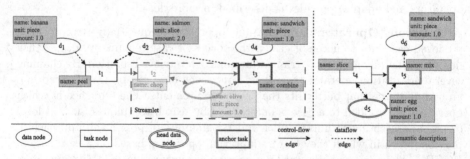

Fig. 2. *NEST* Graph with Learned Streamlet (Left Side) and Substitute Streamlet (Right Side).

be inserted into the graph. In the example, it is determined whether the anchor tasks t_3 and t_5 from the insert streamlet are sufficiently similar to each other and produce the same output, i.e., d_4 and d_6. Assuming that both conditions are satisfied, the head data node of the streamlet d_5 and the task node t_4 are inserted into the graph. Finally, a cleanup function restores the syntactical correctness of the graph by inserting control-flow edges between t_1 and the newly inserted node t_4 and between t_4 and the anchor task t_3. In addition, a dataflow edge between the new head data node d_5 and the anchor task t_3 is inserted. In this context, it is important to note that every time an adaptation operator with either an insert or delete streamlet is applied, only the plain streamlet, i.e., all workflow components except of the anchor task are inserted or deleted to the corresponding graph. During adaptation, each data node in the retrieved graph is considered as head data node and a corresponding streamlet is constructed. Based on this streamlet, suitable and applicable adaptation operators are retrieved and executed. This procedure is repeated until all data nodes have been used once to construct a streamlet.

Adaptation Rules: In contrast to adaptation operators, adaptation rules [4] transform the solution of a case into another solution by exploiting the differences between the given query and the problem description of the retrieved case. Instead of modifying problem description and solution as for adaptation operators, only the solution part of the case is modified. Adaptation rules have a *precondition part* that must be fulfilled to apply the corresponding transformation of the *conclusion part*. For this purpose, the query case, the retrieved case, and the adapted case should be checked for their compatibility. Each adaptation rule whose precondition is fulfilled is then executed on the case [4,27].

2.3   Rule Engines in CBR

In this section, we discuss relevant related approaches for using rule-based adaptation and rule engines in CBR. However, most of the existing work utilizes rule engines in the context of classic CBR, targeting attribute-value based cases, and not procedural cases in POCBR.

Bergmann et al. [8] present an approach of using adaptation and completion rules from general knowledge in CBR. For rule application, they propose the usage of a forward chaining rule interpreter based on a Rete-Network. For this, they use the *NéOpus* system [31], which allows the organization of rules by the means of sub-rule bases and dedicated Rete-Networks according to the structure of the case representation [8]. Bach and Althoff [2] introduce an approach in which they integrate the *Drools* rule engine into the open-source CBR framework *myCBR*. By this, it is possible to use completion and adaptation rules in a wide variety of *myCBR* application domains. Hanft et al. [15] describe the integration of *Drools* within the *SeMantic Information Logistics Architecture (SMILA)*[3]. In their work, the authors link the rule-based adaptation of CBR systems with

---

[3] https://projects.eclipse.org/projects/rt.smila.

business-oriented workflow systems by introducing the *Rule-based Adaptation of Case-based Knowledge (RACK)* for integrating CBR functionalities to *SMILA* [15]. Beyond this, there have been some general approaches that investigate the application of rule engines for the purpose of context-aware workflow adaptation: Döhring et al. [13] develop several adaptation patterns for dynamically changing *BPMN 2.0*[4] workflows along with a prototypical implementation using *Drools*. Similarly, the *CBRflow* system [33] can be used for adaptive workflow management, combining rule-based adaptation representing general knowledge and cases specifying already experienced adaptations in problem situations. Besides the exclusive application of a rule engine within CBR systems, there are also some works that employ a hybrid approach of linking CBR systems with rule-based expert systems for workflow modeling and decision support. In healthcare, for instance, rule engines are also applied within *Clinical Decision Support Systems* [9] for medical diagnosis, as discussed in the work of Cabrera and Edye [11]. In their work, they develop a *Medical Diagnostic System* by combining a rule-based expert system with classical CBR methods.

Although there are related approaches that are used in CBR, they predominantly make use of substitutional adaptation concepts or employ adaptation rules for attribute-value cases. Moreover, only the approach by Bach and Althoff [2] is directly integrated into a CBR framework, although adaptation rules are universally better understandable than own, proprietary adaptation knowledge formats, and, thus, promote the broader usability of CBR frameworks. The presented approaches that incorporate a rule engine for workflow modeling support (e. g., [13,33]) oftentimes deal with event-driven application scenarios and are not necessarily utilizing directly the CBR or POCBR methodology. Thus, it is currently not investigated how rule engines can be used in the context of POCBR to perform complex structural and transformational adaptations of semantic workflow graphs in the *Reuse* phase. In addition, the integration of a rule-based adaptation approach into CBR frameworks is only rarely investigated or not available at all in the context of POCBR. For this reason, this work aims to address this gap and, thus, to provide a first step towards the integration of rule-based adaptation into a POCBR framework.

3   Encoding and Applying Adaptation Rules in POCBR

In this section, we present a rule-based approach for using adaptation rules and a rule engine to perform complex adaptations in POCBR. First, in Sect. 3.1, we describe the predicates used to represent the adaptation operators as adaptation rules. After encoding of the adaptation rules, we discuss in Sect. 3.2 the application of the rules during the *Reuse* phase.

3.1   Encoding Adaptation Operators as Adaptation Rules

As already described in Sect. 2.2, the operator-based adaptation by Müller and Bergmann [30] consists of STRIPS-like adaptation operators. Each operator

---

[4] https://www.omg.org/spec/BPMN/2.0.2/.

contains either an insertion or a deletion streamlet, or both of them. During adaptation, suitable adaptation operators are selected, performing an insertion, deletion, or an exchange in the retrieved workflow graph.

Based on the learning process in which adaptation operators are created, we inspect either the insertion streamlet or the deletion streamlet or, in the case of an exchange operator, both. To generate suitable adaptation rules, the concepts that are currently encoded in the operator-based adaptation algorithm itself (see [30]) must be converted into suitable predicates. This is required to enable the rule engine to perform validation checks or to find best matching positions in the graph. Figure 3 depicts the mapping of the concepts used for adaptation operators to suitable predicates in the adaptation rules. During the mapping process, the predicates are divided into a set of predicates in the form of preconditions that are inevitably required for the execution of a rule, and corresponding effects that specify the modifications of the adapted case after execution of a rule. To satisfy the property of identifying the best matching anchor task in the graph for the insertion streamlet, we introduce the predicate $isBestMatchingAnchor$. The remaining preconditions of the streamlet insertion, i.e., the condition that the head data node should not exist in the graph yet, can be realized by regular pattern matching and do not require special predicates (see Line 3 in Lst. 1). The insertion of the streamlet elements themselves, i.e., the conclusion of the rule, is represented by straightforward predicates, each assigned to a corresponding item type. For deletion, we specify the predicate $isHeadOfMostSimilarStreamlet$ that is used within the precondition. According to the principles outlined in Sect. 2.2, this predicate allows the identification of a data node residing in the graph that acts as the head data node of the most similar streamlet that is con-

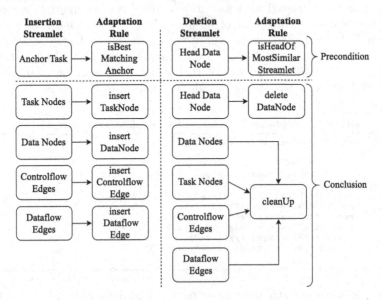

Fig. 3. Mapping Adaptation Operators to Adaptation Rules.

structable out of all data nodes present. Since it is not clear which streamlet is to be identified as the most similar one to the deletion streamlet, the conclusion of a deletion rule makes use of a generic predicate *cleanUp* responsible for the removal of left over streamlet elements as proposed by Müller [27].

Figure 4 illustrates the insertion of a streamlet into a *NEST* graph according to the principles outlined previously. We can represent this insertion procedure by the means of a corresponding adaptation rule. Listing 1 depicts this equiv-

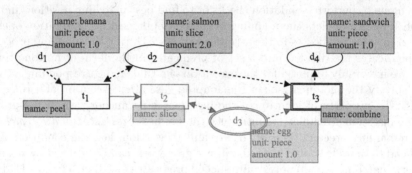

Fig. 4. Adaptation of a *NEST* Graph by Insertion.

alent rule according to the syntax of Drools Rule Language (DRL) after the mapping process. The *when* part describes the preconditions that need to be satisfied for execution, and the *then* part represents the modifications to be performed on the retrieved workflow graph. DRL provides multiple keywords, e. g., *not*, as well as the definition of variables, e. g., *$aC*, which can be matched to objects/facts during the activation of the precondition. In particular, these objects/facts, e. g., nodes and edges, are the items of the *NEST* graph that are inserted into the working memory of the engine. This working memory, also called *Fact Base*, acts as a storage for all facts known to the engine [3].

Listing 1. Adaptation Rule for an Insert Adaptation Operator.

```
1   rule "INSERT === Streamlet 7818 (Egg)"
2     when
3       not DataNode("egg")
4       $aC: TaskNode(isBestMatchingAnchor("mix", $aC, 1.0))
5     then
6       insertDataNode("egg", "piece", 1.0);
7       insertTaskNode("slice");
8       insertDataFlowEdge("slice", "egg");
9       insertDataFlowEdge("egg", "slice");
10      insertDataFlowEdge("egg", $aC);
11      insertControlFlowEdge("slice", $aC);
12  end
```

As already described, a streamlet consists of a head data node, an anchor task, and all other nodes that are linked to the anchor task. To represent adaptation operators that consist of these concepts, we apply the predicates presented in Fig. 3. In the example depicted in Fig. 4, the streamlet on the right side of Fig. 2 is encoded as an adaptation rule. In this example, we use the predicate *isBestMatchingAnchor* to determine the best possible anchor which has a similarity of 1.0 to the streamlet anchor *mix* (see Fig. 2). Assuming that the graph task node *combine* satisfies this condition, it is stored in the variable *$aC*. Subsequently, the plain streamlet consisting of the task *slice* and the data node one piece *egg* is inserted into the graph and connected to the other graph elements, including the newly identified anchor *$aC*. While rules as the one depicted in Lst. 1 are generated automatically, they can also be edited or created manually within the bounds of the domain vocabulary and the DRL syntax. This aspect also elicits explainability of adaptation knowledge, as knowledge encoded in rules is perceived to be more intuitive [20] as well as it provides insights into the adaptation process and its properties.

3.2 Applying Adaptation Rules

After encoding the adaptation rules, they can be applied to a retrieved workflow graph for adaptation. Figure 5 illustrates the general inference mechanism of the *Drools* rule engine for searching and triggering adaptation rules to adapt a retrieved workflow graph.   Each available and encoded rule is part of the *Fact Base* of *Drools*. In addition, the retrieved workflow graph is also part of the fact base, i.e., each graph element can be accessed to check or modify it during adaptation. To perform adaptations, *Drools* internally initiates an inference procedure that consists of several required steps for each adaptation rule contained in the fact base: 1) the preconditions encoded as predicates in a rule are accessed by the rule engine; 2) the graph elements of the retrieved workflow graph are checked whether they satisfy the preconditions of the corresponding rule; 3) if the preconditions of a rule are not satisfied, the next rule is checked. But if the preconditions are satisfied by the retrieved workflow, the rule is triggered by the rule engine; 4) the effects of the adaptation rule are executed, leading to

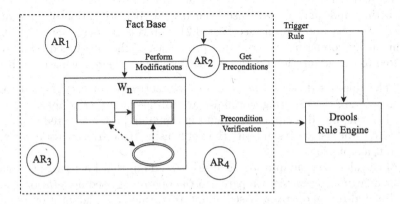

Fig. 5. General Inference Mechanism of the Rule Engine for Applying Adaptation Rules.

modifications performed on the graph elements of the retrieved workflow. The described search process is repeated by the rule engine until no further rule can be triggered, or the process is stopped externally, e. g., if the adaptation goal is already reached or the similarity as approximating function for the utility cannot be increased further. In general, it is difficult to find the best possible sequence of adaptation rules, i.e., the sequence that increases the similarity the most. Therefore, the best possible rules are determined step by step, similar to the application of adaptation operators (see Sect. 2.1). However, the application of adaptation operators considers each fragment of the retrieved graph only once, i.e., streamlets are sequentially created based on the data nodes of the workflow graph. In contrast, during adaptation with adaptation rules, the same fragment in the graph can be adapted more than once, depending on the availability of executable rules in the fact base. Finally, the rule engine needs to be aware of 1) the current state of the workflow (see Fig. 5), this involves all elements of the respective *NEST* workflow graph and, thus, all nodes and edges have to be inserted into the fact base; 2) every adaptation rule contained in the fact base; 3) all applicable adaptation rules for a given workflow state W_n by evaluating the preconditions of the rules; 4) the similarity improvement of the application of a rule w. r. t. the retrieved graph during rule evaluation.

4   Experimental Evaluation

In this section, we evaluate the rule-based approach in the domain of cooking recipes (see Sect. 2.1 for an example). Therefore, a direct comparison between the proposed approach and the existing adaptation operators [30] is conducted. In this context, it is important to note that Müller and Bergmann propose several POCBR adaptation methods (e. g., [28–30]). As the operator-based adaptation has the highest coverage, and it is the most sophisticated adaptation method, we apply it as the basis for the proposed approach in this work. The goal of the evaluation is to determine how well adaptations are performed by the rule-based approach and whether it leads to better and qualitative higher results. Differences in time and quality may arise from the varying utilization of adaptation knowledge in the application (see Sect. 3.2). For this purpose, we conduct an experiment by comparing the runtime properties of the rule-based adaptation compared to the adaptation operators and investigate the following hypotheses:

H1   The rule-based adaptation leads to syntactically correct adapted workflows, i.e., the resulting workflows are consistent *NEST* graphs.

H2   The rule-based adaptation results in equal or better adapted workflows w. r. t. the semantic similarity than only using the retrieved workflow without adaptation.

H3   The rule-based adaptation requires less adaptation knowledge to obtain similar improvements compared to the operator-based adaptation.

H4   Related to the operator-based adaptation, rule-based adaptation requires more time for adaptation, but achieves in relation much higher improvements, i.e., the improvement per time is higher.

Hypothesis **H1** investigates whether the rule-based adaptation maintains syntactically correctness of the workflow graphs. This property is retained by the operator-based adaptation, and, thus, should also be satisfied by the rule approach. Similarly to this, Hypothesis **H2** examines whether the rule-based approach leads to an improvement w.r.t. the similarity and not to a degradation. As the application of adaptation rules is not restricted to certain graph regions, we assume that less adaptation knowledge is required to obtain similar results compared to the adaptation operators (see Hypothesis **H3**). In addition, due to the different utilization of adaptation knowledge, and, thus, more executed rules in total than adaptation operators, we expect that the rule-based adaptation requires significant more adaptation time compared to the adaptation operators (see Hypothesis **H4**). However, it is expected that the improvement is higher in relation to the additional time needed, i.e., the improvement per time is higher.

4.1 Experimental Setup

In the following, we describe the experimental setup to validate the hypotheses. We perform a Leave One Out Cross Validation with a case base of 40 distinct cooking workflows. In this context, the cases in the case base contain on average 21.15 graph nodes and 55.63 graph edges. For the experiment, the rule-based adaptation approach is implemented in the POCBR framework ProCAKE[5] [6] using the *Drools* rule engine[6]. For each of the 40 workflows, we perform a retrieval on the remaining 39 recipes in the case base. Based on that, the retrieved workflows serve as a starting point for adaptation. The required adaptation knowledge is learned automatically based on the remaining case base by using the learning approach for the adaptation operators [30]. In this context, it is important to note that we ensure the separation of training and test cases by constructing a separate operator repository for every evaluation run. More precisely, the particular query workflow is omitted during learning of the respective repository. On average, the resulting repositories contain 2622.85 operators in total, out of which 1840.7 are exchange operators, 740.4 insert operators, and 41.75 delete operators. Based on these operator repositories, adaptation rules are encoded according to the concepts described in Sect. 3.1. To ensure comparable results, the same parameters that have been used during learning are also used for applying the rules and operators. This means that the *Anchor Candidate Threshold* Δ_T and the *Streamlet Similarity Threshold* Δ_S are set to be 0.5 for learning and applying the operators afterwards. Furthermore, the experiment is performed on growing fractions of the learned adaptation knowledge to observe effects related to the existing amount of adaptation knowledge regarding adaptation quality and time. Therefore, 20, 40, 60, and 80 percent of the operator repository are extracted randomly, and the experiment is conducted on each of those fractions independently. Moreover, we perform three runs for each fraction with different

---

[5] https://procake.uni-trier.de.
[6] The implementation can be found at: https://gitlab.rlp.net/procake/procake-rule-engine.

random seeds. For each of those runs, the minimum, maximum, and average as well as the median of the similarity gain and the adaptation time are recorded.

4.2   Experimental Results

Table 1 illustrates the results of the experiment[7]. All differences are statistically significant with $p < 0.05$ for runs conducted with 20% and $p < 0.01$ for the other fractions. We measured the improvement gained by adaptation in percent (see Column *Imp*) based on the semantic similarity measure (see Sect. 2.1), the time needed for adaptation in seconds (see Column *Time*), and the improvement per time, i.e., the improvement per second (see Column *Imp/s*). Furthermore, we evaluate several fractions of potential usable adaptation knowledge, i.e., 20%, 40%, 60%, 80%, and 100%. For every run with 40 adaptations, we calculate the values for all adaptations and represent them as minimum, maximum, average, and median. All performed adaptations either by the rule engine or by the adaptation operators lead to syntactically correct workflows, showing that the knowledge is valid and the application of it is correct. Thus, we accept Hypothesis **H1**. In Hypothesis **H2**, we investigate whether the application of the rule-based adaptation does not lead to a degradation of the retrieval result, i.e., the semantic similarity remains at least the same or increases after adaptation. As can be determined in the first row of Table 1, the minimum improvement is 0, indicating that at worst the adaptation leads to the retrieved workflow without changing anything. The same also holds for the operator-based adaptation. Consequently, we accept Hypothesis **H2**. Considering Hypothesis **H3** which addresses the amount of potential adaptation knowledge, it can be determined that if less adaptation knowledge is available, the rule-based adaptation results in higher improvements regarding the semantic similarity (see Column *Avg* and *Mdn* for 20%). In general, the results also indicate that the quality of adaptation increases with more potential usable adaptation knowledge, but more for the

Table 1. Results of the Experimental Evaluation.

		Amount of Potential Adaptation Knowledge														
		20%			40%			60%			80%			100%		
		Imp	Time	Imp/s	Imp	Time	Imp/s	Imp	Time	Imp/s	Imp	Time	Imp/s	Imp	Time	Imp/s
Rules	Min	0	0.3	0	0	0.6	0	0	2.1	0	0.02	2.6	0	0.02	3.4	0
	Max	29.28	208.3	14.59	31.52	493.6	4.21	30.67	1036.3	2.85	32.25	1497.4	2.12	31.52	1466	1.68
	Avg	9.78	29.1	1.04	11.99	74.6	0.62	13.02	111.7	0.45	13.69	162.4	0.35	14.27	208.4	0.28
	Mdn	9.42	11.47	0.43	11.91	23.93	0.24	13.74	42.3	0.17	14.44	53.2	0.14	14.95	85	0.12
Operators	Min	0	0.3	0	0	0.6	0	0	0.8	0	0	1.1	0	0	1.5	0
	Max	13.9	4.5	20.68	21.82	5.6	10.17	11.53	6.7	6.11	13.12	5.8	4.63	13.58	5.9	2.75
	Avg	2.38	1.1	2.26	2.59	1.6	1.35	2.59	2.2	1.07	2.78	2.6	0.91	2.83	3.2	0.76
	Mdn	0.58	0.8	0.49	0.81	1.3	0.58	1.18	2	0.53	1.51	2.5	0.65	1.62	2.9	0.55

---

[7] All evaluation results and descriptions of how to reproduce the experiment with the proposed implementation can be found at: https://gitlab.rlp.net/procake/publications/procake-rule-engine-iccbr-2024.

rules and only slightly for the operators. Consequently, the adaptation operators only lead to a small increase in improvement, even if the amount of adaptation knowledge increases. As the improvements are much higher for the rule-based adaptation compared to the adaptation operators with 20% of knowledge, we accept Hypothesis **H3**. However, the results also reveal that the rule-based adaptation requires much more time for adaptation than the adaptation operators. Examining the calculated improvements per second, it can be determined that the rule-based adaptation has mostly lower improvements per second than the adaptation operators. As a conclusion, the rule-based adaptation leads to significantly better results, but also requires considerably more time for doing that than the adaptation operators. For this reason, we reject Hypothesis **H4**.

5   Conclusion and Future Work

In this paper, we propose an approach for using adaptation rules and a rule engine for performing complex adaptations in Process-Oriented Case-Based Reasoning (POCBR). Based on previous adaptation methods for POCBR, we develop suitable predicates that are used for encoding adaptation knowledge as adaptation rules. This prevents the modeling and definition of adaptation knowledge in the form of complex graph fragments. Thus, it is now more feasible for domain experts to model workflow adaptation knowledge in POCBR as adaptation rules[8]. In addition, the experimental evaluation results demonstrate that the rule-based adaptation leads to syntactically correct workflows, and indicates that the improvement is significantly higher than for the operator-based adaptation [30]. By the proposed approach, we contribute to the complex task of workflow adaptation in POCBR and help to reduce the laborious and time-consuming task of modeling and maintaining this adaptation knowledge.

In future work, we want to implement further adaptation methods for POCBR (e. g., [28, 29]) by using adaptation rules. Moreover, the current implementation is based on the *Drools* rule engine, but the conceptual idea and the use of special predicates for representing the concepts of adaptation operators is also transferable to other available rule engines. In this context, it is also interesting to investigate how the rule-based approach can be integrated into other CBR and POCBR frameworks developed with other programming languages (e. g., Python [19]) instead of Java. Furthermore, the *Drools* rule engine also offers a graphical user interface for manually modeling and maintaining adaptation rules. Thus, we want to investigate how such a user interface can be integrated into the *ProCAKE* framework. Another topic for further research in this context is to examine how large language models can help in creating and modeling adaptation knowledge in CBR and POCBR [10]. In the experiments, we use the domain of cooking recipes as procedural semantic workflows. In future work, we intend to investigate also other workflow domains, such as for scientific workflows [36] or for

---

[8] An initial user study provides evidence to support this claim. The results of this user study can be found at: https://gitlab.rlp.net/procake/publications/procake-rule-engine-iccbr-2024.

cyber-physical workflows [21,22]. Both domains have in common that they often require complex, structural adaptations to ensure executability of the processes. Moreover, it should be examined how well the proposed rule-based adaptation approach can be applied to other case representations, such as time series in temporal CBR domains [23]. There are also possibilities for further improvement in the evaluation and application of the rules. For example, we are planning to use especially tailored search and optimization techniques for rule engines, which should further improve the use and application of adaptation rules, leading to even better workflow adaptation results.

Acknowledgments. This work is funded by the Federal Ministry for Economic Affairs and Climate Action under grant No. 01MD22002C *EASY*. The authors thank Veronika Kurchyna and Vincent Muljadi for an initial concept and prototypical implementation of the rule-based approach developed during a student research project.

References

1. Aamodt, A., Plaza, E.: Case-based reasoning: foundational issues, methodological variations, and system approaches. AI Commun. **7**(1), 39–59 (1994)
2. Bach, K., Althoff, K.: Developing Case-Based Reasoning Applications Using myCBR 3. In: 20th ICCBR. LNCS, vol. 7466, pp. 17–31. Springer (2012)
3. Bali, M.: Drools JBoss Rules 5.0 Developer's Guide: Develop Rules-based Business Logic Using the Drools Platform. From Technologies to Solutions. Packt Publ, Birmingham (2009)
4. Bergmann, R.: Experience Management: Foundations, Development Methodology, and Internet-Based Applications. LNCS, vol. 2432. Springer , Berlin, Heidelberg (2002). https://doi.org/10.1007/3-540-45759-3
5. Bergmann, R., Gil, Y.: Similarity assessment and efficient retrieval of semantic workflows. Inf. Syst. **40**, 115–127 (2014)
6. Bergmann, R., Grumbach, L., Malburg, L., Zeyen, C.: ProCAKE: a process-oriented case-based reasoning framework. In: 27th ICCBR Workshops (2019)
7. Bergmann, R., Kolodner, J.L., Plaza, E.: Representation in case-based reasoning. Knowl. Eng. Rev. **20**(3), 209–213 (2005)
8. Bergmann, R., Wilke, W., Vollrath, I., Wess, S.: Integrating general knowledge with object-oriented case representation and reasoning. In: 4th German Workshop: Case-Based Reasoning - System Development and Evaluation, pp. 120–126. Humboldt-Universität Berlin, Informatik-Berichte Nr. 55 (1996)
9. Berner, E.S.: Clinical Decision Support Systems: Theory and Practice, 2nd edn. Springer, Cham (2007). https://doi.org/10.1007/978-3-319-31913-1
10. Brand, F., Malburg, L., Bergmann, R.: Large language models as knowledge engineers. In: Proceedings of the Workshops at the 32nd International Conference on Case-Based Reasoning (ICCBR-WS 2024) co-located with the 32nd International Conference on Case-Based Reasoning (ICCBR 2024), Merida, Mexico, 1 July 2024. CEUR Workshop Proceedings, CEUR-WS.org (2024). Accepted for Publication
11. Cabrera, M.M., Edye, E.O.: Integration of Rule Based Expert Systems and Case Based Reasoning in an Acute Bacterial Meningitis Clinical Decision Support System. CoRR **abs/1003.1493** (2010)
12. Craw, S., Wiratunga, N., Rowe, R.: Learning adaptation knowledge to improve case-based reasoning. Artif. Intell. **170**(16–17), 1175–1192 (2006)

13. Döhring, M., Zimmermann, B., Godehardt, E.: Extended workflow flexibility using rule-based adaptation patterns with eventing semantics. In: INFORMATIK 2010. LNI, vol. P-175, pp. 195–200. GI (2010)
14. Fikes, R.E., Nilsson, N.J.: STRIPS: a new approach to the application of theorem proving to problem solving. Artif. Intell. **2**(3–4), 189–208 (1971)
15. Hanft, A., Schäfer, O., Althoff, K.D.: Integration of drools into an OSGI-based BPM-platform for CBR. In: 19th ICCBR Workshops (2011)
16. Hanney, K., Keane, M.T.: Learning adaptation rules from a case-base. In: Smith, I., Faltings, B. (eds.) EWCBR 1996. LNCS, vol. 1168, pp. 179–192. Springer, Heidelberg (1996). https://doi.org/10.1007/BFb0020610
17. Hanney, K., Keane, M.T.: The adaptation knowledge bottleneck: how to ease it by learning from cases. In: Leake, D.B., Plaza, E. (eds.) ICCBR 1997. LNCS, vol. 1266, pp. 359–370. Springer, Heidelberg (1997). https://doi.org/10.1007/3-540-63233-6_506
18. Leake, D.B.: CBR in Context: The Present and Future, chap. 1, pp. 3–30. AAAI Press/MIT Press, Cambridge (1996)
19. Lenz, M., Malburg, L., Bergmann, R.: CBRkit: an intuitive case-based reasoning toolkit for python. In: Recio-Garcia, J.A., et al. (eds.) ICCBR 2024, LNAI 14775, pp. 289–304. Springer, Cham (2024). https://doi.org/10.1007/978-3-031-63646-2_19
20. Ligeza, A.: Logical Foundations for Rule-Based Systems, Studies in Computational Intelligence, vol. 11. Springer, Berlin, Heidelberg (2006). https://doi.org/10.1007/3-540-32446-1
21. Malburg, L., Brand, F., Bergmann, R.: Adaptive management of cyber-physical workflows by means of case-based reasoning and automated planning. In: Sales, T.P., Proper, H.A., Guizzardi, G., Montali, M., Maggi, F.M., Fonseca, C.M. (eds.) Enterprise Design, Operations, and Computing. EDOC 2022 Workshops. EDOC 2022. LNBIP, vol. 466, pp. 79–95. Springer, Cham (2023). https://doi.org/10.1007/978-3-031-26886-1_5
22. Malburg, L., Hoffmann, M., Bergmann, R.: Applying MAPE-K control loops for adaptive workflow management in smart factories. J. Intell. Inf. Syst. 1–29 (2023)
23. Malburg, L., Schultheis, A., Bergmann, R.: Modeling and using complex IoT time series data in case-based reasoning: from application scenarios to implementations. In: 31st ICCBR Workshops, vol. 3438, pp. 81–96. CEUR-WS.org (2023)
24. Minor, M., Bergmann, R., Görg, S., Walter, K.: Towards case-based adaptation of workflows. In: Bichindaritz, I., Montani, S. (eds.) ICCBR 2010. LNCS (LNAI), vol. 6176, pp. 421–435. Springer, .: Towards Case-Based Adaptation of Workflows. (2010). https://doi.org/10.1007/978-3-642-14274-1_31
25. Minor, M., Bergmann, R., Görg, S.: Case-based adaptation of workflows. Inf. Syst. **40**, 142–152 (2014)
26. Minor, M., Montani, S., Recio-García, J.A.: Process-oriented case-based reasoning. Inf. Syst. **40**, 103–105 (2014)
27. Müller, G.: Workflow Modeling Assistance by Case-based Reasoning. Springer, Wiesbaden (2018). https://doi.org/10.1007/978-3-658-23559-8
28. Müller, G., Bergmann, R.: Workflow streams: a means for compositional adaptation in process-oriented CBR. In: Lamontagne, L., Plaza, E. (eds.) ICCBR 2014. LNCS (LNAI), vol. 8765, pp. 315–329. Springer, Cham (2014). https://doi.org/10.1007/978-3-319-11209-1_23
29. Müller, G., Bergmann, R.: Generalization of workflows in process-oriented case-based reasoning. In: 28th FLAIRS, pp. 391–396. AAAI Press (2015)

30. Müller, G., Bergmann, R.: Learning and applying adaptation operators in process-oriented case-based reasoning. In: Hüllermeier, E., Minor, M. (eds.) ICCBR 2015. LNCS (LNAI), vol. 9343, pp. 259–274. Springer, Cham (2015). https://doi.org/10.1007/978-3-319-24586-7_18

31. Pachet, F.: Reasoning with objects: the néopus environment. In: International Conference on East EurOOpe (1991)

32. Schultheis, A., Zeyen, C., Bergmann, R.: An overview and comparison of CBR frameworks. In: Massie, S., Chakraborti, S. (eds.) Case-Based Reasoning Research and Development. ICCBR 2023. LNCS, vol. 14141, pp. 327–343. Springer, Cham (2023). https://doi.org/10.1007/978-3-031-40177-0_21

33. Weber, B., Wild, W., Breu, R.: CBRFlow: enabling adaptive workflow management through conversational case-based reasoning. In: Funk, P., González Calero, P.A. (eds.) ECCBR 2004. LNCS (LNAI), vol. 3155, pp. 434–448. Springer, Heidelberg (2004). https://doi.org/10.1007/978-3-540-28631-8_32

34. Wilke, W., Bergmann, R.: Techniques and knowledge used for adaptation during case-based problem solving. In: Pasqual del Pobil, A., Mira, J., Ali, M. (eds.) IEA/AIE 1998. LNCS, vol. 1416, pp. 497–506. Springer, Heidelberg (1998). https://doi.org/10.1007/3-540-64574-8_435

35. Wilke, W., Vollrath, I., Althoff, K.D., Bergmann, R.: A framework for learning adaptation knowledge based on knowledge light approaches. In: 5th GWCBR, pp. 235–242 (1997)

36. Zeyen, C., Malburg, L., Bergmann, R.: Adaptation of scientific workflows by means of process-oriented case-based reasoning. In: Bach, K., Marling, C. (eds.) ICCBR 2019. LNCS (LNAI), vol. 11680, pp. 388–403. Springer, Cham (2019). https://doi.org/10.1007/978-3-030-29249-2_26

Visualization of Similarity Models for CBR Comprehension and Maintenance

Guillermo Jimenez-Diaz[(✉)] [iD] and Belén Díaz-Agudo[iD]

Department of Software Engineering and Artificial Intelligence Instituto de Tecnologías del Conocimiento, Universidad Complutense de Madrid, Madrid, Spain
{gjimenez,belend}@ucm.es

Abstract. Modeling similarity measures in Case-Based Reasoning systems is a critical and multifaceted task. Typically, similarity measures are manually defined, often with the input of domain experts or utilizing machine learning methods. These measures are then subjected to evaluation processes that include metrics that assess the properties of the retrieval and reuse processes on the case base. In this paper, we present SimViz, an exploratory visualization tool aimed at understanding and identifying errors in both data and similarity measures. Our tool represents an instance of Explainable Case-Based Reasoning, enabling interactive visualization through heatmaps and histograms and assisting in case comparison. These visualizations provide insight into the similarity between local and global attributes across different case representations.

Keywords: Case-Based Reasoning · Similarity · Visualization · Explanations · XCBR

1 Introduction

Case retrieval relies on similarity measures that can be complex and capture the knowledge of experts. The essence of similarity in Case-Based Reasoning (CBR) lies in its ability to encapsulate expert domain knowledge and capture nuanced details that may be challenging to articulate [18]. The similarity modeling in a CBR system can vary from simple to complex knowledge-intensive processes [2, 19] and the formulation of these measures can be a manual task undertaken by domain experts [21] or an automated process through Machine Learning (ML) techniques [9,14].

Although automated methods reduce the burden of knowledge acquisition, they may not comprehensively capture all necessary knowledge or may include errors, such as those stemming from data inaccuracies or empty values. Whether manually defined or learned through ML techniques, similarity measures need to be reviewed and adjusted manually. Visualization has been proven as a useful method for this task in different domains and CBR applications [10,12,13,21].

© The Author(s), under exclusive license to Springer Nature Switzerland AG 2024
J. A. Recio-Garcia et al. (Eds.): ICCBR 2024, LNAI 14775, pp. 67–80, 2024.
https://doi.org/10.1007/978-3-031-63646-2_5

In this paper, we present SimViz, a visualization tool designed to facilitate the comprehension of values, distribution, and calculation of (potentially complex) similarity measures. Visualizing similarity proves invaluable not only within CBR but also for analyzing and elucidating data, particularly their similarity relationships, both at the level of individual attributes and when combined, within any system dealing with structured data. SimViz is a generic and interactive tool that enhances the visualization and understanding of both data and similarity values themselves. SimViz has been successfully employed to investigate similarities between data in the SPICE project [5,6].

SimViz visualizes similarity values for structured data, which can be potentially complex and based on the typical local-global structure [18]. The use of the SimViz tool results in enhanced explainability that increases confidence, transparency, and an explainable approach to CBR (XCBR) [1].

Other tasks may also benefit from data and similarity visualization. For example, maintaining the quality of the case base requires a proactive and interactive approach to address issues such as case redundancy, quality, and diversity [15,16]. Exploring the similarity distribution of the case base also allows us to visually detect dimensions typically used in case-base maintenance, such as the coverage of a case or the reachability of a target problem [11,20], which are key to understanding competence in CBR [22].

The general objective of the research conducted in this paper is to determine how our visualization tool can help to achieve a better understanding of the data and the similarity computation. Additionally, the visualization may help to visually identify some maintenance problems of case bases, like case redundancy (similar or duplicate cases in the case base), case quality (cases that contain missing, incorrect, or irrelevant data), and reachability (the set of cases that can be used to solve a given query or target problem). We have conducted an evaluation on tasks related to understanding, correction, and completeness of a case base. The conclusions of our evaluation with users are very promising and show that SimViz is easy to use and useful for performing exploratory tasks related to the comprehension and maintenance of a case base, as well as the similarity functions developed to work with it.

The paper runs as follows. Section 2 discusses related work on visualization in CBR systems. The requirements for useful visualizations in CBR tasks are established from the literature and described in Sect. 3. We describe the SimViz tool in Sect. 4, using data from case studies in the CBR domain and a case study of the SPICE project. Then, we explain how SimViz is used to address the proposed requirements and evaluate its usability with users. The user evaluation conducted to validate the usability of SimViz according to the previously defined requirements is described in Sect. 5. Finally, the paper discusses limitations, conclusions, and our future work.

2   Related Work

Visualization is an extended approach used in the CBR domain to explore and analyze different aspects of the CBR process. Many authors utilize visualization techniques to explain, comprehend, and refine similarity measures, aiming to make similarities more accessible and to instill confidence in different CBR domains and applications. Several works [3,12] propose visualization methods based on bar charts to explain the similarity-based retrieval in the health domain. These visualizations show the most similar cases for a given query, their similarity values, and the impact of each attribute in a global weighted similarity function. However, the specific attribute values for each case are not visualized. Therefore, this approach does not help to understand the underlying reasons for the observed values. Moreover, these approaches hinder the comparison between the query attribute values with the ones contained in similar cases. These weaknesses have been tackled during the design of SimViz.

The work in [10] describes another alternative to provide visual explanations of the similarity scores between a query and the retrieved cases. These visualizations are based on scatter plots and rainbow boxes and are focused on the final users (medical experts) of the CBR system. This is the main difference with SimViz, which is focused on the experts involved in the development of the similarity measures and some maintenance tasks in the case base. Additionally, we think that the complexity of the used visualization led authors to simplify and reduce the dimensions and the information displayed by the tool. This way, the evaluation with the final users found out that the visualization was easy to understand, but required short training before using it. SimViz focuses on using well-known visualization methods, like heatmaps and histograms, to reduce the learning curve and ease the understanding of the visualization. Additionally, it tries to balance the maximization of the information displayed and the minimization of data overwhelming, using basic tables and interactive filters.

Another visualization-based approach for engineering similarity measures in Process-Oriented Case-Based Reasoning (POCBR) is described in [21]. The authors evaluate various visualization methods concerning derived requirements for visualizations in POCBR with domain experts and conclude that graph mapping visualization is the most suitable for engineering similarity models in POCBR for complex cases. This proposal stands out for the visualization of complex similarities based on nested similarity measures, accessible through visualizations applied to POCBR. Our approach is used for case descriptions in a tabular format. Like the cited work, SimViz visualizes similarity measures based on the local-global principle, although, in our approach, we focus on visualizing the data and the final similarity value (rather than the intermediate values) like in [4], where the focus is not on the similarity measure itself, but rather on the distribution of the individual similarity values. Additionally, our approach is not focused on a specific domain, and it can be used in a broader range of CBR systems. It has been designed starting on more general case descriptions, but it is planned to extend it to more complex cases.

The visualization of the case base content for case base maintenance has been previously investigated in the existing literature. Most of them [17,23] rely on the use of graphs and spring force models to reduce the complexity of representing similarity measures over n-dimensional cases. The distance between cases in a two-dimensional space represents their similarity. This visualization is useful to recognize regions of similar cases, and holes without representative cases or outliers. However, this visualization method is useful only with a small number of cases, due to the complexity of representing all the crossing edges between cases, and the performance of the spring force models with a high number of nodes. Moreover, these graphs can raise the described problems but they are not able to explain the reasons behind them. Our approach displays the similarity values between all cases in the case base using heatmaps. Other works in the literature use heatmaps to visualize similarity distributions in the case base [15,21]. This visualization can also help to detect some of the problems described before, helping with the maintenance tasks associated with the case base. However, we do not discard the use of this visualization method as a complement to the approaches currently used.

Finally, we want to highlight the main difference between SimViz and other visualization tools mentioned in the literature, which is its generality. SimViz has been designed not only to be used for a specific domain, but for a broader range of CBR problems. Currently, it is limited to a global weighted similarity function, but it could be easily extended to more complex ones. Additionally, it can be applied to different case bases and is publicly available for the CBR community, as we will describe in Sect. 4.

3   Visualization Requirements

Based on the literature review and inspired by the requirements identified in [21] for visualization techniques in the POCBR domain, we have formulated our list of requirements that the visualization might fulfill for helping (1) to achieve a better understanding of the data and similarity measures, and (2) to identify some maintenance problems of case bases. This list is more generalized, it removes the requirements that were specific to POCBR, and it adds the requirements related to assisting in some case-base maintenance tasks. These requirements are the following:

Req 1. Generic Visualization for Different Datasets and Similarity Functions: With the visualization, the user could easily compare different similarity functions over the same dataset. Moreover, the visualization should work over different datasets and use some of the standard datatypes employed in case representation.

Req 2. Explanation for Resulting Similarity: As described in [21] "the visualization should comprehensibly justify the calculated similarity value and its composition". The visualization should also explain local similarities by displaying their values and describing the measures used for their calculation.

Req 3. Comparison with other cases: As described in [21] "the visualization should include pairwise visualizations to provide comparison between cases".

Req 4. Exploration of the Similarity Distribution for Individual Cases: It should be easy to explore the similarity distribution for a given case against the other cases in the case base. This will help to understand how similarity measures work on specific cases and if it is consistent in similar/different cases.

Req 5. Exploratory Evaluation of the Case Base Competence: Exploring the similarity distribution of the case base allows us to visually detect dimensions typically used in case base maintenance, such as the coverage of a case or the reachability of a target problem [11,20]. We simplify these dimensions to the observation of the set of similar cases given a target problem. Of course, it should be clear that these metrics are not only dependent on the similarity but also on the characteristics of the particular retrieval and adaptation methods.

Req 6. Detection of Potential Case Issues: The visualization should help to identify errors in cases (for example, missing or redundant values) or *edge-cases*, like cases in cold start –whose similarity with other cases is 0– or redundant cases –which are similar to most of the cases in the case base.

Req 7. Detection of Potential Similarity Issues: The visualization should help to find errors in the similarity calculation (e.g. unexpected global or local similarity values for the whole case base).

Req. 8 Flexible Changes of Similarity Measures: As described in [21] "To be able to estimate the influence of used similarity measures on the overall similarity value, the visualization should provide interactive features for a flexible adjustment of these measures". More specifically, the visualization should provide interactive features for a flexible adjustment of the weights involved in the computation of the global measure to estimate the influence of the local similarity functions.

4 SimViz Tool

Following the requirements described in Sect. 3, we have designed and implemented SimViz (**Sim**ilarity **Vi**suali**Z**ation), a tool focused on the interactive visualization of similarity functions and how they are computed over different case bases. A runnable release of SimViz[1] is available at https://gjimenezucm. github.io/simviz/.

SimViz is an online tool that runs on a web browser. The main interface of SimViz (Fig. 1) is organized in three columns or panels:

– *Similarity selection and description* panel (left): Users employ this panel to select a case base to visualize and to choose a similarity function over this case base.

---

[1] Its source code is also available at https://github.com/gjimenezUCM/simviz under Apache 2.0 License.

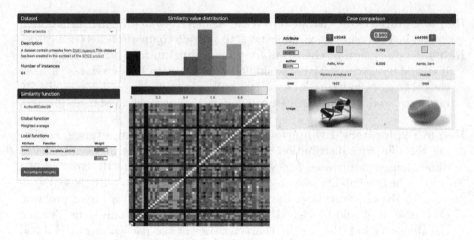

Fig. 1. Overview of SimViz (available at https://gjimenezucm.github.io/simviz/).

- *Similarity value distribution* panel (middle): a heatmap and a histogram show how similarity values are distributed over the case base. Both are interactive and will help to explore the cases and similarity values.
- *Case comparison panel* (right): a table displaying two cases selected using the similarity value distribution panel. The global similarity value is displayed on the header, while the local similarity values and the attributes involved in the similarity calculation are displayed in rows, with a bar indicating the attribute weight in the leftmost cell of each row.

Based on the requirements presented in Sect. 3, we will continue to describe the tool. The use of the *Similarity selection and description* panel (Fig. 2, left) partially fulfills **Req. 1**. Right now, with SimViz users can explore four different datasets. Three of them are usually employed in the CBR domains (Blood Alcohol Domain [7], Breast Cancer Wisconsin [10] and Travel Agent[2]) and they use some basic local similarity metrics for numbers and nominal attribute values. The last two are used to test the tool performance with medium-sized datasets (about 900 cases). An additional case base called *DMH dataset* was created in the context of the SPICE project[3] and it contains 64 artwork descriptions from the Design Museum Helsinki. This dataset was the seed for the design of SimViz because the museum domain imposed the definition of new similarity functions for color perception and emotions [6] and this tool was employed to explore and test these new measures during the development.

Similarity data is computed offline using a weighted average as a global similarity function and predefined local similarity functions over the attributes of the cases contained in a case base. Although we cannot change the local similarity functions or add new datasets, SimViz defines metadata files and structured

---

[2] Available at https://ai-cbr.cs.auckland.ac.nz/cases.html.

[3] https://spice-h2020.eu/.

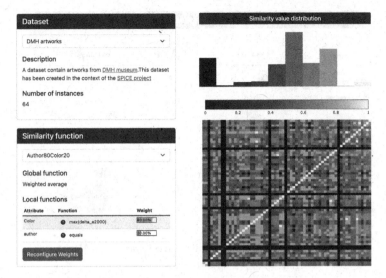

Fig. 2. SimViz interface details: *Similarity selection and description* (left) and *Similarity value distribution* panel (right).

information to easily build similarity data that can be analyzed using this tool. Right now, the case base and the similarity information are enriched with information about attribute datatypes, local similarity functions, weights for global similarity functions, and user explanations,[4] so this model can be reused for other case base exemplars. This process will need further extensions to completely fulfill **Req. 1**.

According to **Req. 2**, the similarity metadata described above is employed in the *Similarity selection and Description* panel to display a description of the global function, the attributes involved in the similarity calculations, and their weights (Fig. 2, bottom left). Additionally, a "question mark icon" next to the local similarity function describes how this function is computed. This information is complemented with actual similarity values for the local and global functions over pairs of cases using the *Case comparison* panel (Fig. 3). This panel is also designed according to **Req. 3** for displaying both cases with their attributes and similarity values in a layout that eases the comparison of them.

The heatmap and the histogram displayed in the *Similarity value distribution* panel (Fig. 2, right) are used to visually explore the distribution of similarity values over the case base, as requested by **Req. 4** and **Req. 5**. Moreover, they are used to select which cases are displayed in the *Case comparison* panel. On one hand, users can click on a cell in the heatmap (Fig. 2, bottom right) to select the pair of cases represented in that cell. With large datasets, users can zoom over the heatmap for more details. On the other hand, clicking on a histogram

---

[4] The **data** folder in SimViz repository contains a notebook with some examples about how the current data was created to be visualized in the tool.

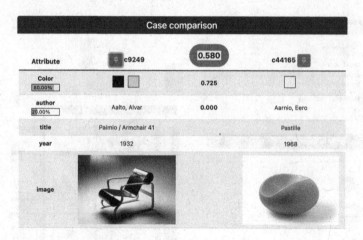

Fig. 3. SimViz interface details: *Case comparison* Panel.

bar (Fig. 2, top right) will randomly select a pair of cases whose similarity fits in the range represented by that bar.

Moreover, an interactive stripe chart (Fig. 4, left) is used for visualizing the similarity values of a specific case against the other cases in the case base (**Req. 4**). This chart is displayed using the "pin icon" next to its case *id* in the *Case Comparison* table header (Fig. 3). The similarity values of this item with the remaining cases in the case base are displayed when the mouse pointer is over the stripes, and more details can be requested by clicking on a stripe and displaying the corresponding case in the *Case comparison* panel.

Req. 6 and **Req. 7** are fulfilled with a combination of the *Similarity value distribution* (Fig. 2, right) and the *Case comparison* (Fig. 3) panels. Darker rows (or columns) in the heatmap represent cases with uniformly low similarity values, and thus missing values. Additionally, according to **Req. 6**, empty values are displayed in the *Case comparison* panel, and the stripe chart helps to find errors in case attributes. According to **Req. 7**, histogram helps to highlight wrongly distributed similarity values, which generally can represent a problem with the similarity function. As darker rows (or columns) represent cases with low similarity values with other cases, light stripes may represent cases with high similarity values with the remaining cases in the case base, thus helping to find edge cases. More details can be observed by selecting random cases using the histogram and analyzing the values displayed on the *Case comparison* panel.

Finally, SimViz fulfills **Req. 8** with a *Similarity configuration panel* (Fig. 4, right), where the user can change the weights of a local similarity function and compare the effect on the global similarity value. This way, we can easily recalculate the global weighted average similarity function on the client side –the browser. As described above, local similarity functions cannot be modified, but this is a feature that will be discussed in the Future Work Section.

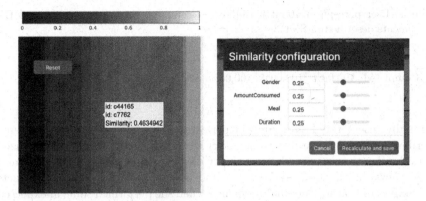

Fig. 4. Additional panels in SimViz: A stripe chart for the Pastille artwork (id: c44165) in the DMH dataset (left), and the Similarity configuration panel (right), for changing the weights on a similarity function.

5 Evaluation

The evaluation examines the hypothesis that the designed visualization tool is suitable for understanding how a similarity model performs over a case base, and for identifying some maintenance problems of case bases, both in cases and in similarity functions.

5.1 Experimental Setup

The evaluation was performed using a task-oriented usability study [8]. This method is built around a real task and scenario to simulate the real user experience and encourage users to interact with the tool naturally. Evaluation participants were provided with a short video tutorial about how to use the tool. Participants were then asked to complete a task using SimViz. Rather than forcing participants to interact with a specific feature, the evaluation scenarios were designed to propose a task in context and see how the user chooses to use the tool. Every evaluation task is correlated with at least one of the requirements described in Sect. 3. The task context was defined by asking the participant to select a case base and to focus on one or more similarity functions for that case base. The tasks were defined in form of user perception questions, like "Can you find cases that have problems when using this similarity function?" or "Do you understand what is the problem with this case?". Participants' responses to these questions allow us to find out whether they feel that they can complete the task successfully.

Each evaluation session was recorded and a facilitator was present throughout the session, taking notes based on observation and providing help if SimViz registered any bug. The facilitator did not help participants to complete any task. Afterwards, notes and recorded videos were analyzed to provide descriptions of problems encountered by users.

Table 1. User perception about if they could complete the tasks, according to the requirements described in Sect. 3

	Req. 2	Req. 5	Req. 3	Req. 4	Req. 6	Req. 7	Req. 8
Completed	100,00%	100,00%	100,00%	100,00%	83,33%	66,67%	83,33%

Finally, users rated how SimViz performs according to the requirements described in Sect. 3 using five-point Likert scale. After that, facilitator finalized the evaluation session with a short interview, to reconstruct the user's mental model –how she thinks SimViz works– and understand why the user interacts with SimViz in that way or what happened when she performed some unexpected behaviours.

5.2   Results and Discussion

The evaluation was completed by a total of 6 researchers, who are experts or familiar with the main concepts of CBR that are involved in the design of SimViz: cases, case bases, and global and local similarity functions. Overall, the tool is easy to use and is highly valued by users, especially after the facilitator-led interview, which helped to resolve questions that arose during the use of the tool.

It is worth noting that Req. 1 was not explicitly evaluated during the evaluation sessions. Most of the tasks consisted of selecting a dataset and one or two similarity functions and nobody had any problem performing this task. Then, we can consider that the users could easily compare different similarity functions and different datasets. However, we did not evaluate if the users could create their similarity functions on their datasets because this is an offline process that involves programming.

According to the rest of the requirements, users rated the tool very positively. Figure 5 shows the results of the Likert scale questionnaire about how users perceive whether SimViz fulfills the proposed requirements. These results are mostly correlated with the task completion figures. Table 1 summarizes the results of users' perception of whether they could complete the tasks that were aligned with the requirements described in Sect. 3. Most of the users could complete most of the tasks. However, some users had issues with the tasks aligned with Req. 6, 7, and 8.

The task aligned with Req. 7 (*Detection of Similarity Issues*) was the lowest percentage of perceived completion, potentially due to task complexity. The task was to find out which similarity function was not working properly for the Travel Agent case base. Both similarity functions were implemented over the Season/Month attribute. The first one was implemented as a common nominal range function (where January-December values have the lowest similarity, as they are the extremes of the range), while the second was implemented taking into account the cyclical nature of the seasons/months (where January-December values have a high similarity value). In the interviews after the evaluation, we

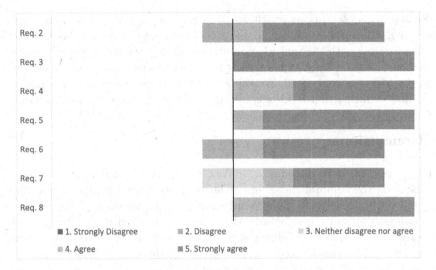

Fig. 5. Distribution of the level of agreement about how SimViz fulfills the requirements described in Sect. 3

found out that most of the users understood which similarity function performed correctly but they were not sure about that when working on the task. We think that the task was complex without a deeper background on the dataset, so we should modify it and run more evaluations to corroborate this statement.

According to Req. 6 (*Detection of Case Issues*), the user who could not complete the task and rated it with a low score explained that she could not find the missing values in the case comparison table. We have improved this visualization by adding a badge in red with a "NULL" label inside to represent missing values and highlight them.

We can also see that one user could not complete the task aligned with Req. 8 (*Flexible Changes of Similarity Measures*). However, if we compare it with the scoring in Fig. 5, we can see that Req. 8 is mostly perceived as fulfilled by all participants. During the final interview, the user who perceived that she could not complete the task related to modifying the weights of the global similarity function explained that it was confusing that the weights could be modified and they could sum to more than 1.0, so she was not sure that she could complete the task correctly (although she perceived that she could adjust the weights to estimate the influence of the local similarity functions).

Other key issues that emerged during the experimental evaluation include challenges in understanding the use of the stripe chart and concerns about the clarity of certain icons, such as the "pin" icon on the *Case Comparison Table* and the "?" icon next to the description of the similarity function. The last one is related to the low score (in yellow) presented in Req. 2 (see Fig. 5), because the user who did not understand the local similarity functions did not have access to its description (displayed when clicking on this icon).

Finally, the observations concluded that SimViz engages users in the exploration of the similarity values and the case base content. As long as the users spent more time with the tool, they interacted more with the different elements of its interface to deeply explore the cases and the similarity functions, even when the task was completed. We think that this engagement is a very positive result that confirms that SimViz is useful for the goals proposed in this paper.

6 Conclusions

In this paper, we have introduced SimViz, a versatile visualization tool aimed at enhancing the comprehension of similarity measures within structured data. The tool not only helps to understand similarity relationships at the attribute level but also provides insight into the combined similarity of data elements. By using it, we increase confidence and transparency in Case-Based Reasoning. Successful applications in projects such as SPICE demonstrate its effectiveness beyond CBR. SimViz shows promise for various tasks, including proactive case base maintenance. By addressing the need for better comprehension and error identification in similarity computation, SimViz contributes to improved data quality and maintenance processes. Evaluation results indicate its ease of use and effectiveness in supporting exploratory tasks related to understanding and maintaining case bases, as well as facilitating the analysis of similarity functions. SimViz is easy to use and available for the CBR community.

Our future research will focus on addressing the challenges inherent in identifying similarities in complex domains such as text, ontologies, graphs, time series, and processes. Key areas for further development include refining local and global similarity measures, improving explanatory capabilities within local similarity functions, and developing interactive tools that allow users to encode similarity functions. This implies the implementation of server-side infrastructure for computing both local and global similarity functions, alongside the establishment of efficient communication protocols between clients and servers. Rigorous evaluations will be conducted to validate the efficacy and applicability of these advancements across diverse domains, fostering practical applications in fields ranging from medicine to engineering.

Acknowledgments. Supported by the UCM (Research Group 921330) and the PERXAI project PID2020-114596RB-C21, funded by the Ministry of Science and Innovation of Spain (MCIN/AEI/10.13039/501100011033).

References

1. XCBR: Workshop on Case-Based Reasoning for the Explanation of Intelligent Systems. In: Proceedings of the Workshops at the 31st International Conference on Case-Based Reasoning (ICCBR-WS 2023) co-located with the 31st International Conference on Case-Based Reasoning (ICCBR 2023), Aberdeen, Scotland, UK, July 17, 2023. CEUR Workshop Proceedings, vol. 3438. CEUR-WS.org (2023)

2. Aamodt, A.: Knowledge-intensive case-based reasoning in CREEK. In: Funk, P., González Calero, P.A. (eds.) ECCBR 2004. LNCS (LNAI), vol. 3155, pp. 1–15. Springer, Heidelberg (2004). https://doi.org/10.1007/978-3-540-28631-8_1

3. Bach, K., Mork, P.J.: On the explanation of similarity for developing and deploying CBR systems. In: Barták, R., Bell, E. (eds.) Proceedings of the Thirty-Third International Florida Artificial Intelligence Research Society Conference, Originally to be held in North Miami Beach, Florida, USA, 17–20 May 2020, pp. 413–416. AAAI Press (2020). https://aaai.org/ocs/index.php/FLAIRS/FLAIRS20/paper/view/18472

4. Batyrshin, I.Z., Kubysheva, N.I., Solovyev, V.D., Villa-Vargas, L.A.: Visualization of similarity measures for binary data and 2 × 2 tables. Computación y Sistemas **20**(3), 345–353 (2016).https://doi.org/10.13053/CYS-20-3-2457

5. Daga, E., et al.: Integrating citizen experiences in cultural heritage archives: requirements, state of the art, and challenges. ACM J. Comput. Cult. Herit. **15**(1), 11:1–11:35 (2022). https://doi.org/10.1145/3477599

6. Díaz-Agudo, B., Jimenez-Diaz, G., Jorro-Aragoneses, J.L.: User evaluation to measure the perception of similarity measures in artworks. In: Sánchez-Ruiz, A.A., Floyd, M.W. (eds.) ICCBR 2021. LNCS (LNAI), vol. 12877, pp. 48–63. Springer, Cham (2021). https://doi.org/10.1007/978-3-030-86957-1_4

7. Doyle, D., Cunningham, P., Coyle, L.: Blood Alcohol Content Domain (2023). https://github.com/gateslm/Blood-Alcohol-Domain. Accessed 30 Apr 2024

8. Hertzum, M.: Usability Testing: A Practitioner's Guide to Evaluating the User Experience. Synthesis Lectures on Human-Centered Informatics, Springer, Switzerland (2020). https://doi.org/10.1007/978-3-031-02227-2

9. Hoffmann, M., Bergmann, R.: Informed Machine Learning for Improved Similarity Assessment in Process-Oriented Case-Based Reasoning. CoRR **abs/2106.15931** (2021)

10. Lamy, J., Sekar, B.D., Guézennec, G., Bouaud, J., Séroussi, B.: Explainable artificial intelligence for breast cancer: a visual case-based reasoning approach. Artif. Intell. Med. **94**, 42–53 (2019). https://doi.org/10.1016/J.ARTMED.2019.01.001

11. Leake, D.B., Smyth, B., Wilson, D.C., Yang, Q.: Introduction to the special issue on maintaining case-based reasoning systems. Comput. Intell. **17**(2), 193–195 (2001). https://doi.org/10.1111/0824-7935.00139

12. Marín-Veites, P., Bach, K.: Explaining CBR systems through retrieval and similarity measure visualizations: a case study. In: Keane, M.T., Wiratunga, N. (eds.) Case-Based Reasoning Research and Development - 30th International Conference, ICCBR 2022, Nancy, France, 12–15 September 2022, Proceedings. LNCS, vol. 13405, pp. 111–124. Springer, Cham (2022). https://doi.org/10.1007/978-3-031-14923-8_8

13. Massie, S., Craw, S., Wiratunga, N.: A visualisation tool to explain case-base reasoning solutions for tablet formulation. In: Macintosh, A., Ellis, R., Allen, T. (eds.) Applications and Innovations in Intelligent Systems XII, LNCS. SGAI 2004, pp. 222–234. Springer, London (2005). https://doi.org/10.1007/1-84628-103-2_16

14. Mathisen, B.M., Aamodt, A., Bach, K., Langseth, H.: Learning similarity measures from data. Prog. Artif. Intell. **9**(2), 129–143 (2020). https://doi.org/10.1007/s13748-019-00201-2

15. McArdle, G., Wilson, D.: Visualising case-base usage. In: Workshop Proceedings of the 5th International Conference on Case-Based Reasoning, pp. 105–114. NTNU (2003)

16. McKenna, E., Smyth, B.: An interactive visualisation tool for case-based reasoners. Appl. Intell. **14**(1), 95–114 (2001). https://doi.org/10.1023/A:1008359125752

17. Namee, B.M., Delany, S.J.: CBTV: visualising case bases for similarity measure design and selection. In: Bichindaritz, I., Montani, S. (eds.) ICCBR 2010. LNCS (LNAI), vol. 6176, pp. 213–227. Springer, Heidelberg (2010). https://doi.org/10.1007/978-3-642-14274-1_17

18. Ontañón, S.: An overview of distance and similarity functions for structured data. Artif. Intell. Rev. **53**(7), 5309–5351 (2020). https://doi.org/10.1007/S10462-020-09821-W

19. Puga, G.F., Díaz-Agudo, B., González-Calero, P.A.: Similarity measures in hierarchical behaviours from a structural point of view. In: Guesgen, H.W., Murray, R.C. (eds.) Proceedings of the Twenty-Third International Florida Artificial Intelligence Research Society Conference, 19–21 May 2010, Daytona Beach, Florida, USA. AAAI Press (2010). http://www.aaai.org/ocs/index.php/FLAIRS/2010/paper/view/1221

20. Reinartz, T., Iglezakis, I., Roth-Berghofer, T.: On quality measures for case base maintenance. In: Blanzieri, E., Portinale, L. (eds.) EWCBR 2000. LNCS, vol. 1898, pp. 247–260. Springer, Heidelberg (2000). https://doi.org/10.1007/3-540-44527-7_22

21. Schultheis, A., Hoffmann, M., Malburg, L., Bergmann, R.: Explanation of similarities in process-oriented case-based reasoning by visualization. In: Massie, S., Chakraborti, S. (eds.) Case-Based Reasoning Research and Development. ICCBR 2023. LNCS, vol. 14141, pp. 53–68. Springer, Cham (2023). https://doi.org/10.1007/978-3-031-40177-0_4

22. Smyth, B., McKenna, E.: Competence models and the maintenance problem. Comput. Intell. **17**(2), 235–249 (2001). https://doi.org/10.1111/0824-7935.00142

23. Smyth, B., Mullins, M., McKenna, E.: Picture perfect - visualisation techniques for case-based reasoning. In: Proceedings of the 14th European Conference on Artificial Intelligence, pp. 65–69. ECAI'00, IOS Press (2000)

Use Case-Specific Reuse of XAI Strategies: Design and Analysis Through an Evaluation Metrics Library

Marta Caro-Martínez(✉) ⓘ, Jesús M. Darias ⓘ, Belén Díaz-Agudo ⓘ,
and Juan A. Recio-García ⓘ

Department of Software Engineering and Artificial Intelligence,
Universidad Complutense de Madrid, Madrid, Spain
{martcaro,jdarias,belend,jareciog}@ucm.es

Abstract. Nowadays, we have access to a good number of eXplainable Artificial Intelligence libraries and techniques aimed at providing explanations for users to comprehend black-box intelligent systems. However, this presents a double-edged sword: while we can access a wide catalogue of explanation possibilities, determining the most suitable explanation method for a specific situation remains a challenging decision-making task. The iSee project was conceived with the primary goal of constructing a platform where users can share their own experiences with explanations and their successful explanation strategies. Through this CBR platform, other users can leverage these solutions for their own explanation needs, obtaining the most suitable explanation solutions regarding their requirements. In this paper, our focus lies on the reuse step of the CBR cycle. We have developed and implemented constructive reuse approaches, consisting of various methods to assist design users in adapting their solutions to specific use cases and end users. We have validated the applicability of the resulting solutions and introduced an evaluation metrics library designed to assess explanation strategies. Using this library, we have evaluated system solutions based on various key features including computational complexity, popularity, uniformity, diversity, serendipity, and granularity.

Keywords: eXplainable Artificial Intelligence · Explanation Strategies · Constructive Reuse · Evaluation Metrics · Case-Based Reasoning

1 Introduction

The concept of eXplainable Artificial Intelligence (XAI) endeavors to increase the interpretability of Artificial Intelligence (AI) systems for human comprehension. The iSee project[1] employs the Case-Based Reasoning (CBR) methodology

---

[1] iSee project web page: https://isee4xai.com/.

J. A. Recio-Garcia et al. (Eds.): ICCBR 2024, LNAI 14775, pp. 81–95, 2024.
https://doi.org/10.1007/978-3-031-63646-2_6

to enhance the AI system explainability by facilitating reuse of XAI experiences elevating the level of abstraction in the explanation processes. The iSee platform [9] facilitates users of AI capturing, sharing, reusing and evaluating their XAI experiences with other users who have similar explanation needs. This way, users can find the previous successful explanation strategies that better fit their needs among the wide offer of explanation techniques available.

Moreover, the iSee project promotes best practices in explainable AI through the use of different algorithms to discover and reuse explanation strategies, which implement the main steps of a CBR cycle (retrieve, reuse, revise and retain). In previous research we have described the case representation structure based on an ontology [3] and different similarity metrics for retrieving explanation strategies [3,4,14,15]. In this paper, we focus on the reuse and evaluation steps. After retrieval, the CBR system needs to adapt the solution of the most similar case to the query. In iSee, the *case solution* is an explanation strategy that is modified to apply to the situation described in the *case description*. This way, we are making our solution use case- and user-specific. Reusable explanation strategies are formalised through Behaviour Trees (BTs) augmented with terminology from the iSee ontology.

The contribution of this paper is twofold. First, we propose use case- and user-specific constructive reuse methods based on the applicability of explanation strategies. These methods are manual, guided and automatic adaptation approaches. Second, we define a set of metrics for the evaluation of the explanation strategies themselves according to different criteria: computational complexity, popularity, uniformity, diversity, serendipity, and granularity. This evaluation metrics library is not specific to the iSee strategies, but it will be useful to evaluate any explanation strategy understood as a combination of explainers and other workflow components. Therefore, it can be a useful tool for the XAI community. In a different paper, we deal with the problem of evaluating the quality of the output (i.e., the explanation itself) generated by post-hoc methods[2]. However, in this current paper, we do not evaluate the explanations outputs, but we have validated the applicability of the explanation strategies obtained with our use case- and user-specific reuse methodology. Moreover, we have used our library to evaluate different features within those XAI strategies. The results lead us to think that these metrics are a powerful tool to personalise the reuse step according to user needs to have strategies with different values for those features.

The paper is structured as follows. First, we study the related work briefly (Sect. 2). Next, we describe the CBR cycle that drives iSee (Sect. 3). In Sect. 4, we describe our reuse approaches, and all the modalities implemented to carry them out. Later, Sect. 5 defines all the explanation strategy evaluation metrics that we propose. We evaluate the reuse results' applicability and the benefits of the metrics library in Sect. 6. We finish the work extracting some conclusions in Sect. 7.

---

[2] Accepted at ICCBR 2024 [5].

2   Related Work

Although there are several libraries of explanation methods, for example, IBM Research's AI Explainability 360[3], none comes with the kinds of representations of applicability and suitability conditions that iSee provides. iSee offers not only a library of algorithms to explain AI, but also with the tools to build personalised XAI experiences. Moreover, none of them are driven by CBR, which makes iSee and its procedures a novelty in the field.

Regarding reuse methodologies, we can find previous work where a new approach to adapt workflows automatically is introduced [10]. However, there are no previous papers in the literature that work on adapting BTs, let alone papers that focus on use case- and user-specific reuse approaches for XAI strategies.

Concerning evaluation metrics for XAI, we can find a quite variety of works that propose metrics to evaluate explanations. They are subjective or objective, centred on online or offline evaluations [1,2]. These works are focused on evaluating explanations themselves, i.e., the result of applying a specific explainer. What we propose in our paper is a set of metrics that evaluate the explanation strategy as a whole, where we include several and different explanation procedures to satisfy users' explanation experiences. That is the novelty of our work since we cannot find previous papers in the state of the art that have looked into this topic.

3   Case-Based Reasoning in the iSee Project

The iSee project platform is based on CBR, which drives the methodology to capture the explanation experience requirements and provide users with the tools to get the best explanation strategy to apply to their experience [15]. iSee also provides tools that allow users to share their own explanation experiences for other users to take advantage of. The main CBR cycle components and procedures are the following:

- **Requirements capture**. To obtain the best explanation strategy to apply in a specific explanation experience, we have developed iSeeOnto [3], an ontology that defines all the concepts and relationships for describing an experience of that kind. The ontology is used to define the requirements that the design users need to include when they want to get a solution (an explanation strategy) that satisfies their explanation needs. These concepts are going to be needed in the retrieval and reuse steps.
- **Case representation**. Cases are defined through the vocabulary from the iSeeOnto ontology [3]. The case description includes knowledge about the AI model, the AI task to explain, the explanation requirements, the explanation evaluation needs, and the user context, intentions, expectations, and satisfaction levels with prior explanations. The case solution is an *explanation*

---

[3] https://aix360.res.ibm.com/.

strategy defined as a BT of XAI methods, that also includes other work-flow definition components, and their further customisation according to the actual users' needs and the explanation context [9]. In iSee BTs, leaves are either explainers or questions that the user wants to answer with explanations. Internal nodes are the following composite nodes: sequence, priority, supplement, replacement, variant, and complement. These nodes will define the explanation workflow and whether there are different perspectives in the explanations provided, and which types of perspectives they are.

- **Retrieval step.** Here, according to the knowledge provided by the design users when requirement capturing, we retrieve the most similar cases' solutions to the design user's experience that we keep in our case base. To find the similarities between our query and the cases in the case base, the system uses different similarity metrics that consider the iSeeOnto hierarchy and concept semantics (see more details in our previous work [15]). At this point in the iSee platform, after including their explanation requirements, design users obtain a list of recommended explanation strategies.
- **Reuse step.** The recommended explanation strategies are not always applicable. Applicability depends on the explainers that the strategy includes and if they fit the explanation requirements. Here resides the novelty of this paper, not published in our previous works about iSee: we propose constructive reuse methods to guide and help users when adapting their recommended solutions to their explanation experience. We have defined different use case- and user-specific procedures to carry out this task. We describe the whole process and details in Sect. 4.
- **Revise and retain steps**. After the reuse, design users can revise the resultant strategy and evaluate it through an interactive conversation [15] while retaining the solution as well.
- **Platform tools**. As part of the iSee platform, the Explanation Experiences Editor (iSeeE^3) [4] allows capturing, editing, and executing explanation strategies through a user-friendly interface based on BTs. iSeeE^3 is also the iSee tool where the reuse procedures that we describe in Sect. 4 are carried out by our design users. Some iSeeE^3 screenshots are also shown in that section.

4   Constructive Reuse

The reuse step in iSee aims at adapting the XAI strategies obtained in the retrieval step for them to be applicable for a specific use case and end user. The applicability of the solutions in iSee is defined based on the knowledge formalised in the ontology. The retrieved solution, represented as a BT, will not be applicable if it includes at least one explainer that: (1) does not fit the AI task and the AI method that we need to explain in the explanation experience query; or (2) cannot manage the same data type that it is accepted by the AI model to explain; or (3) whose implementation framework is not the same as the AI model back-end. Otherwise, when all the explainers in the BT are applicable, we will be able to apply the recommended solution for the query.

The reuse functionality in iSee aims to resolve these limitations. We have defined two alternative reuse techniques following the typical approaches in CBR [6]. On one hand, in Transformational Reuse -or Transformational Adaptation (TA)- the most similar BT to the user requirements is adapted through a transformational process using domain knowledge (that, in our case, is provided by the iSee ontology) [11]. On the other hand, Generative or Constructive Reuse (CR) builds a new solution by using the most similar BTs and domain knowledge as a resource for guiding the constructive process. Here raises the contribution of this paper: two different constructive reuse methods applied on BTs in a use case- and user-specific fashion. One reuse approach is an *explainer-level adaptation*, while the other one is a *BT-level adaptation*. Moreover, both of them can be done by design users in a manual, guided, or automatic way.

4.1   Manual Adaptation

In the manual reuse mode, design users can create BTs from scratch or modify the BTs from the retrieval step just by removing nodes, dragging new nodes, and creating new links thanks to the iSeeE^3 editor. In this mode, iSee does not guide users to build the BT, but iSee aids them in checking if there are explainers that cannot be applied (in that case a red line is shown to tell design users that they cannot use that explainer). Users also can use the *"Check for iSee"* button with which they can see if the BT structure is properly done to be executed for the iSee platform.

4.2   Guided Explainer-level Adaptation

The guided reuse approach allows design users to replace unsuitable explainers with the support of iSeeOnto. Users can see what the non-applicable explainers are and select them. This functionality presents the user with a list with the most similar explainers to the selected ones, that are applicable according to the case description. Users also can see the similarity value between the explainer to be replaced and the recommended one. To calculate the similarity value between explainers, we use the semantic knowledge that defines explainer properties in iSeeOnto. Although there are already semantic metrics in the literature, we decided to create our own metric to be able to compare the different types of knowledge representation within iSee and iSeeOnto. In particular, we use *Depth*, a customised semantic similarity metric that considers explainer property concepts from iSeeOnto and the hierarchy of those concepts in the ontology. For each explainer attribute concept, *Depth* counts the concept depth in terms of its shared parents, comparing it with the maximum concept depth for that attribute. We define depth as the number of levels that we find from the concept class until we get the concept assigned as the explainer property:

$$DP(e_i, e_j, k) = \frac{1}{W} \begin{cases} w_k \cdot equal(e_i(k), e_j(k)), & \text{if } k \in SOP \\ \frac{P(e_i(k)) \cap P(e_j(k))}{maxSize(P(e_i(k)), P(e_j(k)))}, & \text{otherwise} \end{cases}$$

where e_i and e_j are the explainers to compare, values $w_k \in [0..1]$ are weights computed through expert knowledge, SOP represents the set of simple object properties (i.e. the explainer properties that are flattened), k is the explainer property whose depth we are calculating, $P()$ is the function that returns the set of the explainer property's parents in iSeeOnto, and $maxSize()$ calculates the cardinality of the maximum set of parents. To calculate the global $Depth$ similarity value for two explainers e_i, e_j, we add all the values $DP(e_i, e_j, k)$ $\forall k \in explainer\_properties$.

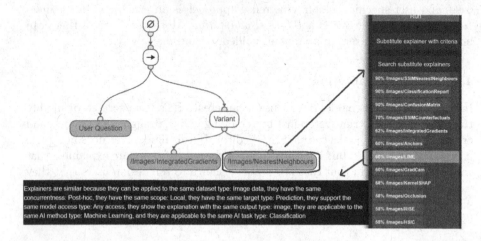

Fig. 1. Example of the constructive reuse functionality to substitute explainers in a guided mode. As we can observe on the screenshot, the users can click on an explainer (/Images/NearestNeighbours), and they receive a list of applicable and similar explainers (on the right side). There, we can see the similarity values between those explainers and the clicked one. If users hover the mouse on a recommended explainer (/Images/LIME [13] on the screenshot), we will see an explanation on the bottom of the screen where users can see the shared properties between both explainers (/Images/NearestNeighbours and /Images/LIME)).

Moreover, this method of reusing explainers, to replace those that are inapplicable, has an extended mode where users fill in a form defining restrictions –from iSeeOnto– for the retrieved explainers. For example, they can say to the system that they want explainers that show counterfactual explanations. Furthermore, users are presented with an explanation about why those explainers are similar. The explanation tells the user what their shared properties are. An example of this adaptation is in Fig. 1.

4.3   Guided Constructive Adaptation

Regarding the BT-level adaptation, in a guided way, the system is going to check within the case base what the most similar BTs to the one to be substituted

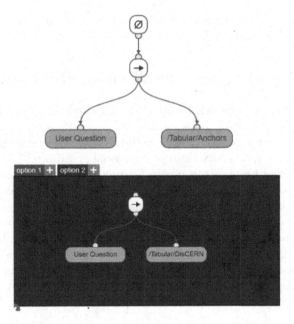

Fig. 2. Example of constructive reuse approach to adapt BTs in a guided mode. At the bottom of the screen, we will see the recommended BTs (the most similar ones with applicable explainers) to replace the original one (at the top).

are (see an example in Fig. 2). Those BTs need to include only explainers that are applicable for that use case. To get the similar BTs we use the Levenshtein edit distance [8]. Although this edit distance is used originally for sequences of strings, we used a library[4] that implements Levenshtein for graphs and trees [12]. This way, Levenshtein computes the difference between two BTs as the number of edits (insertions, deletions, or replacement of nodes) needed to transform one of those BT into the other. Here, we also offer to users the possibility of using a form to tell what the explainers they need in the BT are, and/or what the properties they need the explainers to have in the recommended BTs.

4.4 Automatic Adaptation

The automatic adaptation functionality is the straightforward version of the guided reuse. Design users can apply the explainer-level constructive reuse and change all the explainers that are not applicable in the BT clicking on a button on the iSeeE^3 editor. As a result, we will have exactly the same BT, but all the not applicable explainers will have been replaced by their most similar and applicable explainers from the iSee explainer library. If users want to change all the BT, applying the BT-level constructive reuse, they can click on another button, and it will be replaced by the most similar and applicable BT from the

---

[4] Python Edit Distances: library used to implement the Levenshtein edit distance.

iSee case base solutions. These automatic functionalities are the ones evaluated in this paper (see Sect. 6).

5   Evaluation Metrics for Explanation Strategies

The reuse mechanism proposed in this work and applied to iSee obtains applicable explanation strategies for a specific use case. However, and as we will check in the evaluation section (Sect. 6), these explanation strategies may not be suitable due to several restrictions or additional features related to the users' requirements or the use case's concrete features. For example: computational cost, diversity, popularity, etc. Therefore, we propose different metrics to evaluate these additional dimensions within explanation strategies. These metrics are not only focused on evaluating explanation strategies but also on obtaining more personalised recommendations, enriching the adaptation process. These metrics may guide the user in choosing between the substitute strategies presented in the recommended lists, and, in consequence, decide which of them are the ones they need (not necessarily the most similar substitution to the original strategy suggested by iSee). The metrics that we propose in this work are the following:

Computational complexity. It returns the explanation strategy computational complexity, i.e., the highest computational complexity of all the explainers within the explanation strategy in the normalised range $[0, 1]$. In this metric, we consider the following complexities: constant time ($\mathcal{O}(1)$), logarithmic time ($\mathcal{O}(\log n)$), linear time ($\mathcal{O}(n)$), log-linear time ($\mathcal{O}(n \log n)$), quadratic time ($\mathcal{O}(n^2)$), polynomial time ($\mathcal{O}(n^a)$ when $a > 2$), exponential time ($\mathcal{O}(a^n)$ when $a > 2$), and factorial time ($\mathcal{O}(n!)$). The score is $computational\_complexity = 0$ when the strategy complexity is constant, and $computational\_complexity = 1$ when it is factorial.

$$computational\_complexity(S) = max(cc(e_1^S), ..., cc(e_n^S))$$

where $cc()$ is a function that returns the computational complexity of an explainer and e_i^S are explainers within the explanation strategy S.

Popularity. It returns the mean popularity of all the explainers in the strategy. The explainer popularity must be defined for every use case. For example, in iSee, the explainer popularity is defined as $1, 2$ or 3 depending on the number of times that that explainer was used within explanation solutions in the iSee platform. Therefore, users who want to use the popularity metric must include the minimum and maximum popularity values utilised in their use case. The result is a score in $[0, 1]$.

$$popularity(S) = \frac{mean(pop(e_1^S), ..., pop(e_n^S)) - MIN_P}{MAX_P - MIN_P}$$

where $pop()$ is a function that returns the explainer popularity value, and MIN_P and MAX_P are, respectively, the minimum and maximum possible values in the strategy.

Uniformity. It returns a score that decides the level of the strategy uniformity in terms of explanations provided, and it returns a value between 0 (totally diverse) and 1 (totally uniform). To calculate the uniformity score, the metric takes into account the explainer properties. The uniformity score will be higher if the explainers within the strategy share a higher number of property values. As this metric is based on explainer properties, its application depends on the availability of such knowledge that, in the case of iSee, it is provided by iSeeOnto. Moreover, the uniformity metric also considers other elements (and the number of these elements) in the explanation strategy. It increases its value if the strategy includes explanations that clarify other explanations (we call them variant elements), and/or if the strategy has explanations that add information to other explanations already provided by the strategy (supplement elements). The uniformity score may be also decreased if the strategy includes complement elements (i.e. in the strategy design users point out that there are explanations that provide different perspectives), and/or replacement elements (when the strategy includes explanations that are totally different, so they explain different aspects about the experience). This way, this metric defines four types of elements: variants, supplements, replacements and complements, inspired by the composite nodes that we use in the BTs for the iSee project (see Sect. 3).

$$uniformity(S) = \frac{sum(\forall p_j \in P \frac{sum(\forall v \in V_{p_j} count(v)-1)}{exp(S)-1})}{size(P)} + cSC(S)$$

where $sum()$ is a function that calculates the addition of the elements in a list, P is the set of explainer properties, V_{p_j} is the set of values for a property $p_j \in P$ that the explainers within S have, $count(v)$ is the number of explainers that have the value v for the property p_j, $exp(S)$, the number of explainers in S, and $size()$, the length of a list. We also include an additional score regarding strategy elements that help uniformity: $cSC(S) = w_{unif} * (variantScore(S) + supplementScore(S) - replacementScore(S) - complementScore(S))$. Each of those functions returns a score that counts the number of elements of that type within S regarding all S' elements. w_{unif} is a weight in $[0, 1]$ obtained by expert knowledge.

Diversity. This metric is complementary to uniformity and it measures the variability of the explanations shown by the strategy. Again, this metric returns a value between 0 (totally uniform) and 1 (totally diverse). In this case, complement and replacement elements enhance the diversity score, while the supplement and replacement elements decrease the score.

$$diversity(S) = 1 - uniformity(S)$$

Serendipity. Serendipity is a metric that measures whether the explanation strategy has a surprising element that users may like. It is inspired by the homonym property considered to analyse recommender systems, which declares that a relevant but totally different recommendation from past user interactions sometimes improves user satisfaction [7]. With this metric we can check if an explanation strategy is uniform, but provides a few explanations that are different and might positively surprise the end user. The metric has a binary range, returning true if the strategy has serendipity, or false, if not.

$$serendipity(S) = \begin{cases} True & \text{if } sum([dif(e_1^S), ..., dif(e_n^S)]) < \frac{1}{4} \\ False & \text{otherwise} \end{cases}$$

where $sum()$ is a function that returns the addition of the elements in a list, and $dif(e_i^S)$ is a function that returns whether the explainer e_i^S within the strategy S has a quarter of their properties different from the rest of explainers. We have to consider that the rest of explainers need to have the same property values for the serendipity value to be $True$. $dif()$ is defined as follows:

$$dif(e_i^S) = \begin{cases} 1 & \text{if } size(\forall p_j \in P, [p_j(e_i^S) == p_j(e_k^S), ..., p_j(e_i^S) == p_j(e_n^S)]) < \frac{1}{4} \\ 0 & \text{otherwise} \end{cases}$$

where P is the set of explainer properties. Therefore, $p_j(e)$ returns the property p_j for the explainer e, being $\{e_k^S, ..., e_n^S\} \in S$ not equal to e_i^S.

Granularity. This measure measures the level of detail of the strategy considering the types of nodes and their connections: it increases according to number of connections and nodes. It is a metric that may be useful when end users need to have brief explanations or more detailed explanations. Using granularity, the design user can know whether the explanation is detailed or not in terms of explanations provided. The value that this measure returns is not a $[0, 1]$ interval. It returns a higher score when the granularity is higher.

$$granularity(S) = \frac{adj(S)}{n(S)} * w_a + \frac{exp(S)}{n(S)} * w_e + \frac{comp(S)}{n(S)} * w_c + \frac{quest(S)}{n(S)} * w_q$$

where $n(S)$ returns the number of elements in the strategy S workflow, $adj(S)$ returns the number of links within the strategy S, $exp(S)$, the number of explainers, $comp(S)$, the number of composite elements that define the workflow, and $quest(S)$, the number of questions within S, i.e. the user questions that the strategy answers. The weights w_a, w_e, w_c, w_q are selected using expert knowledge with $w_a > w_e > w_c = w_q$.

All these metrics have been collected into a library available at GitHub. Although these metrics have been designed for the iSee BTs, there are not specific for them. They are suitable for any other explanation strategy representation defined as a combination of explainers, which also can include other elements to define the workflow strategy process. It is important to note that the explanation strategies' format does not need to fit graph or tree format (with the exception of the granularity measure), so the metrics proposed here are flexible in that way. We illustrate how we can use these metrics in Sect. 6, where we evaluate our automatic reuse modality.

6   Evaluation

The main goal of this evaluation is two-fold. On one hand, we want to evaluate the reuse approaches applied on the iSee platform, i.e., we aim to check if every time the system retrieves non-applicable solutions in the iSee platform, we can solve the problem by applying our constructive reuse methods. Therefore, users will be always able to get applicable use case- and user-specific solutions to carry out in their explanation experiences. On the other hand, we want to make use of the evaluation metrics library proposed in this work and check its suitability for evaluating explanation strategies.

To carry out the evaluation, we have generated random BTs for 15 different iSee use cases. These BTs are correctly structured solutions, but not applicable for those use cases. The automatic reuse was applied to make those random BTs applicable in three ways: (1) only replacing non-applicable explainers through our automatic constructive reuse approach to substitute them; (2) replacing the whole tree with another applicable tree, using our automatic constructive reuse method to change BTs; and (3) replacing first only non-applicable explainers and later the whole tree by another applicable tree, using a combination of our automatic adaptation approaches (explainer-level first, BT-level second). To evaluate these reuse approaches, we have compared the number of applicable explainers before and after applying the three options. We have also applied the evaluation metrics from Sect. 5 to all of them. The code generated to make this evaluation as well as the results obtained are available on GitHub. A summary of the results regarding applicability is shown in Table 1.

As we can see in Table 1 and the results uploaded on GitHub, all the BTs generated with our reuse approaches have all of their explainers applicable for their use case. When the system applies the explainer-level adaptation, we can see that the number of explainers in the original BT coincides with the number of applicable explainers after reuse. There are a few cases where the reuse functionality substitutes some non-applicable explainers by using the same explainer, since that explainer is the most similar one for two or more non-applicable explainers in the original BT. We illustrate this showing the use case 2, where that BT originally had three non applicable explainers. The explainer-level reuse functionality has substituted one of them using LIME, and the AI Model Performance explainer to substitute the other two. So, we have two different explainers as a result.

Moreover, as we can see, we obtain totally applicable BTs using the BT-level reuse (alone or combined with the explainer-level reuse). In this case, the BT is new, so the number of explainers does not coincide with the original one's, since its structure has changed. Another point to note is that all of the BTs obtained with this type of reuse have two or one explainers. The reason behind it is that all the solutions in our case base are BTs with one or two explainers at the time of writing. We expect to have larger and more complex BTs in the future when the iSee platform became more popular and users retained their solutions in our case base. In conclusion, we have confirmed that using our reuse functionalities,

Table 1. Results obtained when applying automatic reuse to random BTs. The table shows the number of explainers in each BT (#E) and, from those explainers, the number of applicable explainers for that use case (#AE) in each BT. Remaining columns show the resulting number of explainers after applying the explainer-level adaptation (columns with XM), the BT-level adaptation (columns with BT), and the combined reuse approaches (columns with XM + BT).

Use case	#E Orig	#AE Orig	#E XM	#AE XM	#E BT	#AE BT	#E XM+BT	#AE XM+BT
0	5	3	4	4	2	2	2	2
1	7	1	6	6	1	1	1	1
2	3	0	2	2	1	1	1	1
3	4	0	4	4	1	1	1	1
4	7	0	7	7	2	2	2	2
5	4	1	4	4	2	2	2	2
6	2	1	2	2	1	1	1	1
6	5	0	5	5	1	1	1	1
7	6	1	6	6	1	1	1	1
8	2	0	2	2	1	1	1	1
9	3	0	3	3	1	1	1	1
10	4	3	4	4	1	1	1	1
11	3	0	3	3	1	1	1	1
12	3	1	3	3	2	2	2	2
13	9	2	9	9	2	2	2	2
14	3	0	3	3	1	1	1	1

users can fix their explanation strategies incompatibilities obtained from the retrieval step.

Next, we study the evaluation metrics scores obtained for two different BTs, so we can compare and analyse how the metric scores are useful to evaluate explanation strategies.

6.1   Comparative Example

Following the validation done in previous works when proposing evaluation metrics for XAI [1,2], where other authors analysed the scores obtained with the proposed metrics, we applied our evaluation metrics to all the previous BTs. In this section, we analyse and compare how these scores differ between two different BTs (see them in Fig. 3). Specifically, we have studied the BTs obtained when applying the explainer-level adaptation and the BT-level adaptation, respectively, for a specific random BT. The scores from applying our metrics to evaluate both BTs are shown in Table 2.

Regarding *computational complexity*, we obtained scores where the higher explainer computational complexity in Fig. 3a is exponential time (NearestNeighbours for images explainer's complexity), while the one in Fig. 3b is linear. That is why the scores for this metric are quite separated. *Popularity* scores point out that none of those two BTs contains explainers extremely popular in iSee.

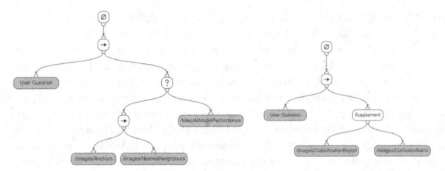

(a) BT obtained after applying the explainer-level adaptation.(b) BT obtained after applying the BT-level adaptation.

Fig. 3. Comparison example.

Table 2. Scores obtained when applying our evaluation metrics to the BTs in Fig. 3.

BT	C. Complexity	Popularity	Uniformity	Diversity	Serendipity	Granularity
Figure 3a	0.86	0.17	0.4	0.6	No	0.42
Figure 3b	0.23	0.25	0.97	0.03	No	0.417

None of those explainers has the maximum popularity value, and the first BT has a score even lower because two of the explainers are ones of the least popular ones in iSee, while in the other BT we have a bit more popular explainer (/Images/ClassificationReport). Evaluating the *uniformity* and *diversity* in our BT example, we can see a big difference between them. The two uniformity and diversity values for Fig. 3a mean that the strategy has explainers that are not very similar, but not very different either. Those explainers have some properties in common (data type to process, scope, target, concurrentness or the AI task that they explain, for example). However, in Fig. 3b, there are two explainers (/Images/ClassificationReport and /Images/ConfusionMatrix) that are extremely similar. They share not only the properties that the previous two have in common, but also, among others, the type of explanation that they show to users, their portability, the AI method to explain, or their implementation framework. In addition, they belong to the same explainability technique type. Furthermore, the other explainer in the strategy (/Misc/AIModelPerformance) also shares some of its properties with them. Finally, the presence of a supplement node, which indicates that one explainer adds information to the explanation provided by the other explainer, increments the uniformity score, while decreases the diversity one. Regarding *serendipity*, the results are also consistent with the expected behaviour. In both BTs, there is no tendency for most of the explainers to be extremely similar, while the remaining ones (which should be a small number of explainers) are completely different from the majority. In the first BT, we can see with the uniformity and diversity metrics, that our explainers are moderately similar. In the second BT, we have two explainers that are remarkably similar, but the other one is not totally different from them, but also moderately similar. Then, there is no serendipity in either BTs. Finally, we have the *granularity* scores, where we can see the level of structural detail of the explanation strategies. Both BTs are quite similar in terms of number of nodes and connections. This explains why their scores are also very close. Moreover, the scores are quite small considering this is a measure that returns unnormalised scores. This result is coherent because these BTs are not huge and there is not a considerable amount of nodes or connections within them. Therefore, we have been able to evaluate our BTs with the metrics proposed. We have even been able to describe different explanation strategy features that could be not only useful to evaluate the strategies, but also to be included as scores to calculate replacement recommendations. This way, we could include new factors to personalise even more our use case- and user specific reuse approaches if we allow users to decide if they want explanations strategies more or less computationally complex, popular, uniform, diverse, surprising or detailed.

7   Conclusions and Future Work

In the context of the iSee project, we aim at building a platform to help users obtain the best explanation solutions for their explanation experiences. The CBR cycle that drives iSee is composed by different tools and methodologies. In this work, we have proposed constructive reuse approaches for iSee that allow users to modify explanation solutions obtained in the retrieval step to be applicable and personalised for specific explanation experiences. iSee constructive reuse approaches offer manual, guided, and automatic methodologies to adapt the solutions in a use case- and user-specific fashion. We have validated and confirmed the applicability of the resulting solutions after executing the reuse procedures.

Moreover, we have proposed an XAI strategy evaluation metrics library used to evaluate the results from the reuse approaches. Using the metrics from this library, we can measure key features within explanation strategies such as computational complexity, popularity, uniformity, diversity, serendipity, and granularity. These metrics are not only useful to evaluate XAI strategies but also to include these feature requirements as part of the iSee constructive reuse, personalising the modifications to be done during this process. We intend to explore this research line in future work. Furthermore, while we used these metrics to evaluate strategies in iSee, we believe that they can be a useful tool for the XAI community to evaluate their explanation strategies as well.

Acknowledgements. This research is a result of the Horizon 2020 Future and Emerging Technologies (FET) programme of the European Union through the iSee project (CHIST-ERA-19-XAI-008, PCI2020-120720-2). Supported by the PERXAI project PID2020-114596RB-C21, funded by the Ministry of Science and Innovation of Spain (MCIN/AEI/10.13039/501100011033) and the BOSCH-UCM Honorary Chair on Artificial Intelligence applied to Internet of Things.

References

1. Bayrak, B., Bach, K.: A twin XCBR system using supportive and contrastive explanations. In: ICCBR 2023 Workshop Proceedings. CEUR Workshop Proceedings (2023)
2. Bayrak, B., Bach, K.: Evaluation of instance-based explanations: an in-depth analysis of counterfactual evaluation methods, challenges, and the CEval toolkit. Under review (2024)
3. Caro-Martínez, M., et al.: Conceptual modelling of explanation experiences through the iSeeOnto ontology. In: Reuss, P., Schönborn, J.M. (eds.) Workshop Proceedings of the 30th ICCBR. CEUR Workshop Proceedings, vol. 3389, pp. 117–128. CEUR-WS.org (2022)
4. Caro-Martínez, M., et al.: iSeeE3 - the explanation experiences editor. SoftwareX **21**, 101311 (2023)
5. Darias, J.M., Bayrak, B., Caro-Martínez, M., Díaz-Agudo, B., Recio-Garcia, J.A.: An Empirical Analysis of User Preferences Regarding XAI metrics. In: ICCBR 2024 Proceedings (2024, in press)
6. Díaz-Agudo, B., Plaza, E., Recio-García, J.A., Arcos, J.-L.: Noticeably new: case reuse in originality-driven tasks. In: Althoff, K.-D., Bergmann, R., Minor, M., Hanft, A. (eds.) ECCBR 2008. LNCS (LNAI), vol. 5239, pp. 165–179. Springer, Heidelberg (2008). https://doi.org/10.1007/978-3-540-85502-6_11
7. Kotkov, D., et al.: A survey of serendipity in recommender systems. Knowl.-Based Syst. **111**, 180–192 (2016)
8. Levenshtein, V.I., et al.: Binary codes capable of correcting deletions, insertions, and reversals. In: Soviet Physics Doklady, vol. 10, pp. 707–710. Soviet Union (1966)
9. Martin, K., et al.: iSee: intelligent sharing of explanation experiences. In: Reuss, P., Schönborn, J.M. (eds.) Workshop Proceedings of the 30th ICCBR. CEUR Workshop Proceedings, vol. 3389, pp. 231–232. CEUR-WS.org (2022)
10. Minor, M., Bergmann, R., Görg, S., Walter, K.: Towards case-based adaptation of workflows. In: Bichindaritz, I., Montani, S. (eds.) ICCBR 2010. LNCS (LNAI), vol. 6176, pp. 421–435. Springer, Heidelberg (2010). https://doi.org/10.1007/978-3-642-14274-1_31
11. Nkisi-Orji, I., et al.: Failure-driven transformational case reuse of explanation strategies in CloodCBR. In: Massie, S., Chakraborti, S. (eds.) Case-Based Reasoning Research and Development. ICCBR 2023. LNCS, vol. 14141, pp. 279–293. Springer, Cham (2023). https://doi.org/10.1007/978-3-031-40177-0_18
12. Paaßen, B., et al.: A toolbox for adaptive sequence dissimilarity measures for intelligent tutoring systems. In: Proceedings of the 8th EDM 2015, p. 632. International Educational Datamining Society (2015)
13. Ribeiro, M.T., Singh, S., Guestrin, C.: Why should I trust you? Explaining the predictions of any classifier. In: Proceedings of the 22nd ACM SIGKDD International Conference on Knowledge Discovery and Data Mining, pp. 1135–1144 (2016)
14. Wijekoon, A., et al.: Behaviour trees for conversational explanation experiences. arXiv preprint arXiv:2211.06402 (2022)
15. Wijekoon, A., et al.: CBR driven interactive explainable AI. In: Massie, S., Chakraborti, S. (eds.) Case-Based Reasoning Research and Development. ICCBR 2023. LNCS, vol. 14141, pp. 169–184. Springer, Cham (2023). https://doi.org/10.1007/978-3-031-40177-0_11

An Empirical Analysis of User Preferences Regarding XAI Metrics

Jesus M. Darias[1,2], Betül Bayrak[1,2], Marta Caro-Martínez[1,2(✉)],
Belén Díaz-Agudo[1,2], and Juan A. Recio-Garcia[1,2]

[1] Department of Software Engineering and Artificial Intelligence, Instituto de
Tecnologías del Conocimiento, Universidad Complutense de Madrid, Madrid, Spain
{jdarias,martcaro,belend,jareciog}@ucm.es
[2] Department of Computer Science Faculty of Information Technology and Electrical
Engineering, Norwegian University of Science and Technology (NTNU), Trondheim,
Norway
betul.bayrak@ntnu.no

Abstract. In this paper, we explore the problem of evaluating explanations in Explainable AI. While there are some objective metrics to measure the quality of explanations, these metrics may not always be fully representative of the quality perceived by end-users. We present an empirical investigation through an online evaluation that gathers data on user preferences regarding explanations generated by three categories of explainers applied to image classification: instance-based explanations (nearest neighbors and counterfactuals), and two families of attribution-based methods (feature-based and segmentation-based methods). Then, we examine the correlation between these objective XAI metrics and user preferences. The results show that certain metrics are strongly correlated with user satisfaction and that the perceived quality of an explanation may vary depending on the background knowledge of end-users.

Keywords: eXplainable Artificial Intelligence · XAI Evaluation Metrics · Case-Based Reasoning

1 Introduction

In the iSee project[1] we have proposed the use of Case-Based Reasoning (CBR) to retrieve and reuse previous experiences of explanations to help users better understand how AI models work. We have proposed capturing complete user-centered explanation experiences and representing complex strategies to recommend what is the explanation strategy that better suits a new explanation situation [13, 55]. In order to capture user explanation experiences and enrich our case base, we require specific metrics to assess the quality of AI explanations and determine whether they are useful for end-users in comprehending and trusting AI systems.

---

[1] iSee project web page: https://isee4xai.com/.

J. A. Recio-Garcia et al. (Eds.): ICCBR 2024, LNAI 14775, pp. 96–110, 2024.
https://doi.org/10.1007/978-3-031-63646-2_7

Regarding evaluation, we are working on two levels. To evaluate the solution structure and semantics, we have defined metrics for assessing different key features (popularity, diversity, serendipity, granularity, etc.) for complex strategies after the reuse process[2]. In this paper, we deal with the problem of evaluating the quality of the output (i.e., the explanation itself). We address the challenge of evaluating final explanations generated by post hoc methods [14,32]. This is a complex process that requires a combination of objective and subjective metrics. Objective metrics such as insertion, deletion, fidelity, stability, sparsity, and diversity can be useful for comparing the quality of explanations provided by different explanation methods and identifying their strengths and weaknesses, but subjective evaluation is essential to understand how users actually perceive these explanations. The reliability of objective metrics depends on several factors, and they may not always represent a trustworthy reflection of user preferences.

In this work, we study how several well-known objective metrics can be useful for evaluating different explanation methods and which metrics capture the quality of the explanation best from a user perspective. To achieve this, we have performed a user study to retrieve users' understanding and satisfaction degree with explanations from three different families of explainers applied to an image classifier: instance-based methods (nearest neighbours and counterfactuals), and two families of attribution-based methods, including feature-based methods (Integrated Gradients [51], GradCAM [43]), and segmentation-based methods (LIME [40] and KernelSHAP [29]).

Our findings indicate that insertion, fidelity, and sparsity metrics are correlated with the subjective perception of explanations as users were more likely to prefer explanations that presented higher values for these metrics. Also, our study shows that while instance-based explanations were preferred in most cases, expert users were more inclined toward attribution-based explanations.

This paper is structured as follows. First, we review the related work in Sect. 2. Section 3 introduces the objective metrics we used in the user study, namely, insertion, deletion, MuFidelity, stability, sparsity, and diversity. Section 4 covers the methodology of our user study. Section 5 summarizes the results of the study. Finally, Sect. 6 concludes the paper and outlines future work.

2 Related Work

The current state of XAI research encompasses various aspects, which can be broadly categorized into notions surrounding XAI, the methods employed, and the evaluation metrics utilized [10].

2.1 XAI Methods

XAI methods can be classified in many ways according to different literature papers [5,49]. One way to define these methods is according to how they obtain

---

[2] This work will be published separately.

the explanations. Based on this, we highlight two families of XAI methods: **attribution-based** methods and **instance-based** methods.

In the attribution-based group, we include all the methods that consider what the AI model uses as key input components to make the prediction. These approaches analyze how the input affects the AI model output, the importance of all its components, and the trade-off between them. Therefore, attribution-based methods make the prediction more transparent by informing users what the important input features are [1,5]. The key components used by attribution-based methods may be data features used by the model (**feature-based** methods) or data components (**segmentation-based** methods). On one hand, feature-based methods analyze how the AI model behaves during the data processing, i.e., they focus on changes in the output (for example in layer outputs) while a specific feature is being processed. Here, we include gradient-based techniques which dive into gradients and their changes for different input features (such as GradCam or Integrated Gradients) [1], and other techniques like HSIC or RISE [35]. The native output of these methods is a saliency map that highlights the features with greater attribution. On the other hand, segmentation-based methods, also called perturbation-based methods, utilize an algorithm to divide the data into small components, e.g., superpixels for image data, and perturb those segments to analyze how each component affects the output [1,5]. This way, we can train a surrogate model to compute explanations as segmented heatmaps that represent what the important components in the prediction are. Some examples of segmentation-based approaches are LIME and SHAP.

As for the instance-based methods, they produce explanations based on examples [16]. These types of explanations show examples of similar data for which the AI model has predicted the same or an opposite outcome than the instance we want to explain. For example, for image classification, we can show examples of similar images to the one being classified that also belong to the same class (nearest neighbours) or a different one (counterfactuals).

2.2 Evaluation Metrics

Related work on XAI metrics has mainly focused on both objective and subjective evaluations to assess the effectiveness and utility of XAI techniques.

Donoso-Guzmán et al. [18] adapted the User-Centric Evaluation Framework [28], a framework that focuses on assessing how objective aspects of the system are subjectively perceived by the user, to the XAI field. Moreover, the authors (re)defined subjective aspects (novelty, coherence with prior knowledge, and plausibility) and objective aspects (certainty, continuity, separability, and consistency) of the system.

Subjective evaluations often revolve around human-centered perspectives, considering factors such as user-based and application-based assessments, which depend on individual perceptions [22,26]. There are diverse studies that conducted user evaluation studies measuring trustworthiness [15,34], usefulness [31,40], and comprehensibility [34,36] by asking users to rank or select the most or least suitable features and explanations.

Objective evaluations are based on the functionality of the XAI methods, which involves assessing how well these methods fulfill their intended purposes [19]. They are commonly preferred in the literature and have been mentioned in reviews, toolkits, applications, and benchmarks [6,33]. These approaches provide structured frameworks and standardized criteria for assessing the performance and capabilities of XAI techniques. For attribution-based methods, the most commonly used metrics include fidelity [54], stability [2], insertion [41], deletion [11], plausibility [42], and fairness [12]. Additionally, there are open-source and easy-to-use toolkits such as Xplique [21] and openXAI [3]. Objective evaluation metrics for instance-based methods, such as validity [25], diversity [23], sparsity [53], and constraint violations [23], are widely used. While most studies have concentrated on counterfactual explanations [33], there are also some that focus on semifactual [27] and alterfactual [30] explanations, generalizing these metrics for all types of instance-based explanations [6].

Overall, while objective evaluations rely on quantitative measurements and statistical analysis, subjective evaluations depend on human judgment and perception. Integrating both objective and subjective evaluation metrics provides a comprehensive understanding of the strengths, limitations, and real-world applicability of XAI methods [46].

3   Evaluation Metrics Summary

In this section, we introduce the XAI metrics we included in the user study. Note that insertion, deletion, MuFidelity, and stability metrics can only be calculated for attribution-based explanations. On the other hand, sparsity and diversity metrics are only applicable to instance-based methods.

- **Insertion:** This metric captures the importance of the pixels in terms of their ability to synthesize an image and is measured by the rise in the probability of the class of interest as pixels are added according to the generated importance map of the explanation [37]. High insertion values indicate that using only the most important pixels of the explanation to make the prediction quickly increases the probability of the target class of the query.
- **Deletion:** As opposed to the insertion metric, the deletion metric measures the drop in the probability of a class as important pixels, given by the saliency map of the explanation, are gradually removed from the image. A sharp drop of the probability, and thus a small area under the probability curve, are indicative of a good explanation [37].
- **MuFidelity:** The MuFidelity metric is based on the premise that, when setting particular features to a baseline value, the change in predictor's output should be proportional to the sum of the attribution scores provided by the explanation [7]. This metric calculates the correlation between a random subset of pixels and their attribution score. For each random subset created, we set the pixels of the subset at a baseline state and obtain the prediction score. Higher MuFidelity scores indicate better explanations.

- **Stability:** This metric ensures that similar inputs with similar predictions should also produce similar explanations [7]. For a given input, sample noise is randomly added and multiple noisy inputs are generated. Next, an explanation is computed for each noisy input to then get the average distance between the original explanations and the noisy explanations. Lower distances are better, as they indicate higher stability among explanations.
- **Sparsity:** The sparsity metric refers to the degree to which the generated explanations focus on altering a limited set of image features or pixels to achieve a desired outcome [6]. A sparse explanation indicates that only a small subset of pixels needs to be modified to transition from the original image to the explanation. This metric quantifies the proportion of modified pixels relative to the total number of pixels in the image. Higher sparsity values suggest explanations that make minimal changes, providing insights into the most influential regions or features driving the model's decision.
- **Diversity:** This metric measures the variety and coverage of different types of modifications applied to generate explanations across a dataset. A diverse set of explanations indicates that the method can capture various ways in which the input image can be altered to achieve different outcomes or classes. Diversity can be quantified by leveraging determinant point processes and calculating the determinant of the kernel matrix of explanations [6]. Higher diversity values suggest a broader range of explanatory capabilities, enhancing the comprehensiveness and robustness of the explanations.

4   Experimental Procedure

For the user study, we developed a questionnaire in which participants are shown an image alongside its respective classification label according to the prediction of a neural network. Next, one explanation of each of the families described in Sect. 2 was presented simultaneously. Users were then asked to select the explanation that best helped them to understand the reasoning behind the classification. The explanation shown for each family was randomly selected from the respective pool of XAI methods, and the order in which these explanations were presented was also randomly defined after each selection. In Fig. 1, a sample question of selection of an explanation extracted from the questionnaire is shown. Additionally, we asked users to indicate their level of knowledge in both AI and XAI on a one-to-five scale.

The model used for the experiment setup was the InceptionV3 [52] network pre-trained on the ImageNet [17] dataset. To limit the duration of the questionnaire, we manually selected 20 images from this dataset, which were clearly classified by the model (accuracy>90%). From these images, we generated the explanations shown to the users using the following methods:

This image has been classified as a(n)

OBELISK

Please, according to your own criteria, <u>click on the approach that best explains this classification</u> from the options below.

Fig. 1. Example of explanation selection in the questionnaire.

- Feature-based: GradCAM++ [9], SmoothGrad [48], SquareGrad [24], Var-Grad [44], Gradient Input [45], Guided Backpropagation [50], HSIC Attribution Method [35], Integrated Gradients [51], Occlusion Sensitivity [4], RISE [38], Sobol Attribution Method [20], and Saliency [47].
- Segmentation-based: LIME [40] and KernelSHAP [29].
- Instance-based: Nearest Neighbours using Euclidean distance, Nearest Neighbours using Structural Similarity Index Measure (SSIM), and In-sample Counterfactuals.

For feature and segmentation-based algorithms, we used the attribution methods module from Xplique [21], an XAI library for Python. The specific execution parameters we used for the experiment can be found in the repository associated with this work[3], along with the implementation of instance-based explanations. It is worth noting that since instance-based explanations required a background dataset for execution, we used a small subset of ImageNet for their generation. Figure 2 illustrates the behaviour of the explanation methods considered for our experiment.

---

[3] https://github.com/jesusdarias/An-Empirical-Analysis-of-User-Preferences-Regarding-XAI-metrics.

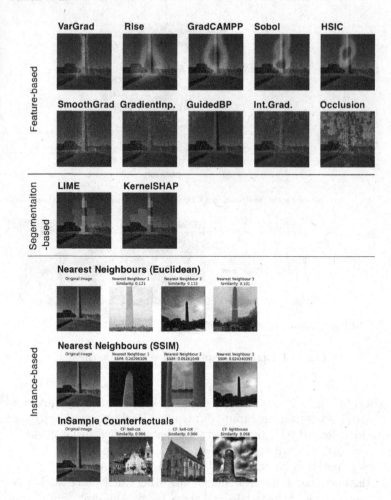

Fig. 2. Explanation methods considered for our experimental setup.

After generating the explanations, we computed the objective metrics described in Sect. 3 for each outcome. For attribution-based explanations, we used the metrics module provided by Xplique. The metrics for instance-based explanations were adapted from a previous study that focused on evaluating instance-based explanations specifically on tabular data [6]. None of these objective metrics were shown to the participants during the questionnaire.

5   Results

The user study counted 62 participants and a total of 1097 responses. While certain users did not get through the 20 questions, we still considered their responses as valid. To determine the most popular explanations among all users, we calculated the selection ratio by counting the number of times an explanation was selected as the best strategy and dividing by the number of times that explanation was presented as a choice during the experiment. The results shown in Fig. 3 indicate that nearest neighbours approaches were preferred in the majority of cases, followed by more sophisticated attribution-based methods such as GradCAM and other gradient-based variations, as well as RISE and HSIC methods.

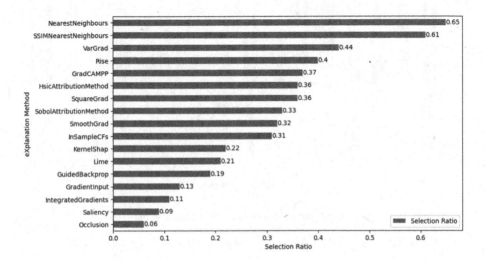

Fig. 3. Average selection ratio per explainer.

While the average selection ratio provides an indication of the most preferred methods, we also studied if the preferences would vary for different user profiles. To achieve this, we divided all the participants into three groups based on the combination of their self-assessed knowledge of AI and XAI. We labeled these user profiles as novice, competent, and expert users. The resulting distribution of the user profiles was balanced with 31.8%, 34.6%, and 33.5% of the total population respectively. Then, we computed a stratified selection ratio that allows us to determine the preferences of different types of users. The results show that both competent and expert users tend to choose nearest neighbours explanations as opposed to expert users, who seem to prefer attribution-based explanations, such as VarGrad and RISE, over instance-based explanations. Figure 4 shows these results, whereas Table 1 presents a summary of the most and least preferred XAI methods for each user profile, including the selection ratio within the group.

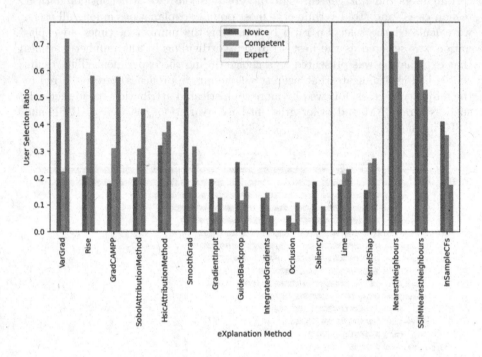

Fig. 4. Stratified selection ratio by user skills

Table 1. Most and least preferred explanation methods by user profile.

	Most Selected Methods		Least Selected Methods	
	Method	Ratio	Method	Ratio
Novice	NearestNeighbours	0.745	KernelShap	0.153
	SSIMNearestNeighbours	0.652	IntegratedGradients	0.125
	SmoothGrad	0.535	Occlusion	0.058
Competent	NearestNeighbours	0.669	GradientInput	0.071
	SSIMNearestNeighbours	0.640	Occlusion	0.030
	HSIC	0.368	Saliency	0.000
Expert	VarGrad	0.718	Occlusion	0.107
	RISE	0.580	Saliency	0.093
	GradCAMPP	0.575	IntegratedGradients	0.058

5.1 Correlation Between User Preferences and Evaluation Metrics

To analyze the relationship between objective metrics for XAI methods and subjective evaluation, we computed the mean value of each proposed metric for every explanation method. Then, we compared these values with the average selection ratio given by the users, and finally, calculated a correlation matrix.

Figure 5 shows the evaluation metrics for the attribution- and segmentation-based explanation methods. As each metric uses a different scale, these values are normalized using a min-max scaler. We can observe that there is a correlation between the selection ratio and the insertion metric. The MuFidelity and Stability metrics also present correlations, albeit weaker. The stability metric presents a positive correlation with the selection ratio although a negative correlation was expected since lower values indicate higher stability among explanations. No correlation was found between the selection ratio and the deletion metric.

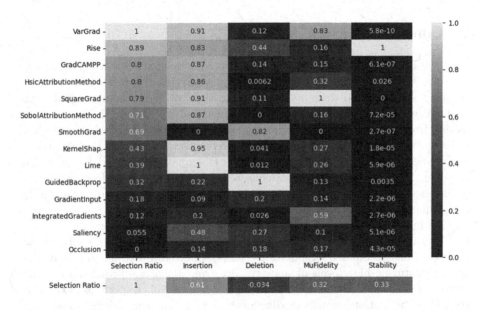

Fig. 5. Correlation matrix for attribution-based methods. The bottom row shows the average correlation.

Regarding instance-based metrics, Fig. 6 shows the corresponding results. We can observe a strong correlation between the sparsity of the explanations and the selection ratio for this family of metrics. However, regarding the diversity metric, we notice an inverse proportion between diversity and the selection ratio among explainers. This implies that less diverse explanations are selected more frequently by users. Commonly, diverse explanations for a sample are considered beneficial because they allow users to compare multiple instances with different characteristics. However, in this case, the inverse ratio may be attributed to

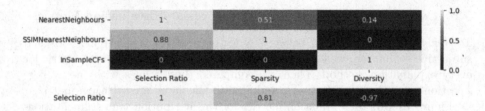

Fig. 6. Correlation matrix for instance- and segmentation-based methods. The bottom row shows the average correlation.

factors such as the application domain or may indicate a distinction from the findings in existing literature, particularly if a sufficient number of user studies have yet to be conducted to validate these observations.

6   Conclusions

This work explores the problem of evaluation of explanations for AI decisions. We have studied several objective metrics, namely insertion, deletion, fidelity, stability, sparsity, and diversity, elucidating their utility in comparing diverse explanation methods and discerning which metrics best capture the explanation quality from a user standpoint. Through user testing, we conducted an empirical investigation, gathering data on user comprehension and satisfaction regarding explanations generated by three categories of explainers applied to an image classifier. It is worth noting that while objective metrics provide quantitative measures, their reliability hinges on numerous factors and may not always fully encapsulate user preferences.

Our findings indicate a preference among users for attribution-based explanations that presented higher values for the insertion metric. Conversely, in the context of instance-based explanations, users exhibited a predilection for explanations featuring high levels of sparsity. Moreover, the study revealed a notable discrepancy in user preferences based on expertise level. Expert users demonstrated an inclination towards attribution-based explanations, whereas less experienced users exhibited their preference for instance-based explanations. The research in this paper is a starting point of explainer evaluation that we intend to use to solve the so-called disagreement problem [39] and deal with the fact that feature attribution methods can be unstable and disagree on the most important features for a model or prediction [8].

Acknowledgements. This research is a result of the Horizon 2020 Future and Emerging Technologies (FET) programme of the European Union through the iSee project (CHIST-ERA-19-XAI-008, PCI2020-120720-2).

Supported by the PERXAI project PID2020-114596RB-C21, funded by the Ministry of Science and Innovation of Spain (MCIN/AEI/10.13039/501100011033) and the BOSCH-UCM Honorary Chair on Artificial Intelligence applied to Internet of Things.

References

1. Abhishek, K., Kamath, D.: Attribution-based xai methods in computer vision: a review. arXiv preprint arXiv:2211.14736 (2022)
2. Agarwal, C., et al.: Rethinking stability for attribution-based explanations. arXiv preprint arXiv:2203.06877 (2022)
3. Agarwal, C., et al.: Openxai: towards a transparent evaluation of model explanations. Adv. Neural. Inf. Process. Syst. **35**, 15784–15799 (2022)
4. Ancona, M., Ceolini, E., Öztireli, A.C., Gross, M.H.: A unified view of gradient-based attribution methods for deep neural networks. CoRR **abs/1711.06104** (2017), http://arxiv.org/abs/1711.06104
5. Arrieta, A.B., et al.: Explainable artificial intelligence (XAI): concepts, taxonomies, opportunities and challenges toward responsible AI. Inf. Fusion **58**, 82–115 (2020)
6. Bayrak, B., Bach, K.: Evaluation of instance-based explanations: an in-depth analysis of counterfactual evaluation methods, challenges, and the CEval toolkit. Under review (2024)
7. Bhatt, U., Weller, A., Moura, J.M.F.: Evaluating and aggregating feature-based model explanations (2020)
8. Brughmans, D., Melis, L., Martens, D.: Disagreement amongst counterfactual explanations: how transparency can be deceptive. arXiv preprint arXiv:2304.12667 (2023)
9. Chattopadhyay, A., Sarkar, A., Howlader, P., Balasubramanian, V.N.: Grad-cam++: generalized gradient-based visual explanations for deep convolutional networks. CoRR **abs/1710.11063** (2017). http://arxiv.org/abs/1710.11063
10. Coroama, L., Groza, A.: Evaluation metrics in explainable artificial intelligence (XAI). In: Guarda, T., Portela, F., Augusto, M.F. (eds.) Advanced Research in Technologies, Information, Innovation and Sustainability. ARTIIS 2022. Communications in Computer and Information Science, vol. 1675, pp. 401–413. Springer, Cham (2022). https://doi.org/10.1007/978-3-031-20319-0_30
11. Covert, I., Lundberg, S., Lee, S.I.: Explaining by removing: a unified framework for model explanation. J. Mach. Learn. Res. **22**(209), 1–90 (2021)
12. Dai, J., Upadhyay, S., Aivodji, U., Bach, S.H., Lakkaraju, H.: Fairness via explanation quality: evaluating disparities in the quality of post hoc explanations. In: Proceedings of the 2022 AAAI/ACM Conference on AI, Ethics, and Society, pp. 203–214 (2022)
13. Darias, J.M., Caro-Martínez, M., Díaz-Agudo, B., Recio-Garcia, J.A.: Using case-based reasoning for capturing expert knowledge on explanation methods. In: Keane, M.T., Wiratunga, N. (eds.) Case-Based Reasoning Research and Development, ICCBR 2022, LNCS, vol. 13405, pp. 3–17. Springer, Cham (2022). https://doi.org/10.1007/978-3-031-14923-8_1
14. Dasgupta, S., Frost, N., Moshkovitz, M.: Framework for evaluating faithfulness of local explanations (2022)
15. Degen, H., Budnik, C., Conte, G., Lintereur, A., Weber, S.: How to explain it to energy engineers?. In: Chen, J.Y.C., Fragomeni, G., Degen, H., Ntoa, S. (eds.) HCI International 2022 - Late Breaking Papers: Interacting with eXtended Reality and Artificial Intelligence, HCII 2022, LNCS, vol. 13518. pp. 262–284. Springer, Cham (2022). https://doi.org/10.1007/978-3-031-21707-4_20
16. Delaney, E., Greene, D., Keane, M.T.: Instance-based counterfactual explanations for time series classification. In: Sánchez-Ruiz, A.A., Floyd, M.W. (eds.) ICCBR 2021. LNCS (LNAI), vol. 12877, pp. 32–47. Springer, Cham (2021). https://doi.org/10.1007/978-3-030-86957-1_3

17. Deng, J., et al.: ImageNet: a large-scale hierarchical image database. In: 2009 IEEE Conference on Computer Vision and Pattern Recognition, pp. 248–255 (2009). https://doi.org/10.1109/CVPR.2009.5206848
18. onoso-Guzmán, I., Ooge, J., Parra, D., Verbert, K.: Towards a comprehensive human-centred evaluation framework for explainable AI. In: Longo, L. (eds.) Explainable Artificial Intelligence, xAI 2023, Communications in Computer and Information Science, vol. 1903, pp. 183–204. Springer, Cham (2023). https://doi.org/10.1007/978-3-031-44070-0_10
19. Doshi-Velez, F., Kim, B.: Towards a rigorous science of interpretable machine learning. arXiv preprint arXiv:1702.08608 (2017)
20. Fel, T., Cadène, R., Chalvidal, M., Cord, M., Vigouroux, D., Serre, T.: Look at the variance! efficient black-box explanations with sobol-based sensitivity analysis. CoRR **abs/2111.04138** (2021). https://arxiv.org/abs/2111.04138
21. Fel, T., et al.: Xplique: a deep learning explainability toolbox. In: Workshop on Explainable Artificial Intelligence for Computer Vision (CVPR) (2022)
22. Gentile, D., Jamieson, G., Donmez, B.: Evaluating human understanding in XAI systems. In: ACM CHI XCXAI Workshop (2021)
23. Guidotti, R.: Counterfactual explanations and how to find them: literature review and benchmarking. In: Data Mining and Knowledge Discovery, pp. 1–55 (2022)
24. Hooker, S., Erhan, D., Kindermans, P., Kim, B.: Evaluating feature importance estimates. CoRR **abs/1806.10758** (2018), http://arxiv.org/abs/1806.10758
25. Hvilshøj, F., Iosifidis, A., Assent, I.: On quantitative evaluations of counterfactuals. arXiv preprint arXiv:2111.00177 (2021)
26. Jalali, A., Haslhofer, B., Kriglstein, S., Rauber, A.: Predictability and comprehensibility in post-hoc XAI methods: a user-centered analysis. In: Arai, K. (ed.) Intelligent Computing, SAI 2023, LNNS, vol. 711, pp 712–733. Springer, Cham (2023). https://doi.org/10.1007/978-3-031-37717-4_46
27. Kenny, E., Huang, W.: The utility of "even if" semifactual explanation to optimise positive outcomes. In: Advances in Neural Information Processing Systems, vol. 36 (2024)
28. Knijnenburg, B.P., Willemsen, M.C., Gantner, Z., Soncu, H., Newell, C.: Explaining the user experience of recommender systems. User Model. User-Adap. Inter. **22**, 441–504 (2012)
29. Lundberg, S.M., Lee, S.: A unified approach to interpreting model predictions. CoRR **abs/1705.07874** (2017). http://arxiv.org/abs/1705.07874
30. Mertes, S., Karle, C., Huber, T., Weitz, K., Schlagowski, R., André, E.: Alterfactual explanations–the relevance of irrelevance for explaining AI systems. arXiv preprint arXiv:2207.09374 (2022)
31. Mohseni, S., Block, J.E., Ragan, E.D.: A human-grounded evaluation benchmark for local explanations of machine learning. arXiv preprint arXiv:1801.05075 (2018)
32. Molnar, C.: Interpretable Machine Learning. 2 edn. (2022). https://christophm.github.io/interpretable-ml-book
33. Nauta, M., et al.: From anecdotal evidence to quantitative evaluation methods: a systematic review on evaluating explainable AI. ACM Comput. Surv. **55**(13s), 1–42 (2023)
34. Nourani, M., Kabir, S., Mohseni, S., Ragan, E.D.: The effects of meaningful and meaningless explanations on trust and perceived system accuracy in intelligent systems. In: Proceedings of the AAAI Conference on Human Computation and Crowdsourcing, vol. 7, pp. 97–105 (2019)
35. Novello, P., Fel, T., Vigouroux, D.: Making sense of dependence: efficient black-box explanations using dependence measure (2022)

36. Papenmeier, A., Englebienne, G., Seifert, C.: How model accuracy and explanation fidelity influence user trust. arXiv preprint arXiv:1907.12652 (2019)
37. Petsiuk, V., Das, A., Saenko, K.: Rise: Randomized input sampling for explanation of black-box models (2018)
38. Petsiuk, V., Das, A., Saenko, K.: RISE: randomized input sampling for explanation of black-box models. CoRR **abs/1806.07421** (2018), http://arxiv.org/abs/1806.07421
39. Pirie, C., Wiratunga, N., Wijekoon, A., Moreno-García, C.F.: AGREE: a feature attribution aggregation framework to address explainer disagreements with alignment metrics. In: Workshops at (ICCBR 2023). CEUR Workshop Proceedings, vol. 3438, pp. 184–199. CEUR-WS.org (2023). https://ceur-ws.org/Vol-3438/paper_14.pdf
40. Ribeiro, M.T., Singh, S., Guestrin, C.: Why should i trust you? explaining the predictions of any classifier. In: Proceedings of the 22nd ACM SIGKDD International Conference on Knowledge Discovery and Data Mining, pp. 1135–1144 (2016)
41. Samek, W., Binder, A., Montavon, G., Lapuschkin, S., Müller, K.R.: Evaluating the visualization of what a deep neural network has learned. IEEE Trans. Neural Netw. Learn. Syst. **28**(11), 2660–2673 (2016)
42. Sato, T., Funayama, H., Hanawa, K., Inui, K.: Plausibility and faithfulness of feature attribution-based explanations in automated short answer scoring. In: Rodrigo, M.M., Matsuda, N., Cristea, A.I., Dimitrova, V. (eds.) Artificial Intelligence in Education, AIED 2022, LNCS, vol. 13355. Springer, Cham (2022). https://doi.org/10.1007/978-3-031-11644-5_19
43. Selvaraju, R.R., Das, A., Vedantam, R., Cogswell, M., Parikh, D., Batra, D.: Grad-cam: why did you say that? visual explanations from deep networks via gradient-based localization. CoRR **abs/1610.02391** (2016). http://arxiv.org/abs/1610.02391
44. Seo, J., Choe, J., Koo, J., Jeon, S., Kim, B., Jeon, T.: Noise-adding methods of saliency map as series of higher order partial derivative. CoRR **abs/1806.03000** (2018). http://arxiv.org/abs/1806.03000
45. Shrikumar, A., Greenside, P., Shcherbina, A., Kundaje, A.: Not just a black box: learning important features through propagating activation differences. CoRR **abs/1605.01713** (2016). http://arxiv.org/abs/1605.01713
46. Silva, A., Schrum, M., Hedlund-Botti, E., Gopalan, N., Gombolay, M.: Explainable artificial intelligence: evaluating the objective and subjective impacts of XAI on human-agent interaction. Int. J. Hum.-Comput. Interact. **39**(7), 1390–1404 (2023)
47. Simonyan, K., Vedaldi, A., Zisserman, A.: Deep inside convolutional networks: visualising image classification models and saliency maps. CoRR **abs/1312.6034** (2013). https://api.semanticscholar.org/CorpusID:1450294
48. Smilkov, D., Thorat, N., Kim, B., Viégas, F.B., Wattenberg, M.: Smoothgrad: removing noise by adding noise. CoRR **abs/1706.03825** (2017). http://arxiv.org/abs/1706.03825
49. Speith, T.: A review of taxonomies of explainable artificial intelligence (XAI) methods. In: Proceedings of the 2022 ACM Conference on Fairness, Accountability, and Transparency, pp. 2239–2250 (2022)
50. Springenberg, J.T., Dosovitskiy, A., Brox, T., Riedmiller, M.A.: Striving for simplicity: the all convolutional net. CoRR **abs/1412.6806** (2014). https://api.semanticscholar.org/CorpusID:12998557
51. Sundararajan, M., Taly, A., Yan, Q.: Axiomatic attribution for deep networks. CoRR **abs/1703.01365** (2017). http://arxiv.org/abs/1703.01365

52. Szegedy, C., Vanhoucke, V., Ioffe, S., Shlens, J., Wojna, Z.: Rethinking the inception architecture for computer vision. CoRR **abs/1512.00567** (2015). http://arxiv.org/abs/1512.00567
53. Verma, S., Boonsanong, V., Hoang, M., Hines, K.E., Dickerson, J.P., Shah, C.: Counterfactual explanations and algorithmic recourses for machine learning: a review. arXiv preprint arXiv:2010.10596 (2020)
54. Wang, Z., Huang, C., Li, Y., Yao, X.: Multi-objective feature attribution explanation for explainable machine learning. ACM Trans. Evol. Learn. **4**(1), 1–32 (2023)
55. Wijekoon, A., et al.: CBR driven interactive explainable AI. In: ICCBR 2023, LNCS, vol. 14141, pp. 169–184. Springer, Cham (2023). https://doi.org/10.1007/978-3-031-40177-0_1

CBR-Ren: A Case-Based Reasoning Driven Retriever-Generator Model for Hybrid Long-Form Numerical Reasoning

Boda Feng, Hui Gao, Peng Zhang[✉], and Jing Zhang

College of Intelligence and Computing, Tianjin University, Tianjin, China
{bodafeng,hui_gao,pzhang,zhang_jing}@tju.edu.cn

Abstract. Numerical reasoning over hybrid data aims to extract critical facts from long-form documents and tables, and generate arithmetic expressions based on these facts to answer the question. Most existing methods are based on the retriever-generator model. However, the inferential power of the retriever-generator model is poor, resulting in insufficient attention to critical facts. To solve these problems, combining Large Language Model (LLM) and Case-Based Reasoning (CBR), we propose a **Ca**se-**B**ased Driven **R**etriever-ge**n**erator model (**CBR-Ren**) to enhance the ability of the retriever-generator model for retrieving and distinguishing critical facts. In the retrieval stage, the model introduces a golden explanation by prompt technology of LLM, which helps the retriever construct explicit templates for inferring critical facts and reduces the impact of non-critical facts on the generator. In the generator stage, the CBR-driven retrieval algorithm enhances the representation learning ability of the encoder and obtains the relevant knowledge in decoder history. In addition, the model proposes fact weighting, which enhances the ability to locate critical facts and helps to generate correct numerical expressions. Experimental results on the FinQA and ConvFinQA demonstrate the effectiveness of CBR-Ren, which outperforms all the baselines.

Keywords: Financial Numerical reasoning · Prompt-based technology · Case-based Reasoning · Encoder-decoder framework

1 Introduction

Numerical reasoning has been extended to more complex application scenarios, with the rise of LLM such as ChatGPT and GPT4 [1]. The previous numerical reasoning datasets focused on simple calculations and reasoning, and mostly only included documents (e.g., MathQA [3] and DROP [9]). In contrast, some new benchmarks are proposed to include longer textual data and more complex data forms, which undoubtedly present greater challenges. As shown in Fig. 1, financial numerical reasoning datasets require models to answer financial analysis questions based on both table and textual data, such as FinQA [7], ConvFinQA [8] and TAT-QA [31].

The mainstream technology for numerical reasoning is the retriever-generator framework, where the retriever identifies relevant information as critical facts from the long documents and tables, and the generator takes the critical facts as the input,

ⓒ The Author(s), under exclusive license to Springer Nature Switzerland AG 2024
J. A. Recio-Garcia et al. (Eds.): ICCBR 2024, LNAI 14775, pp. 111–126, 2024.
https://doi.org/10.1007/978-3-031-63646-2_8

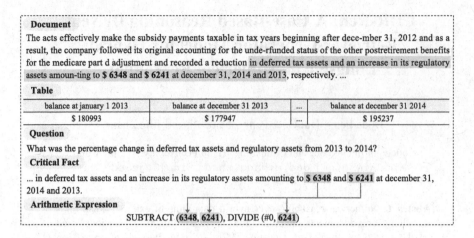

Fig. 1. An example from FinQA dataset.

generates a sequence consisting of numbers and operators. FinQANet [7] proposes this framework, and uses pre-trained language models (RoBERTa [17]) to improve the accuracy. DyRRen [16] extends it to retriever-reranker-generator framework, and proposes a dynamic method for reranking of relevant facts. ELASTIC [27] proposes an adaptive symbolic compiler to handle the hybrid long-form data. Meanwhile, through recognizing phenomena of human beings' behavior, Schank [5] firstly presented the methodology of case-based reasoning (CBR), which revolves around the idea of leveraging past instances to address new problems.

However, the retriever-generator framework lacks inferential capability, resulting in challenges where the retriever may struggle to accurately identify critical facts, and the generator may struggle to effectively distinguish these critical facts. Specifically, two main problems arise:

First, existing methods lack the ability to retrieve critical facts, which is caused by insufficient explicit inference information. The current retrieval paradigm is still centered on the relevance calculation, which leads to retrieve some non-critical facts that may cause significant interference with critical facts. These non-critical facts may contain keyword and numerical information that can lead to cascading errors, affecting the accuracy of the generator.

Second, existing models lack the ability to distinguish between critical facts and relevant knowledge. For critical facts, some work uses a rerank approach to focus on sentences, which containing the number or the relevant facts that can help locate numbers [16]. However, this method introduces redundant information, resulting in a large amount of noise mixed into the generation process. For the relevant knowledge contained in the historical information, the accurate retrieval of relevant knowledge in the generation step is helpful to further optimize the representation learning.

To solve the two problems, we propose a **Case-Based Retriever-generator Model** (**CBR-Ren**). For the retriever, we produce *golden explanation* via prompting, which provides inference information to the retrieve and prepares more reasonable critical facts for the subsequent generator generation. For the generator, we propose a *fact weighting* without excessive information, which combines historical information to enhance the representation of facts, allowing the generator to focus on the correct facts during the inference phase. In addition, we introduce CBR-driven retrieval algorithm for generator decoder, which can enables the generator to obtain more relevant knowledge from historical information, thereby enhancing the representation of the decoder. Experimental result has indicated that CBR-Ren achieves a great performance both on FinQA and ConvFinQA.

The contributions of this work are as follows:

– For the retriever, we introduce the golden explanation by LLM, which uses common sense knowledge to provide explicit reasoning paradigms, and enhance interactions at various levels of granularity to enhance the retriever's ability to retrieve critical facts.
– In the generator, we integrate CBR-driven retrieval algorithm and propose a fact weighting method. The former enhances the ability to represent facts, while the latter helps the model locate the critical facts and generate the correct numerical expression.
– We propose the CBR-Ren, which beyond the state-of-the-art model, and achieves 67.81 execution accuracy (↑ 4.51%), 65.32 program accuracy (↑ 4.03%) on FinQA test set. And CBR-Ren also outperforms all baselines on ConvFinQA (Fig. 3).

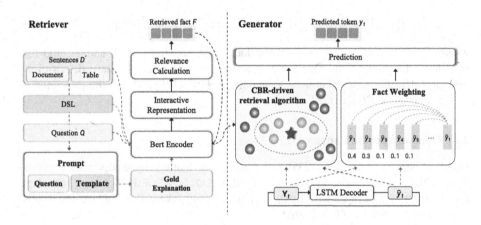

Fig. 2. An overview of CBR-Ren Model.

2 Task Definition

2.1 Problem Formulation

Given a question Q together with a numerical table T which consists of m rows $\{t_1, t_2, ..., t_m\}$ and a long-form document $D = \{d_1, d_2, ..., d_n\}$ which consists of n sentences, the model first aims to retrieve the facts in document

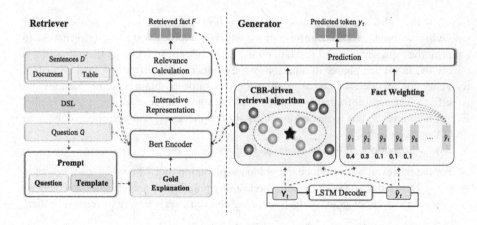

Fig. 3. Flow chart of the CBR-driven retrieval algorithm.

and table. Then the model is asked to generate an arithmetic expression $G = \{op_1(e_0, e_1), op_2(e_2, e_3), ..., EOF\}$, where op_i is a mathematical operator such as ADD or MULTIPLY from domain specific language, and e_i can be a constant token, a register token that can indicate previous operation and a numeric span from Q, T and D. The task can be written as:

$$P(G|Q; T; D) = P(G|F, Q; T; D)P(F|Q; T; D) \tag{1}$$

where $F = \{f_1, f_2, ..., f_k\}$ denotes the facts extracted from Q, T and D, and the facts have the potential to answer the question. In mainstream framework retriever-generator [7], the retriever is used to maximize $P(F|Q; T; D)$, and the generator is used to maximize $P(G|F, Q; T; D)$.

2.2 Domain Specific Language

Domain Specific Language (DSL) consisting of mathematical operations (ADD, MULTIPLY, *etc.*), table operations (TABLE_MAX, TABLE_MIN, *etc.*), constant tokens (CONST_100, CONST_1000, *etc.*) and register tokens that indicate the results of previous operations (#0, #1, *etc.*).

3 Methodology

The CBR-Ren model as shown in Fig. 2, based on the retriever-generator framework. We utilize ChatGPT to generate golden explanations, guiding the retrieval of critical facts, and employ fact weighting to generate correct arithmetic expressions.

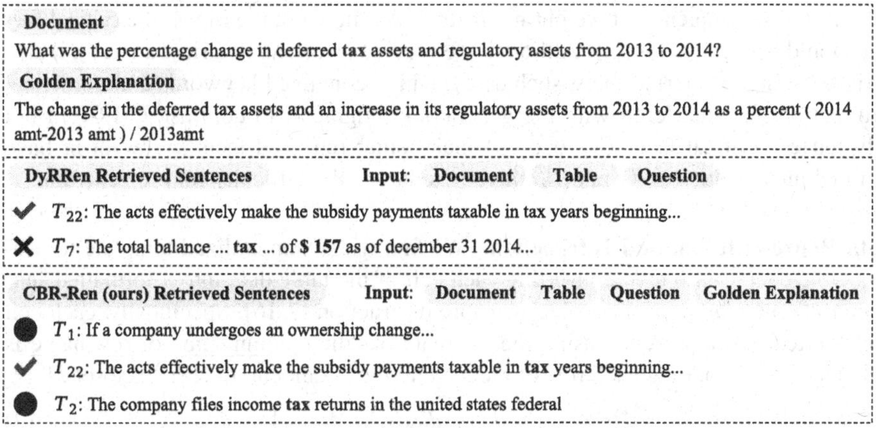

Document

What was the percentage change in deferred tax assets and regulatory assets from 2013 to 2014?

Golden Explanation

The change in the deferred tax assets and an increase in its regulatory assets from 2013 to 2014 as a percent (2014 amt-2013 amt) / 2013amt

---

DyRRen Retrieved Sentences   Input: **Document**   **Table**   **Question**

✔ T_{22}: The acts effectively make the subsidy payments taxable in tax years beginning...

✘ T_7: The total balance ... **tax** ... of **$ 157** as of december 31 2014...

CBR-Ren (ours) Retrieved Sentences   Input: **Document**   **Table**   **Question**   **Golden Explanation**

● T_1: If a company undergoes an ownership change...

✔ T_{22}: The acts effectively make the subsidy payments taxable in **tax** years beginning...

● T_2: The company files income **tax** returns in the united states federal

---

Fig. 4. Comparison between CBR-Ren and previous methods in retriever. The amt is a variable that refers to deferred tax assets and regulatory assets. The X red symbol represents non-critical facts that will cause interference, while the O green symbol represents non-critical facts. (Color figure online)

3.1   The Prompt-Based Inference Retriever

Golden Explanation Production. In order to enhance the inferential capability of the model, we propose a prompt-based golden explanation approach, using ChatGPT to generate paradigmatic answers as Golden Explanations (GE) to guide critical fact retrieval. Specifically, we input only questions into the model without providing the long-form documents and tables, and let the model try to provide a paradigmatic answer. To obtain better GE, develop a template to improve performance and combine 'question + template' as a prompt to obtain a more relevant paradigmatic answer:

Prompt

Question $[x]$:
What was the percentage change in deferred tax assets and regulatory assets from 2013 to 2014?
Template $[t]$:
as a general rule, and give me a formula for calculating it.
Prompt $[x + t]$:
What was the percentage change in deferred tax assets and regulatory assets from 2013 to 2014 as a general rule?
Golden Explanation $[y]$:
The change in the deferred tax assets and an increase in its regulatory assets from 2013 to 2014 as a percent (2014 amt-2013amt)/2013amt

---

Compared to previous work, Golden Explanations help the retriever find critical facts relevant to the question and reduce interference terms for the critical facts. As a result, the extracted non-critical facts have less impact on the critical facts, reducing the difficulty of subsequent fact weighting method. As shown in the Fig. 4, the critical fact that should be retrieved is T_{22}. Although the previous work also retrieved is T_{22}, it also retrieved some interfering facts, such as T_7, which contained keywords and numerical information that interfered with the generator's judgment. In contrast, CBR-Ren not only retrieve critical facts T_{22}, but also make other retrieved facts irrelevant or have minimal impact, such as T_1 and T_2, thereby reducing the difficulty for the generator.

Data Representation and Interaction. We first use a standardized template to process table data T into text, converting each cell of the table data into a formatted sentence to reduce the impact of table structure destruction [7, 16]. Specifically, each cell is converted into a sentence using the template of "the <u>column name</u> of <u>row name</u> is <u>cell value</u>". After adding each row of the table to the document, the sentence set D' is:

$$D' = D \cup \{d_{n+1}, d_{n+2}, ..., d_{n+m}\} \tag{2}$$

where $\{d_{n+1}, d_{n+2}, ..., d_{n+m}\}$ represents the subset of sentences converted from rows.

Next, we encode the sentences set D' and the question Q using BERT transformer:

$$H^{D'} = \text{BERT}(d_1, d_2, ..., d_{m+n})$$
$$H^Q = \text{BERT}(x_1, x_2, ..., x_{|Q|}) \tag{3}$$
$$H^E = \text{BERT}(y_1, y_2, ..., y_{|Q|})$$

where $H^{D'}$ represents the sentence representations, H^Q represents the question representation and H^E represents the GE representation.

Next, we obtain the interactive information between questions, sentences, and GE:

$$Inter_{QD'} = \text{Drop}(H^Q) \cdot \text{Drop}(H^{D'})$$
$$Inter_{QE} = \text{Drop}(H^Q) \cdot \text{Drop}(H^E) \tag{4}$$

where $\text{Drop}(\ )$ denotes the dropout layer, and $(\cdot)$ denotes the matrix multiplication.

Finally, we fuse sentence representation with interactive information by concatenate, and obtain the input representation H^D:

$$H^D = \text{Concat}(H^{D'}, Inter_{QD'}, Inter_{QE}) \tag{5}$$

After fusion with interactive information, the sentence representation is closer to the facts required by the question, leading to more accurate calculations of similarity.

Relevance Calculation. We adopt the cosine function to calculate the similarity between the question and the sentence:

$$\text{Sim}(Q, D) = \sum_{h_i \in H^Q} \max_{h_j \in H^D} \text{Cos}(h_i, h_j) \tag{6}$$

and then we sort the retrieved results based on the similarity score, and obtain the K results with the highest score as the retrieved critical fact $F = \{f_1, f_2, ..., f_k\}$.

By utilizing cosine functions, we can achieve token-level interaction, combined with the encoder section, to achieve interaction of different granularity and promote the retrieval of critical facts.

3.2   The History-Augmented Inference Generator

The generator consists of an encoder and a decoder. In the decoder, we introduce CBR-driven retrieval algorithm to find relevant history information, and propose fact weighting Module to help generator to focus on the facts with numerical information.

Encoder. We feed the critical fact $F_i = (f_1, f_2, ..., f_{|F_i|})$ into BERT, and concatenate them with the question Q:

$$H^{F_i} = \text{BERT}(\text{Concat}(f_1, f_2, ..., f_{|F_i|}, [CLS], Q)) \tag{7}$$

Then, we can get the representation of the question and all the retrieved sentences by concatenating them:

$$H^w = \text{Concat}(H^Q, H^{F_1}, ..., H^{F_k}) \tag{8}$$

In addition, we use H^{DSL} as the representation of DSL, and concatenate H^w and H^{DSL} to calculate the sequence representation of all tokens:

$$H^{seq} = \text{Concat}(H^w, H^{DSL}) \tag{9}$$

Decoder. In the decoding process, it is essential to identify the most relevant information to the current hidden layer state to assist the model in deducing the correct arithmetic expression. In order to achieve this goal, we propose a history-augmented representation based on CBR-driven retrieval algorithm and fact weighting module, and the algorithm is shown in Algorithm 1.

Algorithm 1. The framework of CBR-Ren decoder

Input: LSTM output y_t^{LSTM}, Decoder history Y_t, encoder output H^{seq}
Output: the predicted token representation y_t
  1: $\hat{y}_t = \text{CBR}(Y_t, y_t^{LSTM})$ ▷ Section 3.2
  2: $H^{ht} = \hat{y}_t \circ Y_t$
  3: $H^{all} = \text{Layernorm}(\text{Concat}(H^{seq}, H^{ht}, \hat{y}_t))$
  4: $H^{sc} = W^{sc}(\text{Concat}(H^w, H^{DSL}) \circ H^{seq})$
  5: $s^{con} = H^{sc} \circ H^{all}$
  6: $s = \text{FWR}(Y_t, \hat{y}_t)$ ▷ Section 3.2
  7: $index = \text{argmax}(s)$
  8: $y_t = H^{sc}_{index}$
  9: **return** y_t

Decoder follows LSTM framework, at each decoding step t, which generates a program token representation sequence $Y_t = [y_1, y_2, ..., y_{t-1}]$ as decoding history information, where the decoder output represents $\hat{y}_t$ as:

$$y_t^{LSTM} = \text{LSTM}(y_{t-1}) \tag{10}$$

where y_0 is initialized using Gaussian distribution.

CBR-Driven Retrieval Algorithm. In order to gain more relevant knowledge from the history information, we introduced CBR-driven retrieval algorithm. Within a CBR system, previously encountered scenarios stored in the case library are referred to as base cases, while the current issues at hand are termed target cases. Each case comprises two main components: a problem description section and a corresponding solution segment. First, we train a model without the CBR-driven retrieval algorithm, where use y_t^{LSTM} as $\hat{y}_t$, and use this model to generate a set of key-value pairs, which is sequence representation Y_t' and decoder output $\hat{y}_t'$ generated by this model. During the generation process, we use the CBR-driven retrieval algorithm to find the $top - k$ representations N most relevant to Y_t, and calculate the weighted sum:

$$H^{cbr} = \texttt{Logsumexp}(\hat{y}_t^{k_i}) \tag{11}$$

where $k_i \in N$, and $top - k$ represents the closest k elements.

For the CBR-driven retrieval algorithm, we use the $L2$ norm as the distance function, and use the distance to represent the similarity. Give two cases or vectors a and b, the similarity of them is:

$$Sim(a, b) = \frac{1}{1 + dis(a, b)} \tag{12}$$

Then we fuse the representation with the representation generated by LSTM:

$$\hat{y}_t = (1 - \lambda)\hat{y}_t^{LSTM} + \lambda H^{cbr} \tag{13}$$

where λ is a hyperparameter.

Fact Weighting. In the decoding stage, different steps have different levels of attention to facts. Therefore, we hope to find the facts most relevant to the numerical information for current step t. Specifically, we use an attention mechanism method to obtain h^y for Y_t and $\hat{y}_t$:

$$h^y = \texttt{Softmax}(W^h \hat{y}_t Y_t) Y_t \tag{14}$$

where W^h is a learnable weight matrix.

Meanwhile, we use mean-pooling in token dimension to obtain the representations of all tokens except DSL:

$$h^w = \texttt{MeanPooling}(H^w) \tag{15}$$

Then we concatenate h^w and h^y and fuse them to obtain a more informative representation:

$$h^{inf} = \texttt{Tanh}(\texttt{Concat}(h^w, h^y)) \tag{16}$$

where $\texttt{Tanh}(\ )$ is an activation function.

$\hat{y}_t$ is used as a weight to get more information, and get the weight score of each sentence by:

$$h^{wt} = \hat{y}_t \circ h^{inf}$$
$$s^{wt} = \texttt{Expand}(\texttt{Softmax}(h^{wt})) \tag{17}$$

note that s^{wt} is a score for sentences, and we need to extend it to the token-level, so we need an Expand( ) operation. We fixed the score of tokens in DSL to 1.

Finally, the scores of all tokens are the element-wise product of context scores and weight scores:

$$s = s^{con} \circ s^{wt} \tag{18}$$

Training Loss. Cross-entropy loss is adopted to supervise the generator, and the loss is optimized by s:

$$\mathcal{L} = -log\frac{exp(s^{true})}{\sum exp(s)} \tag{19}$$

where s^{true} is the final score of the ground truth token computed by Eq. (18).

4   Experiments

4.1   Dataset

We evaluate CBR-Ren on FinQA dataset [7] and ConvFinQA dataset [8]. FinQA is a numerical reasoning dataset that contains 8,281 examples with fully annotated numerical reasoning programs, which is developed based on the publicly available earnings reports of S&P 500 companies in 10 years [29].

ConvFinQA is a conversational numerical reasoning dataset that contains 3,892 conversations consisting of 14,115 questions. And the dataset is split into 3,037/421/434 for train/dev/test sets.

4.2   Implementation Details

Our model is implemented on PyTorch and Transformers [24] from Huggingface, and evaluated on a single NVIDIA V100 32GB GPU. In our model, we use pre-trained language model BERT-base-uncased and RoBERTa-large to get the token representation and encoder. For the retriever, we set k = 3 to get three ranked facts as the retriever results, and set epoch = 8, batch size = 4, and maximum sequence length = 256. We optimize the encoder using Adam [14] with learning rate $2e$-5 to update models parameters, and we adopt a linear warmup [23] for the first 10% steps followed by a linear decay to 0 to prevent gradient explosion and over-fitting. For the generator, we set epoch = 500 and batch size = 8 for the two models. We use Adam with learning rate $2e$-5 for BERT-base-uncased and learning rate $1e$-5 for RoBERTa-large, and we set the $K = 3$ for CBR-driven retrieval algorithm. The maximum sequence length is set to 256. We clip the gradients of model parameters to a max norm of 1.0.

4.3   Baselines

We compare CBR-Ren to publicly available methods as the following: (1) **Longformer** [4], which handles the entire long documents to generate arithmetic expressions. (2) **NeRd** [22], which utilizes expression generator based on a pointer

Table 1. Comparison of CBR-Ren and baselines on FinQA. The performances of ChatGPT and GPT4 comes from Xie et al. [26], and they don't contain retrieval module. The pre-trained models that are used in the experiments are BERT-base-uncased and RoBERTa-large.

Model	Dev		Test	
	Exe Acc	Prog Acc	Exe Acc	Prog Acc
Longformer [4]	23.83	22.56	21.90	20.48
NeRd [22]	47.53	45.37	48.57	46.76
ELASTIC [27]	65.00	61.00	62.16	57.54
ChatGPT [20]	–	–	58.00	–
GPT4 [2]	–	–	63.00	–
BERT				
FinQANet [7]	49.91	47.15	50.00	48.00
DyRRen [16]	61.16	58.32	59.37	57.54
CBR-Ren (ours)	**62.62**	**60.13**	**61.92**	**59.96**
RoBERTa				
FinQANet [7]	61.22	58.05	61.24	58.86
DyRRen [16]	66.82	63.87	63.30	61.29
CBR-Ren (ours)	**68.40**	**65.68**	**67.81**	**65.32**
Human Expert	–	–	91.16	87.49
General Crowd	–	–	50.68	48.17

network. (3) **FinQANet** [7], which proposes a retriever-generator framework to generate arithmetic expression over tabular and textual data, and it has BERT and RoBERTa two versions. (4) **ELASTIC** [27], which proposes an adaptive symbolic compiler to get the expression. (5) **DyRRen** [16], which extends the retriever-generator framework and enhances the reasoning by dynamic reranking of retrieved facts. (6) **ChatGPT** [20], which is a large model that excel in numerous fields. (7) **GPT4** [2], which is a further development result of ChatGPT. (8) **Human performance**, which includes both experts and non-experts [7]. (9) **GPT-2** [15], which is similar to GPT4 and use prompts to get the answer. (10) **T-5** [21], which is similar to GPT model and use T-5 model to generate the expressions.

4.4   Metrics

We evaluate CBR-Ren with Program Accuracy (Prog Acc) and Execution Accuracy (Exe Acc). Prog Acc measures the accuracy of whether the generated arithmetic expression and the golden arithmetic expression are the same. Exe Acc measures the accuracy of whether the generated arithmetic expression can obtain the correct result.

Table 2. Comparison of CBR-Ren and baselines on ConvFinQA.

Model	Dev		Test	
	Exe Acc	Prog Acc	Exe Acc	Prog Acc
T-5	58.38	56.71	58.66	57.05
GPT-2	59.12	57.52	58.19	57.00
ChatGPT	–	–	60.00	–
GPT4	–	–	**76.00**	–
RoBERTa				
FinQANet	68.32	67.87	68.90	68.24
CBR-Ren (ours)	**72.61**	**71.03**	71.86	**71.14**
Human Expert	–	–	89.44	86.34
General Crowd	–	–	46.90	45.52

4.5 Main Results

Table 1 displays the performance of CBR-Ren and baseline on FinQA. CBR-Ren achieves the best performance, with 68.40 Exe Acc, 65.68 Prog Acc on dev set and 67.81 Exe Acc, 65.32 Prog Acc on test set. It is obvious that the performance of the model using the RoBERTa is much higher than using BERT. Inspired by the performance of pre-trained language models, we also attempted to use other pre-training language models, such as GPT2 [15], but did not achieve better experimental results than RoBERTa.

Table 2 shows the results on ConvFinQA. Compared with FinQANet, CBR-Ren leads by 3.86% of Exe Acc and 2.90% of Prog Acc on test set and 4.29% of Exe Acc and 3.16% of Prog Acc on dev set. This further demonstrates that our model has a certain degree of robustness and can adapt to different tasks.

Compared to ChatGPT and GPT4, CBR-Ren also outperforms by at least 2.32% of Exe Acc on FinQA, and CBR-Ren outperforms ChatGPT on ConvFinQA. This suggests that while the large language model may have some limitations in the financial reasoning field, with the aid of conversational prompts, it can still demonstrate satisfactory performance. Additionally, the results indicate that our model possesses distinct advantages, enabling it to outperform some large language models in inference tasks.

CBR-Ren outperforms DyRRen both on BERT and RoBERTa, surpassing 4.51% of Exe Acc and 4.03% of Prog Acc on test set and 1.58% of Exe Acc and 1.81% of Prog Acc on dev set. This indicates that improving the inferential capability of the retrieval-generator framework is necessary for financial numerical inference tasks.

For other tasks, the performance of ELASTIC is similar to CBR-Ren in BERT version, this indicates that CBR-Ren better handle long-form data. In addition, CBR-Ren is also much higher than NeRd, indicating the necessity to include a retriever in the model. And it can be noted that CBR-Ren, whether using BERT or RoBERTa, has surpassed the level of the general crowd, but there is still a gap compared to human expert.

Table 3. Ablation study on FinQA.

Model	Dev		Test	
	Exe Acc	Prog Acc	Exe Acc	Prog Acc
BERT				
CBR − Ren	**62.62**	**60.13**	**61.92**	**59.96**
w/o Golden_Exp	61.32	58.28	60.50	58.22
w/o Weight_Reg	59.98	57.29	59.49	57.21
w/o CBR	61.57	59.14	60.83	58.98
RoBERTa				
CBR − Ren	**68.40**	**65.68**	**67.81**	**65.32**
w/o Golden_Exp	67.38	64.67	66.87	64.35
w/o Weight_Reg	65.87	63.01	65.44	62.79
w/o CBR	67.74	64.85	67.26	64.62

4.6   Ablation Study

CBR-Ren consists of three key components: guided explanation module, fact weighting module, and CBR-driven module. The variant w/o Golden_Exp replaces our retriever with the original retriever. w/o Weight_Reg removes the fact weighting, generating arithmetic expressions solely based on retrieval facts. w/o CBR is the model without using CBR-driven retrieval algorithm.

In Table 3, w/o Golden_Exp in BERT leads to a relative drop of Exe Acc and Prog Acc by 1.42%, 1.74% on the test set. And the performance of w/o Golden_Exp in RoBERTa is 0.94% lower in Exe Acc and 0.97% lower in Prog Acc than CBR − Ren. The results also indicate that our guidance method has effect for numerical reasoning and without the help of fact weighting, if we only extract correct facts, but the semantics of facts cannot be correctly understood, correct reasoning cannot be carried out.

Ignoring the fact weighting method leads to a significant drop in performance. In BERT, w/o Weight_Reg performs 2.43% lower in Exe Acc and 2.75% lower in Prog Acc than CBR−Ren$_{BERT}$ on test set. Similarly, in RoBERTa, w/o Weight_Reg results in a performance decrease of 2.37% in Exe Acc and 2.53% in Prog Acc compared to CBR − Ren$_{RoBERTa}$. This highlights the effectiveness of fact weighting and confirms the importance of facts during the inference stage.

For the w/o CBR, in test set, the performance is 0.79% of Exe Acc and 0.98% of Prog Acc over BERT, while the performance is 0.55% of Exe Acc and 0.70% of Prog Acc over RoBERTa, demonstrating the effectiveness of CBR-driven retrieval algorithm.

4.7   Case Study

In Fig. 5, a case is sampled from FinQA. Both CBR-Ren and DyRRen accurately retrieve the critical facts F_2^R and F_3^R. However, CBR-Ren extract another fact that assist in understanding critical facts F_1^R, while DyRRen extracts an irrelevant sentence F_4^R.

Table			
in millions	december 31 2012 amortized cost	december 31 2012 fair value	fair value
...	...	...	...
total securities	$ 59801	**$ 61912**	$ 61018

Question

What would the fair value of total securities available for sale be without the fair value of securities classified as corporate stocks as of december 31, 2012?

Golden Explanation

The fair value of total securities available for sale without the fair value of securities classified as corporate stocks can be calculated using the following formula: *Fair Value of Total Securities Available for Sale=Total Fair Value of Available-for-Sale Securities−Fair Value of Corporate Stocks*

Retrieved Sentences

F_1^R: At december 31, 2012, the securities available for sale portfolio included a net unrealized gain of $ 1.6 billion.

F_2^R: The total securities of december 31 2012 fair value is **$ 61912**; the total securities of fair value is **$ 61018**

F_3^R:Includes **$ 367** million of both amortized cost and fair value of securities classified as corporate stocks and other at december 31, 2012 .

F_4^R:In millions the total securities available for sale of december 31 2012 amortized cost is $ 49447;

CBR-Ren Retrieved: { F_1^R, F_2^R, F_3^R }   **DyRRen** Retrieved: { F_1^R, F_2^R, F_4^R }

Arithmetic Expression	Fact Weight by IGRen				
		Q	F_1^R	F_2^R	F_3^R
✔ **CBR-Ren**: SUBTRACT (61912, 367)	SUBTRACT (61912, 367)	0.002	0.284	**0.638**	0.076
✘ **DyRRen** : SUBTRACT (**61018**, 367) DEVIDE (...)	SUBTRACT(61912, 367)	0.009	0.354	0.090	**0.547**

Fig. 5. Case study from FinQA.

During the inference generation process, both we and DyRRen correctly generated the operator, but on the first parameter, DyRRen was interfered by the interference term 61018. Although it located the correct critical fact, it lacked the assistance of auxiliary facts and could not determine the date of the attribute, resulting in a generation error. Through the weight of facts, it can also be seen that we assign high weights to critical facts. Therefore, we can generate this arithmetic expression correctly.

4.8 Fine-Grained Results

As shown in Table 4, the CBR-Ren achieves the best performance in all fine-grained analysis on dev set and test set. Regarding question types, CBR-Ren outperforms the baselines in all types. Particularly, CBR-Ren exhibits the most improvement in sentence-only questions. This indicates that CBR-Ren not only understands structured table-only questions well, but also handles more challenging sentence-only questions. However, CBR-Ren's performance is not satisfactory for table-sentence questions, suggesting that handling hybrid data remains a challenge.

For expression number, CBR-Ren surpasses other models in all cases. When the number of expressions is 2 or fewer, CBR-Ren performs exceptionally well. However, when the number of expressions exceeds 2, the performance of CBR-Ren shows a cliff-like decline. This phenomenon may be attributed to the fixed number of retrieved facts, which is less than the actual number of crucial facts, leading to significant limitations.

Table 4. Fine-grained comparison with CBR-Ren and DyRRen on question type and expression number. All models use Bert as the encoder.

Model	CBR − Ren(Dev)		CBR − Ren(Test)		DyRRen(Dev)		DyRRen(Test)	
	Exe Acc	Prog Acc	Exe Acc	Prog Acc	Exe Acc	Prog Acc	Exe Acc	Prog Acc
Type								
table-only	73.98	71.74	71.52	69.12	72.51	69.37	68.98	66.71
sentence-only	48.03	46.40	52.10	51.25	46.46	44.44	49.47	48.76
table-sentence	39.72	37.42	36.61	34.58	38.46	35.66	34.18	32.28
Expression Number								
1	67.61	65.44	66.90	65.40	66.16	63.67	64.37	63.00
2	62.54	59.40	60.08	57.24	60.98	57.49	57.46	54.77
> 2	27.42	25.04	32.12	30.93	26.03	23.29	29.76	28.57

5 Related Works

Math Word Problem (MWP) [12] is a challenging task in numerical reasoning, which aims to generate and calculate arithmetic expressions to answer short textual questions. Rule-based methods, such as statistical learning [11], graph-based techniques [25], and tree-based methods [13], are effective due to the regularity and controllability of MWP question descriptions. The HybridQA [6] introduces a new task by combining texts and tables. A BERT-based model proposed by Eisenschlos et al. [10] employs multiple attention mechanisms to tackle the HybridQA task. Then, researchers have shifted their focus to long-form numerical reasoning tasks that involve tabular characteristics, which is more challenging than MWP. TAT-QA [31], FinQA [7] and ConvFinQA [8] are the long-form numerical reasoning hybrid datasets from financial reports. Zhu et al. [30] propose a tree-based method for expression generation. Nararatwong et al. [19] use knowledge injection method to solve the problem of difficult to understand operators, and used GNN to solve the problem of the table data structure being damaged [18].

6 Conclusion

We propose CBR-Ren, comprising three innovative modules to enhance the inferential capability of the model: 1) The golden explanation module improves the quality of retrieved facts by enhancing interactions at different levels of granularity, thereby strengthening the retriever's ability. 2) The fact weighting module enhances the representation of retrieved facts, aiding in the generation of arithmetic expressions. 3) The CBR-driven retrieval algorithm further augments the decoder's representation using historical information. Our model outperforms all baselines on FinQA and ConvFinQA.

Acknowledgments. This work is supported in part by the Natural Science Foundation of China (grant No.62276188), TJU-Wenge joint laboratory funding.

References

1. Achiam, J., et al., et al.: Gpt-4 technical report (2023)
2. Adesso, G.: Gpt4: The ultimate brain. Authorea Preprints (2022)
3. Amini, A., Gabriel, S., Lin, P., Rik, K.-K., Choi, Y., Hajishirzi, H.: MathQA, Towards interpretable math word problem solving with operation-based formalisms (2019)
4. Beltagy, I.: Peters, M.E., Cohan, A.: Longformer, The long-document transformer, (2020)
5. Schank, R.C.: Dynamic Memory: A Theory of Reminding and Learning in Computers and People. Cambridge University Press, Cambridge (1983)
6. Chen, W., Zha, H., Chen, Z., Xiong, W., Wang, H., Wang, W.: HybridQA, A dataset of multi-hop question answering over tabular and textual data (2020)
7. Chen, Z., et al.: et al.: FinQA, A dataset of numerical reasoning over financial data (2021)
8. Chen, Z., Li, S., Smiley, C., Ma, Z., Shah, S., Wang, W.Y.: ConvFinQA, Exploring the chain of numerical reasoning in conversational finance question answering (2022)
9. Dua, D., Wang, Y., Dasigi, P., Stanovsky, G., Singh, S., Gardner, M.: Drop, A reading comprehension benchmark requiring discrete reasoning over paragraphs (2019)
10. Eisenschlos, J.M., Gor, M., Müller, T., Cohen, W.W.: Mate: multi-view attention for table transformer efficiency (2021)
11. Hosseini, M.J., Hajishirzi, H., Etzioni, O., Kushman, N.: Learning to solve arithmetic word problems with verb categorization (2014)
12. Huang, D., Shi, S., Lin, C.-Y., Yin, J., Ma, W.-Y.: How well do computers solve math word problems? large-scale dataset construction and evaluation (2016)
13. Jie, Z., Li, J., Lu, W.: Learning to reason deductively: Math word problem solving as complex relation extraction (2022)
14. Kingma, D.P., Ba, J.: Adam: a method for stochastic optimization (2014)
15. Lagler, K., Schindelegger, M., Böhm, J., Krásná, H., Nilsson, T.: Gpt2: empirical slant delay model for radio space geodetic techniques. Geophys. Res. Lett. **40**(6), 1069–1073 (2013)
16. Li, X., Zhu, Y., Liu, S., Ju, J., Qu, Y., Cheng, G.: Dyrren: a dynamic retriever-reranker-generator model for numerical reasoning over tabular and textual data (2023)
17. Liu, Y., et al.: Roberta, A robustly optimized bert pretraining approach (2019)
18. Nararatwong, R., Kertkeidkachorn, N., Ichise, R.: Enhancing financial table and text question answering with tabular graph and numerical reasoning. In: Proceedings of the 2nd Conference of the Asia-Pacific Chapter of the Association for Computational Linguistics and the 12th International Joint Conference on Natural Language Processing, pp. 991–1000 (2022)
19. Nararatwong, R., Kertkeidkachorn, N., Ichise, R.: Kiqa: knowledge-infused question answering model for financial table-text data. In: Proceedings of Deep Learning Inside Out (DeeLIO 2022): The 3rd Workshop on Knowledge Extraction and Integration for Deep Learning Architectures, pp. 53–61 (2022)
20. Ouyang, L., et al.: Training language models to follow instructions with human feedback (2022)
21. Raffel, C., et al.: Exploring the limits of transfer learning with a unified text-to-text transformer. J. Mach. Learn. Res. **21**(1), 5485–5551 (2020)
22. Ran, Q., Lin, Y., Li, P., Zhou, J., Liu, Z., NumNet, Machine reading comprehension with numerical reasoning (2019)
23. Targ, S., Almeida, D., Lyman, K.: Resnet in resnet, Generalizing residual architectures (2016)
24. Vaswani, A., et al.: Attention is all you need. In: Advances in neural information processing systems, vol. 30 (2017)
25. Wu, Q., Zhang, Q., Wei, Z.: An edge-enhanced hierarchical graph-to-tree network for math word problem solving (2021)

26. Xie, Q., et al.: PIXIU: a large language model, instruction data and evaluation benchmark for finance (2023)
27. Zhang, J., Moshfeghi, Y.: Elastic: numerical reasoning with adaptive symbolic compiler. Adv. Neural. Inf. Process. Syst. **35**, 12647–12661 (2022)
28. Zhao, W., Shang, M., Liu, Y., Wang, L., Liu, J.: Ape210k: a large-scale and template-rich dataset of math word problems (2020)
29. Zheng, X., Burdick, D., Popa, L., Zhong, X., Wang, N.X.R.: Global table extractor (GTE): a framework for joint table identification and cell structure recognition using visual context (2021)
30. Zhu, F., Lei, W., Feng, F., Wang, C., Zhang, H., Chua, T.-S.: Towards complex document understanding by discrete reasoning (2022)
31. Zhu, F., et al.: Tat-QA: a question answering benchmark on a hybrid of tabular and textual content in finance (2021)

A Case-Based Reasoning and Explaining Model for Temporal Point Process

Bingqing Liu[1,2(✉)]

[1] University of Chinese Academy of Science, Beijing, China
liubingqing20@mails.ucas.ac.cn
[2] Academy of Mathematics and Systems Science, CAS, Beijing, China

Abstract. Event sequence data widely exists in real life, where each event can be typically represented as a tuple, event type and occurrence time. Combined with deep learning, temporal point process (TPP) has gained a lot of success for event forecasting. However, the blackbox nature of neural networks makes them lack transparency for their forecasting decision. In this paper, we introduce case-based reasoning (CBR) into the modeling of temporal point process, yielding CBR-TPP. CBR is in line with human intuition and can provide explanation cases for decision-makers. Not using traditional similarity metrics (e.g., edit distance), we propose to employ the type-aware attention mechanism to retrieve the explanation cases as well as for cased-based reasoning. Experimental results on six datasets show that CBR-TPP outperforms existing TPP models on event forecasting task under both extrapolation and interpolation setting. Moreover, the results highlight the generalization ability and interpretability of our proposed model.

Keywords: Case-based reasoning · Interpretability · Event forecasting · Temporal point process · Attention mechanism

1 Introduction

Humans and natural phenomena generate a large number of event sequences. These sequences can be, for example, user behavior sequences, electronic healthcare records, earthquakes and aftershocks in geophysics [2,9,10,15]. In event sequences, there exist strong temporal event dependencies between different types of events that happen in the continuous time domain. Combined with deep learning, neural temporal point process (TPP) has recently become a hot research topic for modeling event sequence data [14,24,32], which is typically an encoder-decoder framework: the encoder is to evaluate the impacts of historical events and the decoder is to compute the probability of the next event. The information retrieval from historical events plays a key role in neural temporal point process modeling. On the one hand, only when the historical information is well summarized can the downstream decoder make better predictions about future events. On the other hand, the interpretability largely comes from the identification of historical events that contribute to the event forecasting.

J. A. Recio-Garcia et al. (Eds.): ICCBR 2024, LNAI 14775, pp. 127–142, 2024.
https://doi.org/10.1007/978-3-031-63646-2_9

Recurrent neural networks are widely utilized [3,8,23,31] to summarize the historical information, which encodes the events history into a low-dimensional semantic vector. Its main drawback comes from the lack of interpretability due to the notorious "black-box" problem of neural networks. Equipped with attention mechanism, Transformers can provide a certain degree of explanation [30,34,36]. However, by using the output vector at the last position as the history vector that encodes the historical information, it only tells which historical events the last event is focusing and can not explain the event forecasting decision. Moreover, existing models only learn from the most recent historical events and cannot utilize the long-term historical experiences when predicting the next event. We now lack a methodology that can better organize and exploit the historical events.

This paper describes CBR-TPP, a case-based reasoning guided method for the modeling of temporal point process. As a history-based problem solving method, guided by similarity [1], case-based reasoning is an appealing paradigm for event forecasting. Historical event sequence is split into different subsequences (case base) and CBR-TPP draws inspirations from the case base, with the historical cases that are most similar with the current situation as references for event forecasting. At the mean time, these historical events can naturally serve as explanation cases for the outcome of the prediction model.

To summarize, our main contributions are as follows: 1) we propose CBR-TPP, a powerful and explainable neural model for event forecasting. As far as we know, we are the first to introduce the case-base reasoning into the field of temporal point process; 2) we evaluate our model over event sequences collected from diverse domains and the empirical results on event prediction task under both extrapolation and interpolation setting demonstrate the superiority of our model; 3) we show CBR-TPP has better generalization ability than conventional TPP models and can provide explanation cases for event prediction.

2   Related Work

2.1   Temporal Point Process

A temporal point process (TPP) is a stochastic process whose realisation is a list of discrete events $\{(k_1, t_1), \cdots, (k_n, t_n), \cdots\}$ [4,5], where $t \in \mathbb{R}^+$ denotes the occurrence time of an event and each event is allocated with a type (aka mark) $k \in \{1, \cdots, K\}$. We typically describe a point process by its conditional intensity function, which can be interpreted as the instantaneous probability of an event occurring at time t conditioned on the history of events, i.e.,

$$\lambda_k^*(t) = \lim_{\Delta \to 0^+} \frac{P\{N_k^*[t, t + \Delta) > 0\}}{\Delta}$$
$$\lambda^*(t) = \sum_{k=1}^{K} \lambda_k^*(t) \tag{1}$$

where $P\{\circ\}$ denotes the probability of $\circ$, $N_k^*[t, t + \Delta)$ is the number of events of type k occurring within the infinitesimal time window $[t, t + \Delta)$ given events history before t, $\lambda_k^*(t)$ is the component intensity and $\lambda^*(t)$ is the total intensity.

Point processes can be specified by choosing a functional form for the intensity function. For example, the Hawkes process [12], one of the simplest interacting point process, is defined as $\lambda_k^*(t) = \lambda_k + \sum_{t_i < t} \varphi_{k,k_i}(t - t_i)$, where λ_k specifies the background intensity and $\varphi_{k,k_i}(t - t_i)$ is the triggering kernel which characterises the excitation effects of prior events (k_i, t_i). As we can see, Hawkes process assumes that the influences from past events are linearly additive towards the current event. These constraints on conditional intensity function limit the expressive power of traditional TPPs. To overcome these limitations, neural point process (NPP [24]) introduces deep learning techniques into point processes, gaining much success. NPPs utilize neural networks to encode the historical events and based on which predict which type of events will happen next and when. Recurrent neural networks (e.g., LSTM [13] and GRU [3]) and attention-based networks (e.g., Transformer [30]) are two most popular history encoders [6, 8, 19, 23, 27, 31, 33–36]. Representing historical events as a vector, known as the history vector, NPPs then construct the conditional intensity function. For example, the intensity function in RMTPP [8] is defined as $\lambda^*(t) = \exp(v^T h + w(t - t_{last}) + b)$, where h is the history vector, v, b are parameters and t_{last} is the occurrence time of the last historical event.

2.2 Cased-Based Reasoning

Case-based reasoning (CBR) bases current decisions on the outcomes of similar decisions that have been made in the past, which makes it a model-agnostic and quite general methodology for event forecasting. Moreover, the benefits of generating predictions based on past cases are the inherent interpretability of the CBR process. CBR has had a long history when it comes to tackling a range of forecasting problems in diverse domains such as sports, weather, finance, and health [7, 11, 21, 25, 29]. For these forecasting problems, a substantial efforts work on the time series data [7, 22]. Not like event sequences that have different event types and irregular inter-event times, time series are sequences of observed values of a variable at equally spaced timestamps. For time series data, a number of similarity metrics has been developed, such as dynamic time warping [20], move-split-merge [28] and time warp edit [17]. However, they can not be applied to event sequences due to the varied sequence settings.

3 Method

In this section, we detail the proposed model CBR-TPP (Case-Based Reasoning guided Temporal Point Process). The overall architecture of the proposed model is shown in Fig. 1 and the work flow of the case-based reasoning for event forecasting is shown in Fig. 2. Given historical events $\{(k_1, t_1), \cdots, (k_i, t_i)\}$, the goal of our model is to predict which type of event will occur next and when. According to the spirit of CBR, we should first gather from events history a case closest to the current situation (query), then based on which, suggest the most likely next event.

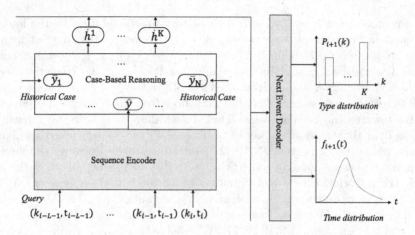

Fig. 1. The proposed Case-Based Reasoning guided Temporal Point Process (CBR-TPP). The mind map of the case-based reasoning for event forecasting is shown in Fig. 2. We first use a sequence encoder to encode the query sequences and historical cases as vector representations. Then, case-based reasoning is utilized to retrieve helpful historical cases, which in the decoding stage will be integrated and decoded to generate the next event distribution for event prediction.

3.1   Preliminary

Before diving into details of case-based reasoning for event forecasting, we firstly define the query (current situation) and historical cases (experiences).

Query. Query stands for the event situation that we are currently facing, also known as current problem. A good description (construction) for the current problem should not miss any historical events that have promoting effects on the next event (k_{i+1}, t_{i+1}). In the absence of domain knowledge, there exist two naive but reasonable problem constructing strategies: 1) (*length-based*) only the most recent L historical events have effects on the next event; 2) (*timespan-based*) only historical events that occurred within time $[t_i - T, t_i]$ have effects, where L and T are both hyperparameters, i.e., the values need to be manually adjusted according to the performance of event prediction.

Historical Cases. The historical cases stand for the earlier problem-solving experiences. Unlike query, which just declares the problem, the historical case must also contain the solution. That is, a historical experience is a tuple (problem, solution), or, (cause, effect) from the perspective of event causality, where cause is also a subsequence like query and the effect is the next event of the subsequence. To construct the cause, we can simply use the sliding-window method and the window can be fixed-length or -timespan according to the problem constructing strategy we previously adopted. For example, every L consecutive events in the past (before t_i) can be considered as a cause.

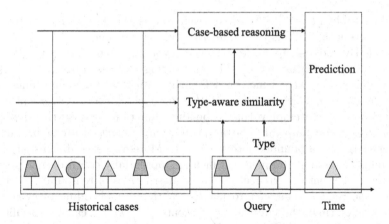

Fig. 2. The work flow of the case-based reasoning for event prediction. Query represents the situation that we are currently facing and historical cases are subsequences in the past that can potentially help predict the next event according to their similarities with the query subsequence.

3.2 Sequence Encoder

Suppose we have N historical cases, we then perform similarity comparison with the query to retrieve the cases that are similar to the current event situation, with the premise that the more similar two problems are, the more similar their solutions will be. An event sequence is a sequence of events with type occurred in continuous time space. This kind of complex setting distinguishes the event sequence from time series or word sequence (sentence) and makes it very challenging to evaluate the similarity. To this end, we turn to the field of deep learning, where there are many techniques that have been testified effective for event sequence processing, e.g., Transformer [30] and recurrent neural network (RNN) [3]. Transformer (and RNN, etc.) is also called sequence encoder, which serves as a flexible function that maps the event sequence to vector representation. With the help of sequence encoder, we can transform the problem of event sequence similarity into a problem of vector similarity. We introduce the sequence encoder in this subsection and leave the introduction of vector similarity for the next subsection.

In this work, we use Transformer to handle the event sequence for it allows the direct "communication" between any two events by the attention mechanism. The Transformer architecture consists of two modules, embedding layer and high-level feature layer. The embedding layer provides each event in the sequence an initial vector representation and the high-level feature layer transforms it into a context-aware vector representation, which is then averaged across all events to obtain the vector representation of the whole event sequence.

Embedding Layer. Given an event $e_j = (k_j, t_j)$, the embedding layer assigns it a vector representation. Specifically, to embed the event type, we train an embedding table $M \in \mathbb{R}^{K \times d}$, where each row is the embedding vector of a particular event type, K is the number of event types and d is the embedding dimension. By looking up table M, event type k_j is embeded as M^{k_j}, here the superscript indicates row k_j. The embedding table is randomly initialized before training. For event time, we define the temporal embedding function as $z(t) = [cos(w_1^t t + b_1^t), \cdots, cos(w_d^t t + b_d^t)]^T$, where $w_1^t, b_1^t, \cdots, w_d^t, b_d^t$ are all trainable parameters. We employ this embedding function because the sinusoidal function $cos(\cdot)$ can map an arbitrary timestamp (sometimes can be numerically very large) to a bounded interval $[-1, 1]$. Moreover, each dimension of $z(t)$ corresponds to an angle frequency, which can potentially capture some periodical patterns of event occurrence. For more alternatives of temporal embedding function, the readers can refer to [34,36]. With the embedding of event type and occurrence time, the embedding of event $e_j = (k_j, t_j)$ can be specified by $X^{e_j} = M^{k_j} + z(t_j)$, where we use $X = [X^{e_1}, \cdots, X^{e_j}, \cdots, X^{e_L}]$ to denote all event embeddings of the given event sequence $\{(k_1, t_1), \cdots, (k_i, t_i)\}$.

High-Level Feature Layer. The embedding layer only assigns each event an initial embedding (identity), without considering any dependencies between different events. To enable the mutual "communication" of events within the given event sequence, attention mechanism is utilized, which is defined as follows,

$$Z = \mathbf{Attn}(Q, J, V) = \mathbf{Softmax}(\frac{QJ^T}{\sqrt{d}})V$$

$$Q = XW_q, J = XW_j, V = XW_v$$

(2)

We explain the attention mechanism as follows: 1) Q, J, V are linear transformations of input $X \in \mathbb{R}^{L \times d}$, projected by weights $W_q, W_j, W_v \in \mathbb{R}^{d \times d}$ respectively; 2) $QJ^T \in \mathbb{R}^{L \times L}$ calculates the relationship between any two events of the given event sequence, scale factor $\sqrt{d}$ and **Softmax** are for the purpose of normalization. This step allows the "communication" of events and each event can find events of its concern; 3) each row vector of the attention output $Z \in \mathbb{R}^{L \times d}$ is a weighted average of row vectors of $V \in \mathbb{R}^{L \times d}$, which means that each row vector of Z has incorporated the context information of the given event sequence and thus can be considered as a more high-level vector representation.

To enhance the model capacity, multi-head self-attention mechanism [30] can be further employed. Then, the attention result Z is fed through a two-layer fully connected neural network described below,

$$Y = (\mathbf{Relu}(ZW_1 + b_1))W_2 + b_2$$

(3)

Here $W_1, W_2 \in \mathbb{R}^{d \times d}$, and $b_1, b_2 \in \mathbb{R}^d$ are trainable parameters of the neural network. To extract higher and higher features, we can construct a deeper neural network by simply repeating the operation in Eq. 2 and 3.

3.3   Similarity and Reasoning

With the help of sequence encoder, the problem of event sequence similarity has been transformed into a problem of vector similarity. In this subsection, we compute the vector-based similarity to retrieve the helpful historical cases, based on which, the case-based reasoning is conducted. Compared with the rule-based similarity, the advantage of neural network-based similarity lies in its flexibility and generality. Given two event sequences, they can have varied similarity from different angles of view. Consider the rule for example: two event sequences should be judged as similar as long as they share the high-risk event type k, regardless of the chronological order. But it can not be that case from the view of other event types. We propose type-aware attention mechanism to capture this difference from the perspective of event types, i.e.,

$$\hat{h}^k = \mathbf{Attn}(q^k, J^k, V^k) = \mathbf{Softmax}(\frac{q^k J^{k^T}}{\sqrt{d}})V^k$$
$$q^k = \hat{y}W_q^k, J^k = \bar{Y}W_j^k, V^k = \dot{Y}W_v^k \tag{4}$$

where $\hat{y}$ is the representation of the query, $\bar{Y} \in \mathbb{R}^{N \times d}$ is representations of the historical cases (N is the number of historical cases). $\dot{Y} \in \mathbb{R}^{N \times d}$ is the effect representations of historical cases (the cause is the historical case and the effect is its next event). In the type-aware attention mechanism, we have K sets of parameters $\{W_q^k, W_j^k, W_v^k\}$ that serve as signals and filters from different event types, and softmax$(q^k J^{k^T}/\sqrt{d}) \in \mathbb{R}^N$ is the normalized similarities between the query and historical cases from the perspective of event type k. Based on the computed similarities, we are not picking the effect of the most similar historical case, rather, we make a weighted average on all the effects $V^k \in \mathbb{R}^{N \times d}$ (transformed from $\dot{Y}$ by weight matrix W_v^k), and obtain the CBR result $\hat{h}^k \in \mathbb{R}^d$.

Given CBR results $H = \{\hat{h}^k\}_{k=1}^K$ from the perspective of different event types, we aggregate them to obtain the final CBR result h, i.e.,

$$h = w_1^g \hat{h}^1 + w_2^g \hat{h}^2 + \cdots + w_K^g \hat{h}^K$$
$$w_1^g, w_2^g, \cdots, w_K^g = \mathbf{Softmax}(Hh^g) \tag{5}$$

where $\{\dot{w}_k^g\}_{k=1}^K$ are the aggregation weights. The trainable vector h^g acts as a measure of the importance of different CBR results. Other widely used aggregation methods like average pooling or max (min) pooling can also be alternatives.

3.4 Next Event Decoder

The next event decoder is to characterize the next event distribution according to the CBR result h. Since an event is a tuple including the event type and occurrence time, we describe it a joint probability distribution, denoted as $P(k,t)$. Following [8,23], we decompose $P(k,t)$ as the multiplication of type distribution $P(k)$ and time distribution $P(t)$. Next, we introduce how these two distributions are modelled.

Modeling of $P(k)$. To infer the probability of various event types occurring at the next event, we can directly compare the CBR result h with the corresponding type embedding vector M^k, i.e.,

$$P(k) \sim \mathbf{Softmax}(Mh) \tag{6}$$

That is, for each event type k, we calculate a score by performing the inner product between the corresponding embedding vector M^k and the case-based reasoning result h. As a result, we get K scores and the type distribution can be obtained by **Softmax** function. To predict the event type of the next event, we can select the one that has the highest probability.

Modeling of $P(t)$. Different from the inference of the probability for event types, the event time is a continuous variable and thus it can not be possible for us to compare the CBR result with each time $t \in \mathbb{R}^+$. In temporal point process, time distribution is typically modeled via the conditional intensity function $\lambda^*(t)$ as introduced in Sect. 2. However, the training of intensity-based models is often a tricky problem as the likelihood contains an integral term, which is usually intractable and requires numerical approximation methods [18,36]. Recently, some works [23,31] showed that the time distribution can be directly modeled by probability density function and as a result, the likelihood can be calculated in closed-form. Commonly used probability density functions for time modeling include exponential distribution, log-normal distribution, Weibull distribution, and etc. The exponential distribution is suboptimal because it's a monotonically decreasing function. As a comparison, the log-normal distribution is a unimodal function and the flexibility of which can be further enhanced to be multi-modal by the mixture method described below,

$$f(t|w, \mu, s) = \sum_{c=1}^{C} w^c \frac{1}{ts^c\sqrt{2\pi}} \exp(-\frac{(\log t - \mu^c)^2}{2(s^c)^2}) \tag{7}$$

where $w, \mu, s \in \mathbb{R}^C$ are the function parameters, serving as the mixture weights, mixture means, and mixture standard deviations, respectively. The probability density function defined in Eq. 7 is called log-normal mixture distribution, with the number of mixture components being C, which has been proven that it is able to approximate any given time distribution as long as C is sufficiently large [23]. Besides, the Weibull mixture distribution can also be alternative [16].

To infer the probability of the occurrence time of the next event, we train a neural network whose input is the CBR result h and output is the function parameters. To this end, we simply use three linear transformations, parameterized by three weight matrices $W_c, W_\mu, W_s \in \mathbb{R}^{C \times d}$, i.e.,

$$w, \mu, s = W_c h, W_\mu h, W_s h \tag{8}$$

To predict the occurrence time of the next event, we can calculate the expectation of log-normal mixture distribution, i.e., $\sum_{c=1}^{C} w_c \exp(\mu_c + s_c^2/2)$.

Training. Suppose we have observed an event sequence S with n events $S = \{(k_i, t_i)\}_{i=1}^n$, our model then can be trained by maximizing the log-likelihood:

$$L(S) = \sum_{i=1}^{n} \log(f_i(t_i - t_{i-1}) + P_i(k_i)) \tag{9}$$

where the subscript i for f and P denotes that they are distributions conditioned on the events history before the i-th event. That is, they have different queries and historical cases. The source code for CBR-TPP, together with the datasets used in the experiment are available at the project website [1].

4   Experiment

4.1   Experimental Setup

Datasets and Baselines Three synthetic datasets and three real-world datasets are used to evaluate the proposed model. Statistics of these six datasets are shown in Table 1. Each dataset has a number of event sequences ("#Seqs"), and each event sequence contains a number of events, the average number of events in an event sequence is denoted as "#Avg. Events". The number of event types for each dataset is denoted as "#Types", and "Max Interval" means the maximum inter-event times. Datasets Hdep2, Hdep3 and Hdep9 are all synthetic datasets generated by multivariate Hawkes process:

$$\lambda_k(t) = \mu_k + \sum_{t_i < t} \alpha_{k,k_i} \beta_{k,k_i} \exp(-\beta_{k,k_i}(t - t_i)) \tag{10}$$

where μ_k is the base intensity for event type k, exciting factor α_{k,k_i} denotes how much event of type k_i will excite the occurrence of event of type k, and time-decaying factor β_{k,k_i} shows how fast this excitation effect is decaying over time. We use tick library [2] to generate Hawkes datasets with three different settings of parameters. HDep2, HDep3 and HDep5 are datasets with 2, 3 and 5 event types respectively. And there exists dependencies between any two event types. For latter evaluation of the explainability on dataset HDep5 [31], we here list the setting of parameters α, which indicates the dependencies among event types:

$$\alpha = \begin{bmatrix} 0.689 & 0.549 & 0.066 & 0.819 & 0.007 \\ 0.630 & 0.000 & 0.457 & 0.622 & 0.141 \\ 0.134 & 0.579 & 0.821 & 0.527 & 0.795 \\ 0.199 & 0.556 & 0.147 & 0.030 & 0.649 \\ 0.353 & 0.557 & 0.892 & 0.638 & 0.836 \end{bmatrix} \tag{11}$$

MIMIC [31], SOflow [8] and MOOC [31] are three publicly available real-world datasets. MIMIC is a dataset concerning the electronic health records and the event type denotes the type of disease. In dataset SOflow, one event sequence represents different badges received by one user over two years. Dataset MOOC records users' actions like taking a course and solving an assignment in an online course system.

To evaluate the effectiveness of our proposed model, we compare against other neural TPP models, including RMTPP [8], NHP [18], SAHP [34], THP

---

[1]   https://github.com/lbq8942/CBR-TPP.
[2]   https://x-datainitiative.github.io/tick/modules/hawkes.html.

Table 1. Dataset statistics and hyperparameters. From left to right columns: name of the dataset, number of event types, number of event sequences in the dataset, average event length per sequence, maximum inter-event time interval, window length L and the number of used historical cases N.

Dataset	#Types	#Seqs	#Avg. Events	Max Interval	L	N
HDep2	2	24576	24.910	4.223	5	10
HDep3	3	3000	256.928	2.423	7	20
HDep5	5	5000	424.765	2.037	10	30
MIMIC	75	715	3.723	5.613	3	30
SOflow	22	6633	72.248	21.033	15	40
MOOC	97	7047	56.284	14.754	20	50

[36], FullyNN [19], LNM [23] and JTPP [31]. Classified by the sequence encoder they used, SAHP and THP are Transformer-based methods while the rest models are RNN-based methods. All baselines don't use the case-based reasoning for event forecasting and instead, they are dedicated to learning a neural network function that directly maps the query to the next event.

Model Configuration. We use Adam to optimize the parameters in CBR-TPP, the learning rate is set to 0.001, and the loss function is the negative log-likelihood. We split each dataset into training data, validation data and testing data according to the number of event sequences, with three parts accounting for 60%, 20% and 20% respectively. The hidden dimension d is set to 32 and the number of mixture components C in Eq. 7 is set to 64 for all datasets. We construct the query and historical cases by length-based strategy. We mainly tune the following two hyperparameters: window length L and the number of used historical cases N. Their settings are reported in Table 1. For all models, we adopt early stop strategy, i.e., stop training if there is no performance (NLL) improvement on the validation data for 10 epochs. For hyperparameters of baselines, we follow the settings in their paper.

4.2   Results

Predictive Ability. In this part, we report the predictive performance of our proposed model. Event type prediction and goodness-of-fit are two tasks that often used to evaluate the predictive performance of an NPP model. Event type prediction is a "hard" prediction task that predicts the most likely event type of the next event and is evaluated by the accuracy. In this paper, we report the accuracy by weighted F1 score. As a complement, goodness-of-fit is a "soft" prediction task that tests whether the type and time distributions are well predicted, the quality of which is quantified by the log-likelihood, as shown in Eq. 9. As with most existing models [18,19,26], we equivalently use negative log-likelihood (NLL) as the metric, the lower the better. In addition to the extrapolation task

Table 2. Comparison of the predictive performance under the extrapolation setting. NLL stands for negative log-likelihood and F1 stands for the weighted F1 score (in percentage). The best and second best model on each dataset have been highlighted in bold and underline respectively.

Model	HDep2		HDep3		HDep5		MIMIC		SOflow		MOOC	
	NLL	F1	NLL	F1	NLL	F1	NLL	F1	NLL	F1	NLL	F1
RMTPP	43.1	51.9	195.2	37.9	322.2	22.9	7.3	63.2	246.1	30.2	226.0	38.9
NHP	43.0	51.7	194.1	37.3	316.6	23.0	7.1	63.4	238.2	30.0	210.3	38.8
FullyNN	42.1	52.7	192.5	37.5	315.4	23.2	6.7	64.0	233.8	30.4	196.6	39.0
LNM	41.8	51.3	190.9	37.7	314.7	23.7	6.5	64.4	232.3	31.3	193.2	39.0
SAHP	42.2	52.8	193.9	37.6	316.5	24.6	6.9	65.3	235.3	31.5	199.4	<u>39.4</u>
THP	42.4	<u>52.9</u>	194.0	<u>37.8</u>	317.8	24.8	6.8	<u>65.5</u>	237.4	31.6	202.4	39.2
JTPP	<u>41.4</u>	51.3	<u>189.5</u>	37.7	<u>310.7</u>	<u>24.9</u>	<u>5.8</u>	65.4	<u>225.3</u>	<u>31.8</u>	<u>181.7</u>	39.3
CBR-TPP	**41.2**	**53.4**	**188.3**	**38.5**	**308.6**	**26.6**	**5.3**	**66.4**	**223.1**	**33.5**	**178.5**	**42.8**

that predict the next event, we introduce a new prediction task, interpolation prediction. Specifically, we randomly select a sequence of events, and then mask off one of the events, our task is to predict the masked event.

Table 3. Comparison of the predictive performance under the interpolation setting.

Model	HDep2		HDep3		HDep5		MIMIC		SOflow		MOOC	
	NLL	F1	NLL	F1	NLL	F1	NLL	F1	NLL	F1	NLL	F1
RMTPP	38.8	52.2	188.6	37.5	309.2	25.1	6.5	66.2	207.7	33.5	177.2	47.8
NHP	38.5	52.6	186.6	37.8	306.5	26.2	6.0	67.1	205.3	33.3	165.8	50.8
FullyNN	37.8	52.7	183.9	37.5	300.4	26.1	5.8	67.4	200.0	33.4	155.6	53.9
LNM	37.4	52.3	180.5	38.0	298.6	26.8	5.5	69.2	195.6	34.5	150.8	54.0
SAHP	38.2	52.9	184.8	38.2	301.9	26.6	6.2	70.1	198.9	34.9	157.7	55.9
THP	37.9	<u>53.4</u>	184.0	38.8	303.0	26.8	6.5	69.3	198.3	35.0	159.4	<u>56.3</u>
JTPP	<u>36.8</u>	52.4	<u>173.7</u>	<u>39.2</u>	<u>290.6</u>	<u>27.5</u>	<u>4.9</u>	<u>70.3</u>	<u>189.3</u>	<u>35.1</u>	<u>142.6</u>	56.2
CBR-TPP	**36.4**	**54.2**	**173.1**	**40.1**	**288.3**	**28.3**	**4.5**	**71.2**	**187.6**	**35.6**	**135.2**	**58.2**

The extrapolation prediction results are shown in Table 2, and the interpolation prediction results are shown in Table 3. For each dataset, larger weighted F1 score indicates better performance and the smaller the negative log-likelihood, the better the fitness. From Table 2, we can see that our proposed model CBR-TPP consistently obtains the best performance over six datasets and we see a significant improvement on some datasets like HDep5 and MOOC, which demonstrates the effectiveness of our proposed case-based reasoning guided neural TPP model. Similar conclusion can be drawn from the comparison of the predictive performance under the interpolation setting.

Generalized Predictive Ability. Conventional TPP models are dedicated to learning neural network functions that directly map the query to the next

Table 4. Comparison of the generalized predictive performance under the extrapolation and interpolation setting (with superscript *).

Model	MIMIC				SOflow				MOOC			
	NLL	F1	NLL*	F1*	NLL	F1	NLL*	F1*	NLL	F1	NLL*	F1*
LNM	15.9	52.8	11.4	59.6	254.2	25.5	216.8	29.5	208.9	31.1	184.6	45.7
THP	17.5	53.9	14.8	60.6	255.9	26.3	220.8	30.7	210.6	31.7	194.4	48.9
JTPP	14.3	53.6	10.5	59.4	250.1	26.9	213.4	30.2	203.5	31.2	178.6	47.3
CBR-TPP	**11.7**	**56.2**	**8.3**	**62.3**	**244.3**	**28.7**	**210.9**	**31.3**	**198.2**	**35.5**	**169.6**	**52.4**

event, which, however, may fail when the query is new, e.g., the query contains new event types that have never been seen during the training phase. As a comparison, CBR-TPP aims at learning a similarity metric that is generally applicable for comparing event sequences (even unseen before). Applying the similarity metric, our model infers the next event of the query from similar historical cases.

To experimentally evaluate the generalization ability, for each dataset, we randomly select 10% of event types and leave all event sequences that contain these event types in the testing set, so that these event types are not visible during the training phase. Since datasets HDep2, HDep3, and HDep5 have very few event types and one event sequence usually contains all the event types, we only conduct this experiment on datasets MIMIC, SOflow and MOOC. The predictive results on testing sets that contain unseen queries are reported in Table 4. As we can see, CBR-TPP outperforms the baselines significantly under both extrapolation and interpolation event prediction setting.

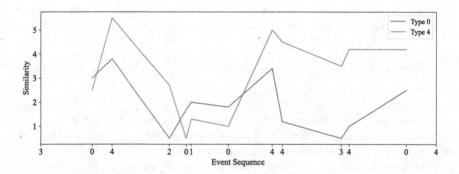

Fig. 3. Similarities between the query and historical cases. The last 2 events is the query (L is set to 2 in this experiment). By sliding the window, every 2 consecutive events before the query forms a historical case and its similarity to the query is computed. The adopted type-aware similarity allows for varied similarity results over the historical cases among different event types, we display the similarities for type 0 and 4.

Interpretability. In this part, we demonstrate the interpretability of CBR-TPP over Hawkes dataset HDep5. Figure 3 displays an event sequence, where the event type is marked on the x-axis and the event time is implicitly indicated by the inter-event distance. The similarities between the query and historical cases are displayed on the y-axis. The curves start from event 0, which stands for the similarity of the query to the first historical case $(3, 0)$.

From the curves, we see our model can well find the similar historical cases. Also, we see varied similarities exist among different event types. According to α_{00} in Eq. 11, type 0 is largely influenced by type 0 but not by type 4, which makes it more interested in historical cases that contains type 0 rather than type 4, see similarities on (4,2) and (2,0). On the contrary, type 4 is interested in both type 0 and type 4 (see α_{40} and α_{44}). Hence, its similarities on historical cases containing the two event types can be very high, regardless of the chronological order, see similarities on (0,4) and (4,0).

4.3   Ablation Study

In this part, we analyze the key ingredients of our model. Specifically, to evaluate the efficacy of the CBR module, we remove the module (the white box in Fig. 2) and then test model's predictive performance. We also validate the contribution of the proposed type-aware similarity by replacing it with type-unaware similarity, i.e., there only exists one similarity between two event sequences (remove the superscript k in Eq. 4). We compare the length- and timespan-based constructing strategy introduced in Sect. 3.1. Besides, we replace our encode and decoder with that used in baseline JTPP and THP.

Table 5. Ablation study: an investigation of the predictive performance of CBR-TPP with some of its modules removed or replaced. TWS denotes type-aware similarity. The prediction is under the extrapolation setting.

Model	HDep3		HDep5		MIMIC		SOflow	
	NLL	F1	NLL	F1	NLL	F1	NLL	F1
don't use CBR	190.4	37.9	312.1	25.3	5.8	65.7	226.1	31.7
don't use TWS	188.8	38.5	310.0	25.9	5.3	66.5	224.3	32.4
use timespan-based construction	187.8	39.2	310.1	27.6	5.7	65.7	225.2	32.5
use RNN as encoder	188.0	38.3	308.2	26.1	5.5	65.8	224.5	31.8
use decoder of THP	191.3	38.0	313.6	25.9	6.1	65.8	230.4	32.1
CBR-TPP	188.3	38.5	308.6	26.6	5.3	66.4	223.1	33.5

We show the ablation results in Table 5. We see that the CBR guided TPP model consistently outperforms the counterpart that doesn't use CBR. This is expected because the conventional TPP model only relies on the query while CBR-TPP further utilizes the historical cases. We also find the type-aware similarity is usually helpful as it can capture more fine-grained information. For the query, we see the length- and timespan-based constructions both have their strengths. By substituting our encoder and decoder, we see RNN is also feasible and the decoder of THP can make worse for it only defines a monotonic intensity function, limiting the flexibility.

5   Conclusion

In this paper, we present case-based reasoning guided temporal point process to model the event sequence data, where CBR serves as a powerful methodology that can learn from the historical events efficiently. CBR-TPP realizes the case-based reasoning during the encoding stage, making the information retrieval from historical events more transparent and understandable, with the explanation cases derived from the similarities between the historical cases and the current situation. Due to the complexity of event sequences, we propose to generally use the type-aware attention mechanism to conduct the similarity comparison as well as the case-based reasoning. Experiments on various synthetic and real-world datasets demonstrate that CBR-TPP achieves state-of-the-art performance on standard prediction tasks under both extrapolation and interpolation setting, has more generalization ability and can provide explanation cases for the prediction.

Despite this success, CBR-TPP does have its drawbacks compared with conventional TPP models that directly map the query to the next event. CBR-TPP additionally utilizes the historical cases, which really enhances the capacity but also makes it much more time-consuming. For example, the running time on MOOC is about 20 times that of conventional models. The key to reducing time complexity is to reduce N, but small N may not be able to recall potentially helpful historical cases, which we leave for future work.

References

1. Aamodt, A., Plaza, E.: Case-based reasoning: foundational issues, methodological variations, and system approaches. AI Commun. **7**, 39–59 (1994). https://api.semanticscholar.org/CorpusID:7069926
2. Bacry, E., Mastromatteo, I., Muzy, J.F.: Hawkes processes in finance. Market Microstruct. Liquidity **1**(01), 1550005 (2015)
3. Chung, J., Çaglar Gülçehre, Cho, K., Bengio, Y.: Empirical evaluation of gated recurrent neural networks on sequence modeling. ArXiv abs/1412.3555 (2014)
4. Daley, D.J., Vere-Jones, D.: An introduction to the theory of point processes: volume I: elementary theory and methods. Springer, New York (2003)
5. Daley, D.J., Vere-Jones, D.: An introduction to the theory of point processes: volume II: general theory and structure. Springer, New York (2007). https://doi.org/10.1007/b97277
6. Dash, S., She, X., Mukhopadhyay, S.: Learning point processes using recurrent graph network. In: 2022 International Joint Conference on Neural Networks (IJCNN), pp. 1–8. IEEE (2022)

7. Dolphin, R., Smyth, B., Xu, Y., Dong, R.: Measuring financial time series similarity with a view to identifying profitable stock market opportunities. In: Sánchez-Ruiz, A.A., Floyd, M.W. (eds.) ICCBR 2021. LNCS (LNAI), vol. 12877, pp. 64–78. Springer, Cham (2021). https://doi.org/10.1007/978-3-030-86957-1_5

8. Du, N., Dai, H., Trivedi, R., Upadhyay, U., Gomez-Rodriguez, M., Song, L.: Recurrent marked temporal point processes: embedding event history to vector. In: Proceedings of the 22nd ACM SIGKDD International Conference on Knowledge Discovery and Data Mining, pp. 1555–1564 (2016)

9. Enguehard, J., Busbridge, D., Bozson, A., Woodcock, C., Hammerla, N.: Neural temporal point processes for modelling electronic health records. In: Machine Learning for Health, pp. 85–113. PMLR (2020)

10. Farajtabar, M., Wang, Y., Gomez Rodriguez, M., Li, S., Zha, H., Song, L.: Coevolve: a joint point process model for information diffusion and network co-evolution. In: Advances in Neural Information Processing Systems, vol. 28 (2015)

11. Feely, C., Caulfield, B., Lawlor, A., Smyth, B.: An extended case-based approach to race-time prediction for recreational marathon runners. In: International Conference on Case-Based Reasoning (2022). https://api.semanticscholar.org/CorpusID: 251648854

12. Hawkes, A.G.: Point spectra of some mutually exciting point processes. J. Roy. Stat. Soc.: Ser. B (Methodol.) **33**(3), 438–443 (1971)

13. Hochreiter, S., Schmidhuber, J.: Long short-term memory. Neural Comput. **9**(8), 1735–1780 (1997)

14. Lin, H., Tan, C., Wu, L., Gao, Z., Li, S., et al.: An empirical study: extensive deep temporal point process. ArXiv abs/2110.09823 (2021)

15. Liu, B., Huang, X.: Link-aware link prediction over temporal graph by pattern recognition. In: International Conference on Industrial, Engineering and Other Applications of Applied Intelligent Systems (2023). https://api.semanticscholar.org/CorpusID:260170307

16. Marín, J.M., Rodriguez-Bernal, M., Wiper, M.P.: Using weibull mixture distributions to model heterogeneous survival data. Commun. Stat.-Simul. Comput. **34**(3), 673–684 (2005)

17. Marteau, P.F.: Time warp edit distance with stiffness adjustment for time series matching. IEEE Trans. Pattern Anal. Mach. Intell. **31**, 306–318 (2007). https://api.semanticscholar.org/CorpusID:10049446

18. Mei, H., Eisner, J.M.: The neural hawkes process: a neurally self-modulating multivariate point process. In: Advances in Neural Information Processing Systems, vol. 30 (2017)

19. Omi, T., Aihara, K., et al.: Fully neural network based model for general temporal point processes. In: Advances in Neural Information Processing Systems, vol. 32 (2019)

20. Sakoe, H.: Dynamic programming algorithm optimization for spoken word recognition. IEEE Trans. Acoust. Speech Sig. Process. **26**, 159–165 (1978). https://api.semanticscholar.org/CorpusID:17900407

21. Sanz-Ramos, Á., Ariza-López, L., Montón-Giménez, C., Sánchez-Ruiz-Granados, A.A.: Retrieval of similar cases to improve the diagnosis of diabetic retinopathy. In: International Conference on Case-Based Reasoning (2023). https://api.semanticscholar.org/CorpusID:260383093

22. Schake, E., Grumbach, L., Bergmann, R.: A time-series similarity measure for case-based deviation management to support flexible workflow execution. In: International Conference on Case-Based Reasoning (2020). https://api.semanticscholar.org/CorpusID:222142477

23. Shchur, O., Biloš, M., Günnemann, S.: Intensity-free learning of temporal point processes. In: International Conference on Learning Representations (2020)
24. Shchur, O., Türkmen, A.C., Januschowski, T., Günnemann, S.: Neural temporal point processes: a review. ArXiv abs/2104.03528 (2021)
25. Smyth, B., Willemsen, M.C.: Predicting the personal-best times of speed skaters using case-based reasoning. In: International Conference on Case-Based Reasoning (2020). https://api.semanticscholar.org/CorpusID:222143572
26. Soen, A., Mathews, A., Grixti-Cheng, D., Xie, L.: Unipoint: universally approximating point processes intensities. In: Proceedings of the AAAI Conference on Artificial Intelligence, vol. 35, pp. 9685–9694 (2021)
27. Song, Z.V., Liu, J.W., Yang, J., Zhang, L.N.: Linear normalization attention neural hawkes process. Neural Comput. Appl. **35**(1), 1025–1039 (2023)
28. Stefan, A., Athitsos, V., Das, G.: The move-split-merge metric for time series. IEEE Trans. Knowl. Data Eng. **25**, 1425–1438 (2013). https://api.semanticscholar.org/CorpusID:12290203
29. Valdez-Ávila, M.F., Bermejo-Sabbagh, C., Díaz-Agudo, B., del Castillo, M.G.O., Recio-García, J.A.: Cbr-fox: a case-based explanation method for time series forecasting models. In: International Conference on Case-Based Reasoning (2023). https://api.semanticscholar.org/CorpusID:260383797
30. Vaswani, A., et al.: Attention is all you need. In: Advances in Neural Information Processing Systems, vol. 30 (2017)
31. Waghmare, G., Debnath, A., Asthana, S., Malhotra, A.: Modeling interdependence between time and mark in multivariate temporal point processes. In: Proceedings of the 31st ACM International Conference on Information & Knowledge Management, pp. 1986–1995 (2022)
32. Yan, J.: Recent advance in temporal point process: from machine learning perspective. SJTU Technical Report (2019)
33. Yang, C., Mei, H., Eisner, J.: Transformer embeddings of irregularly spaced events and their participants. In: Proceedings of the Tenth International Conference on Learning Representations (ICLR) (2022)
34. Zhang, Q., Lipani, A., Kirnap, O., Yilmaz, E.: Self-attentive hawkes process. In: International Conference on Machine Learning, pp. 11183–11193. PMLR (2020)
35. Zhu, S., Zhang, M., Ding, R., Xie, Y.: Deep fourier kernel for self-attentive point processes. In: International Conference on Artificial Intelligence and Statistics (2020)
36. Zuo, S., Jiang, H., Li, Z., Zhao, T., Zha, H.: Transformer hawkes process. In: International Conference on Machine Learning, pp. 11692–11702. PMLR (2020)

Extracting Indexing Features for CBR from Deep Neural Networks: A Transfer Learning Approach

Zachary Wilkerson$^{(\boxtimes)}$, David Leake⓪, Vibhas Vats, and David Crandall

Luddy School of Informatics, Computing, and Engineering, Indiana University,
Bloomington, IN 47408, USA
{zachwilk,leake,vkvats,djcran}@indiana.edu

Abstract. High-quality indices are essential for accurate retrieval in case-based reasoning. However, in some domains, indexing knowledge may be incomplete, unavailable, or unfeasible to obtain by knowledge acquisition, making knowledge-light machine learning methods an appealing alternative for generating indexing features. In response, previous work has developed promising methods for extracting indexing features from deep neural networks trained on case data. However, it has also underlined that CBR using features extracted from a deep neural network achieves low accuracy in domains for which the network itself has low accuracy when trained from scratch. This is a special concern for CBR feature extraction because the ability of CBR to reason successfully in "small-data" domains has been seen as one of its benefits. This paper reports on work investigating the hypothesis that transfer learning may help decrease the data requirements for index extraction. Specifically, it examines how model pretraining affects the quality of extracted indexing features for case-based classification, measured by the performance of a case-based classifier using those features for retrieval. Experimental results suggest that using a pretrained deep learning model for feature extraction can improve classification accuracy and consistency compared to using similar models trained from scratch. An unexpected and intriguing result is that the case-based classifier using extracted features outperformed analogous deep learning classifiers for the tested dataset.

Keywords: Case-Based Reasoning · Deep Learning · Feature Learning · Hybrid Systems · Indexing · Integrated Systems · Retrieval · Transfer Learning

1 Introduction

The performance of case-based reasoning (CBR) systems depends critically on retrieving useful cases from the case base. This retrieval is generally based on a feature vocabulary used to index the cases in the case base. Traditionally, such a vocabulary is developed through knowledge engineering (e.g., [14, 23, 35]), with

J. A. Recio-Garcia et al. (Eds.): ICCBR 2024, LNAI 14775, pp. 143–158, 2024.
https://doi.org/10.1007/978-3-031-63646-2_10

indices assigned to new problems by situation assessment. This knowledge-based approach can be effective in identifying key features and facilitating human-understandable explanations for retrievals. However, knowledge engineering is costly and generating knowledge-engineered feature sets may be unfeasible for some domains, such as image processing.

Deep learning (DL) classification methods avoid traditional knowledge acquisition and provide high accuracy across a variety of domains, including image classification [10]. This stems from the ability of DL models to learn useful feature information from raw data. Consequently, the application of deep learning methods to learning features for case retrieval has received attention from the CBR community (e.g., [3,33,37,38]). DL feature generation for case-based classifiers has three potential benefits: to increase accuracy, to decrease the knowledge engineering burden, and to enable case-based classification in domains for which retrieval features are unfeasible to generate by hand (e.g., image classification). Compared to using a pure DL classifier, the hybrid approach provides an interpretability benefit: The hybrid system can explain its decisions by presenting the retrieved cases for humans to assess their relevance—which can be an effective explanation strategy even when retrieval features are unexplained [16].

Many factors may affect the quality of case retrieval features extracted from a DL model. We have explored how the number of features extracted, network depth at which features are extracted, and extractor model architecture influence feature quality [26,27]. We have also explored how using existing knowledge-engineered and extracted features together improves classification accuracy overall [40]. These experiments provided useful information about how to design feature extraction systems, but the experimental results also pointed to a concern. One of the motivations for using CBR is to enable effective reasoning in "small-data" domains for which only limited numbers of cases may be available or necessary [24]. Consequently, we tested the methods on DL models trained from limited training data to examine performance for small-data domains. Our results showed that DL models trained from scratch on limited training data overfitted or failed to converge, resulting in poor-quality features and suboptimal CBR performance. Thus, in such domains, lack of data limits the effectiveness of feature extraction from DL models. This is problematic for the goal of leveraging DL while retaining the ability of CBR to reason successfully with limited data.

Extensive DL research has shown the benefit of transfer learning, in which DL models thoroughly trained for one domain are leveraged and specialized to new related tasks. This led us to consider whether applying transfer learning to a DL network used for feature extraction could improve the quality of case retrieval features produced with limited domain data. This paper presents experimental results on the use of transfer learning for DL feature extraction, examining the performance achieved for various DL architectures.

The paper begins with an overview of our general DL-CBR feature extraction approach and summary of our previous studies, which provide a baseline for the current work. We then present an evaluation of several DL feature extraction models using networks that have been pretrained and then specialized via training on a novel test domain. Our earlier evaluation of these architectures using training from scratch suggested that more complex DL models (e.g., Inception V3 and DenseNet121) are potentially more prone to overfitting, producing lower-quality features. In contrast, our new experimental results show that using pretrained versions of these same DL models can produce high-quality features, providing high classification accuracy for the CBR system. Surprisingly, the overall DL-CBR system accuracy rivals and occasionally surpasses the classification accuracy of using the pretrained DL architecture end-to-end in our experiments. This potential performance benefit is intriguing, and we discuss potential explanations in Sect. 5.3. The DL-CBR system also appears to be more consistent on average, yielding lower average standard deviation over all tests. Especially when combined with the interpretability of the DL-CBR system, these results appear very promising.

2   Related Work

Integrations of DL with CBR are appealing for goals such as explaining DL and increasing CBR performance. For example, similarity metric learners that focus on class-wise comparison of examples, such as Siamese networks [22], relation networks [36], and matching networks [34], can be used for similarity assessment in CBR (e.g., [4,28,30]), and network architectures can be designed for features to be compared against prototypes to guide the model decision [7,11,29]. Other research has investigated DL-CBR integration to explain DL models, as with *post-hoc* feature-level explanations [5] and "twin systems" [19]. Finally, and of particular interest to this paper, previous research has explored ways that DL systems may be leveraged to extract feature information for CBR systems, as described in Sect. 2.1.

2.1   Extracting DL Features for Case Retrieval

Case retrieval features have traditionally been developed by knowledge engineering [14,23,35]. However, acquiring expert-based feature sets may be unfeasible for some domains, and knowledge engineering can be costly. Symbolic learning methods have successfully been applied to this problem using existing feature vocabularies (e.g., [6,8,9,12,15]), but DL feature extraction is appealing to enable the system to develop its own feature vocabulary (e.g., [3,33,38]) and to develop features for domains such as image classification. For example, Turner et al. use a CBR system to perform relative classification on examples for which the DL system lacks confidence in its decision (esp. for examples from novel classes) [37,38]. In this way, the CBR system leverages features extracted from the DL system and clusters examples to form implicit classes. Sani et al. use a similar approach for feature extraction but always use the CBR system to render model decisions [33]. They highlight that the ability of the hybrid system to explain its decision through case presentation, combined with its accurate performance, make it a promising model for the types of domains in their case study.

These approaches make assumptions that are challenged in our previous work. First, they extract feature vectors from between the convolution and densely-connected layers in the DL model; we found that better quality features may be extracted from between the densely-connected layers and the output layer, where (ideally) features have been combined into more complex indices by the network's densely-connected layers (see Sect. 3.2 for details) [26]. Second, previous work assumes that the DL system is the sole source of features for case retrieval. However, knowledge-engineered features may be available for some domains, even if those features alone are insufficient. We showed that in some cases using a combination of expert-generated and DL-derived features can significantly benefit system performance [27,40]. In addition, we showed sensitivity of feature quality to several model-level parameterizations, such as number of features extracted [26] and DL model architecture [27].

2.2   Transfer Learning

Transfer learning exploits the results of learning for one task to improve performance on another similar task [42]. CBR itself has been advocated as a transfer learning method [21], and knowledge transfer to improve CBR has been studied in contexts such as cross-case-base adaptation [25] and index revision during long-term system operation [17,31].

In deep learning, the need for large datasets and extensive training to achieve strong performance has led to great interest in exploiting prior models to improve training in new domains. In this approach, weights from an already-trained DL model are used to initialize the weights for a new model, which is then specialized on a different dataset during training. Transfer learning by using pretrained models has proven powerful for overcoming issues arising from limited data when training end-to-end DL systems [32]. Because our previous studies of DL feature extraction showed the difficulty of training the networks for small-data domains, we hypothesized that improving the DL model by using pretrained models would improve the quality of extracted features as well.

3   Our Approach to DL Feature Extraction for Case-Based Classification

3.1   Convolutional Neural Network Structure

As context for describing our method, we briefly summarize neural network structure. Neural network models can be broadly conceptualized as a system of layers that use features from previous layers to inform feature combinations that occur in subsequent layers. Taken together, these layers process raw input data into low-level atomic features that are then combined into more complex mid- and high-level features that are used to render the final model decision. In this high-level abstraction of feature learning, successive sub-sampling and feature combination are especially fundamental to convolutional neural network (CNN) models, which are the primary models used in our research.

CNNs extract features by using convolution layers that employ sliding matrix operations to condense multi-dimensional raw input data into numeric features:

$$O_{xy} = \sum_{i=-k}^{k} \sum_{j=-l}^{l} F_{ij}(I_{(x-i)(y-j)}) \tag{1}$$

That is, by applying a convolution filter F of size $(2k+1) \times (2l+1)$ to the input data I, the corresponding output feature O_{xy} is the inner product of the filter, and the region of the input centered on (x, y) and defined by the dimensions of the filter. Thus, successive convolutions map the feature information from the previous layer into increasingly refined feature sets that ideally represent key elements of the original input (e.g., patterns, and shapes for image data). Successive convolutions are flattened into feature vectors and used as input to densely-connected (multi-layer perceptron) layers to generate more complex features. The outputs of these combinations inform the final model decision.

3.2   Extracting Network Features for Case Retrieval

Many CBR systems use feature-vector problem representations. Consequently, the feature vectors generated from convolution in CNNs map naturally to case indices, and post-convolution features have proven useful for case retrieval in CBR [33,37,38]. However, we have found that extracting features after the feature combination step before the output layer can provide higher quality features—that is, features that result in higher classification accuracy [26]. This extraction approach has two potential benefits in addition to increased accuracy: First, the densely-connected layers deeper in the network conveniently may be parameterized to reduce the size of the feature set to mitigate "curse of dimensionality" effects while minimizing side-effects affecting the model's ability to converge, and second, extracting post-combination may be more straightforward than extracting at a shallower location for more complex DL models, whose layers are often more interconnected than more "linear" models such as AlexNet and VGG [20].

Figure 1 illustrates our basic approach to feature extraction [27]. It applies post-combination feature extraction and allows for using extracted features in concert with existing knowledge-engineered features, if they are available.

3.3   Lessons from Our Previous Studies

Building on our basic approach for DL feature extraction for case retrieval, we have explored variants to improve this approach, in the context of image classification tasks. Our work resulted in the following observations:

1. **The number of features extracted significantly impacts classification accuracy.** Comparing high-dimensional feature vectors for CBR similarity calculations can result in a "curse of dimensionality," where individual

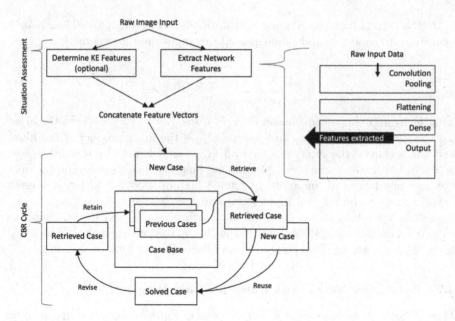

Fig. 1. Features are extracted from the DL model (right), combined with knowledge-engineered features if applicable (top left), and then used to inform case retrieval (figure from Leake et al. [27]; CBR cycle after Aamodt and Plaza [1]). We illustrate CNNs for feature extraction, but this approach may be generalized to other DL models.

features contribute minimally to the overall similarity calculation. Consequently, there exists a point at which increasing the number of features harms case retrieval performance. Conversely, as the number of features extracted decreases, the DL model's representational power also decreases, to the point of failing to converge on a representative feature set, harming classification accuracy as well. Thus, there exists a "sweet spot" for which the number of features extracted is large enough to ensure convergence, but small enough to avoid a curse of dimensionality [26].

2. **Using existing knowledge-engineered features along with extracted features can increase classification accuracy.** When available, knowledge-engineered features can supplement features extracted from the DL system to enable higher classification accuracy [40]. In addition, the inclusion of useful knowledge-engineered features can offset the negative effects of poor model training [27]. However, in both of these cases, overall performance depends on the reliability of the knowledge-engineered features; features whose values are noisy or that do not reliably characterize the case base with respect to the task at hand may have a muted or even harmful impact on model performance.

3. **Small-data domains are challenging for feature extraction, and DL model architecture influences classification accuracy.** Our previous experimental results showed that DL-CBR feature extraction systems trained

from scratch on small-data domains exhibit suboptimal classification accuracy, limiting their applicability to such domains. They also challenged our hypothesis that more recently-developed complex DL models would produce higher-quality features; the deepest model tested (DenseNet121) did indeed have the best relative performance, but it only marginally outperformed the shallowest model tested (AlexNet). These conclusions motivated us to investigate transfer learning to increase robustness for small-data domains, as well as the opportunity for transfer learning to impact the relative performance of different DL feature extractor models.

4 Evaluation

4.1 Hypotheses

We performed computer experiments to evaluate the general hypothesis that pretrained models could result in higher quality feature extraction for small-data domains. Specifically, for a selection of the neural architectures tested in our previous feature extraction research, we investigate the following hypotheses:

H1: **Using transfer learning for feature extraction will produce better quality features than training from scratch.** This will manifest in higher classification accuracy on both train and test data.

H2: **With transfer learning, feature extraction using more complex models (e.g., Inception and DenseNet) will lead to higher classification accuracy.** This hypothesized behavior contrasts with our previous findings without transfer learning [27]. We hypothesize the previous detriment from these models stems predominantly from training from scratch on a small dataset and that transfer learning will address this.

H3: **Using a case-based classifier will lead to lower classification accuracy than using an end-to-end DL system.** DL classifiers can achieve high accuracy, which may be increased through transfer learning. Additionally, our experimental systems are knowledge-light, preventing them from exploiting domain knowledge that can strengthen CBR performance. However, as our method leverages DL to extract case retrieval features, we expect that any accuracy difference between our model and an end-to-end DL system will be sufficiently small that in some domains it may be justified by the benefit of CBR interpretability.

4.2 Evaluation Strategy and Testbed System

Building on our previous work training DL feature extraction models from scratch, we tested three of those DL models that have readily-available pretrained versions through the Tensorflow Applications module [2] (i.e., VGG-19, Inception V3, and DenseNet121 [20]). In contrast with our previous work, we do not consider using supplementary knowledge-engineered features for retrieval, and we modify densely-connected layer structures to keep the number of extracted features constant across all architectures. Furthermore, since this research focuses specifically on retrieval, our CBR system has no adaptation component. It performs classification using a one-nearest-neighbor approach based on Manhattan distance. All extracted features were unweighted, but in principle weights could be learned [39].

We compare the accuracy of the case-based classifiers to a DL classifier baseline. For that baseline, we use the end-to-end classification accuracy of the DL network from which features are extracted for the case-based classifier (i.e., using the DL system's output, rather than extracting features and performing classification with the CBR system). Features are extracted following the densely-connected layers as in our previous work [26].

4.3   Dataset and Experimental Parameters

Each of the models used for feature extraction is pretrained on ImageNet [13] using the built-in functionality provided in the Tensorflow Applications library. Each pretrained model is imported without its top (i.e., the densely-connected layers), which is appended manually so that 1024 features are extracted from every model. Then, each model is further specialized by training on examples from the Animals with Attributes 2 (AwA2) dataset [41] for a maximum of 50 epochs; early stopping with a patience value of two epochs (i.e., halting training if validation accuracy does not improve for two consecutive epochs) is used to minimize overfitting. The number of training examples used for specialization is varied from 1024 to 8192 examples in increments of 1024, and additional experiments with 512 training examples are conducted to enable direct comparison to our previous results. Training examples are selected randomly from the larger dataset. Testing is conducted for both DL and case-based classifiers on both the training set—to estimate an upper bound on classification accuracy—and on an independently-selected test set of the same size and composition to estimate a general classification accuracy. All trials are conducted thirty times to establish reliable mean and standard deviation accuracy values.

5   Results and Discussion

Figure 2 compares our previous experimental results for training from scratch and our results with transfer learning for a similar number of features, and Figs. 3 and 4 show our results using transfer learning for all tested numbers of extracted features. Several broad trends are apparent. First, and most evident, using transfer learning to pretrain DL feature extractors leads to substantially higher classification accuracy across the board than the same models trained from scratch; this supports H1. As the number of extracted features increases, the accuracy advantage of using pretrained models becomes particularly pronounced in some cases, enabling the DL-CBR model accuracy to surpass the accuracy of the DL classifier baseline. This exceeds the expectations set in H3, which predicted that the DL system would maintain superior classification accuracy, potentially with a limited difference. Using DenseNet for feature extraction led to the highest classification accuracy (Figs. 3 and 4). As DenseNet is the most recent/advanced of the DL architectures explored in this work, this is consistent with H2; however, study of other architectures is needed (e.g., larger DenseNet models, ResNet).

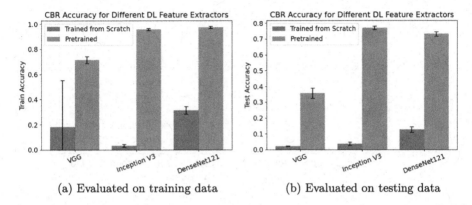

(a) Evaluated on training data   (b) Evaluated on testing data

Fig. 2. AwA2 classification accuracy on train (a) and test (b) data for the DL feature extractor architectures (using the corresponding 512 training example accuracy values from our new data), comparing evaluation on the AwA2 dataset using DL models trained from scratch on AwA2 (as in Leake et al. [27]) and using transfer learning (pretrained on ImageNet and specialized on AwA2, from these experiments). Error bars represent one standard deviation.

5.1   Training from Scratch Versus Transfer Learning

In our previous work, we concluded that the impact of the DL architecture on classification accuracy was overshadowed by the impact of training set size [27]. That is, models across the board overfitted to training data or failed to converge due to the small training set size; some models (e.g., AlexNet and DenseNet) were somewhat resilient to this, but any differences were not dramatic. However, when models are pretrained and specialized on the same limited training data, the results are substantially different (Fig. 2).

At the outset, even using a training set size comparable with the one used in Leake et al. [27], the DL-classification accuracy is significantly higher. This result is especially pronounced when using Inception or DenseNet architectures, both of which significantly outperform VGG-based feature extraction models. Furthermore, while there is an expected decrease between classification accuracy on the training set and the independent test set, the difference is generally more consistent across all models and is smaller in scale (around 30% or less). Our earlier results show that using a case-based classifier does not substantially offset

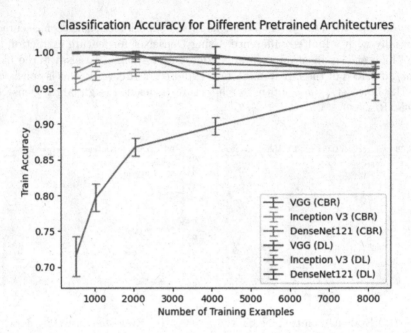

Fig. 3. Accuracy values for tested architectures, evaluated on the training set. Each DL architecture is evaluated both as a feature extractor for a case-based classifier (CBR) or as an end-to-end DL classifier (DL). Error bars represent one standard deviation.

the negative effects of training the DL model from scratch on limited data. Intuitively, such a model may be improved simply by considering more training data and/or training for more epochs. However, our results support transfer learning as an effective means to apply our DL feature extraction approach in data-sparse domains without requiring additional data or training cost.

5.2   Architectural Influences on Feature Quality

When using pretrained models, the choice of architecture significantly impacts extracted feature quality, as evidenced by significantly different classification accuracy values from the experiments. It is immediately apparent that in this context, shallower models such as VGG underperform significantly and are more dependent on having a "critical mass" of training data to achieve reasonable classification accuracy. Presumably, these conclusions may be extrapolated to related models such as AlexNet. Beyond this, the difference between DenseNet and Inception is significantly smaller, but it appears that DenseNet consistently performs better as a feature extraction architecture (Figs. 3 and 4).

Based on these results, it is interesting to consider the factors that might account for DenseNet emerging as the best architecture among those tested in this case study. The answer could be as simple as pointing to the same factors that make DenseNet preferred as an end-to-end DL architecture (i.e., DenseNet's

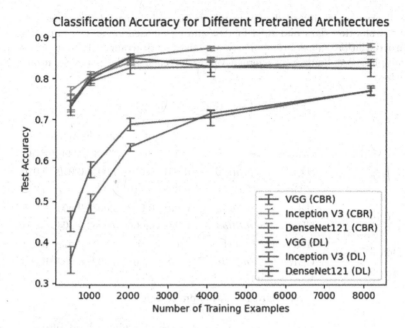

Fig. 4. Accuracy values for tested architectures, evaluated on an independently-selected test set. Each DL architecture is evaluated both as a feature extractor for a case-based classifier (CBR) or as an end-to-end DL classifier (DL). Error bars represent one standard deviation.

greater depth). However, this is potentially less likely due to the comparable performance of the end-to-end models in our experiments (though it is possible that the CBR system is more strongly influenced than the end-to-end performances). It is also reasonable to consider whether the depth-wise parallelism of features afforded via DenseNet's "skip connections" [18] is more useful for CBR feature extraction than the lateral parallelism contained in Inception's inception modules. Further architecture testing (e.g., with ResNet, which also has skip connections) might help isolate any general structural influences.

5.3 Accuracy and Consistency Benefits of Case-Based Classification with DL Features vs. Pure DL

The most unexpected finding in these experiments is that DL-CBR classifiers may perform more accurately than the corresponding end-to-end DL system. In addition, the hybrid models were frequently more consistent, exhibiting a smaller average standard deviation (Table 1). This manifests most dramatically for Inception and DenseNet when given larger training set sizes and tested on an independent test set. However, we also see examples in which the same models show close accuracy correlation across the board with their end-to-end counterparts when evaluated on both the training set and the independent test set.

Table 1. Average standard deviation values for each DL model, organized by train and test evaluation data and then for DL and case-based classifiers. Supporting raw standard deviation values are similarly organized and arranged by number of training examples. Best (smallest) average values for each model per evaluation set are emphasized.

Standard Deviation on Training Set

Model	Classifier	Avg. St. Dev.	# of Training Examples				
			512	1024	2048	4096	8192
VGG	DL	*0.0056*	0.001	0.001	0.004	0.012	0.010
	CBR	0.0174	0.028	0.019	0.012	0.012	0.016
Inception V3	DL	*0.0054*	0.001	0.002	0.007	0.009	0.008
	CBR	*0.0054*	0.008	0.006	0.005	0.004	0.004
DenseNet121	DL	0.0046	0	0	0	0.012	0.011
	CBR	*0.0038*	0.008	0.004	0.002	0.002	0.003

Standard Deviation on Testing Set

Model	Classifier	Avg. St. Dev.	# of Training Examples				
			512	1024	2048	4096	8192
VGG	DL	0.0180	0.025	0.019	0.015	0.019	0.012
	CBR	*0.0164*	0.033	0.024	0.009	0.008	0.008
Inception V3	DL	0.0126	0.019	0.010	0.013	0.013	0.008
	CBR	*0.0058*	0.011	0.007	0.005	0.003	0.003
DenseNet121	DL	0.0164	0.018	0.011	0.010	0.024	0.019
	CBR	*0.0078*	0.014	0.010	0.006	0.005	0.004

The circumstances under which such DL-CBR models may outperform end-to-end models is an interesting question. Ideally, using pretrained models creates a "quality floor" for extracted features, so it is possible that better performance is achieved because the CBR system might be able to reason more effectively from features extracted from a pretrained model that is specialized on a small training set, whereas an analogous pure DL system might require more training data/iterations to reach a similar competency. We note that it appears not to align as well with VGG feature extraction results; this may be due to the relative simplicity/shallowness of the VGG architecture.

The evaluation on the training set was conducted to give an informal "upper bound" indication of how well the methods could capture the data. Intuitively, the training accuracy for an end-to-end DL model might be artificially high due to overfitting on small training sets; this would explain why model training accuracy generally goes down as the amount of training data increases. By contrast, training accuracy values for case-based classifiers using DL features are almost all monotonically increasing with number of training examples (Fig. 3). We suspect that this is another manifestation of the expected benefits of CBR for small data, though that accuracy is often highest for larger numbers of training examples suggests that a "happy medium" number of training examples may exist that produces a relative maximum training accuracy (e.g., as evidenced in the DenseNet extractor trend line, which exhibits the only decrease in training accuracy as training set size increases among case-based classifiers, Fig. 3).

6   Future Research

In the reported experiments, case-based classification using DL-extracted features provided accuracy comparable or superior to the corresponding DL classifiers for image classification. A next step is to solidify these findings with tests across multiple domains and DL architectures.

We are also interested in how training of the DL feature extractor may be better aligned to the needs of the case-based classifier. This could be achieved through in some way incorporating case-based classification error into the backpropagation loss to sensitize DL feature selection to the needs of case-based classification. In addition, where knowledge-engineered features are available to the DL-CBR system [27,40], it may be possible to provide such features to the DL model during training, potentially influencing the DL model to generate features complementary to the knowledge-engineered set. Finally, transfer learning could be applied to the Multi-Net feature extraction architecture [26], to increase accuracy through local feature selection.

7   Conclusions

This paper tests the benefit of using transfer learning when extracting features from DL networks for case retrieval. It presents an evaluation of a selection of pretrained DL models for CBR feature extraction for retrieval; the corresponding results are compared against each other to establish a best-performing architecture, as well as against earlier work on training the same models from scratch [27]. From these comparisons, we conclude that pretraining can significantly improve feature quality over training from scratch on small datasets. Among pretrained models, DenseNet appears to be the best architecture for feature extraction, and using pretraining for feature extraction for the case-based classifier often outperforms the corresponding end-to-end DL classifier (in which instances, the interpretability of case-based classification is a bonus).

We are optimistic that closer DL and CBR system integration for feature extraction, such as incorporating existing knowledge-engineered features into the network directly during training or incorporating case-based classification performance as a loss term during backpropagation, will further improve the resulting classification accuracy. We also intend to revisit our work on localized feature generation [26] with the goal of improving that model using transfer learning. It will be important to confirm the conclusions from this case study through explorations with other domain data, as well as other DL architectures.

Acknowledgments. This work was funded by the US Department of Defense (Contract W52P1J2093009), and by the Department of the Navy, Office of Naval Research (Award N00014-19-1-2655). Authors Wilkerson and Vats led and contributed equivalently to system formulation/experiments, Wilkerson and Leake to paper formulation, and Crandall provided project guidance. We thank Karan Acharya for early contributions.

References

1. Aamodt, A., Plaza, E.: Case-based reasoning: foundational issues, methodological variations, and system approaches. AI Commun. **7**(1), 39–52 (1994)
2. Abadi, M., et al.: TensorFlow: large-scale machine learning on heterogeneous systems (2015). https://www.tensorflow.org/
3. Amin, K., Kapetanakis, S., Althoff, K.-D., Dengel, A., Petridis, M.: Answering with cases: a CBR approach to deep learning. In: Cox, M.T., Funk, P., Begum, S. (eds.) ICCBR 2018. LNCS (LNAI), vol. 11156, pp. 15–27. Springer, Cham (2018). https://doi.org/10.1007/978-3-030-01081-2_2
4. Amin, K., Lancaster, G., Kapetanakis, S., Althoff, K.-D., Dengel, A., Petridis, M.: Advanced similarity measures using word embeddings and siamese networks in CBR. In: Bi, Y., Bhatia, R., Kapoor, S. (eds.) IntelliSys 2019. AISC, vol. 1038, pp. 449–462. Springer, Cham (2020). https://doi.org/10.1007/978-3-030-29513-4_32
5. Bach, K., Mork, P.: On the explanation of similarity for developing and deploying CBR systems. In: Proceedings of the Thirty-Third International Florida Artificial Intelligence Research Society Conference (FLAIRS 2020) (2020)
6. Barletta, R., Mark, W.: Explanation-based indexing of cases. In: Kolodner, J. (ed.) Proceedings of a Workshop on Case-Based Reasoning, pp. 50–60. DARPA, Morgan Kaufmann, Palo Alto (1988)
7. Barnett, A.J., et al.: Interpretable mammographic image classification using case-based reasoning and deep learning. In: Proceedings of IJCAI-21 Workshop on Deep Learning, Case-Based Reasoning, and AutoML (2021). https://arxiv.org/pdf/2107.05605
8. Bhatta, S., Goel, A.: Model-based learning of structural indices to design cases. In: Proceedings of the IJCAI-93 Workshop on Reuse of Design, pp. A1–A13. IJCAI, Chambery, France (1993)
9. Bonzano, A., Cunningham, P., Smyth, B.: Using introspective learning to improve retrieval in CBR: a case study in air traffic control. In: Leake, D.B., Plaza, E. (eds.) ICCBR 1997. LNCS, vol. 1266, pp. 291–302. Springer, Heidelberg (1997). https://doi.org/10.1007/3-540-63233-6_500
10. Chai, J., Zeng, H., Li, A., Ngai, E.W.: Deep learning in computer vision: a critical review of emerging techniques and application scenarios. Mach. Learn. Appl. **6**, 100134 (2021)
11. Chen, C., Li, O., Tao, D., Barnett, A., Rudin, C., Su, J.K.: This looks like that: deep learning for interpretable image recognition. In: Advances in Neural Information Processing Systems, vol. 32, pp. 8930–8941. Curran (2019)
12. Cox, M., Ram, A.: Introspective multistrategy learning: on the construction of learning strategies. Artif. Intell. **112**(1–2), 1–55 (1999)
13. Deng, J., Dong, W., Socher, R., Li, L.J., Li, K., Fei-Fei, L.: Imagenet: a large-scale hierarchical image database. In: 2009 IEEE Conference on Computer Vision and Pattern Recognition, pp. 248–255 (2009)

14. Domeshek, E.: Indexing stories as social advice. In: Proceedings of the Ninth National Conference on Artificial Intelligence, pp. 16–21. AAAI Press, Menlo Park (1991)

15. Fox, S., Leake, D.: Introspective reasoning for index refinement in case-based reasoning. J. Exp. Theor. Artif. Intell. **13**(1), 63–88 (2001)

16. Gates, L., Leake, D., Wilkerson, K.: Cases are king: a user study of case presentation to explain CBR decisions. In: Massie, S., Chakraborti, S. (eds.) ICCBR 2023. LNCS, vol. 14141, pp. 153–168. Springer, Cham (2023). https://doi.org/10.1007/978-3-031-40177-0_10

17. Goldstein, E., Kedar, S., Bareiss, R.: Easing the creation of a multipurpose case library. In: Proceedings of the AAAI-93 Workshop on Case-Based Reasoning, pp. 12–18. AAAI Press, Menlo Park (1993)

18. Huang, G., Liu, Z., van der Maaten, L., Weinberger, K.Q.: Densely connected convolutional networks (2016). https://arxiv.org/abs/1608.06993

19. Kenny, E.M., Keane, M.T.: Twin-systems to explain artificial neural networks using case-based reasoning: comparative tests of feature-weighting methods in ANN-CBR twins for XAI. In: Proceedings of the Twenty-Eighth International Joint Conference on Artificial Intelligence (2019)

20. Khan, A., Sohail, A., Zahoora, U., Qureshi, A.S.: A survey of the recent architectures of deep convolutional neural networks. Artif. Intell. Rev. **53**, 5455–5516 (2019)

21. Klenk, M., Aha, D.W., Molineaux, M.: The case for case-based transfer learning. AI Mag. **32**(1), 54–69 (2011)

22. Koch, G., Zemel, R., Salakhutdinov, R.: Siamese neural networks for one-shot image recognition. In: Proceedings of the 32nd International Conference on Machine Learning (2015)

23. Leake, D.: An indexing vocabulary for case-based explanation. In: Proceedings of the Ninth National Conference on Artificial Intelligence, pp. 10–15. AAAI Press, Menlo Park (1991)

24. Leake, D.: CBR in context: the present and future. In: Leake, D. (ed.) Case-Based Reasoning: Experiences, Lessons, and Future Directions, pp. 3–30. AAAI Press, Menlo Park, CA (1996). http://www.cs.indiana.edu/~leake/papers/a-96-01.html

25. Leake, D., Sooriamurthi, R.: Case dispatching versus case-base merging: when MCBR matters. Int. J. Artif. Intell. Tools **13**(1), 237–254 (2004)

26. Leake, D., Wilkerson, Z., Crandall, D.: Extracting case indices from convolutional neural networks: a comparative study. In: Case-Based Reasoning Research and Development, ICCBR 2022 (2022)

27. Leake, D., Wilkerson, Z., Vats, V., Acharya, K., Crandall, D.: Examining the impact of network architecture on extracted feature quality for CBR. In: Massie, S., Chakraborti, S. (eds.) ICCBR 2023. LNCS, vol. 14141, pp. 3–18. Springer, Cham (2023). https://doi.org/10.1007/978-3-031-40177-0_1

28. Leake, D., Ye, X.: Harmonizing case retrieval and adaptation with alternating optimization. In: Sánchez-Ruiz, A.A., Floyd, M.W. (eds.) ICCBR 2021. LNCS (LNAI), vol. 12877, pp. 125–139. Springer, Cham (2021). https://doi.org/10.1007/978-3-030-86957-1_9

29. Li, O., Liu, H., Chen, C., Rudin, C.: Deep learning for case-based reasoning through prototypes: a neural network that explains its predictions. https://arxiv.org/abs/1710.04806 (2018)

30. Martin, K., Wiratunga, N., Sani, S., Massie, S., Clos, J.: A convolutonal siamese network for developing similarity knowledge in the Selfback dataset. In: Proceed-

ings of the International Conference on Case-Based Reasoning Workshops, CEUR Workshop Proceedings, ICCBR, pp. 85–94 (2017)

31. Oehlmann, R., Edwards, P., Sleeman, D.: Changing the viewpoint: re-indexing by introspective questioning. In: Proceedings of the Sixteenth Annual Conference of the Cognitive Science Society, Atlanta, GA (1994)

32. Ribani, R., Marengoni, M.: A survey of transfer learning for convolutional neural networks. In: 2019 32nd SIBGRAPI Conference on Graphics, Patterns and Images Tutorials (SIBGRAPI-T), pp. 47–57 (2019). https://doi.org/10.1109/SIBGRAPI-T.2019.00010

33. Sani, S., Wiratunga, N., Massie, S.: Learning deep features for KNN-based human activity recognition. In: 25th International conference on case-based reasoning (ICCBR 2017) (2017)

34. Sani, S., Wiratunga, N., Massie, S., Cooper, K.: Personalised human activity recognition using matching networks. In: Cox, M.T., Funk, P., Begum, S. (eds.) ICCBR 2018. LNCS (LNAI), vol. 11156, pp. 339–353. Springer, Cham (2018). https://doi.org/10.1007/978-3-030-01081-2_23

35. Schank, R., et al.: Towards a general content theory of indices. In: Proceedings of the 1990 AAAI Spring Symposium on Case-Based Reasoning. AAAI Press, Menlo Park (1990)

36. Sung, F., Yang, Y., Zhang, L., Xiang, T., Torr, P.H.S., Hospedales, T.M.: Learning to compare: relation network for few-shot learning. In: 2018 IEEE/CVF Conference on Computer Vision and Pattern Recognition (2018)

37. Turner, J.T., Floyd, M.W., Gupta, K.M., Aha, D.W.: Novel object discovery using case-based reasoning and convolutional neural networks. In: Case-Based Reasoning Research and Development, ICCBR 2018, pp. 399–414 (2018)

38. Turner, J.T., Floyd, M.W., Gupta, K.M., Oates, T.: NOD-CC: a hybrid CBR-CNN architecture for novel object discovery. In: Case-Based Reasoning Research and Development, ICCBR 2019, pp. 373–387 (2019)

39. Wettschereck, D., Aha, D., Mohri, T.: A review and empirical evaluation of feature-weighting methods for a class of lazy learning algorithms. Artif. Intell. Rev. 11(1–5), 273–314 (1997)

40. Wilkerson, Z., Leake, D., Crandall, D.: On combining knowledge-engineered and network-extracted features for retrieval. In: Case-Based Reasoning Research and Development, ICCBR 2021, pp. 248–262 (2021)

41. Xian, Y., Lampert, C.H., Schiele, B., Akata, Z.: Zero-shot learning - a comprehensive evaluation of the good, the bad and the ugly. IEEE Trans. Pattern Anal. Mach. Intell. (T-PAMI) 41(9), 2251–2265 (2018)

42. Zhuang, F., et al.: A comprehensive survey on transfer learning. Proc. IEEE 109(1), 43–76 (2021)

Ensemble Stacking Case-Based Reasoning for Regression

Daniel Soto-Forero(✉) [ID], Marie-Laure Betbeder[ID], and Julien Henriet[ID]

DISC, Université de Franche-Comté, CNRS, Institut FEMTO-ST, 16 Route de Gray, 25000 Besançon, France

{daniel.soto_forero,marie-laure.betbeder,julien.henriet}@univ-fcomte.fr

Abstract. This paper presents a case-based reasoning algorithm with a two-stage iterative double stacking to find approximate solutions to one and multidimensional regression problems. This approach does not require training, so it can work with dynamic data at run time. The solutions are generated using stochastic algorithms in order to allow exploration of the solution space. The evaluation is performed by transforming the regression problem into an optimization problem with an associated objective function. The algorithm has been tested in comparison with nine classical regression algorithms on ten different regression databases extracted from the UCI site. The results show that the proposed algorithm generates solutions in most cases quite close to the real solutions. According to the RMSE, the proposed algorithm globally among the four best algorithms, according to MAE, to the fourth best algorithms of the ten evaluated, suggesting that the results are reasonably good.

Keywords: Case-Based Reasoning · Stacking · Regression · Ensemble Methods · Machine Learning

1 Introduction

One of the main issues addressed by case-based reasoning (CBR) is its ability to adapt solutions from source cases to the target ones [16]. Choosing the best adaptation strategy can be based on the prediction of its ability to solve and align with the problem. Thus, its predictive ability can be used to solve a regression problem. In addition, unanticipated events occur during the application of a solution. These events lead the human operator to adapt the proposed solution in real-time quickly.

Ensemble methods use several multiple models performed independently, and their results are combined to obtain a final global prediction. The main idea is to improve the results and generalization ability of individual models [1]. Some ensemble methods use different models with different sets of data; others use the models with the same data but different parameters. The combination of the results of the multiple models can use different strategies as simple rules or more complex approaches [2]. The ensemble methods are useful in classification and regression problems.

J. A. Recio-Garcia et al. (Eds.): ICCBR 2024, LNAI 14775, pp. 159–174, 2024.
https://doi.org/10.1007/978-3-031-63646-2_11

Machine learning methods can be applied to different types of regression problems to predict values by building, evaluating, and training complex linear and non-linear models. However, if it is possible to improve accuracy by integrating them, the most common integration strategies used on ensemble learning are stacking, boosting and bagging [12]. Stacking is a kind of ensemble deep learning meta-learning model, whose purpose is to use various machine learning techniques to overcome the limitations of individual models. The integration generates a final result with improved accuracy [4]. In stacking methods, the base algorithms are called level-0. Generally, they are heterogeneous machine learning models or algorithms, and each works with the same database. The meta algorithm unifying the results from level-0 algorithms using another machine-learning techniques or a set of rules is called level-1 [11].

In this paper, we present a new method for regression based on the ensemble approach combined with the CBR one. Our proposition consists of the enrichment of the knowledge containers defined by M. Richter [15] using the ensemble approach. This paper is organized as follows: Sect. 2 presents the related works about case-based reasoning, ensemble techniques, and regression. The proposed model is explained in Sect. 3. The Sect. 4 shows the experimental description and the results. The results are discussed in section Sect. 5. Finally, the conclusions and future work are discussed in Sect. 6.

2   Related Works

Different strategies for retrieval and adaptation in CBR-systems are proposed in the literature. For example, S. Petrovic *et al.* [13] proposed to use neural networks, Jung *et al.* [7] k-means clustering mixed with RBFN, R. Reyes *et al.* [16] propose a mix with CSP (Constraint satisfaction problems), Y. Lepage *et al.* [9] proposed an alternative retrieve phase based on the LCS (longest common subsequence) metric. Uysal *et al.* [18] implement a CBR with a bootstrap aggregation method (bagging) to improve the CBR accuracy and reduces the variance. D. Leake *et al.* [8] conducted a study analyzing the potential benefits of combining deep learning with CBR to enhance overall performance. All these strategies inspired the work presented in this paper and lead us to the possibility to solve regression problems using CBR. In addition, we studied Ensemble methods and stacking and integrate them to our CBR-based proposition.

2.1   Ensemble Methods

Ju *et al.* [6] study a robust non-parametric regression based on gradient boosting using a linear combination of base learners in two stages. The authors identify the limitations of a classical gradient algorithm: the loss function generally must be convex, but if that is not the case, then the algorithm may not work well. The algorithm behavior is different and has very low efficiency when the data does not contain outliers and, sometimes, the overfitting in the training step. To mitigate these problems, an ensemble model is proposed that combines gradient regression with tree regression in two stages to correct the initial estimator and define an early stopping time with a function that stops the training if the validation error is static after several iterations. The algorithm has been tested in comparison with other boosting regression methods over six database configurations generated with three formula bases, using the RMSE as a metric. The results confirm the good performance and accuracy of the ensemble methods, but only if the good combination of algorithms and aggregation of results is well done.

An ensemble Case-Based Reasoning model is proposed by Yu *et al.* [19] applied to financial prediction and fill missing data. In this case, to retrieve the nearest neighbors, the model uses three different distance metrics and an integration voting stage. The model has been tested with a database with eleven dimensions of financial information from 249 enterprises. The comparison is made with two objectives. First, the filling in missing data with other algorithms like KNN or RandomForest, and second, the prediction comparison with single algorithms using a specific distance metric. Indeed, the results show better performance filling in the missing data and the highest results in prediction.

2.2 Stacking

The work of Mang *et al.* [12] uses stacking method integrating support vector regression (SVR), kernel ridge regression (KRR), and elastic net (ENET) algorithms for prediction in three large genomic datasets. The proposed stacking method is compared with the single algorithms SVR, KRR, ENET, and BayesB using a precision metric over three regression databases. The meta-algorithm for level-1 is an ordinary least squares linear regression (OLS). The algorithms are performed with a 20-fold cross-validation.

Some machine learning algorithms are used for the automatic extraction of building information from images, but Cao *et al.* [3] propose an ensembling method with three neural network models (U-net, SegNet, and FCN-8), whose role is to extract the building features. Each model is optimized with a conditional random fields algorithm, and then all model results are combined with a method based on a sparse autoencoder. The algorithm was evaluated with a database created with 650 satellite images of various Chinese cities with an approximate resolution of 5000×3500 pixels. The algorithm has been compared with the single network models, and the results show that the ensemble method obtains better accuracy, recall, and F1 score than the individual algorithms. Some identified limitations are the computation time, memory, and resources, but it is possible to improve the stacking model to correct these limitations.

Evolutionary iterative techniques can also be used in stacking models as shown in Bakurov *et al.* [2], where the stacking is used to study the impact of changes in genetic programming parameters and improve the genetic programming systems. The focus study is the initialization and selection phases as well as the used operators and stopping criteria. The base learners in this case are multi-linear regression, multi-layer perceptron, random forest regression and support vector regression. Genetic programming has the meta-learning algorithm role in the stacking model. The test was realized with 11 regression databases, seven synthetic and four real-world problems. The experiment was run 60 times with different data partitions. The results yield the optimal hyper-parameters to the genetic programming algorithm according to the best result obtained with MSE and average rank metrics.

3 Proposed Model

The proposed algorithm ESCBR (ensemble stacking case-based reasoning) is based on the generic CBR paradigm associated with several neighbor search and solution generation algorithms that have been integrated according to a stacking model variation in two iterative stages. The integration with the stacking model gives the algorithm the ability to adapt itself to different types of problems, and avoid biases and overtraining. The results of the execution of the stacking levels store knowledge containers in the CBR memory [15] and then help the learning of the algorithm iteratively. In addition, this knowledge container facilitates the generation of solutions to various problems in different databases without the need for a preliminary training phase. Iterative design in two cycles improves the capacity of the CBR system to work and adapt to dynamic problems at run time.

Figure 1 presents the links between the knowledge containers of our CBR system and the different phases of this process. Figure 2 presents the complete workflow of the proposed algorithm. The variables and parameters for the proposed algorithm are shown in Table 1. As shown in these two figures and this table, the retrieve stage uses the search algorithms and the case database (containers C1 and C3) in order to find the nearest neighbors of a given new problem. The reuse stage uses the solution generation algorithms (container C2). The revise stage evaluates the generated solutions and allows the generation of new solutions iteratively according to the parameters stored in the C4 container. The systems invoke the reconfigurate stage in order to change the combination of algorithms. With a selected solution, the renovate stage is called to update the parameters and the container data. Finally, in the retain stage, the case base is updated with the new case and the generated solution.

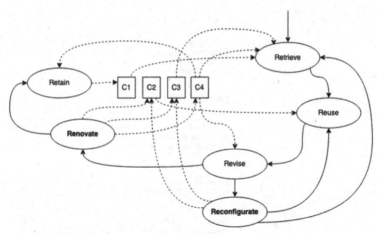

C1 - Container of cases (Database of Cases)
C2 - Container of Adaptation (Ponderation, Copy, Median, Random Selection, Generation from Problem,
     Generation from Problem with PCA, Random Step)
C3 - Container of Similarity (KNN, KMeans, GMM, FuzzyC)
C4 - Container of Vocabulary (Parameters of models, Metrics, Evaluation models)

Fig. 1. Two cycles of proposed CBR

Table 1. Variables and parameters of proposed model (Type: p - parameter, v - variable, f - function)

ID	Type	Description	Domain
it	p	Number of iterations	$\mathbb{N}, it > 0$
np	p	Number of process	$\mathbb{N}, np > 2$
nl	p	Maximum number of local neighbors	$\mathbb{N}, nl > 0$
ng	p	Number of global neighbors	$\mathbb{N}, ng > 2$
n	v	Dimension of problem space	$\mathbb{N}, n > 0$
m	v	Dimension of solution space	$\mathbb{N}, m > 0$
z	v	Database size	$\mathbb{N}, z > 0$
p	v	Problem description	$\mathbb{R}^n$
s	v	Solution description	$\mathbb{R}^m$
r_a	v	Number of Retrieve Models	$\mathbb{N}, r_a > 2$
r_b	v	Number of Reuse Models	$\mathbb{N}, r_b > 2$
at	v	Actions	$[0, 2] \in \mathbb{N}$
nl_i	v	Number of local neighbors for i model	$\mathbb{N}, nl_i \leq nl$
g	v	Global best solution description	$\mathbb{R}^m$
v	v	Global best solution evaluation	$\mathbb{R}$
$d(x_1, x_2)$	f	Distance function between x_1 and x_2	$\mathbb{R}$
$rn(x, y)$	f	Random value with Normal distribution x mean, y standard deviation	$\mathbb{R}_+$
$MP(x_1^z, x_2, a)$	f	Retrieve model function between x_1 and x_2	$\mathbb{R}^{a \times z}$
$MS(x_1^m)$	f	Reuse model function with x_1	$\mathbb{R}^m$
$f_s(p^n, s^m)$	f	Solutions evaluation	$\mathbb{R}$

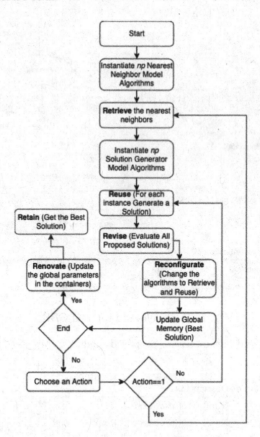

Fig. 2. Flow of stacking CBR

3.1 Retrieve

The first step of the algorithm consists of finding the most similar cases to a new eventual case. Figure 3 shows the different processes used in the stacking model. At level-0, each process selects and executes a different neighbor search algorithm chosen from r_a models into the C3 container, with a number of neighbors nl_i randomly chosen in the interval $[0, nl]$. Then, at level-1, the results are unified by building a global set of similar cases. Five algorithms have been implemented for the retrieve stage: KNN (K-nearest neighbors), K-means, GMM (Gaussian mixture model), fuzzyC-Means and weighted KNN.

KNN is a machine learning algorithm based on learning approach that sort the elements of a dataset considering nearby instances in the feature space [17], this algorithm can be parameterized to consider different weights for each dimension (weighted KNN). K-Means is an algorithm which calculates the sum of distances from each data point to a certain cluster center as optimization objective, and updates the cluster center by using the average value of samples in the cluster. Its goal is to group similar points [10]. GMM is a model that uses a parametric probability density function in order to define a weighted sum of K-Gaussian component densities. The model can be used for regression, classification or clustering problems [14]. FuzzyC-Means is also a clustering algorithm that introduces the fuzzy set theory to quantify the cluster membership uncertainty [5].

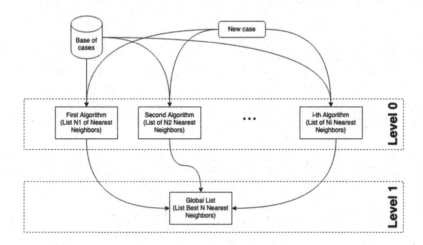

Fig. 3. Stacking for nearest neighbors search

Formally, the first proposed stacking model works with a database of z cases, where a case is composed of the problem description and the solution description $(p^n, s^m)^z$ and a target case (without solution p_w^n). The goal of all level-0 algorithms is to generate a local list of cases similar to the new case using the problem description information. Thus, a set $X_j = \{x_1, x_2, ..., x_z \mid x_i = MP_i((p^n)^z, p_w^n, nl_i)\}$ is generated considering each j model performed. At level-1, a global set $X_g = \biguplus_{n=1}^{ng} min_{distance} ((\cup_{j=1}^{np} X_j))$ using all the j local sets is created, where $\biguplus$ represents an exclusive union (union of elements without repetition). Then, the result of the first stacking model is the X_g set with the ng global nearest neighbors.

3.2 Reuse

Once the global list of similar cases has been constructed, the information corresponding to the solutions of each of those cases is extracted and used to generate a new solution that adapts to the new case using similar cases and similar solutions as shown in Fig. 4. All the generation algorithms must respect the generation rules defined at the beginning of the stacking process. These rules define the restrictions of certain attributes that the generated solutions must have. If no rules are defined, then the algorithms can manipulate the attributes of the solutions freely. The generation is performed with a second stacking model with different processes, as shown in Fig. 5. At level-0, each process selects and executes a different generation algorithm from the r_b models into the C2 container. At level-1, all the different solutions generated are stored in a global memory. Ten algorithms have been implemented for the reuse stage in level-0: weighting with probability, weighting without probability, median values, Copy/Change, voting, interpolation, PCA (principal component analysis), and random step.

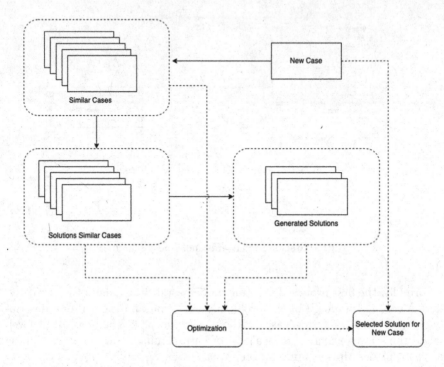

Fig. 4. Automatic generation and verification of solutions

The process that implements the weighting random selection with the probability algorithm builds a solution copying randomly the information of solutions with bigger probability to the associated nearest problem case. The process that executes weighting random selection without the probability algorithm randomly copies the information of solutions according to the uniform distribution. The process that computes median values uses the median value of all the solutions for each dimension. The copy/change-based process copies the information of a random solution and changes a portion with the information of another randomly selected solution. The voting-based process copies the information that is most frequent between the solutions. The interpolation-based process uses random information from a calculated interpolation function. The process based on PCA transforms the problem description to the space of solutions description to establish a relation between the problem and its solution, through a distance metric, with which a possible solution to the new problem can be inferred, considering the solutions that lie within the radius of the distance obtained. The process that executes the random step algorithm chooses a solution and changes the values in one dimension randomly with a small step.

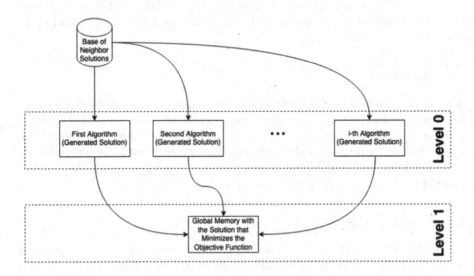

Fig. 5. Stacking for solution generation

This second stacking model works with the solution description s as a parameter with the set $(s^m)^{ng}$. Each performed reuse model can generate a candidate solution $s_{i,c} = MS_i((s^m)^{ng})$. The level-1 is the build of a unification set of all candidate solutions $Y_g = \cup_{i=1}^{np} s_{i,c}$. This set is evaluated with a function to determine the quality of solution.

Finally, the candidate solutions are compared and evaluated. This problem is transformed into an optimization problem, where the objective function is 1.

$$min\ (f_s(p_w^n, s_w^m)) = min\left(\sum_{i=1}^{ng} \frac{d(s_w^m, s_i^t)}{d(p_w^n, p_i^n)^2}\right) \tag{1}$$

$$s_i^t = s_i^m + rn(0, d(p_w^n, p_i^n)) \tag{2}$$

The optimization cycle can execute the retrieve and reuse phases according to the selected random action from $[0, at]$ in each it iteration, saving inside a global memory in each iteration the solution that obtains the minimum value in the evaluation of the objective function.

3.3 Reconfigurate

The internal cycle (retrieve, reuse and revise) has the possibility to dynamically change the combination of algorithms that can be executed in each stage for each process. During this reconfigurate step, information stored in the containers C2 and C3 are used in order to configure and instantiate the new selected algorithms. Each process can change its algorithms randomly during runtime, in any iteration, asynchronously.

3.4 Renovate

After having selected a solution from all the candidates proposed by the process, the renovate phase is executed, which updates the information (used algorithms and their respective parameters) of C2, C3 and C4 containers. This allows the system to learn according to the predictions made, and to propose better results during the next executions. The information inside the containers can be changed in order to fit to a specific problem as best as possible.

3.5 Revise and Retain

As usual, in CBR systems, the revise phase is left to the system user. The retain stage simply takes the best-proposed solution and determines whether it is a new or existing solution and, if it is new, stores it in the database.

4 Results

In order to compare the performance prediction and behavior of the proposed algorithm, ten regression databases with different characteristics has been selected. The databases and their characteristics are shown in Table 2. The values used as parameters to our algorithm are: $it = 100$, $np = 50$, $nl = 10$ and $ng = 10$, the parameters for stacking algorithms are chosen randomly. They are adjusted to get a global convergence during the renovate phase.

The comparison of the proposed algorithm is made with respect to nine well-known regression algorithms widely used in various research and applied problems. The list of algorithms is shown in Table 3. The parameters for each algorithm are shown in Table 4. All the algorithms have been executed 10 times, and their data have been partitioned in k-folds with $k = 100$. The results have been calculated with the best results of ten executions.

Table 2. Description of evaluated datasets. (* After encoding String data)

ID	DataSet	Features	Instances	Output Dimension	Input Domain	Output Domain
DS1	Yatch Hydrodynamics	6	308	1	$\mathbb{R}$	$\mathbb{R}$
DS2	Electrical Grid Stability	12	10000	1	$\mathbb{R}$	$\mathbb{R}$
DS3	Real State Valuation	6	414	1	$\mathbb{R}_+$	$\mathbb{R}_+$
DS4	Wine Quality (Red)	11	1598	1	$\mathbb{R}_+$	$\mathbb{N}$
DS5	Wine Quality (White)	11	4897	1	$\mathbb{R}_+$	$\mathbb{N}$
DS6	Concrete Compressive Strength	8	1030	1	$\mathbb{R}_+$	$\mathbb{R}_+$
DS7	Energy Efficiency	8	768	2	$\mathbb{R}_+$	$\mathbb{R}_+$
DS8	Gas Turbine CO, NOx Emission (2015)	9	7384	2	$\mathbb{R}_+$	$\mathbb{R}_+$
DS9	Student Performance Portuguese	30	649	3	$\mathbb{N}*$	$\mathbb{N}$
DS10	Student Performance Math	30	395	3	$\mathbb{N}*$	$\mathbb{N}$

Table 3. List of evaluated algorithms

ID	Algorithm	ID	Algorithm
A1	Linear Regression	A6	Polinomial Regression
A2	K-Nearest Neighbor	A7	Ridge Regression
A3	Decision Tree	A8	Lasso Regression
A4	Random Forest (Ensemble)	A9	Gradient Boosting (Ensemble)
A5	Multi Layer Perceptron	A10	Proposed Case Based Reasoning

Table 5 shows the detailed results and average ranking for all the databases according to the RMSE (root mean square error) metric. The gradient boosting algorithm (A9) achieves the global best-ranking value, and the proposed algorithm (A10) is placed in fourth position. Table 6 shows the detailed results of the same algorithms and the same databases but compared with the MAE (median absolute error) metric. In that case, the best global average value is for random forest algorithm (A4), and the proposed algorithm (A10) is placed globally in fourth position with the best results in databases DS4 and DS5.

Figure 6 shows the global dispersion, median, and outliers for four representative databases, where it can be seen that the proposed algorithm generates more outliers than other algorithms, but the variance is low and the convergence is close to the real value, better than most of the compared algorithms. These four databases are representative because they have very different characteristics and consider variables to be predicted in different dimensions.

Table 4. Parameters for all compared algorithms

ID	Parameter	Value	ID	Parameter	Value
A1	Intercept	True	A6	Degree	4
	Positive	True		Bias	True
A2	Neighbors	5	A7	Fit Intercept	True
	Weights	Uniform		alpha	0.2
	Metric	Minkowsky		tol	1e-4
	Power Minkowsky	2			
A3	Error	Squared Error	A8	Fit Intercept	True
	Min samples split	2		alpha	[0.00001, 0.4]
				Max iter	1000
				tol	1e-4
A4	Estimators	10	A9	Error	Squarred Error
	Error	Squared Error		Learning Rate	0.1
	Min samples split	2		Estimators	100
	Bootstrap	True		Min Split	2
A5	Hidden Layers	100			
	Activation	Relu			
	Solver	Adam			
	alpha	0.0001			
	Learning Rate	0.001			
	Max Iter	200			
	beta1	0.9			
	beta2	0.999			
	epsilon	1e-8			

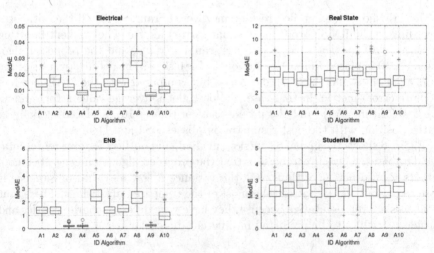

Fig. 6. Results of MAE (median absolute error) for ten algorithms and four representative databases

Table 5. Average ranking of best RMSE (Root Mean Squared Error) for all datasets with machine learning regression algorithms

Dataset	A1	A2	A3	A4	A5	A6	A7	A8	A9	A10
DS1	9.010	10.780	1.224	0.982	3.369	9.009	8.985	9.629	**0.668**	5.871
DS2	0.022	0.025	0.020	0.012	0.017	0.022	0.022	0.037	**0.011**	0.015
DS3	8.633	8.033	9.334	**7.203**	8.470	8.705	8.842	9.009	7.324	8.491
DS4	0.651	0.746	0.782	**0.571**	0.694	0.651	0.651	0.792	0.617	0.762
DS5	0.753	0.806	0.820	**0.599**	0.853	0.754	0.757	0.863	0.688	0.748
DS6	10.439	8.871	6.144	**4.738**	6.553	10.423	10.422	10.428	5.053	8.766
DS7	2.948	2.116	0.541	**0.465**	3.726	2.949	2.979	4.094	0.467	1.973
DS8	1.315	1.161	1.513	**1.109**	1.566	1.303	1.308	1.318	1.125	2.157
DS9	**2.304**	2.624	3.217	2.315	2.898	**2.304**	**2.304**	2.551	2.342	2.802
DS10	3.052	3.404	4.158	**3.014**	3.607	3.061	3.061	3.150	3.020	3.874
Avg. Rank	5.7	6.3	7.2	2.1	6.6	5.6	5.5	8.6	1.8	5.6

Table 6. Comparison of best MAE (median absolute error) for multiple datasets with machine learning regression algorithms

Dataset	A1	A2	A3	A4	A5	A6	A7	A8	A9	A10
DS1	6.776	2.385	0.231	0.207	3.632	6.778	6.307	5.186	**0.162**	1.193
DS2	0.015	0.017	0.012	0.008	0.012	0.015	0.015	0.030	**0.007**	0.011
DS3	5.092	4.320	4.1	3.632	4.435	5.092	5.20	5.132	**3.504**	3.90
DS4	0.413	0.495	0.18	0.325	0.451	0.413	0.412	0.544	0.387	**0.154**
DS5	0.509	0.548	0.285	0.374	0.550	0.509	0.509	0.633	0.456	**0.113**
DS6	6.989	5.709	3.134	**2.839**	4.306	6.989	6.989	6.986	3.084	5.439
DS7	1.393	1.372	**0.217**	0.218	2.523	1.393	1.529	2.346	0.243	1.008
DS8	0.549	0.297	0.365	**0.289**	0.742	0.549	0.549	0.540	0.309	0.861
DS9	**1.496**	1.788	2.080	1.612	2.005	**1.496**	**1.496**	1.714	1.538	1.721
DS10	2.344	2.534	2.910	2.331	2.543	2.344	2.344	2.481	**2.258**	2.602
Avg. Rank	6.45	6.4	4.35	2.3	7.35	6.55	6.6	7.9	2.4	4.7

5 Discussion

The proposed algorithm reveals a competitive performance in comparison with some of the most popular, most used, and recent algorithms for prediction in regression problems. Specifically, in this work, we have run the tests on ten databases with different characteristics, such as the number of instances, the number of features, the domain of the input variables, the dimensions of the output variable, and the subject area demonstrating the versatility of the proposed algorithm and the applicability to different configurations. Given the exploratory and stochastic nature of the proposed algorithm, it presents a great diversity of solutions generating several outliers; but despite, this in most cases, it is possible to reach an approximate solution that converges close to the real solution. It is the reason why in some cases the values of the mean are high but with the median remains low.

It can also be seen that the integration of the search algorithms produces better results than simple algorithms, as in the case of the proposed algorithm compared to KNN or compared to Linear Regression; although, for the proposed algorithm the impact of the first and second stacking on the final results obtained has not been determined exactly.

Globally, for the RMSE, the boosting algorithms perform better overall than the classical algorithms, even though the performance is variable. The proposed algorithm obtains acceptable values in all the databases. According to the average of the ranking positions, it is placed in the fourth place for RMSE, and the algorithm is placed in the fourth place for MAE.

An important aspect of the proposed algorithm is the objective function, which could be evaluated and modified dynamically depending on the characteristics of the evaluated problem, given that in the present study, the tests have been performed with the intuitive function that provides a greater probability of selection and evolution to the solution associated to the nearest neighbors; but, it is possible to complement the evaluation with other relevant terms and in that way improve the results.

In addition to the results, the proposed algorithm presents several advantages with respect to the algorithms with which it has been compared. Among these advantages, it does not require training, it can integrate algorithms and rules in each stacking, and by the design in two cycles, it can work with dynamic problems at runtime.

6   Conclusion

This paper proposes a generic regression technique using case-based reasoning and a stacking model, whose main characteristics are that it does not require training, and that due to the internal iterative cycle, it can adapt to dynamic problems in real time. The numerical results obtained in the tests performed show the potential of the algorithm with varied data and databases of different sizes, as well as the competitiveness with other standard and robust algorithms commonly used in regression problems.

As future work, it is envisaged to use the proposed model in an intelligent learning system to complement the real-time recommendation modules, since the algorithm does not require training and adapts dynamically to the data. Another important modification is to integrate the ESCBR with multi agent systems to improve the performance and precision, reduce the variance, and avoid the generation of outliers. Additionally, further studies could include various retrieve techniques to locate neighbors according to some rules within a given context.

References

1. Ali, M., et al.: Effective network intrusion detection using stacking-based ensemble approach. Int. J. Inf. Secur. **22**, 1781–1798 (2023). https://doi.org/10.1007/s10207-023-00718-7

2. Bakurov, I., Castelli, M., Gau, O., Fontanella, F., Vanneschi, L.: Genetic programming for stacked generalization. Swarm Evol. Comput. **65**, 100913 (2021). https://doi.org/10.1016/j.swevo.2021.100913. https://www.sciencedirect.com/science/article/pii/S2210650221000742

3. Cao, D., Xing, H., Wong, M.S., Kwan, M.P., Xing, H., Meng, Y.: A stacking ensemble deep learning model for building extraction from remote sensing images. Remote Sens. **13**(19) (2021). https://doi.org/10.3390/rs13193898. https://www.mdpi.com/2072-4292/13/19/3898

4. Choi, J., Suh, D., Otto, M.O.: Boosted stacking ensemble machine learning method for wafer map pattern classification. Comput. Mater. Continua **74**(2), 2945–2966 (2023). https://doi.org/10.32604/cmc.2023.033417. http://www.techscience.com/cmc/v74n2/50296

5. Jiao, L., Yang, H., ga Liu, Z., Pan, Q.: Interpretable fuzzy clustering using unsupervised fuzzy decision trees. Inf. Sci. **611**, 540–563 (2022). https://doi.org/10.1016/j.ins.2022.08.077. https://www.sciencedirect.com/science/article/pii/S0020025522009872

6. Ju, X., Salibián-Barrera, M.: Robust boosting for regression problems. Comput. Stat. Data Anal. **153**, 107065 (2021). https://doi.org/10.1016/j.csda.2020.107065. https://www.sciencedirect.com/science/article/pii/S0167947320301560

7. Jung, S., Lim, T., Kim, D.: Integrating radial basis function networks with case-based reasoning for product design. Expert Syst. Appl. **36**(3, Part 1), 5695–5701 (2009). https://doi.org/10.1016/j.eswa.2008.06.099. https://www.sciencedirect.com/science/article/pii/S0957417408003667

8. Leake, D., Crandall, D.: On bringing case-based reasoning methodology to deep learning. In: Watson, I., Weber, R. (eds.) ICCBR 2020. LNCS (LNAI), vol. 12311, pp. 343–348. Springer, Cham (2020). https://doi.org/10.1007/978-3-030-58342-2_22

9. Lepage, Y., Lieber, J., Mornard, I., Nauer, E., Romary, J., Sies, R.: *The French correction*: when retrieval is harder to specify than adaptation. In: Watson, I., Weber, R. (eds.) ICCBR 2020. LNCS (LNAI), vol. 12311, pp. 309–324. Springer, Cham (2020). https://doi.org/10.1007/978-3-030-58342-2_20

10. Li, J., et al.: Hierarchical and partitioned planning strategy for closed-loop devices in low-voltage distribution network based on improved kmeans partition method. Energy Rep. **9**, 477–485 (2023). https://doi.org/10.1016/j.egyr.2023.05.161. https://www.sciencedirect.com/science/article/pii/S2352484723009137. 2022 The 3rd International Conference on Power and Electrical Engineering

11. Liang, M., et al.: A stacking ensemble learning framework for genomic prediction. Front. Genetics **12** (2021). https://doi.org/10.3389/fgene.2021.600040. https://www.frontiersin.org/articles/10.3389/fgene.2021.600040

12. Mang, L., et al.: A stacking ensemble learning framework for genomic prediction. Front. Genet. (2021). https://doi.org/10.3389/fgene.2021.600040

13. Petrovic, S., Khussainova, G., Jagannathan, R.: Knowledge-light adaptation approaches in case-based reasoning for radiotherapy treatment planning. Artif. Intell. Med. **68**, 17–28 (2016). https://doi.org/10.1016/j.artmed.2016.01.006. https://www.sciencedirect.com/science/article/pii/S093336571630015X

14. Rakesh, S., et al.: Moving object detection using modified GMM based background subtraction. Measur. Sens. **30**, 100898 (2023). https://doi.org/10.1016/j.measen.2023.100898. https://www.sciencedirect.com/science/article/pii/S2665917423002349

15. Richter, M.M., Michael, M.: Knowledge containers. In: Readings in Case-Based Reasoning. Morgan Kaufmann Publishers, Burlington (2003)

16. Roldan Reyes, E., Negny, S., Cortes Robles, G., Le Lann, J.: Improvement of online adaptation knowledge acquisition and reuse in case-based reasoning: application to process engineering design. Eng. Appl. Artif. Intell. **41**, 1–16 (2015). https://doi.org/10.1016/j.engappai.2015.01.015. https://www.sciencedirect.com/science/article/pii/S0952197615000263

17. Saxena, N., et al.: Hybrid KNN-SVM machine learning approach for solar power forecasting. Environ. Chall. **14**, 100838 (2024). https://doi.org/10.1016/j.envc.2024.100838. https://www.sciencedirect.com/science/article/pii/S2667010024000040

18. Uysal, F., Sonmez, R.: Bootstrap aggregated case-based reasoning method for conceptual cost estimation. Buildings **13**(3) (2023). https://doi.org/10.3390/buildings13030651. https://www.mdpi.com/2075-5309/13/3/651

19. Yu, L., Li, M.: A case-based reasoning driven ensemble learning paradigm for financial distress prediction with missing data. Appl. Soft Comput. **137**, 110163 (2023). https://doi.org/10.1016/j.asoc.2023.110163. https://www.sciencedirect.com/science/article/pii/S1568494623001813

Retrieval Augmented Generation with LLMs for Explaining Business Process Models

Mirjam Minor[(⊠)] and Eduard Kaucher

Department of Business Informatics, Goethe University Frankfurt,
Frankfurt, Germany
minor@cs.uni-frankfurt.de

Abstract. Large language models (LLMs) and retrieval augmented generation (RAG) are undergoing rapid development. Considering a case base as a memory in a RAG system provides novel opportunities for text generation. In this paper, we investigate the role Case-Based Reasoning (CBR) could play for supporting RAG systems in generating accessible explanations of business process models. We experiment with two different case bases in a RAG system. Case base a) is dedicated to support prompt chaining by reusing index knowledge on the cases with the aim to deal with large process models that do not fit into the context window size of a recent LLM. Second, case base b) contains model-text pairs to serve as in-context examples to enhance prompt templates. Approach b) aims to improve the quality of generated text explanations for process models of normal size. Our contribution opens a novel application area for process-oriented CBR. Further, our case-based RAG system provides a contemporary alternative to traditional Natural Language Processing pipelines. The experimental results contribute to gain some insights on an inherent capability threshold of GPT-4 at which the performance decreases much earlier than having reached the given context window size, on the number of retrieved cases a recent RAG system should use as in-context examples, and on suitable prompt templates.

Keywords: Process-oriented CBR · Large Language models · Retrieval-Augmented Generation

1 Introduction

Most digital transformation projects target at process improvements when investigating the change that digital technologies can bring about in a company [9]. Business processes are "a set of logically related tasks performed to achieve a defined business outcome for a particular customer or market" [3]. Weske claims that business processes are "essential to understanding how companies operate" [27]. The research field of process-oriented case-based reasoning (PO-CBR) [20] addresses those business needs. PO-CBR has achieved considerable

J. A. Recio-Garcia et al. (Eds.): ICCBR 2024, LNAI 14775, pp. 175–190, 2024.
https://doi.org/10.1007/978-3-031-63646-2_12

success in assisting system analysts and further business process professionals [11, 19, 21, 23, 30].

However, many application domain experts and other users lack knowledge
on process modelling languages. They are struggling to understand the graphical process models. Model explanations with plain text can help those users
and save precious hours or days of workshops with system analysts [14]. Early
model-to-text approaches use traditional Natural Language Processing (NLP)
pipes as a process model verbalization technique [14]. Yet, the success of such
methods depends on major knowledge engineering efforts. The coverage of the
generated explanations depends on those efforts. Vidgof et al. [25] discuss the
high potential of Large Language Models (LLMs) for tasks related to business
process management, including model explanation. Hammond and Leake [8] as
well as Watson [26] encourage the research community to experiment with a case-
based memory for LLMS. The role Case-Based Reasoning (CBR) could play for
generating explanations of structural models like business process models is an
interesting research question.

The paper introduces a novel, retrieval augmented generation (RAG) system
with an LLM using PO-CBR for the downstream task of explaining business
process models. The basic idea of RAG systems is to combine a retriever module
with a generator module [16], i.e. to "decouple the capacity that language models have for understanding text from how they store knowledge" [12]. We have
investigated the utility of two alternative case retrieval approaches to support
RAG systems:

a) for prompt chaining to overcome the size restrictions of the LLM's context
   window
b) for enhancing prompt templates with in-context examples for the downstream
   task

Approach a) reuses the indexing knowledge from the case base to tokenize the
prompts into a chain. The retriever component in b) provides problem-solution-
pair cases to fill the prompt templates. Approach b) is following the classical
CBR approach where the case base comprises experiential knowledge to directly
solve a downstream task. Both approaches provide in-context learning [2] when
using the retrieval results to activate the appropriate, task-specific context of the
LLM. A standard LLM has been pre-trained on large amounts of text in a task-
agnostic manner. In contrast to parameter fine-tuning by further pre-training
LLMs for a specific task, in-context learning allows the use of the LLM as it
is [2].

For both approaches, we have conducted experiments with two process-
oriented case bases derived from the same repository of 37 process models.
They describe real business processes from different application areas, including
human resources, insurance claims or supply chains. Case base a) comprises the
business process models per se. In case base b) model-text pairs with a textual
explanation as solution part are recorded. Different variants of prompt templates
and prompting strategies (one-shot, few-shot) per approach are explored. The

experimental results show that RAG following approach b) achieves better process explanations than zero-shot approaches. The results for approach a) are not yet convincing. However, some surprising lessons have been learned for both approaches.

The remainder of the paper is organized as follows. Some foundations of LLMs are reported as background for the work in Sect. 2. Related work is discussed in Sect. 3. The two approaches a) and b) are presented at a conceptual level in Sect. 4 and evaluated by means of a prototypical implementation with a repository of real process models in Sect. 5. A conclusion is drawn in Sect. 6.

2   Foundations of LLMs

LLMs address text generation by a probabilistic model $P(y|x; \theta)$ that predicts an output y for an input x [18]. The parameters θ of the model are learned in a pre-training process. Instead of learning the conditional probability distribution for (x, y)-pairs directly, the model is pre-trained for the probability $P(x; \theta)$ of text x itself from large amounts of text. In a standard language model such as GPT the text is predicted in an autoregressive fashion, predicting the linguistic tokens in the sequence one at a time. This is usually done from left to right [18].

During pre-training [22], each linguistic token u_i from a universe $U = \{u_1, u_2, ...u_n\}$ is assessed within the context of its k predecessor tokens: $P(u_i|u_{i-k}, ..., u_{i-1})$. The target function is to maximize the following likelihood:

$$L(U) = \sum_i \log P(u_i|u_{i-k}, ..., u_{i-1}; \theta)$$

for the context window size of k tokens where P is modeled using a neural network with parameters θ. For details of the pre-training, we refer to the literature [22].

Prompt engineering tries to find the best prompt to solve a downstream task with the LLM [18]. A *prompt template* implements a prompting function f_{prompt} to modify the input text x into a prompt $x' = f_{prompt}(x)$ [18]. A naive example of a prompt template to solve the task of explaining a business process model is the following.

```
Consider the standard BPMN 2.0.2 specification. Please create
a textual process description for following BPMN model
"Example" serialised in XML. [X]
```

where [X] is an input slot that can be filled with x. Further slots can be specified during prompt template engineering, such as slots for an intermediate answer [Z] or slots to shape the answer space [Y].

Prompt augmentation (or demonstration learning) provides answered prompts that can be used to demonstrate how the LLM should provide the answer to the actual prompt instantiated with the input x [18]. Brown et al. distinguish "zero-shot", "one-shot", or "few-shot" learning depending on how many demonstrations (in-context examples) are provided at inference time [2]. *Prompt chaining* is "the process of breaking up complex tasks into smaller steps, where each step can be completed by an independent run of an LLM, and where the output of one or more steps is used as input for the next" [29]. Prompt chaining can be combined with prompt augmentation in a way that the prompt is enriched with a different demonstration example for each iteration in the chain to refine the intermediate answer, for instance. A systematic survey on typical prompting methods for a variety of pre-trained language models is provided in the literature [18].

3   Related Work

Conversational methods have been applied in the literature [13,30] for process modeling tasks. A conversational CBR approach has been used by Zeyen et al. [30] to support users in formulating small process models as queries to a PO-CBR system. LLMs have been applied for conversational process modeling by Klietsova et al. [13]. The conversation with an LLM provides a toolchain to support modelers in extracting tasks from textual descriptions, modeling and refining the logic and layout of a BPMN model.[1] Fill et al. [5] go a step further in fully-automated generating process models from text by means of an LLM. Another text-to-process approach using LLMs is investigated by Grohs et al. [7]. In addition, the authors aim to identify activities within a process model that are suitable to be automated by means of RPA.[2] Bellan et al. [1] use in-context learning to achieve conversational process extraction from text. In contrast to the text-to-model work reported from the literature, our explanation approach addresses the opposite direction of the pipeline namely model-to-text. Further, our RAG system does not require any intermediate representations of the BPMN models.

Explanation has been considered in PO-CBR for the purpose of understanding similarity functions by visualisation [23]. The objective and the explanation type differs from our work where a textual explanation type is used to explain process models. The explanation goal of our work is to increase transparency for the users how a process is described in a BPMN model, e.g. within a PO-CBR system or within a traditional business process management system. In particular, the explanatory texts describe the elements of the process model under consideration and elucidate the semantics of the element types in BPMN.

Somewhat less related is the work of Upadhyay et al. [24] where a data-to-text generation approach is developed based on a neural net. Another type of structural data (database tables on sports events) to be explained and another method is used to create text from data.

---

[1] Business Process Modeling Notation: a standard graphical modeling language for business processes, see Decker et al. [4] for an introduction.
[2] Robotic Process Automation: the automation of tasks which have been performed by human agents so far by means of software robots technology [28].

4   Method

The RAG system comprises a retriever module and a generator module as illustrated in Fig. 1. The input to the RAG includes a BPMN model serialized into XML. The output of the RAG is a text answer that explains the BPMN model to a user who is not familiar with process modeling and BPMN. An example is depicted in Fig. 2 with the graphical representation on the left hand side and the serialized, abbreviated form on the right hand side. The rectangles with the rounded corners depict activities, namely to invoke a risk assessor service first and, in case of a large loan or in need of a review for the risk, to invoke a loan approval service next. The <bpmn:serviceTask ...> on the right hand side corresponds with the first activity "Invoke Risk Assessment" (for a more detailed description including some explanatory remarks on each element type of the BPMN process, see Sect. 4.2).

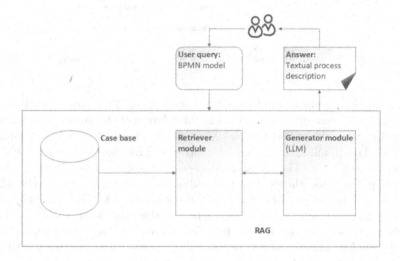

Fig. 1. RAG system for explaining business process models.

The retriever module differs among the approaches. Approach a) is described in Subsect. 4.1 and approach b) in Subsect. 4.2. In contrast to Lewis et al. [16], we do not train the parameters of the entire RAG system end-to-end. Instead, in-context learning is applied for both case-based approaches.

4.1   RAG with Case-Based Prompt Chaining

In this approach, the retrieval of cases provides indexing knowledge for the decomposition of a process model for prompt chaining. The intuition behind this is that process models exceeding the size of the context window can be explained part by part. For each chunk, explanatory texts are generated and merged into an overall explanation of the entire process model.

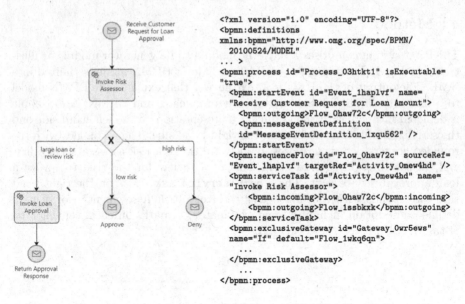

```
<?xml version="1.0" encoding="UTF-8"?>
<bpmn:definitions
xmlns:bpmn="http://www.omg.org/spec/BPMN/
  20100524/MODEL"
... >
<bpmn:process id="Process_03htkt1" isExecutable=
"true">
  <bpmn:startEvent id="Event_1haplvf" name=
  "Receive Customer Request for Loan Amount">
    <bpmn:outgoing>Flow_0haw72c</bpmn:outgoing>
    <bpmn:messageEventDefinition
    id="MessageEventDefinition_1xqu562" />
  </bpmn:startEvent>
  <bpmn:sequenceFlow id="Flow_0haw72c" sourceRef=
  "Event_1haplvf" targetRef="Activity_0mew4hd" />
  <bpmn:serviceTask id="Activity_0mew4hd" name=
  "Invoke Risk Assessor">
      <bpmn:incoming>Flow_0haw72c</bpmn:incoming>
      <bpmn:outgoing>Flow_1ssbkxk</bpmn:outgoing>
  </bpmn:serviceTask>
  <bpmn:exclusiveGateway id="Gateway_0wr5ews"
  name="If" default="Flow_1wkq6qn">
      ...
  </bpmn:exclusiveGateway>
  ...
</bpmn:process>
```

Fig. 2. Sample model for a loan request process in BPMN following [6, p.183].

The case base records serialized BPMN models (see right hand side of Fig. 2). The cases have been automatically sliced into chunks of the same length already. The size of the chunks and the chunk overlap is specified in terms of number of tokens. The chunk overlap aims to inform the LLM how the multiple chunks connect to each other. The set of chunks is sent to a general purpose embedding model that turns the chunks into embedding vectors. Such neural embeddings are a common means in LLM's to represent data. In a RAG system, a similarity metric (e.g., cosine similarity) is calculated on the embedding vectors. A node records an embedding vector and the reference back to the actual textual data from the chunk. These nodes form the index knowledge to represent a BPMN case.

A user query with a BPMN model to be explained could be sliced into chunks in the same manner as described above. However, instead of sequentially prompting the LLM with $chunk_1$ to $chunk_n$, the parts of the process model to be explained first are prioritized by means of retrieval as follows. The k best matching nodes from the case base's index provide the index knowledge for the query, i.e. their embeddings form latent features to draw the attention of the LLM to a particular part of the BPMN model to be explained next. For this, the retrieval result is inserted as context into the prefix of the prompt chunk by chunk for each iteration through prompt chaining until an explanation for the entire process model has been generated.

4.2 RAG with Explanatory Cases as In-context Examples

The retrieval module addresses the explanatory task itself. Process models that have already been explained are prompted to the LLM as in context-examples.

The case base comprises model-text pairs. Figure 2 depicts the problem part of a sample case on a loan request process. The following textual explanation (created by a human expert, with omissions) forms the solution part of the sample case:

```
The "Loan Request" process begins when a customer sends a request for a loan amount via a
    message, which triggers the message start event "Receive Customer Request for Loan
    Amount". A message start event waits for receiving a message from a participant to start
    the process.

Once the request is received, the process moves to the service task "Invoke Risk Assessor".
    A service task is a task that uses some sort of service, which could be a Web service or
    an automated application.

After the risk assessment, the process reaches an exclusive gateway named "If". A diverging
    exclusive gateway (decision) is used to create alternative paths within a process flow,
    whereas only one of the paths can be taken. In this case, the gateway represents a
    decision point in the process where the flow of control will diverge based on the risk
    assessment. This gateway thereby defines a default flow.

If the risk is high, the process will follow the default sequence flow named "high risk",
    and reach the throwing message end event "Deny". This type of end event indicates that
    a message is sent to a participant at the conclusion of the process.

If the risk is low, ...

If the loan is large or the risk needs review, ...

After the loan approval process, the process reaches the throwing message end event "Return
    Approval Response".

In summary, this process model represents a loan request process where the loan request is
    received, the risk is assessed, a decision is made based on the risk assessment, and the
    decision is communicated back to the customer.
```

The explanation is a textual process description that coherently describes all model elements (activities, gateways, events, etc.) and their relationship along the displayed control flow in the given BPMN model. Additionally, it provides explanations of the model elements' semantics, given the underlying defined business need to explain BPMN models to users lacking expertise on BPMN notations. In the above sample, the semantics of the BPMN element types "message start event", "service task" - a special type of activity which is executed by a service, "exclusive gateway", and "throwing message end event" is explained.

The retrieval module of the RAG provides the k best matching cases to the user query. The response is generated in an iterative way following a recommendation from LlamaIndex.[3] First, the best matching case is inserted as context into the prompt template, along with the query, to generate an initial answer. This answer, the query and the second best matching case is then put into a "refine prompt" to generate a refined answer. The refine prompt is applied

---

[3] https://docs.llamaindex.ai/en/stable/api_reference/query/response_synthesizer. html, last access: 03-18-2024.

$k - 1$ times until all cases from the retrieval result have been used as context information.

5   Experiments

The two case-based RAG approaches have been evaluated with a sample repository of BPMN process models. A human expert determined values for some evaluation criteria from the experimental results. At the end of this section, some observations and lessons learned from the experimental runs are discussed.

5.1   Experimental Data

The data underlying the experiments comes from two repositories of process models in BPMN taken from two Master theses [6,10]. The process models describe real business processes from different organisations and application fields, including human resource processes, insurance processes, and production processes. 37 BPMN models have been selected to achieve examples of various model complexity in terms of number of tokens, number of model elements and types of elements. All BPMN flow objects, i.e. events, activities and gateways are counted as model elements. BPMN types such as an XOR split gateway and an AND split gateway are counted as types of elements.

A pre-processor slightly abbreviates the XML files exported from BPMN modeler tools to save tokens as follows. The graphical structuring parts as well as the diagram interchange information are cut off from the XML files. Those parts are specified by means of tool-specific XML tags like <extensionElements> ... </extensionElements> in BizAgi or <bpmndi : BPMNDiagram> ... </bpmndi : BPMNDiagram> in Camunda. That is, the pre-processing of the user query requires a tool-specific filter per modeler tool.

The entire experimental data set can be accessed through a GitHub repository.[4]

5.2   Evaluation Criteria and Performance Metrics

We have defined evaluation criteria to assess the experimental results in a semi-automated manner. Some performance metrics are specified based on the well-known precision and recall formulas introduced by Lesk and Salton in the field of information retrieval in the sixties [15]. The precision metrics identify "hallucinations" by the LLM, which may describe model contents that actually do not occur in the given BPMN model.

Two pairs of metrics aim to measure the accuracy the explanatory texts achieve in terms of covering the model elements `el` and the types of elements `ty` that occur in a process model. A model element mentioned in the explanation, such as the activity "Invoke Risk Assessment", is considered relevant if it

---

[4] https://github.com/hoerb1337/LLMmodel2text/tree/main/Data_set, last access: 03-25-2024.

occurs also in the BPMN model. Irrelevant elements are those that have been hallucinated by the LLM. The accuracy metrics are specified as follows.

$$precision_{el} = \frac{|relevant\ el\ in\ explanation|}{|el\ in\ the\ explanation|} \qquad recall_{el} = \frac{|relevant\ el\ in\ explanation|}{|el\ in\ the\ model|}$$

$$(1)$$

$$precision_{ty} = \frac{|relevant\ ty\ in\ explanation|}{|ty\ in\ the\ explanation|} \qquad recall_{ty} = \frac{|relevant\ ty\ in\ explanation|}{|ty\ in\ the\ model|}$$

$$(2)$$

Further, the extent to which users can easily follow the generated explanation strongly depends on the order of explanatory passages within the text. Thus, the next pair of metrics measures whether the model elements are described at the expected position (pos) within the text following the control flow in the given BPMN model. The performance metrics for the correct positions are specified as follows.

$$precision_{pos} = \frac{|relevant\ el\ in\ explanation\ at\ expected\ position|}{|el\ in\ the\ explanation|}$$

$$recall_{pos} = \frac{|relevant\ el\ in\ explanation\ at\ expected\ position|}{|el\ in\ the\ model|}$$

$$(3)$$

The last pair of formulas measures the additional explanations of the model type's semantics, assuming to facilitate users' understanding of the BPMN model. For instance, the following sentence belongs to these meta model sentences.

```
A diverging exclusive gateway (decision) is used to create
alternative paths within a process flow, whereas only one of
the paths can be taken.
```

We assess the number of explanatory sentences on the meta model of BPMN as follows.

$$precision_{meta} = \frac{|relevant\ meta\ model\ sentences\ in\ explanation|}{|meta\ model\ sentences\ in\ the\ explanation|}$$

$$share_{meta} = \frac{|relevant\ meta\ model\ sentences\ in\ explanation|}{|ty\ in\ the\ model|}$$

$$(4)$$

Please note that $share_{meta}$ is not a metric since it may yield a ratio value above 1.0, potentially indicating longer explanations provided per type of flow object.

5.3   Implementation with LlamaIndex

The implementation of the two RAG approaches described in Sects. 4.1 and 4.2 is based on an open source orchestration framework for RAG systems called *LlamaIndex*[5] [17]. We have used LlamaIndex to bind the general purpose embedding

---

[5] For technical details, see also https://docs.llamaindex.ai/, last access: 03-25-2024.

model *text-embedding-ada-002*[6] by OpenAI to the retriever module to implement the similarity measure within LamaIndex' pre-defined Retriever Query Engine. We bind *chat-GPT4*[7] to the generator module of our RAG system. The tokenizer library tiktoken[8] is integrated to split the texts from the user query and the particular cases into tokens. The interaction between the retriever and the generator is implemented by a LlamaIndex module called *Response Synthesizer*. The latter is able to perform prompt chaining at its core [17]. It allows to feed in any LLM input prompt, get back retrieved context and send knowledge-augmented prompts to the generator module which are created by customized prompt templates. The templates and the configurations of all modules, including the number of cases to be retrieved, the chunk size, the temperature of the generator module (to specify the trade-off in GPT models between creativity and reproducability) are specified in Python scripts.

OpenAI recommends prompting tactics when engineering prompt templates for their GPT models. We have implemented the following model-specific tactics for GPT-4. Delimiters like triple quotation marks or XML tags indicate distinct sections of the prompt to be treated differently. Second, the steps required to complete a task are specified in a step-by-step instruction. Third, the LLM is asked to adopt a persona to set its behavior throughout the conversation. The OpenAI API reference for GPT-4[9] provides a list of pre-defined messages for chat completion. A *system message* describes the perspective that the LLM should consider when generating text, for instance the perspective of a persona like a process modeling expert. Such a system message is followed by a *user message* providing the actual request to respond to. Technically, orchestration frameworks like LlamaIndex can call the OpenAI API via Python code with an array of message objects where each object has a role and content.

We have specified two different templates for the initial (`Text QA Prompt`) and the refine prompts (`Refine Prompt`) per RAG approach. As an example, the Python code for the refine prompt of approach b) (see Sect. 4.2) is depicted in the following.

```
# Refine Prompt
chat_refine_msgs = [
    ChatMessage(
        role=MessageRole.SYSTEM,
        content="""You are an expert Q&A system with expert knowledge on the business process
        modeling language BPMN. You will get presented an exemplary textual process
        description for BPMN model "Example", which you should use as an example for the
        generation of textual process descriptions for given BPMN model "Explain" serialised
        in XML. Additionally, you will get presented your initially generated textual process
        description for the BPMN model "Explain". You therefore strictly operate in two
        modes when refining existing answers:\n1.

        **Add** new information to the original answer, using the exemplary textual process
        description.\n2.
```

[6] https://platform.openai.com/docs/guides/embeddings, last access: 03-25-2024.

[7] https://openai.com/gpt-4, last access: 03-25-2024.

[8] https://cookbook.openai.com/examples/how to count tokens with tiktoken, last access: 03-20-2024.

[9] https://platform.openai.com/docs/api-reference, last access 03-18-2024.

```
        **Repeat** the original answer, if the exemplary textual process description is not
        useful.\n

        Never reference the original answer or the exemplary textual process description
        directly in your answer. When in doubt, just add to the original answer."""
    ),
    ChatMessage(
        role=MessageRole.USER,
        content=(
            """Please create a textual process description for the given BPMN model
            serialised in XML. Add to each type of BPMN element used in the BPMN model a short
            explanation of this element type's semantics.

            Exemplary textual process description for BPMN model "Example": {context_msg}
            BPMN model "Explain" serialised in XML: {query_str}
            Initial textual process description for BPMN model "Explain": {existing_answer}
            Adapted textual process description for BPMN model "Explain": """
        ),
    ),
]
```

Template variables are filled with the case from the retrieval result to be sent along as context in the current prompting iteration (context_msg), the user query ({query_str}) and the intermediate answer from the previous call (existing_answer) to be refined. In the system role, the LLM is instructed to behave in a step-by-step manner through the generation of a refined answer.

5.4 Experimental Setup

We have conducted experiments for both approaches using the LlamaIndex implementation described above in Sect. 5.3. We have chosen a size of 4096 tokens per chunk with a chunk overlap of 800 tokens. The tokens have been created from the XML files following the cl100k_base encoding standard.[10] The chunks are turned into embedding vectors with a maximum size of 8,191 tokens, aligning with GPT-4's context window.

The two case bases have been created from the experimental data as follows. For approach a), the five BPMN models with the highest number of tokens have been selected as queries. Four of them are larger than the context window of 8,191 tokens itself. For the fifth case it is very likely that the template (see previous subsection) filled with the corresponding XML file and any in-context example exceeds the context window size. For approach b) the 33 BPMN models that fit into the context window size have been extended by explanatory texts created by a human expert. Six of them have been arbitrarily selected to form the case base. The remaining 27 are used as query cases for approach b). As a baseline to approach b), each query has been prompted to a zero-shot approach with a template using a system message and a straightforward output instruction. Approach b) has been run in three configurations for $k = 1, 2, 3$. Each run (except for the zero-shot baseline approach) is replicated once to observe the impact of the remaining creativity of the LLM despite the temperature value of 0 is on the experimental results.

---

[10] As implemented in OpenAI's tokenizer library tiktoken, see https://cookbook. openai.com/examples/how_to_count_tokens_with_tiktoken, last access: 20-03-2024.

5.5 Experimental Results

The experimental results for approach a), which tries to overcome the restricted context window size by means of prompt chaining, show a mixed picture. One round for model 8-5 generated output that exhibited a very low performance, reflecting the reason for not evaluating this textual process description. Table 1 depicts the F1 score values of the metric pairs. Especially the two rows for the values of $share_{meta}$ highlight that our approach was not successful in explaining the semantics of BPMN.

Table 1. Experimental results for approach a) on the five largest process models.

	Model 10-2	Model 2-2	Model 8-4	Model 8-5	Model 2-1	Average
No. of tokens	7,018	8,238	8,607	8,634	10,886	8,677
$F1_{el}$	0.6120	0.6283	0.4138	-	0.6227	0.5692
(repeated)	0.6736	0.6	0.4161	0.4824	0.4576	0.5259
$F1_{ty}$	0.6667	0.3571	0.88	-	0.3333	0.5593
(repeated)	0.7143	0.3077	0.7273	0.6316	0.2857	0.5333
$F1_{pos}$	0.6180	0.6147	0.0299	-	0.5208	0.4458
(repeated)	0.5574	0.4356	0.058	0.519	0.2895	0.3719
$share_{meta}$	0.1224	0.04	0.2292	-	0.0169	0.1021
(repeated)	0,	0.02	0.1458	0	0	0.0332
$precision_{meta}$	0.8571	1	0.9167	-	1	0.9435
(repeated)	0	1	1	0	0	0.4

The experimental results for approach b), which uses cases from the case base as in-context examples, are depicted as average values per run in Table 2. The pairs of metrics are combined into F1 scores again. Instead of the 27 models as planned, only 22 models have been considered. The computational time increased tremendously with model complexity, actually requiring a few minutes for only one larger BPMN model with around 5013 tokens and 72 model elements. The quality of the explanations of the larger models decreased rapidly (compare the discussion in Sect. 5.6). Since it would have caused costs of more than 3 US$ for generating a single textual process description, we decided to consider only models with less than 5k tokens.

All RAG rounds achieved better values than the baseline LLM. The differences between two runs in the same configuration are rather small. Surprisingly, the improvements with an increasing number k of in-context examples are marginal on average.

5.6 Lessons Learned

In addition to the measured values, we made some surprising observations in the course of the experiments.

Table 2. Experimental results for approach b) (avg. for 22 models per run).

	LLM (zero-shot)	RAG with k = 1	RAG with k = 2	RAG with k = 3
$F1_{el}$	0.8130	0.8855	0.8790	0.8713
(repeated)	-	0.8646	0.8521	0.8736
$F1_{ty}$	0.7193	0.8676	0.8652	0.8698
(repeated)	-	0.8509	0.8574	0.8625
$F1_{pos}$	0.8071	0.8251	0.8234	0.8301
(repeated)	-	0.8353	0.7995	0.8402
$share_{meta}$	0.2289	0.5575	0.4780	0.5757
(repeated)	-	0.5695	0.4881	0.5556
$precision_{meta}$	0.6307	0.9811	0.9813	0.9924
(repeated)	-	0.9430	0.9738	0.9451

Setting the temperature parameter to 0 did not prevent the RAG from generating variants of output in the different experimental runs. Note that at the end of our work, OpenAI released an updated version of GPT-4 that now includes additional parameters to control non-deterministic behavior.[11] Since different explanations for the same model might even be a benefit for the intended users it is not yet clear whether the additional parameters were useful.

Tests with inserting meta knowledge on BPMN into the prompt instructions did not change the quality of results. This is in contrast to the results reported by Fill et al. [5] who experimented with an older version of GPT. It seems that the meta knowledge on BPMN is an inherent part of GPT-4 already since the training set might have included process model descriptions in BPMN.

The performance decrease with increasing model complexity was steady for any prompting strategy. In particular, we got a sense of increasing difficulty to map the described model elements and their relationships to the original BPMN model. For larger models, typically only parts of the process are correctly described while others - at random locations in the process model - did achieve explanations that are not useful. For instance, the LLM condensed several model elements into a high-level description instead of describing each of them. This makes it very difficult for novice users to understand the process model on the basis of the explanation. There seems to be a hidden capability threshold of somewhere around 3800 tokens which is less than half of GPT-4's context window of 8,191 tokens.

This inherent threshold might also provide a reason for the following, a bit disappointing observation. Increasing the number of in-context examples k achieves only marginal improvements compared to $k = 1$. In the light of energy consumption, the retrieval of a single best matching case seems the most recommendable strategy at the moment to configure the RAG.

---

[11] See   https://openai.com/blog/new-models-and-developer-products-announced-at-devday, last access: 03-26-2024.

6   Conclusion

In this paper, we have presented a RAG system based on the framework LlamaIndex and LLM GPT-4 with the aim to generate explanatory texts describing business process models for users who are not familiar with process modeling. Two alternative approaches of case-based support have been developed. While approach a) addresses reusing the partition of process cases into chunks for prompt chaining approach b) retrieves model-text-pair cases as in-context examples. The experiments for approach a) fail presumably at the limit of current LLM's capability to deal with larger context information. The experiments for approach b) succeed in generating explanations that cover the particular model elements, their control flow as well as the semantics of the BPMN modeling language. Surprisingly, the quality of the results are of nearly the same quality for configurations of one up to three in-context examples retrieved from the case base.

Meanwhile, GPT-4 provides pre-view versions with a context window size of 128k tokens.[12] It is likely that the capability threshold reported above is shifted beyond the 11k tokens of our largest model from the experimental repository. Repeating the experiments for both approaches, prompt case-based chaining (approach a)) and the use of explanatory cases as in-context examples (approach b)) with the new models seems promising. We think that the current experimental results on a case-based memory for model-text-pairs (approach b)) demonstrate the feasibility of using CBR retrieval in RAG systems for generating text explanations of structural models.

References

1. Bellan, P., Dragoni, M., Ghidini, C.: Leveraging pre-trained language models for conversational information seeking from text (2022). http://arxiv.org/abs/2204.03542. arXiv:2204.03542
2. Brown, T.B., et al.: Language Models are Few-Shot Learners. arXiv:2005.14165 (2020). arXiv: 2005.14165
3. Davenport, T.H.: Process Innovation: Reengineering Work Through Information Technology. Harvard Business Press, Brighton (1993)
4. Decker, G., Dijkman, R., Dumas, M., García-Bañuelos, L.: The business process modeling notation. In: Hofstede, A.H.M., Aalst, W.M.P., Adams, M., Russell, N. (eds.) Modern Business Process Automation, pp. 347–368. Springer, Heidelberg (2010). https://doi.org/10.1007/978-3-642-03121-2_13
5. Fill, H.G., Fettke, P., Köpke, J.: Conceptual modeling and large language models: impressions from first experiments with ChatGPT. Enterp. Model. Inf. Syst. Architect. (EMISAJ) **18**, 1–15 (2023)
6. Friedrich, F.: Automated Generation of Business process Models from Natural Language Input. Diplomarbeit, Humboldt-Universität zu Berlin (2010)

---

[12] See   https://openai.com/blog/new-models-and-developer-products-announced-at-devday, last access: 03-26-2024.

7. Grohs, M., Abb, L., Elsayed, N., Rehse, J.R.: Large language models can accomplish business process management tasks. In: De Weerdt, J., Pufahl, L. (eds.) BPM 2023. LNBIP, vol. 492, pp. 453–465. Springer, Cham (2024). https://doi.org/10.1007/978-3-031-50974-2_34

8. Hammond, K., Leake, D.: Large language models need symbolic AI. In: Proceedings of the 17th International Workshop on Neural-Symbolic Learning and Reasoning, La Certosa di Pontignano, Siena, Italy, vol. 3432, pp. 204–209 (2023). https://ceur-ws.org/Vol-3432/paper17.pdf

9. Hess, T., Matt, C., Benlian, A., Wiesböck, F.: Options for formulating a digital transformation strategy. MIS Q. Executive 15(2), 123–139 (2016)

10. Hoffmann, D.: Ontology-based transfer learning for the digitization of administrative processes. Master thesis, Goethe University, Frankfurt (2022)

11. Kendall-Morwick, J., Leake, D.: A study of two-phase retrieval for process-oriented case-based reasoning. In: Montani, S., Jain, L.C. (eds.) Successful Case-based Reasoning Applications-2, vol. 494, pp. 7–27. Springer, Heidelberg (2014). https://doi.org/10.1007/978-3-642-38736-4_2

12. Khattab, O., Potts, C., Zaharia, M.: Building Scalable, Explainable, and Adaptive NLP Models with Retrieval (2021). https://ai.stanford.edu/blog/retrieval-based-NLP/. Accessed 24 Apr 2024

13. Klievtsova, N., Benzin, J.V., Kampik, T., Mangler, J., Rinderle-Ma, S.: Conversational process modelling: state of the art, applications, and implications in practice. In: Di Francescomarino, C., Burattin, A., Janiesch, C., Sadiq, S. (eds.) BPM 2023. LNBIP, vol. 490, pp. 319–336. Springer, Cham (2023). https://doi.org/10.1007/978-3-031-41623-1_19

14. Leopold, H., Mendling, J., Polyvyanyy, A.: Supporting process model validation through natural language generation. IEEE Trans. Softw. Eng. 40(8), 818–840 (2014)

15. Lesk, M.E., Salton, G.: Relevance assessments and retrieval system evaluation. Inf. Storage Retrieval 4(4), 343–359 (1968)

16. Lewis, P., et al.: Retrieval-augmented generation for knowledge-intensive NLP tasks. In: Advances in Neural Information Processing Systems, vol. 33, pp. 9459–9474 (2020)

17. Liu, J.: LlamaIndex (2022). https://doi.org/10.5281/zenodo.1234. https://github.com/jerryjliu/llama_index. Accessed 23 Apr 2024

18. Liu, P., Yuan, W., Fu, J., Jiang, Z., Hayashi, H., Neubig, G.: Pre-train, prompt, and predict: a systematic survey of prompting methods in natural language processing. ACM Comput. Surv. 55(9), 1–35 (2023)

19. Minor, M., Herold, M., Rubbe, J., Dufner, S., Brussas, G.: Transfer learning operators for process-oriented cases. In: Proceedings of 2021 IEEE Fourth International Conference on Artificial Intelligence and Knowledge Engineering AIKE 2021, pp. 9 – 16. IEEE Computer Society Press (2021)

20. Minor, M., Montani, S., Recio-García, J.A.: Editorial: process-oriented case-based reasoning. Inf. Syst. 40, 103–105 (2014)

21. Minor, M., Tartakovski, A., Bergmann, R.: Representation and structure-based similarity assessment for agile workflows. In: Weber, R.O., Richter, M.M. (eds.) ICCBR 2007. LNCS (LNAI), vol. 4626, pp. 224–238. Springer, Heidelberg (2007). https://doi.org/10.1007/978-3-540-74141-1_16

22. Radford, A., Narasimhan, K., Salimans, T., Sutskever, I.: Improving language understanding by generative pre-training. Technical report (2018). https://openai.com/research/language-unsupervised. Accessed 23 Apr 2024

23. Schultheis, A., Hoffmann, M., Malburg, L., Bergmann, R.: Explanation of similarities in process-oriented case-based reasoning by visualization. In: Massie, S., Chakraborti, S. (eds.) ICCBR 2023. LNCS, vol. 14141, pp. 53–68. Springer, Cham (2023). https://doi.org/10.1007/978-3-031-40177-0_4

24. Upadhyay, A., Massie, S.: CBR assisted context-aware surface realisation for data-to-text generation. In: Massie, S., Chakraborti, S. (eds.) ICCBR 2023. LNCS, vol. 14141, pp. 34–49. Springer, Cham (2023). https://doi.org/10.1007/978-3-031-40177-0_3

25. Vidgof, M., Bachhofner, S., Mendling, J.: Large language models for business process management: opportunities and challenges. In: Di Francescomarino, C., Burattin, A., Janiesch, C., Sadiq, S. (eds.) BPM 2023. LNBIP, vol. 490, pp. 107–123. Springer, Cham (2023). https://doi.org/10.1007/978-3-031-41623-1_7

26. Watson, I.: A case-based persistent memory for a large language model. CoRR abs/2310.08842 (2023). https://doi.org/10.48550/ARXIV.2310.08842. https://doi.org/10.48550/arXiv.2310.08842

27. Weske, M.: Business Process Management: Concepts, Languages, Architectures, 2nd edn. Springer, Heidelberg (2012). https://doi.org/10.1007/978-3-662-59432-2

28. Willcocks, L.P., Lacity, M., Craig, A.: The it function and robotic process automation. Technical report (2015)

29. Wu, T., Terry, M., Cai, C.J.: AI chains: transparent and controllable human-AI interaction by chaining large language model prompts. In: CHI Conference on Human Factors in Computing Systems, New Orleans, LA, USA, pp. 1–22. ACM (2022). https://doi.org/10.1145/3491102.3517582. https://dl.acm.org/doi/10.1145/3491102.3517582

30. Zeyen, C., Müller, G., Bergmann, R.: Conversational process-oriented case-based reasoning. In: Aha, D.W., Lieber, J. (eds.) ICCBR 2017. LNCS (LNAI), vol. 10339, pp. 403–419. Springer, Cham (2017). https://doi.org/10.1007/978-3-319-61030-6_28

The Intelligent Tutoring System AI-VT with Case-Based Reasoning and Real Time Recommender Models

Daniel Soto-Forero$^{(\boxtimes)}$ [iD], Simha Ackermann[iD], Marie-Laure Betbeder[iD],
and Julien Henriet[iD]

DISC, Université de Franche-Comté,CNRS, institut FEMTO-ST, 16 Route de Gray,
25000 Besançon, France
{daniel.soto_forero,marie-laure.betbeder,julien.henriet}@univ-fcomte.fr

Abstract. This paper presents a recommendation model coupled on an existing CBR system model through a new modular architecture designed to integrate multiple services in a learning system called AI-VT (Artificial Intelligence Training System). The recommendation model provides a semi-automatic review of the CBR, two variants of the recommendation model have been implemented: deterministic and stochastic. The model has been tested with 1000 simulated learners, and compared with an original CBR system and BKT (Bayesian Knowledge Tracing) recommender system. The results show that the proposed model identifies learners' weaknesses correctly and revises the content of the ITS (Intelligent Tutoring System) better than the original ITS with CBR. Compared to BKT, the results at each level of complexity are variable, but overall the proposed stochastic model obtains better results.

Keywords: Real Time Revision · Intelligent Training System · Thompson Sampling · Case-Based Reasoning · Bayesian Knowledge Tracing · Automatic Adaptation

1 Introduction

The AI-VT system is a generic ITS that aims to accompany learners by proposing sheets of exercises called sessions. Inside each session, the expected abilities are divided into skills themselves broken down into subskills. The learner chooses a skill to work on, and the system generates a session composed of exercises associated with several subskills of the chosen skill. The system offers a list of exercises at the beginning of a session using the case-based reasoning paradigm with a database of questions [8].

Actually, the AI-VT system has a database of questions. Each of them is associated with a context, the text of a question, and a complexity level. The questions belong to a subskill level, and the subskills belong to a skill level. The teacher and the learner are the principal actors in the system. The teacher has the capacity to configure the whole system, number of skills, subskills in a skill,

J. A. Recio-Garcia et al. (Eds.): ICCBR 2024, LNAI 14775, pp. 191–205, 2024.
https://doi.org/10.1007/978-3-031-63646-2_13

number of questions, complexity of each of them, number of complexity levels, and time per session. The learner can start the series of a specific subskill, access complementary support resources, and answer the test questions in the sessions proposed by the system.

Using the CBR philosophy, the global AI-VT system assumes that there are learners with similar learning performances, needs, and abilities. It is then possible to group them and thus improve the general learning process for all of them. The case base comprises exercises associated with multiple skills.

CBR phases in AI-VT are used as described below. The retrieve phase involves finding exercises previously proposed for the same skill to other learners. The reuse phase modifies this list according to the sessions previously proposed to the learner. The revision phase, presented in this paper, involves modifying this list of exercises in real time. The retain phase maintains this new session [9]. To improve the functionality of AI-VT, two real-time recommendation models have been developed and the necessary architecture has been designed to integrate all the elements without significantly affecting the internal structure of the original system.

The two main types of software architecture to integrate modules and functionalities are monolithic and modular. In monolithic architecture, the software system is considered as a single unit with only one code source, one database, and one deployment for the whole system. This type of system is simple to develop and test but is not good for updating and scaling because of its rigidity. Modular architecture divides the system into independent modules that can communicate with each other. Each module then contains everything needed to work. Actually, there are many software systems designed with modular architecture because of the multiple advantages it offers [3,19].

The recommendation systems in ITS generally pretend to find the weakness of learners and try to help them to improve the knowledge adapting the system. A common recommender algorithm is Bayesian Knowledge Tracing (BKT). This algorithm use four parameters for each learner to estimate the learned probability. Then with a defined threshold, it is possible to adapt a specific system to personal calculated knowledge [12]. Formally, the model defines four parameters $P(k)$ is the parameter to estimate the knowledge probability in a specific skill. $P(w)$, is the probability of the learner demonstrating knowledge. $P(s)$, is the probability the learner makes a mistake. $P(g)$, is the probability that the learner guessed a response. For each response given by the learner, the $P(k)$ value is updated as shown in Eqs. 1, 2 and 3. With these equations, it is possible to see the knowledge progression in a skill [16].

$$P(k_{t-1}|Correct_t) = \frac{P(k_{t-1})(1 - P(s))}{P(k_{t-1})(1 - P(s)) + (1 - P(k_{t-1}))P(g)} \tag{1}$$

$$P(k_{t-1}|Incorrect_t) = \frac{P(k_{t-1})P(s)}{P(k_{t-1})(P(s)) + (1 - P(k_{t-1}))(1 - P(g))} \tag{2}$$

$$P(k_t) = P(k_{t-1}|evidence_t) + (1 - P(k_{t-1}|evidence_t))P(w) \tag{3}$$

The *evidence* represents the response to a specific question. If the response is *correct* then the Eq. 1 is used, but if the response is *incorrect* the Eq. 2 is used. The BKT equations calculate the values for each step of time t sequentially.

This work focuses on the CBR revise step. Indeed, in our proposition a training session is proposed to the learner after the reuse step. This initial training session is adapted to the learner level *a priori*. Then, the new module described in this paper analyses the answers given by the learner in real-time during the training session and proposes some modifications in real-time. For this reason, we consider the contribution of this paper is situated in the revise phase of the classic CBR-cycle. The recommendation module is integrated into the AI-VT CBR system by means of a modular architecture.

This paper presents two main contributions: (i) a modular distributed architecture that allows integration of multiple artificial intelligence models in CBR in an asynchronous manner, (ii) two recommender models based on rules and reinforcement learning to improve the revision CBR system for learner needs. These models have been compared to common BKT algorithm used in others ITS.

The structure of this paper is as follows: Sect. 2 presents related works on recommender systems, Bayesian Knowledge Tracing, Case-Based Reasoning and adaptation methods. The proposed model is explained in Sect 3. Section 4 describes the experiments and results. Finally, Sect 5 presents the conclusions.

2   Related Works

In the field of ITS, recommender systems have been shown to have a positive impact on learners as they aid in finding relevant resources and maintaining motivation. Additionally, the application of artificial intelligence techniques to personalize recommendations has made these systems more efficient. These effects were validated by Huang *et al.* [10], who measured the difference between preliminary tests and tests taken after the completion of a course, with and without recommender system. In intelligent tutoring systems, the architecture is also important to define the actors, services, functionalities, and scenarios while taking into account the information corresponding to each learner, such as the uncertainty of progress, specific needs, and defined objectives. Xu and Zhao [15] propose a modular architecture for adjusting an educational system with artificial intelligence, where the authors show the flow of request and answer information between modules and actors to perform a specific task, as well as the layers and their functionalities.

The work of Bradác *et al.* [4], designs a system that allows for adaptation through the collection of complementary information from the learner throughout the learning process. The modules have been defined to obtain information from the learner and after processing and analyzing it, to transmit it to other modules whose purpose is to adapt the learning objects.

Recommender systems require information about the learner and their requirements so that a module can define a profile and perform a set of algorithms to produce a recommendation. The work of Lalitha and Sreeja [11] uses the KNN algorithm to identify the common characteristics between the learners and to extract the adapted resources from the web using Random Forest. There are various methods for creating and suggesting personalized resources and paths. For instance, in Zhao et al. [17], learner data is collected and classified into groups with similar characteristics to determine the performance of each learner using the data envelopment analysis (DEA) method.

The recommendation may suggest resources, themes, or exercises. In Zhou and Wang [18] an exercise recommendation system for learning English was developed. The system includes a main module that represents learners as vectors based on the DINA model. For instance, if in the vector $k_1 = 1$, the learner has mastered knowledge point k_1. On the other hand, if $k_2 = 0$, the learner needs to study knowledge point k_2 as they have not yet acquired mastery in that area.

Some recommendation and personalization works consider complementary variables to the grades, as in Ezaldeen et al. [7], which combines the analysis of the learner's behavior and semantic analysis. The first step is to collect the necessary data to create a learner profile. The profile is assigned to a set of predefined learning categories according to their preferences and historical data. Then, the system generates a guide to obtain resources that the system can recommend on the web.

In Zhang and Yao [16] a variant of the BKT algorithm for a specific type of problem with three possible answers is proposed. Basically, the work divides the learning process into three states by changing the equations and defining new parameters to obtain the learning state with more precision. Using the AUC, RMSE and standard deviation, the BKT for three answers show better results compared with original BKT.

The work of Xu et al. [14] uses the BKT model to recommend personalized training materials according to learner progress in a system of educational safety behaviors in the construction industry. The model was tested with real participants using the results of several quizzes performed throughout the training as a metric. The model help to acquire a higher level of mastery of the knowledge associated with a specific competency and the students present better results than the students who used the system without a recommendation system.

Other techniques and algorithms were applied to improve the ITS as a CBR. The use of CBR in ITS shows positive results as indicated by the work of Supic [13] whose model follows the traditional cycle of CBR by combining traditional and digital learning models. The main contributions are the representation of cases and the recommendation of personalized learning paths according to other learners' information. To demonstrate the effectiveness of the model, an initial case base was created to recommend courses to 120 learners. The results were obtained with the help of exams before and after following the course recommended by the model.

Recommendation systems are generally used in commerce and on the market to recommend products to customers, but these techniques may be used in other fields to recommend training exercises, planning paths, study resources, etc. These recommendations are based on historical data and user feedback. In Eide *et al.* [6], a Recurrent Neural Network as a recommender system is proposed for a marketplace. The network had been tested in combination with several variants of the Thompson Sampling (TS) algorithm because it allows maximization of the explorative opportunities and ensures a machine learning process.

The recommendation of products for e-commerce with an extension of the Bernoulli Thompson Sampling algorithm is proposed in Brodén *et al.* [5], where combinations of TS with sleeping bandit and dynamic partitioning are tested with information belonging to a single user in the same session. The results of metrics precision and recall show high values of accuracy for three different types of products.

Another application of TS appears in Akerblom *et al.* [1], where a variant of TS is implemented to find the minimax paths in a network with stochastic weights and partial knowledge. The work with three different test scenarios demonstrates the algorithm effectiveness despite the complexity and lack of information.

3 Proposed Model

3.1 Proposed Architecture

The proposed model[1] belongs to an architecture shown in Fig. 1, where the solid lines represent a bidirectional information flow, the solid lines with an arrow represent the unidirectional flow and the dashed lines represent the information dependency between the modules. The external devices that can be used by the modules to execute their functionalities and the labels that indicate what kind of information the module sends to the central system are also shown, as well as some of the artificial intelligence algorithms implemented in each module and the stage of development each one of them is in. Some devices are necessary for the execution of modules requiring getting data from external sources. The NAO robot, sensors, video camera, and microphone are represented in the architecture diagram. This kind of architecture preserves the original AI-VT CBR system functionality, and thus, the system can make use of complementary functions simply by activating the corresponding module by sending and receiving the necessary information for its operation, which extends the original global functionality of the system and facilitates integration with the designed modules and even new modules. The modular design also facilitates code maintenance, development and integration of new extensions, and configuration and adaptation of the system to different scenarios all reducing risks and costs. The modularity also enables the functionalities of each module to be executed asynchronously in parallel or distributed mode if required.

The architecture consists of two main elements: the central system (AI-VT CBR System) and the functional modules. The central system manages all the learning processes; generates and starts the sessions; stores the data for skills,

---

[1] https://disc.univ-fcomte.fr/gitlab/daniel.soto_forero/ai-vt-recommender-system/tree/main.

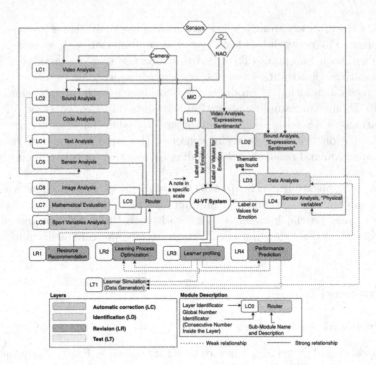

Fig. 1. Proposed Architecture to Integrate AI-VT CBR with AI Algorithms

questions, resources, learners, and responses; contains the controls and general interface; manages the flow of information; and activates the necessary modules. Modules are a set of independent functionalities implemented with artificial intelligence algorithms that receive and send data from the central component. Each module operates according to specific criteria related to its own particular purpose. The modules are grouped in layers according to their functionality: automatic correction, identification, adaptation, revision, and testing. The teacher and learner do not use the modules directly. The modules are used by the system to complement some functionalities.

The automatic correction layer (LC) corresponds to the modules in charge of receiving the learner's answers. According to the defined algorithms and criteria, they establish a grade consistent with a reference answer to a specific question. In this layer, the router module (LC0) is in charge of identifying the type of correction needed and instantiating the appropriate module to execute the specific task. The identification layer (LD) contains the modules that identify the learner's weaknesses or external variables when performing the exercises proposed by the system or after analyzing the results. These modules help to customize the learner's processes according to the results obtained from the analyses. The revision layer (LR) includes the modules that take the data from the results obtained in the LC layer and the results of the analysis in the LD layer to modify the learner's path by trying to reinforce the learning in the detected weaknesses. The modules that obtain information from the learners and try to predict their results according to different skills and levels of complexity are in the revision layer (LR).

Specifically, the recommender model belongs to the revision layer (LR1, LR2), where the modules use the information generated by the automatic correction and identification layer modules, as well as the learner's complementary information stored in the system's database. All this information helps establish the best way to guide the learner towards better understanding by overcoming the weaknesses and gaps that have been identified. In this case, the recommender model attempts to change the list of exercises using CBR and according to the learner's partial results. The architecture with modular design also facilitates code maintenance, development and integration of new extensions, and configuration and adaptation of the system to different scenarios all reducing risks and costs. The modularity also enables the functionalities of each module to be executed asynchronously in parallel or distributed mode if required.

3.2 Proposed Models of Recommendation

For adaptation and revision modules, the model requires the grades, time of answers, and complexity of questions to perform the recommendation for the learner, this information is represented as a numeric vector. The model variables and parameters are detailed in Table 1. The model is proposed in two versions, one deterministic and the other stochastic.

The proposed deterministic model calculates the mastery rate with Eqs. 4, 5 and 6. The mastery rate helps to guide the learner within the complexity levels using historical grades and to recommend the complexity level closest to the current one where weaknesses have been detected. Mastery rate m_c is a value on a scale of 0 to 100 that reflects the level of proficiency attained by the learner in a subskill. It serves to condense the learner's scores for each subskill. It is calculated based on the (latest) scores and weighted by the complexity of the exercises. The mastery rate must take into account the complexity of the exercises as follows: a 100% mastery rate cannot be achieved solely with low-complexity exercises; conversely, it can be achieved with maximum-complexity exercises alone. We then propose a tiered system. With c_n levels of complexity, exercises of complexity c should enable the attainment of a maximum mastery rate of $c * 100/c_n$. Finally, the mastery rate is calculated recursively.

$$f(g) = <g> - \left(<g> * \lambda * \frac{<t_c>}{t_m} \right) \tag{4}$$

$$m_1 = \frac{10}{c_n} * f(g_1)_{n_q} \tag{5}$$

$$m_c = max \left(m_{c-1} + \frac{10}{c_n} * f(g_c)_{n_q}, \frac{c * 10}{c_n} * f(g_c)_{n_q} \right) \tag{6}$$

Table 1. Variables and parameters of the proposed model

ID	Description	Domain
c_n	Complexity levels	$\mathbb{N} \mid c_n > 0$
g_m	Max value into the scale of grades	$\mathbb{N} \mid g_m > 0$
g_t	Grade threshold	$(0, g_m) \in \mathbb{R}$
s	Number of defined paths	$\mathbb{N} \mid s > 0$
s_c	Defined fixed current path	$[1, s] \in \mathbb{N}$
Δs	Step for beta distribution parameters in path s	$(0, 1) \in \mathbb{R}$
t_m	Max value in time answer	$\mathbb{R} \mid t_m > 0$
nv	Number of intervals for each path	$\mathbb{N} \mid nv > 0$
g_c	Grade for a learner for a question with complexity c	$[0, g_m] \in \mathbb{R}$
ng_c	Grade of learner with time penalization	$[0, g_m] \in \mathbb{R}$
t_c	Time to answer a question with complexity c	$[0, t_m] \in \mathbb{R}$
m_c	Mastery rate of learner for a complexity c	$[0, 100] \in \mathbb{R}$
$v_{s,nv}$	Limits for each nv interval	$[0, 100]$
n_q	Number of questions to consider of history	$\mathbb{N}$
$f(g)$	Function to calculate the mean of grades g	$\mathbb{R}_+$
ncl	New calculated complexity level	$\mathbb{N}$
α_c	Value for α in complexity c	$\mathbb{R} \mid \alpha_c > 0$
β_c	Value for β in c complexity	$\mathbb{R} \mid \beta_c > 0$
$\Delta\beta$	Step of beta parameter initialization	$\mathbb{N} \mid \Delta\beta > 0$
λ	Weight of time penalization	$(0, 1) \in \mathbb{R}$
G_c	Set of d grades in complexity level c	$\mathbb{R}^d , d \in \mathbb{N} \mid d > 0$
x_c	Normalized average grades	$[0, 1] \in \mathbb{R}$
n_c	Number of total questions in a session	$\mathbb{N} \mid n_c > 0$
ny_c	Number of questions in complexity level c	$\mathbb{N} \mid 0 < ny_c \leq n_c$
y_c	Proportion of questions in complexity level c	$[0, 1] \in \mathbb{R}$
r	Total value for adaptability defined metric	$[0, c_n] \in \mathbb{R}$
sc	Total value for cosine similarity metric	$[-1, 1] \in \mathbb{R}$
th_1	First threshold for BKT system	$[0, 1] \in \mathbb{R}$
th_2	Second threshold for BKT system	$[0, 1] \in \mathbb{R}$

With the calculation of the mastery rate for the last level of complexity it is possible to recommend an adapted complexity level using a predefined strategy. Equation 7 uses an indicator function I_c to determine the adapted complexity level using a table $v_{s,nv}$ of predetermined intervals.

$$ncl = I_c(inf(v_{s,nv}) <= m_c <= sup(v_{s,nv})), \forall nv \tag{7}$$

The proposed stochastic model uses the Beta family of distribution of probability to define dynamically the new complexity level inspired by the Thompson Sampling algorithm. This model version allows recommendation of non-contiguous complexity levels, but the priority is to recommend levels where faults have been detected. The initial parametrization of all distributions of probability can force the model to recommend contiguous complexity levels.

In this case, the grade threshold variable g_t is necessary to determine the variability of distribution of probability for each complexity level. Equations 8 and 9 show the correlated update rules. These rules modify the values by inverse reward. Each complexity level has an associated Beta distribution of probability with predefined initial values for the parameters α and β.

$$ng_c = g_c - \left(g_c * \lambda * \frac{t_c}{t_m} \right) \tag{8}$$

$$ng_c \geq g_t \rightarrow \begin{cases} \beta_c = \beta_c + \Delta_s \\ \beta_{c-1} = \beta_{c-1} + \frac{\Delta_s}{2} \\ \alpha_{c+1} = \alpha_{c+1} + \frac{\Delta_s}{2} \end{cases} \quad ng_c < g_t \rightarrow \begin{cases} \alpha_c = \alpha_c + \Delta_s \\ \alpha_{c-1} = \alpha_{c-1} + \frac{\Delta_s}{2} \\ \beta_{c+1} = \beta_{c+1} + \frac{\Delta_s}{2} \end{cases} \tag{9}$$

The new complexity level is the maximum random value index for all the complexity levels (Eq. 10).

$$ncl = max_x(\mathbb{E}[Beta(\alpha_x, \beta_x)]), 0 <= x <= c_n \tag{10}$$

4   Evaluation

The model was tested with a generated dataset that contains the grades and response times of 1000 learners for five different levels of complexity. The approximation of each learner's grades are generated with the logit-normal distribution of probability because it is experimentally the best representation model [2], and response times with normal distribution of probability. The generated dataset is a simulation of learners grades for answers to fifteen questions at each of the five levels of complexity. The dataset simulates a weakness in each level of complexity for 70% of learners in the first ten questions. The difficulty of the complexity is also simulated by reducing the average score and increasing the variance.

The defined general testing parameters for the model are detailed in Table 2. The specific parameters for all models have been estimated based on *Optuna* hyperparameter optimization for Python, to get the best possible global configuration. The parameters for the deterministic variant are in Table 3. Using these parameters, the model is formally written as Eqs. 11, 12, 13, 14 and 15. Table 4 shows the definition v of intervals. The stochastic variant parameter values are in Table 5, and parameters with an unique subjective configuration for BKT are in Table 6.

$$m_1 = \frac{10}{5} * f(g_1)_3 \tag{11}$$

Table 2. Values for tested scenarios

ID	c_n	g_m	t_m	s	s_c	λ
Value	5	10	120	3	2	0.25

Table 3. Initial values for the deterministic recommendation model

ID	nv_1	nv_2	nv_3	n_q	$v_{s,nv}$
Value	8	7	7	3	Table 4

Table 4. Table v with the values for three paths ($s = 3$), seven to eight intervals ($nv_1 = 8, nv_2 = 7$ and $nv_3 = 7$) and five CL (Complexity Levels)

Path 1		Path 2		Path 3	
Interval	CL	Interval	CL	Interval	CL
[0, 20]	0	[0, 15]	0	[0, 10]	0
[21, 30]	1	[16, 25]	1	[11, 20]	1
[31, 45]	1	[26, 35]	2	[21, 30]	2
[46, 50]	2	[36, 42]	2	[31, 36]	2
[51, 65]	2	[43, 50]	3	[37, 43]	3
[66, 75]	3	[51, 75]	3	[44, 65]	3
[76, 90]	3	[76, 100]	4	[66, 100]	4
[91, 100]	4				

Table 5. Initial values for the stochastic recommendation model (x represents all learners, y represents all complexity levels greater than 1)

ID	g_t	$\alpha_{x,1}$	$\alpha_{x,y}$	$\beta_{x,1}$	$\Delta\beta_{x,y}$	Δ_1	Δ_2	Δ_3
Value	6	2	1	1	1	0.3	0.5	0.7

Table 6. Initial values for the BKT recommendation model

ID	p_k	p_{wl}	p_s	p_g	th_1	th_2	g_t
Value	0.3	0.2	0.4	0.2	0.5	0.95	6

$$m_2 = max\left(m_1 + \frac{10}{5} * f(g_2)_3, \frac{20}{5} * f(g_2)_3\right) \tag{12}$$

$$m_3 = max\left(m_2 + \frac{10}{5} * f(g_3)_3, \frac{30}{5} * f(g_3)_3\right) \tag{13}$$

$$m_4 = max\left(m_3 + \frac{10}{5} * f(g_4)_3, \frac{40}{5} * f(g_4)_3\right) \tag{14}$$

$$m_5 = max\left(m_4 + \frac{10}{5} * f(g_5)_3, \frac{50}{5} * f(g_5)_3\right) \tag{15}$$

To compare the models, three scenarios has been defined, where the progression of learners are simulated. The first scenario is the recommendation without initial data (cold start). The second scenario is the learner data for the first complexity level and the third scenario contains grades for all learners in the first and second complexity levels.

Equation 16 describes a quality metric to compare the original system, two recommendation model variants and BKT numerically. The goal of this metric is to measure the system's ability to adapt in dynamically in real-time the navigation between levels of complexity. The metric calculates a value for each complexity level according to grade averages and the number of recommended questions in that complexity level. The purpose of this metric is to give a high score to the recommender systems that propose more exercises at the complexity level where the learner has registered a lower average grade with the idea of reinforcing the knowledge at that complexity level. If they propose fewer exercises at complexity levels where the average grade is high it is assumed that the student has already acquired sufficient knowledge at those complexity levels. Low scores are assigned to systems that recommend few exercises at complexity levels with low average grades and, conversely, if they propose many exercises at complexity levels with high average grades.

$$r = \sum_{c=0}^{c_n-1} e^{-2(x_c+y_c-1)^2}; \ x_c = \frac{<g_c>_{G_c}}{g_m}; \ y_c = \frac{ny_c}{n_c} \tag{16}$$

In Eq. 16, x_c is the normalized average of grades in complexity level c, and y_c is the normalized number of answered questions in complexity level c. The global equation for the metric rp is inside the domain of two variables x_c and y_c. The maximum value for r in a specific complexity level is 1. The global maximum value for the tested scenarios is 5; therefore a good recommender system should have a high r value.

5 Results and Discussion

A first comparison between the recommender models (deterministic, stochastic and BKT) is shown in Fig. 2 where it is possible to see the different state

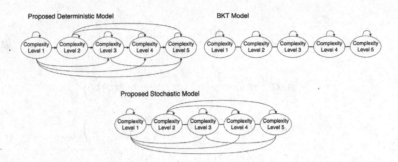

Fig. 2. Possible transitions for the three different recommender models (lines without arrow mean that the flow can be bi-directional)

transitions for the test scenarios, with five states corresponding to the levels of complexity.

The results of the comparison without historical data (cold start) between the two versions of the proposed model, BKT and the original system (CBR) are shown in Fig. 3, where different transition numbers and scales appear. The original system does not have transitions, this behavior motivates the development of a real-time adaptation module, as it allows to adjust the system more efficiently to the needs of each individual learner. All the learners are evaluated inside complexity level 0. Grades obtained during the session are not considered. The deterministic model generates four big transitions with a large number of learners in Questions 5, 6, 8 and 12 all of them between contiguous complexity levels. The trends are downward for levels 0, 1, and 2 after the eighth question and upward for levels 1 and 3. The mean after 20 executions for stochastic model show that it starts by proposing all the possible levels of complexity but focuses on level 0. The transitions are constants, but for a small number of learners, the trends after the tenth question are downward for levels 0 and 4 and upward for levels 1, 2 and 3. The BKT model starts stable for the first 5 questions. After that, it is less stable and propose big changes between complexity levels. In the cold start the trend is very similar to the deterministic model, but the progression is faster. In the first session almost 800 learners pass to complexity level 1 and 100 to level 4, that behavior can be explained by the values of the configuration parameters. Then it is possible to see that Deterministic and BKT systems are very sensible to small changes in the value of grades and that can difficult the precision in the weakness identification.

The results of quality metric calculations for the original system, BKT, and the two proposed models in the three defined scenarios are shown in Table 7. According to these results, it can be said that each model can be used in specific situations, BKT obtains good results for each level of complexity in the cold start scenario, but only allows advancement between contiguous levels of complexity. The deterministic model allows passing between different levels of complexity, but since the defined scales are closed intervals only advancement is possible, which allows the model to guarantee level passage. The stochastic model obtains

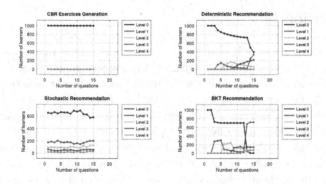

Fig. 3. Recommended complexity levels with two version models, first session case without historical grades data (cold start)

better overall results in scenarios 1 and 2. In addition it provides transitions between different levels forward and backward generating greater diversity in the proposed exercises.

Table 7. Results Metric Table (CBR - System without recommendation model, DM - Deterministic Model, SM - Stochastic Model)

	c_0	c_1	c_2	c_3	c_4	Total (r)	Total (%)
Scenario 1							
CBR	0.5388	–	–	–	–	0.5388	10.776
DM	0.8821	0.7282	0.9072	0.8759	-	3.3934	67.868
SM	0.9463	0.8790	0.7782	0.7108	0.6482	3.9625	79.25
BKT	**0.9996**	**0.9981**	**0.9262**	**0.8769**	**0.8023**	**4.6031**	**92.062**
Scenario 2							
CBR	0.9445	**0.9991**	–	–	–	1.9436	38.872
DM	–	0.9443	0.8208	**0.9623**	–	2.7274	54.548
SM	**0.9688**	0.9861	0.8067	0.7161	0.6214	**4.0991**	**81.982**
BKT	–	0.9954	**0.9910**	0.893	**0.8233**	3.7027	74.054
Scenario 3							
CBR	–	0.8559	0.7377	–	–	1.5936	31.872
DM	–	–	0.5538	0.7980	–	1.3518	27.036
SM	**0.9089**	0.9072	0.9339	0.7382	0.6544	**4.1426**	**82.852**
BKT	–	**0.9988**	**0.9882**	**0.9102**	**0.8478**	3.745	74.9

6   Conclusion

The proposed architecture is based on concepts and patterns commonly used to design complex systems that use artificial intelligence algorithms and tools in some way. This kind of design allows the implementation of a functional system with the adaptability necessary for the execution of one of the main requirements of intelligent learning systems. Moreover, as the referenced works indicate, modular architecture allows more flexible implementation and gives the system the possibility to scale quickly and even add complementary functionalities.

The recommendation module implemented tries to identify learners' weaknesses in order to propose coherent revisions, the algorithms in each of the cases tend to use few subjective and individual parameters for each learner unlike in the case of with the BKT model. The results show that it is indeed possible to identify the weaknesses of the learners and to revise the content of the training session in a personalized way for each learner. Compared to the global unique best BKT subjective parameter settings, the results are differents depending on the level of complexity and the initial situation. In some configurations, the best results have been obtained globally with the stochastic model. Therefore, it is determined that the proposed model can be complementary and used according to the specific situation of each learner.

Future work includes an analysis of architecture with other parameter values and other configurations, a complementary module to verify the changes proposed by the recommender model before sending them to the learner and analyze the specific pedagogical situations.

References

1. Akerblom, N., Hoseini, F.S., Haghir Chehreghani, M.: Online learning of network bottlenecks via minimax paths. Mach. Learn. **122**, 131–150 (2023). https://doi.org/10.1007/s10994-022-06270-0
2. Arthurs, N., Stenhaug, B., Karayev, S., Piech, C.: Grades are not normal: improving exam score models using the logit-normal distribution. In: International Conference on Educational Data Mining (EDM), p. 6 (2019). https://eric.ed.gov/?id=ED599204
3. Auer, F., Lenarduzzi, V., Felderer, M., Taibi, D.: From monolithic systems to microservices: an assessment framework. Inf. Softw. Technol. **137**, 106600 (2021)
4. Bradáč, V., Smolka, P., Kotyrba, M., Prudek, T.: Design of an intelligent tutoring system to create a personalized study plan using expert systems. Appl. Sci. **12**(12) (2022). https://doi.org/10.3390/app12126236. https://www.mdpi.com/2076-3417/12/12/6236
5. Brodén, B., Hammar, M., Nilsson, B.J., Paraschakis, D.: Ensemble recommendations via thompson sampling: an experimental study within e-commerce. In: 23rd International Conference on Intelligent User Interfaces, IUI '18, pp. 19–29. Association for Computing Machinery, New York (2018). https://doi.org/10.1145/3172944.3172967

6. Eide, S., Leslie, D.S., Frigessi, A.: Dynamic slate recommendation with gated recurrent units and thompson sampling. Data Min. Knowl. Disc. **36** (2022).https://doi.org/10.1007/s10618-022-00849-w

7. Ezaldeen, H., Misra, R., Bisoy, S.K., Alatrash, R., Priyadarshini, R.: A hybrid e-learning recommendation integrating adaptive profiling and sentiment analysis. J. Web Semant. **72**, 100700 (2022)

8. Henriet, J., Christophe, L., Laurent, P.: Artificial intelligence-virtual trainer: an educative system based on artificial intelligence and designed to produce varied and consistent training lessons. Proc. Inst. Mech. Eng. Part P: J. Sports Eng. Technol. **231**(2), 110–124 (2017). https://doi.org/10.1177/1754337116651013

9. Henriet, J., Greffier, F.: AI-VT: an example of CBR that generates a variety of solutions to the same problem. In: Cox, M.T., Funk, P., Begum, S. (eds.) ICCBR 2018. LNCS (LNAI), vol. 11156, pp. 124–139. Springer, Cham (2018). https://doi.org/10.1007/978-3-030-01081-2_9

10. Huang, A.Y., Lu, O.H., Yang, S.J.: Effects of artificial intelligence-enabled personalized recommendations on learners' learning engagement, motivation, and outcomes in a flipped classroom. Comput. Educ. **194**, 104684 (2023)

11. Lalitha, T.B., Sreeja, P.S.: Personalised self-directed learning recommendation system. Procedia Comput. Sci. **171**, 583–592 (2020). https://doi.org/10.1016/j.procs.2020.04.063. https://www.sciencedirect.com/science/article/pii/S1877050920310309

12. Sun, J., Wei, M., Feng, J., Yu, F., Li, Q., Zou, R.: Progressive knowledge tracing: modeling learning process from abstract to concrete. Expert Syst. Appl. **238**, 122280 (2024)

13. Supic, H.: Case-based reasoning model for personalized learning path recommendation in example-based learning activities. In: 2018 IEEE 27th International Conference on Enabling Technologies: Infrastructure for Collaborative Enterprises (WETICE), pp. 175–178 (2018). https://doi.org/10.1109/WETICE.2018.00040

14. Xu, S., Sun, M., Fang, W., Chen, K., Luo, H., Zou, P.X.: A bayesian-based knowledge tracing model for improving safety training outcomes in construction: an adaptive learning framework. Dev. Built Environ. **13**, 100111 (2023)

15. Xu, X., Zhao, H.: Artificial intelligence education system based on feedback-adjusted differential evolution algorithm. Soft. Comput. 1–12 (2023)

16. Zhang, K., Yao, Y.: A three learning states bayesian knowledge tracing model. Knowl.-Based Syst. **148**, 189–201 (2018)

17. Zhao, L.T., Wang, D.S., Liang, F.Y., Chen, J.: A recommendation system for effective learning strategies: an integrated approach using context-dependent dea. Expert Syst. Appl. **211**, 118535 (2023)

18. Zhou, L., Wang, C.: Research on recommendation of personalized exercises in English learning based on data mining. Sci. Program. **2021**, 5042286 (2021). https://doi.org/10.1155/2021/5042286

19. Zuluaga, C.A., Aristizábal, L.M., Rúa, S., Franco, D.A., Osorio, D.A., Vásquez, R.E.: Development of a modular software architecture for underwater vehicles using systems engineering. J. Marine Sci. Eng. **10**(4) (2022). https://doi.org/10.3390/jmse10040464. https://www.mdpi.com/2077-1312/10/4/464

Explaining Multiple Instances Counterfactually: User Tests of Group-Counterfactuals for XAI

Greta Warren[1,2,3], Eoin Delaney[4], Christophe Guéret[5],
and Mark T. Keane[1,2(✉)]

[1] School of Computer Science, University College Dublin, Dublin, Ireland
grwa@di.ku.dk
[2] Insight Centre for Data Analytics, University College Dublin, Dublin, Ireland
mark.keane@ucd.ie
[3] Department of Computer Science, University of Copenhagen,
Copenhagen, Denmark
[4] Oxford Internet Institute, Oxford University, Oxford, UK
eoin.delaney@oii.ox.ac.uk
[5] Accenture Labs, Dublin, Ireland
christophe.gueret@accenture.com

Abstract. Counterfactual explanations have become a major focus for post-hoc explainability research in recent years, as they seem to provide good algorithmic recourse solutions, people can readily understand them, and they may meet legal regulations (such as GDPR in the EU). However, this large literature has only addressed the use of counterfactual explanations to explain single predictive-instances. Here, we explore a novel use case in which groups of similar instances are explained in a collective fashion using "group counterfactuals" (e.g., to highlight a repeating pattern of illness in a group of patients). Group counterfactuals potentially provide broad explanations covering multiple events/instances. A novel case-based, group-counterfactual algorithm is proposed to generate such explanations and a user study is also reported to test the psychological validity of the algorithm.

Keywords: XAI · Explainability · Counterfactuals · User-Centered

1 Introduction

In recent years, the literature on eXplainable AI (XAI) has focused significantly on the use of counterfactual explanations to explain the predictions of opaque machine learning (ML) models [14,19,22,24,30], as they show what changes to input-features can alter a model's output decisions (e.g., "if only the bank customer had applied for a lower loan amount of $10,000, their loan application would have been approved"). Interest in counterfactuals as explanations has been boosted by arguments made in philosophy and psychology about the formal

J. A. Recio-Garcia et al. (Eds.): ICCBR 2024, LNAI 14775, pp. 206–222, 2024.
https://doi.org/10.1007/978-3-031-63646-2_14

analysis of causality [28] and people's causal thinking [4, 30], respectively. Furthermore, legal analyses have suggested that counterfactual explanations comply with General Data Protection Regulation (GDPR) requirements [39], leading to their extensive use in algorithmic recourse [19].

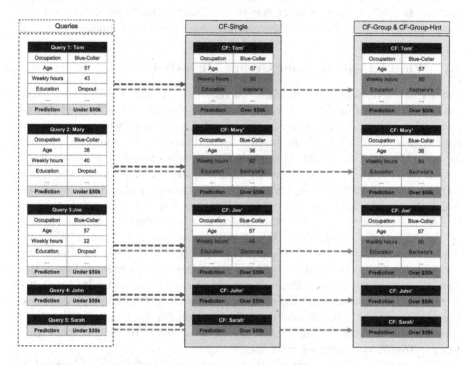

Fig. 1. Sample Queries with Single or Group Counterfactual Explanations. Five summary queries are shown paired with single or group counterfactual explanations (n.b., John and Sarah details are finessed). Note that target-values for Weekly Hours and Education in the single counterfactuals vary in each explanation, whereas those for the group counterfactuals are the same in each explanation; critically, all of the feature-differences in these pairings create valid counterfactuals that flip the outcome class.

However, counterfactual XAI has been criticised for not paying sufficient attention to suitable use cases, to determining when counterfactual explanations work well [3, 21]. Indeed, mixed results from recent user studies may arise from inappropriate usages (see e.g., [7, 8, 26, 38, 40]). Most counterfactual use-cases assume scenarios in which a *single* prediction for a *single instance* is explained using a *single* explanation (e.g., a loan application). However, AI systems also make *multiple* predictions for *similar instances with the same outcome*, predictive-instances that could be explained in a grouped way using the "same" counterfactual explanation (i.e., feature-differences with identical target-values, see Fig. 1). The current work came from end-user feedback trialling XAI models for disease prediction [32,36]. When we showed farmers disease predictions for a cow explained by a counterfactual (e.g., "if this animal had a lower cell count, it would be healthy"), they said that typically several animals fall ill at a time and explaining the whole group together would be better (e.g., "if these four animals had lower cell counts and were younger then they would be healthy"); that is, they felt a group counterfactual could surface patterns of disease in the herd, leading to better disease interventions (e.g., isolating animals).

1.1 When Explanations for Groups Might Help

Different stakeholders may have different requirements and desiderata for explanations [27]. Previous work on counterfactual explanations has focused on end-users affected by automated decisions (e.g., a bank customer who has applied for a loan), where a single explanation or a set of diverse explanations are provided for a single prediction [31,39]. However, other stakeholder users may want explanation for patterns of predictions for similar queries. For example, the farmer wanting one explanation for a group of sick animals (rather than a different counterfactual for each animal) or a bank manager might want single explanation for a group of customers to determine if they are being discriminated against by the AI system. For example, in our use-case we assume the stakeholder is a risk analyst assessing groups of bank customers to determine if they have been correctly treated in automated decisions, a real use-case in the home loan sector. Hence, we used the Adult (Census) dataset [11] to build a classifier that predicted whether individuals earned under or over $50,000 in annual income (see Fig. 1). We note that people seem to have a reasonable level of knowledge about this domain; without training, they are quite accurate in their classifications (e.g., ~70–80% accurate; see later user tests).

Our novel case-based algorithm for group counterfactuals (**Group-CF**) explains binary classifications for similar individuals from the same class using a group counterfactual with common feature-values (see Fig. 1). In contrast, a traditional single-counterfactual method (**Single-CF**) explains each instance using a different counterfactual; that is, "if Tom worked *50* hours per week instead of 43, he would have earned over $50k", "if Mary worked *62* h per week instead of 40, she would have earned over $50k", "if Joe worked *45* h per week instead of 22, he would have earned over $50k" and so on. Group-CF generates a group counterfactual re-using the same target-value in the feature-differences for instances; that is, "if Tom worked *50* h per week instead of 43, he would have earned over $50k", "if Mary worked *50* h per week instead of 40, she would have earned over $50k", "if Joe worked *50* hours per week instead of 22, he would have earned over $50k" and so on. Note, here, we do not consider how pools of queries are selected to be explained; they could identified by the user or by clustering similar cases to present to the user. For present purposes, we randomly selected a seed-query, then created a pool of k-nearest instances (usually, $k = 5$), computing a group counterfactual for them.

1.2   Related Work

Single-counterfactual methods provide *local* (or quasi-local) explanations rather than *global* ones (that explain the whole dataset), in that they attempt to explain a circumscribed region of the decision space (sometimes called *cohort* explanations). Local explanations using single-counterfactuals for XAI have been studied extensively (see e.g., [18,21,37] for reviews), with probably 150+ distinct algorithms. However, work on group counterfactuals is recent and rare. Kanamori et al. [17] proposed Counterfactual Explanation Trees (CETs) that covered multiple instance predictions from decision trees as a "summary of local explanations". In a 2023 workshop paper, Warren, et al. [41] proposed the instance-based, CBR method for group-counterfactuals reported here. More recently, several other papers have formally described group counterfactuals along with optimisation methods for their computation [1,2,5,6]). Artelt & Gregoriades [1,2] compute group counterfactuals for a human resources dataset dealing with employee attrition; their group counterfactuals explain what needs to happen to prevent employees leaving an organisation (e.g., "If these employees had a salary increase of 20%, AND increased job satisfaction of 50%, attrition would be unlikely"). They also competitively tested their method against other methods (i.e., [17,41]), showing that it was more *cost effective* (in its sparsity) and *correct* (in instance coverage) [2]. In a related vein, hyperbox methods for forming general descriptions of collections of instances, called Actionable Recourse Summaries [34], Global Counterfactual Explanations [33], and Interpretable Regional Descriptors [9]) – have been advanced though they tackle somewhat different problems.

The rapid growth in counterfactual methods for explaining multiple instances underscores their potential utility in XAI. However, a major gap in this work is a failure to consider psychological validity. There are no existing user tests of group counterfactuals or methodologies proposed for testing them. Although these papers tend to agree on the form of group counterfactuals (i.e., stated as specific-value differences for a group of instances), we do not know if people can comprehend this type of explanation and if so, whether they are better than using several single-counterfactuals. However, there are hints in the cognitive literature that group-counterfactuals might work; good explanations tend to be more general [23,29] and people prefer broad scope explanations covering several observations [12,16,35]. For instance, explanations for disease diagnoses that account for three observed symptoms are judged to be better than those that account for just one [29]. A major contribution of this paper is a methodology for user testing the group-counterfactuals idea and its application in a concrete testing situation.

1.3   Paper Outline and Contributions

The present paper proposes a novel case-based algorithm for group counterfactuals (called Group-CF) and a first user test of group counterfactuals. As such, it makes two key contributions:

- *Algorithmic Development*: the development of a novel case-based counterfactual XAI algorithm that groups explanations of similar predictive-instances, along with a methodology for presenting these to end-users (see Sect. 2)
- *User Study*: the first user evaluation of the group-counterfactual idea, carefully designed to assess its impact on objective (i.e., accuracy) and subjective (i.e., confidence, satisfaction and trust) psychological measures of human understanding, relative to traditional single counterfactuals (see Sect. 3)

In the final section of the paper, we consider some of the caveats, limitations and future directions in this area that need to be addressed (Sect. 4).

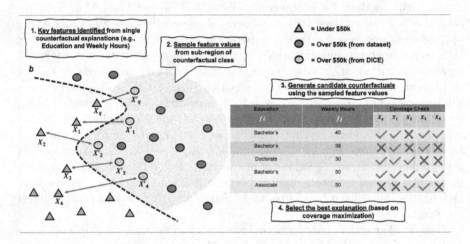

Fig. 2. A group of queries, $(X_q, X_1, X_2, ..., X_n)$, are classed as being on one side of a decision boundary (e.g., Under \$50k). Single counterfactuals are generated for each of these points, forming several individual explanations revealing two feature differences commonly used (i.e., Education and Weekly Hours are $[f_i, f_j]$). New values for the identified features are sampled from a region of training instances in the contrasting class (i.e., Over \$50k) and substituted into the query instances to create candidate group-counterfactuals ($X_{sub_1}, X_{sub_2}, ..., X_{sub_n}$) checked for validity, the best being chosen on coverage.

2   A Group-Counterfactual Algorithm: Group-CF

Figure 2 illustrates the main steps in the **Group-CF** algorithm developed to compute a group counterfactual for some selected pool of instances (see Algorithm 1 for formalization). The algorithm starts from a set of related training instances that have been correctly classified as being from the same class[1]; for example, a pool containing a query instance, X_q, and its nearest-like-neighbours

---

[1] It is not enough just to select training instances with class label c as the model may not agree with this label due to regularization of the classifier to prevent over-fitting.

$(X_1, X_2, ..., X_{n-1})$ (n.b., pool size is a hyperparameter, here set to 5). So, we adopt a simple solution to the pool selection issue mentioned earlier.

Taking these inputs, the four main steps of the method are: (i) *identifying key difference-features* by generating individual counterfactuals for each related instance and analysing the feature differences on which they rely, and then (ii) *sampling feature-values* for key difference-features from data-points in the contrasting class for (iii) *generating candidate group-counterfactuals* based on substituting these feature-values into the original instances before (iv) *selecting the best group-counterfactual* based on its valid coverage of all the instances in the pool. Note, this method does *not* generalise the individual counterfactuals for the instances, rather it uses them to guide feature-selection towards good group-counterfactuals (see https://github.com/e-delaney/group_cfe). As the method leverages class labels, it is supervised and not a form of unsupervised learning (e.g., clustering).

2.1   Step 1: Key-Feature Identification

Given a pool of to-be-explained instances (of size n) – a query, X_q, and its nearest-like-neighbours $(X_1, X_2, ...X_{n-1})$ – and an opaque black-box model, b, ensure that $b(X) = c$, where c is the predicted class. Then, generate individual counterfactuals for all instances in the pool, forming a set of counterfactual instances $(X'_q, X'_1, X'_2, ..., X'_{n-1})$ such that $b(X') = c'$. Any "traditional" counterfactual method can be used to generate these diverse counterfactuals; we used DiCE [31] due to its popularity, above baseline performance, and open source-code availability (n.b., DiCE, as a generative method, is known to periodically produce implausible counterfactuals; so, these were filtered out when selecting items in the user study). The feature labels that are altered in the individual counterfactual generation are counted across all counterfactuals to determine the most commonly used features. For example, Education and Weekly Hours emerge here as the most frequently used difference-features that flip the classification (see Figs. 1 and 2), so these would be chosen as the two key features (i.e., $[f_i, f_j]$) to modify in generating candidate group-counterfactuals (n.b., majority voting is just one way to do this). This step also identifies the direction-of-difference in the key features (e.g., increase/decrease for a continuous feature) that flips the classification, that is used in step 2.

2.2   Step 2: Sample Feature Values

Having identified the key features in the single counterfactuals, we need to perturb their values to create candidate group counterfactuals, from which we will select one that has a common set of feature-difference values for them all. To constrain possible selections, we sample from training data in a sub-region of the **contrasting class** (e.g., the Over \$50k class). For example, for the Education feature, this sampling identifies candidate values such as Bachelor's, Doctorate or Associate's degree (see Fig. 2). Importantly, these sampled instances are known, valid data-points, and therefore, are more likely to yield feature-value transformations that result in valid counterfactuals. Obviously, it makes sense to reduce the size of this sub-region (e.g., only consider data points with same direction-of-difference such as a higher educational qualification than the to-be-explained instances or data-points that are within a certain distance). In addition, using feature-values from prototype-like instances in this sub-region works well (e.g., medoids from k-medoids clustering).

2.3   Step 3: Generating Candidates

The feature-values from the sub-region's data-points are interpolated into the original counterfactuals to create candidate group counterfactuals (i.e., X_{sub}; see Fig. 2). Next, each of the candidate counterfactuals is passed to the model to verify that they are indeed valid and predicted to be in the counterfactual class (coverage check).

2.4   Step 4: Selecting the Best Explanation

The feature-value substitutions that create the candidate group-counterfactuals are checked for validity and coverage. The validity check determines whether the feature-changes do indeed flip the classification of a given instance to the

---

Algorithm 1. Group-CF Method

Require: $b(.)$; to-be-explained black-box model
Require: D_c; Instances in the training data with class label c
Require: $D_{c'}$; Instances in the training data with class label c'
Require: X_q; Query instance with features $[f_1, f_2, ..., f_k]$ s.t. $b(X_q) = c$
Require: n; the size of the group (including the query, X_q)
   Retrieve $X_{NLN} \in D_c$, the Nearest Like Neighbour subset pool, $\{X_1, X_2, ..., X_{n-1}\}$, for the query are selected such that $b(X) = c \, \forall \, X \in X_{NLN}$.
   for $X \in \{X_q, X_1, X_1, ..., X_{n-1}\}$ **do**
      Generate individual CFE, X', s.t. $b(X') = c'$.
      Note the feature change and the direction of change if applicable.
   end for
   The most commonly perturbed feature set, $[f_i, f_j]$, from the individual counterfactuals informs the features to-be-changed in the Group-CF.
   Randomly sample feature pairs $[f_i, f_j]$ from sub-region, R, of the training data in the counterfactual class $R \in D_{c'} \rightarrow samples$
   for $[f_i, f_j]$ in samples **do**
      for $X \in \{X_q, X_1, X_1, ..., X_{n-1}\}$ **do**
         substitute feature values with $[f_i, f_j] \rightarrow X_{sub}$
         If $b(X_{sub}) \neq c'$ **Stop**
      end for
      Return sample feature pair that maximises coverage,
   end for
   Stop

---

contrasting class (i.e., $b(X_{sub}) = c'$). The coverage check determines whether this classification change holds over all the original instances in the pool (i.e., the number of valid counterfactuals created when substituting the feature values $[f_i, f_j]$ into the original group of instances). The group counterfactual with the highest coverage is chosen to explain multiple instances (see Fig. 2). In this step, if this "best" candidate fails to cover all instances in the pool, then those that are not covered would be excluded from the original to-be-explained set (perhaps, to be explained as part of a different pool).

3   Group Counterfactuals: A User Study

Most current methods produce group-counterfactuals that look like those generated by our instance-based, Group-CF method. However, we do not know whether people can comprehend this type of counterfactual and whether they work better than several, single counterfactuals. Hence, we designed a user study to measure whether group counterfactuals improved people's understanding of an AI decision-making system compared to single counterfactuals. The study had two phases: a (i) *training phase*, in which people were shown instances from a dataset and asked to predict their outcomes before being shown the AI system's prediction along with an explanation (see Fig. 3), and a (ii) *testing phase*, in which people were shown instances and asked to predict their outcomes with no feedback or explanation as to their correctness (akin to solely getting part-a of Fig. 3 on its own). The main measure was *accuracy*, the proportion of instance-items correctly predicted in the testing phase (i.e., corresponding to the model's prediction). Subjective measures of confidence, satisfaction and trust were also recorded. Participants were shown 40 instances in each phase of the study (i.e., 80 unique items in total), with no overlap between the items in each phase. In the training phase, the 40 items were made up of eight 5-item groups of similar instances for which group counterfactuals were generated (in the relevant conditions). To control for possible order effects, the material sets were randomly re-ordered in each phase for each participant. Participants were assigned to one of three conditions – CF-Single, CF-Group, or CF-Group-Hint – that were matched in every respect except for the type of counterfactual explanations provided during the training phase (see Sect. 3.1 for details). Participants in the CF-Single condition were presented with classifications that were explained using diverse, single counterfactual explanations. Participants in the CF-Group and CF-Group-Hint conditions were presented with the same classifications, which were explained using group counterfactuals for related classified instances. The participants in the CF-Group-Hint condition received an additional "hint" along with each explanation that informed users that the individual belonged to a related group of people, to explicitly signal the commonality between the counterfactual instances.

So, this design tests whether the experience of seeing single/group counterfactuals in the training phase, improves their knowledge of the model's predictions in the test phase. This was a hard test of the group-counterfactual proposal, as we did not present the pool of queries together as a group in the test phase (i.e., queries with a common group counterfactual were randomly distributed in the 40 presented items). So, participants had to spontaneously notice that some items had common explanations. We chose this procedure as it seemed to, perhaps, better correspond to some real-life use-cases (e.g., where an analyst is sequentially assessing several customer-decisions and the model has determined in the background that some are part of similarly-treated pool). If we had presented the pool of queries together, the study could be criticised for making the group counterfactuals too obvious.

3.1   Method: Design and Procedure

The study had a 3 (Explanation: CF-Single vs CF-Group vs CF-Group-Hint) x 2 (Phase: Training vs Testing) mixed design with Explanation as a between-participant and Phase as a within-participant variable. The three Explanation conditions varied the counterfactual explanations provided in the training phase: *CF-Single* gave people instance-predictions explained using a single counterfactual unique to that instance (e.g., "If Joe's *Weekly hours* had been *45* and his *Education level* had been *Doctorate degree*, he would have earned Over $50k"; see Fig. 1), *CF-Group* gave people instance-predictions explained using group-counterfactuals with common target-values, implicitly grouping the similar instances in a given 5-item set (e.g., "If Joe's *Weekly hours* had been *50* and his *Education level* had been *Bachelor's degree*, he would have earned Over $50k"; see Fig. 1), and *CF-Group-Hint* presented people with the same group-counterfactuals as in CF-Group along with an explicit "hint" saying the instance was "part of a group of people with similar characteristics" (see Fig. 3). CF-Single

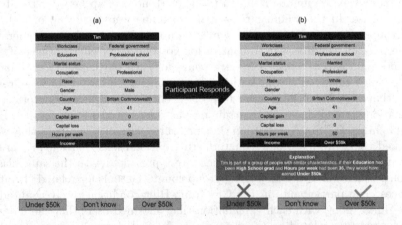

Fig. 3. Sample Material from Training Phase of the User Study. The participant first sees (a) with the task of providing their own prediction for the item (3 options). After they respond, they are presented with (b), showing feedback on the correctness of their response along with an explanation (in this case for the CF-Group-Hint condition).

is essentially the control condition, with CF-Group and CF-Group-Hint being the experimental conditions, all three being matched in other respects.

At the beginning of the study, participants were informed that they would be testing an AI system designed to predict people's annual income from available information about them. Participants read detailed instructions about the task and provided informed consent. After completing practice trials for each phase of the study, participants progressed through both phases of the main task, and subsequently completed the subjective measures (i.e., Explanation Satisfaction and Trust scales). During the training phase, on each screen participants were presented with an instance without the class prediction and asked to make an *income* prediction from three options – Under $50k / Don't know / Over $50k – as shown in Fig. 3(a). Button order was randomised for each item, to prevent users from repeatedly selecting the same response. After making their prediction, users were shown feedback, with the AI model's prediction (correct answer) shown in green with a tick-mark, and the incorrect answer shown in red with a cross-mark. Figure 3(b) shows an example from the Group-CF-Hint condition where a correct prediction was made and explained using a group-counterfactual with a hint. After completing the 40 items in the training phase, people progressed to the testing phase, in which they were shown 40 further instances without outcomes shown and asked to choose one of the three options to make their prediction (as in part (a) of Fig. 3 with no further feedback). Here, after each response, participants rated their confidence in their prediction (using a 5-point Likert scale, from 1 (*Not at all confident*) to 5 (*Extremely confident*). In the testing phase, participants progressed through the 40 items, providing their predictions and confidence judgments without receiving feedback or explanations. After the testing phase, participants completed the satisfaction and trust measures before concluding the study. All the items presented in both phases were randomly re-ordered for each participant to control for possible order effects. On completion, participants were debriefed on the background of the study and paid £ 2.50 for taking part. Ethics approval for the study was granted by University College Dublin with the reference code *LS-E-20-11-Warren-Keane*. Task instructions and data for the study are at https://osf.io/smupq/.

3.2   Method: Participants

Participants (N = 207) were recruited using *Prolific Academic* (https://www.prolific.co), and assigned in a fixed order to three between-participant conditions: CF-Single (n = 68), CF-Group (n = 70) and CF-Group-Hint (n = 69). The sample consisted of 122 women, 84 men and one non-binary participant aged 18–76 years (*M* = 40.86, *SD* = 14.31), with respondents pre-screened to select native English speakers from Ireland, the United Kingdom, the United States, Australia, Canada and New Zealand, who had not participated in previous related studies. Prior to analysis, 19 participants were removed as they failed >1 attention or memory check. An *a priori* power analysis with G*Power indicated that 207 participants were required to achieve 90% power for a medium effect size with alpha <.05 for two-tailed tests.

3.3   Materials: Dataset and Implementations

The Adult (Census) dataset describes census information[2] and contains a mixture of continuous (age, weekly work hours, capital gain, capital loss), and categorical variables (employment type, occupation, marital status, country of birth, gender, race). A model that predicted a binary outcome, whether a person is earning over or under $50k/year, was implemented using a Gradient Boosting Classifier [13], as the to-be-explained black-box model. The default sklearn hyperparameters are used with a log loss implemented and a learning rate of 0.1 achieving an accuracy of 0.874 on the task. Training and test data were split and pre-processed according to Klaise et al. [25], where categorical features were encoded ordinally when possible. Instances were randomly selected from the dataset as query-items for the study. The instances selected were all correct classifications, with low predicted class confidence (within 0.15 of the other class) to make the classifications non-obvious to participants, and the selection was balanced with equal numbers for each class. For the training phase, 8 seed-instances were randomly selected (balanced across classes) and 4 nearest-like-neighbours were found for these seeds (using Hamming distance) to create the 40 queries used (i.e., eight 5-item sets of related instances). For the testing phase, all 40 items were randomly selected from the dataset as the queries to be used, balanced across classes. The single counterfactual explanations for each of the 40 training phase queries for the CF-Single condition were generated using DiCE [31][3]. For the CF-Group conditions, the Group-CF method (see Algorithm 1) was applied to the 5-item sets to find good group-counterfactuals to cover them. If a group-counterfactual was found then the five instances with their paired single- and group-counterfactuals were used as an item-set in the study. Finally, the sets of counterfactuals used in the CF-Single and CF-Group conditions were matched on proximity and sparsity. Proximity was measured using ℓ_1 distance scores, scaled by the median absolute deviation (MAD) of the feature's values in the training set (for continuous features), and a metric that assigns a distance of 1 if the features differ from the original input or zero otherwise (for categorical features). These distance scores were computed for the matched query-explanation pairs used in the control and experimental conditions; a paired two-tailed t-test indicated that they were not significantly different to one another, $t(39) = 1.30, p = .197$. Sparsity was measured as the number of feature-differences between counterfactual pairs which was always 2 for all query-explanation pairs used.

---

[2] The New Adult Datasets by Ding et al. [10] could be preferred here if examining group counterfactual explanations through the lens of fairness in XAI (see also [20]).

[3] We used the original random sampling variant of DiCE implemented using an sklearn backend and a sample size of 1000. The default post-hoc sparsity parameter of 0.1 and stopping threshold of 0.5 were implemented. Also, counterfactuals that we judged to be implausible were excluded from the materials.

3.4 Measures: Objective and Subjective Measures

A mix of objective and subjective measures was used (see [40] for a discussion of this distinction). The key objective measure was *accuracy*, which measured the extent to which exposure to the model's predictions and explanations in the training phase improved their knowledge of the domain/model; specifically, it was measured as the proportion of correct responses made in the training and testing phases (i.e., consistent with the model's predictions). The subjective measures evaluated people's self-assessments of their (i) *confidence* in their own predictions made in the testing phase, (ii) *satisfaction* with explanations used overall by the AI system, (iii) *trust* in the overall AI system. The latter two measures were made after people completed the training and testing phases of the study using the Explanation Satisfaction and Trust scales [15]. Four attention checks were deployed at randomised intervals (two during the training phase, and two during the testing phase) and participants were also asked to recall and select a subset of the features used by the system from a list of 10 options (5 correct, 5 incorrect) at the end of the experiment.

3.5 Results and Discussion

Figure 4 and Table 1 show the results across the three conditions in the study – CF-Single, CF-Group, and CF-Group-Hint – for the different measures used. On all the measures, the relative differences show a trend favoring the use of group counterfactuals but the conditions were not significantly different. Hence, as a first test of the idea, this experiment does *not* confirm that group counterfactuals are better than single counterfactuals in this task. Though this result may be initially disappointing to proponents of group-counterfactuals, it highlights the importance of performing human evaluations in XAI and incorporating

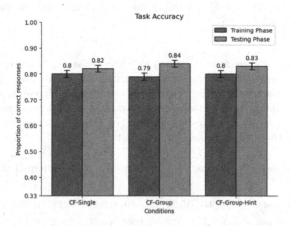

Fig. 4. Task Accuracy (proportion of correct answers) for the three conditions (CF-Single, CF-Group, CF-Group-Hint) in the Training and Testing Phases of the Study (showing standard error of the mean; y-axis begins at 0.33, chance-level for responding).

them in the development process of new methods, in order to ensure that explanations achieve their intended purpose. Furthermore, we explore the results in more detail to reveal some interesting insights into the conditions under which group counterfactuals might work. Specifically, this exploration shows that group counterfactuals may need to be presented (i) together as a consecutive group of explained instances rather than being randomly mixed up (as was done in the experiment), and/or (ii) in a task context where the group is explicitly assessed as a data pattern (e.g., as a risk analyst might do).

3.5.1   Objective Measure: Accuracy

A 3 (Explanation: CF-Single vs CF-Group vs CF-Group-Hint) x 2 (Phase: Training vs Testing) mixed ANOVA with repeated measures on the second factor was carried out on the proportion of correct responses given by each participant (i.e., accuracy; see Fig. 4). There was no main effect of Explanation $F(2, 204)=.174$, $p=.840$, however, there was a main effect of Phase, $F(1, 204)=25.153$, $p<0.001$, $\eta_p^2=.11$. As one would expect, participants in all three conditions were more accurate in the testing phase ($M=.829$, $SD=.096$) than in the training phase ($M=.795$, $SD=.111$). The two factors did not interact $F(2, 204)=1.608$, $p=.203$. Notably, response accuracy was quite high from the outset in the training phase ($\sim$80% in all three conditions), potentially leading to ceiling effects in the testing phase. However, in the testing phase, there was still evidence of a trend in increasing accuracy across conditions with the following order: CF-Single < CF-Group < CF-Group-Hint conditions, Page's $L(40)=500.0$, $p=.013$ (see Fig. 4). This trend indicates that when people were given group counterfactual explanations (without and with a hint), their accuracy progressively improved. Indeed, the improvement in accuracy (the difference between a given participant's training accuracy and their testing accuracy), shows the CF-Single condition to be the least improved ($M=0.019$, $SD=.089$), with the CF-Group ($M=0.049$, $SD=.083$) and CF-Group-Hint conditions showing more improvement ($M=0.034$, $SD=.117$).

Table 1. Means and standard deviations for each measure in the conditions of the user study (CF-Single, CF-Group, CF-Group-Hint) for (i) *Accuracy* (proportion of correct answers in the testing phase), (ii) *Confidence* (ratings on a 5-point scale of each answered item in the testing phase), (iii) *Explanation Satisfaction* (summed ratings from the 8-item scale after the testing phase), (iv) *Trust* (summed ratings from the 8-item scale after the testing phase).

Measure	CF-Single		CF-Group		CF-Group-Hint	
	M	SD	M	SD	M	SD
Accuracy	0.816	0.104	0.839	0.085	0.832	0.100
Confidence	3.956	0.432	3.936	0.437	4.047	0.432
Satisfaction	26.632	6.462	25.800	6.826	28.493	6.910
Trust	24.324	5.454	24.786	5.522	25.899	5.480

3.5.2   Subjective Measures

A series of subjective evaluations were made by participants in the study, comprising confidence in their responses and satisfaction and trust in the AI system (see Table 1 for means and standard deviations). Overall, these measures show no main effects between conditions, though reliable trends are found in increasing scores across conditions with the following order: CF-Single < CF-Group < CF-Group-Hint. This trend was significant for *Confidence*, Page's $L(40) = 513.5$, $p < .001$, *Explanation Satisfaction*, Page's $L(8) = 105.0$, $p = .012$, and *Trust*, Page's $L(8) = 108.0$, $p = .001$.

3.5.3   Effects of Grouping on Accuracy

These weak effects could have emerged from the fact that the item-sets were not explicitly presented together in a group (recall, order was randomised). To address this question, we analysed the specific item-sets used in the training phase of the study. In the training phase, participants were presented with eight distinct 5-item-sets (i.e., 40 items in total); that is, sets of 5 similar instances and predictions that were explained with the same group counterfactual in the experimental conditions (CF-Group and CF-Group-Hint) and matched with respect to the control condition (CF-Single). For each participant, the 40 items were randomly re-ordered to control for possible order effects between item-sets. However, due to this randomisation, different participants would have seen more and less favourable sequences for a given item-set; that is, the 5 items in a set could happen to be presented together in the randomised sequence (with no gaps between them) whereas another item-set could be mixed in with other item-sets (with many gaps between items from the same set). Hence, some participants could have been presented with five (grouped) counterfactual explanations one after the other using the same target-feature values, presumably making it easier for them to benefit from the group-counterfactual. So, if a given item-set has lower gap-scores, one would expect higher accuracy for that set in both CF-group conditions. Accordingly, we analysed the order of items presented and calculated gap-scores for each item-set presented to each participant in the three conditions of the study to check whether favourable orderings had any effect. Spearman's correlations were computed between these gap-scores for item-sets in the training phase and the accuracy observed in that phase. This analysis showed that there were moderate-to-high, negative correlations between gap-scores and accuracy in all three conditions, the lower the gap-score between items from the same set, the higher the accuracy: CF-Single ($r_S(6) = -0.43$), CF-Group ($r_S(6) = -0.38$), and CF-Group-Hint ($r_S(6) = -0.69$). Notably, the CF-Group-Hint condition had the highest correlation, where participants were told that certain items were part of a group. Though these correlations do not imply causality, they present a consistent picture of the effects of group counterfactual explanations with a hint. It may be that instances need to be grouped in an unbroken sequence, to allow end-users to benefit from these group explanations.

4 Conclusion and Future Directions

This paper tested counterfactual explanations for multiple instances, or group counterfactuals, a new and emergent area of XAI. Proponents of this explanation strategy have argued that there are many real-world contexts in which various stakeholder users require predictions to be explained as meaningful groupings to provide additional insights (e.g., identifying disease patterns in a dairy herd, patterns of attrition in employees, risk profiles in mortgage holders). We advanced a case-based method for computing these explanations and carried out the first user tests of this group counterfactual concept. The results of this study showed weak support for the learning impacts of using group counterfactuals over single counterfactuals. However, group counterfactuals may work better in task contexts aimed at showing patterns in data (e.g., explicitly presenting pools of queries together). Specifically, the present study shows that the predictive-instances grouped in the explanation may need to be presented together to impact human learning. It is clear that more attention needs to be given to framing the task in which group counterfactuals are used. Our findings underscore the need for XAI research to move beyond traditional, simplified scenarios to more complex real-world, user-driven solutions.

Acknowledgements. This research was supported by Science Foundation Ireland via the Insight SFI Research Centre for Data Analytics (12/RC/2289-P2). For the purpose of Open Access, the author has applied a CC BY copyright to any Author Accepted Manuscript version arising from this submission.

References

1. Artelt, A., Gregoriades, A.: "how to make them stay?"–diverse counterfactual explanations of employee attrition. arXiv preprint arXiv:2303.04579 (2023)
2. Artelt, A., Gregoriades, A.: A two-stage algorithm for cost-efficient multi-instance counterfactual explanations. arXiv preprint arXiv:2403.01221 (2024)
3. Barocas, S., Selbst, A.D., Raghavan, M.: The hidden assumptions behind counterfactual explanations and principal reasons. In: Facct-20, pp. 80–89 (2020)
4. Byrne, R.M.: Counterfactuals in explainable artificial intelligence (XAI): evidence from human reasoning. In: IJCAI-19, pp. 6276–6282 (2019)
5. Carrizosa, E., Ramírez-Ayerbe, J., Morales, D.R.: Generating collective counterfactual explanations in score-based classification via mathematical optimization. Expert Syst. Appl. **238**, 121954 (2024)
6. Carrizosa, E., Ramírez-Ayerbe, J., Morales, D.R.: Mathematical optimization modelling for group counterfactual explanations. Eur. J. Oper. Res. (2024)
7. Celar, L., Byrne, R.M.: How people reason with counterfactual and causal explanations for artificial intelligence decisions in familiar and unfamiliar domains. Memory Cogn. **51**, 1481–1496 (2023)
8. Dai, X., Keane, M.T., Shalloo, L., Ruelle, E., Byrne, R.M.: Counterfactual explanations for prediction and diagnosis in XAI. In: Proceedings of the 2022 AAAI/ACM Conference on AI, Ethics, and Society, pp. 215–226 (2022)
9. Dandl, S., Casalicchio, G., Bischl, B., Bothmann, L.: Interpretable regional descriptors: hyperbox-based local explanations. arXiv preprint arXiv:2305.02780 (2023)

10. Ding, F., Hardt, M., Miller, J., Schmidt, L.: Retiring adult: new datasets for fair machine learning. Adv. Neural Inf. Process. Syst. **34**, 6478–6490 (2021)
11. Dua, D., Graff, C.: UCI machine learning repository (2017)   .
12. Edwards, B.J., Williams, J.J., Gentner, D., Lombrozo, T.: Explanation recruits comparison in a category-learning task. Cognition **185**, 21–38 (2019)
13. Friedman, J.H.: Greedy function approximation: a gradient boosting machine. Ann. Stat. 1189–1232 (2001)
14. Guidotti, R., Monreale, A., Ruggieri, S., Turini, F., Giannotti, F., Pedreschi, D.: A survey of methods for explaining black box models. ACM Comput. Surv. (CSUR) **51**(5), 93 (2018). https://doi.org/10.1145/3236009
15. Hoffman, R.R., Mueller, S.T., Klein, G., Litman, J.: Metrics for explainable ai: challenges and prospects. arXiv preprint arXiv:1812.04608 (2018)
16. Johnson, S.G., Johnston, A.M., Toig, A.E., Keil, F.C.: Explanatory scope informs causal strength inferences, pp. 2453–2458 (2014)
17. Kanamori, K., Takagi, T., Kobayashi, K., Ike, Y.: Counterfactual explanation trees: transparent and consistent actionable recourse with decision trees. In: AISTAT-22, pp. 1846–1870. PMLR (2022)
18. Karimi, A.H., Barthe, G., Schölkopf, B., Valera, I.: A survey of algorithmic recourse: contrastive explanations and consequential recommendations. ACM Comput. Surv. **55**(5), 1–29 (2022). https://doi.org/10.1145/3527848
19. Karimi, A.H., Schölkopf, B., Valera, I.: Algorithmic recourse: from counterfactual explanations to interventions. In: Facct-21, pp. 353–362 (2021)
20. Kasirzadeh, A., Smart, A.: The use and misuse of counterfactuals in ethical machine learning. In: Facct-21, pp. 228–236 (2021)
21. Keane, M.T., Kenny, E.M., Delaney, E., Smyth, B.: If only we had better counterfactual explanations: five key deficits to rectify in the evaluation of counterfactual xai techniques. In: IJCAI-21, pp. 4466–4474 (2021)
22. Keane, M.T., Smyth, B.: Good counterfactuals and where to find them: a case-based technique for generating counterfactuals for explainable AI (XAI). In: Watson, I., Weber, R. (eds.) ICCBR 2020. LNCS (LNAI), vol. 12311, pp. 163–178. Springer, Cham (2020). https://doi.org/10.1007/978-3-030-58342-2_11
23. Keil, F.C.: Explanation and understanding. Ann. Rev. Psychol. **57**, 227–254 (2006)
24. Kenny, E.M., Keane, M.T.: On generating plausible counterfactual and semi-factual explanations for deep learning. In: AAAI-21, vol. 35, no. 13, pp. 11575–11585 (2021)
25. Klaise, J., Van Looveren, A., Vacanti, G., Coca, A.: Alibi: algorithms for monitoring and explaining machine learning models (2020)
26. Kuhl, U., Artelt, A., Hammer, B.: Keep your friends close and your counterfactuals closer. In: Facct-22, pp. 2125–2137 (2022)
27. Langer, M., et al.: What do we want from explainable artificial intelligence (xai)?- a stakeholder perspective on xai and a conceptual model guiding interdisciplinary xai research. Artif. Intell. **296**, 103473 (2021)
28. Lewis, D.: Counterfactuals. John Wiley & Sons, Hoboken (2013)
29. Lombrozo, T.: Explanatory preferences shape learning and inference. Trends Cogn. Sci. **20**(10), 748–759 (2016)
30. Miller, T.: Explanation in artificial intelligence: insights from the social sciences. Artif. Intell. **267**, 1–38 (2019)
31. Mothilal, R.K., Sharma, A., Tan, C.: Explaining machine learning classifiers through diverse counterfactual explanations. In: Facct-20, pp. 607–617 (2020)
32. Pakrashi, A., et al.: Early detection of subclinical mastitis in lactating dairy cows using cow level features. J. Dairy Sci. **106**, 4978–4990 (2023)

33. Plumb, G., Terhorst, J., Sankararaman, S., Talwalkar, A.: Explaining groups of points in low-dimensional representations. In: Proceedings of the 37th International Conference on Machine Learning, ICML 2020, pp. 7762–7771 (2020)
34. Rawal, K., Lakkaraju, H.: Beyond individualized recourse: interpretable and interactive summaries of actionable recourses. Adv. Neural. Inf. Process. Syst. **33**, 12187–12198 (2020)
35. Read, S.J., Marcus-Newhall, A.: Explanatory coherence in social explanations: a parallel distributed processing account. J. Pers. Soc. Psychol. **65**(3), 429–447 (1993)
36. Ryan, C., Guéret, C., Berry, D., Corcoran, M., Keane, M.T., Mac Namee, B.: Predicting illness for a sustainable dairy agriculture: predicting and explaining the onset of mastitis in dairy cows. arXiv preprint arXiv:2101.02188 (2021)
37. Verma, S., Dickerson, J., Hines, K.: Counterfactual explanations for machine learning: a review. arXiv preprint arXiv:2010.10596 (2022)
38. van der Waa, J., Nieuwburg, E., Cremers, A., Neerincx, M.: Evaluating xai: a comparison of rule/example-based explanations. Artif. Intell. **291**, 103404 (2021)
39. Wachter, S., Mittelstadt, B., Russell, C.: Counterfactual explanations without opening the black box: automated decisions and the GDPR. Harvard J. Law Technol. **31**, 841 (2018)
40. Warren, G., Byrne, R.M.J., Keane, M.T.: Categorical and continuous features in counterfactual explanations of AI systems. In: IUI '23 (2023)
41. Warren, G., Keane, M.T., Gueret, C., Delaney, E.: If Only...If Only...If Only...we could explain everything. In: IJCAI-23 XAI Workshop (2023)

Olaaaf: A General Adaptation Prototype

Erwan Diebold[1], Yan Kabrit[2], Axel Kril[2], Jean Lieber[3(✉)], Paul Malvaud[2],
Emmanuel Nauer[3], and Jules Sipp[2]

[1] Université de Lorraine, Master Informatique, 54000 Nancy, France
[2] Université de Lorraine, Master Sciences Cognitives, 54000 Nancy, France
[3] LORIA, Université de Lorraine, CNRS, Inria, 54000 Nancy, France
`jean.lieber@loria.fr`

Abstract. Adaptation is often considered a complex issue during the design of a case-based reasoning system. Various approaches can be found in the literature, but their scopes are often limited to a relatively narrow range of applications.However, a general approach to adaptation based on belief revision has been developed over the years and applied in several formalisms, these formalisms being chosen for particular needs. This article presents the first version of Olaaaf, a general adaptation prototype based on belief revision whose long-term objective is to cover a wide range of adaptation processes. It is based on a formalism that covers both attribute-value pairs (often used for representing cases) and taxonomies (often used for representing domain knowledge). It is shown through an example how this system works, and it is discussed how it can be used for other complex adaptations.

Keywords: case-based reasoning · adaptation · general prototype

1 Introduction

Case-based reasoning (CBR [1,27]) aims to solve problems by retrieving and reusing previous problem-solving episodes (or cases). The reuse step consists either (a) in reusing as such the solution of the retrieved case(s) (and this is appropriate for some applications), (b) in leaving to the user the adaptation of this solution (this is often acceptable, since, for a human being, retrieval is often considered as tedious, while adaptation sometimes appears as a simple task for humans while more difficult to implement), or (c) by implementing an automatic adaptation procedure. The approach (c) requires some work to design and implement such a procedure. Indeed, to the best of our knowledge, very little work has been done on the development of domain-independent adaptation engines. In particular, in a recent survey on general frameworks for CBR [28], the adaptation procedures of the described frameworks were, at best, limited to null adaptation, ontology-based substitutions, handling adaptation rules, or adaptation methods defined by the developers using such a framework, hence domain dependent.

© The Author(s), under exclusive license to Springer Nature Switzerland AG 2024
J. A. Recio-Garcia et al. (Eds.): ICCBR 2024, LNAI 14775, pp. 223–239, 2024.
https://doi.org/10.1007/978-3-031-63646-2_15

Now, a general approach to adaptation has been developed, studied and applied. This approach is based on belief revision operators and requires the implementation of such operators in a formalism in which cases and domain knowledge are defined. The first study on this work was published in 2007 [18] and it has been developed from there (see e.g. [6]), with applications to adaptation processes for the Taaable system in the cooking domain [8], in three different formalisms [5,12,23]. This was the first motivation for developing Olaaaf,[1] a revision-based inference engine in a general formalism.

This article presents Olaaaf, a domain-independent case adaptation prototype in a formalism that is general enough to express various kinds of knowledge, including attribute-value pairs and taxonomies. This has a certain level of generality since, in CBR, cases are often represented in an attribute-value representation, and domain knowledge is often represented by taxonomies, i.e., class hierarchies organized under the subclass-of relation. More precisely, this formalism is based on constraints (e.g. linear numerical constraints or propositional variables) and on the connectives of propositional logic ($\neg$, $\wedge$, $\vee$, etc.).

A running example, in the cooking domain that illustrates the case adaptations in Olaaaf is introduced now. The target problem is "I want a recipe of milkshake with kiwis." The retrieved case is a recipe for a banana milkshake, consisting in mixing the following ingredients: 2 bananas, 4 tablespoons of granulated sugar, 2 packets of vanilla sugar, 1 liter of cow milk, 4 ice cubes. To perform the adaptation, the following domain knowledge is used:

DK1 Bananas and kiwis are fruits.

DK2 For each food type and unit, there is a known correspondence of one unit of this food type to its mass, e.g. the mass of 1 banana and the mass of 1 tablespoon of granulated sugar.

DK3 There are relations between quantities of one type of food and its subtypes in a taxonomy (e.g. the mass of fruits is the sum of the masses of bananas, kiwis, etc.). In the same line of idea, the sweetening power is known for every food type, e.g. 1 for granulated sugar, 0.158 for bananas (1 gram of banana has the same sweetening power as 0.158 gram of granulated sugar), etc.[2]

DK4 Almond milk, cow milk and soy milk are 3 types of milks (and, to make it simpler, it is assumed that there are no other types of milk in my fridge).

DK5 Cow milk and soy milk associated with kiwis give a bitter taste.

DK6 A milkshake is a dessert, and a dessert must not be bitter.

The expected adaptation consists of substituting bananas for kiwis and, to avoid bitterness (forbidden in desserts), substituting cow milk for almond milk which does not taste bitter when associated with kiwis. It also consists in changing quantities (number of fruits, mass of ingredients), in order to conserve the

---

[1] The Olaaaf system, available at https://github.com/OlaaafEngine/Olaaaf, is distributed under a free MIT license. This repository also contains a video demo and the examples presented in this paper.

[2] Numerical information about conversions for DK2 and DK3 has been found on the Web, in particular, at https://fdc.nal.usda.gov.

mass of fruits and total mass of the milkshake, and to preserve the sweetening power.

In the Taaable system, this adaptation was performed in two steps, using two adaptation engines, working with two different formalisms: propositional logic to compute substitutions of ingredient types and conjunction of linear constraints to adapt ingredient quantities once the substitutions of ingredient types are known. On the contrary, Olaaaf solves this adaptation problem in a single step.

Section 2 recalls some general notions related to CBR, in particular, to adaptation, and to the general approach to adaptation that is used in our system. Olaaaf is presented in Sect. 3: how it can be used to solve adaptation problems and the main principles of its algorithm. As Olaaaf has been announced as a general tool for case adaptation, Sect. 4 discusses its scope: What are the adaptation inferences that it can or cannot (yet) draw? Finally, Sect. 5 concludes and gives some future direction of work for the development of future versions of Olaaaf.

2 Preliminaries

In Sect. 2.1, some basic notions about CBR are recalled, together with the notations used throughout the article. The general approach to adaptation by Olaaaf is revision-based adaptation (described in Sect. 2.4), which is based on belief revision (whose principles are recalled in Sect. 2.3), which requires a few reminders about formal logics (Sect. 2.2).

2.1 Case-Based Reasoning: Notions and Notations

In this paper, a problem is denoted by x and a solution by y. In particular, the target problem is denoted by x^{tgt} and the solution proposed by the CBR system by y^{tgt}. A case is the representation of an episode of problem solving, often given only by a problem-solution pair (x, y) where y is a solution of x. Note that, in the context of this article (and of the examples), this a priori distinction between the problem part and the solution part of a case is not necessary. Two kinds of cases are distinguished: correct and incorrect cases; a case is correct if it leads to an acceptable solution to the problem it solves. It should be noted that this distinction between correct and incorrect cases is usually incompletely known by the CBR system. A *source case*, denoted by c^s, is a case available to a CBR system, and the set of source cases constitutes the *case base* CB. The source cases are supposed to be correct.

In this article, only single case reuse is considered, that is, the process model of CBR consists in (1) retrieving a $c^s \in$ CB deemed similar to x^{tgt}, (2) adapting c^s in order to propose a solution y^{tgt} to x^{tgt}. Other CBR steps are not considered in this article. In fact, this article is primarily concerned with step (2), adaptation.

The knowledge model of a CBR system usually consists of four containers [26]: the case base CB, the *domain knowledge* DK, the *adaptation knowledge*

AK, and the *retrieval knowledge* RK. CB has been introduced above and RK, is not considered in this article.

DK concerns cases and may be seen as a set of integrity constraints. In particular, DK often contains a taxonomy, i.e., a set of ordered pairs (A, B) where A is a subclass of B and such a pair corresponds to the constraint that prohibits having an instance of A that is not an instance of B: written in propositional logic, the constraint $A \rightarrow B$ means that $A \wedge \neg B$ cannot be true. Thus, DK can be seen as a set of necessary conditions for the correctness of a case.

AK concerns the way cases relate in the case space: given a case that is supposed to be correct (e.g. a source case), it gives knowledge about other cases that *should* be correct, with some uncertainty. This uncertainty is often measured by a number. In this article, this number is called a *cost*: given c^1 and c^2 two cases, the former known to be correct (e.g. $c^1 \in CB$), AK gives an estimation of this cost c, which can be interpreted, e.g., in a probabilistic way: $c = -\log P$ where P estimates the probability that c^2 is correct (knowing that c^1 is). For example, AK may contain adaptation rules. Such an adaptation rule states that if a case c^1 and a problem x^2 are related according to the condition of the rule, then the rule is triggered and gives a modification of c^1 into c^2, such that c^2 represents a solving of the problem x^2 and the correctness of c^2 is estimated according to the cost associated with the adaptation rule.

It is important to distinguish the roles of DK and of AK. Indeed, DK is about cases considered in isolation, whereas AK concerns variations between cases.

2.2 Some Basic Notions About Some Monotonic Logics

A monotonic logic, in all generality, is an ordered pair $(\mathcal{L}, \models)$ where $\mathcal{L}$ is a language defined by a formal syntax (a *formula* is by definition an element of $\mathcal{L}$) and $\models$ is a binary relation that relates a set of formulas B to a formula α where $B \models \alpha$ reads "B entails α."

For some logics (including propositional logic and the formalism of the Olaaf system), the relation $\models$ is defined as follows. A fixed set Ω is given, and an *interpretation* is an element of Ω. A fixed mapping $\mathcal{M}$ is given, which associates to a formula α a subset $\mathcal{M}(\alpha)$ of Ω (the definitions of Ω and of $\mathcal{M}$ depend on the chosen logic). For a set of formulas $B = \{\alpha_1, \alpha_2, \ldots, \alpha_p\}$, $\mathcal{M}(B)$ is defined by $\mathcal{M}(B) = \mathcal{M}(\alpha_1) \cap \mathcal{M}(\alpha_2) \cap \ldots \cap \mathcal{M}(\alpha_p)$ (if $B = \emptyset$, $\mathcal{M}(B) = \Omega$). Then $\models$ can be defined for B, a set of formulas, and $\alpha \in \mathcal{L}$ by $B \models \alpha$ if $\mathcal{M}(B) \subseteq \mathcal{M}(\alpha)$. Given $\alpha, \beta \in \mathcal{L}$, α is equivalent to β, denoted by $\alpha \equiv \beta$, if $\mathcal{M}(\alpha) = \mathcal{M}(\beta)$. A formula α is inconsistent if $\mathcal{M}(\alpha) = \emptyset$. A formula α is inconsistent with a formula β if $\mathcal{M}(\alpha) \cap \mathcal{M}(\beta) = \emptyset$. The principle of irrelevance of syntax means that two equivalent formulas are interchangeable within an inference.

Finally, in the following, it is assumed that $\mathcal{L}$ uses the unary connective $\neg$ and the binary connectives $\wedge$ and $\vee$, and that these connectives have the following semantics: for $\alpha, \alpha_1, \alpha_2 \in \mathcal{L}$, $\mathcal{M}(\neg \alpha) = \Omega \setminus \mathcal{M}(\alpha)$, $\mathcal{M}(\alpha_1 \wedge \alpha_2) = \mathcal{M}(\alpha_1) \cap \mathcal{M}(\alpha_2)$ and $\mathcal{M}(\alpha_1 \vee \alpha_2) = \mathcal{M}(\alpha_1) \cup \mathcal{M}(\alpha_2)$. So, in particular, α_1 is inconsistent with α_2 iff $\alpha_1 \wedge \alpha_2$ is insatisfiable.

2.3   Belief Revision

Consider an agent whose set of beliefs represented by a formula ψ is confronted with new beliefs represented by a formula μ, and that these new beliefs are supposed to take priority over the old ones. If ψ is consistent with μ (i.e., $\mathcal{M}(\psi \wedge \mu) \neq \emptyset$), then the revised set of agent beliefs is the union of old and new beliefs, represented by $\psi \wedge \mu$. Otherwise, $\psi \wedge \mu$ is insatisfiable, so some changes must be made in ψ (not in μ since it takes priority over ψ) in ψ' so that $\psi' \wedge \mu$ is consistent. Then, the result of belief revision of ψ by μ is $\psi + \mu = \psi' \wedge \mu$. According to the principle of minimal change defended in the so-called AGM theory of belief revision [2], the modification $\psi \mapsto \psi'$ must be "minimal" in some sense, and, since the measure of change to assess this minimality is not unique, there are in general many *revision operators* $+$.

Let $(\mathcal{L}, \models)$ be a monotonic logic whose semantics is given by the set of interpretations Ω and the mapping $\mathcal{M}$, and let dist be a distance function on Ω. Technically, dist is only assumed (1) to return a nonnegative real number and (2) to verify, for $\mathcal{I}, \mathcal{J} \in \Omega$, that $\mathrm{dist}(\mathcal{I}, \mathcal{J}) = 0$ iff $\mathcal{I} = \mathcal{J}$. Thus, neither symmetry nor triangular inequality is required for dist. A revision operator $+^{\mathrm{dist}}$ can be semantically defined, up to syntax, as follows: $\mathcal{J} \in \mathcal{M}\left(\psi +^{\mathrm{dist}} \mu\right)$ if $\mathcal{J} \in \mathcal{M}(\mu)$ and $\mathcal{J}$ is maximally close to elements of $\mathcal{M}(\psi)$ according to dist. Formally:

$$\mathcal{M}\left(\psi +^{\mathrm{dist}} \mu\right) = \{\mathcal{J} \in \mathcal{M}(\mu) \mid \mathrm{dist}\left(\mathcal{M}(\psi), \mathcal{J}\right) = \mathrm{dist}\left(\mathcal{M}(\psi), \mathcal{M}(\mu)\right)\}$$

where $\mathrm{dist}\left(\mathcal{M}(\psi), \mathcal{J}\right) = \inf_{\mathcal{I} \in \mathcal{M}(\psi)} \mathrm{dist}(\mathcal{I}, \mathcal{J})$ and $\mathrm{dist}\left(\mathcal{M}(\psi), \mathcal{M}(\mu)\right) = \inf_{\mathcal{I} \in \mathcal{M}(\psi), \mathcal{J} \in \mathcal{M}(\mu)} \mathrm{dist}(\mathcal{I}, \mathcal{J})$.

2.4   Revision-Based Adaptation

In [18], an approach to adaptation based on belief revision has been introduced. It presupposes that the cases and the domain knowledge are represented in the same monotonic logic $(\mathcal{L}, \models)$. The idea is to use a revision operator $+$ on this logic to modify the retrieved source case c^s so that it becomes consistent with the target problem. Now, both c^s and x^{tgt} must be considered with the domain knowledge, so the revision to be performed is of $\psi = \mathrm{DK} \wedge c^s$ by $\mu = \mathrm{DK} \wedge x^{\mathrm{tgt}}$. Finally, the choice of the revision operator for that purpose is of importance in the same way as the choice of a similarity measure is important for case retrieval: a basic choice often gives interesting results, but a better choice gives better results. The idea is to choose a revision operator $+^{\mathrm{AK}}$ parametrized by the available adaptation knowledge AK. Therefore, the revision-based adaptation of c^s to a problem x^{tgt} is defined by:

$$c^{\mathrm{tgt}} \quad = \quad (\mathrm{DK} \wedge c^s) \quad +^{\mathrm{AK}} \quad (\mathrm{DK} \wedge x^{\mathrm{tgt}}) \tag{1}$$

where c^{tgt} is a solving of x^{tgt} that leads to the solution y^{tgt}. It can be noted that an operator $+^{\mathrm{AK}}$ can often be written as an operator $+^{\mathrm{dist}}$, for a distance function that takes into account adaptation knowledge, for example, adaptation rules.

Various distance-based revision engines have been defined for revision-based adaptation in several formalisms, in particular, to be used in different versions of the Taaable system, a contestant of every edition of the Computer Cooking Contest (see [8] for a first synthesis of Taaable). The first engines were developed for propositional logic: first with no adaptation knowledge, using an arbitrary distance function dist [18], then for adaptation knowledge using adaptation rules [23]. This was used in Taaable to adapt a recipe represented at the level of its food types and recipe types. To be able to adapt the quantities of ingredients in Taaable, a revision engine has been developed in the formalism of conjunctions of linear constraints. It should be noted that both propositional logic and this latter formalism are fragments of the formalism of Olaaaf as presented in the next section. Then, a belief revision engine was developed for qualitative algebras (i.e. a family of formalisms including Allen algebra [3] and RCC8 [24], for reasoning on temporal or spatial constraints) and applied, in particular, to the preparation part of the recipes in Taaable [12]. Then, this has been extended to belief revision in the propositional closure of qualitative algebras [10]. Finally, it has been shown that analogical extrapolation (that is, case-based inference based on analogical proportion) can be related to revision-based adaptation [20].

3   Olaaaf: How it Can be Used and How it is Implemented

The formalism used by Olaaaf is described in Sect. 3.1. Section 3.2 explains how this adaptation system can be used on the running example and Sect. 3.3 specifies it. The complete description of Olaaaf algorithm is beyond the scope of this article (and its description is long), but its principles are given in Sect. 3.4.

3.1   Olaaaf Formalism for Representing Cases and Domain Knowledge

Syntax. Let $\mathbb{B} = \{F, T\}$ be the set of Booleans. Let $\mathbb{Z}$, $\mathbb{Q}$ and $\mathbb{R}$ be the set of integers, of rational numbers and of real numbers. A *variable* is a symbol x associated with a type $\tau(x)$, where $\tau(x)$ is either $\mathbb{Z}$, $\mathbb{R}$ or a finite set S defined in an enumerated way (e.g. $S = \{a, b, c\}$ or $S = \mathbb{B}$). The finite set of variables is denoted by $\mathcal{V}$.

The atoms of Olaaaf's formalism, called *constraints*, are:

- Linear constraints: expressions of the form $a_1 x_1 + a_2 x_2 + \ldots + a_n x_n \leq b$ where $a_1, a_2, \ldots, a_n \in \mathbb{Q}$ and, for each $k \in [\![1, n]\!]$, x_k is a numerical variable (i.e. either $\tau(x_k) = \mathbb{Z}$ or $\tau(x_k) = \mathbb{R}$) if $a_k = 0$ then the term $a_k x_k$ can be omitted;
- Constraints of the form $x = v$ where $\tau(x)$ is a finite set S and $v \in S$.

A formula of Olaaaf's formalism is either a constraint or an expression of one of the forms $\neg\alpha$, $\alpha \wedge \beta$ and $\alpha \vee \beta$ where α and β are formulas.

The following abbreviations are made (where *iaaf* stands for "is an abbreviation for"):

$$a_1 x_1 + a_2 x_2 + \ldots + a_n x_n \geq b \ \underline{iaaf} \ (-a_1)x_1 + (-a_2)x_2 + \ldots + (-a_n)x_n \leq -b$$

$$a_1 x_1 + a_2 x_2 + \ldots + a_n x_n < b \ \underline{iaaf} \ \neg(a_1 x_1 + a_2 x_2 + \ldots + a_n x_n \geq b)$$

$$a_1 x_1 + a_2 x_2 + \ldots + a_n x_n > b \ \underline{iaaf} \ \neg(a_1 x_1 + a_2 x_2 + \ldots + a_n x_n \leq b)$$

$$a_1 x_1 + a_2 x_2 + \ldots + a_n x_n = b \ \underline{iaaf} \ \begin{vmatrix} (a_1 x_1 + a_2 x_2 + \ldots + a_n x_n \leq b) \\ \wedge (a_1 x_1 + a_2 x_2 + \ldots + a_n x_n \geq b) \end{vmatrix}$$

$$a_1 x_1 + a_2 x_2 + \ldots + a_n x_n \ \boldsymbol{R} \ a'_1 x_1 + a'_2 x_2 + \ldots + a'_n x_n + b$$

$$\underline{iaaf} \ (a_1 - a'_1)x_1 + (a_2 - a'_2)x_2 + (a_n - a'_n)x_n \ \boldsymbol{R} \ b \qquad (\boldsymbol{R} \in \{<, \leq, \geq, >, =\})$$

$$\alpha \to \beta \ \underline{iaaf} \ \neg\alpha \vee \beta$$

$$\alpha \leftrightarrow \beta \ \underline{iaaf} \ (\alpha \to \beta) \wedge (\beta \to \alpha)$$

$$\begin{matrix} x \ \underline{iaaf} \ x = \mathrm{T} \\ \neg x \ \underline{iaaf} \ x = \mathrm{F} \end{matrix} \ \bigg| \ \text{for a variable } x \text{ such that } \tau(x) = \mathbb{B}$$

Semantics. An *Interpretation* $\mathcal{I}$ is a mapping of every variable x to a value $\mathcal{I}(x) \in \tau(x)$. For an interpretation $\mathcal{I}$ and a formula α, the relation $\mathcal{I} \models \alpha$ ($\mathcal{I}$ satisfies α) is defined inductively as follows:

- $\mathcal{I} \models a_1 x_1 + a_2 x_2 + \ldots + a_n x_n \leq b$ if $a_1 \mathcal{I}(x_1) + a_2 \mathcal{I}(x_2) + \ldots + a_n \mathcal{I}(x_n) \leq b$;
- $\mathcal{I} \models x = v$ for $\tau(x)$ be a finite set if $\mathcal{I}(x) = v$;
- $\mathcal{I} \models \neg\alpha$ if $\mathcal{I} \not\models \alpha$;
- $\mathcal{I} \models \alpha \wedge \beta$ if $\mathcal{I} \models \alpha$ and $\mathcal{I} \models \beta$;
- $\mathcal{I} \models \alpha \vee \beta$ if $\mathcal{I} \models \alpha$ or $\mathcal{I} \models \beta$.

The set of all interpretations is denoted by Ω and $\mathcal{M}$ is a mapping defined by $\mathcal{M}(\alpha) = \{\mathcal{I} \in \Omega \mid \mathcal{I} \models \alpha\}$ for any formula α of Olaaaf's formalism. Then, the notions related to deductive reasoning (entailment, (in)satisfiability, contradiction, etc.) are defined as in Sect. 2.2.

The running example can be formalized in the Olaaaf formalism with the following naming conventions:

- Given a food type f, say kiwi, the fact that f is an ingredient of the recipe is represented by a Boolean variable whose name is just f (e.g. `kiwi`), its mass in grams in the recipe is given by the real variable of name f_g (e.g. `kiwi`$_g$), its number of units is given by an integer variable of name f_u (e.g. `kiwi`$_u$).
- In a similar way, variables corresponding to volumes of ingredients can be defined in L (liter) or tbsp (tablespoon), e.g. `granulatedSugar`$_{tbsp}$.
- The Boolean variable `milkshake` states that this is a milkshake recipe.

The target problem $\mathbf{x}^{\text{tgt}}$ and the retrieved case c^s are represented as follows:

$$\mathbf{x}^{\text{tgt}} = milkshake \wedge kiwi$$
$$c^s = milkshake \wedge (banana_u = 2) \wedge (granulatedSugar_{\text{tbsp}} = 4)$$
$$\wedge (vanillaSugarBag_u = 2) \wedge (cowMilk_L = 1.) \wedge (iceCube_u = 4) \wedge \dots$$

The "$\dots$" indicates that for every ingredient not stated in the recipe, its mass is interpreted as 0 (e.g., $c^s \models (kiwi_g = 0)$). The domain knowledge considered in the example is $DK = DK_1 \wedge DK_2 \wedge DK_3 \wedge DK_4 \wedge DK_5 \wedge DK_6 \wedge DK_7$ where DK_1 to DK_6 corresponds to the DK1 to DK6 in Sect. 1 and DK_7 relates propositional variables and numerical variables.[3]

$$DK_1 = (banana \rightarrow fruit) \wedge (kiwi \rightarrow fruit)$$
$$DK_2 = (banana_g = 115\, banana_u) \wedge (granulatedSugar_g = 15\, granulatedSugar_{\text{tbsp}})$$
$$\wedge (kiwi_g = 100\, kiwi_u) \wedge (cowMilk_g = 1030\, cowMilk_L) \wedge \dots$$
$$DK_3 = (fruit_g = banana_g + kiwi_g + \dots)$$
$$\wedge (milk_g = almondMilk_g + cowMilk_g + soyMilk_g)$$
$$\wedge \begin{pmatrix} sweeteningPower_g &= 0.158\, banana_g & + 0.0899\, kiwi_g \\ & + 1.\, granulatedSugar_g & + 0.98\, vanillaSugar_g \\ & + \dots \end{pmatrix}$$
$$DK_4 = (almondMilk \vee soyMilk \vee cowMilk) \leftrightarrow milk$$
$$DK_5 = (soyMilk \vee cowMilk) \wedge kiwi \rightarrow bitter$$
$$DK_6 = (milkshake \rightarrow dessert) \wedge (dessert \rightarrow \neg bitter)$$
$$DK_7 = (banana \leftrightarrow banana_g > 0) \wedge (cowMilk \leftrightarrow cowMilk_g > 0) \wedge \dots$$

3.2   Using Olaaaf Through an Example

Once c^s, $\mathbf{x}^{\text{tgt}}$, DK and the parameters of the distance used (see Sect. 3.3 below), with respective Python variable names `srce_case`, `tgt_problem` and `dk`, the adaptation can be computed by Olaaaf:

```
min_dist, tgt_case = adaptator.execute(srce_case, tgt_problem, dk)
```

where `min_dist` is the minimal distance between source and target cases and `tgt_case` corresponds to c^{tgt}.

With the running example, the computation time of Olaaaf took about 40 s on a simple laptop. An excerpt of the display of the result is as follows:

---

[3] Complete Python example available at https://github.com/OlaaafEngine/Olaaaf/tree/main/examplesICCBR2024/example1.KiwiMilkshake.py.

```
          cowmilk_L = 0              kiwi_u = 1
      almondMilk_L = 0.95          banana_u = 1
granulatedSugar_tbsp = 6
```

For the sake of readability, the lines of the variables whose values can be deduced from other variables, such as $almondMilk_g$, and the variables whose values have not changed from the source case to the target case, such as $iceCube_u$, have been removed. Furthermore, the order of the lines have been changed. This adaptation shows that 1 banana has been substituted with 1 kiwi, that cow milk has been substituted with almond milk (to avoid the bitterness of this dessert), and that the amount of some ingredients (in particular, granulated sugar) has been changed in order to preserve the sweetening power.

Now, the result of this adaptation can be debated: some persons would expect to have all the bananas removed and replaced by kiwis. This result is consistent with the minimal change principle of the revision process, though: it has been required that there is some kiwi in the recipe (hence the minimal non null number of units of kiwis) but nothing is said about bananas. In order to achieve an adaptation removing all the bananas and replacing them with a similar amount of kiwis (in term of masses, while respecting the fact that the number of kiwis is an integer), one quick fix is to add the conjunct ¬$banana$ to the target problem.[4] However, this may be an unsatisfactory way to solve the problem, as it appears to be an a posteriori adjustment of the target problem. Another way to formulate that all the bananas must be replaced could be to add a variable that counts the number of different fruit types, variable whose preservation would make a substitution of all the bananas by kiwis. More precisely, every variable x such that $\tau(x) = \mathbb{B}$ is associated with an integer variable $b2i\_x$ that is bound to 0 (resp., 1) whenever x is bound to F (resp., T): $b2i\_$ stands for "Boolean to integer". Then the following formula is added to the domain knowledge:[5]

$$\mathrm{DK}_8 = \left(numberOfFruitTypes = b2i\_banana + b2i\_kiwi + \ldots\right)$$

Both variations of the example give the same result:

```
    kiwi_u = 2              banana_u = 0              (etc.)
```

3.3 Olaaaf's Specification

Olaaaf takes as input the domain knowledge DK, a case c^s, a problem x^{tgt} and returns a solved case c^{tgt}. It is based on revision-based adaptation (cf. Sect. 2.4, equality (1)) and the revision operator used is distance-based, so, it is specified by a distance function $dist_w^\varepsilon$ described below.

---

[4] https://github.com/OlaaafEngine/Olaaaf/blob/main/examplesICCBR2024/example2.KiwiMilkshakeNoBanana.py.

[5] https://github.com/OlaaafEngine/Olaaaf/blob/main/examplesICCBR2024/example3.KiwiMilkshakeSameNumberOfFruitTypes.py.

Distance functions between interpretations. Let $\mathcal{I}, \mathcal{J} \in \Omega$ and $x \in \mathcal{V}$. Let

$$\Delta_{\mathcal{I}\mathcal{J}}x = \begin{cases} \mathcal{J}(x) - \mathcal{I}(x) & \text{if } \tau(x) = \mathbb{Z} \text{ or } \tau(x) = \mathbb{R} \\ 0 & \text{if } \tau(x) \text{ is an enumerated type and } \mathcal{I}(x) = \mathcal{J}(x) \\ 1 & \text{if } \tau(x) \text{ is an enumerated type and } \mathcal{I}(x) \neq \mathcal{J}(x) \end{cases}$$

Now, let w be a mapping from $\mathcal{V}$ to the positive real number: w is called a *weighting function*. For $x \in \mathcal{V}$, $w(x)$ is denoted by w_x. The distance function dist_w is defined as follows, for $\mathcal{I}, \mathcal{J} \in \Omega$:

$$\text{dist}_w(\mathcal{I}, \mathcal{J}) = \sum_{x \in \mathcal{V}} w_x \cdot |\Delta_{\mathcal{I}\mathcal{J}}x| \tag{2}$$

An issue with this distance function is that the revision operator $\dotplus^{\text{dist}_w}$ associated with it does not satisfy all the postulates of the AGM theory, in particular, the postulate stating that if μ is satisfiable then $\psi \dotplus \mu$ has also to be satisfiable. For example if $x \in \mathcal{V}$ with $\tau(x) = \mathbb{R}$, $\psi = (x \leq 0)$ and $\mu = (x > 1)$, then there is no interpretation $\mathcal{J} \in \mathcal{M}(\mu)$ that is the closest one to $\mathcal{M}(\psi)$ according to dist_w, due to the fact that $\mathcal{M}(\mu)$ is not a closed set of the metric space (Ω, dist_w). Since this postulate is important for revision-based adaptation, another distance function $\text{dist}_w^\varepsilon$ is defined as the upper approximation of dist_w to multiples of ε, where ε is a positive real number:

$$\text{dist}_w^\varepsilon(\mathcal{I}, \mathcal{J}) = \varepsilon \cdot \left\lceil \frac{\text{dist}_w(\mathcal{I}, \mathcal{J})}{\varepsilon} \right\rceil \qquad (\text{for } \mathcal{I}, \mathcal{J} \in \Omega)$$

where $\lceil r \rceil$ is the ceil function applied to $r \in \mathbb{R}$.[6]

Remark. According to the specification of distance-based revision, the output of revision is a satisfiable formula ϱ such that $\mathcal{M}(\varrho)$ may be infinite. By default, the adaptation process of Olaaaf provides only one model of ϱ, thus ϱ can be written as a conjunction of formulas of the form $x = v$ where $x \in \mathcal{V}$ and $v \in \tau(x)$, which is in general more readable than any formula ϱ. However, it is possible to ask for a formula ϱ with potentially many models, at the costs of an important additional computing time and a less readable result.

3.4   Algorithmic Principles of Olaaaf

According to the specification of Olaaaf given below, Olaaaf consists in finding the solution(s) of the following optimisation problem:

$$\mathcal{I} \in \mathcal{M}(\text{DK} \wedge c^s) \tag{3}$$
$$\mathcal{J} \in \mathcal{M}(\text{DK} \wedge x^{\text{tgt}}) \tag{4}$$
$$\text{minimize } \text{dist}_w^\varepsilon(\mathcal{I}, \mathcal{J})$$

---

[6] Since $\text{dist}_w^\varepsilon$ is a discrete distance function, every subset of Ω is a closed set of $(\Omega, \text{dist}_w^\varepsilon)$.

Such a solution is a pair $(\mathcal{I}^*, \mathcal{J}^*)$ and the output of Olaaf is given by a formula equivalent to $\text{DK} \wedge x^{tgt} \wedge y^{tgt}$ where y^{tgt} is a proposed solution to x^{tgt} and $\mathcal{J}^* \in \mathcal{M}(\text{DK} \wedge x^{tgt} \wedge y^{tgt})$.

Technically, the above optimization problem is based on (a) transforming the formulas in the constraints (3) and (4), in particular, putting them in disjunctive normal form, and (b) calling a mixed integer linear optimization system.[7] A comprehensive version of Olaaf's algorithm is given in [19].

3.5   Towards a Methodology for Choosing the Weights of $\text{dist}_w^\varepsilon$

The appropriate choice of weights for similarity measures for retrieval is a long-standing issue in CBR research (see e.g. [29]). A similar issue occurs here: how can the weights w_x be adequately chosen? This issue deserves some future work, though we have applied two heuristic principles that led us to a choice of weights consistent with our expectation of the adaptation results of the examples without having to perform many trial and error tests. These heuristics are:

- Strongly weighting more "abstract" variables, e.g. $w_{fruit} \gg w_{kiwi}$.
- Giving a weight for variables associated to a unit conversion, which takes into account this conversion, e.g. since 1 liter of cow milk has a mass of $1030\,\text{g}$, so $w_{cowMilk_L} = 1030\, w_{cowMilk_g}$.

4   Discussion and Related Work

Building a general adaptation system such as Olaaf requires studying the adaptation processes proposed in previous CBR works. Various types of adaptation have been studied in the past, in addition to the revision-based adaptation approach used in this article. Is Olaaf able to integrate other adaptation approaches? Sect. 4.1 shows how Olaaf could be helpful for generic CBR systems. Section 4.2 discusses how Olaaf could take into account common adaptation approaches. Section 4.3 discusses this issue for various formalisms of case representation.

4.1   Adaptation in Generic Tools

For many years, the CBR community has developed and distributed some generic tools. In [28], Schulteis et al. compare five systems that are still currently available: CloodCBR, eXiT*CBR, jColibri, myCBR and ProCAKE. For these systems, many features are analyzed, including the reuse step feature. The null adaptation (aka adaptation by copy) is provided by all these systems; it consists simply in using as such the solution of the retrieved case as a solution to the target problem. However, even if some of these systems provide some other adaptation possibilities, these adaptation processes are still limited and could benefit from the addition of Olaaf.

---

[7] We have used the scipy wrapper for HiGHS [16], https://highs.dev.

jColibri [25] computes ontology-based adaptations and adaptations based on numerical proportions. myCBR [4] uses adaptation rules. CloodCBR and Pro-CAKE use adaptation methods defined outside of these generic systems. The ontology-based adaptation of jColibri is similar to the one introduced in our running example, exploiting the hierarchical organization that can be expressed using Olaaaf logical expressions of the form $a \rightarrow b$ (where a and b are two propositional variables). Numerical proportions, as implemented in jColibri, are used to adapt numerical values exploiting dependencies within cases. For example, if the cost of a hotel 1 night is 80 €, the cost of 2 nights will be 160 €. This type of dependency can be expressed in Olaaaf according to a logarithmic change of variables (turning equalities of proportions into equalities of differences, which are linear constraints). Adaptation rules used, in particular, by myCBR are studied below in the context of Olaaaf.

4.2 Common Adaptation Approaches

Rule-based adaptation, used e.g. by myCBR and in the Taaable system [8], is a way to apply adaptation knowledge in the form of adaptation rules (that are acquired either from experts or using adaptation learning methods generally based on differences between source case pairs [14,22]). Revision-based adaptation using such rules has already been studied in the past, in a propositional logic setting [23], but can it be applied with the Olaaaf formalism? Although answering precisely this question would require the specification of an adaptation rule formalism, an example can be used to give an idea of how Olaaaf could integrate such an adaptation rule. Let us consider the adaptation rule AR informally defined by "In a salad dish recipe, 1 g of vinegar can be substituted by 0.5 g of lemon juice and 0.5 g of water, and reciprocally." Now, assume that the source case recipe c^s contains 4 g of vinegar and that vinegar is forbidden in the target problem $\mathtt{x^{tgt}}$ ($c^s \models_{DK} (vinegar_g = 4)$ and $\mathtt{x^{tgt}} \models_{DK} \neg vinegar$). A first idea to use AR to adapt c^s would consist of modifying the distance $\text{dist}_w(\mathcal{I}, \mathcal{J})$ defined in Eq. (2), Sect. 3.3, by adding the following terms:

$$w_{\text{AR}} \left| \Delta_{\mathcal{I}\mathcal{J}} vinegar_g + \Delta_{\mathcal{I}\mathcal{J}} lemonJuice_g + \Delta_{\mathcal{I}\mathcal{J}} water_g \right| \\ + w_{\text{AR}} \left| \Delta lemonJuice_g - \Delta water_g \right| \tag{5}$$

The addition of these terms is conditioned by the fact that the source case is a salad dish ($c^s \models_{DK} saladDish$). In this situation, if the weight w_{AR} is large enough, these two terms are equal to 0 when $\text{dist}(\mathcal{I}, \mathcal{J})$ is minimal, so the result of Olaaaf adaptation will give 2 g of lemon juice and 2 g of water (or 2 additional grams of each, if there is already lemon juice or water in c^s).

Since adaptation rules are not (yet) integrated into Olaaaf, this has been performed in the current version of this engine by introducing two additional real variables AR_1 and AR_2 with weights both equal to w_{AR}, with the following additional domain knowledge:

$$saladDish \rightarrow \left(\begin{array}{c} (AR_1 = vinegar_g + lemonJuice_g + water_g) \\ \wedge\ (AR_2 = lemonJuice_g - water_g) \end{array} \right)$$

Olaaaf adaptation using this additional piece of domain knowledge translating the adaptation rule AR has given the expected result on an example of carrot and cabbage salad recipe.[8]

Now, beyond these examples, two issues remain. First, what is the language of adaptation rules that Olaaaf could manage in a similar way as in this example? Second, how would such adaptation rules interact? This second issue is related to the way adaptation rules can be composed (one after the other) and to the way they interact (when two adaptation rules applicable to the same adaptation problem are based on common variables). These complex issues are left for future work.

Case-based adaptation, introduced in [17] and reused further in [9], consists in applying CBR to adaptation, using *adaptation cases*, which capture previous successful adaptation episodes. One might consider adaptation cases as specific adaptation rules (at least in some applications). Thus, the use of adaptation cases in Olaaaf might be related to the previous issue of integrating adaptation rules into this engine, though this issue deserves much more work to be studied in a proper way.

Differential adaptation [13] is a methodology for acquiring adaptation knowledge as well as a numerical adaptation approach. It relies on linear relations between the variations of the problem variables and the variations of the solution variables. Using the notation of the current article, with $x_1, \ldots, x_m$ problem variables, and y_ℓ a solution variable, it relies on pieces of adaptation knowledge given by linear constraints of the form $\Delta_{IJ} y_\ell = \sum_{k=1}^{m} a_{k\ell} \Delta_{IJ} x_k$ (with $a_{k\ell}$, numerical constants). This is similar to the example given above of the adaptation rule AR and this can be managed in a similar way. Actually, it has been shown in [6] how such piece of adaptation knowledge can be taken into account by a revision-based adaptation approach in a setting such as the Olaaaf formalism.

4.3   Adaptation in Various Case Representation Formalisms

Adaptation in Process-Oriented CBR (PO-CBR) Systems. In PO-CBR systems, cases represent processes. The most common representation of process cases in PO-CBR is the formalism of workflows. For example, in [21], adaptation cases are used to adapt workflows. Unfortunately, no obvious way has been found (yet) to translate workflows into the Olaaaf formalism. Now, in [11], revision-based adaptation is studied in qualitative algebra formalisms, and one of these algebras, $\mathcal{INDU}$, is used to represent and adapt process cases (this has been applied to the adaptation of recipe preparations within the Taaable system). Since there are translations of qualitative algebras into propositional logic that can be used for belief revision and other belief change operations (see [7]), and since Olaaaf formalisms contains propositional logic, adapting processes represented in a qualitative algebra can theoretically be computed by Olaaaf.

---

[8] https://github.com/OlaaafEngine/Olaaaf/tree/main/examplesICCBR2024/
example4.CarrotCabbageSalad.py.

Geometric Adaptation. The CADRE system [15], aims at assisting computer-aided design, using CBR, to adapt architectural plans. In this system, the goal is to optimize a set of constraints that represent different geometric views. The variables used to express the constraints are continuous numerical variables. However, some of the constraints are quadratic (hence nonlinear). Therefore, the current approach of Olaaaf is insufficient to fully simulate the adaptations of CADRE. Taking into account some nonlinear constraints within Olaaaf is a future work.

Textual Adaptation. Textual CBR is CBR where cases are (at least partially) composed of texts in a natural language. When textual cases are handled directly, there is little hope that Olaaaf can be used for their adaptations. By contrast, when textual cases are handled through a structured representation, then Olaaaf might be used to adapt them. For example, in Taaable, textual preparations of recipes have been formalized using the qualitative algebra $\mathcal{INDU}$ (see above) and the adaptation is made at that representation level and then applied to the text of the source case. Other textual CBR systems use structured representation associated with texts (see e.g. [30]) and thus, a revision-based adaptation for them might be usable in these contexts.

5   Conclusion

This article has presented the first version of Olaaaf, an adaptation engine for CBR in a formalism that contains both attribute-value pair representations for cases and taxonomies for domain knowledge (and beyond). It should be noted that Olaaaf uses the available domain and adaptation knowledge: if there is little of this knowledge, then it behaves as a knowledge-light approach, otherwise it behaves as a knowledge-intensive one. The generality of Olaaaf has been discussed in Sect. 4. This work contributes to the development of generic tools for CBR, specifically, for a phase of CBR whose development is often little considered or considered ad hoc.

One strength of CBR compared to more fashionable AI approaches (deep learning, LLMs) is that it requires much less electrical energy and much less data than these approaches. On the downside, designing a CBR system is often more complex than using such a heavy machine learning approach, which often requires only to pick up some tools "from the shelf". Therefore, the development of general systems for CBR or for some CBR steps, such as adaptation in Olaaaf, contributes to reducing this weakness of CBR and thus making it more attractive, which should reduce the negative ecological impact of AI technologies.

A first direction of future work on Olaaaf is to reduce its computing time. For this purpose, some ongoing work aims to use optimization techniques from the field of algorithmics for logic. Another optimization approach will aim to circumscribe the set of variables required for a given adaptation problem.

Another direction of future work is the extension of Olaaaf. In particular, as explained in Sect. 4.2, we are looking now at ways to take into account adaptation rules, which can be seen as shortcuts in the case space. An example has shown that this idea is promising, though it requires some work to be adequately generalized. Another extension of Olaaf is motivated by the discussion about the CADRE system (Sect. 4.3). In this system, some nonlinear constraints are used to represent cases, so the question is whether Olaaf could be extended for a formalism with such constraints. From a theoretical point of view, as soon as an optimization system is available to solve optimization problems working with these kinds of constraints, this should be feasible, and this would further extend the scope of Olaaf.

References

1. Aamodt, A., Plaza, E.: Case-based reasoning: foundational issues, methodological variations, and system approaches. AI Commun. **7**(1), 39–59 (1994)
2. Alchourrón, C.E., Gärdenfors, P., Makinson, D.: On the logic of theory change: partial meet functions for contraction and revision. J. Symb. Log. **50**, 510–530 (1985)
3. Allen, J.F.: Maintaining knowledge about temporal intervals. Commun. ACM **26**(11), 832–843 (1983)
4. Bach, K., Althoff, K.-D.: Developing case-based reasoning applications using myCBR 3. In: Agudo, B.D., Watson, I. (eds.) ICCBR 2012. LNCS (LNAI), vol. 7466, pp. 17–31. Springer, Heidelberg (2012). https://doi.org/10.1007/978-3-642-32986-9_4
5. Cojan, J., Lieber, J.: Conservative adaptation in metric spaces. In: Althoff, K.-D., Bergmann, R., Minor, M., Hanft, A. (eds.) ECCBR 2008. LNCS (LNAI), vol. 5239, pp. 135–149. Springer, Heidelberg (2008). https://doi.org/10.1007/978-3-540-85502-6_9
6. Cojan, J., Lieber, J.: Applying belief revision to case-based reasoning. In: Prade, H., Richard, G. (eds.) Computational Approaches to Analogical Reasoning: Current Trends. SCI, vol. 548, pp. 133–161. Springer, Heidelberg (2014). https://doi.org/10.1007/978-3-642-54516-0_6
7. Condotta, J.-F., Kaci, S., Marquis, P., Schwind, N.: Merging qualitative constraints networks using propositional logic. In: Sossai, C., Chemello, G. (eds.) ECSQARU 2009. LNCS (LNAI), vol. 5590, pp. 347–358. Springer, Heidelberg (2009). https://doi.org/10.1007/978-3-642-02906-6_31
8. Cordier, A., et al.: Taaable: a case-based system for personalized cooking. In: Montani, S., Jain, L.C. (eds.) Successful Case-based Reasoning Applications-2, vol. 494, pp. 121–162. Springer, Heidelberg (2014). https://doi.org/10.1007/978-3-642-38736-4_7
9. Craw, S., Jarmulak, J., Rowe, R.: Learning and applying case-based adaptation knowledge. In: Aha, D.W., Watson, I. (eds.) ICCBR 2001. LNCS (LNAI), vol. 2080, pp. 131–145. Springer, Heidelberg (2001). https://doi.org/10.1007/3-540-44593-5_10
10. Dufour-Lussier, V., Hermann, A., Le Ber, F., Lieber, J.: Belief revision in the propositional closure of a qualitative algebra. In: 14th International Conference on Principles of Knowledge Representation and Reasoning, p. 4. AAAI Press, Vienna (2014)
11. Dufour-Lussier, V., Le Ber, F., Lieber, J., Martin, L.: Case adaptation with qualitative algebras. In: Rossi, F. (ed.) International Joint Conferences on Artificial Intelligence (IJCAI-2013), pp. 3002–3006. AAAI Press, Pékin (2013)

12. Dufour-Lussier, V., Le Ber, F., Lieber, J., Martin, L.: Adapting spatial and temporal cases. In: Agudo, B.D., Watson, I. (eds.) ICCBR 2012. LNCS (LNAI), vol. 7466, pp. 77–91. Springer, Heidelberg (2012). https://doi.org/10.1007/978-3-642-32986-9_8

13. Fuchs, B., Lieber, J., Mille, A., Napoli, A.: Differential adaptation: an operational approach to adaptation for solving numerical problems with CBR. Knowl.-Based Syst. **68**, 103–114 (2014)

14. Hanney, K., Keane, M.T.: Learning adaptation rules from a case-base. In: Smith, I., Faltings, B. (eds.) EWCBR 1996. LNCS, vol. 1168, pp. 179–192. Springer, Heidelberg (1996). https://doi.org/10.1007/BFb0020610

15. Hua, K., Fairings, B., Smith, I.: CADRE: case-based geometric design. Artif. Intell. Eng. **10**(2), 171–183 (1996)

16. Huangfu, Q., Hall, J.A.J.: Parallelizing the dual revised simplex method. Math. Program. Comput. **10**(1), 119–142 (2018)

17. Leake, D.B., Kinley, A., Wilson, D.: Acquiring case adaptation knowledge: a hybrid approach. In: Proceedings of the Thirteenth National Conference on Artificial Intelligence, AAAI 1996, vol. 1, pp. 684–689. AAAI Press (1996)

18. Lieber, J.: Application of the revision theory to adaptation in case-based reasoning: the conservative adaptation. In: Weber, R.O., Richter, M.M. (eds.) ICCBR 2007. LNCS (LNAI), vol. 4626, pp. 239–253. Springer, Heidelberg (2007). https://doi.org/10.1007/978-3-540-74141-1_17

19. Lieber, J.: Révision des croyances dans une clôture propositionnelle de contraintes linéaires. In: Maudet, N., Zanuttini, B. (eds.) Journées d'intelligence artificielle fondamentale, plate-forme intelligence artificielle, Rennes, France (2015)

20. Lieber, J., Nauer, E., Prade, H.: When revision-based case adaptation meets analogical extrapolation. In: Sánchez-Ruiz, A.A., Floyd, M.W. (eds.) ICCBR 2021. LNCS (LNAI), vol. 12877, pp. 156–170. Springer, Cham (2021). https://doi.org/10.1007/978-3-030-86957-1_11

21. Minor, M., Bergmann, R., Görg, S., Walter, K.: Towards case-based adaptation of workflows. In: Bichindaritz, I., Montani, S. (eds.) ICCBR 2010. LNCS (LNAI), vol. 6176, pp. 421–435. Springer, Heidelberg (2010). https://doi.org/10.1007/978-3-642-14274-1_31

22. Nauer, E., Lieber, J., d'Aquin, M.: lazy adaptation knowledge learning based on frequent closed itemsets. In: Massie, S., Chakraborti, S. (eds.) International Conference on Cased-Based Reasoning (ICCBR 2023). Lecture Notes in Computer Science, Aberdeen, United Kingdom, vol. 14141, pp. 309–324. Springer, Switzerland (2023). https://doi.org/10.1007/978-3-031-40177-0_20

23. Personeni, G., Hermann, A., Lieber, J.: Adapting propositional cases based on tableaux repairs using adaptation knowledge. In: Lamontagne, L., Plaza, E. (eds.) ICCBR 2014. LNCS (LNAI), vol. 8765, pp. 390–404. Springer, Cham (2014). https://doi.org/10.1007/978-3-319-11209-1_28

24. Randell, D.A., Cui, Z., Cohn, A.G.: A spatial logic based on regions and connection. In Nebel, B., Rich, C., Swartout, W.R. (eds.) 3rd International Conference on Knowledge Representation and Reasoning (KR-92), pp. 165–176. Morgan Kaufmann (1992)

25. Recio-García, J.A., González-Calero, P.A., Díaz-Agudo, B.: jcolibri2: a framework for building case-based reasoning systems. In: Experimental Software and Toolkits (EST 4): A Special Issue of the Workshop on Academic Software Development Tools and Techniques (WASDeTT-3 2010), vol. 79, pp. 126–145 (2014)

26. Richter, M.M., Michael, M.: Knowledge containers. Readings in case-based reasoning. Morgan Kaufmann Publishers (2003)

27. Riesbeck, C.K., Schank, R.C.: Inside Case-Based Reasoning. Lawrence Erlbaum Associates Inc., Hillsdale (1989)
28. Schultheis, A., Zeyen, C., Bergmann, R.: An overview and comparison of case-based reasoning frameworks. In: Massie, S., Chakraborti, S. (eds.) ICCBR 2023. LNCS, vol. 14141, pp. 327–343. Springer, Heidelberg (2023). https://doi.org/10.1007/978-3-031-40177-0_21
29. Stahl, A.: Learning similarity measures: a formal view based on a generalized CBR model. In: Muñoz-Ávila, H., Ricci, F. (eds.) ICCBR 2005. LNCS (LNAI), vol. 3620, pp. 507–521. Springer, Heidelberg (2005). https://doi.org/10.1007/11536406_39
30. Upadhyay, A., Massie, S., Clogher, S.: Case-based approach to automated natural language generation for obituaries. In: Watson, I., Weber, R. (eds.) ICCBR 2020. LNCS (LNAI), vol. 12311, pp. 279–294. Springer, Cham (2020). https://doi.org/10.1007/978-3-030-58342-2_18

Identifying Missing Sensor Values in IoT Time Series Data: A Weight-Based Extension of Similarity Measures for Smart Manufacturing

Alexander Schultheis[1,2]($\boxtimes$) , Lukas Malburg[1,2] , Joscha Grüger[1,2] ,
Justin Weich[1,2] , Yannis Bertrand[3] , Ralph Bergmann[1,2] ,
and Estefanía Serral Asensio[3]

[1] German Research Center for Artificial Intelligence (DFKI), Branch University of
Trier, Behringstraße 21, 54296 Trier, Germany
`{alexander.schultheis,lukas.malburg,joscha.gruger,justin.weich,ralph.`
`bergmann}@dfki.de,`
`{schultheis,malburg1,grueger,s4juweic,bergmann}@uni-trier.de`
[2] Artificial Intelligence and Intelligent Information Systems, University of Trier,
54296 Trier, Germany
[3] Research Centre for Information Systems Engineering (LIRIS), KU Leuven,
Warmoesberg 26, 1000 Brussels, Belgium
`{yannis.bertrand,estefania.serralasensio}@kuleuven.be`
`https://www.wi2.uni-trier.de`

Abstract. Smart Manufacturing integrates methods of Artificial Intelligence and the Internet of Things into processes to enhance efficiency and flexibility. However, analysis of time series sensor data, crucial for process optimization, is susceptible to Data Quality Issues (DQIs) and can lead to operational problems. Traditional Machine Learning approaches struggle with limited error data availability in addressing DQIs. The knowledge-driven approach of Case-Based Reasoning targets this issue by reusing experiences regarding already identified DQIs. While some DQIs can be detected using conventional similarity measures, the common, frequently occurring DQI type of missing sensor values pose challenges that cannot be solved using established measures. To address this, this paper proposes a weight-based extension of similarity measures for time series data. This extension aims at the identification and handling of missing sensor values in smart manufacturing processes. Furthermore, analog extensions of established time series measures are presented and possible areas of application outside the DQI domain are outlined.

Keywords: Temporal Case-Based Reasoning · Time Series Data · Time Series Similarity Measures · Data Quality Issues

J. A. Recio-Garcia et al. (Eds.): ICCBR 2024, LNAI 14775, pp. 240–257, 2024.
https://doi.org/10.1007/978-3-031-63646-2_16

1   Introduction

Smart Manufacturing [49] refers to the integration of advanced technologies such as *Artificial Intelligence* (AI) and the *Internet of Things* (IoT) into manufacturing processes to increase their efficiency, improve their flexibility and enable data-based decisions. In the course of this development, more companies are integrating sensors into their processes to achieve tighter control and a more profound understanding of the processes, based on which these processes can be optimized [42]. The sensor data generated during the process serves as a valuable resource for analysis and control purposes. However, due to the presence of *Data Quality Issues* (DQIs) [17], the reliability of this data can occasionally be compromised. These can lead to problems during process execution, such as production downtimes due to defects, or falsify process analyses, resulting in possible incorrect action recommendations. Therefore, it is important to identify and eliminate DQIs before an analysis is carried out based on this data. Several types of data quality issues are already investigated in preliminary work [6], such as time shifts, complete missing sensor time series, or missing sensor values in a recorded time series. Traditional approaches focus on *Machine Learning* (ML) methods for this purpose. However, DQIs are a domain in which little error data is available, as they have to be recognized and processed mostly manually [12]. It is often not possible to train suitable ML models on such small databases. Therefore, instead of a data-driven AI method, the usage of a knowledge-driven approach is suitable that does not attempt generalization based on the limited data, but instead directly reuses experience [34]. An established AI method for reusing collected experience is *Case-Based Reasoning* (CBR) [1,4]. To apply this technique, a case base can be created in which similar problem situations with already detected faults are stored. During runtime, queries are generated, and similar cases are retrieved from the case base. If a similar case is found, the solution of the case determines whether the current time series data from the IoT sensors is faulty and, if this applies, how this fault effects resulting event logs or other higher-level systems.

In CBR retrieval of time series, established similarity measures are utilized to assess the resemblance between the time series of a query and that of a case [29]. Some types of data quality issues, such as time shifts and complete missing sensor time series, can be detected and classified using conventional time series measures in combination with traditional local-global approaches [4]. In contrast, individual missing sensor values in a recorded time series pose a particular challenge. These are common across domains and often occur frequently so that it is necessary to identify them. Due to the length of the time series, individual outliers usually do not have a significant impact on the similarity calculation, making it difficult to detect whether this type of DQI is present based on established similarity measures alone. If this data is recorded at fixed intervals, a simple algorithm for determining this type of DQI would be suitable, which would take place outside a CBR system. However, this underlying assumption does not always hold, as in some domains, for example, only value changes are recorded (cf. [29]). While this anomaly of missing values can be easily recognizable for simple value domains (e. g., Boolean values), they are hardly visible for more complex domains such as coordinates. Furthermore, a simple, integrated algorithm would only indicate the presence of such an error without providing information about its possible origin. Identifying such an error using similarity measures in CBR, on the other hand, identifies cases that provide information about the source of the error and thus contain a certain explanation in themselves [45]. This process can also include suggested solutions from past cases that improve the decision-making process and provide insight into possible actions for event log repair [10]. Another advantage of using CBR is its interactive character that enables that humans remain in the loop [51] and stay responsible for the decision, which is based on the results of the CBR application.

Due to the described limitations of traditional similarity measures, it is necessary to investigate suitable similarity measures for the DQI type of missing sensor values. This paper's contribution lies in introducing a weight-based enhancement to current similarity measures for time series, aimed at effectively detecting this specified DQI. These similarity measures are developed based on the requirements of the DQI domain and evaluated based on these. However, the area of application of the extension of the traditional measures is not limited to this use case, but can also be relevant for other domains such as speech recognition, financial data or medical diagnoses.

The further structure of the paper is as follows: In Sect. 2, the theoretical foundations and related work are presented. The use case of the DQI is then presented in Sect. 3. On this basis, the problem of why traditional similarity measures are not suitable is explained, and other possible fields of application that benefit from an extended measure are named. In Sect. 4, the approach for integrating weights into established similarity measures is presented and illustrated using selected measures. Section 5 deals with an evaluation of these similarity measures based on DQI data. Finally, a conclusion is drawn in Sect. 6 and an outlook on future work is given.

2   Foundations and Related Work

The application of CBR methods to time series falls within the sub-research area of *Temporal Case-Based Reasoning* (TCBR) [16,23]. This deals with how temporal relationships can be expressed in cases. A case expressing temporal relationships is a sequence of certain attributes related to the time dimension. The most common form of representation for such attributes is a time series [29], which is introduced in Sect. 2.1 and illustrated using an example from the DQI domain. Subsequently, similarity measures are presented and categorized in Sect. 2.2 that are used in CBR to address time series.

2.1   Representation of Time Series Data

For modeling similarity measures, it is necessary to fill the knowledge containers [35] of the vocabulary and, on this basis, of the case base [29]. While there are also rarely used representation forms such as episodes, graphs, and event sequences, time series are an established and most basic representation for a temporal case. A time series stands for a measured real value over a time course, where concrete time points are referred to. For the IoT domain, present in the DQI use case, such time points are contained in sensor data [12]. To represent the time series, we use a symbolic representation, which can vary depending on the use case, and which represents the real values. These values are summarized and mirrored as a feature vector [29]. There are simplified representation types, such as temporal abstractions [38,43] or Allen intervals [2,16], which are intended to reduce the complexity of the time series and thus that of the subsequent similarity calculation. However, such a change to the time series is not suitable for the DQI use case of missing sensor values, as abstraction results in a loss of information. So, the explicit consideration of the individual time points is no longer possible. Therefore, unchanged feature vectors are used, which can be embedded in other objects at higher levels if necessary. The individual values within the sequence are also objects that contain, on the one hand, the timestamp and, on the other hand, the symbolically represented value at this time.

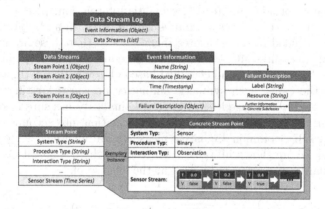

Fig. 1. An Exemplary Object-Oriented Data Stream Case From the DQI Domain Containing Time Series at a Lower Level, with an Exemplary Concrete Instance of a Lower Class.

Figure 1 shows an example of a vocabulary that originates from the DQI domain. An object-oriented case is shown here, which is an instance of the Data Stream Log class. This aggregates several attributes that describe information on the global level of the event (class Event Information), which in turn contains a specific instance to describe the DQI (class Failure Description). This specific object forms the solution part of the case. The data stream log case also contains several data stream points (class Stream Point), which represent a sensor with its attributes and the specific time series. Figure 1 shows an example instance of such a stream point. This is a sensor that measures the breaking of a light barrier and accordingly contains a time series of Boolean values. This time series consists of attribute-value pairs, each of which contains a time point (here, the time in milliseconds since the start of the process) and the corresponding value. In addition to Boolean values, other time series from other sensors may contain, for example, coordinate values, weight measurements, speeds, or other sensor values. In this specific case representation from the DQI domain, the time series are at the lowest, local level of the vocabulary.

2.2 Similarity Measures for Time Series Data

The calculation of similarity between time series is an area of research that is investigated in CBR [29, 37] as well as in other research areas [13, 22]. In preliminary work [29], we divide the syntactic similarity measures already used in research into three categories that are shown in Table 1. For all of these categories, the similarity calculation is based on the local-global principle [4, pp. 106–107]. In this context, similarities are calculated at the level of individual attributes and then aggregated globally for the complete case. Semantic similarity measures can be integrated at the local level to determine the similarities of the individual attribute values and the time points. However, the time series measures do not consider any further semantic information, such as dependencies (cf. [21]) of the time series attributes within cases. In addition, no domain knowledge is included in the measures themselves so that these are knowledge-poor similarity measures [46, pp. 59–62]. In domains such as DQI, in which an anomaly is to be recognized and classified based on semantic information stored elsewhere in the cases, such syntactic similarity measures for time series are sufficient. At the overall case level, the global similarity measure is knowledge-intensively enriched by taking this domain information into account. In preliminary work [29, 37], common similarity measures are identified for each of the categories. These are shown in Table 2. For each of these similarity measures, a suitable similarity measure can be used at the local level.

Table 1. The Three Categories of Similarity Measures for Time Series (according to Malburg et al. [29]).

Cat. 1	Cat. 2	Cat. 3
Similarity measures that can only be applied to time series of the same length. These compare only the values at the corresponding times	Similarity measures that can be applied to time series of different lengths and consider not only the values, but the time points themselves	Similarity measures, like those in Cat. 2, but that can detect stretching and compression in addition

Table 2. Established Algorithms From the Literature [29,37] for the Three Categories of Similarity Measures for Time Series.

Cat. 1: List Mapping	Cat. 2: *Smith-Waterman-Algorithm* (SWA)	Cat. 3: *Dynamic Time Warping* (DTW)
To compare two sequences of equal length, a direct mapping of the time series elements is conducted [29], disregarding time points. This method can also assess time series of differing lengths by treating the shorter sequence as a subset of the longer one and finding a corresponding subsequence of equal length	An algorithm to determine the sequence matching based on required insertion or deletion operators is SWA [37,44]. This is done based on a scoring matrix in which operations are penalized so that the best possible similarity value can be determined from the matrix	An algorithm that can also deal with the stretching and compression of time series common in many domains is DTW [36,37]. Analogous to SWA, scoring matrices are created that determine the steps from one sequence to another. The maximum value is the best possible similarity

3   Use Case and Requirement for Extended Measures

To understand the limitations of traditional similarity measures and the associated need to extend them, the use case of the DQI domain is first presented in Sect. 3.1. On this basis, the problem of identifying missing sensor values using CBR is introduced in Sect. 3.2 and the necessity for the weight integration is explained. Section 3.3 describes further use cases in which the application of weighted time series measures can also be worthwhile.

3.1   Data Quality Issues

Addressing data quality in the IoT domain is a research area that ranges from detecting such data quality issues to addressing them through cleaning methods [6,17,48]. In particular, low-cost sensors with limited battery and processing power used in harsh environments can lead to sensor problems [48]. These include failures such as low sensing accuracy, calibration loss, sensor failures, incorrect device placement, range limitation and data packet loss. Such sensor failures in turn cause various types of errors in the generated data, which complicates further analysis. For example, these errors are reflected in the data often as outliers, missing values, bias, drift, noise, constant value, uncertainty or stuck-at-zero. Bose et al. [7] list missing, incorrect, imprecise and irrelevant data as superordinate categories for such DQIs. Verhulst [50] examines other dimensions of DQIs in a taxonomy, such as the completeness or correctness of the time series in event logs. Leaving these errors untreated leads to incorrect data, and the subsequent analysis may provide unreliable results that ultimately could cause incorrect decisions [6]. To avoid wrong decisions, it is important to evaluate the underlying data quality. For this purpose, measures of quality such as completeness, timeliness, plausibility, and concordance are addressed [20].

The DQI failure of missing sensor values occurs if one or more values that should have been observed are not contained in the time series. Therefore, it falls into the category of missing data [7] and addresses a completeness issue [50]. This error can originate from the sensor itself or occur due to a loss in data transmission. Depending on the cause, the failure must be rectified in different ways, for example by manual recalibration or data imputation. The error can become apparent in the final time series in two ways: In the first way, the time series logs the data at fixed intervals and one or more values are missing. In the second way, only value changes are logged, so that missing values can only be noticed if a state transition or value change has not been logged.

3.2   Identification Problem of Missing Sensor Values

Missing values can also occur intentionally due to sensor calibrations or similar, so that it does not necessarily have to be an error that can be determined by a pattern. To identify a suitable, similar error case, similarities to the currently available sensor time series must be calculated. Since a syntactic similarity of the time series is sufficient and semantic information can be taken from the attribute values of the case (see Fig. 1), the similarity measures presented in Sect. 2.2 are suitable in general.

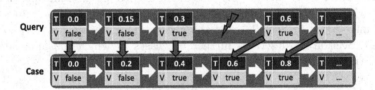

Fig. 2. Mapping of a Time Series With the Missing Sensor Failure to Another, Error-Free Time Series.

Figure 2 shows two time series, for which a similarity is calculated. A sensor value is missing in the query time series, but not in the one from the case. Here, there would be different mapping methods applied depending on the similarity measure used. With the list mapping from Cat. 1, a similarity comparison of the time series with unequal lengths would not be possible. Due to the different intervals the values are recorded in this example, the application would not be possible even with two error-free time series if both had run for the same length of time. To calculate the similarity of one time series as a subsequence of the other, would not be suited as well, as the different time points would result in an unrealistic similarity value. When using SWA as a Cat. 2 measure, penalties could be applied for insertions or deletions that occur when one time series is to be transferred to the other. Using these, missing values would have a significant impact on global similarity. However, if the penalties were too high, the algorithm would prefer to accept very low local similarities during mapping instead of maximizing the local similarities, as this would nevertheless increase the global similarity. In addition, SWA cannot deal with stretching and compression, which occurs in the example in Fig. 2. DTW as a Cat. 3 measure, on the other hand, would be suitable for mapping the stretched upper time series to the compressed lower time series. Depending on the local similarity measure, the different time points would hardly matter, and the two time series would be identified as similar. However, the missing value would also go unnoticed, as DTW would map several elements of the query to one element of the case and achieve similarity values minimally below 1.0. Even with a selective local similarity measure for the time points and an equal weighting with the actual attribute value there, the resulting relatively low local similarity value would hardly carry any weight in the global time series measure.

As described, none of the time series measures presented is therefore suitable for the use case of the DQI type of missing sensor value. To identify such an error using a time series measure, a further factor is therefore required in addition to a selective local measure enabling a significant influence on the global similarity. The integration of weights into the presented similarity measures is a possibility to achieve the desired selectivity. In the case of missing sensor values, DTW is a suitable similarity measure. However, this is not the only possible use case for this nor the other categories. Since CBR has not yet been used as an anomaly detection method for a use case such as the DQI, there is no time series similarity measure that is suitable for this purpose. As described, this must penalize a small deviation from the good case to such an extent that this deviation manifests itself in the global time series similarity.

3.3 Further Use Cases

In addition to the described missing sensor failure from the DQI domain, possible use cases can be derived for weighted similarity measures of the various categories to detect anomalies. A weighted list mapping as a Cat. 1 measure is suitable for use cases in which time series of the same length are available, but where individual, local differences can be serious. In an industrial context, if two sensors log their time series at the same interval, individual outliers can indicate incorrectly calibrated sensors or other errors. These can be clearly highlighted using weights so that abnormal cases can be better distinguished from error-free cases. Furthermore, in medical monitoring, where time series are already being analyzed using CBR [47], individual outlier values can indicate poor health conditions that would hardly be noticed when using classic measurements. For Cat. 2 with SWA, for example, weights in text syntax checking would make it possible to emphasize errors caused by individual letters or characters when detecting spelling errors. CBR is already used for spell and grammar checking with SWA as one of the measures [3]. In addition, mutations in biology, analogous to the original purpose of SWA [44], could be better distinguished from healthy genes and thus identified. DTW as a measure of Cat. 3 could also be used for the areas of application already covered by the TCBR of speech recognition [26] or motion detection [14], for example, to identify individual errors caused by background noise. Conversely, in the already investigated area of financial data [9,15], market volatility or seasonal trends, for example, could be intercepted using weights so that these would be less significant in terms of global similarity. Another area in which TCBR is already being used is the home monitoring of elderly people in a smart home [25]. Here, too, short-term anomalies can be highlighted much better using weights. In an industrial environment, this weighted measure may be of interest in the context of predictive maintenance where in the CBR context expert knowledge is already used [19,29] to detect anomalies and identify their causes based on case knowledge.

The suitability of the measures for the respective domains must be examined and evaluated. This list merely serves as an example to show that this contribution is not limited to the DQI domain and reaches beyond this.

4   Approach of Weighted Time Series Similarity Measures

The similarity measures for time series presented in Sect. 2.2 all have in common that an unweighted mean value is used when aggregating the local similarity values. For longer time series, low local similarity values due to individual deviations have a minimal influence on the global similarity value at the time series level and thus also on possible object levels above it. The SWA approach also prefers to accept poor local similarity values instead of a penalty to maximize similarity, so that higher penalty values have no influence in many domains. Therefore, we introduce weights for the individual local similarities in this contribution, which we present in the following. Thereby, we describe how these weights can be integrated into the respective global time series measures.

Some definitions that are essential for understanding the approach are introduced in the following. The definitions are partly based on the CBR definitions by Bergmann [4, pp. 48–60].

Definition 1 (case). *Let c be a time series case, represented as a tuple (d, l), where d denotes the problem description and l as corresponding solution. For both hold that they are represented by the vocabulary container: $(d, l) \in VOC$. Each element in the time series at a position h is referred to with c_j for which holds $q_j \in c$.*

In the DQI use case, the description contains the measured time series and the meta information, while the solution is the failure classification, such as a missing sensor value (see Fig. 2).

Definition 2 (query). *Let q be the time series query for which a retrieval is executed. Like every case c, q is also represented using the same vocabulary, but* *contains no solution part, i.e.,* $q = (d) \in VOC$. *Each element in the time series at a position* i *is referred to with* q_i *for which holds* $q_i \in q$.

The following definitions are specific to the proposed approach and build on the above definitions. The relationship of an element from the query to a corresponding element of the case is described using a mapping.

Definition 3 (mapping). *Let* m *be a mapping function* $\forall q_i \in q \; \exists c_j \in c \; m(q_i) :$ $q_i \rightarrow c_j$ *that maps an element of the query* q *to a corresponding element from the case* c. *The function is injective, there is only one mapping partner for each element* $q_i \in q$. *In turn, several elements from the query can point to* $c_j \in c$.

For time series, such a mapping is always calculated based on the query. Each mapping pair has a local similarity. The aggregation of the local similarities leads to the global similarity value.

Definition 4 (similarity). *Let the similarity between query* q *and case* c *be denoted by* $sim(q,c) \in [0,1]$. *The function* $sim_{local}(q_i, m(q_i)) \in [0,1]$ *is defined as the local similarity of two values for the value* $q_i \in q$ *with its corresponding mapping partner* $m(q_i) \in c$. *These local similarities are aggregated in a global time series similarity measure. The value range of each similarity function is bound to the interval* $[0,1]$.

The local and global similarities are calculated based on functions that assign a similarity value to two elements. At a global level, this is based on the aggregation of the local similarities. For the integration of the weights, the original mappings are calculated by the similarity measures to be extended. For each of the similarity measures presented in Sect. 2.2, the integration is performed in the same way. Therefore, the weights are integrated into the local similarities for the already computed mappings. This is because the mappings would be different if the weights had been applied beforehand, since new local similarities exist. This would contradict the idea of weighted time series measures, that outliers have a greater influence on the global time series similarity due to penalties. Therefore, the mappings and similarities are first calculated based on the traditional measures, only the global aggregation is not carried out.

Definition 5 (traditional similarity measure). *Let* $sim_{trad}(q,c)$ *be the function for traditional time series similarity measure. For the weighted approach, this similarity measure returns a set containing each mapping with a local similarity value instead of the aggregated global similarity value. Therefore, it holds:*

$$sim_{trad}(q,c) = \{((q_1, m(q_1)), sim_{local}(q_1, m(q_1))), ..., ((q_n, m(q_n)), sim_{local}(q_n, m(q_n)))\}$$

The mapping partners calculated here can be accessed with the function $m(q_i)$. *The local similarity values are also accessed with* $sim_{local}(q_i, m(q_i))$.

To apply weights depending on local similarity values, weights must be set for intervals of similarity values. These can be defined manually or, depending on the domain, learned by ML methods. Therefore, the following definition is introduced.

Definition 6 (weighted local similarity, maximum weight). *Let* w : $[0,1] \rightarrow \mathbb{R}_0^+$ *be a function. Then* w *maps from the closed interval 0 to 1 to the set of positive real numbers* $\mathbb{R}_0^+$. max_w *denotes the maximum weight for a given weight function* w, *such that for all* $x \in [0,1]$, *it holds that* $w(x) \le max_w$.

The sum of the weights does not have to be 1.0 at this point. To implement penalties for low similarity values, high weights are suitable for low similarities and low weights for high similarities. For example, the similarity value interval $[0.0, 0.2]$ can be weighted with a factor of 10, the interval $(0.2, 0.5]$ with a factor of 5, and the interval $(0.5, 1.0]$ with a factor of 1.

Overall, the entire interval range of possible similarity values of $[0.0, 1.0]$ must be covered. A weighting of 0.0 should be assumed for all interval ranges that are not defined. The weights for the individual intervals are normalized using the highest possible weight value so that they are contained in the interval $[0,1]$. Therefore, the following definition is introduced.

Definition 7 (normalized weights). *The normalized weight for each local similarity value is referred to as* $w_{norm}(sim_{local}(q_i, m(q_i))) \in [0,1]$. *This is calculated by the following formula:*

$$w_{norm}(sim_{local}(q_i, m(q_i))) = \frac{w(sim_{local}(q_i, c_i))}{max_w}$$

Each normalized weight $w_{norm}(sim_{local}(q_i, c_i))$ *is bound after normalization to the interval* $[0,1]$.

For the example, all weights are normalized using the highest weight, in this case 10. The normalized weights are therefore 1.0 for the similarity values in interval range $[0.0, 0.2]$, 0.5 for the range $(0.2, 0.5]$, and 0.1 for the range $(0.5, 1.0]$.

To calculate the global weighted similarity, the local similarity values are recalculated based on the normalized weights, and aggregated to a global similarity value. Therefore, the following similarity function is defined.

Definition 8 (weighted global similarity). *Let the global weighted similarity be referred to as* $sim_{weighted}(q, c) \in [0,1]$. *For this, it holds:*

$$sim_{weighted}(q, c) = \frac{\sum_{q_i \in q, m(q_i) \in c} sim_{local}(q_i, m(q_i)) * w_{norm}(sim_{local}(q_i, m(q_i)))}{\sum_{q_i \in q, m(q_i) \in c} w_{norm}(sim_{local}(q_i, m(q_i)))}$$

The application of the formula and the difference it makes is illustrated in the following example. If we have one case with a similarity of 0.1 and five others with 1.0, the traditional average similarity value would be 0.85. The similarity value would be high and would cushion the one outlier. If the weights introduced as examples are used, the similarity value would be reduced. If the weights introduced as examples are used, the similarity value would be reduced. The local similarity for the case with the output similarity 0.1 is still 0.1 as the weight for this interval range is 1.0. For the cases with local similarities 1.0, the local similarity decreases to 0.1 by multiplication with the weight of 1.0 in each case. Thus, the global similarity for the weighted DTW measure is $sim_{weighted}(q, c) = 0.4$. By applying the weights, in this case, to the interval with low similarity values, the penalty ultimately has an impact and allows individual outliers to have a significant influence on the global similarity of two time series.

5   Evaluation

The presented extension of the similarity measures for time series using weights was evaluated using the DQI domain. The hypothesis to be investigated is that the integration of weights enables a better classification of the DQI type of missing sensor values. For this purpose, the underlying data and the methodology of the evaluation are presented in Sect. 5.1. The results of the evaluation are then presented in Sect. 5.2 and discussed in Sect. 5.3.

5.1   Experimental Setup

The presented extensions of the time series similarity measures are implemented in the CBR framework ProCAKE [5], which already contains the traditional measures [41] and is already used for time series applications [24,29,37]. The evaluation of these measures takes place in the DQI domain and is therefore limited to the extended version of DTW. The suitability of the other measures must be checked separately. For the evaluation, we used the Fischertechnik Smart Factory from the IoT Lab Trier[1] [30] as application. The error-free data used is publicly available [27] and is represented in the DataStream format [31]. In addition, data was generated containing three different DQI types: Missing sensor value, as well as time shift and missing sensors. A reduced case base was used for the evaluation, which contains 425 error-free cases and 25 cases of each respective DQI type, all randomly chosen. This means that a total of 500 cases are available, 25 of which are cases containing a missing sensor failure. To show the generalizability of this method, a cross validation is performed. A 10-fold is used as a setup which is performed separately for both, the DTW measure and the weighted DTW measure (in the configuration listed as an example in Sect. 4). Based on the five most similar cases and an additional threshold value of 0.9, which ensures that only sufficiently similar cases are considered, a majority vote is carried out to determine whether the failure type is present or not.

---

[1] https://iot.uni-trier.de/.

5.2 Experiment Results

The evaluation has been carried out on a server with 34 processors, a clock frequency of 2850 MHz, and 400 GB of RAM. As some cases contained several long time series and due to the quadratic runtime of the DTW measure [37], some calculations took a long time. Consequently, a ten-minute time limit per retrieval has been imposed, resulting in the termination of some queries that exceeded this duration. This resulted in 288 retrieval runs of the 500 being carried out. The average time per run has been 8 min and 40 s. The further 212 cases are therefore not considered in the evaluation.

Based on the most similar cases, a majority vote has been carried out after the retrieval. The resulted classification determined by the CBR system was then compared with the actual presence of the missing sensor failure. The traditional approach has been able to classify two of the 13 DQI error cases correctly and two false-positive misclassifications. The weighted approach, on the other hand, has been able to identify five of the error cases correctly and three false positives under the above conditions. On this basis, accuracy, precision, recall, specificity and F1 score are calculated as performance measures. In terms of accuracy, precision, recall and thus the F1 score, the weighted DTW measure is minimally better, while the specificity for the traditional measure is higher. The comparison shows that while the weighted DTW measure performs better on the correct failure classification measures, it lags the traditional measure on other performance measures. Due to the sample size of 288 requests, of which only 13 are failure cases, the relative numbers are susceptible to small absolute number changes. Overall, the classifications only change in three cases when the different measures are applied.

5.3 Discussion

As explained before, the weighted time series measure improves the classification of missing sensor values compared to the traditional measure. However, it also does not make it possible to find the majority of failure cases. While the traditional DTW measure classifies only two out of 13 failure cases, the weighted measure detects five of them. Thus, eight failure cases are still incorrectly not found, while the risk of false positive classification also increases. Due to these results, which fall short of expectations, the error cases set as queries in the evaluation and their retrieval results were examined more closely. It is noticed that two types can occur:

a) There are one or more error cases that have a missing sensor value at a similar point. The weighted DTW measure can provide discriminatory power by penalizing small deviations from good cases and enable correct classification.
b) There are only fault cases that have missing sensor values in other places. The application of the similarity measure reduces the similarities to all cases, so that the ranking of the most similar cases does not change and at most cases are taken outside by the threshold value.

As the evaluation data set was selected at random, it is not possible to ensure that there were enough cases with similar faults. However, this corresponds to the real conditions in production plants, where faults occur infrequently and have to be recorded manually. Type b) is therefore the one that occurs much more frequently. For this case, the weighted similarity measures are only suitable to a limited extent. It can also happen that the similarity values to actually similar cases also fall due to the high penalties. If it can be ensured that type a) is present, the similarity measure presented is suitable for the application. In general, however, it cannot be shown that the weighted similarity measures are appropriate for the specific use case of missing sensor failures. Therefore, the hypothesis cannot be entirely confirmed, but neither can it be refuted. Further research may need to investigate a hybrid approach [11,39] combining CBR and ML techniques to investigate how the performance of the measure can be optimized for the DQI domain. At the very least, the weighted DTW measure can be used for DQI to identify a suitable case to explain a failure that has already been identified based on the case [32]. Furthermore, it should also be investigated how the relatively high runtime of the calculations can be reduced to be able to use the procedures for real-time diagnostics. An evaluation of the suitability for other domains, as described in Sect. 3.3, can also be carried out.

6 Conclusion and Future Work

In this paper, the DQI problem of missing sensor values is presented, and it is explained why addressing by CBR is appropriate. Therefore, an approach for the integration of weights into similarity measures for time series is provided. For each category of similarity measures from the TCBR domain, the integration is presented conceptually as well as prototypically implemented and evaluated in ProCAKE. For the DQI use case, it is shown that these adapted similarity measures enable a more accurate identification of anomalies due to missing values, as well as classification. However, this improvement is not sufficient to reliably detect such failures in time series, if there are not enough suitable error cases. As this is not the case in most use cases, further optimizations of this approach or research into other methods are necessary.

From the evaluation of this measure, the runtime optimization of the time series measures is derived as further research potential. For other case representations, GPU methods are used for retrieval in preliminary work [28], which significantly accelerated the retrieval phase. It can be investigated how these can be adapted to time series and what influence they have on the retrieval for this case representation. Distributed CBR approaches [33] can also be used to shorten the computing time. Such distributed computing in edge-cloud architectures is particularly suitable for production environments [42]. Alternatively, case-based maintenance methods [8] can also be used for runtime optimization, which can be investigated for the DQI domain or TCBR in general. Another possibility would be to research a hybrid CBR approach [39]. This could integrate embeddings as ML methods that are trained based on the weighted DTW measure, thereby significantly accelerating retrieval. Similar approaches are already applied to complex similarity measures for other case representations [18].

Additional to this, we want to extend the DQI investigation by designing a CBR framework that provides to analyze sensor data for different failure types, such as additional time shifts and complete missing sensor time series. This CBR construct is expected to further elaborate the already presented advantages of CBR over ML methods due to the small amount of data. Within this framework, the similarity measures presented in this paper or an extended version may be applied to identify the one type. In addition, an explanatory component can be investigated, analogous to approaches for other representations [40]. Furthermore, it can be researched whether the extended weighted similarity measures presented in this work can also be used for other types of anomaly detection, as presented in this contribution. Hybrid AI approaches are also named as possible extensions to be investigated. As an alternative to the presented weighted measure, embeddings for the detection of missing sensor values can be investigated by training them to recognize this type of DQI and then be included as a similarity measure in CBR.

Acknowledgments. This work is funded by the Federal Ministry for Economic Affairs and Climate Action under grant No. 01MD22002C *EASY*.

References

1. Aamodt, A., Plaza, E.: Case-based reasoning: foundational issues, methodological variations, and system approaches. AI Commun. **7**(1), 39–59 (1994)
2. Allen, J.F.: Maintaining knowledge about temporal intervals. Commun. ACM **26**(11), 832–843 (1983)
3. Bacca, J., Baldiris, S., Fabregat, R., Ávila, C.: A case-based reasoning approach to validate grammatical gender and number agreement in Spanish language. Int. J. Interact. Multimed. Artif. Intell. **2**(1), 73–81 (2013)
4. Bergmann, R.: Experience Management: Foundations, Development Methodology, and Internet-Based Applications. LNCS, vol. 2432. Springer, Heidelberg (2003). https://doi.org/10.1007/3-540-45759-3
5. Bergmann, R., Grumbach, L., Malburg, L., Zeyen, C.: ProCAKE: a process-oriented case-based reasoning framework. In: 27th ICCBR Workshop Proceedings, vol. 2567, pp. 156–161. CEUR-WS.org (2019)
6. Bertrand, Y., Belle, R.V., Weerdt, J.D., Serral, E.: Defining data quality issues in process mining with IoT data. In: Montali, M., Senderovich, A., Weidlich, M. (eds.) ICPM 2022. LNBIP, vol. 468, pp. 422–434. Springer, Cham (2022). https://doi.org/10.1007/978-3-031-27815-0_31
7. Jagadeesh Chandra Bose, P.R., Mans, R.S., van der Aalst, W.M.P.: Wanna improve process mining results? In: CIDM 2013 Proceedings, pp. 127–134. IEEE (2013)
8. Chebel-Morello, B., Haouchine, M.K., Zerhouni, N.: Case-based maintenance: structuring and incrementing the case base. Knowl. Based Syst. **88**, 165–183 (2015)
9. Chun, S.H., Jang, J.W.: A new trend pattern-matching method of interactive case-based reasoning for stock price predictions. Sustainability **14**(3), 1366 (2022)
10. Conforti, R., La Rosa, M., ter Hofstede, A.: Timestamp repair for business process event logs. Technical report, University of Melbourne, Melbourne, Australia (2018)

11. Corchado, J.M., Lees, B.: Adaptation of cases for case based forecasting with neural network support. In: Pal, S.K., Dillon, T.S., Yeung, D.S. (eds.) Soft Computing in Case Based Reasoning, pp. 293–319. Springer, London (2001). https://doi.org/10.1007/978-1-4471-0687-6_13

12. Grüger, J., Malburg, L., Bergmann, R.: IoT-enriched event log generation and quality analytics: a case study. it - Inf. Technol. 65(3), 128–138 (2023)

13. Gunopulos, D., Das, G.: Time series similarity measures and time series indexing. In: SIGMOD 2001 Proceedings, p. 624. ACM (2001)

14. Ho, Y., Sekine, N., Sato-Shimokawara, E., Yamaguchi, T.: Motion pattern recognition using case-based reasoning for information providing. In: SICE Annual Conference 2011, pp. 1284–1289. IEEE (2011)

15. Ince, H.: Short term stock selection with case-based reasoning technique. Appl. Soft Comput. 22, 205–212 (2014)

16. Jære, M.D., Aamodt, A., Skalle, P.: Representing temporal knowledge for case-based prediction. In: Craw, S., Preece, A. (eds.) ECCBR 2002. LNCS (LNAI), vol. 2416, pp. 174–188. Springer, Heidelberg (2002). https://doi.org/10.1007/3-540-46119-1_14

17. Karkouch, A., Mousannif, H., Al Moatassime, H., Noel, T.: Data quality in Internet of Things: a state-of-the-art survey. JNCA 73, 57–81 (2016)

18. Klein, P., Malburg, L., Bergmann, R.: Learning workflow embeddings to improve the performance of similarity-based retrieval for process-oriented case-based reasoning. In: Bach, K., Marling, C. (eds.) ICCBR 2019. LNCS (LNAI), vol. 11680, pp. 188–203. Springer, Cham (2019). https://doi.org/10.1007/978-3-030-29249-2_13

19. Klein, P., Weingarz, N., Bergmann, R.: Enhancing siamese neural networks through expert knowledge for predictive maintenance. In: Gama, J., et al. (eds.) ITEM/IoT Streams -2020. CCIS, vol. 1325, pp. 77–92. Springer, Cham (2020). https://doi.org/10.1007/978-3-030-66770-2_6

20. Kuemper, D., Iggena, T., Toenjes, R., Pulvermüller, E.: Valid.IoT: a framework for sensor data quality analysis and interpolation. In: 9th MMSys Proceedings, pp. 294–303. ACM (2018)

21. Kumar, R., Schultheis, A., Malburg, L., Hoffmann, M., Bergmann, R.: Considering inter-case dependencies during similarity-based retrieval in process-oriented case-based reasoning. In: 35th FLAIRS Proceedings, Florida OJ (2022)

22. Lhermitte, S., Verbesselt, J., Verstraeten, W.W., Coppin, P.: A comparison of time series similarity measures for classification and change detection of ecosystem dynamics. RSW 115(12), 3129–3152 (2011)

23. López, B.: Case-Based Reasoning: A Concise Introduction. Synthesis Lectures on Artificial Intelligence and Machine Learning. Morgan & Claypool Publishers (2013)

24. López, B., et al.: Tutorial on CBR frameworks. In: 31st ICCBR Workshop Proceedings, vol. 3438, pp. 216–217 (2023)

25. Lupiani, E., Juarez, J.M., Palma, J., Marin, R.: Monitoring elderly people at home with temporal case-based reasoning. KBS 134, 116–134 (2017)

26. Maier, V., Moore, R.K.: The case for case-based automatic speech recognition. In: 10th INTERSPEECH Proceedings, pp. 3027–3030. ISCA (2009)

27. Malburg, L., Grüger, J., Bergmann, R.: An IoT-enriched event log for process mining in smart factories. Zenodo (2023). https://doi.org/10.6084/m9.figshare.20130794

28. Malburg, L., Hoffmann, M., Trumm, S., Bergmann, R.: Improving similarity-based retrieval efficiency by using graphic processing units in case-based reasoning. In: 34th FLAIRS Proceedings, Florida OJ (2021)

29. Malburg, L., Schultheis, A., Bergmann, R.: Modeling and using complex IoT time series data in case-based reasoning: from application scenarios to implementations. In: 31st ICCBR Workshop Proceedings, vol. 3438, pp. 81–96 (2023)

30. Malburg, L., Seiger, R., Bergmann, R., Weber, B.: Using physical factory simulation models for business process management research. In: Del Río Ortega, A., Leopold, H., Santoro, F.M. (eds.) BPM 2020. LNBIP, vol. 397, pp. 95–107. Springer, Cham (2020). https://doi.org/10.1007/978-3-030-66498-5_8

31. Mangler, J., et al.: DataStream XES extension: embedding IoT sensor data into extensible event stream logs. Future Internet **15**(3), 109 (2023)

32. Olsson, T., Gillblad, D., Funk, P., Xiong, N.: Case-based reasoning for explaining probabilistic machine learning. IJCSIT **6**(1), 87–101 (2014)

33. Plaza, E., McGinty, L.: Distributed case-based reasoning. Knowl. Eng. Rev. **20**(3), 261–265 (2005)

34. Power, D.J.: Decision Support Systems: Concepts and Resources for Managers. Quorum Books (2002)

35. Richter, M.M.: Knowledge containers. In: Readings in Case-Based Reasoning. Morgan Kaufmann Publishers (2003)

36. Sakoe, H., Chiba, S.: Dynamic programming algorithm optimization for spoken word recognition. IEEE Trans. Acoust. Speech Sig. Process. **26**(1), 43–49 (1978)

37. Schake, E., Grumbach, L., Bergmann, R.: A time-series similarity measure for case-based deviation management to support flexible workflow execution. In: Watson, I., Weber, R. (eds.) ICCBR 2020. LNCS (LNAI), vol. 12311, pp. 33–48. Springer, Cham (2020). https://doi.org/10.1007/978-3-030-58342-2_3

38. Schmidt, R., Gierl, L.: A prognostic model for temporal courses that combines temporal abstraction and case-based reasoning. Int. J. Med. Inform. **74**(2–4), 307–315 (2005)

39. Schultheis, A.: Exploring a hybrid case-based reasoning approach for time series adaptation in predictive maintenance. In: 32nd ICCBR Workshop Proceedings. CEUR-WS.org (2024). Accepted for Publication

40. Schultheis, A., Hoffmann, M., Malburg, L., Bergmann, R.: Explanation of similarities in process-oriented case-based reasoning by visualization. In: Massie, S., Chakraborti, S. (eds.) ICCBR 2023. LNCS, vol. 14141, pp. 53–68. Springer, Cham (2023). https://doi.org/10.1007/978-3-031-40177-0_4

41. Schultheis, A., Zeyen, C., Bergmann, R.: An overview and comparison of case-based reasoning frameworks. In: Massie, S., Chakraborti, S. (eds.) ICCBR 2023. LNCS, vol. 14141, pp. 327–343. Springer, Cham (2023). https://doi.org/10.1007/978-3-031-40177-0_21

42. Schultheis, A., et al.: EASY: energy-efficient analysis and control processes in the dynamic edge-cloud continuum for industrial manufacturing. Künstliche Intelligenz (2024). Submitted for Review

43. Shahar, Y.: A framework for knowledge-based temporal abstraction. Artif. Intell. **90**(1–2), 79–133 (1997)

44. Smith, T.F., Waterman, M.S.: Identification of common molecular subsequences. JMB **147**(1), 195–197 (1981)

45. Sørmo, F., Cassens, J., Aamodt, A.: Explanation in case-based reasoning - perspectives and goals. Artif. Intell. Rev. **24**(2), 109–143 (2005)

46. Stahl, A.: Learning of knowledge-intensive similarity measures in case-based reasoning. Ph.D. thesis, University of Kaiserslautern (2004)

47. Szczepanski, T., Bach, K., Aamodt, A.: Challenges for the similarity-based comparison of human physical activities using time series data. In: 31st ICCBR Workshop Proceedings, vol. 1815, pp. 173–177 (2016)

48. Teh, H.Y., Kempa-Liehr, A.W., Wang, K.I.: Sensor data quality: a systematic review. J. Big Data **7**(1), 11 (2020)
49. Tran, K.P.: Artificial intelligence for smart manufacturing: methods and applications. Sensors **21**(16), 5584 (2021)
50. Verhulst, R.: Evaluating quality of event data within event logs: an extensible framework. Master's thesis, Eindhoven Univ. of Technology, Netherlands (2016)
51. Zanzotto, F.M.: Viewpoint: human-in-the-loop artificial intelligence. J. Artif. Intell. Res. **64**, 243–252 (2019)

Examining the Potential of Sequence Patterns from EEG Data as Alternative Case Representation for Seizure Detection

Jonah Fernandez[1], Guillem Hernández-Guillamet[1,2], Cristina Montserrat[1], Bianca Innocenti[1], and Beatriz López[1(✉)]

[1] eXiT Research Group, University of Girona, Girona, Spain
{jonah.fernandez,bianca.innocenti,beatriz.lopez}@udg.edu,
ghernandezgu.germanstrias@gencat.cat
[2] Research Group on Innovation, Health Economics and Digital Transformation, Institut Germans Trias i Pujol (IGTP), Cami de les Escoles, Badalona, 08916 Catalunya, Spain

Abstract. The management of EEG signals for disease diagnosis has been traditionally addressed by extracting features from the bio-signal data, either in the time domain, frequency domain, or time-frequency domain; and recently, deep learning has been used to find patterns that are later used for a classification method. In this work, we propose the use of sequence pattern mining algorithms combined with case-based reasoning (CBR). First, patterns are mined from EEG data. Next, cases are built based on binary features representing the patterns. A CBR system uses the cases to detect epileptic seizures. Experimentation is carried out with the CHB-MIT scalp EEG database of Physionet concerning epileptic seizures. The study reveals distinctive patterns related to the preictal phase of EEG signals, indicating the potential for accurate prediction of epileptic seizures.

Keywords: Sequence pattern mining · Temporal abstraction · Case representation · EEG

1 Introduction

Electroencephalography (EEG) has become a fundamental tool for the analysis of brain activity to support the diagnosis of neurological and mental diseases. In particular, it has become a key tool for studying epilepsy, a disease suffered by a huge number of people (50 million people according to WHO [31]). Approximately 70% of patients diagnosed with epilepsy can be fully controlled with antiepileptic drugs. Unfortunately, the remaining 30% are drug-resistant and continue to suffer crises [31]. Monitoring people suffering from drug-resistant epilepsy with EEG wearable devices is a challenging work that drives biomedical research in order to improve the quality of life of such people.

© The Author(s), under exclusive license to Springer Nature Switzerland AG 2024
J. A. Recio-Garcia et al. (Eds.): ICCBR 2024, LNAI 14775, pp. 258–272, 2024.
https://doi.org/10.1007/978-3-031-63646-2_17

The manual analysis of the EEG signal, however, is highly complex and subject to subjective interpretations, and AI techniques are of paramount importance in supporting EEG analysis. Among the different AI techniques, case-based reasoning (CBR) provides advantages over other techniques, such as allowing the individualization of the result, the management of the context, and the uncertainty of different alternatives or recommendations [11]. For example, [5] uses CBR on EEG data for early depression detection. CBR allows managing historical data from a personal point of view, which is important for seizure detection since no two persons are alike with the same EEG register (there is a high inter-subject variability).

The nature of EEG, however, is longitudinal and high dimensional. Most of the approaches opt to reduce dimensionality by transforming the data to a tabular representation, in which each column corresponds to some feature extracted from the EEG data. For example, [5] considered the center frequency, inclination, and kurtosis in the whole band (0.5–50 Hz) of the EEG signal, as well as the relative center frequency, absolute gravity frequency, relative power, and absolute power in theta (4–8 Hz), alpha (8–13 Hz), beta (13–30 Hz), and gamma (30–50 Hz) bands. Recently, deep learning (DL) methods have also been employed for dimensionality reduction [28].

An alternative representation of EEG signals is [23], which uses sequential patterns combined with DL for predicting emotional states. We follow a similar approach. To that end, we are using sequential pattern mining to find frequent patterns in EEG signals, which are then used as binary features from which cases are represented. To our knowledge, no previous work has applied sequence pattern mining on EEG data for representing cases in CBR. This work is a preliminary study to analyze the potential of such representation regarding seizure detection.

This paper is organized as follows. We continue in Sect. 2 some basic EEG concepts for understanding the research are provided, and next, in Sect. 3, the related work to this study is presented. Afterwards, in Sect. 4 the methodological contribution of this paper is described. In Sect. 5 the experimental results are provided and discussed. The paper ends with some conclusions in Sect. 6.

2   Background

In the EEG of a person diagnosed with epilepsy, four phases can be distinguished (see Fig. 1): interictal, preictal, ictal, and post-ictal. In the interictal phase, although the patient does not present symptoms of a seizure, the brain may present abnormalities in electrical activity, called Interictal Epileptiform Discharges (see Fig. 2). In the preictal phase, it is possible to read abnormalities in the electrical activity of the brain that indicate the possibility of a future seizure. This can be useful in anticipating and preventing an epileptic seizure. In the ictal phase, the seizure occurs. Finally, in the post-ictal phase, the brain may temporarily exhibit abnormal electrical activity due to the previous phase.

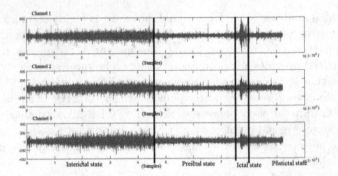

Fig. 1. Interictal, preictal, ictal and post-ictal states. From [29]

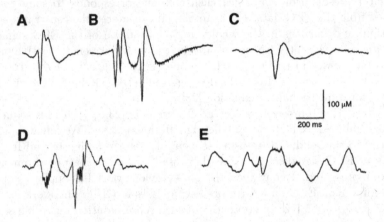

Fig. 2. Interictal epileptiform discharges. From [9]

Detecting epilepsy from EEG signals involves recognizing preictal states from the remainder, mainly, interictal states that precede the preictal phase. The use of EEG raw data for AI decision tools requires a preprocessing pipeline that includes noise removal (notch noise and artifacts), and other steps that are explained elsewhere [15, 20].

3   Related Work

The use of CBR for predictive tasks from EEG data has been a matter of study in the recent years. [5] used linear (center frequency, inclination, kurtosis) and non linear features (power spectral entropy, Kolmogorov entropy) for characterizing EEG data; next K-Nearest Neighbors (KNN) is applied with a normalized Euclidean distance to generate predictions for early depression detection. [1] transformed EEG data into time-domain (as power spectral density) and frequency (as fast Fourier transform) features. Afterwards, the impact of both sets of features is analyzed with CBR for predicting the cognitive load of driving.

In so doing, [1] used the Euclidean distance (as we do), and learned the weight of each feature with a neighborhood component analysis. [26] combined J48 for dimensionality reduction, and CBR for predicting several diagnoses from EEG data. In this work, we are not considering extracting features as a summary of the dynamic behaviour of the biosignal but finding sequence patterns to characterize EEG data.

One close work is [13], which proposes a methodology to combine CBR and sequence learning. Different from us, CBR is used to match the pattern corresponding to the information from a channel of a signal among a set of available patterns. Next, the patterns of the full signal are used to compose a sequence, and sequence pattern matching is applied to determine the class. [13] represents an interesting foundational work, and the results are provided based on a toy problem. Another work, [8] combines sequence learning with CBR as we do, but applies to complex medical equipment failure detection. In that regard, the dimensions of the input data to be managed are different, making the EEG larger and more challenging, as described in this paper.

Another interesting work is [10], which used the Ngram algorithm for the detection and prediction of epileptic seizures. Ngram tries to segment text into words [7]; in the case of EEG data, Ngram was applied to identify patterns in time instants of EEG data, with some determined length (1-gram, 2-gram, ...). In this work we use sequence pattern mining, and the length of the patterns depends on their frequency on the available data.

There is a major number of works of CBR for other physiological signals than EEG. One of the pioneers' works was [3], in which longitudinal data of diabetic patients monitored at home were represented by means of temporal abstractions (TA). Similarly, [21] used TA for representing dialysis data, and then, define a similarity metric among them. In this work we are going a step further, so after applying TA we learn sequential patterns, so as our cases are binary representations of sequential patterns. A work related to the research in physiological signals with CBR is [27], which applied the bag of words method to characterize the signal before being used by a KNN algorithm for classification in a rehabilitation problem.

Regarding the management of longitudinal data with CBR, one pioneering work was Ceaseless [19]. However, the approach proposed in [19] focused on continuous monitoring based on episodes, and activating different cases accordingly. In this work we focus on a more eager approach, by learning patterns; the huge dimension of EEG data requires this effort. Other interesting approaches concern the use of CBR for explaining black box decisions (as DL methods) from time series, as proposed in [30].

Concerning predictive models with EEG data with machine learning models, and in particular, for epilepsy detection, there is an increasing number of works due to the impact of the disease on the quality of life of the people suffering it (see for example [6,14]). On the other hand, we use CBR that, as stated in the introduction, provides some advantages regarding other machine learning approaches, such as managing context, uncertainty, and personalized diagnosis

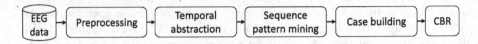

Fig. 3. Overview of the methodology.

[11]. Nevertheless, the combination of DL and CBR, so that DL reduces the dimensionality of the input data, is also a matter of interest. For example, [4] used an autoencoder to reduce the dimensionality, and an LSTM architecture to learn the similarity between cases, in the context of dealing with sequential data for patient survival analysis.

About finding patterns for EEG data, [23] proposed the use of sequential patterns for representing EEG data, and used the patterns to characterize input data for a DL architecture, in order to predict emotional states. This is a close work to us, through using a similar data representation, but we are using CBR instead of DL, according to the advantages suggested by [11]. [28] used a DL schema (convolutional neural network) together with cosine similarity between EEG channels, to characterize the data. Next, graph clusters are used to detect alcoholic persons versus control ones. [17] discovered patterns of epilepsy from EEG data, meaning the relation of the excitatory and inhibitory set of neurons, and the self-excitation coefficient of the brain activity related to the seizure. In that regard, patterns are found with the purpose of interpreting EEG data. In this work, we are also working towards results interpretability by using sequential patterns, in combination with CBR.

4   Materials and Method

The methodology proposed in this paper is shown in Fig. 3. Our aim is to detect the preictal phases in EEG data, as a prediction of a possible seizure. To that end, we start with a dataset of EEG recordings. First, preprocessing is applied to the EEG data to clean, segment, and label it according to the annotations provided in the EEG recordings (preictal versus non-preictal segments), and select the most appropriate channels. Next, a symbolic representation of the EEG data is obtained through a temporal abstraction process, which enables the application of a sequence pattern mining algorithm. From the discovered patterns, cases are built by using a binary representation. Finally, a simple CBR method is applied to detect preictal states.

4.1   Dataset Description

The public database of the Physionet repository called CHB-MIT Scalp EEG Database [16] was used. It consists of EEG recordings of 23 subjects[1], 5 men

---

[1] Two EEG recordings, chb01 and chb21, correspond to the same person, and have been considered as a single subject.

aged between 3 and 22 years, and 17 women aged between 1.5 and 19 years. Each case contained a variable number of records ranging from 9 to 42. Generally, each record contains one hour of EEG data, except for case chb10 which contains two hours, and cases chb4, chb6, chb7, chb9, and chb23 which lasted more than two hours. The recording of the signals was carried out with the placement of the electrodes corresponding to the international 10–20 system (see Fig. 4). These signals were stored according to the bipolar system and each case has a number of channels between 23 and 26. For the sake of uniformity, it was decided to remove all records that did not have the full number of channels. All signals were sampled at the same frequency, 256 Hz.

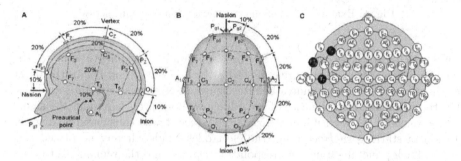

Fig. 4. A–B. International 10–20 System for placement of extracranial electrodes. The letters indicate the area (F_p, prefrontal; F, frontal; C, central; P, parietal; T, temporal and O, occipital), while the numbers designate the hemisphere (evens on the right, nones on the left) and the electrodes of the midline are marked with a "z". Initially, the system 10–20 only considered 19 electrodes. C. Currently, it is possible to place up to 70 electrodes. From [25].

In total, the records include 198 epileptic seizures. During the first exploration of the data, an uneven distribution of the seizures among cases was observed. There was a significant number of EEG signals without a seizure period compared to those containing a crisis. For example, patient chb03 had 33 records without a seizure period and only 7 with a seizure period.

4.2   EEG Data Preprocessing

Four main steps have been performed in this stage. Firstly, a notch and a pass band filter, so to finally have clean data on 1–70 Hz, the typical range of frequencies related to the neural activities [15,20]. Secondly, downsampling is applied, reducing from 250 samples per second to 1 sample per second. This heavily reduction is due to the computational cost of the algorithms to be applied downstream. Thirdly, each EEG recording was cut to select the relevant signal segment for the study. To that end, each EEG recording has a summary line containing the number of preictal states registered in the session, and the starting time of

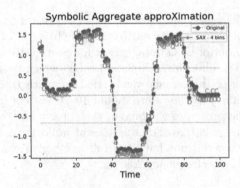

Fig. 5. Example of symbolic transformation of a time series.

each preictal state. In the case of records containing an epileptic seizure, the focus of interest was on the preictal state, which is the period before the onset of the seizure. The five minutes before seizure onset were selected for analysis. On the other hand, in the case of recordings without a crisis period, the signal was segmented between minutes 15 and 20, since it was considered that, after 15 min of starting the recording, the electrodes would already be placed correctly. Each preictal segment corresponds to class 1, and the remainder, to class 0. It is important to remark that segmentation reduces the size of the samples in a different way than a windowing process does: while windowing keeps data for the whole EEG signal, with segmentation we kept only a single piece of the signal regarding each preictal and non-preictal state.

Lastly, to further reduce the number of samples, it was decided to continue working only with two channels: F7-T7 and T7-FT9 (see black electrodes in Fig. 4.C). The main reason for such a decision was because the epileptic attacks have been demonstrated to be focused on the signal obtained from the temporal lobe which is measured by these channels [10].

4.3   Temporal Abstraction

Sequential pattern algorithms are applied to discrete data and temporal abstraction methods are required to transform EEG time point series into a symbolic representation by using cut points regarding the signal value [24] (see Fig. 5). Cut points can be defined based on different strategies (equal with, quantiles, etc.).

In this work, it was decided to divide the sample space into 4 bins with the aim of differentiating four possible scenarios:

– Positive or negative polarity: each sample of the signal could have a positive polarity with respect to the reference point, which is the zero value, or a negative polarity. Two values are dedicated to distinguishing whether the corresponding sample was positioned above or below zero.

Symbolic representation of F7-T7	1 2 4 2 1 3
Symbolic representation of F7-FT9	5 7 8 6 5 8
Sequence of the both channels	1 5 -1 2 7 -1 4 8 -1 2 6 -1 1 5 -1 3 8 -1 -2

Fig. 6. From EEG signal to a symbolic representation. Delimiters are in blue: The value '−1' indicates the end of an itemset, while the value '−2' indicates the end of a sequence. (Color figure online)

- Considerably high or low value: We sought to recognize if there was any sample or set of samples with a value that was considered significantly high or low in relation to the baseline or to other samples in the same segment. This could help identify patterns or notable features in the signal.

Moreover, we use numerical symbols instead of the alphabet. Thus, values 1–4 correspond to the F7-T7 channel, and 5–8 to the T7-FT9 one. We use the SAX algorithm [18] with some modifications according to our purposes. The algorithm is applied to all of the channels at once. At the end, we get a sequence of itemsets: in the first itemset the symbols corresponding to the first value of each of the channels symbols are represented; in the second itemset the symbols corresponding to the second value; and so on (see Fig. 6).

4.4 Sequence Pattern Mining

Sequence pattern mining discovers frequent subsequences (or patterns) in a sequence database (i.e. collections of data represented sequentially) [22]. For example, in Fig. 7 an example is provided. The third pattern, [[1], [2, 5]] can be read as follows: first, symbol 1 happens, and next, 2 and 5 altogether. Sequence pattern mining algorithms depend on several constraints, including the minimum support required for a sequence to be considered a pattern. In the example of Fig. 7, we required a minimal support of 0.8; 4 of 5 sequences support the pattern [[1], [2, 5]].

Among the different sequence pattern mining algorithms, VEPRECO was selected, as a state-of-the-art algorithm that uses some strategies for efficient computation [22]. We opt for a minimal support of 0.8 and a maximum pattern length of 6.

Frequent pattern algorithms are applied to each class separately. Once applied, only the different patterns of each class were saved (mutual exclusion).

4.5 Case Building

Each case is represented by a set of binary features, with a total amount equal to the number of patterns obtained from the previous phase. This is a common approach for using temporal patterns for classification purposes [2]. The feature value is 1 if the signal matches the pattern; otherwise is 0. Figure 8 shows an example of the process.

SEQUENCES	PATTERNS
1 6 -1 2 5 -1 1 8 -1 -2	[[1]] # 4
	[[1], [2]] # 4
1 6 -1 2 5 -1 4 5 -1 -2	[[1], [2, 5]] # 4
3 8 -1 1 7 -1 2 5 -1 -2	[[1], [5]] # 4
	[[2]] # 5
2 7 -1 3 6 -1 2 8 -1 -2	[[2, 5]] # 4
	[[5]] # 4
4 8 -1 1 7 -1 2 5 -1 -2	[[8]] # 4

Fig. 7. Sequence pattern mining example. Delimiters in blue: The value '−1' indicates the end of an itemset, while the value '−2' indicates the end of a sequence. Green color: third pattern and sequences that support it (with minimal support of 0.8). (Color figure online)

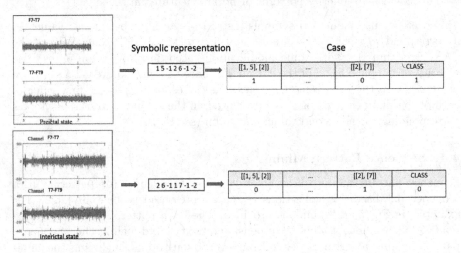

Fig. 8. From EEG signal to case representation. Top: case corresponding to a preictal segment (class 1). Bottom: case corresponding to an interictal segment (class 0). Column names are the patterns.

4.6   CBR

In this work, we implement the first phase of CBR, retrieve. To that end, we employ a KNN algorithm, with the Euclidean distance (and uniform weights), and supported by a kd-tree. The metrics for the binary features are then the number of patterns per instance that matches the query case.

4.7   Experimental Set Up

To test our methodology, two experiments have been carried out:

- Intra-subject. The methodology is applied separately to the data of each subject. The results of the intra-subject analysis should demonstrate the ability

of CBR to manage the individual variations of the EEG data regarding the classification within each subject.
- Inter-subject. The methodology is applied to the whole available data. The results of the inter-subject analysis would provide some insights into the effectiveness of CBR with sequential patterns in the detection of group variations and the classification of biomedical signals between different subjects.

5   Results and Discussion

Results are analyzed in terms of accuracy, precision, recall, and f1-score. Moreover, the number of patterns found is related to the final dimension of the cases.

5.1   Intra-subject

Table 1 top shows the results for each individual. Accuracy achieves in general good scores, but the key issue is recall, meaning how many times a seizure has been detected. Few individuals have a score different than zero, with the exceptions of chb06, chb08, chb10, chb13 and chb22. Complementary, Fig. 9 and 10 show the total number of instances and patterns found per subject, correspondingly. It is worthy to observe, that individuals with a high recall, have no patterns for the interictal signals, while they have for the preictal ones.

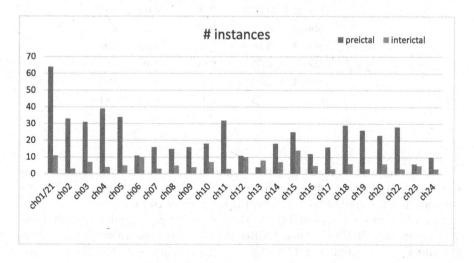

Fig. 9. Instances per subject.

Table 1. Experimental results.

Experiment	Patient	Accuracy	Precision	Recall	f1-score
Intra-subject	chb01/21	0.89	0.00	0.00	0.00
	chb02	0.89	0.00	0.00	0.00
	chb03	0.88	0.00	0.00	0.00
	chb04	0.90	0.00	0.00	0.00
	chb05	0.89	0.00	0.00	0.00
	chb06	0.50	0.67	**1.00**	0.80
	chb07	0.80	0.00	0.00	0.00
	chb08	0.75	0.50	**1.00**	0.67
	chb09	0.80	0.00	0.00	0.00
	chb010	0.40	0.25	**1.00**	0.00
	chb011	0.89	0.00	0.00	0.00
	chb012	0.50	0.00	0.00	0.00
	chb013	0.67	0.67	**1.00**	0.80
	chb014	0.80	0.00	0.00	0.00
	chb015	0.56	0.00	0.00	0.00
	chb016	0.75	0.00	0.00	0.00
	chb017	0.80	0.00	0.00	0.00
	chb018	0.88	0.00	0.00	0.00
	chb019	0.86	0.00	0.00	0.00
	chb020	0.81	0.00	0.00	0.00
	chb022	0.88	0.00	0.00	0.00
	chb023	0.50	0.50	**1.00**	0.67
	chb024	0.67	0.00	0.00	0.00
	mean	0.75	0.11	0.23	0.14
Inter-subject	NA	0.75	0.00	0.00	0.00

Another interesting result is that for some of the subjects (chb06, chb13), the seizure can be detected with a high score; and with a good balance of f1-score, meaning that the rate of false positives is kept under control.

Regarding case dimensionality, we started with EEG signals of 921,600 values on average (256 Hz, one hour); after preprocessing, each case downloads to 300 values (undersampled at 1 Hz, segmented in 5 min each). The binary representation proposed in this work is unevenly distributed. The average number of patterns is 35,806 (18,890 for preictal data and 16,915 for interictal), but with an enormous standard deviation. In Fig. 10 we can see big differences among cases. There are up to 10 cases with a number of patterns lower than 300 (including 7 cases with a number lower than 100).

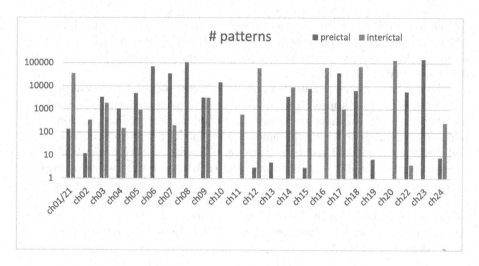

Fig. 10. Patterns per subject.

5.2 Inter-subject

Table 1 bottom contains the results for the inter-subject experiment. In that case, the input was 135 preictal records and 517 interictal ones. From them, a total of 30,432 patterns for the interictal signals were discovered, and 28,198 for the interictal data. In this experiment, accuracy achieved a similar result to the mean accuracy value for the intra-subject experiment.

5.3 Discussion

Several conclusions can be drawn from the results obtained. First, though the results in the inter-subject experiment equal the mean of the intra-subject experiment regarding accuracy, the results with all of the subjects fail in the recall. Conversely, intra-subject results show better performance regarding seizure detection. This is particularly important regarding the importance of building personalized systems, and CBR is a key methodology for this purpose.

For some of the subjects, the results achieved are promising. The results seem to be related to the amount of patterns found, and in particular, in the presence of patterns in the preictal phase. However, there is no relation between the number of available records and the patterns that can be found. Subject variability (see Sect. 2) is huge, and further work is required to understand the patterns found regarding the different EEG data available; in particular, the relation between the presence of interictal epileptiform discharges (see Fig. 2) and the performance of the system.

Concerning the complexity and scalability of the approach, although the extraction of sequence patterns is time-consuming, this process could be kept in offline mode. On the other hand, when having a query case, a pattern matching calculation must be performed to obtain its binary representation, the cost of which will depend on the final number of patterns that represent a case. To diminish this cost, pattern selection methods could be applied to reduce the dimensionality of cases [12].

The results obtained are, however, far to be good enough for clinical practice. This work is the first approach to obtain sequence patterns from EEG data and use them in CBR. We have made several assumptions regarding the downsampling, the channels selected, the amount of symbols for temporal abstraction, and other parameters of sequence learning. Therefore, future work should consider deepening the different alternatives of each step of the methodology. One possible direction under study is, for example, to analyze alternative metrics for CBR, to consider a partial matching of sequential patterns, that is, features representing patterns be in the [0, 1] range instead of being binary. Moreover, design methods for the remainder phases of CBR, that is, reuse, revise, and retain should be explored too.

6   Conclusions

Epilepsy affects a considerable amount of people worldwide, and it is necessary to provide doctors with the necessary tools to treat them. EEG is one of the fundamental tools, and AI is the key to interpreting the data collected. In this work, we propose learning sequence pattern mining from EEG data, and next, building cases based on binary representations of the patterns. A simple CBR, fed with such cases and with a KNN for the retrieval phase, assists in detecting epileptic seizures.

The results show that sequence patterns have some potential for representing EEG data while using CBR for dealing with individual management of the recommendations. Nevertheless, the results are quite preliminary and require continued work with different parameters of the proposed methodology. One possible direction is to refine the metrics used in the retrieve phase of CBR.

Acknowledgements. This work received joint funding from the EU, Next Generation EU, the Spanish Ministry of Science and Innovation, under grant no. CPP2021-008311. This work was conducted with the support of the Secretary of Universities and Research of the Department of Business and Knowledge at the Generalitat de Catalunya 2021 SGR 01125, and founded by the Industrial Doctorate Plan 2021 DI 106, provided by the Agència de Gestió d'Ajuts Universitaris i de Recerca (AGAUR).

References

1. Barua, S., Ahmed, M.U., Begum, S.: Classifying drivers' cognitive load using EEG signals. In: Studies in Health Technology and Informatics, vol. 237, pp. 99–106 (2017). https://doi.org/10.3233/978-1-61499-761-0-99
2. Batal, I., Valizadegan, H., Cooper, G.F., Hauskrecht, M.: A temporal pattern mining approach for classifying electronic health record data. ACM Trans. Intell. Syst. Technol. **4**, 1–22 (2013). https://doi.org/10.1145/2508037.2508044

3. Bellazzi, R., Larizzav, C., Riva, A.: Temporal abstractions for interpreting diabetic patients monitoring data. Intell. Data Anal. **2**, 97–122 (1998). https://doi.org/10.1016/S1088-467X(98)00020-1

4. Bichindaritz, I., Liu, G.: Synergies between case-based reasoning and deep learning for survival analysis in oncology. In: Massie, S., Chakraborti, S. (eds.) ICCBR 2023. LNCS (LNAI), vol. 14141, pp. 19–33. Springer, Cham (2023). https://doi.org/10.1007/978-3-031-40177-0_2

5. Cai, H., Zhang, X., Zhang, Y., Wang, Z., Hu, B.: A case-based reasoning model for depression based on three-electrode EEG data. IEEE Trans. Affect. Comput. **11**, 383–392 (2020). https://doi.org/10.1109/TAFFC.2018.2801289

6. Chen, W., et al.: An automated detection of epileptic seizures EEG using CNN classifier based on feature fusion with high accuracy. BMC Med. Inform. Decis. Making **23**, 1–17 (2023). https://doi.org/10.1186/S12911-023-02180-W

7. Cohen, P., Heeringa, B., Adams, N.M.: An unsupervised algorithm for segmenting categorical timeseries into episodes. In: Hand, D.J., Adams, N.M., Bolton, R.J. (eds.) Pattern Detection and Discovery. LNCS (LNAI), vol. 2447, pp. 49–62. Springer, Heidelberg (2002). https://doi.org/10.1007/3-540-45728-3_5

8. Compta, M., López, B.: Integration of sequence learning and CBR for complex equipment failure prediction. In: Ram, A., Wiratunga, N. (eds.) ICCBR 2011. LNCS (LNAI), vol. 6880, pp. 408–422. Springer, Heidelberg (2011). https://doi.org/10.1007/978-3-642-23291-6_30

9. de Curtis, M., Jefferys, J.G.R., Avoli, M.: Interictal Epileptiform Discharges in Partial Epilepsy: Complex Neurobiological Mechanisms Based on Experimental and Clinical Evidence. National Center for Biotechnology Information (US) (2012). https://www.ncbi.nlm.nih.gov/books/NBK98179/

10. Eftekhar, A., Juffali, W., El-Imad, J., Constandinou, T.G., Toumazou, C.: Ngram-derived pattern recognition for the detection and prediction of epileptic seizures. PLoS ONE **9**, e96235 (2014). https://doi.org/10.1371/JOURNAL.PONE.0096235

11. Eskridge, T.C., Weekes, T.R.: Opportunities for case-based reasoning in personal flow and productivity management. In: Watson, I., Weber, R. (eds.) ICCBR 2020. LNCS (LNAI), vol. 12311, pp. 349–354. Springer, Cham (2020). https://doi.org/10.1007/978-3-030-58342-2_23

12. Estiri, H., et al.: Transitive sequencing medical records for mining predictive and interpretable temporal representations. Patterns **1**, 100051 (2020). https://doi.org/10.1016/J.PATTER.2020.100051

13. Funk, P., Xiong, N.: Extracting knowledge from sensor signals for case-based reasoning with longitudinal time series data. In: Perner, P. (ed.) Case-Based Reasoning on Images and Signals. SCI, vol. 73, pp. 247–284. Springer, Heidelberg (2008). https://doi.org/10.1007/978-3-540-73180-1_9

14. Gadda, A.A.S., Vedantham, D., Thomas, J., Rajamanickam, Y., Menon, R.N., Ronickom, J.F.A.: Optimization of pre-ictal interval time period for epileptic seizure prediction using temporal and frequency features. In: Studies in Health Technology and Informatics, vol. 302, pp. 232–236 (2023). https://doi.org/10.3233/SHTI230109

15. Gil-Ávila, C., et al.: DISCOVER-EEG: an open, fully automated EEG pipeline for biomarker discovery in clinical neuroscience. Sci. Data **10**, 613 (2023). https://doi.org/10.1038/s41597-023-02525-0

16. Guttag, J.: CHB-MIT scalp EEG database v1.0.0 (2010). https://doi.org/10.13026/C2K01R. https://physionet.org/content/chbmit/1.0.0/

17. Kim, S.H., Faloutsos, C., Yang, H.-J.: EEG-MINE: mining and understanding epilepsy data. In: LI, J., et al. (eds.) PAKDD 2013. LNCS (LNAI), vol. 7867, pp. 155–167. Springer, Heidelberg (2013). https://doi.org/10.1007/978-3-642-40319-4_14

18. Lin, J., Keogh, E., Lonardi, S., Chiu, B.: A symbolic representation of time series, with implications for streaming algorithms. In: Proceedings of the 8th ACM SIGMOD Workshop on Research Issues in Data Mining and Knowledge Discovery, DMKD 2003, pp. 2–11 (2003). https://doi.org/10.1145/882082.882086

19. Martin, F.J., Plaza, E.: Ceaseless case-based reasoning. In: Funk, P., González Calero, P.A. (eds.) ECCBR 2004. LNCS (LNAI), vol. 3155, pp. 287–301. Springer, Heidelberg (2004). https://doi.org/10.1007/978-3-540-28631-8_22

20. Massana, J., Raya, Ò., Gauchola, J., López, B.: Signaleeg: a practical tool for EEG signal data mining. Neuroinformatics 19, 567–583 (2021). https://doi.org/10.1007/s12021-020-09507-2

21. Montani, S., Portinale, L.: Case based representation and retrieval with time dependent features. In: Muñoz-Ávila, H., Ricci, F. (eds.) ICCBR 2005. LNCS (LNAI), vol. 3620, pp. 353–367. Springer, Heidelberg (2005). https://doi.org/10.1007/11536406_28

22. Mordvanyuk, N., Bifet, A., López, B.: VEPRECO: vertical databases with pre-pruning strategies and common candidate selection policies to fasten sequential pattern mining. Expert Syst. Appl. 204, 117517 (2022). https://doi.org/10.1016/j.eswa.2022.117517

23. Mordvanyuk, N., Gauchola, J., Lopez, B.: Understanding affective behaviour from physiological signals: feature learning versus pattern mining. In: Proceedings - IEEE Symposium on Computer-Based Medical Systems, pp. 438–443 (2021). https://doi.org/10.1109/CBMS52027.2021.00049

24. Moskovitch, R.: Multivariate temporal data analysis - a review. Wiley Interdisc. Rev. Data Min. Knowl. Discov. 12, e1430 (2022). https://doi.org/10.1002/WIDM.1430

25. Novo-Olivas, C., Guitiérrez, L., Bribiesca, J.: Mapeo Electroencefalográfico y Neurofeedback, pp. 371–412 (2010)

26. Pandey, B., Kundra, D.: Diagnosis of EEG-based diseases using data mining and case-based reasoning. Int. J. Intell. Syst. Des. Comput. 1, 43 (2017). https://doi.org/10.1504/IJISDC.2017.082851

27. Pla, A., López, B., Nogueira, C., Mordvaniuk, N., Blokhuis, T., Holtslag, H.: Bag-of-steps: predicting lower-limb fracture rehabilitation length (2016)

28. Romanova, A.: Time series pattern discovery by deep learning and graph mining. In: Kotsis, G., et al. (eds.) DEXA 2021. CCIS, vol. 1479, pp. 192–201. Springer, Cham (2021). https://doi.org/10.1007/978-3-030-87101-7_19

29. Usman, S.M., Khalid, S., Aslam, M.H.: Epileptic seizures prediction using deep learning techniques. IEEE Access 8, 39998–40007 (2020). https://doi.org/10.1109/ACCESS.2020.2976866

30. Valdez-Ávila, M.F., Bermejo-Sabbagh, C., Diaz-Agudo, B., del Castillo, M.G.O., Recio-Garcia, J.A.: CBR-fox: a case-based explanation method for time series forecasting models. In: Massie, S., Chakraborti, S. (eds.) ICCBR 2023. LNCS (LNAI), vol. 14141, pp. 200–214. Springer, Cham (2023). https://doi.org/10.1007/978-3-031-40177-0_13

31. WHO: Epilepsy (2024). https://www.who.int/news-room/fact-sheets/detail/epilepsy

Towards a Case-Based Support for Responding Emergency Calls

Lisa Grumbach[1]([✉]) [iD], Alexander Winzig[1] [iD], and Ralph Bergmann[1,2] [iD]

[1] German Research Center for Artificial Intelligence (DFKI), Branch Trier University, Behringstraße 21, 54296 Trier, Germany
{lisa.grumbach,alexander.winzig,ralph.bergmann}@dfki.de,
bergmann@uni-trier.de
[2] Artificial Intelligence and Intelligent Information Systems, Trier University, 54296 Trier, Germany

Abstract. In emergency situations, the quick and precise initiation of rescue measures is crucial. Dispatchers are responsible for answering emergency calls and deciding about measures and resources. However, currently there is no support on the basis of an intelligent system that is able to exploit experiences from previous situations. Therefore, we propose a concept for a case-based support for emergency call handling in this work. First, we investigate where case-based reasoning can be applied in the decision process and sketch our vision of a hybrid intelligent approach that combines expert and experiential knowledge. For the case-based approach, we focus on deriving adequate measures and resource types. Furthermore, we propose a mechanism that supports the dispatcher in the choice of the questions such that precise decisions can be derived. The approach is prototypically implemented and will be evaluated with experts in future work.

Keywords: Case-Based Reasoning · Knowledge Management · Hybrid Artificial Intelligence · Emergency Management

1 Introduction

Public Safety Answering Points (PSAP) are the first point of contact for individuals in situations that pose a danger to life and limb seeking professional emergency assistance. PSAP operators are trained to handle emergency situations through gathering essential information from callers to initiate appropriate measures and dispatch the necessary resources efficiently. They have to make precise decisions under time pressure, as some diagnoses, e.g. stroke or heart attack, are life-threatening and every second reduces the chance of survival. In addition, the capacities regarding resources and personnel of the control centers are limited. The problem is further exacerbated by the ever-increasing volume of calls. In 2021, there were nearly 17 million calls in Germany to the emergency number "112", which excludes issues addressing the police [1]. This includes a

J. A. Recio-Garcia et al. (Eds.): ICCBR 2024, LNAI 14775, pp. 273–288, 2024.
https://doi.org/10.1007/978-3-031-63646-2_18

large number of calls that do not count as emergencies and therefore unnecessarily tie up capacity [13]. For these reasons, the optimal use of control center resources is a major challenge. Nowadays, the PSAP operators in Germany are currently supported by a very rigid and rudimentary system based on a decision tree that covers the most necessary aspects of emergency call inquiries, but lacking intelligent and flexible support.

The SPELL[1] project addresses decision support in the context of emergency management. To this end, a semantic platform is developed that integrates data from various sources and manifold services based on Artificial Intelligence (AI). One of those services is a rule-based approach towards an intelligent support for emergency call handling that exploits acquired medical and firefighting-related expert knowledge. To this end, rules are manually modeled on the basis of an ontology pursuing a data-driven approach [17,24]. Nevertheless in some cases, the ideal handling of emergency situations goes beyond this modeled knowledge, and experience is helpful. In order to systematically exploit the experience of the PSAP operators, this paper presents an approach that utilizes experiential knowledge to support decisions made during emergency call handling in order to increase performance. The result is a first step towards a hybrid AI approach that integrates rule- and Case-Based Reasoning (CBR) for emergency call handling with a focus on the case-based approach.

In Sect. 2 relevant foundations, such as emergency management and preliminary work are explained. Section 3 presents the conducted expert interviews in order to derive requirements. The proposed concept is introduced in Sect. 4 and the paper concludes with a summary and suggestions for future work in Sect. 5.

2   Foundations

First, emergency management in general is introduced and the aspect of emergency call response and its state of the art is described in detail. The subsequent section outlines the semantic platform of SPELL and the existing rule-based support for emergency call handling. The section concludes with related work on the use of CBR in emergency management.

2.1   Emergency Management

Emergency management refers to the organization and coordination of resources and responsibilities for dealing with all aspects of emergencies and disasters, whether natural or human-made. It consists of four phases: preparedness, response, recovery, and mitigation [26]. Preparedness refers to all activities taken in advance, like training. Response concerns immediate reactions to the incident such as dispatching resources. In the recovery phase, the affected objects are restored after the concrete hazard has passed. Mitigation considers long-term measures to increase resilience in case of future incidents.

---

[1] SPELL is the acronym for semantic platform for intelligent decision and operations support in control and situation centers (https://spell-plattform.de).

In this work, we focus on the response phase and on the partial aspect of medical emergency call handling. Furthermore, as emergency call handling is different in each country, we focus on Germany, but due to the same core objective, a potential transfer of results to other countries is highly probable.

In Germany, the central emergency number "112" can be called when encountering medical or firefighting-related issues. These calls are forwarded to the nearest PSAP based on the location of the caller. Emergency call handling is a highly complex process consisting of several different tasks and decisions. Call-takers are responsible for assessing the situation in dialog with the caller. This process of interaction between caller and call-taker can be sketched as an iterative cycle [21] (see left side in Fig. 1). With the given information and expert knowledge of the call-taker, a mental picture is created. Through this, it is decided about how the situation is handled in terms of measures to be implemented and resources to be dispatched, like an ambulance.

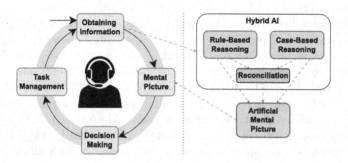

Fig. 1. Iterative Procedure of Emergency Call Handling by Call-Takers based on Møller et al. [21] (left) extended with Hybrid AI based on [16] (right)

In some cases, depending on each emergency control center, the task of deciding for measures and resource types is assigned to the call-taker, whereas dispatching a specific resource is the responsibility of a dedicated dispatcher. For the sake of simplicity, we will not go into the separation of these two responsibilities any further, but instead use the term dispatcher for both.

This process of emergency call response is time-critical and the recommendation is that a maximum of 90 s elapse before resources are dispatched so that help arrives in good time in critical situations [11]. In addition, these decisions are usually made by a single person as it is a one-to-one connection between caller and dispatcher, such that they are based on personal medical knowledge and experience. This concerns several aspects [16]:

- deriving specific diagnoses or threats from paraphrases by a caller who has no specialist knowledge (e.g. chest pain as a sign of a heart attack)
- risk estimation through assessing the situation (e.g. surroundings of a fire)
- identifying the best measure to initialize and an adequate resource type (e.g. transport by an ambulance for a dialysis patient)
- choosing a specific available resource

Whereas in some countries, standardized emergency call handling systems are established, in Germany there is no such use due to a lack of acceptance of the dispatchers, as these standardizations are inflexible and induce a lack of scope of action [18]. In some PSAPs, structured emergency call responses are implemented through questionnaires that base on decision trees. These are specified by experts, but only cover certain sub-areas, such as particularly critical conditions. However, there is a strict order of questions to which the call-taker needs to adhere to or ask questions without support with the risk of forgetting important aspects and ultimately worsen the incident [17]. For this reason, there are situations, especially those that occur infrequently, where inexperienced dispatchers in particular are not optimally guided by the system and the integration of experiential knowledge seems promising and indispensable.

2.2   Intelligent Emergency Call Response

In the context of the SPELL project, first steps towards an intelligent emergency call handling have been done. The overall aim is to incorporate different kinds of knowledge, such as expert (e.g. rules) and experiential knowledge (e.g. cases). Thus, the iterative procedure of Møller et al. [21] is enhanced with hybrid AI methods that build up an artificial mental picture (see right side in Fig. 1). Here, new knowledge can be inferred by both AI methods, CBR and Rule-Based Reasoning (RBR), and thereby support the dispatcher by suggesting decisions. For emergency call handling, we propose a hybrid AI approach that *co-processes* the information, which refers to a parallel application of RBR and CBR with the same objective [22]. Thus, both approaches could result in different decisions. To this end, a reconciliation step (see Fig. 1) might be necessary to decide for a best suggestion and not proposing contradicting results to the dispatcher. However, the reconciliation is not part of this work, but will be investigated in future research as essential part of the support for the dispatcher. Nevertheless, some decision might also be derived from only one AI method without using the hybrid approach but acting standalone.

The framework for this hybrid AI approach is given by Maletzki et al. [17] by proposing an Ontology- and Data-Driven Expert System (ODD-ES) for dispatchers with a focus on medical emergency calls. Here, the knowledge base is represented as semantically modeled functions for the integration of symbolic and subsymbolic AI. These functions are described through input and output which refer to individuals of an ontology concept. The functions itself range from simple logical functions to more complex AI-based services, like RBR or CBR.

In this work, we focus on the specific integration of RBR and CBR with a detailed concept for the case-based support for the regarded domain. The existing rule-based support is based on rules that are modelled in cooperation with medical experts. For instance, the three symptoms shortness of breath, cough and fever lead to a suspected diagnosis of pneumonia. As a rule, this can be expressed as follows: IF shortness_of_breath AND cough AND fever THEN hint_pneumonia, such that a hint for the diagnosis is given to the dispatcher. However, emergencies are highly individual such that the rules cannot cover everything. To this end, we propose a hybrid approach that combines implicit as well as explicit knowledge.

The foundation for such a hybrid AI approach is a common ontology that is used by both methods to enable communication. In the context of the SPELL project, a knowledge graph was build that semantically describes the emergency management domain. Thereby, emergency call handling with a special focus on medical knowledge was modelled in detail. This expert knowledge was acquired manually in cooperation with experts. The main concepts, derived from the tasks and decisions of the dispatcher, are illustrated in Fig. 2.

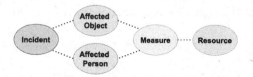

Fig. 2. Main Concepts of the SPELL Knowledge Graph - Abstract View

The overall knowledge graph contains all relevant information, in total more than 1000 concepts, that could come up during a call. Semantics contained in the graph, which can be exploited for similarity assessment, are several taxonomies, e.g. symptoms. Furthermore, publicly accessible context information like weather conditions or water levels is also represented in the knowledge graph. Since the SPELL platform serves as a central data pool through which data can be exchanged on the basis of the concepts of the knowledge graph, both approaches from the proposed hybrid AI approach can exploit the information obtained from the caller as well as context information by connecting to the platform.

2.3   Related Work

In preliminary work, we investigated how different AI-based methods can be used for decision support in emergency call handling [16]. In particular, we focused on hybrid intelligence, that refers to the combination of human and artificial intelligence. We identified exemplary integrations of AI methods in ODD-ES to support emergency call handlers, and outlined a mechanism for calculating reliabilities for conclusions based on experience in similar situations.

In the context of emergency management, several related approaches have been researched [6]. Most of them focus on larger incidents such as crises or environmental disasters [5,8,9,20,27,28], but not on smaller daily occurring emergencies and rather regard organisational instead of operational aspects [4].

Althoff et al. [3] propose an approach for the support of medical decision tasks and focus on short response times and dealing with incomplete information, which are basic characteristics in the medical domain [3]. The authors introduce a novel data structure, named Inreca-Tree, for indexing large case bases. Attribute values are used to traverse the tree structure leading to diagnosis in the leaf nodes, similar to a decision tree. As rather few information is available in the emergency management domain, this data structure is not suitable, because in the worst case many symptoms would be assumed to be unknown, even if they are present leading to wrong results or otherwise if asking all attributes on the path in the tree, loosing valuable time until dispatching resources.

3   Analysis

Before designing a concept for a case-based decision support in emergency call handling, the process was analysed in detail for identifying the biggest potential for an improvement through an integration of experiential knowledge.

3.1   Interviews

In order to gain a deeper understanding of the possibilities of supporting the call handling and dispatching process with CBR, an explorative qualitative interview study was designed. We conducted four interviews with experts from the control center domain, two of whom are dispatchers. One participant is a medical director of the rescue service and responsible for quality management and developing guidelines for the dispatchers. The fourth participant is a specialist nurse for intensive care medicine, who additionally is studying in the management of health care services and in this context analyzed emergency calls. These experts have a minimum of ten years of professional experience. The semi-structured interviews were conducted using a designed interview guide, which consists of three topic blocks: information about emergency call handling in general, identifying current problems and potentials based on experiential knowledge, and presenting specific example scenarios where CBR could be useful.

Analyzing the results of the interviews, we find that there are significant challenges with a major impact on the effectiveness of decision-making. Of particular importance here is that decisions are largely based on the individual knowledge and experience of a single person. However, according to the respondents, a serious shortcoming is the lack of systemic support for decision making.

The most important aspect is the communication between caller and dispatcher. One of them uses a layman's language, while the other is responsible to translate it into expert terms. The information provided is unstructured and most of the times does not fit to the order of the questions in the existing questionnaire. Furthermore, in some cases the described symptoms do not fit into the specified schemes in the questionnaire, but are rather diffuse, rare or unknown disease patterns. In such cases the dispatcher tries to narrow down in order to find adequate measures and resources.

Another mentioned issue for emergency call response are so-called fixation errors, which describe the overly rapid commitment to a diagnosis or disposition decision and are a common problem for experts. Here, the next questions focus on confirming the assumed diagnosis, ignoring other aspects and possibly resulting in inappropriate measures. The interviewees confirmed that for all these decisions experience is beneficial in addition to acquired knowledge. The challenge lies in dealing with each individual situation appropriately.

The results of the study are reflected by the work of Møller et al. [21], in which most dispatchers emphasize that their medical knowledge and experience are the critical factors in their emergency management decision-making.

3.2   Requirements

Based on the results of the qualitative study, requirements are derived in order to create a concept for a useful case-based support for emergency call handling.

(R1) Response Time: Due to the time criticality, the proposals for a disposition decision should be in less than a few seconds.

(R2) Precise Decision: The proposed decisions should be precise or a hint should be given to the dispatcher on how to refine the query.

(R3) Flexibility: The order of the information entered into the system is not prescribed and a changed order does not affect the resulting decision.

(R4) Support: The proposed decision is not prescribed, but can be changed by the dispatcher.

(R5) Minimize Fixation Errors: The case-based component should not only output one result in case there are alternative ones.

(R6) Complex Case Representation: The case representation should be able to include several data types, such as numerical or taxonomical values.

(R7) Unknown Values: As unknown values are common, they should not have any effect on the result.

(R8) Unknown Diagnoses: Unknown diagnoses should be supported through finding similar ones from the past.

4   Case-Based Support for Emergency Calls

The overall proposed concept, which was developed based on the previously described requirements, is shown in Fig. 3. The main objective is to reliably propose measures and resource types based on a similar incident from the past. To this end, in case a decision cannot be proposed with high certainty at the current state of information, which means other similar cases lead to a contrasting measure than the most similar case, a partial aspect of the concept is deriving further reasonable and targeted questions about unknown information.

As initial setup of the case-based component, the case base is initialized in step 0 through transferring all historical emergency calls that are available in the knowledge graph to the chosen case representation. Steps 1 and 2 indicate the standard communication between caller and dispatcher, where the dispatcher asks questions in order to obtain information from the caller. The dispatcher enters this information into the emergency call handling service, which persists all data in the knowledge graph (see step 3). In the fourth step, the case-based component accesses this information and transfers it to the chosen case representation (see Subsect. 4.1), initializing the query. This can be done at any time, but

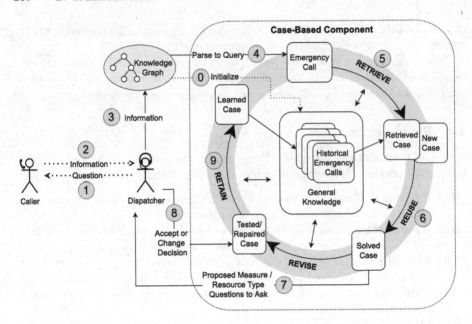

Fig. 3. Concept for a Case-Based Support for Emergency Call Response

it is reasonable to await a minimum state of information, such that the results are meaningful, rather than initiating the retrieval with the first information such as name of the caller. Afterwards, the CBR cycle begins. First in step 5, the most similar cases to the query are retrieved from the case base (see Subsect. 4.2). These cases are compared to the query and decisions are derived with the overall goal of reliably proposing a measure and resource type (see step 6), which is described in Subsect. 4.3. These suggestions are presented to the dispatcher in combination with questions that could be asked in order to increase the certainty of the decision (cf. step 7), which is explained in Subsect. 4.4. The revise phase is done manually by the dispatcher, who either accepts the suggested decision for measures and/or resource types or declines them and decides for something else (see step 8), addressing requirement **R4**. In the last step, when the emergency call is terminated, such that measures are chosen and resources are dispatched, this completed case can either be retained in the case base or be discarded. In case the dispatcher chooses to ask for more information, the cycle is triggered again, starting in step 4 with an enhanced query.

The focus of this work is on retrieve and reuse. Revise and retain were not elaborated beyond the abstract description above, but are part of future work.

4.1   Case Representation

The input data for the case-based component is transferred from the knowledge graph as instances. While some attributes are stored in the cases as references to their elements in the knowledge graph, other attributes are translated into a data structure that can be used for a meaningful semantic comparison such as numerical values or address data, referring to requirement **R6**. Therefore, these instances are parsed into an object-oriented representation. In this paper, not all details of the case representation are introduced, but selected parts are explained to get an overview and some detailed insights.

One case represents one incident. There is no explicit differentiation between case and solution, but the case itself contains the solution, as it depends on which information is specified, which information is the solution. If no measure is specified, then the focus is on identifying a measure in combination with resource types. If a measure is specified, then only resource types are derived.

One `incident` contains the following elements:

- Incident Type ∈ {*Fire Operation, Medical Operation, Traffic Accident, Hazardous Substances, Person in Predicament, Other Operations*}
- Number of Affected Persons
- Set of Affected Persons
- Set of Affected Objects
- Position
- Date and Time

The main attributes on the top level are specified on the basis of the concepts in the knowledge graph mentioned earlier in Fig. 2, such as `affected persons`. Additionally, some other specific and relevant information is stored in the `incident` object, such as `incident type` or `position`. The attribute `incident type` is used for a categorization of the incident. The `position` attribute is stored as geocoordinates. In case the caller provides an address of the incident, it is translated to geocoordinates as those can be meaningfully compared.

As the affected person plays a special role, when considering medical cases, a detailed description is provided. One `affected person` is constructed as follows:

- Age
- Gender ∈ {*male, female, diverse*}
- Vital Signs
- Suspected Diagnosis

The same strategy was followed for this object as for `incident`. Some attributes are mapped explicitly due to their importance. For instance, `age` and `gender` are a decisive aspect for the suspected diagnosis [13] and are therefore specified explicitly. Here, `age` is parsed into a numerical value for a more sophisticated comparison, whereas `suspected diagnosis` is stored as reference to the instance in the knowledge graph. `Vital signs` is stored as boolean and is translated from the existence of several attributes in the knowledge graph, such as breathing, pulse or consciousness. If none of these are available, the attribute is set to false and an immediate reaction with emergency ambulance is necessary.

Additionally, `measures` and `resources` can be stored as well on the level of the incident itself, but also on the level of one affected person, to ensure a mapping in case several persons are affected. On the top level, those assigned measures and resources are aggregated, because for larger or unclear incidents no information is existent about single affected persons.

These explicitly defined attributes do not account for all possible details in the conversation. Due to the variety of information, it is also not reasonable to map everything explicitly. However, it must be assumed that all information in an emergency situation has an influence on the measure or resources and therefore, all information provided by the caller should be taken into account and processed by the case-based system. To this end, a `set of additional information` is introduced in both objects, `incident` and `affected person`, which contains all information that is not explicitly mentioned as attribute. Each element in this set is defined as key-value pair, that contains the concept ID and the instance value in the knowledge graph. All remaining information that is connected to the incident or an affected person in the knowledge graph is stored in this set.

During parsing of the incidents that are contained in the knowledge graph, several cases are created. For each incident one case is created with all available information in the knowledge graph. Furthermore, if details of single affected persons are available, they are extracted and also saved as one case in order to abstract from the overall incident (see example for a query in Fig. 4). Through this, it is possible to transfer partial solutions in the sense of individual measures and resource types from incidents with several affected persons to an emergency with only one affected person. Otherwise the incident and the number of affected persons and each affected person needs to be similar to be considered during retrieval. As can be seen in Fig. 4, the division into several cases is done analogously with one incident that is used as query. Therefore, several retrievals and disposition decisions are derived for each person for whom detailed information is available and for the rest of the incident without available details.

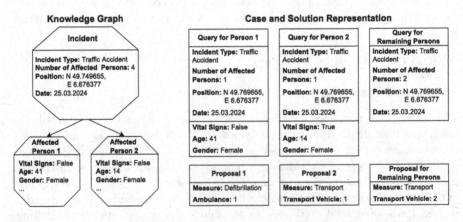

Fig. 4. Knowledge Representation in the Knowledge Graph and its Translation to Cases

4.2   Retrieve

During similarity computation, the attributes are compared according to their data type. For numerical attributes, such as `age`, a numerical similarity measure is used, that calculates the distance between two numbers and transforms it into a similarity value, where a high distance refers to a small similarity and vice versa. The time attribute is compared using the cyclic distance in order to match similar time of day. All attributes, that refer to an instance in the knowledge graph, in particular those that are arranged in a taxonomic order, are compared using semantic similarity [12]. The elements in the set of additional information are mapped to each other through using the local similarity functions. Here, the best mapping is searched for, such that if an additional information is present in both cases, the global similarity value increases. All local similarity values are provided with weights and aggregated to one global *incident* similarity.

Based on these defined similarity measures, a retrieval is performed to determine the most relevant cases for the query. The efficiency of the retrieval algorithm is one of the decisive factors for achieving a short response time due to the time-critical nature of emergency call response, addressing requirement **R1**. A suitable method that can be well applied to the concept is MAC-FAC retrieval. MAC-FAC stands for "Many Are Called - Few Are Chosen" and is a two-stage retrieval approach [10]. The MAC stage consists of a preselection that is done through an efficient similarity assessment. In the presented concept, the case base is searched for cases, that have the same value for `incident type`, while other attributes are not considered at all, as these cases differ rather than those of the same incident type. In the second stage, the FAC stage, the selected cases are sorted in descending order of similarity to the entire query with all its information. Here, we chose to determine those cases that have a similarity value with a maximum variance of 5% of the highest similarity value in order to prevent fixation errors and include other options depending on the further development of the information situation.

Furthermore, we included a weighting of attributes depending on the type of incident, as certain information has a higher influence on the measure and resource type, for e.g. *traffic accidents*, the position can indicate the severeness of the crash, like a busy intersection with potential hazards, and imply the need for stronger rescue equipment. For individual medical emergencies the age, gender and suspected diagnosis is of higher relevance.

Another important aspect of comparing cases in the emergency domain as sketched before is that there are many possible attributes and many unknown attribute values. Here, we apply the strategy of excluding values in the similarity assessment for addressing requirement **R7**, as an optimistic or pessimistic strategy would distort the global similarity value.

4.3   Reuse

As described before, those cases with a similarity value with a maximum variance of 5% of the highest similarity value are selected for reuse. As solution for the dispatcher, either measure and resource type or, if the measure is already available in the query, only the resource type of the most similar case is proposed.

In some cases, adaptation is necessary. We identified some straightforward rules that are applied. One aspect that was mentioned in the interviews where future situations can learn from historical cases was re-disposition, which means that initially too few or inadequate resources were sent, such that at a later time, additional or other resources had to be dispatched. These situations are implicitly covered by the used data structure, as there are no timestamps for when resources were sent, but only the total amount of dispatched resources are stored. Thus, if a case is reused, the total amount of resources is directly adopted without knowing if it was a result of a re-disposition in the past.

One simple adaptation rule that is applied concerns the amount of resources, as for each affected person one resource should be sent. For instance, in case of a traffic accident with a number of affected persons that differs slightly, but the rest of the case is highly similar, the resource types are adopted, but the number of resources is adapted accordingly.

Another adaptation rule prevents under-disposition. If the vital signs specified in the query are false, such that not all vital signs of the affected person are given, but the vital signs in the retrieved and most similar case are true and no emergency service vehicle or a rescue helicopter was dispatched in that case, then the reused resources are overwritten through either an emergency ambulance or a rescue helicopter. This rule is derived from the dispatcher aid of the Kaiserslautern Integrated Control Center [25], which describes, that threats for vital signs always require an emergency physician.

4.4   Deriving Relevant Questions

Furthermore, it is analyzed how certain this proposed decision is according to the available historical cases, referring to requirements **R2** and **R5**. Therefore, all cases in the retrieved set of cases are used for validating the decision, which means it is checked whether all cases share the same measure and resource type. If this is not the case, then the decision might be altered if more information is available. An example for such a situation is shown in Fig. 5. Here, three cases are retrieved with almost the same similarity value, but differing measures. If the most similar case would only be consulted for a disposition decision, an under-disposition might happen. However, the given information whether diabetes is present would lead to an unmistakable decision according to the cases. If the affected person suffers from diabetes, this would indicate a silent heart attack and an emergency medication is necessary. Otherwise the diagnosis would be far less severe and a transport would be sufficient.

To this end, we propose a mechanism that is applied for deriving attributes with so far unknown values in the query, that might be decisive for a decision. Through identifying relevant questions, the proposed approach is extended to a conversational CBR (CCBR) approach [2]. Here, the dispatcher decides whether to ask further questions and subsequently triggering the case-based component again in order to support the decision, in contrast to traditional CCBR

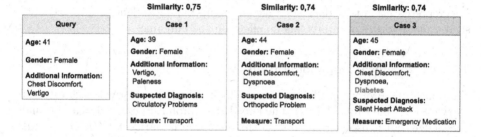

Fig. 5. Retrieval with Similar Cases and a Decisive Information

approaches, where the systems decide by themselves whether to stop asking for more information and propose decisions. Therefore, the following steps are made:

1. Identify the goal of decision which is either the measure or resource type in case the measure is already specified in the query.
2. Evaluate, whether this goal differs in the retrieved cases. If not, the decision based on the cases is certain and no attribute to question is proposed.
3. Otherwise identify all attributes, that are unknown in the query, but specified in one of the cases.
4. Apply an attribute selection strategy for all these attributes considering the goal of decision.
5. Propose this identified attribute to the dispatcher to ask the caller about its value in order to increase the certainty for the decision.
6. If the dispatcher decides to ask about the attribute value and obtains a new information, the retrieval is triggered again for a revision of the proposals for a disposition decision.

Several existing strategies could be applied for identifying the attribute that allows for a more efficient discrimination of similar cases and thus, increase the certainty of the decision. Some first ideas are sketched in the following.

An established measure from information theory that could be applied is the entropy that could be assessed for each attribute [23]. Through this, the expectation of the information gain of a known value for an attribute is measured.

Kohlmaier et al. developed an approach specifically for CCBR that utilizes the similarity influence of an attribute in order to determine relevant information [14]. Furthermore, McSherry proposes a lightweight local feature selection strategy based on n similar retrieved cases through computing the discriminating power of one attribute in the medical domain [19]. Which strategy fits the domain of emergency call handling best and which small adjustments are necessary, needs to be evaluated in future work.

While requirements **R3** and **R8** were not considered until now through integrating specific aspects in the concept, they are met through the case-based approach itself. Requirement **R8** is addressed through using the concept of similarity that is able to assess similar results, rather than rules that are hardly able to allow vagueness. Furthermore, requirement **R3** is implicitly met through the case representation that does not take any temporal dependencies into account, such that the order of inputs has no effect on the outcome.

4.5   Prototypical Implementation

The concept is prototypically implemented with the process-oriented case-based knowledge engine ProCAKE [7]. The knowledge graph is integrated as additional knowledge that is used for computing the semantic similarity. ProCAKE itself is connected to the SPELL platform through an implemented API that can receive and send data. This implementation was used so far as proof-of-concept, while all requirements could be met at least partially. For this, we modelled several exemplary emergency calls as cases in cooperation with experts and simulated different aspects of the concept. The experiment showed that the integration of the MAC-FAC approach led to decreased retrieval times (85%) compared to a sequential retrieval. Nevertheless, an evaluation of utility with the rating of experts remains open and will be addressed in future work.

5   Conclusion

In this paper we presented an approach towards a case-based support for emergency call handling, that proposes measures to be taken and resources to be dispatched. Furthermore, we described a mechanism to provide information to the dispatcher about what question to ask to increase the certainty of the proposed decisions. Moreover, we sketched the pursued hybrid AI approach towards integrating rule-based and case-based reasoning for emergency call handling. The presented work focused on the technical implementation of the case-based decision support. In future work, we plan to investigate the necessary reconciliation mechanism for this hybrid AI approach in case both single approaches deliver different results.

A so far ignored aspect is the acceptance and trust of the dispatcher. Therefore, a further focus will be laid upon an adequate visual integration of the decision proposals in the existing user interface of the rule-based emergency call handling. To this end, the mental workload of the call-taker should be at the center of attention in terms of not overloading but focus on the most important information with explanation in order to increase trust [15].

Besides, the prototypical implementation of the approach will be evaluated in real scenarios with experts that simulate an emergency call handling process.

So far, the approach mainly focused on medical emergencies. A possible transfer of the proposed approach to non-medical emergencies, such as firefighting-related ones, will be investigated.

Acknowledgements. This work is funded by the Federal Ministry for Economic Affairs and Climate Action (BMWK) under grant no. M01MK21005A *SPELL*.

References

1. Report from the commission to the European parliament and the council on the effectiveness of the implementation of the single European emergency number '112'. Technical report, European Commission (2022)
2. Aha, D.W., Breslow, L., Muñoz-Avila, H.: Conversational case-based reasoning. Appl. Intell. **14**(1), 9–32 (2001)
3. Althoff, K., et al.: Case-based reasoning for medical decision support tasks: the Inreca approach. Artif. Intell. Med. **12**(1), 25–41 (1998)
4. Amailef, K., Lu, J.: Ontology-supported case-based reasoning approach for intelligent m-Government emergency response services. Decis. Support Syst. **55**(1), 79–97 (2013)
5. Bannour, W., Maalel, A., Ghézala, H.H.B.: Case-based reasoning for crisis response: case representation and case retrieval. In: Cristani, M., Toro, C., Zanni-Merk, C., Howlett, R.J., Jain, L.C. (eds.) Knowledge-Based and Intelligent Information & Engineering Systems: Proceedings of the 24th International Conference KES-2020, Virtual Event, 16–18 September 2020 (2020). Procedia Comput. Sci. **176**, 1063–1072. Elsevier (2020)
6. Bannour, W., Maalel, A., Ghézala, H.H.B.: Emergency management case-based reasoning systems: a survey of recent developments. J. Exp. Theor. Artif. Intell. **35**(1), 35–58 (2023)
7. Bergmann, R., Grumbach, L., Malburg, L., Zeyen, C.: ProCAKE: a process-oriented case-based reasoning framework. In: Kapetanakis, S., Borck, H. (eds.) Workshops Proceedings for the Twenty-Seventh International Conference on Case-Based Reasoning Co-Located with the Twenty-Seventh International Conference on Case-Based Reasoning (ICCBR 2019). CEUR Workshop Proceedings, Otzenhausen, Germany, 8–12 September 2019, vol. 2567, pp. 156–161. CEUR-WS.org (2019)
8. Chang, D., Fan, R., Sun, Z.: A deep belief network and case reasoning based decision model for emergency rescue. Int. J. Comput. Commun. Control **15**(3) (2020)
9. Feng, Y., Xiang-Yang, L.: Improving emergency response to cascading disasters: applying case-based reasoning towards urban critical infrastructure. Int. J. Disaster Risk Reduction **30**, 244–256 (2018). Understanding and mitigating cascading crises in the global interconnected system
10. Forbus, K.D., Gentner, D., Law, K.: MAC/FAC: a model of similarity-based retrieval. Cogn. Sci. **19**(2), 141–205 (1995)
11. Hackstein, A., Sudowe, H.: Handbuch Leitstelle: Strukturen - Prozesse - Innovationen. Stumpf + Kossendey Verlag (2017)
12. Harispe, S., Ranwez, S., Janaqi, S., Montmain, J.: Semantic Similarity from Natural Language and Ontology Analysis. Synthesis Lectures on Human Language Technologies. Morgan & Claypool Publishers (2015)
13. Hegenberg, K., Trentzsch, H., Prückner, S.: Differences between cases admitted to hospital and discharged from the emergency department after emergency medical services transport. BMJ Open **9**(9), e030636 (2019)
14. Kohlmaier, A., Schmitt, S., Bergmann, R.: A similarity-based approach to attribute selection in user-adaptive sales dialogs. In: Aha, D.W., Watson, I. (eds.) ICCBR 2001. LNCS (LNAI), vol. 2080, pp. 306–320. Springer, Heidelberg (2001). https://doi.org/10.1007/3-540-44593-5_22

15. Maletzki, C., Elsenbast, C., Reuter-Oppermann, M.: Towards human-AI interaction in medical emergency call handling. In: Bui, T.X. (ed.) 57th Hawaii International Conference on System Sciences, HICSS 2024, Hilton Hawaiian Village Waikiki Beach Resort, Hawaii, USA, 3–6 January 2024, pp. 3374–3383. ScholarSpace (2024)

16. Maletzki, C., Grumbach, L., Rietzke, E., Bergmann, R.: Towards hybrid intelligent support systems for emergency call handling. In: Martin, A., et al. (eds.) Proceedings of the AAAI 2023 Spring Symposium on Challenges Requiring the Combination of Machine Learning and Knowledge Engineering (AAAI-MAKE 2023). CEUR Workshop Proceedings, Hyatt Regency, San Francisco Airport, California, USA, 27–29 March 2023, vol. 3433. CEUR-WS.org (2023)

17. Maletzki, C., Rietzke, E., Bergmann, R.: Utilizing expert knowledge to support medical emergency call handling. In: Beierle, C., Ragni, M., Stolzenburg, F., Sauerwald, K., Thimm, M. (eds.) Proceedings of the 8th Workshop on Formal and Cognitive Reasoning Co-Located with the 45th German Conference on Artificial Intelligence (KI 2022). CEUR Workshop Proceedings, Virtual Event, Trier, Germany, 19 September 2022, vol. 3242, pp. 79–89. CEUR-WS.org (2022)

18. Mayr, B.: Strukturierte bzw. standardisierte Notrufabfrage. Notfall + Rettungsmedizin 23(7), 505–512 (2020)

19. McSherry, D.: Conversational case-based reasoning in medical decision making. Artif. Intell. Med. 52(2), 59–66 (2011)

20. Möhrle, S.: Case-based decision support for disaster management. Ph.D. thesis, Karlsruhe Institute of Technology, Germany (2020)

21. Møller, T.P., Jensen, H.G., Viereck, S., Lippert, F., Østergaaard, D.: Medical dispatchers' perception of the interaction with the caller during emergency calls - a qualitative study. Scand. J. Trauma Resuscitation Emerg. Med. 29(1), 45 (2021)

22. Prentzas, J., Hatzilygeroudis, I.: Categorizing approaches combining rule-based and case-based reasoning. Expert Syst. J. Knowl. Eng. 24(2), 97–122 (2007)

23. Quinlan, J.R.: C4.5: Programs for Machine Learning. Morgan Kaufmann (1993)

24. Rietzke, E.: Modellierung, Visualisierung und Ausführung wissensintensiver Prozesse unter Verwendung Semantischer Technologien. Doctoralthesis, Universität Trier (2021)

25. Stadt Kaiserslautern: Die qualifizierte Notrufabfrage der Integrierten Leitstelle Kaiserslautern. Referat Feuerwehr und Katastrophenschutz, Abt. 37.5 Information und Kommunikation - Integrierte Leitstelle pp. 1–9. Accessed 31 Dec 2023

26. Vivacqua, A.S., Borges, M.R.S.: Taking advantage of collective knowledge in emergency response systems. J. Netw. Comput. Appl. 35(1), 189–198 (2012)

27. Wang, D., Wan, K., Ma, W.: Emergency decision-making model of environmental emergencies based on case-based reasoning method. J. Environ. Manag. 262, 110382 (2020)

28. Yao, X., Guo, H.X., Zhu, J., Shi, Y.: Dynamic selection of emergency plans of geological disaster based on case-based reasoning and prospect theory. Nat. Hazards 110, 2249–2275 (2021)

CBRkit: An Intuitive Case-Based Reasoning Toolkit for Python

Mirko Lenz[1,2(✉)] ⓘ, Lukas Malburg[1,2] ⓘ, and Ralph Bergmann[1,2] ⓘ

[1] Trier University, Universitätsring 15, 54296 Trier, Germany
`info@mirko-lenz.de`, {`malburgl,bergmann`}`@uni-trier.de`
[2] German Research Center for Artificial Intelligence (DFKI), Branch Trier University, Behringstraße 21, 54296 Trier, Germany
{`mirko.lenz,lukas.malburg,ralph.bergmann`}`@dfki.de`

Abstract. Developing Case-Based Reasoning (CBR) applications is a complex and demanding task that requires a lot of experience and a deep understanding of users. Additionally, current CBR frameworks are not as usable as Machine Learning (ML) frameworks that can be deployed with only a few lines of code. To address these problems and allow users to easily build hybrid Artificial Intelligence (AI) systems by combining CBR with techniques such as ML, we present the CBRkit library in this paper. CBRkit is a Python-based framework that provides generic and easily extensible functions to simplify the creation of CBR applications with advanced similarity measures and case representations. The framework is available from GitHub and PyPI under the permissive MIT license. An initial user study indicates that it is easily possible even for non-CBR experts and users who only have limited Python programming skills to develop their own customized CBR application.

Keywords: Case-Based Reasoning · Machine Learning · Hybrid AI · CBR Frameworks · Python Library

1 Introduction

Building Case-Based Reasoning (CBR) [1,17] applications is a demanding and complex task. In addition to the fact that a lot of expertise and knowledge is required to encode cases, similarity measures, possible adaptations, and vocabulary, it is also a challenge to use a CBR framework itself. This is particularly relevant when teaching novices, such as students, the use of CBR with the help of frameworks. With the recent rise in Machine Learning (ML) applications, Python has become an increasingly popular choice due to its simple yet expressive syntax combined with the wide selection of libraries such as NumPy and PyTorch. However, we observe a lack of Python-based CBR frameworks that are easy to use and powerful enough to suit more advanced use cases. This disparity leads to a situation where CBR researchers cannot experiment with up-to-date ML approaches without resorting to complex workarounds, such as using web

J. A. Recio-Garcia et al. (Eds.): ICCBR 2024, LNAI 14775, pp. 289–304, 2024.
https://doi.org/10.1007/978-3-031-63646-2_19

requests to integrate custom models. At the same time, data scientists and ML engineers are missing out on features that most CBR systems naturally provide, including complex case representations and similarity measures.

In an effort to make ML techniques easier to use by CBR researchers and expand the CBR community to more users, including students and data scientists, we present the CBRKIT library. This Python-based toolkit aims to reduce the effort needed to build a case-based application and instead allows the user to focus on solving the problem at hand. CBRKIT is available from PyPI and can be easily installed via pip without requiring any further configuration. The library allows for simple import of existing case bases in various formats, provides an extensive set of similarity measures, and allows the definition of custom functionality by a fully typed and generic Application Programming Interface (API). In the first version of CBRKIT, we focus on the retrieval step in the CBR cycle—that is, finding the most relevant cases given some query from a user. This paper contains the following contributions: (i) An analysis of existing Python-based CBR libraries/frameworks, (ii) a high-level overview of the CBRKIT framework and usage examples, and (iii) a user study comparing the proposed CBRKIT with the established Java-based PROCAKE [4] framework.

The remainder of this paper is structured as follows: Sect. 2 introduces the integration of CBR and ML, followed by a discussion of related work in Sect. 3. Section 4 introduced the CBRKIT framework that is evaluated by a user study in Sect. 5. Finally, Sect. 6 concludes the paper and presents future work.

2   Foundations

Recently, ML frameworks are widely used in academia and practice because they are easy to use. Particularly in research, hybrid Artificial Intelligence (AI) systems combining ML with other AI techniques are gaining importance, limiting, for example, the need for a large amount of qualitative data for ML or for increasing the accuracy of the complete hybrid AI system. One possibility of creating a hybrid AI system is to combine ML and CBR. In the following, we describe how CBR can benefit from the integration of ML and vice versa.

Integrating ML in CBR. As CBR is an analogy-based reasoning method [1], it inherently relies on a suitable definition of a vocabulary and the corresponding similarity measures based on the defined vocabulary. Consequently, CBR applications benefit from the knowledge defined in similarity measures during inference, as they are specially tailored to certain attributes and their types [3]. In addition, the similarity assessment is more precise because it is based on the local-global principle, which states that the similarity between cases is calculated based on the similarity of individual attributes (i.e., local similarities), and subsequently the overall similarity is calculated by an aggregation function (i.e., global similarity) [1]. Using this principle, it is possible to individually decide which similarity measures should be used and applied for certain attributes. ML can be used in this context to automatically learn similarity measures [8,9,19,20] or weights for local similarities during the retain phase.

These structure-aware measures can be expensive to compute, which is why the MAC/FAC *(many are called, but few are chosen)* pattern [7] may be used to discard irrelevant cases early in the retrieval phase. Here, ML could be used as the backbone of the MAC phase—for instance, through a custom classifier that predicts the similarity values of the FAC phase. Another possible integration of ML into the CBR methodology is the use of methods from Natural Language Processing (NLP) [2] in the context of textual CBR—for instance, by computing the similarity of textual attributes with embeddings [5]. With Large Language Models (LLMs) becoming more advanced, it also becomes possible to integrate them in other stages such as the reuse step [10], leading to the development of hybrid CBR applications.

Integrating CBR in ML. The revival of using ML is mainly driven by the high data availability in the context of Big Data today. Based on that data, a suitable ML model can be trained and used in an application. For this purpose, several ML frameworks such as PyTorch or Scikit-learn are publicly available and can be easily used. However, only a few methods are available for using analogy-based reasoning techniques in these frameworks—for instance, Scikit-learn only provides simple nearest-neighbor algorithms for regression tasks. In this context, the ML community could profit from using CBR in ML for having more sophisticated techniques in analogy-based reasoning. One such technique that goes beyond the use of classic nearest-neighbor algorithms is the application of adaptation methods in CBR by which ML can significantly benefit. Furthermore, the retrieval techniques of CBR can be combined with Retrieval-Augmented Generation (RAG) [11] to improve the capabilities of generative LLMs. Finally, CBR may be part of Explainable Artificial Intelligence (XAI) approaches—for instance, to help explain black-box models like deep neural networks [16,21].

3 Requirements and Related Work

Before presenting our proposed CBRKIT library, we first present requirements that must be satisfied by a Python-based CBR framework to be easy to use and applicable in the use cases sketched in Sect. 2. For this purpose, we analyze existing Python-based CBR frameworks in the context of these requirements.

3.1 Requirements

Due to the lack of literature, we systematically derived requirements that should be satisfied by a Python-based CBR library in brainstorming sessions. We also searched for existing Python libraries and collected available features to complete our requirements list. In the following, we first present two general requirements (GR) in the context of software engineering principles, followed by three requirements (R) for CBR software and its integration with ML.

GR 1 (Software Engineering). The software should be available from PyPI to enable easy installation and use type annotations to make the code more maintainable. Its correctness should be ensured by a comprehensive test suite, and documentation to help users get started should be available.

GR 2 (Interoperability). The software should be interoperable with other systems by providing some API. In addition to programmatic access—enabling the use in other Python projects—there should be a Representational State Transfer (REST) API—simplifying the integration in existing systems.

R 1 (High-Level Abstractions). The software should provide built-in functionality for common CBR tasks, such as predefined similarity measures and case representations. Furthermore, the complete CBR cycle should be available in high-level function calls—for instance, through generic retrieval functions that allow for the combination of sequential retrievals such as MAC/FAC, generic adaptation functions that are applied automatically, or generic retain methods that adapt weights and similarities measures through ML techniques.

R 2 (Low-Level Customization). In addition to high-level functions, the software should enable advanced use cases through custom extensions—for instance, through abstract interfaces for similarity measures and the ability to use complex case representations with validation logic. It should be possible to combine such extensions with the built-in ones in the same application.

R 3 (Integration with ML Frameworks). The software should allow easy integration with established ML frameworks, such as NumPy, pandas, and PyTorch. It should be possible to combine established CBR measures such as taxonomies with ML-based ones such as embeddings, depending on the case representation. The framework should provide a programmatic interface that allows deep integration with ML libraries—for instance, by accepting data types such as NumPy arrays and using similar function signatures.

3.2 Analysis of Related Work

The selection and evaluation of the CBR frameworks is based on the review of GitHub and PyPI for CBR frameworks.[1]. In addition, we include Python-based CBR frameworks from the study of Schultheis et al. [18] in our analysis.[2] The results are summarized in Table 1 and described in the following. A detailed analysis of CBRKIT is provided in Sect. 4.2.

Clood CBR. The cloud-based CBR framework CLOOD CBR [15] can be used to develop textual and structural CBR applications. It provides several built-in similarity measures (e. g., for strings, numerics, and categorical values). In addition, it supports the complete CBR cycle with generic methods—for instance,

---

[1] PyArgCBR (https://github.com/jaumejordan/pyargcbr) is not considered as it is not actively maintained, lacks documentation, and specializes in argumentation.

[2] With our goal of integrating CBR and ML, tools in other languages are excluded.

Table 1. Requirement analysis of existing Python-based CBR frameworks with ✓ meaning *fulfilled*, ✓/✗ meaning *partially fulfilled*, and ✗ meaning *not fulfilled*.

Framework	Engineering (GR1)	Interoperability (GR2)	Abstraction (R1)	Customization (R2)	ML (R3)
Clood CBR	✓/✗	✓/✗	✓	✓/✗	✓/✗
pycbr	✗	✓/✗	✓/✗	✓	✓/✗
cbrlib	✓/✗	✓/✗	✓/✗	✓	✓/✗
CBRKIT	✓	✓	✓/✗	✓	✓

a MAC/FAC retriever is available (R1). Creating customized case representations is possible, but support for custom similarity measures and generic retrieval pipelines is lacking (R2). Some ML frameworks like sentence-transformers are natively integrated with the application, but adding new ones is not straightforward (R3). Documentation is available on a dedicated website, but the code does not use type annotations, and tests are only available for the frontend part of the application (GR1). For accessing the framework, a REST API is available. Being optimized for the cloud use case, the library does not include support for programmatic use and is also not available from PyPI (GR2).

pycbr. The library pycbr[3] describes itself as a microframework for CBR applications and, as such, is built for microservice architectures. It provides a set of predefined similarity measures for common data types such as strings and numbers and includes ways to import data, but does not support retrieval pipelines and is limited to the retrieval step (R1). The pycbr library exposes an abstract method for custom similarity measures/attribute types (R2). The framework integrates with some ML libraries (e. g., nltk and Scikit-learn), but more advanced libraries such as transformers are missing, and its programmatic interface is based mainly on classes (R3). The source code does not use type annotations, the documentation must be built manually, and end-to-end tests are missing (GR1). Developed as a microframework, pycbr offers a REST API for interoperability, but programmatic usage is not a focus (GR2).

cbrlib. There exist two versions with a major difference in their overall design: While cbrlib v1 uses a class-based interface with a relatively verbose syntax, cbrlib v2[4] has a functional interface with a more concise syntax. The release of v2 was in March 2024—three months *after* the first public version of CBRKIT. With v1 not receiving updates since 2021, we will focus on v2 in our analysis.

The framework includes some similarity measures, but they are limited in scope (e. g., no specialized functions for strings), and the user is responsible for loading the case base. The library is focused on the retrieval step and provides no straightforward way to implement the MAC/FAC pattern (R1). However, it provides an interface for defining custom similarity measures (R2). Native

---

[3] https://github.com/dih5/pycbr.
[4] https://github.com/cdein/cbrlib.

integration with ML frameworks is not provided, but the functional approach leads to a programmatic interface that should be familiar to data scientists (R3). The code uses type annotations and is tested, but no documentation is available except for a few examples. The framework makes extensive use of the Python method `functools.partial` to parameterize the built-in measures, which may be less intuitive for inexperienced Python users (GR1). A REST API is not available, but the library can be used programmatically (GR2).

4   CBRkit Framework

Based on our requirements and the analysis of existing Python-based CBR systems, we developed the CBRKIT framework. It has been engineered from the ground up for modern Python features and is designed to be easy to use, yet flexible enough to support advanced use cases. CBRKIT uses a *compositional* and *functional* approach of declaring similarity measures, which means that complex ones can be built from simple building blocks. The source code is publicly available on GitHub under the MIT license with releases published to PyPI.[5] In the following section, we first provide an overview of the main components of CBRKIT followed by an analysis of the requirements defined in Sect. 3.

4.1   Conceptual Overview

The overall goal of CBRKIT is to provide a Python-based framework that simplifies the development of CBR applications. In the first version of the framework, we focus on the retrieval step and, thus, address three main aspects: (i) The representation of cases and queries, (ii) the definition of similarity measures, and (iii) the retrieval of similar cases. These fundamental building blocks will eventually allow for the implementation of more advanced features, such as a generic interface for adaptation techniques.

In the following, we demonstrate how CBRKIT can be used to retrieve similar cases based on a query. As an application scenario, we use the cars domain from previous work [13]. The case base consists of millions of cars and their attributes, such as paint color, mileage, and manufacturer. Due to the large number of cases, the MAC/FAC pattern [7] is used. In the following, we provide a fully working example in Listing 1, containing both simple and advanced patterns, which are discussed in the following section. It also shows that CBRKIT makes it possible to implement a two-stage retrieval with a custom similarity measure in approximately 50 lines of code, regardless of whether the user wants to use simple knowledge-poor similarity measures or knowledge-intensive ones based on taxonomies or ontologies [19].

Case Representation. In CBRKIT, a case base is modeled as a dictionary— that is, a collection of key-value pairs. The keys represent the name (or unique

---

```
1   import cbrkit
2   import pandas as pd
3
4   df = pd.read_csv("casebase.csv")
5   casebase = cbrkit.loaders.dataframe(df)
6   query = pd.Series({
7     "miles": 20000,
8     "year": 2010,
9     "model": {"make": "a4", "manufacturer": "audi"},
10    "engine": {"fuel": "gas"},
11    "paint_color": "red",
12  })
13
14  def miles_similarity(x: int, y: int) -> float:
15    if abs(x - y) < 10000:
16      return 1.0
17    elif abs(x - y) < 25000:
18      return 0.7
19
20    return 0.0
21
22  mac_sim = cbrkit.sim.attribute_value(
23    attributes={
24      "paint_color": cbrkit.sim.generic.equality(),
25    },
26  )
27
28  fac_sim = cbrkit.sim.attribute_value(
29    types={
30      str: cbrkit.sim.strings.spacy("en_core_web_lg"),
31      int: cbrkit.sim.numbers.linear(max=9999999),
32    },
33    attributes={
34      "miles": miles_similarity,
35      "model": cbrkit.sim.attribute_value(
36        attributes={
37          "make": cbrkit.sim.strings.levenshtein(),
38          "manufacturer": cbrkit.sim.strings.taxonomy.load(
39            "cars-taxonomy.yaml",
40            measure=cbrkit.sim.strings.taxonomy.wu_palmer(),
41          ),
42        }
43      ),
44      "engine": cbrkit.sim.attribute_value(
45        types={str: cbrkit.sim.strings.openai("text-embedding-3-large")}
46      ),
47    },
48    aggregator=cbrkit.sim.aggregator(
49      pooling="mean",
50      pooling_weights={"miles": 0.5, "model": 0.3},
51      default_pooling_weight=1.0,
52    ),
53  )
54
55  mac_retriever = cbrkit.retrieval.build(mac_sim, min_similarity=1.0)
56  fac_retriever = cbrkit.retrieval.build(fac_sim, limit=10)
57
58  result = cbrkit.retrieval.apply(casebase, query, [mac_retriever,
        fac_retriever])
```

Listing 1. Full example of a retrieval with CBRkit. The case base uses an object-oriented representation with nested attributes. The code contains two advanced patterns: A custom similarity function for the attribute miles and the use of multiple retrievers to apply the MAC/FAC pattern.

```
1   def threshold_sim(threshold: float):
2     def wrapped_func(x: int, y: int) -> float:
3       return 1.0 if abs(x - y) <= threshold else 0.0
4
5     return wrapped_func
```

Listing 2. Example definition of a similarity function for integers showcasing the functional pattern used in CBRKIT.

identifier) of a case, while the value may have an arbitrary structure. A fundamental assumption of CBRKIT is that the query has the same type as the cases—otherwise, the similarity measure would not be applicable. In the application scenario used, an object-oriented case representation with nested attributes is used, such as the model and engine of a car. The cases are stored in a CSV file that is first loaded into a pandas DataFrame (Line 4) and then converted (Line 5). The query could also be loaded from a file, but is defined directly in the code for simplicity (Line 6). The structure of cases can be validated through an integration with the popular Pydantic library (omitted for brevity).

Similarity Measures. The library provides a set of built-in similarity measures for common data types, such as strings and numbers, but also allows the definition of custom ones. In CBRKIT, a similarity measure is defined as a mathematical function f that receives two arguments $x, y \in T$ of the same type T and returns a similarity value between 0 and 1—that is, $f: T \times T \to [0, 1]$. To improve efficiency when working with ML models, CBRKIT allows for batch processing of multiple values at once. In this case, the function f' expects a list with tuples of values and returns an ordered list of similarity values—that is, $f': \{T \times T, \ldots\} \to \{[0, 1], \ldots\}$. Implementation-wise, similarity measures are implemented as nested functions, allowing for the parameterization of the measure. An example of a relatively simple numeric measure is shown in Listing 2. Here, the outer function expects a threshold value and returns an inner function that implements the actual similarity measure and thus conforms to the previously defined signature $f: T \times T \to [0, 1]$. As a result, the function `threshold_sim` needs to be called twice:(i)to create a similarity measure with a specific threshold and (ii) to actually calculate the similarity between two values.

The same pattern is used in CBRKIT to implement seemingly more complex similarity measures, especially the one for attribute-value data types. Since the cars domain uses an object-oriented case representation, this function is used both for the MAC phase (Line 22) and for the FAC phase (Line 28). It allows the user to apply similarity functions based on an attribute's type (Line 29) and/or name (Line 33). Local similarities can be aggregated into a global one using an aggregation function (Line 48). In the given example, the unweighted arithmetic mean is used as an aggregation function in the MAC phase, while a weighted version is applied in the FAC phase. The result of the attribute-value similarity function is a method that complies with the previously defined signature, which means that it can even be used for nested attributes (Line 35). This definition style has the additional advantage of providing visual cues for the structure of the similarity measure, making it easier to understand and maintain.

CBRKIT comes with numerous built-in similarity measures, including generic objects, collections, numbers, and strings. With the rise of language models, the latter category has seen numerous changes. Consequently, we include not only *traditional* measures such as Levenshtein distance-based or taxonomy-based ones, but also more recent approaches such as text embeddings from popular NLP libraries like spaCy (Line 30) and OpenAI (Line 44). At the same time, we are aware that it is never possible to cover all available similarity measures, so we provide an easy way to define custom ones: Users simply need to define a function that conforms to the previously defined signature and can be used in the same way as the built-in ones. In the example used, the car dealer wanted to use a non-standard measure to compare the attribute *miles* and thus defined a custom function (Line 14). Note that instead of calling the function in Line 34, it is passed as a reference since it does not contain an inner function.

Retrieval. With both the cases loaded and the similarity measures defined, the final step is to perform the actual retrieval. In our two-stage scenario, we first apply the MAC phase with a minimum similarity of 1.0 (Line 55). In this pre-filter, we only consider cars that have exactly the same paint color that the user is searching for (i. e., red) and enforce this by setting the minimum similarity to 1.0. The FAC retriever is set to return at most ten cars (Line 56) so that the user is not overwhelmed with too many results. The result of the retrieval (Line 58) is an object containing the global similarity scores and the imposed ranking. For advanced use cases, it is also possible to inspect the result of each retriever individually and even obtain the local similarity values for each attribute.

4.2   Requirements Analysis

Having introduced the central concepts of CBRKIT through an end-to-end example, we now analyze the framework based on the requirements defined in Sect. 3.1. The library offers a suite of built-in similarity measures that may be parameterized to fit the user's needs, includes abstractions to implement the MAC/FAC pattern, and also offers methods to load case bases in common data formats. Our library focuses on the retrieval step, which means that the remaining phases need to be implemented manually (R1). Custom similarity functions are first-class citizens in CBRKIT and can be easily defined and used in conjunction with built-in ones. By providing multiple retrieval functions, it is possible to build arbitrarily complex pipelines that go beyond the two-stage MAC/FAC pattern (R2). CBRKIT is designed to be used in conjunction with established ML frameworks and provides native integrations with pandas, spaCy, sentence-transformers, and other popular libraries. Its functional design resembles the programmatic interface of these frameworks to make it easier for data scientists to start (R3). The code is fully typed and makes extensive use of generics for best-in-class type safety and completion support in modern Integrated Development Environments (IDEs). The library contains a comprehensive test suite—including end-to-end ones—and contains documentation for its public interface.

Together with a detailed tutorial, the documentation is available as a static website. CBRKIT uses NIX [6] to ensure reproducibility and utilizes a Continuous Integration (CI) pipeline to automatically publish new releases based on conventional commit messages (GR1). The framework can be consumed through a REST API, a Command Line Interface (CLI), or directly imported into other Python projects, making it interoperable with third-party systems. To simplify deployment, a ready-to-use Docker image is provided (GR2).

5   User Study

While in theory, CBRKIT meets the requirements of data scientists, CBR researchers, and students, it is essential to evaluate the usability of the framework in practice. As part of our investigation of related work, we identified a lack of evaluations: In many cases, new tools are only introduced but not tested in a real-world scenario. To address this, we conducted a user study comparing the proposed CBRKIT with the established Java-based PROCAKE framework, which is also developed in our department. While a complete evaluation would only be possible once CBRKIT has matured and has been used in a variety of projects, this first study tries to assess whether our library is even considered to be a suitable CBR framework by our target audience. After analyzing what requirements are met by PROCAKE, in the following we will describe the experimental setup, present the results, and discuss the implications of the findings.

Among the frameworks discussed by Schultheis et al. [18], PROCAKE has been selected because it has extensive documentation and tests (GR1), and provides a programmatic interface as well as a REST API (GR2). In addition, it includes a suite of similarity measures, but does not provide generic functions for the complete CBR cycle (R1). The MAC/FAC pattern is supported, but support for generic pipelines is missing, and even though complex case representations can be used, custom similarity measures are difficult to integrate, as they must be registered in proprietary classes (R2). Being a Java-based framework, integration with ML frameworks is not straightforward (R3). Choosing our internal framework enables us to recruit people with three different backgrounds: Core developers of PROCAKE, computer science students familiar with PROCAKE, and data science students having (almost) no prior experience with CBR.

5.1   Experimental Setup

The study has been conducted in a controlled environment through a reproducible Virtual Machine (VM) built using NIX. The image contained all the necessary software: A desktop environment, the JetBrains IDEs PyCharm and IntelliJ, and the CBRKIT and the PROCAKE libraries with their respective documentation. The study was carried out with v0.6.1 of CBRKIT and v5.0 of PROCAKE. The code to generate the image is publicly available on GitHub[6] in

---

[6] https://github.com/wi2trier/cbr-vm.

an effort to simplify the setup of future user studies in the CBR community. It can be used to create VMs that are compatible with VirtualBox, QEMU/KVM, and Proxmox. In the study, we used Proxmox to host the VM on a server in our department, which was accessible via Remote Desktop Protocol (RDP).

In total, we recruited twelve participants, each receiving a voucher worth 10€ as compensation. The survey was conducted on-site for two days with six participants each. Based on the car domain application scenario, we have specified a set of tasks designed to test the features that both CBRKIT and PROCAKE provide. Since CBRKIT and PROCAKE are implemented in different programming languages, we provided code templates for both of them in an effort to abstract them from the underlying implementation.[7] There have been three tasks for both frameworks and one additional task that should only be solved with CBRKIT: (i) Create a structured query for a car with specific attributes, (ii) implement missing similarity measures for two attributes, (iii) create a retrieval pipeline with a MAC and a FAC retriever, and (iv) implement a custom similarity measure for one attribute (only CBRKIT). Since we are dealing with a quite heterogeneous group of participants, we set strict time limits for each task to ensure that all participants had the opportunity to get an impression of both frameworks. Except for the first task (i. e., defining the query), all assignments were designed to be independent of each other so that participants could skip those they had been struggling with. We provided help to those who struggled with the query definition so that they could proceed with the other tasks.

After completing all assignments, the participants were asked to complete a questionnaire. Among others, we asked whether they have been able to solve the tasks, what issues they encountered, and what aspects they liked or disliked about the frameworks. Furthermore, we collected some information about their prior knowledge of Java/Python/CBR. These rating-based questions must be answered on a 5-point Likert scale [12]. Finally, participants could provide free-text feedback on the libraries and the study itself.

5.2 Results and Discussion

The participants' ratings are shown in Fig. 1. In general, the participants rated themselves as more proficient in Java than in Python, while the self-assessment of CBR skills tended to be more balanced (Fig. 1a). CBRKIT has been considered the more viable option for the initial development/prototyping stage and small-scale deployments for individual users or small teams, while PROCAKE has been considered the better choice for large-scale deployments and possibly cloud use cases (Fig. 1b). The responses to the four tasks are mixed (Sect. 5.2): Although the first task has been considered to be easy by most participants, the third has been rated as the most difficult. For all tasks, the scores given to CBRKIT are slightly higher than those given to PROCAKE, for task three, the difference is even more pronounced. Here, no user assigned the highest 5 rating

---

[7] https://github.com/wi2trier/cbrkit-demo and https://gitlab.rlp.net/procake/publications/procake-demos-for-cbrkit-eval-iccbr-2024.

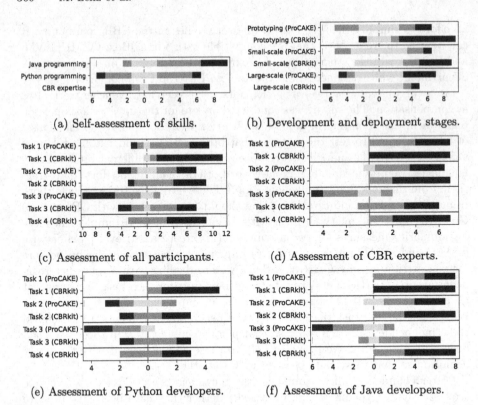

(a) Self-assessment of skills.

(b) Development and deployment stages.

(c) Assessment of all participants.

(d) Assessment of CBR experts.

(e) Assessment of Python developers.

(f) Assessment of Java developers.

Fig. 1. Survey results of Likert scale questions as diverging stacked bar charts centered on neutral responses. Red tones towards the left represent negative scores, whereas blue tones towards the right represent positive scores. (Color figure online)

to PROCAKE, meaning the distribution of the scores ended up skewed towards the left, while the distribution of the scores for CBRKIT has been distributed more evenly. In addition to the difficulty of the tasks, we also asked the participants about the usefulness of the documentation. We found that the scores are almost identical to the difficulty assessed, indicating that documentation plays a central role in making the frameworks accessible to users and even enabling them to solve more complex tasks. With PROCAKE, five participants needed help with the query definition, while only one participant was unable to solve the task on their own with CBRKIT.

To gain additional insights into the results, we also analyzed the responses of the participants based on their self-assessed skills. In the context of this analysis, a participant is deemed an expert if they rated themselves with a 4 or 5 in the respective category. Consequently, there may be some overlap between the groups—for instance, a participant may be equally proficient in Java and Python. When analyzing the ratings of CBR experts (Sect. 5.2), we still see a slight preference for CBRKIT over PROCAKE with a notable difference for task three:

Although there is only a single score below 4 for CBRKIT, only one participant rated PROCAKE with a 4 or higher. The Java developers' ratings (Sect. 5.2) are very similar to those of the CBR experts, with the only difference being that the ratings are slightly lower overall. Python developers (Sect. 5.2) tend to favor CBRKIT even more, with the differences between the systems being more pronounced and no participant rating PROCAKE with a 5 for any task. We also see that familiarity with Python has no direct influence on the ability to implement custom measures (task 4): No CBR expert or Java developer rated the task as difficult, while two Python experts did.

In addition to the Likert scale questions, we also asked the participants about the best and worst aspects of the frameworks and gave them the opportunity to provide free-text feedback. The most common positive aspects of PROCAKE include the Java programming language (namely the type system and the IDE support), the built-in similarity measures, and its modularity. The most common negative aspects have been the large amount of boilerplate code, its overall complexity (e. g., the need for custom classes to declare similarities) and the issues of starting with the framework. The response to the documentation has been mixed, with some participants praising the detailed explanations and others criticizing the lack of examples. Feedback regarding the XML-based configuration has also been twofold: Some liked the clear modeling, but others found it cumbersome to work with.

For CBRKIT, the most common strengths include ease of use, the few lines of code required to implement tasks, and its intuitive design. The most common weaknesses have been Python-related issues (e. g., potential performance issues compared to Java and its general syntax) and the smaller scope compared to PROCAKE (e. g., no adaptation support). Similarly to PROCAKE, the documentation received mixed reviews, with praise from some participants and criticism from others. One user without prior CBR experience reported problems with the use of built-in similarity measures and the implementation of custom ones. Consistent with previous findings, one respondent mentioned that they are more proficient in Java, but still found CBRKIT easy to handle.

In free-text feedback, one participant noted that custom classes have been used for the domain model in PROCAKE, but not for CBRkit. This is a direct consequence of the way similarities are defined in the two frameworks: In PRO-CAKE, similarity measures are linked directly to classes, meaning that custom classes are required if one wants to use different measures for objects of the same type. In CBRKIT, similarities can also be assigned based on an attribute's name, meaning that custom classes are not necessary. As mentioned in Sect. 4, CBRKIT can be integrated with specialized tools such as Pydantic to add schema validation in the case representation if desired.

The same participant also noted that the simple interfaces for common CBR tasks in CBRKIT could in principle be implemented in Java and, thus, PRO-CAKE as well. We fully agree with this assessment and believe that the functional approach used in CBRKIT could serve as a blueprint for future versions of established CBR frameworks. Although there may be certain limitations in Java that make it harder to implement a similar design—mostly due to Java being a compiled language that is centered around classes—such abstract interfaces have already been successfully implemented in the past (e.g., Keras as a high-level API for TensorFlow). At the same time, such a redesign would not solve the lack of support for Python-based ML frameworks, which is a major reason for the development of CBRKIT.

5.3   Limitations

The study has been conducted with a limited number of participants who have been recruited from a single university. Although participants have been selected to represent a wide range of backgrounds, the results may not be generalizable to the broader CBR and ML communities. Furthermore, the study has been based on solving a set of predefined CBR tasks, which may not fully capture the complexity of real-world CBR applications, especially when combined with other ML techniques. Consequently, the results should not be taken as a definitive assessment of the usability of CBRKIT and PROCAKE, but rather as a first indication of how the frameworks are perceived by potential users. To gain a more comprehensive understanding of the frameworks, more studies with a larger and more diverse group of participants are needed.

6   Conclusion and Future Work

The CBRKIT library proposed in this paper is a simple to use Python-based framework, which enables users to easily combine CBR and ML applications. Current Python-based CBR frameworks are partly cumbersome to use and do not provide full support for users—for instance, missing documentation and interoperability difficulties. CBRKIT is based on modern software engineering principles and comes with a comprehensive testing suite and documentation. In an initial user study, we compare CBRKIT with the PROCAKE framework, which is also developed in our department. The study indicates that CBRKIT enables users to easily build their own CBR applications, even if they only have limited knowledge of CBR or the Python programming language. CBRKIT is available from GitHub and PyPI under the permissive MIT license. Moreover, we are open to any kind of contribution to further develop CBRKIT.

In future work, we want to investigate how well CBRKIT can be used to develop hybrid AI systems. For this purpose, we plan to acquire ML experts and give them CBRKIT as an additional tool. In this context, we examine how CBRKIT is used in the future and what feedback we receive from the community and users. Another starting point for future work is the implementation of additional functions for the library. We aim to provide functions for the remaining CBR phases—for instance, a reuse method that enables users to easily adapt retrieved cases. In addition, further similarity measures could be added to the library, including those from popular ML libraries like Scikit-learn. This generic adaptation function could be based on our recent work of using adaptation rules in conjunction with rule engines [14]. Finally, a web interface could be provided to allow novices to develop CBR applications.

Acknowledgments. This work was partly funded by the Deutsche Forschungsgemeinschaft (DFG) within the projects *ReCAP* and *ReCAP-II* (№ 375342983, 2018–2024) as part of the priority program *RATIO* (Robust Argumentation Machines, SPP-1999), the *Studienstiftung*, and the Federal Ministry for Economic Affairs and Climate Action within the project *EASY* (№ 01MD22002C).

References

1. Aamodt, A., Plaza, E.: Case-based reasoning - foundational issues, methodological variations, and system approaches. AI Commun. (1994). https://doi.org/10.3233/AIC-1994-7104
2. Allen, J.F.: Natural language processing. In: Encyclopedia of Computer Science, pp. 1218–1222. Wiley, GBR (2003)
3. Bergmann, R., Goos, G., Hartmanis, J., Van Leeuwen, J., Carbonell, J.G., Siekmann, J. (eds.): Experience Management, Lecture Notes in Computer Science, vol. 2432. Springer, Heidelberg (2002). https://doi.org/10.1007/3-540-45759-3
4. Bergmann, R., Grumbach, L., Malburg, L., Zeyen, C.: ProCAKE: a process-oriented case-based reasoning framework. In: Kapetanakis, S., Borck, H. (eds.) Workshops Proceedings for the Twenty-seventh International Conference on Case-Based Reasoning. CEUR Workshop Proceedings, vol. 2567, pp. 156–161. CEUR, Otzenhausen (2019)
5. Bergmann, R., Lenz, M., Ollinger, S., Pfister, M.: Similarity measures for case-based retrieval of natural language argument graphs in argumentation machines. In: Barták, R., Brawner, K.W. (eds.) Proceedings of the Thirty-Second International Florida Artificial Intelligence Research Society Conference. pp. 329–334. AAAI Press, Sarasota (2019)
6. Dolstra, E.: The purely functional software deployment model. Ph.D. thesis, Utrecht University, Utrecht, The Netherlands (2006)
7. Forbus, K.D., Gentner, D., Law, K.: MAC/FAC - a model of similarity-based retrieval. Cogn. Sci. **19**(2), 141–205 (1995). https://doi.org/10.1207/s15516709cog1902_1
8. Hoffmann, M., Malburg, L., Klein, P., Bergmann, R.: Using Siamese graph neural networks for similarity-based retrieval in process-oriented case-based reasoning. In: Watson, I., Weber, R. (eds.) ICCBR 2020. LNCS (LNAI), vol. 12311, pp. 229–244. Springer, Cham (2020). https://doi.org/10.1007/978-3-030-58342-2_15
9. Klein, P., Malburg, L., Bergmann, R.: Learning workflow embeddings to improve the performance of similarity-based retrieval for process-oriented case-based reasoning. In: Bach, K., Marling, C. (eds.) ICCBR 2019. LNCS (LNAI), vol. 11680, pp. 188–203. Springer, Cham (2019). https://doi.org/10.1007/978-3-030-29249-2_13
10. Lenz, M., Bergmann, R.: Case-based adaptation of argument graphs with wordnet and large language models. In: Massie, S., Chakraborti, S. (eds.) ICCBR 2023. LNCS, vol. 14141, pp. 263–278. Springer, Cham (2023). https://doi.org/10.1007/978-3-031-40177-0_17
11. Lewis, P., et al.: Retrieval-augmented generation for knowledge-intensive NLP tasks. In: Advances in Neural Information Processing Systems, vol. 33, pp. 9459–9474. Curran Associates, Inc. (2020)

12. Likert, R.: A technique for the measurement of attitudes. Arch. Psychol. **22**(140), 55 (1932)
13. Malburg, L., Hoffmann, M., Trumm, S., Bergmann, R.: Improving similarity-based retrieval efficiency by using graphic processing units in case-based reasoning. In: The International FLAIRS Conference Proceedings, Florida, vol. 34 (2021). https://doi.org/10.32473/flairs.v34i1.128345
14. Malburg, L., Hotz, M., Bergmann, R.: Improving complex adaptations in process-oriented case-based reasoning by applying rule-based adaptation. In: Recio-Garcia, J.A., et al. (eds.) Case-Based Reasoning Research and Development. LNAI, vol. 14775, pp. 50–66. Springer, Cham (2024). https://doi.org/10.1007/978-3-031-63646-2_4
15. Nkisi-Orji, I., Wiratunga, N., Palihawadana, C., Recio-García, J.A., Corsar, D.: CLOOD CBR: towards microservices oriented case-based reasoning. In: Watson, I., Weber, R. (eds.) ICCBR 2020. LNCS (LNAI), vol. 12311, pp. 129–143. Springer, Cham (2020). https://doi.org/10.1007/978-3-030-58342-2_9
16. Recio-García, J.A., Parejas-Llanovarced, H., Orozco-del-Castillo, M.G., Brito-Borges, E.E.: A case-based approach for the selection of explanation algorithms in image classification. In: Sánchez-Ruiz, A.A., Floyd, M.W. (eds.) ICCBR 2021. LNCS (LNAI), vol. 12877, pp. 186–200. Springer, Cham (2021). https://doi.org/10.1007/978-3-030-86957-1_13
17. Richter, M.M., Weber, R.: Case-Based Reasoning: A Textbook. Springer, Heidelberg (2013). https://doi.org/10.1007/978-3-642-40167-1
18. Schultheis, A., Zeyen, C., Bergmann, R.: An overview and comparison of case-based reasoning frameworks. In: Massie, S., Chakraborti, S. (eds.) ICCBR 2023. LNCS, vol. 14141, pp. 327–343. Springer, Cham (2023). https://doi.org/10.1007/978-3-031-40177-0_21
19. Stahl, A.: Learning of knowledge-intensive similarity measures in case-based reasoning. Ph.D. thesis, University of Kaiserslautern, Kaiserslautern (2004)
20. Stahl, A.: Learning similarity measures: a formal view based on a generalized CBR model. In: Muñoz-Ávila, H., Ricci, F. (eds.) ICCBR 2005. LNCS (LNAI), vol. 3620, pp. 507–521. Springer, Heidelberg (2005). https://doi.org/10.1007/11536406_39
21. Wijekoon, A., et al.: CBR driven interactive explainable AI. In: Massie, S., Chakraborti, S. (eds.) ICCBR 2023. LNCS, vol. 14141, pp. 169–184. Springer, Cham (2023). https://doi.org/10.1007/978-3-031-40177-0_11

Experiential Questioning for VQA

Ruben Gómez Blanco, Adrián Pérez Peinador, Adrián Sanjuan Espejo,
Antonio A. Sánchez-Ruiz⁽✉⁾ , and Belén Díaz-Agudo

Department of Software Engineering and Artificial Intelligence, Instituto de
Tecnologías del Conocimiento, Universidad Complutense de Madrid, Madrid, Spain
{rubgom03,adpere08,adrisanj,antsanch,belend}@ucm.es

Abstract. Visual Question Answering (VQA) is a task born out of the
need to answer queries regarding images or videos. Unlike simpler tasks
such as classification or regression, VQA requires expertise from both
computer vision and language modeling domains. These systems typically mimic human reasoning by detecting objects and establishing their
relationships within the image using different techniques such as object
detection, fine-grained recognition, action detection, and common-sense
reasoning. VQA systems generally assume that the user initiates the
interaction by asking specific questions about the image, but this can be
problematic for some people with visual impairments. In this paper, we
present a case-based approach to help users formulate relevant questions
about an image based on questions that other users asked about similar images. We evaluate the use of different similarity measures between
images and propose a way to cluster and filter the retrieved questions.

Keywords: Case-Based Reasoning · Visual Question Answering ·
Similarity

1   Introduction

Visual Question Answering (VQA) is a task that emerged from the necessity
of answering questions about an image or video. Unlike simpler tasks such as
classification or regression, VQA requires expertise from two key domains: computer vision and language modeling. It seems in general VQA systems do follow
human reasoning in the sense that they detect objects in the image and then
establish the relations between those objects [3]. Research in VQA has identified
different types of questions regarding the knowledge needed to answer them [2]:
object detection, like *Are there dogs in the picture?*, fine-grained recognition, like
What type of dog breed appears in the picture?, action or activity detection and
recognition, like *Is the dog eating?*, others knowledge-intensive or common-sense
questions, like *Is the dog breed the favorite dog breed of Queen Elizabeth II?* or
Does the dog love her humans? [4].

VQA is also useful in helping the visually impaired describe or understand
the content of a photo and is invaluable in fostering independence and enriching
experiences by allowing users to interact with visual content independently [14].

J. A. Recio-Garcia et al. (Eds.): ICCBR 2024, LNAI 14775, pp. 305–320, 2024.
https://doi.org/10.1007/978-3-031-63646-2_20

However, most VQA systems tend to assume that it is the user who initiates the interaction by asking specific questions about the image. This assumption can be problematic for some people, particularly those with visual impairments, who, unable to see the image, can only ask very general questions and may need several iterations of questions and answers to get the relevant information from the image.

In this paper, we present a case-based approach to help users formulate relevant questions about an image based on questions that other users asked about similar images. The formulation of relevant questions is a complex problem because it may depend on factors external to the image itself, such as the user's intention or the context in which the image is analyzed. This type of knowledge is difficult to elicit and model but can be essential to provide a satisfactory user experience. For this reason, we hypothesize that a case-based reasoning approach will be useful for this problem because cases represent past experiences and might implicitly capture part of this knowledge. In this paper, we propose and evaluate the use of different similarities to retrieve similar images and propose a method to cluster and filter all the questions associated with those images so that we do not ask the same using different formulations.

The rest of the paper is organized as follows. Section 2 presents related work on VQA. Section 3 describes the proposed case-based approach to retrieve relevant questions about an image. Sections 4 and 5 present the dataset and the different measures of similarity between images that we used in the study. Section 6 describes the experiment that have been carried out and the results obtained. Finally, Sect. 7 discusses our conclusions and proposes future lines of work.

2   Related Work

In the literature, VQA has been achieved using both knowledge-light [9, 20] and knowledge-intensive methods [18, 19]. Both approaches typically involve the following steps: 1) object detection in an image with high accuracy with fine-grained details; 2) language comprehension of the question; and 3) compilation of the answer utilizing the information from steps 1 and 2, and external knowledge sources (mostly in knowledge-intensive systems) [3]. Step 3 is the most challenging one due to the complex reasoning we have to carry out. Depending on the questions and the type of images, questions are very easy to answer from the objects detected in the image. However, often, there is a need to infer knowledge from other knowledge sources to find the coincidences between our question and the objects detected in our image [13]. This is especially relevant for open-ended or ambiguous questions, questions with multiple answers or questions that require additional information not available on the image [19]. Besides, knowledge-intensive approaches infer knowledge from other knowledge sources to disambiguate the uncertainties between our question and the objects detected in our image [13].

Some data-driven models encapsulate all three steps. Deep vision-language (VL) models that perform VQA using sequence-to-sequence models are trained on extremely large datasets. A key component of VL models is learning the alignment between images and paired text in an unsupervised manner using contrastive losses. Given an $<image, question>$ pair, VL models generate answers using auto-regressive sequence generation models by using the granular alignments between the question and the image as well as linguistic proficiency acquired in pre-training. Some recent models are the ALIGN model trained using contrastive loss [8], ALBEF model trained using the inter-modal alignment [9]; VL model trained using Triple Constrastive Loss [20]; and VinVL [21] which integrates improved object detection with VL modeling. Overall, these data-driven methods treat VQA as an end-to-end task instead of a pipeline of sub-tasks as in knowledge-intensive approaches. VQA is one of the many downstream tasks for a fine-tuned VL model. To support VQA, the VL model is further trained using a dataset of $<image, question, answer>$ triplets where the input is the $<image, question>$ pair, and the ground truth is the answer in textual format. VQA can be modeled as a generative task and a classification task. A generative VQA model will employ a text generator such as GPT [15] to generate the answer. Conversely, a classification model will employ a softmax layer at the end of the fusion encoder to predict the answer from a given set of answers [20].

While deep learning models are limited by the knowledge they have learned from the training data, knowledge-intensive methods [13,19] get an answer using also external knowledge from different complementary knowledge sources apart from the images and the questions. Using additional knowledge sources can be remarkable in VQA tasks for *complex* or common sense questions. For example, in a question like "How many types of fruits are in the picture?". The algorithm should recognize not only the foods that we have in the image but also identify and understand which foods are fruits and which ones are not. Different approaches use complementary knowledge like the *Grounded Visual Question Answering* model (GVQA) [1] that use different algorithms depending on the type of question that we come across (yes/no or non-yes/no question). They also divide the model's behaviour process to get the answer in different steps (getting important parts in the image, retrieving concepts from the question, classifying the type of questions, or predicting the answer). VLC-BERT [16] is a VQA model that uses COMET (Commonsense Transformer) a commonsense reasoning generation transformer model that given a subject and a relation, predicts a possible object. An example from the authors is if the subject is "taking a nap" and the relation is "causes" a possible object is "have energy". It is trained and tested on ATOMIC [17] and ConceptNet knowledge graphs both of which consist of social commonsense knowledge. Commonsense reasoning extracted from the COMET is used in VLC-BERT to improve answer generation making it knowledge-intensive.

In this paper, we propose an approach using Case-based reasoning to reuse questions for similar images and avoid the use of other additional knowledge sources while maintaining a good performance of the question-answering process.

3   A Case-Based Reasoning Model for VQA

The generation of relevant questions to describe an image is a complex problem because it may depend on factors external to the image itself, such as the user's intention or the context in which the image is analyzed. For example, a history student may visit an exhibition of classical painting to see historical figures and events, while another art student may visit the same exhibition paying special attention to the use of color and the organization of the elements in the scene. Each of these students would ask different questions about the same paintings because of their objective and, therefore, the type of information they seek is different.

This type of knowledge is difficult to elicit and model but can be essential to provide a satisfactory user experience. In this context, case-based reasoning techniques can be useful because cases, representing past experiences, capture, to some extent, this type of knowledge. We propose to describe images by retrieving and reusing questions that have been relevant to describe similar images in past situations.

The description of the *cases* is composed, in its simplest version, of an image. This description could be extended with knowledge about the user who interacted with the image and his context. The case solution consists, in its simplest version, of the questions that the user considered relevant to describe the image. This information could be extended with the answers to those questions or the user's reactions to the answers obtained.

When a user wants to get the description of an image, we search for similar cases in our experience base, to reuse the questions that were asked back then. Once the k most similar cases are retrieved, we must adapt the retrieved questions to the current context. This adaptation process must consider, in addition to the differences between the past situations and the current ones, the possible overlaps between questions retrieved from different similar cases.

sizeIn the current version of our system, cases contain images and their associated questions (see Fig. 1). The retrieval of the most similar cases is performed using different similarity measures between images, with lower or higher semantic load, which will be introduced in Sect. 5. The adaptation process is in charge of selecting the most relevant questions from all the retrieved images. We must consider that being similar images, there will be many repeated questions (even if they are not formulated the same) that must be filtered. For example, from two similar images we could retrieve the questions "What time of the day is it?" and "Is it daytime or nighttime?", and we should not ask both. To solve this problem, we propose to generate embeddings of the questions using a language model, apply a clustering algorithm, and select the question closest to the centroid of each cluster. In our case, we use *gte-small* [10] to generate the embeddings, a language model based on BERT, and the DBSCAN [5] algorithm to generate the clusters.

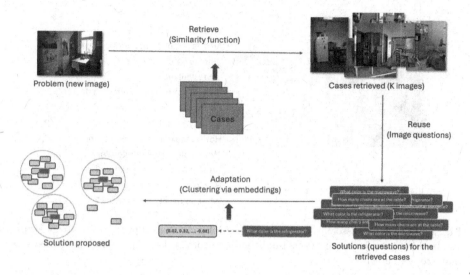

Fig. 1. Question retrieval CBR system. The retrieval phase finds the K most similar images (based on a predefined metric) to the query image. Questions associated with these retrieved images are then extracted. The adaptation phase generates embeddings for these questions and groups them into clusters. Finally, the system proposes questions associated with the most representative embedding from each cluster.

4   The Visual Question Answering Dataset

The Visual Question Answering Dataset and Challenge[1] (VQA v2.0) [6] contains open-ended questions about images requiring an understanding of vision, language, and commonsense knowledge to answer. The dataset contains over 200k COCO dataset images, 5.4 questions per image on average and 10 correct answers for each question.

The images show a wide variety of scenes including landscapes, house interiors, everyday objects, wild and domestic animals, people doing different activities, etc. Each of the images contains information about the entities that appear in it, in particular their categories and their bounding boxes. There are 80 different types of entities (person, umbrella, dog, car, bed, clock...) [12]. Each image also has a variable number of questions associated with it (at least 3) and for each of them 10 answers in natural language. The questions, in turn, are tagged with a type from among 65 possible categories. The number of questions in each category is highly variable, the most numerous categories being *how many*, *is the*, *what*, *what color is the*, and *what is the*.

For example, Fig. 2 shows one of the images in the dataset and its associated information. In this case, it is a domestic kitchen in which 11 objects have been identified. The image has 12 associated short questions that will require different types of answers (yes/no, colors, numbers...). It is interesting to note that some

---

[1] https://visualqa.org/ (last accessed on 04/26/24).

Questions:
- What color is the table?
- Are the lamps turned on?
- What is sitting on the table?
- Is the wall red?
- Is there a pretty decoration on the table?
- Does the table appear messy?
- What type of doorway is shown?
- How many chairs are at the table?
- What color is the refrigerator?
- Is there a bowl in the picture?
- How many chairs are there?
- What color is the microwave?

Objects:
{ refrigerator, oven, oven, chair, couch
chair, chair, chair, chair, dining table, vase }

Fig. 2. Information associated with an image: objects that appear in the image (type and bounding box) and questions (and their categories). Each question has 10 answers that are not shown for clarity.

of the questions cannot be answered with the labeled objects (*Is there a pretty decoration on the table?, Is the wall red?*).

In this work, we have selected a subset of the dataset consisting of 5000 images so that their questions follow a similar distribution to those in the original dataset in terms of question types as depicted in Fig. 3.

5   Similarity Between Images

Let us recall that our goal is to describe an image using questions that have been relevant to describe similar images in the case base. Therefore, the quality of the retrieved questions will depend on how we measure the similarity between images. Next, we introduce several similarity measures that attempt to capture different aspects that we can take into account when considering whether two images are similar. We will also show examples of similar and dissimilar images to the target image in Fig. 4 according to each of them.

5.1   Pixel Similarity Metric

Pixel-level image comparison is performed by comparing pixels at the same position in both images. This type of similarity measure can be useful, for example, when comparing landscape images where color plays a key role. Pixel similarities require that both images have the same size, so we resized the images in the dataset to 640×480 pixels, the modal size in the dataset, constituting 20.26% of the original images. There are different ways to compare two images based on the pixels composing them. We opted for mean square error between pixels due to its simplicity and interpretability.

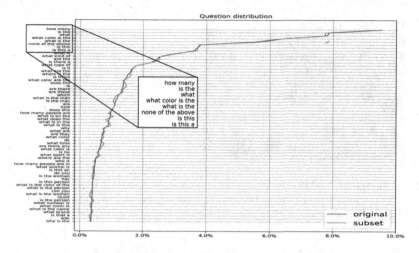

Fig. 3. Question type distributions.

Fig. 4. Target image used to exemplify the different similarity measures.

Normalized Root Mean Squared Error. This metric calculates the average squared distance between pixels in the same position, then takes the square root to get a value in the same color units. Then, values are normalized. The similarity is computed as 1 minus this distance.

$$sim(\mathbf{im_A}, \mathbf{im_B}) = 1 - \frac{\|\mathbf{im_A} - \mathbf{im_B}\|}{\|\mathbf{im_A}\|} \tag{1}$$

where $\mathbf{im_A}$, $\mathbf{im_B}$ are both images represented as pixel matrices and $\|.\|$ is the Frobenius norm. Figure 5 shows an example of similar and dissimilar images using this metric.

5.2 Object Detection Similarity Metrics

We can consider two images to be similar when they show similar objects. The images in the dataset already contain annotations about the entities in them

Fig. 5. Example of NRMSE based similarity calculation against image in Fig. 4: First image has a similarity of 0.4535 being the most similar in our dataset. The second image has a similarity of −0.4771 being the least similar in our dataset.

and their bounding boxes, but we need to use some object recognition model to use images external to the dataset. We delegate that task to the Retina Net [11] model, a convolutional neural network (CNN) trained on the COCO dataset. Next, we define two different similarity measures based on the entities appearing in the images, depending on whether we use their labels or their bounding boxes.

Tag-Based Similarity. Given the set of object tags (without duplicates) in both images, we compute the similarity as the intersection over the union between the two sets.

$$sim(\mathbf{im_A}, \mathbf{im_B}) = \frac{|obj_A \cap obj_B|}{|obj_A \cup obj_B|} \tag{2}$$

where obj_A, obj_B are the sets of objects in both images and $|.|$ is the cardinality of the set. An example of similar and dissimilar images using this metric is shown in Fig. 6.

Bounding Box-Based Similarity. This similarity is intended to capture the idea that larger objects tend to have more importance in an image than smaller ones. First, we calculate how much of the image area the objects of each class occupy relative to the total area occupied by all objects. These values represent the relative importance of the object class in the image. Next, we sum the minimum value for each class in both images. It is easy to see that this value is between 0 and 1.

$$sim(\mathbf{im_A}, \mathbf{im_B}) = \sum_{c \in C} min\left(\frac{r_A^c}{r_A}, \frac{r_B^c}{r_B}\right) \tag{3}$$

where C is the set of object classes defined in COCO, r_A^c (resp. r_B^c) is the sum of the areas of objects belonging to the class c in the image A (resp. B), and r_A is the sum of the areas of all the objects in the image A (resp. B). An example of similar and dissimilar images using this metric can be seen in Fig. 7.

Fig. 6. Example of tag-based similarity calculation against the image in Fig. 4: The first image has a similarity of 0.75, being the most similar in our dataset. The second image has a similarity of 0, the lowest value.

Fig. 7. Example of bounding boxes based similarity calculation against image in Fig. 4: First image has a similarity of 0.82898, being the most similar in our dataset. The second image has a similarity of 0, the lowest value.

5.3   Embedding-Based Similarity Metric

Image embeddings are low dimensional representations in a *latent space* that capture, to some extent, semantic features of the images. They are extracted from internal layers of already trained neural networks and tend to group closer images with common features. Embedding-based similarities consider that two images are more similar the closer their embeddings are.

We use the Img2Vec model from the PyTorch library with the DenseNet [7] architecture to obtain a 1024 feature embedding of each image. DenseNet is a CNN architecture characterized by having dense connections between layers, which means that each layer is directly connected to all subsequent layers in the model. This allows the flow of information through the different layers to be more fluent and direct, which can result in better performance and better generalization ability compared to other architectures. DenseNet architecture achieves state-of-the-art performance on various benchmark image classification datasets and it is also suggested it can be a good feature extractor for various computer vision tasks [7].

Fig. 8. Example of cosine similarity among image embeddings against the image in Fig. 4: The first image has a cosine similarity of 0.6958 being the most similar in our dataset. The second image has a cosine similarity of −0.0939 being the least similar in our dataset.

Http Similarity. Cosine similarity is particularly useful when working with high-dimensional data such as image embeddings because it considers both the magnitude and direction of each vector. This makes it more robust than other measures like Euclidean distance, which only considers the magnitude.

$$sim(\mathbf{im_A}, \mathbf{im_B}) = \frac{\mathbf{v_A} \cdot \mathbf{v_B}}{\|\mathbf{v_A}\|\|\mathbf{v_B}\|} \tag{4}$$

where $\mathbf{v_A}$, $\mathbf{v_B}$ are the embeddings of the images $\mathbf{im_A}$ and $\mathbf{im_B}$, $\cdot$ represents the dot product between them, and $\|.\|$ is defined as the norm of a vector. Figure 8 shows an example of similar and dissimilar images using this metric.

6   Experiment and Results

The goal of the experiment is to assess the effectiveness of different similarity measures to retrieve images with semantically relevant associated questions. Our initial hypothesis are:

- Pixel similarity metrics, lacking semantic information, will exhibit poor performance in retrieving images with relevant questions. We expect to retrieve images with a high degree of pixel similarity but potentially low semantic relevance to the query.
- Object detection similarity metrics, while incorporating semantic information through object category recognition, will be limited by the predefined categories within the training dataset. Additionally, we believe that images with few or no objects to detect, such as landscapes, will demonstrate a weakness of these metrics.

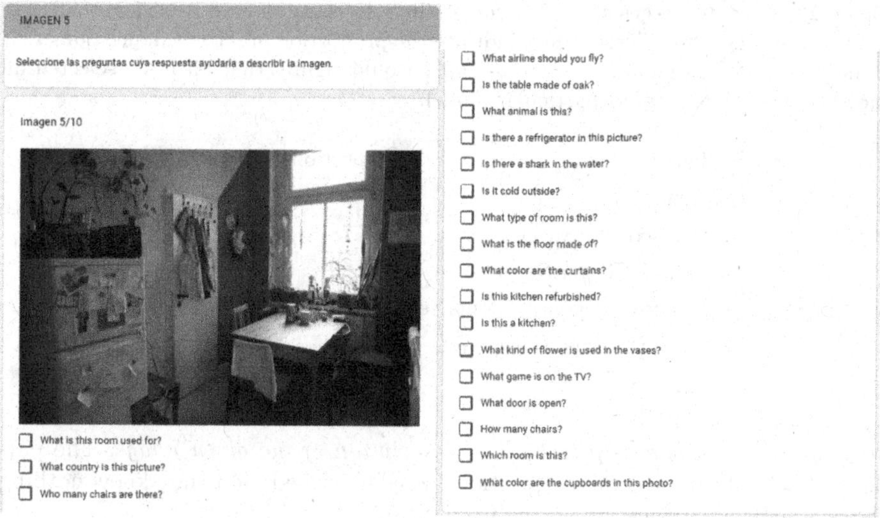

Fig. 9. Example of image and questions in the conducted experiment.

– Embedding-based similarity metrics, in the same way as object detection, incorporate semantic information. We hypothesize they will perform more consistently across a wider range of image types than pixel-based or object-detection-based metrics.

6.1 Experiment Set-Up

We selected 20 new images from Pixabay[2] with different topics (animals, landscape, street, transport, technology, rooms, sports, and food) so that they would not be related to the ones present in the case base. Then we used the 4 similarity metrics introduced in the previous section (pixel-based, tag-based, bounding box-based, and embedding-based) to retrieve 4 questions associated with each one of them. The retrieval was performed using the 50 most similar images according to each similarity and the clustering method described in Sect. 3. We also introduced a baseline composed of the 4 most typical types of questions in the entire dataset (we used clustering over all the questions and selected representatives of the 4 largest clusters). Therefore, the experiment was performed with 20 images and a pool of 20 randomly ordered questions for each of them: 4 questions using each similarity and 4 baseline questions. An example is shown in Fig. 9.

The 20 images were divided into 2 online tests with 10 images each to enhance participation so that each test could be completed in less than 10 min. The participants were asked to choose among the pool of questions those *whose answers*

---

[2] https://pixabay.com/ (last accessed on 04/26/24).

Table 1. The percentages shown represent the selectivity of each model, rather than an overall success rate. These values indicate the proportion of retrieved questions that users chose for each model. A score of 100% would signify that all users selected all questions presented by that particular model.

Similarity	Questions selected (%)
Baseline	6.43%
Pixel-based (NRMSE)	17.78%
Tag-based (RetinaNet)	48.22%
Bounding box-based (RetinaNet)	54.58%
Embedding cosine (DenseNet)	65.53%

they considered would help to build a description of the given image. The participants could select as many questions as they wished, and they knew nothing about where those questions came from.

6.2 Experiment Results

A total of 80 people answered to test A and 68 to test B. The average number of questions selected per person and image was 7.08 out of 20. The evaluation was carried out by analyzing the selection rates of questions retrieved using each similarity metric. This way, we aimed to identify the model that consistently retrieved the most relevant questions. The results are summarized in Table 1.

As expected, the naive approach of selecting the most common questions in the dataset does not work for this type of problem. Pixel-based similarity is a little better but not much more than the baseline. The similarity metrics that consider the semantic information contained in the image are a better choice. In the detected object similarities is interesting that the size of the objects in the picture seems to be relevant. Finally, the similarity based on embeddings is the clear winner. We believe that leveraging DenseNet embeddings for image retrieval goes beyond simple object recognition and likely captures additional features that contribute to semantic similarity (as stated in Sect. 5.3), potentially leading to the retrieval of more relevant images.

It is interesting to analyze the results by dividing the set of test images into different categories. A first distinction can be made between indoor and outdoor images. Within the indoor images we can distinguish between those inside rooms and those focusing on specific items. As for outdoor images, they can be divided into images of nature and images of the urban environment. We analyze the results of the experiment according to this classification as follows (see Table 2):

- **Indoor room images (4 test images).** Similarities based on object detection perform reasonably well because the images contain several recognizable objects such as chairs, beds, or animals. On the other hand, pixel-based similarities are usually not useful because of the diversity of sizes and, especially,

Table 2. Selection rate for each model divided by test image type. Analogous to Table 1.

Similarity	Questions selected (%)					
	Interior			Exterior		
	Room	Items	All	Urban	Nature	All
Baseline	16.54%	5.37%	10.34%	2.48%	5.27%	3.24%
Pixel-based (NRMSE)	17.28%	4.49%	10.18%	21.32%	31.13%	24.00%
Tag-based (RetinaNet)	51.10%	46.99%	48.82%	54.04%	30.88%	47.73%
Bounding box-based (RetinaNet)	66.54%	53.09%	59.07%	54.46%	41.42%	50.90%
Embedding cosine (DenseNet)	76.38%	61.62%	68.18%	62.50%	65.68%	63.37%

colors of these objects. Similarity based on embedding is the most effective in most cases, except for one of the images in this category.

- **Indoor images focused on specific items (5 test images).** Similarity based on embedding again performs best in this group. Similarities based on object detection are limited by the predefined categories and objects that the model can recognize, and that is especially important for these images. Pixel-based similarity performs poorly in this group, probably due to the variability of colors in everyday objects.
- **Images of urban environments (8 test images).** In this group, we appreciate two types of images. Object detection-based similarity obtains the best results only in some images that are not saturated with objects and certain elements are clear protagonists. Otherwise, embedding-based similarity performs better probably because it considers more objects that are important in the image. Pixel-based similarity only works well when the tone of the image is important for meaning (rainy days will have more grayish tones, and sunny days will have warmer tones).
- **Images of nature environments (3 test images).** Similarities based on object detection perform worse in this group than in the previous ones because there are usually not many objects in open, outdoor landscapes, although they improve if animals are present. Pixel-based similarity performs better in images where the color is very uniform, such as the sea, the sky or a meadow, although it still performs worse than bounding-box-based and embedding-based similarities. Embedding-based similarities continue to be the top performers with this type of image.

Our evaluation demonstrates that embedding cosine similarity offers the best sim metric for question recommendation. This approach retrieved a user-reported suitability rate exceeding 60%. Object-based similarity metrics achieved a modest performance when the model identified recognizable objects within the images. However, this approach exhibited limitations with landscape imagery or scenes lacking identifiable object categories. Notably, incorporating relative object size improved object-based similarity by over 10% in certain scenarios. Pixel-based similarity metrics consistently underperformed, even operating below baseline results in some cases.

7 Conclusions and Future Work

In this paper we have proposed a case-based reasoning approach to help users, especially those with visual impairments, to formulate relevant questions about an image based on questions that other users previously asked about similar images. In particular, we evaluated the use of different similarity measures to retrieve similar images and proposed a method to cluster and filter the questions associated with those images so that the same question is not asked multiple times using different formulations.

The results of our user experiment suggest that pixel-based similarities do not suit this type of problem, except for images where color or hue is a dominant semantic feature (e.g., snowy landscapes or water scenes). Similarity based on detected objects works well when the image contains a few important elements that can be recognized by the detection model but fails when there are too many elements in the image, none, or the detection model is not able to recognize the relevant entities. Embedding-based similarity depends on the quality of the embeddings (and thus the model and dataset used to create them) but seems to work better on a wider range of image types. Embeddings are a very effective way to encode the general semantic information present in the image, but they are also less transparent and difficult to interpret. For example, the embedding-based similarity performed worse than expected in one image of the experiment, but we cannot explain why this is the case. These results encourage us to study the possible combination of different similarity measures to improve the relevance of the retrieved images in different situations. This is an interesting and challenging line of research, as it is not straightforward to characterize the information used when calculating similarity based on embeddings.

There are several lines of research to improve this work. One of the most important problems that we have not yet addressed concerns how to adapt the retrieved questions to the current image. Two different images could show similar scenarios with different contexts and that could make some questions relevant to the first image absurd for the second one. We also used a very simple representation of the cases in this work that could be enriched with knowledge about the user who asked the question, such as her intention and context (physical, temporal, social, etc.), and her reactions to the answers obtained. All this new information could be taken into account to retrieve more relevant cases and make more complex adaptations. Finally, once the relevant questions about the image have been retrieved, we should compose a description based on the answers to those questions and evaluate whether that description is useful for visually impaired people.

Acknowledgements. This work has been partially funded by the Ministry of Science, Innovation and Universities (PID2020-114596RB-C21, PID2021-123368OB-I00) and the Complutense University of Madrid (Group 921330).

References

1. Agrawal, A., Batra, D., Parikh, D., Kembhavi, A.: Don't just assume; look and answer: overcoming priors for visual question answering. In: Proceedings of the IEEE Conference on Computer Vision and Pattern Recognition, pp. 4971–4980 (2018)

2. Antol, S., et al.: VQA: visual question answering. In: Proceedings of the IEEE International Conference on Computer Vision, pp. 2425–2433 (2015)

3. Basu, K., Shakerin, F., Gupta, G.: AQuA: ASP-based visual question answering. In: Komendantskaya, E., Liu, Y.A. (eds.) PADL 2020. LNCS, vol. 12007, pp. 57–72. Springer, Cham (2020). https://doi.org/10.1007/978-3-030-39197-3_4

4. Caro-Martínez, M., Wijekoon, A., Díaz-Agudo, B., Recio-García, J.A.: The current and future role of visual question answering in explainable artificial intelligence. In: Malburg, L., Verma, D. (eds.) Proceedings of the Workshops at the 31st International Conference on Case-Based Reasoning (ICCBR-WS 2023) Co-located with the 31st International Conference on Case-Based Reasoning (ICCBR 2023), Aberdeen, Scotland, UK, 17 July 2023. CEUR Workshop Proceedings, vol. 3438, pp. 172–183. CEUR-WS.org (2023). https://ceur-ws.org/Vol-3438/paper_13.pdf

5. Ester, M., Kriegel, H., Sander, J., Xu, X.: A density-based algorithm for discovering clusters in large spatial databases with noise. In: Simoudis, E., Han, J., Fayyad, U.M. (eds.) Proceedings of the Second International Conference on Knowledge Discovery and Data Mining (KDD-96), Portland, Oregon, USA, pp. 226–231. AAAI Press (1996). http://www.aaai.org/Library/KDD/1996/kdd96-037.php

6. Goyal, Y., Khot, T., Summers-Stay, D., Batra, D., Parikh, D.: Making the V in VQA matter: elevating the role of image understanding in visual question answering. In: Proceedings of the IEEE Conference on Computer Vision and Pattern Recognition, pp. 6904–6913 (2017)

7. Huang, G., Liu, Z., van der Maaten, L., Weinberger, K.Q.: Densely connected convolutional networks. In: Proceedings of the IEEE Conference on Computer Vision and Pattern Recognition (CVPR), pp. 4700–4708 (2016)

8. Jia, C., et al.: Scaling up visual and vision-language representation learning with noisy text supervision. In: International Conference on Machine Learning, pp. 4904–4916. PMLR (2021)

9. Li, J., Selvaraju, R., Gotmare, A., Joty, S., Xiong, C., Hoi, S.C.H.: Align before fuse: vision and language representation learning with momentum distillation. Adv. Neural. Inf. Process. Syst. **34**, 9694–9705 (2021)

10. Li, Z., Zhang, X., Zhang, Y., Long, D., Xie, P., Zhang, M.: Towards general text embeddings with multi-stage contrastive learning. CoRR abs/2308.03281 (2023). https://doi.org/10.48550/ARXIV.2308.03281

11. Lin, T., Goyal, P., Girshick, R.B., He, K., Dollár, P.: Focal loss for dense object detection. CoRR abs/1708.02002 (2017). http://arxiv.org/abs/1708.02002

12. Lin, T.-Y., et al.: Microsoft COCO: common objects in context. In: Fleet, D., Pajdla, T., Schiele, B., Tuytelaars, T. (eds.) ECCV 2014. LNCS, vol. 8693, pp. 740–755. Springer, Cham (2014). https://doi.org/10.1007/978-3-319-10602-1_48

13. Marino, K., Rastegari, M., Farhadi, A., Mottaghi, R.: OK-VQA: a visual question answering benchmark requiring external knowledge. In: Proceedings of the IEEE/CVF Conference on Computer Vision and Pattern Recognition, pp. 3195–3204 (2019)

14. Patil, A.P., Behera, A., Anusha, P., Seth, M., Prabhuling: speech enabled visual question answering using LSTM and CNN with real time image capturing for

assisting the visually impaired. In: TENCON 2019 - 2019 IEEE Region 10 Conference (TENCON), Kochi, India, 17–20 October 2019, pp. 2475–2480. IEEE (2019).https://doi.org/10.1109/TENCON.2019.8929263

15. Radford, A., et al.: Language models are unsupervised multitask learners. OpenAI Blog **1**(8), 9 (2019)
16. Ravi, S., Chinchure, A., Sigal, L., Liao, R., Shwartz, V.: VLC-BERT: visual question answering with contextualized commonsense knowledge. In: Proceedings of the IEEE/CVF Winter Conference on Applications of Computer Vision, pp. 1155–1165 (2023)
17. Sap, M., et al.: ATOMIC: an atlas of machine commonsense for if-then reasoning. In: Proceedings of the AAAI Conference on Artificial Intelligence, vol. 33, pp. 3027–3035 (2019)
18. Wang, P., Wu, Q., Shen, C., Dick, A., Van Den Henge, A.: Explicit knowledge-based reasoning for visual question answering. In: Proceedings of the 26th International Joint Conference on Artificial Intelligence, pp. 1290–1296 (2017)
19. Wu, Q., et al.: Visual question answering: a survey of methods and datasets. Comput. Vis. Image Underst. **163**, 21–40 (2017)
20. Yang, J., et al.: Vision-language pre-training with triple contrastive learning. In: Proceedings of the IEEE/CVF Conference on Computer Vision and Pattern Recognition, pp. 15671–15680 (2022)
21. Zhang, P., et al.: VinVL: revisiting visual representations in vision-language models. In: Proceedings of the IEEE/CVF Conference on Computer Vision and Pattern Recognition, pp. 5579–5588 (2021)

Autocompletion of Architectural Spatial Configurations Using Case-Based Reasoning, Graph Clustering, and Deep Learning

Viktor Eisenstadt[1,2]([✉]), Christoph Langenhan[3], Jessica Bielski[3], Ralph Bergmann[2], and Klaus-Dieter Althoff[1,2]

[1] Institute of Computer Science, University of Hildesheim, Hildesheim, Germany
[2] German Research Center for Artificial Intelligence (DFKI), Kaiserslautern, Germany
{viktor.eisenstadt,ralph.bergmann,klaus-dieter.althoff}@dfki.de
[3] Technical University of Munich, Munich, Germany
{christoph.langenhan,jessica.bielski}@tum.de

Abstract. This paper presents an approach for autocompletion of architectural building designs in the form of graph-based floor plans during the early design phase. We utilize established case-based reasoning methods, such as subgraph matching and transformational adaptation, further we employ supervised and unsupervised machine learning techniques, such as graph clustering and graph neural networks. Combining those methods into a single approach, the goal is to predict possibly missing spaces in architectural designs of housing buildings, supporting the acceleration of the early design process of architects to make it more sustainable, while enriching it with the recent developments of artificial intelligence. The approach was validated by a performance evaluation and a user study with participation of representatives of the architecture domain.

Keywords: artificial intelligence · case-based-reasoning · deep learning · graph matching · graph neural networks · architectural design process

1 Introduction

The process of designing a building in architecture can be described as a non-linear ill-structured workflow without a clear definition, timeline, or sequence of design steps [10]. It consists of many stages of creative and decision-making iterations that aim to produce a complex prototype of a functional, properly laid out, and sustainable construction unit, e.g., in the form of a *building information modeling* (BIM) model. Nevertheless, a common feature of all individual architectural design processes is the *early conceptual design phase* which is crucial for creation of the first design ideas and directions, e.g., in the form of digital

J. A. Recio-Garcia et al. (Eds.): ICCBR 2024, LNAI 14775, pp. 321–337, 2024.
https://doi.org/10.1007/978-3-031-63646-2_21

floor plan sketches that represent different variations of the design for implementation in the BIM model. According to the *Official Scale of Fees for Services by Architects and Engineers in Germany* (Honorarordnung für Architekten und Ingenieure, HOAI) [15], the early conceptual design phase (labeled as 'schematic design' phase) takes up to around 30% of the overall design development process.

Artificial intelligence (AI) is an established computational technology, nowadays ubiquitous in many industrial areas as well as everyday life with services such as text-based chatbots, image and video generation, automatic translation and transcription, or completion of text messages on mobile devices. In architectural design, however, AI is still not widely applied, being limited to research projects in academia and rudimentary automation tasks [19], and hardly present in the established commercial design software, such as Revit, Allplan, or ArchiCAD.

In order to explore the potential and further establish AI in architecture, the DFG research project Metis-II, investigates AI methods such as *deep learning* (DL) or *case-based reasoning* (CBR) for support of the early design phase. One of the main goals of the project is the autocompletion of graph-based representations of floor plans using semantic data of the building. Being similar to the suggestions of the next word in a text message on the mobile devices, AI-based autocompletion of floor plans helps the architects to accelerate the early design process by making well-informed suggestions for missing spaces (coherent rooms and their interconnections) of the current floor plan. Furthermore, being compliant with the basic rules of the specific architectural design domains (e.g., housing buildings), such autocompletion makes the results of the early conceptual design phase more sustainable and cost-efficient, establishing a longer building lifecycle [14].

In this paper, we describe the first complete solution for AI-based graph autocompletion system for support of the early conceptual design phase in architecture. The approach was developed in the context of the project Metis-II and is based on the established and recent AI methods: case-based reasoning, graph clustering, and deep learning with graph neural networks. In the following sections, we present the AI foundations of the system, its basic data structures and algorithms, conducted evaluations, and an outlook to the future research.

2   Foundations and Concepts of the System

2.1   Case-Based Reasoning

The established AI method case-based reasoning can be described as an analogy to natural human behavior in situations where past experiences provide a basis for present decision-making, if the current problem is similar to one or more previous problems [18]. The most important basic foundation of CBR is the concept of *case* which can be described as a combination of *problem and solution*. Cases are collected in specific datasets, known as *case bases*, from which they can be retrieved for transfer of the solution to the current problem.

Within the context of the research work presented in this paper, case-based reasoning was previously applied for support of design process in architecture, originating in the hypothetic-deductive reasoning practices present in the early architectural design process [4]. Mostly, the CBR-based solutions were developed for retrieval of similar building designs. Previously developed systems, e.g., CaseBook [16] or CBArch [5] can be named as some notable examples. For the research project Metis-II and its predecessor Metis-I, other case-based retrieval systems for graph-based architectural designs were developed [9,22].

2.2   Deep Learning

Deep learning can be considered a family of algorithms within the field of *machine learning* (ML) that are able to 'acquire their own knowledge, by extracting patterns from raw data' [13, pp. 2f]. DL is mostly utilized for supervised ML using apriori labeled large datasets. Frequently, 'deep learning' is used as an umbrella term for different kinds of artificial *neural networks* (NN), such as convolutional NN or *graph neural networks* (GNN). DL-based approaches relevant for this paper, i.e., for support of the early design phase in architecture, investigate the (physical) design actions performed by architects during the design process to suggest the next design step [3,20]. Besides the evaluation of the design steps data, it is also possible to utilize the current *design state*, e.g., the underlying graph of the current floor plan sketch [8]. Other DL approaches for the early design phase include optimization of urban configurations [27] or prediction of space probability using the model BHK (Bedroom, Hall, Kitchen) [21].

2.3   Clustering

Clustering is an unsupervised ML method that is able to investigate a dataset for coherent internal dependencies and correlations [23, p. 14]. The main task of all clustering algorithms is the automatic segmentation of the provided data entities into coherent groups (clusters) in order to explore the cluster data separately from the entire dataset. Clustering is widely applied in many domains and services (e.g., in marketing to build customer clusters using features, such as purchasing preferences or demographics). A well-known clustering algorithm is *k-Means*.

Graph clustering methods work with graphs instead of, e.g., categorical attributes, making use of graph-specific information (e.g., the shortest path between two nodes). Different methods were proposed to date for graph clustering. While in some cases it is hard to define if the method was developed specifically for graph clustering (e.g., k-Means can be utilized for this task too), several method families can be named as typical for application to graph clustering.

The density-based methods group together nodes of the graph that are dense, i.e., have the closest absolute distance to each other. Different distance functions can be used to detect dense clusters, e.g., *Manhattan, Euclidean,* or *Cosine* distance. A well-known density-based clustering method is *DBSCAN* (Density-based Spatial Clustering of Applications with Noise) [11]. Hierarchical graph

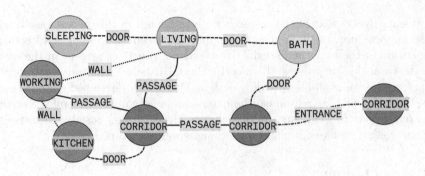

Fig. 1. An example of a graph-based room configuration.

clustering methods apply either an *agglomerative* or *divisive* approach. Agglomerative approaches consider each data point a standalone cluster and merge points with the closest distance, while divisive approaches consider the entire dataset an initial big cluster, subdividing based on distance. A representative of such approaches is *Anderberg Hierarchical Clustering* [1, pp. 131ff]. *Betweenness*-based graph clustering approaches measure how often an edge is passed through on the shortest path between two nodes. *Girvan-Newman* [12] is one of the most well-known representatives of the betweenness-based graph clustering methods.

2.4 Room Configuration

During the early design phases in architecture, it is common to sketch the early ideas for the future floor plan using a simplified schematic representation. Commonly, such schematic representations are called *room configurations* (also: *spatial configurations*). Architects draw such spatial configurations using either digital devices (e.g., Wacom tablet or iPad) or traditional sketching means (pen and paper). Room configurations usually consist of abstract representations of *rooms* (e.g., living or sleeping) and their *connections* (also: *relations*, e.g., door or passage) depicting the general layout of the upcoming floor plan. Bubbles, rectangles, or similar shapes that do not provide data on detailed geometry can be used to represent rooms, while connections are represented by lines of different thickness or style (e.g., solid or dashed). For use in architectural AI methods, the most frequent formalization of a spatial configuration is a graph-based representation, where *nodes* (rooms) and *edges* (relations) are labeled with relevant semantic information. Being a suitable representation of early design sketches, room configurations are used as cases throughout all CBR-based approaches of the projects Metis-I and Metis-II. To formalize such cases, a specific set of room types was defined for the project Metis-I, based on the architecture domain-specific space description language *Space Syntax*. Some examples of such room types are LIVING, SLEEPING, KITCHEN, BATH, WORKING, or CORRIDOR. They are complemented by the corresponding set of relation types, some examples are DOOR, PASSAGE, ENTRANCE, or WALL. Figure 1 demonstrates an example of a room configuration graph as a simplified schematic early design sketch.

3   The Autocompletion Approach

In this section, we present the AI-based autocompletion approach for room configurations that makes use of the concepts and foundations described in Sect. 2. As mentioned previously, the main purpose of this approach is to support architects during the early design phases by providing automatic suggestions for possibly missing spaces in the current floor plan design. The showcase domain of the approach is design of *housing buildings*. Figure 2 shows a visual overview of the approach. The following section describes the operation phases of the approach.

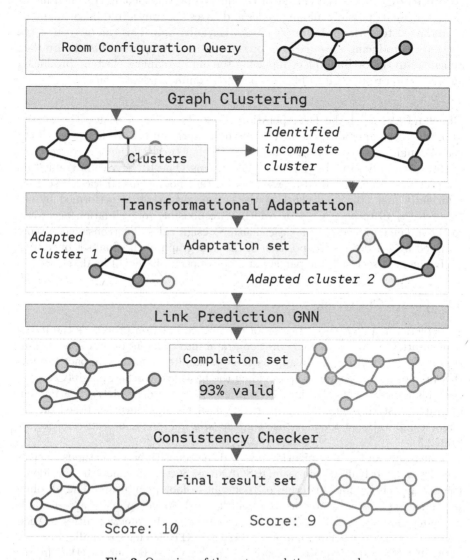

Fig. 2. Overview of the autocompletion approach.

3.1   Operation Phases

Clustering Phase. In the first operation phase, the current room configuration (query) initially gets divided into different spatial segments (clusters) followed by the detection of *incomplete* query clusters, i.e., those that might have missing rooms and connections. A cluster is incomplete if it is a subgraph of one of the clusters of a graph in the system's case base that contains *consistent* graphs, i.e., those checked for adherence to a list of basic housing design rules.

Adaptation Phase. If a cluster of the query graph is incomplete, then in the second phase its possibly missing nodes and edges are transferred (also: adapted) from the clusters where this query cluster is a subgraph. This can be seen as the process of producing a *completion* for this cluster. Completed clusters are then appended to the original query replacing the old incomplete clusters, producing an adaptation result. All results are put in a common adaptation set.

Checks Phase. In the last operation phase, in order to ensure the quality of produced completions, the results of the adaptation set are first sent to the deep learning service of *Link Prediction* (LP) that checks if the new connections might potentially exist in consistent floor plans. The LP service is trained on the previously mentioned case base of consistent floor plans. If the LP score is sufficiently high, the final check of the entire new graph is performed by the *Consistency Checker* (CC) tool, which is responsible for validation according to the aforementioned list of basic housing design rules. The consistency score returned by CC defines the position of the new graph in the final set of results.

In the next sections, the particular steps of each phase will be described.

3.2   Graph Clustering

As depicted in Fig. 2, the first step of the autocompletion process is the initial segmentation of the room configuration graph into coherent cluster spaces. This step is the key feature of the approach as its results essentially impact the further process of autocompletion providing the basis for search of possibly missing floor plan components. During the runtime of the project Metis-II, a number of graph clustering methods were investigated for this purpose, based on different computational foundations (e.g., *density*, *hierarchy*, or *betweenness*, see Sect. 2.3).

The results of this investigation revealed that density-based methods, such as the very frequently used approach DBSCAN (see Sect. 2.3), cannot be considered the optimal choice for clustering of rooms in a floor plan graph. The absolute positions (e.g., room center as x, y coordinates) do not provide a reasonable grouping foundation, i.e., might not correlate with the functionalities of their respective room types. For example, if BATH and KITCHEN have a smaller distance between their respective room centers, then they can be put together in one cluster, instead of BATH being clustered together with TOILET (a more reasonable choice) whose center coordinates have a bigger calculated distance. Hierarchical methods, dividing data points into groups using distance functions as well (see Sect. 2.3), have identical clustering problems with room configuration graphs.

Excluding both density-based and hierarchical methods, a clustering approach was required which is able to reliably find reasonable segments within spatial configuration graphs using *non-distance-based* techniques. Girvan and Newman [12] proposed a method able to produce coherent clusters of a graph using *betweenness*, a metric that calculates a numerical value for each edge based on how frequently the shortest path between two nodes passes through this edge. Using the max. number of clusters as a parameter and running multiple iterations of betweenness calculation for each edge, the *Girvan-Newman* algorithm removes edges with the highest betweenness values, separates the graph, and returns coherent clusters.

The Girvan-Newman approach is often applied in online social network services, where its algorithm is used to cluster the network into separate communities in order to make friend suggestions [6]. Adapting this method to architectural room configuration graphs, a hypothesis can be drawn that connections (edges) predominantly used as pathways between rooms (nodes) can be considered proper separators of room clusters. The implementation of the algorithm should ignore blocking connections, i.e., those physically not traversable (e.g., WALL or SLAB).

In Fig. 3, an example of graph clustering using the Girvan-Newman method is shown, applied to a room configuration graph, where the central PASSAGE relation between the LIVING and CORRIDOR rooms has the highest betweenness value of 9.

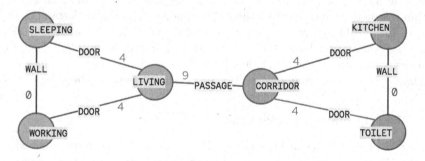

Fig. 3. Clustering of a room configuration by the Girvan-Newman [12] method.

As it is the most frequented connection in the floor plan to get from one room to another, removing this edge creates two coherent spatial clusters (subgraphs). The left (orange) cluster can be seen as a habitation zone, whereas the right one (pink) can be considered a utility zone. By the end of the investigation of clustering methods for Metis-II, the Girvan-Newman approach provided the best arguments for implementation for clustering of spatial configuration graphs.

Having detected the room clusters with the Girvan-Newman method, the autocompletion approach continues with identification of *structurally incomplete* clusters in the context of the architectural domain of the system, e.g., our show-case domain of housing buildings. In general, such context is highly dependent on the floor plan dataset (here: case base) provided to the system. The following Definition 1 was developed for Metis-II to define what is an incomplete cluster.

Definition 1. *Given a cluster set S in a room configuration graph $G = (R, C)$, a room cluster $s \in S$ is an incomplete cluster if it represents an exact or inexact subgraph of at least one cluster of any spatial configuration from the dataset, provided that all spatial configurations in the dataset are compliant with its architectural design domain and query and case graphs were processed by a clustering algorithm that ensures non-randomized segmentation results.*

From Definition 1, it can be concluded that the clustering method for auto-completion should reliably guarantee that, structurally and quantitatively, it always produces the same clusters for the room configuration graph it was provided with, given that the topological structure of this graph allows for such non-randomized segmentation. An example of a topology that does not support non-randomized clustering results is a 'rectangular' graph that contains non-blocking edges only (physically traversable connections, e.g., DOOR or PASSAGE). For such structures, it is nearly impossible to determine which of the edges has the highest betweenness value. However, as the Girvan-Newman algorithm meets this requirement, no arguments were left to look for other graph clustering methods.

Additionally, Definition 1 suggests that the system requires a subgraph matching method able to process a potentially high amount of cluster graphs within reasonable time, avoiding the NP-completeness problem of graph isomorphism. Such problems are identical to those of the CBR-based floor plan retrieval using (sub)graph matching developed for Metis-I and Metis-II [9,22]. Therefore, to identify incomplete clusters, a decision in favor of the (sub)graph isomorphism method *VF2* [7] was made, successfully applied for retrieval in these approaches.

3.3 Transformational Adaptation

After the identification of incomplete clusters and their corresponding *super-graphs* (complete clusters that enclose the incomplete ones), the rooms and relations from the supergraph that are missing in the subgraph are appended, basically applying the *transformational structural adaptation* strategies from CBR [25]. Figure 4 demonstrates an example process of transformational adaptation. In this figure, it is shown that both query clusters are incomplete, such that they both are subgraphs of complete clusters within other room configuration cases.

Algorithm 1: Transformational adaptation for room configurations.

Data: queryGraph, caseBase
Result: completedGraphs
// *Remove all walls, windows, or slab connections*
removeBlockingEdges(queryGraph);
// *Set max. number of clusters and min. number of rooms per cluster*
clusterCount = 2; minRoomsCluster = 3;
// *Get clusters using provided parameters*
queryClusters = GirvanNewmanClustering(queryGraph, clusterCount);
removeIfSmallerMinRooms(queryClusters, minRoomsCluster);
// *Find incomplete clusters*
completionIndex = [];
for *caseGraph in caseBase* **do**
  removeBlockingEdges(caseGraph);
  caseClusters = GirvanNewmanClustering(caseGraph, clusterCount);
  removeIfSmallerMinRooms(caseClusters, minRoomsCluster + 1);
  for *queryCluster in queryClusters* **do**
    for *caseCluster in caseClusters* **do**
      // *Run VF2 subgraph matching to identify inconmpleteness*
      graphIncomplete = VF2(queryCluster, caseCluster);
      if *graphIncomplete* **then**
        entry = completionIndex.getOrCreate(caseGraph.id);
        completionIndex.update(entry, caseCluster, queryCluster);

// *Sort the completion index by count of clusters matched per case*
sortByClusterMatchCount(completionIndex);
// *Append rooms and connections from matched clusters*
completedGraphs = [];
for *caseGraphId in completionIndex* **do**
  matchedClusters = completionIndex.get(caseGraphId);
  caseGraph = caseBase.get(caseGraphId);
  appendNodesAndEdges(queryGraph, caseGraph, matchedClusters);
  if *matchedClusters.size ¡ queryClusters.size* **then**
    ac = getAdditionalClusters(completionIndex, matchedClusters);
    appendNodesAndEdges(queryGraph, ac);
  completedGraphs.add(queryGraph);
return completedGraphs;

While in Fig. 4 rooms and relations from two different cases are appended, the adaptation Algorithm 1 implemented in the autocompletion approach (see Fig. 2) prefers cluster matches from the same case, effectively adapting the query as much as possible to one case, starting with cases with the highest number of cluster matches. To this end, Algorithm 1 makes use of a *completion index* created for the current matching process with case entries sorted by the number of case cluster matches in descending order. If matched clusters from one case

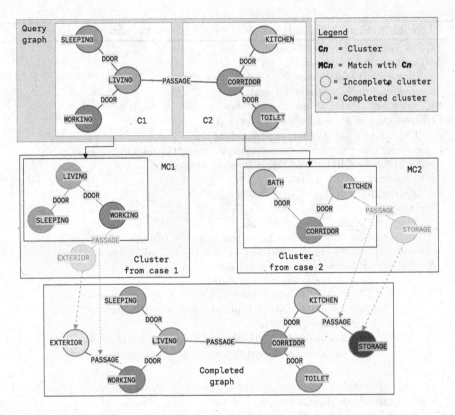

Fig. 4. An example of transformational adaptation of room clusters.

cannot complete the entire query (i.e., all incomplete query clusters), then the remaining incomplete clusters are completed by other cases using the index.

Algorithm 1 suggests that for the proper clustering and adaptation processes, several pre-processing operations are required at the start. The first such operation is the removal of the blocking edges from the graph, currently these are WALL, WINDOW, and SLAB. It is necessary to remove such relations as they break the intended use of the Girvan-Newman clustering method, being physically non-traversable to get from one room to another. Additionally, the Girvan-Newman method requires the value of max. number of clusters that should be detected.

Furthermore, to generate a reasonable number of adaptations, it was decided to introduce the min. number of rooms per cluster to be qualified for completion. Basically, this means that clusters with less rooms than the min. number will not be completed/adapted as they would produce too many matches and slow down the entire autocompletion procedure without adding a significant number of useful autocompletion results. The max. number of clusters and the min. number of rooms per cluster are set heuristically. Algorithm 1 shows the default values.

3.4   Link Prediction

After the completion process for the entire query graph has been performed by the adaptation Algorithm 1, the completion results (i.e., the new graphs) need to be checked for architectural consistency within the basic rules of designing for the domain of the autocompletion system (e.g., housing). To this end, all completion results are first put in a common *adaptation set* (see Fig. 2) which is sent to the specific deep learning service of *Link Prediction*.

The LP service [8] was developed for the project Metis-II to check if the connections between the rooms of a spatial configuration might potentially exist in domain-consistent floor plan graphs. The link prediction approach is trained on a dataset of such consistent, partly AI-generated, graphs. LP returns a *probability score* in the range 0–1 that predicts the domain consistency of the connections for the entire adaptation set, which becomes a *completion set* (see Fig. 2) if the score is sufficiently high (e.g., >0.5).

Technically, the LP service is built upon a graph neural network, a DL model developed to work specifically with unbiased graph data. In the previously published research works, GNNs were already investigated for link prediction [17,26]. Utilizing graph neural networks, it is possible to learn semantic data in spatial configuration graphs to predict if the suggested rooms can be connected to the existing ones in different spatial contexts.

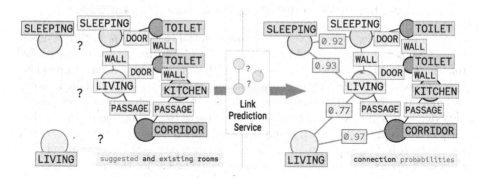

Fig. 5. Link prediction approach for spatial configurations.

In Fig. 5, the general approach of the LP method of Metis-II is demonstrated. On the left side, two new rooms (LIVING and SLEEPING), were suggested by the autocompletion process. On the right side, their probabilities to be connected to the existing rooms are depicted.

To implement LP for floor plan graphs, the framework *Deep Graph Library* (DGL) [24] was selected that provides a number of integrated graph-specific ML methods. The eventually implemented DGL-based GNN for LP [8], is a modified variant of the original network by the DGL developers. It provides an optimal use of LP for room configurations and was developed using the description language Space Syntax (see also Sect. 2.4) to formalize the training dataset. The basic foundation of the original as well as modified GNN is *negative sampling*, a method that investigates similarity of objects in the identical or similar contexts (e.g., rooms in spatial configuration graphs), trying to maximize similarity values between objects closer to each other. To this end, graph neural networks implemented in DGL learn contextual *relation triples* (e.g., LIVING<-DOOR->SLEEPING in room configuration graphs) to predict linkages between potential node neighbors.

3.5   Consistency Checker

In the last step of the autocompletion approach, provided that the LP score is sufficiently high, the final entire check of each new graph from the completion set is performed by the *Consistency Checker* [2]. CC is a rule-based approach that makes use of specific *floor plan consistency rules*, defined by the architecture domain experts from the project Metis-II, to evaluate if the room configuration complies with the spatial structure conventions of the architectural domain of the system. For the domain of housing buildings, the following rules can be used:

- Spatial configuration contains at least 3 rooms
- No direct access via PASSAGE or DOOR from BATH or TOILET to KITCHEN
- Each room has at least one relation to another room using one connection type from the set {DOOR, PASSAGE, ENTRANCE, WALL}
- No PASSAGE from BATH or TOILET (except it connects to SLEEPING)

Overall, 11 rules were implemented in the initial release *v1.0.0* of the Consistency Checker [2] and reduced to 10 in *v1.1.0*. CC returns the *consistency score* that indicates the number of positive rule checks, with the release-dependent max. value of 11 or 10. Further result data is a list of passed and failed checks to report possible spatial convention problems. Additionally, the *spatial class* is provided indicating the number of habitable spaces (e.g., sleeping, living, or children's rooms) in the floor plan graph and if it is 'open' (there is a passage between the kitchen and the living room) or 'closed' (no such passage). An example of such class is "2_open". The higher is the score returned by CC for the completed graph the higher is its position in the final set of autocompletion results.

4   Evaluation

To evaluate the autocompletion system, a performance evaluation was conducted first to explore if the approach is able to fulfill its primary purpose, i.e., autocompletion of incomplete clusters within room configuration graphs. That is, the main question to be answered was if the approach is able to produce floor plan completions that comply with *architectural consistency* in terms of *structure* and *relations*. An automatic workflow that involves all components of the autocompletion system (see Fig. 2) was developed for this evaluation process, designed as a loop that runs 10 times to exclude the possible interpretation as a random outcome. Each run of the workflow loop consists of the following steps:

Step 1. Create the run-specific evaluation dataset of room configurations that should be completed using the method of generating a validation dataset from the LP approach (see Sect. 3.4). This method ensures that all available spatial classes (see Sect. 3.5) are represented at least once within this dataset.

Step 2. Using the graphs from the evaluation dataset as queries, apply Algorithm 1 to perform completion. Use the case base of 2544 complete floor plan graphs as the adaptation basis from which completions should be appended to the detected incomplete clusters.

Step 3. Conclude the run by calculating the scores for probability of links in the adaptation set of each query using the LP service and, if qualified, structural/relational consistency of each graph from the completion set of each query.

For each run of the evaluation loop, a number of essential evaluation values for later analysis are recorded by the system; they are described in Table 1.

Table 1. Values recorded for the performance evaluation.

Value	Description
$|Q|$	Number of query graphs in evaluation dataset Q
$|R|$	$R \subset Q$, queries with results eligible for LP (valid spatial housing classes)
v_{avg}	Average number of variants (completions) produced per query $q \in Q$
l_{avg}	Average LP score per adaptation set (1.0 = highest)
l_{sel}	Cumulated LP score for a representative selection from all adaptation sets
c_{avg}	Average consistency score per completion set (10 = highest)

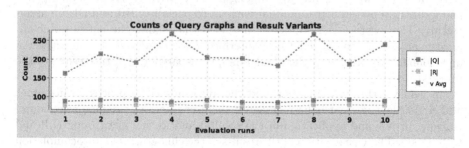

Fig. 6. Graph counts for queries, LP results, and variants averages.

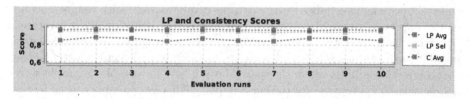

Fig. 7. LP and consistency scores (normalized to range 0–1).

In Fig. 6, the main quantitative results of the performance evaluation are shown. For all evaluation runs, the average number of completion variants per query v_{avg} is higher than the overall number of query graphs $|Q|$. It is also higher than $|R|$, the number of queries with results for which only valid spatial housing classes were detected by the Consistency Checker and therefore were selected for the adaptation set for LP (trained on valid class labels only). These results show that the system, despite removing some clusters from the completion process due to insufficient size (see Sect. 3.3), was able to generate sufficient numbers of completion suggestions, providing a big variety of completions to select from.

In Fig. 7, scores achieved for LP and CC are presented. Regarding the LP scores, all runs of the evaluation loop resulted in an average score of 0.84–0.88%, while l_{sel}, the LP score for the representative selection from all results (max. 100 results per spatial housing class) lies in a higher value range of 0.94–0.96%. This can be interpreted as a clear indication that in the representative selection results of higher quality are included. Finally, the average scores c_{avg} of the Consistency Checker response are high as well, between 9.6–9.8, which proves that the completion of clusters based on transformational adaptation has no effect on the architectural consistency in terms of structure and spatial relations.

The results of the performance evaluation allow the conclusion for the automatic evaluation process that the system was able to reach its goal, that is, to produce consistent completions of incomplete room configuration graphs. However, while the link prediction service and the Consistency Checker can be interpreted as evaluation systems with expert knowledge included, a separate user study was conducted in addition to the performance evaluation.

The character of the user study can be described as preliminary, due to the limited number of participants ($n = 4$) and evaluation materials. For this pilot study, a video[1] was disseminated among selected architecture domain experts and industry representatives familiar with AI (especially CBR and DL) in architecture. They were asked to follow the video that shows the entire autocompletion process in the specific user interface *RoomConf Editor* and answer a questionnaire to rate the self-explainability, transparency, and the results of the process.

In general, the participants found the autocompletion process transparent and could identify what is happening on the user interface (manual selection of clusters, review and application of the results) and in the background (LP and CC checks). The visualization of the results of the clustering and autocompletion process was rated positively by all participants and some participants suggested improvements for a more vivid visual feedback. Explainability of results (e.g., which CC checks have failed) was rated positively as well, with suggestions on how to improve it to match architects' language better. Additionally, it was rated positively that the system informs if for the current design no autocompletion is possible (no incomplete clusters detected). Problems were detected mostly for the autocompletion results, where the spatial layouts of some completed graphs were not considered appropriate for the current query. This was possibly caused by the

---

[1] https://www.youtube.com/watch?v=FR7EToQQcJw

partly AI-generated case base of consistent room configurations (see Sect. 3.4). Overall, the study resulted in positive feedback for the autocompletion approach.

5   Conclusion and Outlook

This paper presented an AI-based approach for autocompletion of architectural floor plans in the form of graph-based room configurations. Methods of case-based reasoning (subgraph matching and transformational adaptation), deep learning (link prediction with graph neural networks), and graph clustering (the Girvan-Newman method) are applied to identify incomplete spatial clusters in housing floor plans and complete them with the suggested rooms and connections. An additional rule-based approach is applied to check the autocompletion results for architectural consistency in terms of structure and spatial relations. The performance evaluation revealed that the autocompletion approach is able to produce room configurations compliant with the design conventions of the architectural domain of housing buildings. Further, a pilot user study revealed that users are able to understand and follow the presented autocompletion process.

For the future of the project Metis-II, the research context of the autocompletion approach, a larger user study is planned. Incorporating the feedback of the domain experts received during the pilot study, an improved setting should reveal if AI-based autocompletion methods are mature for architectural practice.

Acknowledgments. Research work presented in this paper was conducted for the research project Metis-II, funded from 2020 to 2024 by the DFG (German Research Foundation).

References

1. Anderberg, M.R.: Cluster Analysis for Applications: Probability and Mathematical Statistics: A Series of Monographs and Textbooks. Probability and mathematical statistics. Academic Press, Cambridge (1973)
2. Arora, H., et al.: Consistency checker - an automatic constraint-based evaluator for housing spatial configurations. In: Proceedings of the 39th eCAADe Conference, vol. 2, pp. 351–358 (2021)
3. Bayer, J., Bukhari, S.S., Dengel, A.: Interactive LSTM-based design support in a sketching tool for the architectural domain - floor plan generation and auto completion based on recurrent neural networks. In: Proceedings of ICPRAM 2018, pp. 115–123 (2018)
4. Bielski, J., Langenhan, C., Eisenstadt, V., Petzold, F.: Lost in architectural designing - possible cognitive biases of architects during the early design phases. In: Sociedad Iberoamericana de Gráfica. SiGraDi, Lima, Peru (2022)
5. Cavieres, A., Bhatia, U., Joshi, P., Zhao, F., Ram, A.: CBArch: a case-based reasoning framework for conceptual design of commercial buildings. Papers from the AAAI 2011 Spring Symposium (SS-11-02), pp. 19–25 (2011)

6. Chiang, J.: Girvan-newman - the clustering technique in network analysis part 1 (2021). https://medium.com/analytics-vidhya/girvan-newman-the-clustering-technique-in-network-analysis-27fe6d665c92. Accessed 27 Mar 2024

7. Cordella, L., Foggia, P., Sansone, C., Vento, M.: A (sub)graph isomorphism algorithm for matching large graphs. IEEE Trans. Pattern Anal. Mach. Intell. **26**, 1367–1372 (2004)

8. Eisenstadt, V., Bielski, J., Langenhan, C., Althoff, K.D., Dengel, A.: Autocompletion of design data in semantic building models using link prediction and graph neural networks. In: Proceedings of the 40th eCAADe Conference, vol. 1, pp. 501-510 (2022)

9. Eisenstadt, V., Langenhan, C., Althoff, K.-D., Dengel, A.: Improved and visually enhanced case-based retrieval of room configurations for assistance in architectural design education. In: Watson, I., Weber, R. (eds.) ICCBR 2020. LNCS (LNAI), vol. 12311, pp. 213–228. Springer, Cham (2020). https://doi.org/10.1007/978-3-030-58342-2_14

10. Elango, M., Devadas, M.: Identification of parameters for evaluating architectural design. a case of housing in hot and humid region, Chennai, India. In: ARCHDESIGN '14 (2014)

11. Ester, M., Kriegel, H.P., Sander, J., Xu, X.: A density-based algorithm for discovering clusters in large spatial databases with noise. In: Proceedings of the Second International Conference on Knowledge Discovery and Data Mining, pp. 226–231. AAAI Press (1996)

12. Girvan, M., Newman, M.E.J.: Community structure in social and biological networks. Proc. Natl. Acad. Sci. **99**, 7821–7826 (2002)

13. Goodfellow, I., Bengio, Y., Courville, A.: Deep Learning. MIT Press, Cambridge (2016). http://www.deeplearningbook.org. Accessed 24 Mar 2024

14. Haeusler, M.H., Butler, A., Gardner, N., Sepasgozar, S., Pan, S.: Wasted... again-or how to understand waste as a data problem and aiming to address the reduction of waste as a computational challenge. In: Proceedings of the 26th CAADRIA Conference, pp. 371–380 (2021)

15. HHH GbR: Verordnung über die honorare für architekten- und ingenieurleistungen (honorarordnung für architekten und ingenieure - hoai) - in der fassung von 2021 - (2021). https://www.hoai.de/hoai/volltext/hoai-2021/. Accessed 18 Mar 2024

16. Inanc, B.S.: Casebook. an information retrieval system for housing floor plans. In: Proceedings of the 5th CAADRIA Conference, pp. 389–398 (2000)

17. Kipf, T.N., Welling, M.: Variational graph auto-encoders. arXiv preprint arXiv:1611.07308 (2016). https://doi.org/10.48550/arXiv.1611.07308

18. Kolodner, J.: Case-Based Reasoning. Morgan Kaufmann, Burlington (1993)

19. Mercer, A.: Artificial Intelligence in BIM and renovation. buildingSMART International (2022)

20. Mete, B., Bielski, J., Langenhan, C., Petzold, F., Eisenstadt, V., Althoff, K.D.: Predicting semantic building information (BIM) with recurrent neural networks. In: ECPPM 2022. CRC Press (2022)

21. Rajasenbagam, T., Jeyanthi, S., Uma Maheswari, N.: Floor plan designer application by predicting spatial configuration using machine learning. In: Joshi, A., Mahmud, M., Ragel, R.G., Thakur, N.V. (eds.) Information and Communication Technology for Competitive Strategies (ICTCS 2020). LNNS, vol. 191, pp. 665–673. Springer, Singapore (2022). https://doi.org/10.1007/978-981-16-0739-4_63

22. Sabri, Q.U., Bayer, J., Ayzenshtadt, V., Bukhari, S.S., Althoff, K.D., Dengel, A.: Semantic pattern-based retrieval of architectural floor plans with case-based and graph-based searching techniques and their evaluation and visualization. In: Proceedings of ICPRAM 2017, vol. 1, pp. 50–60 (2017)
23. Smola, A.J.: An Introduction to Machine Learning with Kernels. Lecture 1 (2004). lecture slides. Australian National University. http://alex.smola.org/teaching/kernelcourse/day_1.pdf. Accessed 29 Mar 2024
24. Wang, M., et al.: Deep graph library: a graph-centric, highly-performant package for graph neural networks. arXiv preprint arXiv:1909.01315 (2019). https://doi.org/10.48550/arXiv.1909.01315
25. Wilke, W., Bergmann, R.: Techniques and knowledge used for adaptation during case-based problem solving. In: Pasqual del Pobil, A., Mira, J., Ali, M. (eds.) IEA/AIE 1998. LNCS, vol. 1416, pp. 497–506. Springer, Heidelberg (1998). https://doi.org/10.1007/3-540-64574-8_435
26. Zhang, M., Chen, Y.: Link prediction based on graph neural networks. In: Advances in Neural Information Processing Systems (NeurIPS), vol. 31, pp. 5171–5181. Curran Associates, Inc. (2018)
27. Zhang, Y., Grignard, A., Aubuchon, A., Lyons, K., Larson, K.: Machine learning for real-time urban metrics and design recommendations. In: Proceedings of the 38th ACADIA Conference, pp. 196–205 (2018)

A Case-Based Reasoning Approach to Post-injury Training Recommendations for Marathon Runners

Ciara Feely[✉], Brian Caulfield, Aonghus Lawlor, and Barry Smyth

Insight Centre for Data Analytics, University College Dublin, Dublin, Ireland
{ciara.feely,b.caulfield,aonghus.lawlor,barry.smyth}@ucd.ie

Abstract. Recreational running is a popular way for people to exercise, but it attracts a high rate of injury. The widespread adoption of wearable sensors has led to a large volume of real-world data about how people train and recover. While such data has been used for performance prediction and injury risk assessment, little attention has been paid to how recreational runners return to training after an injury. We consider this novel application by recommending a suitable training workload when they return to training, based on how similar runners have returned to training in the past. Our results indicate that, contrary to the conventional wisdom, a conservative return to training may not always be the best option for a runner. Higher initial workloads are associated with improved race-day performance, but without materially increasing the risk of future injuries, compared to lower training workloads.

Keywords: marathon running · CBR for health and fitness

1 Introduction

As we come to better appreciate the vital role that exercise plays in improving our lives [1], more people are engaging in various forms of endurance exercise to improve their cardiovascular fitness, mental health and overall wellbeing [2,3]. Running is one of the most popular forms of activity because of its low barrier to entry and well-documented physiological and mental health benefits [4–8].

The marathon is one of the ultimate running challenges and every year marathons around the world attract millions of runners who are motivated to tackle these challenging 26.2 mi (42.2 km) events. This interest, combined with the widespread adoption of mobile devices and wearable sensors, makes marathon running an appealing domain to explore from a machine learning perspective [9–12]. The activity data produced has enabled better race-time prediction [13–15], training plan recommendation [15–17], injury prediction [18,19], as well as several data analysis of marathon training and racing [20–23].

Although running is a popular form of exercise it is not without its problems. It is a high impact sport (each stride delivers a force equivalent to 2.5 times

J. A. Recio-Garcia et al. (Eds.): ICCBR 2024, LNAI 14775, pp. 338–353, 2024.
https://doi.org/10.1007/978-3-031-63646-2_22

a runner's body weight [24]) and it is associated with a high rate of injury, particularly over longer distances [25]. As a result, researchers have become increasingly interested in using a runner's training activity data to predict their current level of injury risk and to recommend preventative actions (e.g. reducing training volume or intensity) when appropriate [18]. While such approaches have the potential to help runners train more safely and effectively, better prediction accuracy is needed, and it is likely that many other lifestyle and historical factors are in play when it comes to the relationship between running and injury risk.

In this work, instead of trying to predict when, or if, a runner will become injured, we aim to support runners as they *return to training* after period of injury. This novel topic has received much less attention in the literature [26], but nevertheless represents an important challenge faced by many runners. Consider a runner who has been diligently following a training plan to achieve a marathon finish-time of 4 h. Unfortunately, 8 weeks before race-day they become injured and need to take a two-week break from training. Now, when the runner returns to training, there are only 6 weeks remaining to race-day. This creates a dilemma for our runner as they consider several possible return-to-training options. 'Plan A' might be to return to training as if nothing has happened – because they still want to achieve their original goal-time – so they rejoin their training programme at the 6-week point, adopting its increased training load relative to when they became injured. 'Plan B' might be more conservative: they rejoin their training programme at week 6 but perhaps with a reduced training load, at least for a week or two, and they might also reconsider their goal-time aspirations; Feely et. al [23] determined that a two week break from training was associated with a 5–8% performance cost (slow down in marathon finish-time). Finally, 'Plan C' might involve a more drastic reduction to training and a more conservative reset of their goal-time. The conventional wisdom often leans towards a more conservative return to training [26] – runners are usually cautioned against doing too much too soon – but, as we shall discuss, the data suggest that many runners adopt more aggressive strategies and perform better on race-day. To date there has been little work on how these alternatives are likely to impact performance or future injury risk and how this relates to a particular set of injury circumstances. Thus, the question of how a given runner should return to training, given their training history and race goal, remains an open problem.

Here, we use data from wearable sensors tracked using the mobile fitness application Strava[1], to study the *return-to-training* strategies of runners following a *disruption* to their training in the lead-up to a marathon race. Using ideas from case-based reasoning (CBR) [27], we create a case base of training disruptions, that is, periods with several (≥ 7) consecutive days without training indicative of injury. Each case represents a training disruption (≥ 7 days) experienced by a runner during their training. Each case is also associated with a return-to-training strategy – the relative workload in the weeks that follow injury as they return to training – their subsequent marathon finish-time and any further disruptions before race-day. For a target runner who has experienced

---

[1] www.Strava.com.

a training disruption, we identify similar cases and use their return-to-training workload as the basis for a workload recommendation for the target runner. We also predict their marathon finish-time and future disruption risk.

The remainder of this paper is organised as follows. In the next section we review related work on running-related injuries paying particular attention to recent work on the use of data-driven and machine learning techniques to predict the occurrence of such injuries during training. In Sect. 3, we describe the details of our CBR approach: we describe the structure of the cases used and we outline two different case-based approaches to support runners as they return from injury. Before concluding, in Sect. 4 we describe the results of a large-scale evaluation, based on historical training data, to evaluate the efficacy of these recommendations and predictions.

2   Related Work

Running related injuries (RRIs) are common among recreational runners. They run the gamut from bothersome "iggles"to career ending problems [28]. There have been numerous studies about the risk factors involved, from physiological factors related to the mechanics of running gait [29,30] to a runner's experience [31–33], and even their personality traits [34,35]. Most studies are limited in several ways, such as using a small numbers of participants [25] or relying on varying definitions of what constitutes an injury, even though a consensus definition usually defines an injury to be a physical problem which requires a runner to abstain from training for at least 7 days [36]. Suffice to say that when it comes to a better understanding of the relationship between training practices and injury risk, considerable further research is required.

Two factors that are often cited as risk factors for injury are a runner's history of injuries – past RRIs are strongly predictive of future RRIs [37] – and their training load [38,39], particularly sudden and significant increases in training load [40–44]. One common metric to measure training load is the so-called *acute-chronic workload ratio (ACWR)*, which is the ratio of the current week's (*acute*) training load to the average of the past 4 weeks (*chronic*). Total weekly distance is often used as a basic training load measure and previous studies have often found links between periods of high training load (ACWR>1) and injury; See [43–45].

With the widespread adoption of wearable sensors and mobile devices, there is growing optimism that the resulting activity data has the potential to revolutionise our understanding of the customs and practices of recreational runners, from the activities they engage in (e.g. timing, distance, effort) to their rest and recovery practices (e.g. using sleep trackers), and many other aspects of their overall health and wellbeing (e.g. nutrition, blood glucose etc.). Already, the availability of large-scale datasets about how recreational runners train and compete, have been used to shed fresh light on several research questions, from analysing the pacing and performance differences between male and female marathoners [21], to better understanding how and why some marathoners "it the wall"[22,46], to determining the best *tapering* strategy [20] as runners prepare for race-day.

Recently, such data-driven approaches have been used to explore the prevalence of training disruptions related to injuries during marathon training. For example, Feely et. al [23] found that 15% of runners experienced a 14-day training disruption 3–12 weeks before their marathon and that such disruptions were associated with a 5–8% performance cost on race-day. Another study found that high training load (ACWR>1.5) was associated with higher rates of injury among runners training for, and competing in, the 2019 New York City marathon [47]. In the future, it may be possible to more reliably model the relationship between fitness, training, recovery and injury risk, across many sports, to develop more effective early-warning systems for athletes; see [40,48–50]. Ultimately, the aim should be to alert runners if and when their current training practices are indicative of a greater risk of injury [51–53] and to recommend actions that they can take to reduce this risk [18].

One of the contributions of this work, which distinguishes it from what has come before, is the identification of a novel intervention to further support marathon runners. Rather than trying to predict when, or if, a runner will become injured, we instead focus on helping injured runners return to training safely and effectively. In what follows, we will describe how we do this using ideas from case-based reasoning and a large-scale, real-world dataset of marathon training activities, by recommending different return-to-training approaches.

3   A CBR System to Support Injured Runners as They Return to Training

In this section we describe our case-based approach to supporting runners as they return from an injury. We will use a large-scale dataset containing the training activities of runners during the period 2014–2017. This dataset was made available to the authors under a data sharing agreement with Strava Inc. Most runners will typically log 3–5 training sessions per week in the 12–16 weeks before race-day. Each logged activity record includes detailed time-series information about the distance, duration, pace, and elevation of the activity as described in [13,18]. The details of this dataset are described in Sect. 4.

An important limitation of this dataset is that it does not contain any explicit injury data and so, in line with [36] and [18] we use *training disruptions* as proxies for injury. Specifically, we focus on disruptions of at least 7 consecutive days without any logged training activities. However, it is worth noting that it is possible (and quite likely) that in many cases these disruptions may be for reasons other than injury, such as illness or taking a holiday. In future, we aim to validate the findings of this work with injury labelled data. In what follows, we describe how we identify and represent so-called *injury cases* from this dataset and how we can use the cases of similar runners to generate return-to-training advice for a target runner who has been recently injured, or who has had their training otherwise disrupted.

3.1   Case Representation

To begin with, we identify runners who experience training disruptions of at least 7 days during their training; shorter disruptions are unlikely to be associated with meaningful injuries although it is worth noting that some runners will experience some level of running injury without taking a complete break from training.

$$C(r, w, d, m) = \left\langle F_{pre}(r, w, m) \mid F_{post}(r, w, m), FT, Max \right\rangle \tag{1}$$

For a runner r training for marathon m, who experiences a training disruption of d days ($d \geq 7$) w weeks before race-day, we generate an injury case $C(r, w, d, m)$; see Eq. 1. Such a case is made up of the following components:

1. $F_{pre}(r, w, m)$ – refers to a feature based representation of r's training for the 4 weeks directly before the training disruption.
2. $F_{post}(r, w, m)$ – refers to a representation of their training in the period directly after the training disruption, when r returns to regular training.
3. FT – the eventual finish-time for r in marathon m.
4. $Max(d)$ – the maximum length of any future disruption (consecutive days without training) before m; longer values could indicate subsequent injury.

Thus, $F_{pre}(r, w, m)$ serves as the *case description* – used during case retrieval to identify runners with similar pre-injury training characteristics – whereas $F_{post}(r, w, m)$, FT and $Max(d)$ are elements of the *case solution* and used as prediction targets. Concretely, $F_{pre}^{w_i}(r, w, m)$ is made of the average values of the features below for the 4 weeks ($w - 1, ..., w - 4$) before the disruption.

1. $NumActivities(r, w_i)$ – the number of training activities in week w_i
2. $TotalDistance(r, w_i)$ – the total distance covered by r in w_i of training, measured in kms.
3. $MeanPace(r, w_i)$ – the mean pace for training week w_i, measured in mins/km.
4. $Fastest10kmPace(r, w_i)$ – the fastest 10km pace (mins/km) run in week w_i.

In this work, the post-injury strategy implemented by r, $F_{post}(r, w, m)$, is given by the relative difference in training load, δ, when we compare the 2 weeks pre- and post-injury. For simplicity, we use total weekly distance as a proxy for training load, and thus δ is calculated as the relative difference between the average weekly training distance in the two weeks after (*post*) and before injury (*pre*), as shown in Eq. 2.

$$\delta(r, w, m) = \frac{post(r, w, m) - pre(r, w, m)}{pre(r, w, m)} \tag{2}$$

For example, if r was running an average of 50 km per week for the two weeks before injury, and they averaged 45 km per week for the two weeks after returning to training, then $delta = \frac{45-50}{50} = -.1$ indicating a 10% reduction in training load on their return. If instead, they returned with a 60 km average training week then $\delta = \frac{60-50}{50} = 0.2$, indicating a 20% increase in training load.

It is important to note that by using relative training load, $F_{post}(r, w, m)$, we avoid the need to prescribe a specific set of training activities. This would have been inappropriate in any event since different runners will be following different training programmes, the details of which are not explicitly present in our Strava dataset. By recommending a relative training load, we instead allow the runner to translate this into a modified version of their training plan and the activities it includes for their next training weeks. If we recommend a 10% reduction in training load then the runner can decide how to implement this in a manner that best suits their needs. For example, they may reduce the distance of each of the next week's activities by 10% or they may drop an activity entirely.

3.2 A Baseline CBR Approach

Our objective is to support a target runner r_t who is planning a return to training after a break caused by injury or illness. We do this in several different ways:

1. Recommending a suitable relative training load δ allows r_t to calibrate their return-to-training relative to their training directly before their injury-break; as mentioned above, δ is the average training load in the two weeks after injury relative to the average training load in the two weeks prior to injury.
2. Predicting an eventual marathon finish-time.
3. Estimating r_t's risk of future disruptions (after they return to training and before race-day) in terms of the maximum number of days for any future disruptions they might experience.

We first present our simple baseline strategy which is to recommend a particular return-to-training strategy or workload to r_t and convey the implications of this in terms of predicted race-day performance and future injury-risk, and so help the runner to better evaluate their return-to-training options. Each of these three tasks can be implemented using a conventional kNN/CBR approach, given a target r_t, as follows:

1. Identify a set of *relevant cases*, R, by filtering the injury cases by sex, week of training, and injury duration (1–2 weeks, 2–3 weeks, >3 weeks).
2. Compare r_t's pre-injury features to the relevant cases in R – here we use standard Euclidean distance – and select the k most similar relevant cases.
3. Use these k cases to calculate the mean values for the return-to-raining strategy (using δ), estimated marathon finish-time (using FT), and predicted maximum duration of future training disruptions (using $Max(d)$).

One disadvantage of this baseline approach is that it is limited to predicting a single return-to-training workload (δ), finish-time (FT) and injury risk ($Max(d)$) for r_t to "take it or leave it". In our dataset, we find that different runners adopt very different return-to-training strategies after a break, depending on where they are in their training, the duration of their injury, and their goal-time expectations; presumably, personality and experience also play an important role in this regard. Some runners are more conservative: they return to training carefully with a reduced training load ($\delta < 0$). Others are more optimistic, preferring to pick up training from where they left off ($\delta \approx 0$). Yet others will try to make up for lost training by increasing their training load ($\delta > 0$). This suggests an alternative approach to supporting runners, one that more explicitly acknowledges these different strategies, which we discuss in the next section.

3.3   A Stratified CBR Approach

Given that runners adopt a variety of return-to-training strategies, we consider a *stratified* CBR approach to more explicitly account for this variation and to help the target runner to make a more informed decision about which approach best suits their circumstances. Instead of making a single recommendation to r_q, we recommend several different return-to-training strategies based on the range of values for $\delta(r, w, m)$ found among the injury cases that are similar to r_q. To do this we adapt our (*baseline*) CBR approach (see Fig. 1) as follows:

1. Identify a set of *relevant cases*, R, by filtering the injury cases by sex, week of training, and injury duration (1–2 weeks, 2–3 weeks, >3 weeks).
2. Stratify these relevant cases into sets of cases based on their relative return-to-training workload. Specifically, we split R into three (approximately) equal size sets of cases corresponding to *low*, *medium*, and *high* values of δ. This produces 3 sets of relevant cases, R_{low}, R_{med} and R_{high}.
3. Compare r_t's pre-injury features to the relevant cases in R_{low}, R_{med} and R_{high} and select the k most similar cases from each set: k_{low}, k_{med}, k_{high}.
4. Using these cases, calculate the weighted mean values for the return-to-raining strategy (using δ), estimated marathon finish-time (using FT), and predicted maximum duration of future training disruptions (using $Max(d)$). Thus we generated predicted δ, FT, and $Max(d)$ values from these low, medium, and high return-to-training workload strategies.

In this way, r_q is presented with a set of three different return-to-training recommendations – and their corresponding finish-times and future injury risk predictions – based on how similar runners have returned from similar injuries in the past. These recommendations reflect different levels of relative training load (low, medium, high) in the weeks that follow injury. Using this information the target runner can better understand the different return-to-training strategies (in terms of training load adjustments) that were used by runners similar to them and the corresponding performance implications on race-day.

For example, in Fig. 1 we can see that the target runner is presented with 3 return-to-training strategies with values of δ ranging from -0.10 (most conservative) to +0.16 (most aggressive). In this example, the approach that is associated with the fastest marathon time is $\delta = +0.05$. If the runner adopts this modestly aggressive approach then they will increase their training volume by about 5%

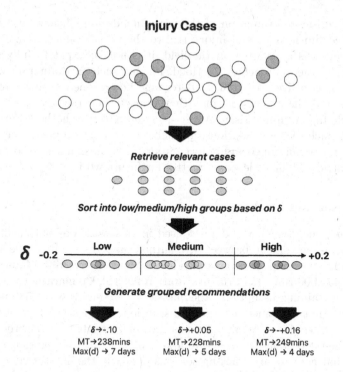

Fig. 1. Stratified CBR approach to recommending return-to-training strategies for a target runner. In this example, the recommendations include several return-to-training approaches from a conservative $\delta = -0.10$ (a 10% reduction in training load) to an aggressive $\delta = +0.16$ (16% increase in training load). In this case, we can see that the medium strategy ($\delta = +0.05$) leads to the fastest finish-time prediction (228 min) and a moderate risk of future disruption ($Max(d) = 5$ days).

over the next two weeks, relative to the two weeks before injury, to make up for their missed training time. In the past, similar runners who have taken a similar approach have achieved an average finish-time of 228 min versus the longer finish-times of more conservative and more aggressive strategies. And runners adopting this $\delta = +0.05$ workload have experienced an average future disruption of 5 days, which compares favourably with the more conservative and more aggressive alternatives. It will be up to the target runner to decide which, if any, of these approaches is appropriate to their needs, circumstances and goals, and how they wish to translate it for their particular training plan.

4   Evaluation

In this section we consider the extent to which our different CBR approaches can be used to support runners as they return from injury. We first present an analysis of the typical recommendations/predictions generated by each strategy.

Then we describe an evaluation of the recommendation efficacy by comparing the predicted finish-times and injury risk to the actual values. While this *retrospective* analysis is common in the field, it is not sufficient to fully evaluate the benefits of the approaches described. Ideally, such an evaluation would be accompanied by a live-user trial, to determine how runners respond to recommendations and the extent to which they impact their race-day performances and/or their future injury risks. A key question will be whether runners, presented with such recommendations, are liable to choose a course of action that leads to better performance and reduced injury risk, in comparison to what they might do unaided. This is left as a matter for future work.

4.1   Dataset and Methods

As previously mentioned, the dataset used in this work was obtained through a data sharing agreement between the authors and Strava Inc. The complete dataset contains training sessions uploaded to Strava between 2014 and 2017 by more than 400,000 runners in the preparation for 800,000 marathons. As we are interested in training disruptions, the dataset was reduced to 103,580 marathon training sets that contained a training disruption of at least 7 days in the 6–12 weeks before race day. This dataset was further restricted to marathon finish-times between 3–6 hours, as there are fewer runners outside this range. Finally, to ensure that runners are tracking sessions regularly the dataset contains only runners who completed at least 2 sessions per week on average for the 4 weeks prior to their disruption. A summary of the final dataset is shown in Table 1.

Table 1. The Strava dataset used in this work showing the number of injury cases available for different break/disruption durations, sex, and for different training weeks.

Break Length	Sex	w = 6	w = 7	w = 8	w = 9	w = 10	w = 11	w = 12
7–13 Days	F	813	665	685	595	597	547	451
	M	3710	3088	2921	2538	2365	2254	1932
14–20 Days	F	62	64	49	44	37	36	39
	M	304	254	245	227	216	204	197
21+ Days	F	45	43	40	38	36	34	28
	M	177	167	139	128	136	123	129

A standard 5 fold cross validation procedure is used to generate and test the recommendations/predictions produced for test runners. For each sex, training week, and break duration category, 80% of the data is used as injury cases and the remaining 20% is used for target runners/queries. For each test case we generate FT and $Max(d)$ predictions, and determine the error when comparing the predictions to their actual values. This is repeated 5 times, such that each runner is used as a test runner exactly once, and the results were averaged.

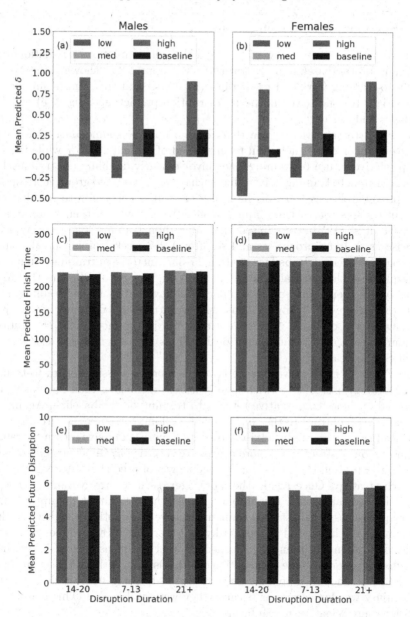

Fig. 2. The average predicted values for the relative change in training load (δ), marathon finish-time and future disruption across the baseline and stratified subgroups: low, medium and high.

4.2   Summary Recommendations

First we provide an overview of the typical recommendations/predictions that are made by the baseline and stratified CBR approaches showing the average return-to-training workload predictions (Fig. 2 (a) and (b)), finish-time predictions (Fig. 2 (c) and (d)), and future disruption predictions (Fig. 2 (e) and (f)), for males and females.

In Fig. 2 (a) and (b) we see that the workload recommendations from the *low* group involve a reduction in training load of around 20–25% while the *high* group relative return to training loads involve nearly doubling the training load upon returning to training. Given that each of these stratified groups corresponds to approximately one-third of the injury cases it is surprising to see that one-third of runners return from injury by effectively doubling their training load. However, it should be recognised that marathon training load does typically increase as training progresses and so after a 2–3 week training break, late in training, a runner might be faced with a 25–35% increase in training volume as a consequence of this natural inflation. In addition, it might also be true that in the weeks before their injury break a runner will have reduced their training, in an effort to recover while training. Thus, while returning to a doubling of their prior training load is certainly aggressive – and flies in the face of the conventional wisdom to return to training cautiously – it is perhaps not as excessive as it might first appear.

In Fig. 2 (c) and (d) we can see how this more aggressive return-to-training (high) strategy is associated with slightly faster finish-times than the finish-times predicted by more conservative returns to training or the baseline. Again, this suggests that, contrary to the conventional wisdom, there may be circumstances in which the runners can be advised to adopt a more aggressive return to training because in our dataset these more aggressive returns pay dividends on race-day.

Figure 2 (e) and (f) shows the average length of predicted future disruptions for each strategy. Once again, the more aggressive return-to-training strategy (high) is associated with favourable (slightly shorter) future disruptions than other approaches. Again, this is counter-intuitive as adopting a higher workload would normally be viewed as more risky and therefore be associated with longer future disruptions if the injury returned or other problems occurred. Yet this is not what is reported. One explanation for this is that perhaps those runners in our data who adopt a more aggressive return-to-training strategy do so because their injury was less severe or because they were well healed. This is worthy of additional investigation in the future.

4.3 Prediction Error

The results so far illustrate the different approaches runners take when returning to training, and their associated finish-time and future disruption predictions. But how accurate are these predictions? In this section we compare the prediction error rates by varying k and the training week where injury occurs (Fig. 3).

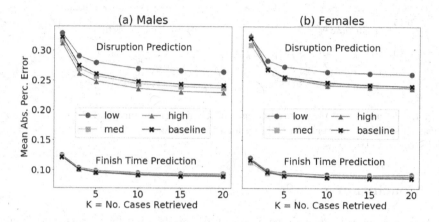

Fig. 3. The average error in predicting marathon performance and future disruption duration for different values of k (the number of cases retrieved) for (a) males and (b) females, for the baseline, and stratified strategies.

Next, using $k = 10$ we consider the finish-time and future disruption predictions generated for each week of training. The results are presented in Fig. 4 for (a) males and (b) females. In general all of the baseline and stratified approaches perform similarly when it comes to finish-time predictions but there are some differences in the accuracy of the future disruption predictions, with the high group more accurate than more cautious groups, particularly among males. There is some marginal improvement in the accuracy of finish-times as we approach race-day, but not as much as might be expected. This may be due to the fact that injury cases are based on a relative narrow snapshot of training prior to injury (4 weeks), some of which might be impacted by the impending injury, and so in the future an enriched representation may be worthwhile to consider. Finally, we notice that the accuracy of future disruptions deteriorates as we approach race-day. It is not clear why this should be the case but it may be complicated by the so-called taper period in the last 2–4 weeks in which runners gradually reduce their training load and naturally take more rest days.

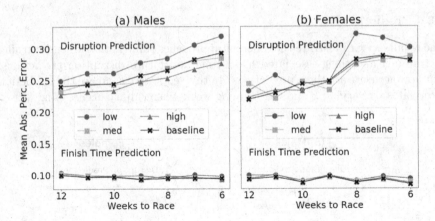

Fig. 4. The average error in predicting marathon performance and future disruption duration for different weeks in training for (a) males and (b) females, for the baseline, and stratified strategies.

5   Conclusion

In this work we have considered a novel CBR application for marathon runners: helping them to return to training after an injury by recommending them a suitable training load and by predicting their finish-times and future disruption risk. We have described an approach that presents runners with more or less conservative strategies so that they may choose the strategy that best fits their circumstances. The results of a retrospective analysis on a large-scale marathon dataset suggest that this approach may be useful to runners because the conventional wisdom, which advocates a cautious return to training, may not always be suitable. In particular, we presented evidence that a more aggressive return to training can be associated with faster finish-times on race-day and reduced risk for future disruptions for the remainder of training.

Future work will involve a user study with runners to validate the findings and to determine the efficacy of our post training disruption strategy recommendations and whether runners choose to adopt the findings or not. This work could be adapted for other endurance sports such as cycling or swimming.

Acknowledgements. Supported by Science Foundation Ireland through the Insight Centre for Data Analytics (12/RC/2289_P2).

References

1. Lieberman, D.E.: Is exercise really medicine? An evolutionary perspective. Curr. Sports Med. Rep. **14**(4), 313–319 (2015)
2. Sharma, A., Madaan, V., Petty, F.D.: Exercise for mental health. Prim. Care Companion J. Clin. Psychiatry **8**(2), 106 (2006)

3. Vina, J., Sanchis-Gomar, F., Martinez-Bello, V., Gomez-Cabrera, M.: Exercise acts as a drug; the pharmacological benefits of exercise. Br. J. Pharmacol. **167**(1), 1–12 (2012)
4. Cantwell, J.D.: Cardiovascular aspects of running. Clin. Sports Med. **4**(4), 627–640 (1985)
5. Grunseit, A., Richards, J., Merom, D.: Running on a high: parkrun and personal well-being. BMC Publ. Health **18**(1), 1–11 (2018)
6. Shipway, R., Holloway, I.: Running free: embracing a healthy lifestyle through distance running. Perspect. Publ. Health **130**(6), 270–276 (2010)
7. Szabo, A., Ábrahám, J.: The psychological benefits of recreational running: a field study. Psychol. Health Med. **18**(3), 251–261 (2013)
8. Pedisic, Z., et al.: Is running associated with a lower risk of all-cause, cardiovascular and cancer mortality, and is the more the better? A systematic review and meta-analysis. Br. J. Sports Med. **54**(15), 898–905 (2020)
9. Dunne, L.E., Ashdown, S.P., Smyth, B.: Expanding garment functionality through embedded electronic technology. J. Text. Apparel Technol. Manag. **4**(3), 1–11 (2005)
10. Willy, R.W.: Innovations and pitfalls in the use of wearable devices in the prevention and rehabilitation of running related injuries. Phys. Ther. Sport: Official J. Assoc. Chartered Physiotherapists Sports Med. **29**, 26–33 (2018)
11. Kiernan, D., et al.: Accelerometer-based prediction of running injury in national collegiate athletic association track athletes. J. Biomech. **73**, 201–209 (2018)
12. Brady, S., Dunne, L. E., Tynan, R., Diamond, D., Smyth, B., O'Hare, G.M.: Garment-based monitoring of respiration rate using a foam pressure sensor. In: Ninth IEEE International Symposium on Wearable Computers (ISWC'05), pp. 214–215, IEEE (2005)
13. Feely, C., Caulfield, B., Lawlor, A., Smyth, B.: Using case-based reasoning to predict marathon performance and recommend tailored training plans. In: Watson, I., Weber, R. (eds.) ICCBR 2020. LNCS (LNAI), vol. 12311, pp. 67–81. Springer, Cham (2020). https://doi.org/10.1007/978-3-030-58342-2_5
14. Feely, C., Caulfield, B., Lawlor, A., Smyth, B.: An extended case-based approach to race-time prediction for recreational marathon runners. In: Keane, M.T., Wiratunga, N. (eds.) Case-Based Reasoning Research and Development. Lecture Notes in Computer Science(), vol. 13405, pp. 335–349. Springer, Cham (2022). https://doi.org/10.1007/978-3-031-14923-8_22
15. Berndsen, J., Smyth, B., Lawlor, A.: Fit to run: Personalised recommendations for marathon training. In: Fourteenth ACM Conference on Recommender Systems, pp. 480–485 (2020)
16. Feely, C., Caulfield, B., Lawlor, A., Smyth, B.: Providing explainable race-time predictions and training plan recommendations to marathon runners. In: Fourteenth ACM Conference on Recommender Systems, RecSys '20, (New York, NY, USA), pp. 539-544. Association for Computing Machinery (2020)
17. Feely, C., Caulfield, B., Lawlor, A., Smyth, B.: Modelling the training practices of recreational marathon runners to make personalised training recommendations. In: Proceedings of the 31st ACM Conference on User Modeling, Adaptation and Personalization, pp. 183–193 (2023)
18. Feely, C., Caulfield, B., Lawlor, A., Smyth, B.: A case-based reasoning approach to predicting and explaining running related injuries. In: Sánchez-Ruiz, A.A., Floyd, M.W. (eds.) ICCBR 2021. LNCS (LNAI), vol. 12877, pp. 79–93. Springer, Cham (2021). https://doi.org/10.1007/978-3-030-86957-1_6

19. Smyth, B., Lawlor, A., Berndsen, J., Feely, C.: Recommendations for marathon runners: on the application of recommender systems and machine learning to support recreational marathon runners. User Model. User-Adap. Inter. **32**(5), 787–838 (2022)

20. Smyth, B., Lawlor, A.: Longer disciplined tapers improve marathon performance for recreational runners. Front. Sports Active Living., 275 (2021)

21. Smyth, B.: Fast starters and slow finishers: a large-scale data analysis of pacing at the beginning and end of the marathon for recreational runners. J. Sports Analyt. **4**, 229–242 (2018)

22. Berndsen, J., Lawlor, A., Smyth, B.: Exploring the wall in marathon running. J. Sports Analyt. **6**, 1–14 (2020)

23. Feely, C., Smyth, B., Caulfield, B., Lawlor, A.: Estimating the cost of training disruptions on marathon performance. Front. Sports Active Living **4**, 507 (2022)

24. Mann, R.: Biomechanics of running. Running Injuries, 1–20 (1989)

25. Kluitenberg, B., van Middelkoop, M., Diercks, R., van der Worp, H.: What are the differences in injury proportions between different populations of runners? A systematic review and meta-analysis. Sports Med. (Auckland, N.Z.) 45, 1143–1161 (2015)

26. World, R.: How to run a half marathon - and half marathon training plans for every runner. https://www.runnersworld.com/uk/training/half-marathon/a764179/half-marathon-training-plans/. Accessed 01 Mar 2024

27. Kolodner, J.: Case-Based Reasoning. Morgan Kaufmann, Burlington (2014)

28. Lacey, A., Whyte, E., O'Keeffe, S., O'Connor, S., Burke, A., Moran, K.: The running injury continuum: a qualitative examination of recreational runners' description and management of injury. PLoS ONE **18**, e0292369 (2023)

29. Napier, C., MacLean, C.L., Maurer, J., Taunton, J.E., Hunt, M.A.: Kinetic risk factors of running-related injuries in female recreational runners. Scand. J. Med. Sci. Sports **28**, 2164–2172 (2018)

30. Vannatta, C.N., Heinert, B.L., Kernozek, T.W.: Biomechanical risk factors for running-related injury differ by sample population: a systematic review and meta-analysis. Clin. Biomech. **75**, 104991 (2020)

31. Damsted, C., Parner, E.T., Sørensen, H., Malisoux, L., Nielsen, R.O.: ProjectRun21: do running experience and running pace influence the risk of running injury-A 14-week prospective cohort study. J. Sci. Med. Sport **22**, 281–287 (2019)

32. Kemler, E., Blokland, D., Backx, F., Huisstede, B.: Differences in injury risk and characteristics of injuries between novice and experienced runners over a 4-year period. Phys. Sportsmed. **46**, 485–491 (2018)

33. Agresta, C.E., Peacock, J., Housner, J., Zernicke, R.F., Zendler, J.D.: Experience does not influence injury-related joint kinematics and kinetics in distance runners. Gait Posture **61**, 13–18 (2018)

34. Fields, K.B., Delaney, M., Hinkle, J.S.: A prospective study of type a behavior and running injuries. J. Fam. Pract. **30**, 425–429 (1990)

35. Nielsen, R.O., et al.: Predictors of running-related injuries among 930 novice runners: a 1-year prospective follow-up study. Orthop. J. Sports Med. **1**(1), 2325967113487316 (2013)

36. Yamato, T.P., Saragiotto, B.T., Lopes, A.D.: A consensus definition of running-related injury in recreational runners: a modified Delphi approach. J. Orthop. Sports Phys. Ther. **45**, 375–380 (2015)

37. Fokkema, T.: Prognosis and prevention of injuries in recreational runners. PhD thesis, University of Rotterdam (2020)

38. Nielsen, R.O., Buist, I., Sørensen, H., Lind, M., Rasmussen, S.: Training errors and running related injuries: a systematic review. Int. J. Sports Phys. Ther. **7**, 58–75 (2012)

39. Baltich, J., Emery, C., Whittaker, J., Nigg, B.: Running injuries in novice runners enrolled in different training interventions: a pilot randomized controlled trial. Scand. J. Med. Sci. Sports **27**, 08 (2016)

40. Thornton, H.R., Delaney, J.A., Duthie, G.M., Dascombe, B.J.: Importance of various training-load measures in injury incidence of professional rugby league athletes. Int. J. Sports Physiol. Perform. **12**, 819–824 (2017)

41. Malisoux, L., Nielsen, R.O., Urhausen, A., Theisen, D.: A step towards understanding the mechanisms of running-related injuries. J. Sci. Med. Sport **18**, 523–528 (2015)

42. Lazarus, B.H., et al.: Proposal of a global training load measure predicting match performance in an elite team sport. Front. Physiol. **8**, 930 (2017)

43. Barros, E.S., et al.: Acute and chronic effects of endurance running on inflammatory markers: a systematic review. Front. Physiol. **8**, 779 (2017)

44. Bowen, L., Gross, A.S., Gimpel, M., Bruce-Low, S., Li, F.X.: Spikes in acute: chronic workload ratio (ACWR) associated with a 5–7 times greater injury rate in English premier league football players: a comprehensive 3-year study. Brit. J. Sports Med. **54**, 731–738 (2019)

45. Hulin, B.T., Gabbett, T.J., Lawson, D.W., Caputi, P., Sampson, J.A.: The acute: chronic workload ratio predicts injury: high chronic workload may decrease injury risk in elite rugby league players. Br. J. Sports Med. **50**, 231–236 (2016)

46. Smyth, B.: How recreational marathon runners hit the wall: a large-scale data analysis of late-race pacing collapse in the marathon. PLoS ONE **16**(5), e0251513 (2021)

47. Toresdahl, B.G., et al.: Training patterns associated with injury in New York city marathon runners. Brit. J. Sports Med. **57**, 146–152 (2022)

48. Rossi, A., Pappalardo, L., Cintia, P., Iaia, F., Fernández, J., Medina, D.: Effective injury forecasting in soccer with GPS training data and machine learning. PLoS ONE **13**, e0201264 (2018)

49. Carey, D. L., Ong, K., Whiteley, R., Crossley, K.M., Crow, J., Morris, M.E.: Predictive modelling of training loads and injury in Australian football. arXiv preprint: arXiv:1706.04336 (2017)

50. Kampakis, S.: Comparison of machine learning methods for predicting the recovery time of professional football players after an undiagnosed injury. MLSA@PKDD/ECML (2013)

51. Gabbett, T.J.: The training-injury prevention paradox: should athletes be training smarter and harder? Br. J. Sports Med. **50**(5), 273–280 (2016)

52. López-Valenciano, A., et al.: A preventive model for muscle injuries: a novel approach based on learning algorithms. Med. Sci. Sports Exerc. **50**, 915–927 (2018)

53. Claudino, J.G., Capanema, D.D.O., de Souza, T.V., Serrão, J.C., Machado Pereira, A.C., Nassis, G.P.: Current approaches to the use of artificial intelligence for injury risk assessment and performance prediction in team sports: a systematic review. Sports Medi. - Open 5, 28 (2019)

Towards Network Implementation of CBR: Case Study of a Neural Network K-NN Algorithm

Xiaomeng Ye[1]([⊠]), David Leake[2] [ID], Yu Wang[2], Ziwei Zhao[2], and David Crandall[2]

[1] Department of Mathematics and Computer Science, Berry College, Mount Berry, GA 30149, USA
xye@berry.edu
[2] Luddy School of Informatics, Computing, and Engineering, Indiana University, Bloomington, IN 47408, USA
{leake,yw173,zz47,djcran}@iu.edu

Abstract. Recent research brings the strengths of neural networks to bear on CBR tasks such as similarity assessment and case adaptation. This paper further advances this direction by implementing both retrieval and adaptation as a single neural network. Such an approach has multiple goals: From the perspective of CBR, it enables harmonizing the interaction between feature extraction, retrieval/similarity assessment, and case adaptation through end-to-end training. From the perspective of neural networks, a neural network implementing CBR processes ceases to be a black box and provides the natural interpretability of CBR. As a first step towards this goal, this paper presents *neural network based k-nearest neighbor* (NN-kNN), a network architecture that can be interpreted as a k-NN method. Unlike other network architectures, NN-kNN's decisions can be fully explained in terms of surface features, feature/case weights and nearest neighbors. It can be trained or fine-tuned using existing neural network methods. This study illustrates its feasibility and examines its strengths and limitations. The approach is evaluated for classification and regression tasks comparing NN-kNN, a standard neural network, and k-NN models using state-of-the-art distance metric learning algorithms. In these tests, NN-kNN achieves equal or less error when compared to the other models, while being fully interpretable as a k-NN method. The study also considered the limitations of NN-kNN and future directions to alleviate them.

1 Introduction

Neural network (NN) techniques are powerful but often uninterpretable black boxes. Tremendous effort has been devoted to opening the black box with post-hoc explanation [11]. As observed since the early days of CBR research, case-based reasoning provides interpretability [17], suggesting benefits of hybrid systems where a CBR system provides cases as explanations for network decisions

J. A. Recio-Garcia et al. (Eds.): ICCBR 2024, LNAI 14775, pp. 354–370, 2024.
https://doi.org/10.1007/978-3-031-63646-2_23

[20]. However, Rudin [27] contends that post-hoc explanations have fundamental flaws and that intrinsically interpretable methods are needed for critical tasks.

An alternative to abandoning networks or relying on post-hoc explanation is to develop network architectures that are more interpretable. An interesting approach to this is to design network architectures so that their processes parallel CBR [20]. Li et al. [22] propose a neural network model in which predictions are based on learned prototypes, which that can subsequently be used to explain network decisions. Their model uses an autoencoder to encode features and reconstruct samples from features, and a special prototype layer which stores the features of prototypes found through training. The prototype layer calculates the distance between the input and each prototype, which then feeds to a fully connected layer for a final classification output. The model is trained with a loss function that encourages (1) high classification accuracy, (2) faithful reconstruction from the autoencoder, (3) every prototype being similar to at least one encoded input and every encoded input being similar to at least one prototype. In summary, the model learns prototypes in a low dimensional space, which are then used in distance-based classification.

Their approach enables explaining using learned prototypes and achieves strong accuracy. However, it has limitations as well. First, the system learns the prototypes through an autoencoder, which is a black box itself. Second, there is no guarantee that sufficiently similar prototypes exist to explain all or most of the possible situations, or that the prototypes will correspond to actual situations in the world, or that they will be comprehensible to humans (e.g., if a prototype were to blend several conflicting classes). Our goal is to develop a fully interpretable network model based on cases rather than prototypes. As a fully interpretable model, it is at one endpoint of the interpretability spectrum. Researchers can integrate it with black-box approaches to trade off interpretability for accuracy, ease of use, prepocessing, multi-modal learning, scalability or other benefits of black-box models.

Our model, called *Neural network based k-nearest neighbor*, is a neural network that compares a query with stored cases, activates neighboring cases, and makes a prediction based on the labels and activations of the neighboring cases, It can function like a classical k-NN system, with full interpretability. It can be chained with a feature extractor to learn features that best serve k-NN or that are harmonized with a network case adaptation module, or to be combined with other neural network modules for decisions based on the nearest neighbors found. Unlike CBR systems where feature extraction, similarity metrics, or adaptation methods are independent neural/symbolic components, our model does everything in a single neural network. Therefore, the different stages of CBR are trained from end to end to minimize a single loss function combining factors such as explainability, adaptation distance, and even case maintenance cost, achieving better overall system performance. Previous work has show the benefit of harmonizing similarity and adaptation knowledge [18,29]; we hypothesize that analogous benefits can accrue to other CBR processes as well.

This paper is organized as follows. Section 2 discusses related research in learning for k-NN, ANN-CBR hybrid methods, and interpretable AI. Section 3 explains NN-kNN from the perspectives of neural networks and k-NN. Section 4 compares NN-kNN and other models in computational experiments. The paper concludes with discussion and future directions.

2   Background

2.1   K-Nearest Neighbor and Distance Metric Learning

K-NN can be viewed as a simple form of CBR with minimal adaptation (e.g., averaging of case values). In its most basic form, k-NN, for classification tasks, takes the majority vote of the top k nearest neighbors' class labels, and for regression tasks, averages the labels. [6]. K-NN models are appealing because they are easy to interpret and often provide good accuracy [2].

A simple k-NN approach assumes that all features are equally important in the calculation of distances between cases, and that all cases carry equal weight in the voting of the final prediction. Wettschereck et al. [34] relax both assumptions with a general distance calculation. Following that, research on distance metric learning has yielded many variants of k-NN [1,16,24,33]. Feature-weighted k-NN weights each feature differently (e.g. house age and number of rooms are more important in deciding a house's price that its longitude and latitude). Methods such as neighborhood components analysis (NCA) and large margin nearest neighbor (LMNN) learn a linear transformation of the feature space to enhance classification accuracy [10,33]. Distance-weighted k-NN weights cases based on their distance from the query. Instance-weighted k-NN weights cases based on their own significance (e.g. a run-down house in a good neighborhood is an outlier and carries less weight) [3].

This paper proposes a general model wherein the calculations of feature distances, case distances, and target activations are implemented by layers in a neural network that can be trained together.

2.2   Hybrid ANN-CBR Models

ANN-CBR integrations have been proposed both to provide explanations for neural systems and to improve the performance of CBR. In twin systems, cases retrieved using features extracted from networks are used as post-hoc explanations of network decisions [14]. The goal of such systems is to illustrate the types of cases the network might consider similar, but the explanation is decoupled from the network processing. NN-kNN contrasts in providing an interpretable network: it retrieves cases and then adapts them towards the final prediction.

Hybrid ANN-CBR models have also used neural networks to implement different CBR stages [5,28], with the goal of increasing the scope of CBR system applicability (e.g., to image-based data [31] or increasing the performance of CBR). For example, Mathisen et al. [23] used a siamese network to implement the similarity measurement in case retrieval, and Ye et al. [35] trained a neural network to carry CBR adaptation using case difference heuristics. Following this work, Leake and Ye built a CBR system that uses a siamese network for retrieval and another neural network for adaptation, and then trained the two stages using alternating optimization [21]. The goal of their approach was to harmonize retrieval and adaptation, enabling automated refinement of the coupling of retrieval and adaptation knowledge that had been shown important in the research on adaptation-guided retrieval [30] and case-based coupling similarity and adaptation learning [18]. NN-kNN combines both retrieval and adaptation in a single neural network model (instead of two) and trains both processes end to end to harmonize them. This is especially beneficial when the training needs to coordinate many independent components (e.g. feature extractor, retrieval, adaptation, and case base maintenance).

2.3   Interpretable Neural Networks

Rudin [27] argues that post-hoc explanation of neural networks is inadequate for critical applications. In response, Li et al. [22] propose a neural network model for image classification which can explain each prediction with a set of learned prototypes. Their model includes an autoencoder to encode features and reconstruct samples from features. A special prototype layer stores the features of prototypes found through training, and reconstructed images of prototypes are used for explanation. Their system is interpretable in that network classifications are based on prototypes, and explanations reveal the prototypes used by the system. However, using learned prototypes has potential limitations: the learned prototypes are not guaranteed to correspond to any real example and may blend several conflicting classes, making them less understandable or convincing to a user, and a case may not be covered by any prototype sufficiently similar to be a convincing explanation. Another approach, taken by Chen et al. [4] in ProtoPNet, focuses on explanation based on component extraction: the network "dissects the image by finding prototypical parts, and combines evidence from the prototypes to make a final classification".

Logical Neural Networks [26] address interpretability by endowing each node in a network with the meaning of a logical operator or proposition, and performing logical inference through the network process. They reflect the neuro-symbolic perspective that neural net and logic statements are two renderings of the same model. Our model has an analogous duality: the neural network and k-NN are two renderings of NN-kNN.

3   The NN-kNN Architecture

Neural network based k-nearest neighbor (NN-kNN) is a neural network with special structures and parameters to capture properties of k-NN. Similar to traditional k-NN algorithms, an NN-kNN stores a set of training cases. The basic process is: NN-kNN calculates the case distance between the query and

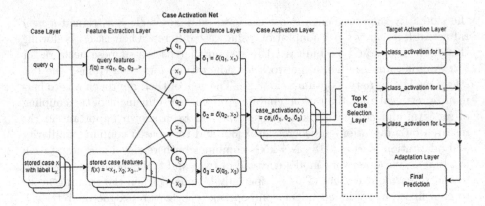

Fig. 1. The Model of NN-kNN.

each stored case; The closer cases gain higher activation values; Activated cases contribute to a weighted voting of the final prediction. A sample NN-kNN model is shown in Fig. 1. Its workflow is as follows (this is an intuitive description of the general process, which we specify in the following section):

1. Given a query q, a copy of q is paired with each stored case x and passed to the feature extraction layer.
2. The feature extraction layer uses a feature extractor f to get the features of the query and cases. This corresponds to the CBR situation assessment process [15].
3. The feature distance layer δ measures distance between corresponding features as $\delta_i = \delta_i(q_i, x_i)$
4. The case activation layer sums up all feature distances δ_is between q and x and calculates a case activation value representing how much the case x activates for the query q.
5. The steps 1–4 are repeated for the query q and each stored cases. The NN-kNN produces one case activation value for each stored case.
6. An optional top k case selection layer then selects the top k activated cases.
7. The target activation layer activates the target output neuron by considering the case activation values. Then a final adaptation layer produces the output based on activated labels.

3.1 Default Implementation of NN-kNN

We consider NN-kNN for classification and regression tasks where each case x contains multiple features and a label L_x. Below we describe a default implementation of the model layers and explain why it is a k-NN method.

1. Feature extraction layer: As for traditional CBR situation assessment, when input cases are already represented as desired features, no processing is needed. In such case, this layer can be omitted. Let $f(x) = <x_1, x_2, x_3...>$ and $f(q) = <q_1, q_2, q_3...>$, where x_i and q_i are the i-th feature of x and q. Potentially, the feature extraction layer can be a ResNet model for images, a doc2vec model for documents, or any neural feature extractor.

2. Feature distance layer: For $\delta_i()$ we use weighted mean square difference

$$\delta_i(q_i, x_i) = w_{xi}(q_i - x_i)^2$$

where w_{xi} is the feature weight for the case x's feature x_i. Here we assume non-nominal attributes, which requires alternative weightings. The function $\delta_i(q_i, x_i)$ outputs a non-negative number and bigger differences are weighted more after the square operation.

3. Case activation layer: This layer calculates

$$case\_activation(x) = ca_x(\delta_1, \delta_2, \delta_3...) = \sigma(w_{x\delta_1} * \delta_1 + w_{x\delta_2} * \delta_2 + ... + b_x)$$

where $w_{x\delta_i}$ is the weight for feature distance δ_i and b_x is the bias for the case x. The sigmoid function $\sigma(ca) = \frac{1}{1+e^{-ca}}$ limits $case\_activation$ within $[0, 1]$.

NN-kNN calculates the distance between the query and a stored case as a weighted combination of feature distances. Because higher feature distances decrease case activation, feature distance weights $w_{x\delta_i}$ are less than or equal to zero. Thus b_x can be considered as a baseline activation of the case x while $w_{x\delta_i} * \delta_i$ is an inhibitor reducing the activation. The case activation layer uses a sigmoid function to limit all $case\_activations$ in the range of $[0, 1]$. The lower limit prevents negative activations while the upper limit of (≤ 1) prevents any case from being overly active and overshadowing the influence of other cases.

In the two layers above, cases may share feature weighting, or each case may have its own feature weighting. To illustrate, consider two cases x and y:

1. Their feature distance functions may share a feature weight for the same feature, or $w_{xi} = w_{yi}$.
2. Their case activation functions may share the same feature distance weights, or $w_{x\delta_i} = w_{y\delta_i}$.

If all weight sharing is disabled, each case has its own set of weightings. It is as if each case has its own NN-kNN model with unique weights and biases. If all weight sharings are enabled, all cases share a single NN-kNN model. Case biases b_x and target activation weights $w_{(x,L)}$ (described later) are never shared.

Our choices of feature distance function δ and case activation function ca produce overlapping effects between the weight w_{xi} in the feature distance layer and the weight $w_{x\delta_i}$ in the case activation layer. Consequently, disabling weight sharing for either is effectively disabling both. We therefore regard the two weight sharing settings as a single "weight sharing" flag in Tables 1 and 2. This is not necessarily true for other choices of δ and ca functions.

4. Top k case selection layer: This layer keeps the top k activated cases' activation values and resets other activation values to 0. If this layer is disabled, all activation values are considered for the next step. It is recommended to disable this layer during training for classification, or altogether for regression, as explained later in the Sect. 5.

The optional top k case selection layer imitates a k-NN model selecting the top k nearest neighbors. When this layer is disabled, NN-kNN behaves more like a standard neural network classifier/regressor where all activations are considered.

5. Target Activation Layer and Final Adaptation Layer: In classification, the target activation layer has multiple neurons, each representing an unique class L. A neuron's output is a weighted sum of all *case_activations* as

$$class\_activation_L = \Sigma_x(w_{(x,L)} * case\_activation(x)) + b_L$$

where $w_{(x,L)}$ is the weight of the case x for the class L, *case_activation*(x) is the *case_activation* of the case x and b_L is the bias of the class L. A rule is set that $w_{(x,L)} > 0$ if the case x is of class L and $w_{(x,L)} = 0$ otherwise, because a case is supposed to only contribute to its correct class label but not to other labels. The adaptation layer chooses the label L with the maximum *class_activation*.

In regression, the target activation layer and adaptation layer is a single neuron. Its output *num_prediction* is a numeric value representing the final prediction. Case activations are normalized based on the sum of all case activations and then they all contribute to the final prediction to the extent of their own labels.

$$normalized\_CA(x) = \frac{case\_activation(x)}{\Sigma_i case\_activation(i)} \quad num\_prediction = \Sigma_i(normalized\_CA(i) * L_i)$$

where $\Sigma_i case\_activation(i)$ is the total of all case activations and L_i is the correct label (numerical value) for case i.

During training, the loss is calculated as the error of the final output (cross entropy loss for classification and mean squared error for regression) and backpropagated to all layers in NN-kNN.

In distance-based k-NN, cases are weighted based on their distance to the query. Closer cases carry more weight in deciding the final label. In NN-kNN, a high *case_activation* indicates a closer case and contributes more to the downstream *class_activation* or *num_prediction*. In Regression, all case activations collectively contribute to one target node. The final prediction is a weighted average of the cases' labels, weighted by their *case_activations*. In instance-weighted k-NN, regardless of their distances to the query, some cases are more important (e.g. a prototype) than others (e.g. an outlier). Instance-weighted k-NN assigns a weight for each case. NN-kNN imitates this behavior with the weight $w_{(x,L)}$ in classification, where a higher weight means the case contributes more to the final prediction.

3.2   NN-kNN Is a k-NN Method

In its simplest form, NN-kNN can be tuned to act as a vanilla k-NN classifier by choosing the following parameters for each case x: $w_{xi} = w_{x\delta_i} = 1$ for any feature i, so all features are weighted equally; $b_x = 1$ so all cases are weighted equally; The top k case selection layer is enabled; $w_{(x,L)} = 1, b_L = 0$ if the case x is of class L, so each case contributes equally to the final label.

The parameter settings above can also be tuned for NN-kNN to act as a k-NN regressor. A vanilla k-NN regressor selects the top k cases and then takes their average values as its final prediction. The required NN-kNN parameter settings are: $w_{xi} = w_{x\delta_i} = 1$ for any feature i, $b_x = 1$, the top k case selection layer is enabled, and the final adaptation layer sets non-zero case activations to $1/k$. Therefore the top k cases will be selected and their numeric labels averaged.

When weights and biases are preset as described above, NN-kNN replicates a vanilla k-NN. When certain weights are not fixed, NN-kNN can imitate the behavior of k-NN variants using feature weightings, distance weightings, instance weightings, or any combination of them.

We note that NN-kNN's default implementation contains no fully connected layers or other structures that would be considered black boxes. The whole model can be fully interpreted as a CBR system using k-NN for retrieval and a final neural layer for adaptation. However, the model is still a neural network and compatible with network training techniques and with black-box models. Therefore, this formulation of NN-kNN can serve as an endpoint in the spectrum of interpretability, and future variants might combine NN-kNN with black-box models to trade interpretability for accuracy, ease of use, adaptability, scalability or other benefits of black-box models.

3.3   The Benefits of a Network Architecture for k-NN

In addition to its interpretability and high accuracy (which are examined in Sect. 4), NN-kNN offers the following benefits:

Simple Training: Because NN-kNN is trained by backpropagation regardless of its configuration, it is simple to train compared to traditional k-NN variants. Such variants can use combinations of several categories of weights but require several training schemes to train different weights separately. For example, Jie et al. [12] calculate the weighting of a feature based on accuracy of the data without a feature and then use class distributions to predict based on nearest neighbors. To our knowledge, no prior kNN variant trains multiple categories of weightings simultaneously using a single procedure, because different weightings interact with and influence each other in the model's final prediction. All the weights and biases in NN-kNN can be trained from end to end using back-propagation, as for any other neural network.

Harmonization Across CBR Knowledge Containers: CBR systems are often built with retrieval and adaptation steps in independent but interacting modules. Harmonization between the two steps is not guaranteed. For example, the retrieval step might retrieve a case seemingly similar to the query, but whose solution is hard to adapt to solve the query [30]. NN-kNN encapsulates both retrieval and adaptation. NN-kNN achieves retrieval by all layers until the case activation layer, and adaptation by the target activation layer and a final adaptation layer. The two stages are trained together using backpropagation to minimize a total loss (e.g. prediction accuracy) for the whole system.

NN-kNN can easily chain with other network methods. Traditional k-NN methods struggle with high dimensional or complex data sets. Existing works may use a feature extractor such as a VGG net to extract facial features first and use those features as case features in k-NN [36]. There is no guarantee that the features extracted are useful for the k-NN method in predicting the target label. However, when the feature extractor and the NN-kNN model are trained together from end to end and if the performance of the combined model is good, we know that the feature extracted are actually useful features for NN-kNN to identify nearest neighbors and make a final prediction.

4   Evaluation

We carried out experiments to compare NN-kNN, a neural network of similar complexity and k-NN using state-of-the-art metric learning algorithms. We addressed two questions: 1) Does NN-kNN provide accuracy comparable to other models? 2) Are the cases activated by NN-kNN good explanations for the model's final decision? Potentially, NN-kNN as a neural network could make correct predictions based on combinations of evidence that do not align with the most similar cases, making their explanations unintuitive (human subjects studies show that the similarity of a case to a new situation affects user trust [9]). Consequently, here we examine if NN-kNN falls into this trap by checking if the top activated cases' labels are close to the real target.

4.1   Implementation Details

Our testbed implementation of NN-kNN followed Sect. 3.1. We omitted the feature extraction layer and used the features provided in the data sets.

Parameter Settings: We tested four different settings of NN-kNN, with feature weight sharing enabled/disabled and its top k case selection layer enabled/disabled. We compared NN-kNN with k-NN models using three distance metric learning algorithms (from sklearn [25] and metric-learn [32] implementation): Euclidean distance, Neighborhood Components Analysis (NCA) [10] and Large Margin Nearest Neighbor (LMNN) [33]. NCA and LMNN only work with classification data sets. For NN-kNN, NCA and LMNN we set $k = 5$ because it works well on all data sets. For LMNN we used a default learning rate of $1e - 6$. Other parameters for NCA and LMNN are set to their default values. We also compare with standard neural network models. For classification tasks, the neural network comprises four hidden layers using the LeakyReLU activation function. For regression tasks, it includes three hidden layers with the ReLU activation function, and dropout layers with a 0.5 probability incorporated in the final two hidden layers. The number of parameters of the linear layers is slightly increased for data sets of higher complexity. Each network model (NN-kNN or a neural network) is trained until its testing performance does not improve for 40 epochs, and the best-so-far model is chosen. The training procedure uses the Adam optimizer (we used learning rate = 0.01 for NN-kNN and 0.0001 for a neural network because the settings produced the best average result) based on cross entropy loss for classification and mean square error loss for regression.[1]

Data Sets and Procedure: Experiments used 10-fold cross validation for six classification data sets and four regression data sets. Classification data sets are Olivetti faces, digits, iris, wine, breast cancer, and balance. Regression data sets are diabetes, california housing, abalone, and body fat and their feature values are normalized befor experiments. They are all available from the UCI ML repository [7] or integrated in scikit-learn [25]. To investigate the performance of NN-kNN with instance-based feature weighting, we also created two data sets, Zebra (a) and Zebra (b) (shown in Fig. 2), which contain cases with (x, y) coodinates and one of two class labels. In Zebra (a), two classes (100 cases) alternate along the x axis, analogously to a zebra stripe pattern. In Zebra (b), two classes (100 cases) appear in a vertical zebra stripe pattern when $x < 100$ and (100 cases) in a horizontal zebra stripe pattern when $x \geq 100$. The data set Zebra (b) is more difficult than Zebra (a) as it requires the classifier to learn local patterns instead of a single global pattern.

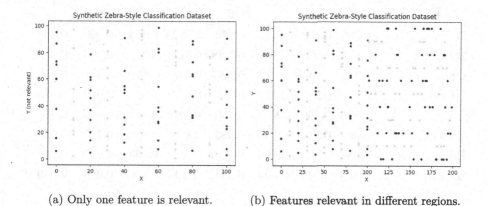

(a) Only one feature is relevant.   (b) Features relevant in different regions.

Fig. 2. Two Zebra-Style Data Sets

---

[1] Code is available at https://github.com/Heuzi/NN-kNN/tree/main.

4.2 Experimental Results

Tables 1 and 2 summarize the experimental results. Numbers for classification are classification accuracy (the higher the better). Numbers for regression are mean square error (the lower the better). For regression, the errors of the top k cases' average in NN-kNN are also shown. We first consider results on the zebra data sets, then classification, and finally regression.

Generated Zebra Stripe Data Sets: Many methods struggle in the generated zebra data sets as data are sparse and one of the two dimensions is irrelevant (row 1 and 2 in Table 1). Methods with feature weightings and instance weightings, such as NN-kNN, can potentially solve Zebra data sets well. For data set 2a, NN-kNN achieves highest accuracy when all training cases are used to train a shared set of feature weightings. For data set 2b, NN-kNN achieves highest accuracy when feature weighting is not shared. This is because the importance of a give feature varies in different regions of the data landscape. It is interesting to note that NN-kNN still functions well for data set 2b when feature weight sharing is on. We hypothesize that this is because it also learns a case weighting $w_{(x,L)}$, which can lower the importance of cases that are too close to class boundaries or are in ambiguous regions. Note that the neural network over-fits and performs poorly on these data sets.

Table 1. Accuracy (the Higher the Better) on Classification Data Sets

NN-kNN					NNet	K-NN	NCA	LMNN
Weight Sharing	On	On	Off	Off				
Top K	On	Off	On	Off				
Zebra (a)	0.909	0.918	0.872	0.872	0.782	0.363	**0.981**	0.336
Zebra (b)	0.850	0.850	**0.968**	**0.968**	0.673	0.368	0.395	0.354
OFace	0.862	0.945	0.934	**0.987**	0.938	0.850	0.9375	0.975
Digits	0.988	0.987	0.979	0.988	0.983	0.987	0.989	0.988
Iris	0.926	0.966	0.953	0.960	**0.987**	0.966	0.966	0.953
Wine	0.961	**0.994**	0.966	0.983	0.836	0.680	0.747	0.954
Breast Cancer	0.940	0.943	0.929	**0.959**	0.951	0.933	0.927	0.947
Balance	0.894	0.929	0.894	0.944	**0.994**	0.8463	0.960	0.849

Table 2. Mean Squared Error (the Lower the Better) for Regression Data Sets. NN-kNN provides both weighted average of activated cases ("Wtd"), or plain average of top k activated cases ("Top k").

NN-kNN									NNet	K-NN
Wt Sharing	On		On		Off		Off			
Top K	On		Off		On		Off			
	Wtd	Top k	Wtd	Top k	Wtd	Top k	Wtd	Top k		
Diabetes	0.558	0.616	0.563	0.606	0.558	0.571	0.549	0.594	**0.513**	0.615
California	0.690	0.958	0.537	0.912	0.931	1.564	**0.358**	0.783	0.705	1.079
Abalone	0.500	0.530	0.442	0.918	0.455	0.944	0.436	1.229	**0.414**	0.483
Body Fat	0.671	0.531	0.493	0.663	0.741	0.616	**0.423**	1.013	0.585	0.609

Classification Data Sets: When top k case selection is enabled, NN-kNN achieves relatively good accuracy, indicating that the top activated cases generally share the same class label as the query and are indeed good explanations for its prediction. Turning off the top k case selection generally improves NN-kNN's classification accuracy as the model can utilize all cases' activations. Turning off the feature weight sharing also improves its accuracy as the model can generalize over local patterns.

The best performing models are either NN-kNN or the traditional neural network. NCA learns a metric well when certain features are obviously important (e.g., zebra (a)). Both NCA and LMNN perform relatively well on most data sets but struggle on some, most notably zebra (b). The standard k-NN suffers for harder data set while NN-kNN maintains performance.

Regression Data Sets: Enabling the top k case selection layer can lead to bad performance for regression tasks, as we explain in detail in Sect. 5. In addition to the NN-kNN model's error, which is based on a *weighted average* of the labels of the activated cases, we show the average error of the top k cases' *plain average*. We note: (1) The weighted average generally has lower error than the plain average, suggesting that NN-kNN learns to activate cases for a proper activation-based weighting. (2) Sometimes the error of the NN-kNN's plain average is worse than the error of k-NN. This is because NN-kNN may activate cases with labels far from the true label. However, NN-kNN can correct this by weighting them by their activation and also by considering all cases' activations, leading to a lower error than that of k-NN.

Discussion of Experimental Results

Accuracy. Different methods excel at different data sets: The baseline neural network performs well when it captures a hidden rule (e.g. in the balance data set, a balance is achieved if the products of weight and distance are equal on two sides); NCA learns a metric that captures the underlying structure (certain features are obviously important such as in zebra (a)); LMNN performs well when local patterns matter by maximizing the margin between classes. NN-kNN performs the best or relatively well across all data sets. The best performing NN-kNN variant feature weight sharing disabled—for maximum degrees of freedom and has the top k case selection layer disabled, to use all cases.

NN-kNN is inherently a neural network with preset neuron meanings (in the case layer), connections (e.g. one case only activates a corresponding class) and preset-but-tunable parameters (weights and biases). It might appear that NN-kNN would sacrifice a fraction of performance because the preset connections and parameters constraints limit the degrees of freedom, in comparison to a neural network where all neurons and weights may vary freely. However, we observe that NN-kNN can perform equally good or even better than a neural network, as the preset neurons and connections function as case base knowledge infused into the network model

Interpretability. NN-kNN offers interpretability through its top activated cases. In classification, the accuracy of NN-kNN when the top k case selection layer is enabled is only slightly worse than or the same as when the layer is disabled, suggesting that the top k cases already provides a good estimation of the final label. In regression, this is not the case as the error of the plain average of the top k cases is potentially much worse than the weighted average. This is due to the nature of regression problems: Neighboring cases in classification likely share the same label, while neighboring cases in regression can have vastly different labels. Currently NN-kNN takes a weighted average based on case activations, correcting the error of the plain average. NN-kNN can offer explanations for regression by providing the top activated cases and their corresponding activations. A future direction is to lower the error of the plain average by including it as an additional term in the loss function, so that the training process may minimize it.

Moreover, the internal function of NN-kNN can be fully interpreted as a k-NN model. Given a query and a case in the NN-kNN system case base, (1) The feature distance layer's activations indicate which features are similar between the query and the case. (2) The feature weights indicate which feature is important in activating cases. (3) The case activation layer's activations indicate which case is most relevant for decision making for the particular query. (4) The case bias b_x and class bias b_L indicate the default significance of the case and a class respectively. (5) The weight $w_{(x,L)}$ indicates the weight of contribution from the case to the prediction of a class.

5   Discussion: Effect of Top K Case Selection

The effect of the top k case selection layer varies according to circumstances. We disabled it during training, because of potential detrimental effects during training. If the layer is enabled during training, each training query would only provide gradient descent information for the top k cases. Only a small set of cases are activated and a small portion of the network is trained. Moreover, the weights of one activated case are only trained to work with weights of $k - 1$

other cases in that small set of top k cases. Given a new query during testing, NN-kNN is likely to activate a small set of nearest neighboring cases, that might have never activated together before during training. Therefore their weights are never trained to work in harmony. This last point is especially an issue for regression, where case activations are used to produce a weighted average of the final prediction. As supported by the experimental results in Sect. 4, we recommend disabling the top k case selection layer for regression.

Interestingly, we note that top k cases are always selected in k-NN and its variants, yet no other reports on k-NN to our knowledge have mentioned that selecting top k cases is an issue. This is due to the hidden assumption in most k-NN methods that all cases share the same feature weights (the feature x_i in case x is as important as the feature y_i in case y) and instance weights. Because cases are equally important, k-NN classifier can take a majority vote of the top k cases' class label in classification; k-NN regressor can take an average of the top k cases' numeric label in regression. This assumption does not hold in NN-kNN and enabling top k cases layer generally lowers the model's accuracy.

6   Challenges and Future Directions

NN-kNN can be considered as k-NN algorithm or as a neural network. It follows that NN-kNN unavoidably inherits some limitations from both sides, but we also see potential to circumvent these limitations with techniques from both sides.

Online Learning: A neural network does not have online learning ability: adding a training case means, in principle, that the whole model needs retraining. When weight sharing is disabled, adding a new case creates a separate NN-kNN and the whole model (other NN-kNNs along with the newly added NN-kNN) needs to be retrained. However, this drawback can be offset by turning on all weight sharing, so that the newly added cases reuse weights already trained. This can be seen as equivalent to simply adding cases to a kNN system with fixed weights. A next step is to build variants of NN-kNN with online learning ability.

Scaling Up and Case Base Maintenance: For extremely large data sets, the cost of NN-kNN becomes an issue. This may be partially alleviated by maintaining only the prototypical cases instead of all cases, as it was done by Li et al. [22]. Other solutions involve case base maintenance techniques [13, 19] or neural network pruning techniques [8].

Hyperparameters and Settings for Training NN-kNN: Like any neural network, NN-kNN depends on hyperparameters that may be tuned. Common settings for regular networks do not directly apply to NN-kNN. For example: 1) A learning rate of 1e-5 is common for neural networks, but it leads to underfitting in NN-kNN. Our NN-kNN used 1e-2 for learning rate in all experiments; 2) L2 regularization normally prevents overfitting, but it impedes the learning of NN-kNN, because for NN-kNN some cases/features should be learned to be (non-)important and L2 regularization defeats this learning purpose. An important future direction is finding a hyperparameter optimization strategy for NN-kNN's structure.

Case Adaptation: The model presented here uses simple case adaptation. The reasoning of CBR depends on rich adaptation capabilities. NN-kNN may be chained with an adaptation network [35], but if that network is uninterpretable it undermines the interpretability of the overall architecture. Thus making network adaptation architectures more interpretable is an interesting future task.

7 Conclusion

NN-kNN combines perspectives of connectionist and symbolic machine learning approaches. This method serves as an endpoint on a spectrum of interpretability, and new models can be built upon it by integrating additional interpretable, explainable, or black-box modules. NN-kNN has the potential to coordinate learning for multiple CBR processes, from feature extraction to retrieval and adaptation to case base maintenance, in a single coherent model.

References

1. Bellet, A., Habrard, A., Sebban, M.: Metric Learning. Synthesis Lectures on Artificial Intelligence and Machine Learning. Morgan & Claypool Publishers, New York (2015)
2. Beyer, K., Goldstein, J., Ramakrishnan, R., Shaft, U.: When is "Nearest Neighbor" meaningful? In: Beeri, C., Buneman, P. (eds.) ICDT 1999. LNCS, vol. 1540, pp. 217–235. Springer, Heidelberg (1999). https://doi.org/10.1007/3-540-49257-7_15
3. Bicego, M., Loog, M.: Weighted k-nearest neighbor revisited. In: Twenty-Third International Conference on Pattern Recognition (ICPR), pp. 1642–1647. IEEE (2016)
4. Chen, C., Li, O., Tao, D., Barnett, A., Rudin, C., Su, J.K.: This looks like that: deep learning for interpretable image recognition. In: Advances in Neural Information Processing Systems, vol. 32. Curran (2019). https://proceedings.neurips.cc/paper_files/paper/2019/file/adf7ee2dcf142b0e11888e72b43fcb75-Paper.pdf
5. Chen, J., Hsu, S.C.: Hybrid ANN-CBR model for disputed change orders in construction projects. Autom. Constr. **17**(1), 56–64 (2007)
6. Cover, T., Hart, P.: Nearest neighbor pattern classification. IEEE Trans. Inf. Theory **13**(1), 21–27 (1967)
7. Dua, D., Graff, C.: UCI machine learning repository (2017). http://archive.ics.uci.edu/ml
8. Frankle, J., Carbin, M.: The lottery ticket hypothesis: finding sparse, trainable neural networks. In: 7th International Conference on Learning Representations, ICLR 2019, New Orleans, LA, USA, 6–9 May 2019. OpenReview.net (2019). https://openreview.net/forum?id=rJl-b3RcF7
9. Gates, L., Leake, D., Wilkerson, K.: Cases are king: a user study of case presentation to explain CBR decisions. In: Massie, S., Chakraborti, S. (eds.) Case-Based Reasoning Research and Development. Lecture Notes in Computer Science(), vol. 14141, pp. 153–168. Springer, Cham (2023). https://doi.org/10.1007/978-3-031-40177-0_10

10. Goldberger, J., Hinton, G.E., Roweis, S., Salakhutdinov, R.R.: Neighbourhood components analysis. In: Advances in Neural Information Processing Systems, vol. 17. MIT Press (2004). https://proceedings.neurips.cc/paper_files/paper/2004/file/42fe880812925e520249e808937738d2-Paper.pdf

11. Guidotti, R., Monreale, A., Ruggieri, S., Turini, F., Giannotti, F., Pedreschi, D.: A survey of methods for explaining black box models. ACM Comput. Surv. **51**(5), 1–42 (2018)

12. Huang, J., Wei, Y., Yi, J., Liu, M.: An improved KNN based on class contribution and feature weighting. In: 2018 10th International Conference on Measuring Technology and Mechatronics Automation (ICMTMA), pp. 313–316 (2018)

13. Juarez, J.M., Craw, S., Lopez-Delgado, J.R., Campos, M.: Maintenance of case bases: Current algorithms after fifty years. In: Proceedings of the Twenty-Seventh International Joint Conference on Artificial Intelligence, IJCAI-18, pp. 5457–5463. IJCAI (2018)

14. Keane, M.T., Kenny, E.M.: How case-based reasoning explains neural networks: a theoretical analysis of XAI using *Post-Hoc* explanation-by-example from a survey of ANN-CBR twin-systems. In: Bach, K., Marling, C. (eds.) ICCBR 2019. LNCS (LNAI), vol. 11680, pp. 155–171. Springer, Cham (2019). https://doi.org/10.1007/978-3-030-29249-2_11

15. Kolodner, J., Leake, D.: A tutorial introduction to case-based reasoning. In: Leake, D. (ed.) Case-Based Reasoning: Experiences, Lessons, and Future Directions, pp. 31–65. AAAI Press, Menlo Park, CA (1996)

16. Kulis, B.: Metric learning: a survey. Found. Trends Mach. Learn. **5**, 287–364 (2013). https://api.semanticscholar.org/CorpusID:55485900

17. Leake, D.: CBR in context: The present and future. In: Leake, D. (ed.) Case-Based Reasoning: Experiences, Lessons, and Future Directions, pp. 3–30. AAAI Press, Menlo Park, CA (1996). http://www.cs.indiana.edu/~leake/papers/a-96-01.html

18. Leake, D., Kinley, A., Wilson, D.: Learning to integrate multiple knowledge sources for case-based reasoning. In: Proceedings of the Fourteenth International Joint Conference on Artificial Intelligence, pp. 246–251. Morgan Kaufmann (1997)

19. Leake, D.B., Wilson, D.C.: Categorizing case-base maintenance: dimensions and directions. In: Smyth, B., Cunningham, P. (eds.) EWCBR 1998. LNCS, vol. 1488, pp. 196–207. Springer, Heidelberg (1998). https://doi.org/10.1007/BFb0056333

20. Leake, D., Crandall, D.: On bringing case-based reasoning methodology to deep learning. In: Watson, I., Weber, R. (eds.) ICCBR 2020. LNCS (LNAI), vol. 12311, pp. 343–348. Springer, Cham (2020). https://doi.org/10.1007/978-3-030-58342-2_22

21. Leake, D., Ye, X.: Harmonizing case retrieval and adaptation with alternating optimization. In: Sánchez-Ruiz, A.A., Floyd, M.W. (eds.) ICCBR 2021. LNCS (LNAI), vol. 12877, pp. 125–139. Springer, Cham (2021). https://doi.org/10.1007/978-3-030-86957-1_9

22. Li, O., Liu, H., Chen, C., Rudin, C.: Deep learning for case-based reasoning through prototypes: a neural network that explains its predictions. In: Proceedings of the Thirty-Second AAAI Conference on Artificial Intelligence, pp. 3530–3537. AAAI Press (2018)

23. Mathisen, B.M., Aamodt, A., Bach, K., Langseth, H.: Learning similarity measures from data. Prog. Artif. Intell. **9**, 129–143 (2019)

24. Park, J., Im, K.H., Shin, C.K., Park, S.: MBNR: case-based reasoning with local feature weighting by neural network. Appl. Intell. **21**, 265–276 (2004)

25. Pedregosa, F., et al.: Scikit-learn: machine learning in Python. J. Mach. Learn. Res. **12**, 2825–2830 (2011)

26. Riegel, R., et al.: Logical neural networks. arXiv preprint: arXiv:2006.13155 (2020)
27. Rudin, C.: Stop explaining black box machine learning models for high stakes decisions and use interpretable models instead. Nat. Mach. Intell. **1**, 206–215 (2019)
28. Sarabia, Y., Lorenzo, M., Perez, R., Martinez, R.: Extending CBR-ANN hybrid models using fuzzy sets. In: 2005 International Conference on Neural Networks and Brain, vol. 3, pp. 1755–1760 (2005)
29. Smyth, B., Keane, M.: Design à la Déjà Vu: reducing the adaptation overhead. In: Leake, D. (ed.) Case-Based Reasoning: Experiences, Lessons, and Future Directions. AAAI Press, Menlo Park, CA (1996)
30. Smyth, B., Keane, M.: Adaptation-guided retrieval: questioning the similarity assumption in reasoning. Artif. Intell. **102**(2), 249–293 (1998)
31. Turner, J.T., Floyd, M.W., Gupta, K., Oates, T.: NOD-CC: a hybrid CBR-CNN architecture for novel object discovery. In: Bach, K., Marling, C. (eds.) ICCBR 2019. LNCS (LNAI), vol. 11680, pp. 373–387. Springer, Cham (2019). https://doi.org/10.1007/978-3-030-29249-2_25
32. de Vazelhes, W., Carey, C., Tang, Y., Vauquier, N., Bellet, A.: metric-learn: metric learning algorithms in python. J. Mach. Learn. Res. **21**(138), 1–6 (2020). http://jmlr.org/papers/v21/19-678.html
33. Weinberger, K.Q., Saul, L.K.: Distance metric learning for large margin nearest neighbor classification. J. Mach. Learn. Res. **10**, 207–244 (2009)
34. Wettschereck, D., Aha, D., Mohri, T.: A review and empirical evaluation of feature-weighting methods for a class of lazy learning algorithms. Artif. Intell. Rev. **11**(1–5), 273–314 (1997)
35. Ye, X., Leake, D., Crandall, D.: Case adaptation with neural networks: capabilities and limitations. In: Keane, M.T., Wiratunga, N. (eds.) Case-Based Reasoning Research and Development. Lecture Notes in Computer Science(), vol. 13405, pp. 143–158. Springer, Cham (2022). https://doi.org/10.1007/978-3-031-14923-8_10
36. Ye, X., Zhao, Z., Leake, D., Wang, X., Crandall, D.J.: Applying the case difference heuristic to learn adaptations from deep network features. CoRR abs/2107.07095 (2021). https://arxiv.org/abs/2107.07095

Aligning to Human Decision-Makers in Military Medical Triage

Matthew Molineaux[1](✉), Rosina O Weber[2], Michael W. Floyd[3],
David Menager[1], Othalia Larue[1], Ursula Addison[1], Ray Kulhanek[1],
Noah Reifsnyder[1], Christopher Rauch[2], Mallika Mainali[2], Anik Sen[2],
Prateek Goel[2], Justin Karneeb[3], JT Turner[3], and John Meyer[3]

[1] Parallax Advanced Research, Beavercreek, OH 45431, USA
{matthew.molineaux,david.menager,othalia.larue,ursula.addison,
ray.kulhanek,noah.reifsnyder}@parallaxresearch.org
[2] Drexel University, Philadelphia, PA, USA
[3] Knexus Research LLC, National Harbor, MD, USA
http://parallaxresearch.org

Abstract. Expert human decision makers do not make optimal decisions in realistic domains; their decisions are affected by preferences, ethics, background experience, and contextual factors. Often there is no optimal decision, or any consensus on what makes a decision good. In this paper we consider the problem of aligning decisions to human decision makers. To this end, we introduce a novel formulation of an aligned decision-making problem, and present the Trustworthy Algorithmic Delegate (TAD), an integrated AI system that learns to align its decision-making process to target decision-makers using case-based reasoning, Monte Carlo simulation, Bayesian diagnosis, and Naturalistic decision-making. We apply TAD in a military triage domain, where experts make different decisions, and present experimental results showing that it outperforms baselines and ablations at alignment in this domain. Our primary claims are that the combined components of TAD allows for aligned decision-making using a small, learned case base and that TAD outperforms simpler strategies for alignment in this domain.

Keywords: Case-based Decision-making · Alignment · Integrated AI · Case-based Agents

1 Introduction

In some decision-making domains, there is no consensus about how to judge correct or best decisions. Conflicting priorities, uncertainty caused by partial observations, time pressure, and diverse values lead to situations where experts often disagree on the correct action to be taken. When delegating decision-making to others in these domains, humans make reference to experience, ethics, and trust in choosing appropriate decision-makers. An important domain illustrating this kind of *difficult* decision-making is military medical triage, where

J. A. Recio-Garcia et al. (Eds.): ICCBR 2024, LNAI 14775, pp. 371–387, 2024.
https://doi.org/10.1007/978-3-031-63646-2_24

human decision-makers must decide who will receive life-saving care when there is insufficient time and resources to save everyone [1]. For such contexts, there is no agreement on metrics for success, and no way to generate ground truth data evaluating decisions.

Because there is no object definition of success in these domains, we consider how to align to subjective definitions. In this work, we examine the problem of demonstrating alignment to a target profile made up of human decision-maker features. Such profiles assign values to a decision-maker along certain key features. For triage, examples are desire to maximize available information before making choices, and dedication to seeing that the "morally deserving" receive care first. We hope to allow non-experts the choice to delegate decisions to a system aligned to the decision-making model of trusted experts in emergency situations when an expert cannot be present.

The Trustworthy Algorithmic Delegate (TAD) system is a case-based agent designed to align to specific human experts on demand. The time of these experts is valuable, and the amount of data available for alignment is restricted. To do so, TAD uses case-based reasoning techniques that generalize well based on a small number of examples, leveraging robust similarity measures for retrieving relevant experience. Cases in TAD attach a decision-making *profile* that describes expert human decision-making characteristics to a situation and decision. At learning time, TAD creates a case base using available profile information for a group of experts and certain situations. Online, TAD estimates the profile of possible decisions by comparing to nearby cases in this case base.

A primary contribution of this work is the development of an autonomous CBR agent that performs user-aligned decision-making, which, to the best of our knowledge, has not previously been explored in the CBR literature.

In the rest of this paper, we: (1) detail the aligned decision-making problem and the triage problem, the context where TAD is described in this work; (2) discuss related work that solves similar problems; (3) describe the operation of TAD and its subsystems and components; and (4) describe experiments and results showing that the alignment of decisions produced by TAD in triage provides improvements over other decision-making strategies.

2   Aligned Decision Making Problem

In aligned decision making, there is no description of success in terms of goals or utilities (i.e., there is no single correct answer). Instead, there is a target decision-making *profile* to align to that represents characteristics of a human decision-maker, decision-making is judged based on how well a set of decisions satisfy that decision-making profile.

Formally, we characterize the general *alignable decision making problem* (ADMP) as a tuple $\langle S, S', A, \lambda, R(S'), P, pdet, pdist \rangle$. Given:

- a space of states S,
- a set of known starting states $S' \subset S$,
- a space of actions A,

- a transition function $\lambda : S \times A \to S$,
- a reachability function, $r : S \times S \to [0,1]$ that separate states which have a trajectory between them in λ, and those that don't
- an alignment profile space P,
- a profile detection function over the reachable states $pdet : r(S') \times A \to P$, and
- a profile distance function $pdist : P \times P \to \mathbb{R}^{[0,1]}$,

Find: an *alignable decision maker* $\mathbb{ADM} : P \to (S \to A)$ that, given a profile $p \in P$, returns a policy $\pi : S \to A$ that minimizes

$$alignment(p, \pi) = \frac{\sum_{s \in S} pdist\left(pdet\left(s, \pi\left(s\right)\right), p\right)}{|S|}.$$

This function guides a learner toward reducing error between its responses and the responses dictated by a target profile. A key difference between the ADMP context and general optimal decision-making is that truth comes from the profile detection function *pdet* defined over actions rather than a goal or utility defined over states. We refer to decisions that minimize distance to a target profile as *aligned decisions*.

An important subclass of profiles represents humans considered to be experts by other humans; we refer to these as *admissible* profiles. An ADMP is *difficult* when there is a set of distinct admissible profiles $P_A \subseteq P$ such that for any pair of profiles $(p_1, p_2) \in P$, any policy π_1 that minimizes $alignment(p_1, \pi_1)$ cannot also minimize p_2, and vice versa. This can be thought of as two experts who have differing views on how a problem should be solved. If a single policy works for all experts, the ADMP devolves to an optimal decision-making problem.

$$difficult(S, S', A, \lambda, R(S'), P, pdet, pdist) \equiv \exists P_A \subset P, |P_A| > 1 : \forall p_1, p_2 \in P_A :$$
$$p_1 \neq p_2 \implies \forall \pi : \exists \pi' : alignment(p_1, \pi') < alignment(p_1, \pi)$$
$$\vee \, alignment(p_2, \pi') < alignment(p_2, \pi) \quad (1)$$

2.1 Military Medical Triage

We investigate the difficult decision-making problem of military medical triage, specifically point of injury medical care. In the American military, personnel receive training to provide care beyond first aid, but have less medical education than a practicing doctor or medic. Decisions are life-changing, both for care providers and patients, and must be made rapidly, often in dangerous environments with limited resources. Personal accounts indicate that these are some of the hardest decisions to make and live with in a provider's entire life. We hope that in the future, tools for aligned decision-making will lift some part of these burdens.

In this work, we consider a simulated version of triage that allows exploration of this topic. Observations of the environment are complex, containing information about the world as well as the various people involved in the scenarios. In each state, there may be one or more patients, each with measurable vitals and possible injuries of various severity. The simulation supports 11 classes of injury and 14 types of medical supplies that can be used for treatments. Injuries can be immediately visible (e.g., amputation), discoverable (e.g., low blood pressure), or hidden (e.g., brain trauma). Seven characteristics make up patient vitals: consciousness, responsiveness to stimuli, ability to walk, mental status, breathing rate, heart rate, and blood oxygen level. In addition, the state includes a number of environmental factors, mission status, patient demographics, and patient status features. Actions include *situation report* (SITREP), which asks for patients' own description of their status, *vitals check* (CHECK_ALL_VITALS), in which all available vitals are recorded for a patient, *patient tagging* (TAG_CHARACTER), in which a triage tag is applied to a patient to indicate their status, and *treatment* (APPLY_TREATMENT), in which a medical procedure is performed to care for a patient (possibly using medical supplies). In TAG_CHARACTER, a triage tag describes injury severity and care prioritization, and includes *minimal* (i.e., minor injuries not requiring immediate care), *delayed* (i.e., serious injuries for which treatment can be delayed), *immediate* (i.e., severe, life threatening injuries requiring prioritized care), and *expectant* (i.e., unrecoverable injuries). In APPLY_TREATMENT, medical supplies to use for treatment must be selected, as well as the location on a patient's body to be treated (e.g., apply splint to left leg).

2.2   Specific Decision Maker Attributes

All decision-makers are assumed to have requisite skills to make good decisions (i.e., all trained in medicine), and each decision-maker attribute describes one aspect that affects decision selection when multiple reasonable decisions exist to choose from. In this work, we consider two attributes of triage decision-makers: *moral desert*, the degree to which a medic will prioritize patients whose moral culpability in injuries to others is lesser (i.e., the most morally deserving); and *maximization*, the degree to which a medic will prioritize actions that gain information over beginning treatment immediately [2].

An alignable decision-maker (ADM) does not attempt to achieve "correct" values on an attribute; instead, an ADM must be capable of aligning to a profile describing arbitrary features of human behavior. Decision-makers profiles contain values between 0 and 1 for each of a set of decision-maker attributes. Each profile may represent an individual decision-maker, cluster of decision-makers, or a theoretical decision-maker. Our current work has focused on decision-making profiles consisting of a single real-valued decision-maker attribute.

3   Related Work

The task of aligning an algorithmic decision maker with reference decision makers for contexts where a correct decision is unknown is relatively novel [3]. To address it, TAD innovates by incorporating other methods within CBR and by using data points obtained from those methods to add features to a case base.

CBR has a long history of integrations with other methods (*e.g.*, [4,5]). It is the way in which TAD integrates CBR with other methods that is unusual. Previously, due to machine learning underspecificity, [6] other work has proposed to obtain features using methods other than CBR for identifying new features to be added to a case base [7,8]. When doing this, [8] found in three different data types that average accuracy can be improved.

The topic of user preferences influencing decision making when multiple possible solutions exist has been previously explored using trust-guided behavior adaptation [9,10]. In this work, a CBR agent performs adaptive autonomy using both explicit and implicit feedback from a user. The agent uses an inverse trust estimate to keep a real-time measurement of its perceived trustworthiness and adapts its behavior when it believes its trust has fallen below a threshold. This work differs from ours in that it requires constant user feedback, which is unlikely to be available in high-pressure domains like medical triage.

The alignment profiles stored in our cases are similar to the idea of case provenance [11], where the source of a case is recorded such that more or less trust can be placed on it. The decision-maker attributes serve a similar role, allowing decision selection to be biased towards cases that come from decision-makers that more closely align with our desired behavior. However, in our work we do not explicitly record the case's source but instead use higher-level decision-maker attributes to record properties about the source.

4   Technical Approach

TAD's functions are divided across two distinct subsystems. The offline **training** subsystem (see Fig. 1) learns case knowledge from observations and a profile detection function. The online **decision-making** subsystem (see Fig. 2) uses the learned case base to select aligned decisions in response to observations. The online system is designed to operate quickly, and the offline system is designed to maximize performance. TAD components are orange, data input and output by TAD are blue; external sources (observations and the profile detection function) are shown in black.

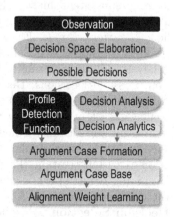

Fig. 1. TAD offline training subsystem creates the case base and weights

4.1   Subsystems

Offline Training Subsystem. The TAD training subsystem uses examples of known user decisions to create cases. Based on the **Observations** of the environment (e.g., the state and any contextual information), **Decision Space Elaboration** generates a set of candidate decisions (**Possible Decisions**) that are feasible in the current situation. As an example, consider a situation with two patients with known injuries requiring treatment. Decision Space

Elaboration would produce a set of possible APPLY_TREATMENT actions based on the patients, possibly injuries, and available medical treatments.

Decision Analysis. Considers features of a decision in various ways that are analogous to human considerations and produces **Decision Analytics** for each decision. *Monte Carlo Simulation* explores possible futures and effects of decisions; *Bayesian Diagnosis* considers hypotheses about what causes could underlie observations; and *Bounded Rationalizer* conducts fast and frugal methods to compare possible treatment and resource use decisions.

The **Profile Detection Function** is a black box that serves as a source of profile information during training. Profile information and decision analytics are fed into *Alignment Case Formation*, which outputs a case into the *Alignment Case Base*. Each case is made up of features describing a single observation, a decision made following that observation, decision analytics, and the decision-maker profile. After an entire case base is collected, the training subsystem performs **Alignment Weight Learning** to learn **Distance Function Weights** used to estimate decision-maker attributes.

Online Decision-Making Subsystem. The decision-making subsystem reuses many similar TAD components to the training subsystem, with the primary difference being that the input Observations do not have known decisions associated with them (i.e., they are not training examples of past decision-making). Instead, the decision-making subsystem must select an appropriate aligned decision to perform based on a specified *Alignment Profile*. Each Observation is run through Decision Space Elaboration and Decision Analysis, similar to during training. The Observation, Possible Decisions, Decision Analytics, and Alignment Profile are used to query the Alignment Case Base (learned by the training subsystem) using the Distance Function Weights to find a case that is most similar to the current situation (i.e., Observation, Possible Decisions, and Decision Analytics) while aligning with the target decision-maker (i.e., Alignment Profile). The **Decision Selection** component then returns an **Aligned Decision** by selecting the decision that minimizes alignment distance, as estimated based on that case's neighbors.

Fig. 2. TAD online decision-making subsystem makes aligned decisions

4.2 Components

Decision Space Elaboration. TAD generates decisions in the triage domain by enumerating actions over all patients, treatments, categories, and injury locations. Each decision is checked to see whether it is compatible with the current state using domain-specific logic, and all reasonable decisions are retained. Nonsensical decisions (such as putting a tourniquet on a patient without a bleed) are removed. Future work will focus on extracting knowledge about reasonable decisions from domain documents.

Decision Analysis. TAD analyzes decisions using analogues to how humans might consider them. It uses a variety of analysis techniques, each of which provides different types of analyses, which are run in parallel. We currently have implementations of three forms of decision analysis, described below: *Monte Carlo Simulation*, *Bayesian Diagnosis*, and *Bounded Rationalizer*. Each decision analysis component is primarily responsible for generating case features that describe aspects of a situation and possible decision analogous to what a human would consider in evaluating a possible decision. We enumerate these features for each component below; descriptions of these features may refer to a target patient or treatment specified by a decision. Because not all decisions involve treatments, features that refer to a treatment or target patient are left blank for decisions not involving them.

Monte Carlo Simulation:

A key factor in human decision making is considering the *effects* of our actions. Simplistically, that may only involve considering the immediate effects. However, there are also potentially delayed or longer-term effects. For example, consider having a small paper cut on your finger. One action that could be taken is to put an adhesive bandage over the cut, stopping the bleeding and protecting the wound. A potentially unforeseen impact of that action is that if there was only a single adhesive bandage, future treatments of additional injuries will not have adhesive bandages available.

To account for action effects, uncertainty, and longer-term impacts, we use a Monte Carlo Simulation approach. For each possible action that can be taken in the current environment state (i.e., from the Decision Space Elaboration component), a light-weight simulation is performed to measure the effects of taking that action. The Monte Carlo Simulation process performs the following steps:

1. Simulate performing a single action a_0 (i.e., the next action to perform) from among the set of possible actions to take.
2. Update the state from s_0 to s_1 based on performing action a_0.
3. Select another action a_1 to perform.
4. Update the state from s_1 to s_2 based on performing action a_1.
5. Continue selecting actions and updating the state until a completion criterion is reached (e.g., a fixed number of actions were performed).

Actions may have non-deterministic outcomes (e.g., applying a bandage may only stop bleeding some of the time, based on the severity of the cut) or the space of possible actions may be so large that considering all potential action sequences may be infeasible. Instead, Monte Carlo sampling is used where a set number of rollouts are performed, with each rollout examining a single action sequence given the non-deterministic action effects (i.e., a sequence s_0, a_0, s_1, a_1, ...). The results of all performed rollouts are combined to provide an estimate of an action's long-term effects given the environmental uncertainty that exists.

The Monte Carlo Simulation creates the following case features describing the expected state after a decision:

- Target Patient Severity (injury severity of the target patient)
- Severest Severity (injury severity of the most severely injured patient)
- Overall Severity (aggregate severity value for all patients)
- Target Patient Severity Change (expected change in Patient Severity)
- Severest Severity Change (change in Severest Severity)
- Overall Severity Change (change in Overall Severity)
- Death Probability – Immediate (probability at least one patient dies)
- Death Probability – 1 min (probability a patient dies within a minute)
- Injury Per Second ("amount" of injury occurring to patients each second: blood loss, lung damage, burn damage, and shock)
- Supplies Used (number of supplies used)
- Supplies Remaining (number of supplies remaining)
- Weighted Supplies Used (no. of supplies used weighted by importance)
- Time Taken (average time taken)
- Information Gained (reduction in uncertainty due to the action)

Bayesian Diagnosis: To handle uncertainty with respect to the current state of each patient, we use a Bayesian Network that describes the interrelation between various medical conditions and symptoms. This permits us to efficiently compute the joint posterior distribution of these variables given a set of (partial) observations provided by the triage simulator, which in turn allows us to provide two broad types of information to the Decision Selector:

- The probability of variables that are difficult or impossible to directly observe. This permits the operator to rapidly identify (and treat) immediately life-threatening conditions that are especially likely given the observations without first needing to perform additional (time-consuming) diagnostic actions.
- The entropy of either the network as a whole or of individual variables. By measuring the entropy before a proposed diagnostic action, and the *expected* entropy after, we can determine whether the expected reduction in uncertainty that the diagnostic provides is sufficient to justify the time it takes.

The conditional probability tables are currently rough estimates based on known causal links between medical conditions, and will be replaced by probabilities learned from records of trauma cases in the MIMIC-IV health record dataset on PhysioNet [12–14]. Inference is performed using the pyAgrum toolkit [15].

The Bayesian diagnosis analyzer outputs the following metrics for each action. Each is conditioned on the set of provided observations.

- P(death): Probability of death if no further action is taken
- P(pain): Probability of severe pain
- P(brain injury): Probability of brain injury
- P(airway): Probability of blocked airway
- P(internal hemorrhage): Probability of internal hemorrhage
- P(external hemorrhage): Probability of external hemorrhage
- H(full): Entropy of the joint distribution over the full network
- H(death): Entropy of the death random variable

Bounded Rationalizer When faced with a vast amount of information, human decision-makers rely on heuristic decision-making and simplified search strategies rather than perfect rationality [16]. The Bounded Rationalizer simulates human-like automated search strategies that provide naturalistic solutions in general domains [17] and, in particular, medical decision-making [18].

Inputs for the different heuristics of the Bounded Rationalizer include decision feature selections, *predictors* of known preferences, and order of validity (for some heuristics). The Bounded Rationalizer generates all possible combinations of these inputs that could lead to a given decision. A set M of *predictors* is used by the Bounded Rationalizer, features of a decision that may be central to its ranking with respect to other decisions. Predictors for patient priority include age, rank, relationship, and injury_severity. Predictors for treatment selection include risk_reward_ratio, resources, time, and system.

The Bounded Rationalizer uses case features to describe for each human search strategy and each selection of predictors, which patients and treatments are preferred. For each strategy, the case features are:

- **Target Patient Selection** is a single feature per strategy that describes whether the strategy would prioritize the target patient.
- **Treatment Selection** is a set of features per strategy that describes what treatments would be selected, given different predictor subsets $m \in M$.

Each strategy compares possible patients and treatments pairwise, then selects one or more options that maximize its heuristic. In the *exhaustive* strategy, the winner is selected based on a total ranking using all predictors in M. The *tallying* strategy considers predictors in m. In *take-the-best*, options are compared on predictors *in order of validity*, stopping as soon as one option has an advantage. The *satisfactory* strategy considers predictors in m in a random order, stopping as soon as any predictor shows an advantage. In the *one-bounce* strategy, "potential winners" are found in random pairwise comparisons using all predictors in M. One-bounce selects the first potential winner that improves against k other choices on the predictor subset m.

Alignment Case Formation. Alignment cases are based on states, decisions, decision analytics, and attribute values. All decision analysis features described above are included in each case, as well as features of the state and decision. State features include:

- `unexamined_count`: Number of patients who have not been examined yet, other than the action target;
- `injured_count`: Number of injured patients, other than the action target;
- `others_tagged_or_uninjured_count`: Number of patients, other than the action target, who have received a triage tag or are uninjured;
- `aid_available`: True if evacuation is available or will be;
- `environment_type`: A high-level description of the treatment environment; one of *submarine*, *urban*, *desert*, or *jungle*.

Case action features are as follows:

- Action category:
  - `questioning`: Includes actions such as SITREP in which the medic talks to one or more patients.
  - `assessing`: Includes actions such as CHECK_ALL_VITALS in which the medic measures vital characteristics.
  - `treating`: Includes actions such as APPLY_TREATMENT in which the medic gives care to a patient.
  - `tagging`: Includes actions such as TAG_CHARACTER in which the medic applies a triage tag to a patient.
  - `leaving`: Includes actions such as END_SCENARIO which ends all further interaction with patients.
- Target patient demographics: `age`, `sex`, `rank`
- Target patient status:
  - `examined`: True if and only if a medic has checked the patient close enough to see visible injuries (typically after a CHECK_ALL_VITALS)
  - `tagged`: True if and only if target patient has a trauma tag
  - `relationship`: Describes an existing relationship between the medic and the patient; one of "friend", "relation", or "neutral"
  - `intent`: Describes whether the patient intended any participation in a harmful act. One of "intend major harm", "intend minor harm", "no intent", "intend minor help", "intend major help"
  - `directness_of_causality`: Describes a patient's role in causing an injury. One of "direct", "somewhat direct", "somewhat indirect", "indirect", or "none"
- patient vitals: `consciousness`, `responsiveness`, `ability_to_walk`, `mental_status`, `breathing_level`, `heart_rate`, `blood_oxygen_level`
- `category`: Triage tag category applied during a tagging action; one of "minimal", "delayed", "immediate", or "expectant"
- `treatment`: Specific treatment given during a treating action; includes 14 types medical supplies which can be applied to different areas of the body

Alignment Weight Learning. CBR research and practice has long incorporated weighted similarity measures, distinguishing it from vanilla forms of k-nearest neighbors (kNN) algorithms. Seminal work from the 1990s [19–21] has established that feedback methods (*e.g.*, [22] those that assess the output produced by intermediary weights as feedback) are likely to lead to higher retrieval accuracy. Methods such as gradient descent [23], Relief [22] and its variations [24], decision trees [25], and genetic algorithms [26] have been used as alternatives for learning to represent the relative relevance of features for case-based similarity [27]. However, in the past 10 years, gradient boosted decision trees have substantially improved the performance of decision trees (*e.g.*, [28,29]). XGBoost [28] was found to improve accuracy of CBR retrieval when adopting as weights the importance factors from XGBoost in a regression task [30]. Our preliminary experiments confirm the higher accuracy of XGBoost over alternatives in TAD's classification task.

Decision Selection. For each possible decision, the Decision Selector constructs a new case with features based on that decision, the current state, and the decision analytics. In current experiments, the decision-maker profile consists of a single decision maker attribute. To estimate the value of this attribute, the Decision Selector first finds the 4 nearest neighbors of each decision case as shown in Eqs. 2–4. The Euclidean distance function is computed with weights found by the alignment weight training component for the particular decision-maker feature.

$$nearestNeighbor(c, CB) = \arg\max_{c' \in CB} euclidean(c, c') \tag{2}$$

$$NN(c, CB, 0) = \emptyset \tag{3}$$

$$NN(c, CB, Size > 0) = nearestNeighbor(c, CB)$$
$$\cup\, NN(c, CB/nearestNeighbor(c, CB), Size - 1) \tag{4}$$

The Decision Selector estimates the value of the target attribute by averaging the known attribute values of the nearest neighbors. Each neighbor provides a weighted contribution to this average based on its distance from the current case, as seen in Eqs. 5 and 6.

$$contribution(n, c, N) = \left(\sum_{n' \in N} \frac{euclidean(n, c)}{euclidean(n', c)} \right)^{-1} \tag{5}$$

$$attributeValueEstimate(feature, c, CB) =$$
$$\sum_{n \in NN(c, CB, 4)} contribution(n, c, NN(c, CB, 4)) \times feature(n) \tag{6}$$

The Decision Selector chooses a single decision with a minimum difference between the estimated attribute value and the target attribute value.

5 Methodology and Results

We evaluated TAD in two settings, a *maximization*[1] and a *moral deserts*[2] setting. In each setting, we were provided with a profile detection function defined over a set of initial states in the space defined by our triage simulator. These states were partitioned into a training set and a test set in advance. We prepared our algorithms without knowledge of the test set. To train the case base, we recorded (1) the behavior of a random agent, (2) the agent's observations, (3) decision analytics for its actions, and (4) the profile detected for its actions by the provided profile detection function, on each of the training states 1,000 times. For each unique pair of observed state and selected action, we created a single case containing the state, decision, and decision analytic features corresponding to that unique pair, as well as two values concerning the decision-maker attribute profile found. One value was the detected attribute score, which had an undefined value for some state-action pairs; the other value was an approximation of the value of an action based on the detected attribute score of later actions. To approximate the action value, we averaged over the observed later outcomes of the action, discounting the late received value of an unscored action using an exponential decay (see Eq. 7).

$$valueApprox(s_t, a_t) = \begin{cases} pdet(s_t, a_t) \neq \bot : & pdet(s_t, a_t) \\ pdet(s_t, a_t) = \bot : & 0.99 \times valueApprox(s_{t+1}, a_{t+1}) \end{cases}$$
(7)

After obtaining this case base, we found weights that predicted detected attribute scores without unscored actions (where *pdet* had an undefined value). To evaluate, we ran the TAD decision-making subsystem using the case base and weights created during training. Decisions were selected using the *approximated action values* of neighbor cases, as relevant neighbors did not always receive a defined score. We ran TAD for each scored initial state in the test set exactly once. For comparison, we ran two ablated versions of the system. The *informed baseline* used an ablated case base without the decision analytic features, and a uniform weighting scheme. The *uninformed baseline* considered the same decisions as TAD, but selected decisions based only on likelihood of survival, as determined by the projected "Overall Severity" value given by the Monte Carlo simulation, which describes how bad a state is after an action is taken. The informed baseline represents a naive attempt to approximate decision-maker attributes with no decision analysis. The uninformed baseline represents a typical decision-making system that does not attempt to align at all.

---

[1] Initial states and profile detection function for maximization were provided by Alyssa Tanaka and colleagues with Soar Technology, LLC. Contact nicholas.paul@soartech.com to obtain.

[2] Initial states and profile detection function for moral deserts were provided by RTX BBN Technologies. Code can be downloaded from https://gitlab.com/itm-ta1-adept-shared/adept_server.

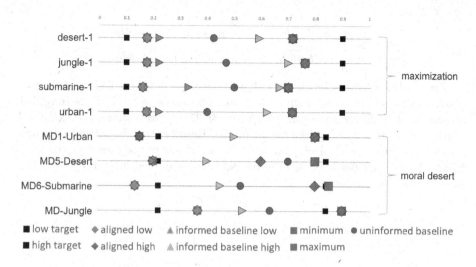

Fig. 3. Per-scenario alignment chart depicting the average maximization/moral deserts value attained by multiple versions of TAD (Color figure online)

The alignment chart (Fig. 3) shows a visual depiction of how TAD and its two baselines compare on initial state groupings. Four scenarios are given for each setting, each with a set of initial states; 13 initial states are described in each group for maximization and 7 in each for moral desert. On each line, black squares give the target profile positions for each attribute on a 0 to 1 scale. Grey squares show the minimum and maximum values achievable on those initial states. Profiles detected for our three conditions are shown by different shapes; green diamonds for TAD, yellow triangles for the informed baseline, and red circles for the uninformed baseline. Both low (near 0) and high (near 1) targets are used in separate evaluation conditions, so we depict low and high values for both aligned TAD and the informed baseline. Since the initial states are the same for both evaluation conditions, and the uninformed baseline ignores the profile targets, only one value is shown for the uninformed baseline.

This chart gives an idea of how TAD and the baselines perform relative to one another at aligning to profile targets. In most cases, TAD's performance is closer to the profile target than either baseline, and often it is as close as possible (shown as a grey minimum or maximum square on top of green diamond in the chart). This gives an intuitive representation of what performance looks like.

To measure performance more objectively, we consider how often the decision picked by TAD in evaluation scenarios is maximally aligned to the target profile. The percentage of aligned decisions simply considers whether any alternative decision available to TAD had a profile closer to the target profile than the decision selected. We also consider the percentage achieved of possible alignment. Given a target profile p^*, this value is calculated as:

$$\sum_{s\in S, a\in A} \frac{pdist(p^*, pdet(s, a)) - \min_{a'\in A} pdist(p^*, pdet(s, a))}{\max_{a'\in A} pdist(p^*, pdet(s, a)) - \min_{a'\in A} pdist(p^*, pdet(s, a))} \tag{8}$$

Figure 4 shows the percentage of aligned decisions made by TAD and the two baselines. These are statistically significant differences, with TAD > Informed Baseline > Uninformed Baseline, with $p \approx .0037$. Figure 5 shows the extent to which each system matches the target profile. Results are different from aligned decisions because some misaligned decisions are closer to the target profile than others. For both figures, error bars indicate 95% confidence intervals over the mean for each condition.

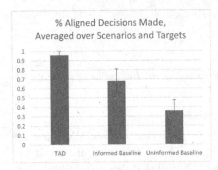
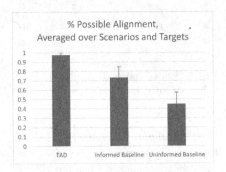

Fig. 4. % Aligned Decisions   **Fig. 5.** % Possible Alignment

6   Conclusions and Future Work

Experimental results so far are promising, showing the ability of a system with representations of human-like behavior to mimic opposed decision-making profiles given a relatively small amount of data. We can conclude that a naive approach is not sufficient to solve the problem. However, we have not shown generality, and future steps are necessary to make the TAD system approximate profiles in a larger range of domains.

We are enthusiastic about examining profiles based on multiple decision-maker attributes and their tradeoffs; data gathered so far does not support the study, but we expect to have such data soon. Local weighting strategies, where the presence of different context characteristics affect the distance function, are likely to come up with more complex attributes, and we expect to examine methods for acquiring local weights given sparse data. Ongoing work on case base augmentation will examine whether performance at aligned decision-making given sparse data can be improved by augmenting a case base with counterfactual data. Finally, we would like to reduce our dependence on knowledge engineering in decision space elaboration and the data analysis components, where human-generated probabilities, rules, and transition functions are used to help generate both possible decisions and decision analysis features.

Code. Code to replicate the experiments described in this paper can be downloaded from https://github.com/Parallax-Advanced-Research/ITM.

Acknowledgements. We'd like to thank scientists from RTX BBN Technologies and Soar Technology, LLC, who created the profile detection functions and datasets used in our experiments. We'd also like to thank CACI International, Inc., for creating the triage simulation used in our experiments.

This research was developed with funding from the Defense Advanced Research Projects Agency (DARPA) In the Moment program, contract number FA8650-23-C-7317. In the Moment (ITM) is assessing whether aligning AI to human values will make humans more willing to delegate decision-making in complex, time-sensitive situations where human experts disagree, such as battlefield triage. The views, opinions and/or findings expressed are those of the authors and should not be interpreted as representing the official views or policies of the Department of Defense or the U.S. Government.

References

1. Shortland, N.D., Alison, L.J., Moran, J.M.: Conflict: How Soldiers Make Impossible Decisions. Oxford University Press, Oxford (2019)
2. Shortland, N., Alison, L., Thompson, L.: Military maximizers: examining the effect of individual differences in maximization on military decision-making. Personality Individ. Differ. **163**, 110051 (2020)
3. Turek, M.: In the Moment (ITM) (2022). Contract Opportunity Type: Presolicitation (Original). BAA Number (Notice ID): HR001122S0031
4. Marling, C., Rissland, E., Aamodt, A.: Integrations with case-based reasoning. Knowl. Eng. Rev. **20**(3), 241–245 (2005)
5. Ali, R., et al.: Multimodal hybrid reasoning methodology for personalized wellbeing services. Comput. Biol. Med. **69**, 10–28 (2016)
6. D'Amour, A., et al.: Underspecification presents challenges for credibility in modern machine learning. J. Mach. Learn. Res. **23**(226), 1–61 (2022)
7. Weber, R.O., Johs, A.J., Li, J., Huang, K.: Investigating textual case-based XAI. In: Cox, M.T., Funk, P., Begum, S. (eds.) ICCBR 2018. LNCS (LNAI), vol. 11156, pp. 431–447. Springer, Cham (2018). https://doi.org/10.1007/978-3-030-01081-2_29
8. Weber, R.O., Shrestha, M., Johs, A.J.: Knowledge-based XAI through CBR: there is more to explanations than models can tell. In: Borck, H., Eisenstadt, V., Sanchez-Ruiz, A., Floyd, M. (ed.) Workshop Proceedings for the 29th International Conference on Case-Based Reasoning, vol. 3017, p. 103. CEUR Workshop Proceedings (2021)
9. Floyd, M.W., Drinkwater, M., Aha, D.W.: How much do you trust me? Learning a case-based model of inverse trust. In: Lamontagne, L., Plaza, E. (eds.) ICCBR 2014. LNCS (LNAI), vol. 8765, pp. 125–139. Springer, Cham (2014). https://doi.org/10.1007/978-3-319-11209-1_10

10. Floyd, M.W., Aha, D.W.: Incorporating transparency during trust-guided behavior adaptation. In: Goel, A., Díaz-Agudo, M.B., Roth-Berghofer, T. (eds.) ICCBR 2016. LNCS (LNAI), vol. 9969, pp. 124–138. Springer, Cham (2016). https://doi.org/10.1007/978-3-319-47096-2_9

11. Leake, D., Whitehead, M.: Case provenance: the value of remembering case sources. In: Weber, R.O., Richter, M.M. (eds.) ICCBR 2007. LNCS (LNAI), vol. 4626, pp. 194–208. Springer, Heidelberg (2007). https://doi.org/10.1007/978-3-540-74141-1_14

12. Johnson, A., Bulgarelli, L., Pollard, T., Horng, S., Celi, L.A., Mark, R.: MIMIC-IV (version 2.2). PhysioNet. https://doi.org/10.13026/6mm1-ek67 (2023)

13. Johnson, A.E., et al.: MIMIC-IV, a freely accessible electronic health record dataset. Sci. Data 10(1), 1 (2023)

14. Goldberger, A.L., et al.: PhysioBank, PhysioToolkit, and PhysioNet: components of a new research resource for complex physiologic signals. Circulation 101(23), e215–e220 (2000)

15. Ducamp, G., Gonzales, C., Wuillemin, P.H.: aGrUM/pyAgrum: a toolbox to build models and algorithms for probabilistic graphical models in python. In: International Conference on Probabilistic Graphical Models. PMLR (2020)

16. Mosier, K.L.: Searching for coherence in a correspondence world. Judgm. Decis. Mak. 4(2), 154–163 (2009)

17. Gigerenzer, G., Todd, P.M.: Fast and frugal heuristics: the adaptive toolbox. In: Simple Heuristics that Make us Smart, pp. 3–34. Oxford University Press, Oxford (1999)

18. Marewski, J.N., Gigerenzer, G.: Heuristic decision making in medicine. Dialogues Clin. Neurosci. 14(1), 77–89 (2012)

19. Wettschereck, D., Aha, D.W.: Weighting features. In: Veloso, M., Aamodt, A. (eds.) ICCBR 1995. LNCS, vol. 1010, pp. 347–358. Springer, Heidelberg (1995). https://doi.org/10.1007/3-540-60598-3_31

20. Wettschereck, D., Aha, D.W., Mohri, T.: A review and empirical evaluation of feature weighting methods for a class of lazy learning algorithms. Artif. Intell. Rev. 11, 273–314 (1997)

21. Aha, D.W.: Feature weighting for lazy learning algorithms. In: Liu, H., Motoda, H. (ed.) Feature Extraction, Construction and Selection: a Data Mining Perspective, pp. 13–32. Springer US, Boston (1998). https://doi.org/10.1007/978-1-4615-5725-8_2. ISBN: 978-1-4615-5725-8

22. Kira, K., Rendell, L.A.: A practical approach to feature selection. In: Machine Learning Proceedings 1992, pp. 249–256. Elsevier (1992)

23. Intelligence, B.: Hepatitis diagnosis using case-based reasoning with gradient descent as feature weighting method. J. Inf. Syst. Eng. Bus. Intell. 4(1), 25 (2018)

24. Kononenko, I.: Estimating attributes: analysis and extensions of RELIEF. In: Bergadano, F., De Raedt, L. (eds.) ECML 1994. LNCS, vol. 784, pp. 171–182. Springer, Heidelberg (1994). https://doi.org/10.1007/3-540-57868-4_57

25. Richardson, M.M., Warren, J.R.: Induced decision trees for case-based reasoning. In: 1996 Australian New Zealand Conference on Intelligent Information Systems. Proceedings. ANZIIS 96, pp. 52–55. IEEE (1996)

26. Chang, P.C., Lai, C.Y., Lai, K.R.: A hybrid system by evolving case-based reasoning with genetic algorithm in wholesaler's returning book forecasting. Decis. Support Syst. 42(3), 1715–1729 (2006)

27. Richter, M.M., Weber, R.O.: Case-Based Reasoning. Springer, Heidelberg (2013). https://doi.org/10.1007/978-3-642-40167-1. ISBN 978-3-642-40166-4

28. Chen, T., Guestrin, C.: XGBoost: a scalable tree boosting system. In: Proceedings of the 22nd SCM SIGKDD International Conference on Knowledge Discovery and Data Mining, pp. 785–794 (2016)
29. Ke, G., et al.: LightGBM: a highly efficient gradient boosting decision tree. In: Advances in Neural Information Processing Systems, vol. 30 (2017)
30. Ahmed, M.U., Barua, S., Begum, S., Islam, M.R., Weber, R.O.: When a CBR in hand is better than twins in the bush. In: ICCBR XCBR'22: 4th Workshop on XCBR: Case-Based Reasoning for the Explanation of Intelligent Systems at ICCBR-2022. CEUR-WS.org (2022)

Counterfactual-Based Synthetic Case Generation

Anik Sen[1]($\boxtimes$), Mallika Mainali[1], Christopher B. Rauch[1], Ursula Addison[2],
Michael W. Floyd[3], Prateek Goel[1], Justin Karneeb[3], Ray Kulhanek[2],
Othalia Larue[2], David Ménager[2], Matthew Molineaux[2], JT Turner[3],
and Rosina O. Weber[1]

[1] Drexel University, Philadelphia, PA 19104, USA
`as5867@drexel.edu`
[2] Parallax Advanced Research, 4035 Colonel Glenn Hwy, Beavercreek, OH 45431,
USA
[3] Knexus Research, 174 Waterfront Street, Suite 310, National Harbor, Oxon Hill,
MD 20745, USA

Abstract. Case augmentation is often desirable when applying case-based reasoning to real-world problems. Initially explored for explainability, counterfactuals were recently recommended as a strategy to augment data. In this work, we implement an existing approach for generating counterfactuals, propose one variant of the original approach, and propose a third approach based on the literature on algorithmic recourse. We apply these three approaches to two datasets in military medical triage. To assess generalization, we also examine one of our approaches on three publicly available datasets. We compare the approaches based on the number of counterfactuals they produce, their resulting accuracy, overlapping counterfactuals, and domain knowledge. Experimental results are encouraging for the proposed approaches and bring up opportunities for future research.

Keywords: Counterfactuals · Counterfactual Generation · Synthetic Cases · Case-Based Reasoning (CBR) · Data Augmentation · Synthetic Data

1 Introduction

Case-based reasoning (CBR) leverages past experiences to solve new problems [11]. Despite its usefulness in various contexts, limited data poses challenges for CBR. One domain where data is often limited is in medical decision-making, due to privacy and ethical concerns [12]. Within computer science, counterfactuals (CFs) have extensive use for explainable artificial intelligence (XAI).

Recently, Temraz and Keane [14] demonstrated the use of Keane and Smyth's [5] approach to CF generation to attenuate problems with class imbalance. CF-based synthetic case generation relies on the factual-CF relationship between cases to identify regions of the data space that may be filled with new instances. In this paper, we limit the scope of our examination to CF-based synthetic case generation for data augmentation.

J. A. Recio-Garcia et al. (Eds.): ICCBR 2024, LNAI 14775, pp. 388–403, 2024.
https://doi.org/10.1007/978-3-031-63646-2_25

When applying Keane and Smyth's [5] approach for augmenting medical triage cases, the number of generated synthetic cases was insufficient for our needs. For this reason, we explored variations of said approach. In this paper, we implement Keane and Smyth's [5] approach, which we henceforth refer to as Keane's-CF, analyze it, and compare it with two other approaches. Approach 2 is inspired by Keane's-CF; we call it Direct-CF. Approach 3, denoted by High-Weights-CF, is a novel approach inspired by research in algorithmic recourse (*e.g.*, [3,6]). This paper's intended contribution is to present an analysis of these three approaches.

The analysis methodology we employ anticipates that all approaches receive as input an *original case base* with an average accuracy previously recorded via leave-one-out cross-validation (LOOCV). The new cases generated by the approaches are then used to build a new case base that we test by assessing its ability to classify the cases from the *original case base*. The average accuracy of the synthetic cases is one of the aspects used in the analysis. Other aspects include a further ablation of those cases to determine if the quality of individual cases differs, the number of synthetic cases generated, whether the generated cases overlap, and an analysis of their plausibility based on domain knowledge.

In the next section, we describe related work. Section 3 describes the three approaches we analyze. Section 4 presents the experimental design. Next are results and discussion, then conclusion in Sect. 6.

2 Related Work

CFs were originally proposed to provide explanatory information in XAI to users (*e.g.*, [4,16,17,20,21]). Given the relationship between a factual and its CF, generating synthetic CFs for data augmentation is a suitable approach. Data augmentation based on CF generation [1,2,10,14] using actual feature values rather than interpolating between instances have been demonstrated to increase the number of plausible cases [14].

Keane and Smyth highlighted the challenges in finding *good* CFs and proposed a case-based technique to generate plausible CFs by reusing the patterns of good CFs present in a case base [5]. This approach generates CFs based on similarity metrics rather than random perturbations so that the CFs are likely to be inherently plausible and sparse. Similarly, to generate sparse and diverse CFs, Smyth and Keane proposed a method to adapt native CFs existing in the original dataset to generate synthetic CFs from naturally occurring features [13].

CFs are the basis of algorithmic recourse (AR) where the distinction lies in that AR requires changes made to the instances to be *feasible* [15]. Karimi et al. highlighted the inadequacy of CF explanations in offering actionable recommendations capable of positively altering model predictions due to a lack of consideration of causal relations [3]. To address this limitation, they reformulated the framework proposed by Ustun et al. [15] by adding a plausibility constraint to generate optimal CFs. Building upon this foundation, Konig et al. introduced a method to constrain AR to recommend only actions deemed *meaningful*, which aimed to improve both the prediction of the model and the target

[6]. They proposed that by generating causal instances, the resulting CFs would be meaningful, ensuring that the algorithm's performance remains intact.

Conversely, generating instances that lack causality would not provide a guarantee that the resulting CFs lie within the data manifold, thereby jeopardizing the classifier's predictability [16]. Taking all these factors into consideration, O'Brien et al. devised a novel algorithm called Causal Augmented Sparse Classification Algorithm to implement causality and generate CFs solely by using causal features [8]. Given the implementation of causality requires ground truth and domain rules, which were unavailable in our synthetic cases, we resorted to the next best approach: correlation. In our High-Weights-CF approach, we use correlation indicated by feature weights to prioritize the features to be altered while generating CFs, as elaborated in Sect. 3.3.

3   Three Approaches for Synthetic Case Generation

Common to the approaches we describe next is the identification of *native* and *non-native* CF sets. A native CF is a pair of cases where one is the *factual*

Algorithm 1: Pseudocode for Keane's-CF approach.

Input: Case base
Output: A set of synthetic cases
1 *similarity_threshold*, *feature_difference* ← set similarity threshold and feature difference
2 *native_cf* ← [], *non_native_cf* ← []
3 **for** *case1 in Case base* **do**
4   Compare *case1* with the other cases
5   Calculate local similarity, global similarity, and feature difference between *case1* and all the other cases
6   Create a list for *case1* with all the retrieved cases
7   Put *case1* in the *non_native_cf* if it has no native CF (within threshold). Otherwise put *case1* in the *native_cf*
8 *new_cases* ← []
9 **for** *case_non_cf in non_native_cf* **do**
10   **for** *case_cf in native_cf* **do**
11   *global_sim* ← Calculate global similarity between case_non_cf and case_cf
12   **if** *global_sim* ≥ *similarity_threshold* **then**
13   *similar_cases* ← Find all of the similar cases of *case_cf*
14   **for** *sim_case in similar_cases* **do**
15   **if** *sim_case* **has different label than** *case_non_cf* **then**
16   *diff_attr_names* ← Find which attributes have different values between *case_cf* and *sim_case*
17   *sim_attr_names* ← Set the remaining attributes as similar
18   *new_case* ← Copy *diff_attr_names* from *sim_case* and *sim_attr_names* from *case_non_cf*
19   Set label of *sim_case* to *new_case*
20   **if** *new_case* **Not Exists In** Case base **then**
21   Append *new_case* to *new_cases*
22 **return** *new_cases*

---

and one is its CF (*i.e.*, similar but with a different decision label). The term native expresses that the pair occurs naturally in the data rather than it is created artificially. *Non-native* CF pairs indicate sets of cases for which there are no native CFs naturally occurring in the data for the factual cases. These definitions are based on the previous usage of the term [14] but in this paper we use a looser definition of similar from that used before [5,14].

3.1   Keane's-CF Approach

This approach is mostly based on previous work by Keane and Smyth [5], with two differences. First, we relax the notion that a CF has only two feature differences by exploring CFs with more than two feature differences. Second, we do not submit the synthetic CF to the model for classification. Instead, we simply reuse the label. For these differences, this is not really the same as Keane and Smyth approach; though the remaining steps are the same. In Algorithm 1, we outline the process of generating synthetic cases based on a similarity threshold and feature differences. We compile two sets of cases: native CFs (*native_cf*) and non-native CFs (*non_native_cf*) (lines 3–7). We then iterate through each case

---

Algorithm 2: Pseudocode for Direct-CF approach.

Input: Case base
Output: A set of synthetic cases

1 *similarity_threshold, feature_difference* ← set similarity threshold and feature difference
2 *native_cf* ←[], *non_native_cf* ←[]
3 **for** *case1* in *Case base* **do**
4 | Compare *case1* with the other cases
5 | Calculate local similarity, global similarity, and feature difference between *case1* and all the other cases
6 | Create a list for *case1* with all the retrieved cases
7 | Put *case1* in the *non_native_cf* if it has no native CF for a certain threshold. Otherwise put *case1* in the *native_cf*
8 *new_cases* ← []
9 **for** *case* in *non_native_cf* **do**
10 | *non_cf_cases* ← Find all cases with similar labels within a certain feature difference.
11 | Find a native CF case (*native_cf*) of *case* with the lowest feature difference
12 | *different_attributes* ← Compute which attribute values are different between *case* and *native_cf*
13 | **for** *case2* in *non_cf_cases* **do**
14 | | Create case (*new_case*) by taking the attribute from *native_cf* that differ between *case* and *native_cf* and remaining attributes from *case2*
15 | | Make the label of *native_cf* the label of *new_case*
16 | | **if** *new_case* **Not Exists In** *Case base* **then**
17 | | | Append *new_case* to *new_cases*
18 **return** *new_cases*

---

in *non_native_cf*, comparing it with every case in *native_cf* to assess similarity between them (lines 13–14). For similar cases found, we first take the CF of the similar case and identify varying attributes between this CF and the case from the *non_native_cf* set. We then create a CF case based on attributes from both the case from the *non_native_cf* set and the CF of the similar case (*case_non_cf*). The label of the new case corresponds to the similar case's (*sim_case*) label. To clarify the attributes used, we classify the features of the two cases as *different-features*, denoting features with distinct values in them, and *match-features*, representing features with identical values. Then, we create the synthetic CF by transferring the *different-features* values from the native CF and *match-features* from the case from the *non_native_cf* set.

3.2   Direct-CF Approach

The intuition behind this approach is that when cases have a lot of similar cases that include both CFs and similar cases with the same label, that the variability of similar cases with the same label could be used to increase the opportunities of creating synthetic CFs than by creating synthetic CFs indirectly by using the CF of a similar case,as in Keane's approach. This is why we call this *Direct-CF*.

   Algorithm 2 starts by creating native CF (*native_cf*) and non-native CF (*non_native_cf*) sets (Lines 3–7). Then, for each case (*case* in line 9) in the second set, we find the first occurrence of a CF case (*native_cf* in line 11) to extract attributes with the lowest feature difference (line 12). Subsequently, we iterate through each case in the second set (*case2* in line 13) to identify similar cases. A new case is generated by combining feature values from *native_cf* and similar attribute values from *case2*. The label of the new case follows that of *native_cf*. This new case is considered if it does not already exist in the case base. The process is outlined in Fig. 1.

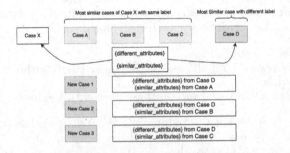

Fig. 1. Visualization of the process of Direct-CF approach.

3.3   High-Weights CF Approach

Our third approach, as outlined in Algorithm 3, is based on the feature importance of the attributes. Based on the notion that causal features are better choices of features to change to obtain a different label, as discussed in Sect. 2, in lack of which features are causal, we focus on the features that are likely to have higher correlations to the label, those with highest weights to consider differences between cases as basis of CFs. By high weights, we mean weights above a set threshold. The remainder of the process is similar to Keane's-CF.

Algorithm 3: Pseudocode for High-Weights-CF approach.

Data: Case base

Result: A set of synthetic cases

1 *similarity_threshold, feature_difference, weight_threshold* ← set similarity threshold, feature difference, and weight threshold

2 *native_cf, non_native_cf* ← [], []

3 *feature_importance* ← Extract feature importance of the attributes by executing the weight learning algorithm

4 **for** *case1 in Case base* **do**

5   Compare *case1* with the other cases

6   Calculate local similarity and global similarity between *case1* and all the other cases

7   Computer feature differences for those attributes where the value is greater than *feature_importance*

8   Create a list for *case1* with all the retrieved cases

9   Put *case1* in the *non_native_cf* if it has no native CF. Otherwise put *case1* in the *native_cf*

10 (Lines 8-22 are same as Algorithm 1)

---

4   Experimental Design

Given a dataset, we implement preprocessing, case base creation and evaluation, then execute case augmentation and evaluate synthetic cases, and finally evaluate the resulting case base after adding augmented cases. The next sections describe these steps.

4.1   Datasets

We use five datasets. Two datasets, A and B, describe decisions of medical triage. The other three datasets are from the UCI repository[1], which we included to assess generality of the approaches. The characteristics of the datasets are presented in Table 1.

---

[1] The UCI repository is available at: https://archive.ics.uci.edu/datasets.

Table 1. Characteristics of the datasets used in the study.

Dataset	Instances	Features	Unique Labels	Feature Types	Missing Values
A	792	169	68	Binary, Categorical, Numeric	Yes
B	4138	141	74	Binary, Categorical, Numeric	Yes
Votes	435	16	2	Categorical	Yes
Ecoli	336	7	7	Binary, Categorical, Continuous	No
Soybean	307	35	19	Categorical	Yes

Datasets A and B entail decisions collected from medical decision-makers presented with battlefield triage scenarios. These scenarios probe the decision-making process in austere combat situations where medics must quickly assess the condition of wounded soldiers and decide on the most appropriate course of action, such as immediate treatment, evacuation priority, or deferment of care based on the severity of injuries and available resources. These datasets were created by performers in the ITM DARPA Project [7].

Cases represent a combination of scenario features, supplemented features [19] added by decision analysis [7], and a decision. We consider these cases as ground truth, as they are developed with domain experts. Next are descriptions of some of the important features of this data.

Action: decision chosen by medical decision-makers in response to triage scenarios. Possible values include *apply treatment, check all vitals, check pulse, check respiration* and *move to evacuation*.

Supplies: medical resources and equipment available to carry out treatments. Examples of possible values are *tourniquet, pressure bandage, hemostatic gauze, burn dressing, and nasopharyngeal airway*.

Treatment: particular medical intervention selected as a result of the *action* attribute. It is based on the administration of an available supply.

Severity of injury: is categorized from low to extreme, indicating the urgency of medical attention needed.

Casualty tag: *tagging* a casualty involves assessing each individual's injuries or condition to give a tag that indicates the priority for receiving medical treatment. Tag values range from *minor*, which requires minimal care, to *expectant*, which indicates survival is unlikely even with optimal medical resources.

Soldier's status: including combat role, vital signs, and potential for recovery with immediate care.

Environmental factors: such as the proximity of ongoing combat, weather conditions, the likelihood of safely evacuating the wounded, and the delay of delivering aid.

Decision Analytics: are data generated from the observed scenario using a variety of algorithms. The values are not themselves observed data but represent analytical results produced by the application of evaluative metrics, such as the probable severity change of an injury over time, or the probabilities of events such as death by asphyxia, depending on the values in the dataset [7].

4.2 Preprocessing

Preprocessing addresses missing values, attributes lacking distinct values, and duplicate samples. Initially, we replace all empty values with -999. Attributes with fewer than ten distinct values are considered categorical, while those with ten or more distinct values are treated as numerical. We use this unless available domain rules dictate a different scale. We calculate the range between the highest and lowest values for numerical attributes as a measure of feature variability. This feature variability is used to assess the local similarity between cases and informs subsequent steps in the CF generation process.

4.3 Create and Evaluate Case Bases

To create case bases from data, we define similarity assessment through local similarity functions, learning feature weights, and global similarity for aggregation. We calculate local similarity between two cases by using functions based on their feature type. For categorical features, the algorithm checks for exact equality. For numerical features, similarity is calculated based on the absolute difference between the feature values, scaled by the difference of maximum and minimum values occurring in the data for that feature. The process of calculating local similarity is highlighted in Algorithm 4. Then, we use a weight learning method to obtain weights for each attribute. To compute the global similarity score between an input case and candidate cases, we aggregate local similarity and weights with the weighted mean.

Algorithm 4: Local similarity calculation between two cases.

Input: case1, case2, feature type
Output: Similarity between two cases

1   $local\_sim \leftarrow []$, $i \leftarrow 0$
2   **for** $c1, c2$ **in** $zip(case1, case2)$ **do**
3   **if** $feature\_type[i][0]$ **is** *Categorical* **then**
4   **if** $c1$ **is equal to** $c2$ **then**
5 | append 1 to $local\_sim$
6   **else**
7 | append 0 to $local\_sim$
8   **else**
9         $temp \leftarrow 1 - \left(\frac{|c1-c2|}{feature\_type[i][1]} \right)$
10   append $temp$ to $local\_sim$
11      $i \leftarrow i + 1$
12 **return** $local\_sim$

Once we have a case base, then we assess the average accuracy using LOOCV.

4.4   Case Augmentation and Evaluation of Synthetic Cases

This is where we execute Algorithms 1, 2, and 3 from Sect. 3. They all use a case base as input. Once an approach produces augmented cases, we evaluate the quality of the augmented cases by assessing how well they predict the original case base (*i.e.*, using original cases as a test set).

4.5   Combined Evaluation of Original and Augmented Cases

Average Accuracy. We evaluate each approach and each feature difference. To assess the quality of the synthetic cases, we predict the cases in the original case base by considering all the newly generated synthetic cases as the training samples. We only consider testing cases from the case base if the labels are present in the new cases, as we do not generate new cases for all labels. After these results, we conduct ablation studies, which we detail with the results. For comparison and comprehension of the value of the approach, we evaluate the overall accuracy of the resulting case base after adding all the synthetic cases to the original case base, which was our original goal.

Overlap analysis. Overlap analysis compares the cases generated by each approach to check whether different approaches would produce the same case.

Plausibility analysis. The evaluation method used to assess the plausibility of counterfactual cases generated in our study focused on ensuring that each data point adhered to certain logical rules reflecting the domain. This systematic checking of data plausibility involved both automatic and manual reviews.

Automatic validation processes ensured that the data points conformed to predefined constraints derived from the nature of the data. For instance, in the medical triage context of the examined probes, specific treatments are only applicable to certain conditions or anatomical locations, and a treatment cannot be applied if the required supplies are unavailable. Given the discrete choices of data on actions, treatments, and supplies, the categorical components of the dataset, these checks could be programmatically enforced, ensuring that each data point was plausible within the operational constraints of the dataset. This method reflects a common practice in synthetic data generation, where constraints are defined based on domain knowledge to ensure the generated data maintains logical consistency. In addition to automated checks, samples of the data were manually reviewed to ensure they adhered to common sense and exhibited logical consistency. This manual checking involved assessing if the treatment and actions applied were plausible and did not result in contradictory or impossible actions. Such manual review provides an additional layer of assurance that the automated processes did not overlook non-feasible or implausible results.

Generalizability. The datasets from the UCI repository are evaluated to assess the generality of the approaches, as described in Sect. 5.4. As the UCI datasets have fewer attributes as compared to our triage datasets, we restrict the analysis to two and three feature difference. We measure performance using the number of cases generated and average accuracy (Acc.) in predicting the cases with similar labels. For the Ecoli dataset, we restrict our analysis to single precision floating point values. Initially, we partition the case base into non-CFs and CFs by employing feature differences of two and three. Subsequently, in Direct-CF approach, to identify the most similar CF case-for each non-CF case, we incrementally adjust the feature difference by one unit, thereby ensuring the plausibility of the generated new cases.

5 Results and Discussion

5.1 Accuracy

The results of three different approaches for two datasets are shown in Table 2. We consider the number of new cases generated and average accuracy (Acc. %). We observe that the new cases are created only for certain labels. While calculating the average accuracy, we only predict those instances that have the same labels as the original cases. We compare the performance for two, three, and four feature differences. There are times when neither dataset generates a new case, making it impossible to calculate the average accuracy. Keane's-CF records the highest, 100% accuracy using a feature difference of two for Case Base A. This approach records only 35.29% accuracy using three feature differences on Case Base B. For Case Base A, Direct-CF is 92.74% accurate using both two and three feature differences, while for Case Base B, the highest accuracy is 95.85%. High-Weights-CF achieves 100% accuracy for Case Bases A (three feature differences) and B (four feature differences). Direct-CF generated a good number of cases for all feature differences. For the third approach, there is an additional parameter, feature importance, for which we set the value 0.015. It is also apparent that Direct-CF generates more cases than the other two approaches. That is because it is considering one most similar CF case for each non-CF case. For some non-CF cases, the most similar case has a higher number of feature differences and for some cases, the most similar case has fewer feature differences with high similarity.

The original case base accuracy for both the triage datasets are shown in second column (Base Acc. %) of Table 2. Then, we calculate the overall accuracy of both case bases, including all the new cases. Keane's-CF enhances the accuracy of Case Base A from 87.25% to a maximum of 88% with two feature differences, while there is no improvement for Case Base B. Direct-CF improves the overall accuracy for both case bases across all feature difference values. For Case Base A, accuracy increases to 89.60% with two feature differences, and for Case Base B, it rises to 99.98% with four feature differences. High-Weights-CF increases the accuracy of Case Base A to 89.66% with three feature differences and Case Base B to 98.68% with four feature differences.

Although the Keane's-CF and High-Weights-CF approaches produced a limited number of CF cases, employing these methodologies can still be advantageous. By presenting a broad spectrum of scenarios for the model to learn from,

Table 2. Results of three different approaches on two case bases.

Case Base	Base Acc. (%)	Exact. Feat. Diff	Keane's-CF		Direct-CF		High-Weights-CF	
			New Cases	Acc. (%)	New Cases	Acc. (%)	New Cases	Acc. (%)
A	87.25	2	1	100	131	87.06	8	81
		3	4	33.33	141	92.74	1	100
		4	None	N/A	142	92.74	None	N/A
B	98.65	2	None	N/A	1071	90.71	None	N/A
		3	6	35.29	1381	88.93	None	N/A
		4	None	N/A	1733	95.85	90	100

Table 3. Results for ablation study by randomly dropping new cases using Direct-CF from Dataset A. The results are based on five iterations.

New Cases	Drop Rate.	Max Acc. (%)	Min Acc. (%)
131	10%	95.4	86.73
	20%	95.1	84.62
141	10%	94.7	89.8
	20%	92.7	88.8

these techniques may significantly improve its ability to generalize across heterogeneous datasets. The absence of case overlap in our experiments underscores the complexity of integrating various augmentation techniques into a comprehensive augmentation strategy. However, it also highlights the value of experimenting with different approaches, as some may be more effective than others depending on the specific characteristics of the data in question.

Keane's-CF for Case Base A creates four cases. In an ablation study, we remove each instance and compare average accuracy. Removing the first case improves accuracy to 66.67%. Removing the second, third, and fourth cases individually does not change average accuracy. In the second ablation study, as highlighted in Table 3, we randomly drop 10% and 20% of the cases generated by Direct-CF from Case Base A (131, 141). Although there is evidence of a 20% reduction in cases, the average accuracy increases to 94% for some experiments. These two ablation studies suggest further refinement of the newly generated cases.

5.2   Overlap Analysis

This section describes the overlapping CFs resulting from three approaches. We observed that each approach produced a distinct set of new cases. A comparison between the new cases generated from Case Base B by Direct-CF and High-Weights-CF, considering a feature difference of four, revealed that High-Weights-CF produced 29 new cases with label 35 and 61 new cases with label 36. On the other hand, among the 1733 new cases produced by Direct-CF, 101 were labeled as 35 and 130 as 36. Remarkably, no overlaps or subsets were found between the datasets from the two approaches. This was also the case with Case Base A, where we examined the new cases generated by each approach for feature differences two and three and discovered that none of the approaches had overlapping cases for any number of feature differences. The lack of overlap suggests that each approach generates distinct cases.

5.3 Domain Analysis and Plausibility

Plausibility in CFs is defined as the realism and relevance of these hypothetical alternatives to actual events or data points. For CFs to be considered plausible, they must meet several criteria, including relevance to the domain, adherence to causal relationships presented in the empirical data, and the ability to be actionable or achievable under the constraints set by the nature of the case. The synthetic examples should also reflect the underlying distribution and characteristics of the original datasets [9,18].

In our experiments, we generate CFs from the reference datasets developed by domain experts. When these datasets are used as a basis for generating CFs, our initial assumption is that they accurately represent observed real-world scenarios, patterns, and distributions.

The original datasets capture decisions made under a variety of conditions and have native CF cases. By methodically varying between two and four attributes of these cases, such as the severity of injuries, availability of resources, or environmental factors, new CF cases are constructed for those cases in the original case base that do not already have them. In order to evaluate the plausibility of these CFs without specific domain expertise, we examine four criteria:

Consistency with the Reference Data: CFs should maintain consistency with the patterns, relationships, and distributions found in the reference datasets. This ensures that the CF scenarios or augmented data points they represent are within the realm of possibility for the given domain.

Adherence to Known Causal Relationships: Even without domain-specific knowledge, CFs can be assessed for their plausibility based on their adherence to causal relationships that are either evident within the dataset or established through general knowledge. This involves evaluating whether the changes proposed by CFs make logical sense given the observed cause-and-effect dynamics in the original data.

Feasibility and Actionability: CFs should propose changes or scenarios that are actionable within the constraints of the domain, even as understood by a non-expert. For example, if a limb has been amputated, a treatment that requires the application of a supply to that (nonexistent) limb is not actionable or feasible.

Alignment with Domain Goals and Values: Even without in-depth domain expertise, the evaluation of CFs can consider their alignment with the overarching goals, values, and ethical standards of the domain. This includes the obvious criteria that the application of treatment should not cause harm but does not extend to the trade off between harm and mission accomplishment. Here, we mean obvious harm, such as denying a patient care completely rather than prioritizing the order of care.

We analyze the plausibility of example CFs created from the case base, as shown in Table 4. It would be tempting to present a comparison of original cases and their CFs showing the feature change of two or three and thereby inferring a causal relationship of those features directly to the change in the decision. However, the high dimensionality of the source data complicates the direct identification of specific feature differences responsible for the transition from one decision outcome to the next. The heterogeneity of intra-feature correlations that are involved in the triage medical dataset further obscures the relationship between specific features and changes in the predicted action and treatment. Generated cases are created by altering the original data are not real-world observations themselves, so we can only discuss correlation, not causation, as we have done in analyzing feature weights for class prediction. Additional observations are as follows. The CF is consistent with the reference dataset. The CF generated appears as an available treatment in the original dataset. The adherence to the causal relationship known from the base data is also preserved by virtue of its existence in the original dataset. There is no obvious misalignment with the domain goals and values. For example, no CF case contains an instance of administering pain medication to someone who is not injured. The result is actionable. For example, the suggested case does not create a situation that would not be feasible given the domain knowledge represented by the original case base. Possible features that are not actionable would be those that defy logic; for example, applying a treatment such as a tourniquet to *left face*.

Table 4. An example case and a CF represented in abbreviated form. The relationship between the original and CF cases will not necessarily be directly apparent from the feature differences, but the derived case should be plausible.

Base Case	name: TAG_CHARACTER, params: (category: MINIMAL, casualty: CASUALTY_X), environment: DESERT, outcome_probability: 0.93
CF	name: APPLY_TREATMENT, params: (treatment: NASOPHARYNGEAL AIRWAY, casualty: CASUALTY_V, location: LEFT FACE), environment: JUNGLE, outcome_probability: 0.95

5.4   Performance on Other Datasets

The results are presented in Table 5. It is apparent that Keane's-CF performs better for all three datasets in predicting the cases while using the new cases as the training samples. The base accuracies of the Votes, Ecoli, and Soybean datasets are 95.40%, 73.51%, and 91.53%, respectively. We analyze whether the new cases increase base accuracy. None of the approaches record an accuracy increase for the Votes dataset. Keane's-CF, using three feature differences, increases the base accuracy of the Ecoli dataset to 90.39%. It also increases the base accuracy of the Soybean dataset to 92.81% using two feature differences. Direct-CF and High-Weights-CF both record about a 1% accuracy increase using two and three feature differences.

Table 5. Performance of the three approaches on three UCI datasets.

Dataset	Base. Acc. (%)	Exact Feat. Diff.	Keane's-CF		Direct-CF		High-Weights-CF	
			New Cases	Acc. (%)	New Cases	Acc. (%)	New Cases	Acc. (%)
Votes	95.40	2	1340	80.92	None	N/A	None	N/A
		3	6389	72.18	None	N/A	None	N/A
Ecoli	73.51	2	363	77.51	104	38.90	402	70.82
		3	2141	87.72	93	51.09	1975	59.28
Soybean	91.53	2	13	49.17	60	41.67	3	2.00
		3	238	65.38	66	54.44	40	64.29

While the Direct-CF approach produces more cases for the triage datasets, it exhibits different behavior for the UCI datasets, as illustrated in Table 5. UCI datasets are standardized to some extent, whereas our medical triage datasets require additional standardization techniques. Furthermore, we acknowledge that each approach may behave differently based on the nature of data and pre-processing techniques. Further exploration will provide insight into these behaviors.

6 Conclusion and Future Work

In this research, we proposed two novel approaches based on an established framework [5] for generating CF-based synthetic cases. The approaches help to address data scarcity issues often present in the medical domain. For the two medical triage datasets, our Direct-CF approach demonstrates better results in predicting the cases in the original case base by taking all the new cases as the training set. This approach also increases overall accuracy by combining new cases with original cases. Despite the low number of CFs generated by two of the approaches using triage datasets, the exploration of alternative approaches produces synthetic data with high levels of accuracy.

Our studies reveal opportunities for future research. It is clear that not all new cases generated are equally accurate, but without close examination and consideration of domain knowledge, we cannot automatically distinguish which ones to keep. High-Weights-CF approach was conceived based on the notion that correlation is the closest we can come in the absence of ground truth for causality. In future work, it would be beneficial to examine how feature weights may affect the consideration of feature differences.

Acknowledgements. This research was conducted as part of the In the Moment (ITM) project, supported by the Defense Advanced Research Projects Agency (DARPA) under contract number HR001122S0031. We acknowledge other performers from ITM who provided the datasets in the military medical triage. Dataset A was based on data provided by Alyssa Tanaka and colleagues with Soar Technology, LLC. Dataset B was based on work provided by RTX BBN Technologies.

References

1. Gowtham Reddy, A., Bachu, S., Dash, S., Sharma, C., Sharma, A., Balasubramanian, V.N.: Rethinking counterfactual data augmentation under confounding. arXiv e-prints, pp. arXiv–2305 (2023)
2. Hasan, M.G.M.M., Talbert, D.A.: Counterfactual examples for data augmentation: a case study. In: The International FLAIRS Conference Proceedings, vol. 34 (2021)
3. Karimi, A.H., Schölkopf, B., Valera, I.: Algorithmic recourse: from counterfactual explanations to interventions. In: Proceedings of the 2021 ACM Conference on Fairness, Accountability, and Transparency, FAccT '21, pp. 353–362 (2021)
4. Keane, M.T., Kenny, E.M., Delaney, E., Smyth, B.: If only we had better counterfactual explanations: five key deficits to rectify in the evaluation of counterfactual XAI techniques. In: Proceedings of the Thirtieth International Joint Conference on Artificial Intelligence, IJCAI-21, pp. 4466–4474 (2021)
5. Keane, M.T., Smyth, B.: Good counterfactuals and where to find them: a case-based technique for generating counterfactuals for explainable AI (XAI). In: Watson, I., Weber, R. (eds.) ICCBR 2020. LNCS (LNAI), vol. 12311, pp. 163–178. Springer, Cham (2020). https://doi.org/10.1007/978-3-030-58342-2_11
6. König, G., Freiesleben, T., Grosse-Wentrup, M.: A causal perspective on meaningful and robust algorithmic recourse. arXiv preprint: arXiv:2107.07853 (2021)
7. Molineaux, M., et al.: Aligning to human decision-makers in military medical triage. In: Juan, A.D.B., Mauricio, R.G., Orozco-del-Castillo, G. (ed.) ICCBR 2024, Lecture Notes in Computer Science. Springer, Cham (2024)
8. O'Brien, A., Kim, E., Weber, R.: Investigating causally augmented sparse learning as a tool for meaningful classification. In: 2023 IEEE Sixth International Conference on Artificial Intelligence and Knowledge Engineering (AIKE), pp. 33–37. IEEE (2023)
9. Par, Ö.E., Sezer, E.A., Sever, H.: Small and unbalanced data set problem in classification. In: 2019 27th Signal Processing and Communications Applications Conference (SIU), pp. 1–4 (2019)
10. Pitis, S., Creager, E., Garg, A.: Counterfactual data augmentation using locally factored dynamics. In: Advances in Neural Information Processing Systems, vol. 33, pp. 3976–3990 (2020)
11. Richter, M.M., Weber, R.O.: Case-Based Reasoning: A Textbook. Springer, Berlin (2013)
12. Rodriguez-Almeida, A.J., et al.: Synthetic patient data generation and evaluation in disease prediction using small and imbalanced datasets. IEEE J. Biomed. Health Inform. **27**(6), 2670–2680 (2023)
13. Smyth, B., Keane, M.T.: A few good counterfactuals: generating interpretable, plausible and diverse counterfactual explanations. In: Keane, M.T., Wiratunga, N. (eds.) Case-Based Reasoning Research and Development. Lecture Notes in Computer Science(), vol. 13405, pp. 18–32. Springer, Cham (2022). https://doi.org/10.1007/978-3-031-14923-8_2

14. Temraz, M., Keane, M.T.: Solving the class imbalance problem using a counterfactual method for data augmentation. Mach. Learn. Appl. **9**, 100375 (2022)

15. Ustun, B., Spangher, A., Liu, Y.: Actionable recourse in linear classification. In: Proceedings of the Conference on Fairness, Accountability, and Transparency, pp. 10–19 (2019)

16. Verma, S., Dickerson, J., Hines, K.: Counterfactual explanations for machine learning: challenges revisited. arXiv preprint: arXiv:2106.07756 (2021)

17. Wachter, S., Mittelstadt, B., Russell, C.: Counterfactual explanations without opening the black box: automated decisions and the GDPR. Harv. JL Tech. **31**, 841 (2017)

18. Warren, G., Smyth, B., Keane, M.T.: "better" counterfactuals, ones people can understand: psychologically-plausible case-based counterfactuals using categorical features for explainable AI (XAI). In: Keane, M.T., Wiratunga, N. (eds.) Case-Based Reasoning Research and Development. Lecture Notes in Computer Science(), vol. 13405, pp. 63–78. Springer, Cham (2022). https://doi.org/10.1007/978-3-031-14923-8_5

19. Weber, R., Shrestha, M., Johs, A.J.: Knowledge-based XAI through CBR: there is more to explanations than models can tell. arXiv preprint: arXiv:2108.10363 (2021)

20. Wiratunga, N., Wijekoon, A., Nkisi-Orji, I., Martin, K., Palihawadana, C., Corsar, D.: DisCERN: discovering counterfactual explanations using relevance features from neighbourhoods. In: 2021 IEEE 33rd International Conference on Tools with Artificial Intelligence (ICTAI), pp. 1466–1473. IEEE (2021)

21. Yang, W., Li, J., Xiong, C., Hoi, S.C.H.: Mace: An efficient model-agnostic framework for counterfactual explanation. arXiv preprint: arXiv:2205.15540 (2022)

On Implementing Case-Based Reasoning with Large Language Models

Kaitlynne Wilkerson and David Leake[✉]

Luddy School, Indiana University, Bloomington, IN 47408, USA
{kwilker,leake}@indiana.edu

Abstract. Systems based on Large Language Models (LLMs), such as ChatGPT, have impressive performance but also well-known issues with erroneous output. Retrieval Augmented Generation (RAG), which typically presents the LLM with text snippets of additional knowledge retrieved from an external knowledge base, is a popular method for increasing LLM accuracy. This paper presents initial studies exploring augmenting LLMs with cases rather than snippets and prompting LLMs towards performing case-based reasoning. The studies consider four possible scenarios, exploring the potential benefit of LLMs performing different subparts of the CBR process: (1) a scenario in which the LLM is prompted to adapt a presented case, (2) a scenario in which the LLM is first prompted to perform similarity assessment to select a case from a set of candidates, and then to adapt the selected case, (3) a scenario in which the LLM is prompted to select the two most similar cases to a problem and generate an adapted/combined solution in light of both, and (4) a scenario in which the LLM selects the nearest neighbor and nearest unlike neighbor and generates an adapted/combined solution based on both. Results of tests using Llama and ChatGPT are encouraging for the accuracy benefits of providing LLMs with cases and raise questions for future study.

Keywords: Case-Based Reasoning · ChatGPT · Llama · Large Language Models · Retrieval Augmented Generation

1 Introduction

In 2022, ChatGPT captured public attention. Not only did it demonstrate remarkable capabilities but it became notorious for incorrect, confusing and disruptive output—including output the system simply "hallucinated". As competing systems became publicly available it became clear that such problems were not just characteristics of ChatGPT, but instead results of fundamental characteristics of the Large Language Models (LLMs) underlying such systems [5,19]. Nevertheless, LLMs are rapidly being assimilated into everyday technologies, resulting in a pressing need to develop methods to alleviate LLM errors.

A promising method for reducing factual errors by LLMs is to provide them with external knowledge regarding the prompt topic. Retrieval Augmented Generation (RAG) operates by retrieving text related to a query and adding it to the

© The Author(s), under exclusive license to Springer Nature Switzerland AG 2024
J. A. Recio-Garcia et al. (Eds.): ICCBR 2024, LNAI 14775, pp. 404–417, 2024.
https://doi.org/10.1007/978-3-031-63646-2_26

prompt. This approach has been shown to improve LLM responses [3,18]. RAG typically provides the LLM with knowledge in the form of snippets reflecting individual facts. However, providing knowledge in the form of cases is an appealing alternative [18]. This paper proposes going beyond augmenting LLM knowledge with cases, by specifically prompting the LLM to perform CBR on those cases. Watson [17] observed that Case Based Reasoning (CBR) is a methodology of reasoning from experiences rather than a specific technology: it can be implemented with any technology. In that vein, this paper explores implementing a case-based classification process using LLMs.

LLM-based implementations of CBR—or of specific parts of the CBR cycle—might provide benefits both to LLMs and to CBR. Having LLMs perform CBR could potentially improve both the accuracy and explainability of LLM-based systems, for three reasons. First, ideally, grounding LLM reasoning in similar cases might reduce the risk of hallucination when generating solutions. Second, guiding an LLM through a CBR-like process might increase system accuracy by helping focus the LLM on reasoning related to similar problems. Third, because cases are naturally intuitive explanations for human users [6], grounding LLM reasoning in cases might aid explanation of system decisions: humans find cases useful as explanations [2,4]. Being able to present the user of an LLM not only with a solution but with a relevant case to compare would help in assessing solutions, and might increase user trust when both are consistent [4].

Conversely, for certain task domains, LLM-based implementations of CBR processes could benefit CBR. If the parts of the CBR process depending on rich knowledge could be performed by an LLM, it could have transformative impact for increasing the scope of CBR applications, by facilitating applying CBR to knowledge-rich domains for which formally encoded knowledge is unavailable, expensive, or difficult to encode. We note the limitation that LLMs could still produce erroneous results. However, part of the CBR process is for CBR systems to assess proposed results for correctness, and when final system results are presented to users, users can assess them in light of the cases on which they were based—which has been shown effective for building justified trust [4].

To explore the effects of providing retrieved cases to an LLM and prompting it to perform parts of the CBR process, we performed an experiment using two LLMs, ChatGPT 3.5 and Llama 2 [15], for a classification task in a medical triage domain. Triage decisions require rich world knowledge; this task illustrates a use of LLMs to bypass knowledge acquisition for a complex real-world task. We tested performance with three types of prompts: (1) the baseline of prompting the LLM for a direct solution without providing any case information, (2) prompting for a solution after providing a similar case to the LLM, and (3) prompting for the LLM to do similarity assessment to select case(s) and then prompting it to adapt them to generate a solution. We also tested whether the LLM using different numbers and types of cases (using only similar cases, or using both a similar case and the nearest unlike neighbor) affected accuracy.

We found that using cases could improve the classification performance of the LLM, which demonstrates cases as a source of useful information for our testbed task, and that the adaptation ability of an LLM impacted the best methods for utilizing cases. We also found that while ChatGPT and Llama 2 both performed similarity assessment poorly, their adaptation rates were quite different and this led to certain prompts performing better than others. Overall, we consider the results an encouraging beginning. We close the paper by discussing next steps for building on these first results.

2   Background

Issues with LLMs: LLMs combine remarkable conversational capabilities with limitations such as hallucinations, and, unless combined with other systems, a lack of episodic and causal knowledge (e.g., [5]). Their facility at generating language can give the appearance of reasoning [8,12], but they struggle at tasks such as planning [16]. Because LLMs rely on statistical profiles of human language and tasks such as identifying facts are not statistical in nature, LLMs are inherently ill-suited to them [5]. In addition, their reasoning is based on generalizations, which are necessarily lossy, and can be distorted by the LLM when generating a response [13]. Issues may also stem from prompts asking for information beyond the LLM's training data, such as time-sensitive information [3]. Such issues are well known and current efforts aim at alleviating them, e.g., with augmented models that draw on additional methods when needed [10].

One approach to increasing LLM accuracy is to integrate external knowledge into the model, either by integrating the information into the prompt or by providing the LLM with a knowledge base that it can query on its own [3,9]. This has been shown to improve LLM performance [3,9] and reduce many of the issues discussed above, including identifying potential hallucinations by comparing the response to the retrieved knowledge [13]. While this does not (and cannot) fix the fact that LLMs are limited by their statistical nature, it does help to address the knowledge problem by providing the LLM with additional knowledge on a topic that has not been distorted or generalized. The usefulness of cases as a form of knowledge in CBR applications [1] and prevalence of case-based reasoning by people [7] suggests the potential promise of providing a different type of knowledge—case knowledge—to LLMs from an external case base.

Knowledge Integration Improves LLM Responses: Retrieval Augmented Generation is one of the most widely adopted strategies for integrating external knowledge into LLMs [3]. RAG can be implemented in many ways, but the core process contains three main steps: First, partition a corpus of text into n chunks and vectorize. Second, given some query, assess similarity between the query and each of the vectorized n chunks. Third, present the retrieved information to an LLM so that it can be used to generate a response [3]. A demonstration of the benefit of retrieved information can be found through the study of LLM performance on commonsense reasoning benchmarks when contextual knowledge was provided [9]. Retrieval-based methods for integrating knowledge improved the accuracy of LLMs on each of the benchmark datasets.

The spirit of RAG relates to CBR, but RAG differs in the type of knowledge retrieved and how that knowledge is used. RAG tends to focus more on knowledge statements that can add context to a prompt [3,9,12], while CBR uses cases aimed at the task at hand. Also, RAG may provide general information, while CBR provides specific concrete episodes. We seek to understand the impact of providing cases and prompting the LLM to provide solutions by CBR.

3   Questions for Implementing CBR with LLMs

This paper presents the start of a research program to better understand the capabilities of LLMs with respect to CBR and whether previous research showing gains in accuracy from external knowledge [3,9] extends not only to providing cases to an LLM (e.g., [18]), but to guiding the LLMs through a CBR-like process. Understanding the potential of case-augmented generation and of implementing CBR with LLMs will require answering questions such as:

1. Do LLMs benefit from having a similar prior case as a starting point?
2. Do LLMs benefit from having multiple cases for a single problem?
3. Do LLMs benefit from having both example and counterfactual cases?
4. How well can LLMs assess case similarity?
5. How well can LLMs perform case adaptation?
6. What types of prompts are most effective for guiding LLM similarity assessment and case adaptation?
7. To what extent, and how, do the above depend on characteristics of specific LLMs and types of task domains?

Each of these questions is a substantial topic for which a definitive answer would require extensive studies. The purpose of this paper is to open the door to future investigations by gathering initial experimental data and observations relevant to questions 1–5.

4   Experimental Design

As a first step towards answering questions 1–5 in the previous section, we conducted an experiment comparing the baseline accuracy of OpenAI's ChatGPT and Meta's Llama 2 to their accuracy when provided with cases and either (1) prompted to perform a sort of implicit CBR—to solve the new problem based on the case—or (2) prompted to follow the CBR cycle more explicitly, by providing cases and prompting the LLM to first perform similarity assessment and then case adaptation.

4.1   Large Language Models Used

OpenAI's ChatGPT 3.5[1] and Meta's Llama 2 70b-chat [15], which hereafter will be referred to as ChatGPT and Llama 2 respectively, were used in this experiment. ChatGPT was selected to give an illustration of the current commercial

---

[1] https://openai.com/blog/chatgpt.

state of the art. However, because it is not possible to set parameters or control possible updates, the ChatGPT results should only be seen as suggestive—they are not replicable. For replicability, the experiments were also run on the open source LLM, Llama 2, for which we could control the model parameters.

All interactions with ChatGPT were done by hand through the ChatGPT website over the course of a single day. Llama 2 was hosted locally and automatically invoked on Indiana University's Big Red 200 supercomputer using the Llama.cpp[2] and llama-cpp-python projects.[3] We tested several combinations of parameters but found the best performance with a temperature of 0. The top_p value was set at 0.9, but this was not found to be as impactful as temperature.

All cases were presented to the LLMs via prompts. Because of limitations on prompt size, we did not present the entire case base to the LLM. Instead, a subset of cases was selected from the case base by an initial retrieval phase, using the retrieval component of a k-NN system, and that subset was provided to the LLM. The full k-NN system was also used as a baseline for our experiments.

4.2 Test Case Base

Experiments used a case base for medical triage classification. This task is an existing medical AI task area; the use of AI in medical triage increased as a result of the Covid-19 pandemic [14]. Both LLMs tested in this paper have been applied to medical domains [11]. Triage depends on extensive rich real-world knowledge, making it the type of domain for which bypassing traditional CBR knowledge acquisition by using LLM knowledge would be desirable. We note that supporting triage using public LLMs is problematic for medical applications due to data privacy concerns. Real application would require using local versions that do not retain query data.

Cases were constructed using data collected from a primary triage dataset posted on Kaggle.[4] The original dataset contained cases for 1,267 patients and tracked 24 different vital signs and medical assessments. Each patient was assigned a Korean Triage and Acuity Scale (KTAS) number of 1 through 5, with 1 indicating patients most in need of immediate medical attention and 5 indicating patients least in need of immediate medical attention. When the data set was generated, this value was obtained by three triage experts reviewing the patient's condition and assigning a number. We narrowed the case data down to seven features commonly discussed in triage literature [20]: sex and age of the patient, heart rate, respiratory rate, mental state, blood pressure and the patient's chief complaint upon entrance to the Emergency Room. These features tend to be the most commonly used by a range of different triage methods [20]. Sex, mental state and chief complaint were non-numerical values, with sex and mental state being categorical while chief complaint was a simple string value. Mental state contained four different values: Alert, Verbal Response, Pain Response,

---

[2] https://github.com/ggerganov/llama.cpp.

[3] https://github.com/abetlen/llama-cpp-python.

[4] https://www.kaggle.com/datasets/ilkeryildiz/emergency-service-triage-application.

and Unresponsive. The original dataset contained many missing values, especially for heart rate, respiratory rate, blood pressure and chief complaint. We removed instances with missing values from the pool of candidate cases. The remaining cases were divided by class and 5 cases per class were used to create the testing set (25 total), with the rest being assigned to the training pool. From the pool of training cases, a random sample of 102 cases was selected, with at least one case representing each class, to form the case base. This was done to streamline the retrieval and weight configuration processes.

We note that because the dataset was released in 2019, it is possible that either of the test LLMs was trained with this data. If so, that training could be expected to produce a favorable setting for direct LLM performance, potentially reducing the benefit of providing cases. However, given the lossy nature of LLM learning, the specific information provided by cases might still be valuable.

4.3 Case Retrieval

A k-NN system was used as a performance baseline and its retrieval mechanism was used to retrieve cases to present to the LLM. The k-NN based retrieval used weighted Euclidean distance, with weights selected by hill climbing to maximize k-NN accuracy. The best accuracy was 48% when the weights were set at Sex = 0.001, Age = 0.001, Heart Rate = 0.001, Respiratory Rate = 1.0, Mental State = 0.25, Chief Complaint = 0.25, and Blood Pressure = 0.001. Categorical data distance was 1 for non-matching categories and 0 for matching categories. Textual data was compared by semantic similarity implemented using HuggingFace's sentence transformer library and the all-mpnet-base-v2 model.[5] Vectorized text was assessed for semantic similarity using pyTorch's cosine similarity function.

4.4 Prompt Types

We tested three prompt types, all of which were in textual format:

- **Direct Solution:** Directly asks LLM for a solution without providing any additional information. LLM prompt form: *[instructions + problem case]*
- **Implicit CBR (ICBR):** Uses k-NN to provide LLM with one or more prior cases. LLM prompt form: *[instructions + problem case + prior case(s)]*
- **Explicit CBR (ECBR):** Uses k-NN to obtain the 10 most similar cases to the problem case and provides those to LLM for similarity assessment (only 10 cases were provided, to control prompt size). Instructions and additional information are designed to have LLM step through the CBR process. LLM prompt form: *[instructions + problem case + set of prior cases]*

The Direct Solution prompts establish a non-CBR LLM performance baseline for the triage task. ICBR prompts are designed to test how well an LLM can derive an answer from a nearest neighbor case without explicit instructions

---

[5] https://huggingface.co/sentence-transformers/all-mpnet-base-v2.

on how to do so. Tests of ICBR prompts assess (1) the LLM's capability to apply a previous case without specific guidance, and (2) whether the knowledge embedded in the LLM can lead to improved performance over that of the baseline knowledge-light k-NN system. Finally, the ECBR prompts aim to guide an LLM through a CBR process of similarity assessment and adaptation.

For both the ICBR and ECBR prompt types, we tested three different formulations that differed by the cases provided to the LLM:

- **1NN formulation:** Provides only the Nearest Neighbor
- **2NN formulation:** Provides the top two Nearest Neighbors
- **NUN formulation:** Provides the Nearest Neighbor and a counterfactual (the Nearest Unlike Neighbor)

The 2NN formulation was included to potentially increase the robustness of the model's response by providing more cases, and potentially helping alleviate issues in selecting the most similar case. The NUN formulation provided a counterfactual, to potentially help delineate the border between triage categories.

4.5 Prompt Instructions

Depending on the prompt type and the formulation of case information provided, each test used a slightly different set of instructions (Table 1). The instructions for all tests were crafted during an extensive round of pre-testing to assess how different prompt wordings affected the response given. For reasons of space, the pre-testing will not be discussed in this paper, but the prompts below were designed following the lessons learned from the best performing prompts during pre-testing. All prompts started with instructions and then provided the current patient's status and the cases of previous patient(s), if applicable, presented in a textual attribute-value form, for example:

> *Patient Status: Sex: Female, Age: 50, Chief complaint: Blood Pressure. Low, Mental state: Pain Response, Heart Rate: 37, Respirations: 28, Blood Pressure: 50/33*

Direct and Indirect Solution: The Direct Solution prompt was designed to provide the system with a base set of information about the classification task, in the context of a task scenario. The ICBR prompts all started with the same instructions, but, depending on the formulation, contained different amounts of case information. The system was explicitly told to use the similarities and differences between the current case and prior case(s) to make a decision on the classification of the current case. Thus, it can be seen as a prompt for performing adaptation.

Explicit CBR: The ECBR prompts differed depending on the number and type of cases the LLM was asked to select. For each formulation, the LLM was provided with 10 cases and asked to select some case(s) to work with. For the 1NN formulation, it was only asked to select the most similar previous patient. The

Table 1. Prompt(s) used for each prompt type and formulation.

Type and Formulation	Prompt(s)
Direct Solution	*Instructions: You are helping triage patients following a disaster and have limited medical personnel and resources. Given the following information about a patient in a triage situation, assign them a triage number of 1, 2, 3, 4 or 5, where 1 is assigned to the patients most in need of immediate medical attention and 5 is assigned to patients least in need of medical care.*
ICBR (All Formulations)	**Adaptation:** *Instructions: You are helping triage patients following a disaster and have limited medical personnel and resources. You need to assign the current patient with a specific tag number of 1, 2, 3, 4 or 5, where 1 is assigned to the patients most in need of immediate medical attention and 5 is assigned to patients least in need of medical care. Each tag number indicates the likelihood of the patient dying without immediate medical treatment. Given a previous patient and their condition, use the similarities and differences in vital signs to assign a tag number to the current patient.*
ECBR 1NN	**Similarity Assessment:** *Instructions: Given a current patient status, choose a previous patient whose condition is most similar to the current patient.* **Adaptation:** *Instructions: You are helping triage patients following a disaster and have limited medical personnel and resources. You need to assign the current patient with a specific tag number 1, 2, 3, 4 or 5, where 1 is assigned to the patients most in need of immediate medical attention and 5 is assigned to patients least in need of medical care. Each tag number indicates the likelihood of the patient dying without immediate medical treatment. Given the most similar previous patient's condition and associated triage number, use the similarities and differences in vital signs to assign a triage number to the current patient.*
ECBR 2NN	**Similarity Assessment:** *Instructions: Given a current patient status, choose a previous patient whose condition is most similar to the current patient.* **Similarity Assessment:** *What is the next most similar patient?* **Adaptation:** *Instructions: You are helping triage patients following a disaster and have limited medical personnel and resources. You need to assign the current patient with a specific tag number 1, 2, 3, 4 or 5, where 1 is assigned to the patients most in need of immediate medical attention and 5 is assigned to patients least in need of medical care. Each tag number indicates the likelihood of the patient dying without immediate medical treatment. Using the two most similar previous patients condition's and associated triage numbers, use the similarities and differences in vital signs to assign a triage number to the current patient.*
ECBR NUN	**Similarity Assessment:** *Instructions: Given a current patient status, find the nearest neighbor to the current patient. Assuming the tag number from the nearest neighbor could be the tag number for the current patient, find the nearest unlike neighbor to the current patient.* **Adaptation:** *Instructions: You are helping triage patients following a disaster and have limited medical personnel and resources. You need to assign the current patient with a specific tag number 1, 2, 3, 4 or 5, where 1 is assigned to the patients most in need of immediate medical attention and 5 is assigned to patients least in need of medical care. Each tag number indicates the likelihood of the patient dying without immediate medical treatment. Given the similarities and differences between the current patient, the nearest neighbor and the nearest unlike neighbor and assuming that the current patient tag number is unknown, assign a triage number to the current patient.*

2NN formulation asked for the most similar previous patient and then followed up with a second question asking for the next most similar previous patient. The NUN formulation specifically asked for the Nearest Neighbor and Nearest Unlike Neighbor in the same prompt. Then the LLM was provided with the triage scenario and asked to provide a solution that took into account the similarities and differences between the current patient and selected case(s).

A slight difference from the NUN prompt is that the similarity assessment prompt told the LLM to use the NN's classification as the current patient's classification, to find the NUN. During pre-testing, it was unclear if the LLM knew how to find the NUN, so instructions were added. To avoid biasing results, the LLM is instructed to assume it does not know the current patient's classification.

4.6   Procedure and Analysis

For each of the 25 test cases, a prompt was created for each of the prompt and formulation types, resulting in seven prompts per test case. Each of the 175 prompts was input by hand into the ChatGPT web interface and automatically delivered to Llama 2 via a python script. Responses were catalogued and checked to ensure that each LLM had not hallucinated any additional information that it ascribed to the input case. Any response in which a hallucination was found was discarded and the test was repeated until no hallucinations occurred in the response. We note that the ability to filter out such hallucinations follows from having the original case to compare; thus, asking an LLM to reason from a prior case enables a basic form of "sanity check" on the LLM output.

The LLM-generated classifications were compared to the KTAS expert values to judge accuracy using each prompt type. LLM responses were also compared to the expert value of the nearest neighbor (selected by the k-NN similarity metric for ICBR or LLM-chosen for ECBR) to assess whether the LLM performed adaptation occurred. For the ECBR prompt types, the LLM's ability to perform similarity assessment was evaluated by comparing the cases the LLMs selected as most similar to those selected as most similar by k-NN retrieval.

5   Results and Discussion

Triage is a challenging real-world domain; a patient's status may change rapidly and different levels of expertise or experience may result in slightly different categorizations [20]. Consequently, we included three different categories of "correctness" with varying amounts of latitude:

- *Strict Accuracy*: The LLM's response matched the correct classification
- *Correct or within 1 class (higher)*: Given the risks associated with erroneously lower triage scores, this category accepts safe near misses.
- *Correct or within 1 class (higher or lower)*: The LLM's response either matched the correct classification exactly or was within one category on the triage scale. This category includes near misses that might entail risk.

Table 2 shows the results from the prompt type accuracy tests.

Strict Accuracy Results: Direct Solution correctly classified triage patients 28% of the time, which was on par with the unweighted k-NN classifier. Both implicit and explicit CBR prompt types performed on par with or better than the Direct

Table 2. Accuracy by prompt type, case provided, and LLM. This table includes strict accuracy, accuracy with including responses 1 class higher than correct, and accuracy including responses 1 class higher or lower than correct. The best performing prompt type in each column is in bold.

Prompt Type and Formulation	Strict Accuracy	Correct within 1 class (higher)	Correct within 1 class (higher or lower)	Strict Accuracy	Correct within 1 class (higher)	Correct within 1 class (higher or lower)
Baselines						
Unweighted 1-NN	28%	56%	64%	28%	56%	64%
Weighted 1-NN	48%	60%	76%	48%	60%	76%
ChatGPT				Llama 2		
Direct Solution	28%	64%	72%	28%	52%	**72%**
ICBR 1NN	**60%**	68%	**80%**	**56%**	**60%**	68%
ICBR 2NN	40%	48%	64%	44%	56%	**72%**
ICBR NUN	44%	56%	68%	28%	40%	48%
ECBR 1NN	36%	56%	64%	44%	48%	60%
ECBR 2NN	44%	**72%**	76%	40%	48%	68%
ECBR NUN	28%	28%	44%	28%	40%	56%

Solution prompts for both LLMs. This suggests that in the test domain, providing cases can increase the accuracy of LLMs. It also suggests that even if one or both of the LLMs tested were trained on the dataset, providing the specific information on cases improves the LLM response over generating a solution with only network embedded information.

The ICBR prompts performed on par with or better than their ECBR counterparts, with the ICBR 1NN prompt formulations performing the best of all prompt types and outperforming the weighted k-NN classifier for both LLMs tested. Performance with the 2NN and NUN formulations differed slightly based on the LLM used for testing. With ChatGPT, ICBR NUN slightly outperforms ICBR 2NN. However, this is reversed for Llama 2. Among the ECBR prompts, the 2NN formulation performs well, but depending on the model may not be best. With ChatGPT, 2NN outperforms 1NN and NUN. However, with Llama 2, 1NN and 2NN perform very similarly, with 2NN slightly under performing. This seems to suggest that less knowledge is more when the case provided is the case selected as most similar using the k-NN weights (ICBR). When the LLM is used to judge similarity, additional cases generally yield higher accuracy, with slight differences in performance for different LLMs.

A surprising result was the relatively poor performance of ECBR prompts compared to their ICBR counterparts. We hypothesized that this may be the result of poor similarity assessment by LLMs. To test this, LLM-chosen and k-NN-chosen most similar case(s) were compared against each other for each test case for each prompt type. Table 3 displays the rate at which each LLM selected the same case as the optimized retrieval of the k-NN classifier. Both have comparably low performance, though Llama 2 outperformed ChatGPT when selecting the 2NN case for the ECBR 2NN prompt and the NUN for the ECBR NUN prompt.

Table 3. Similarity Assessment performance for ChatGPT and Llama 2. The ECBR 2NN and NUN rows show the percentage of correctly selected Nearest Neighbor (NN) and either second Nearest Neighbor (2NN) or Nearest Unlike Neighbor (NUN).

Target cases		ChatGPT	Llama 2
ECBR 1NN		20%	28%
ECBR 2NN	NN	24%	28%
	2NN	4%	16%
ECBR NUN	NN	16%	12%
	NUN	16%	32%

Correct within One Class: As discussed in the strict accuracy results, cases generally improved LLM performance, but only one prompt type and case formulation outperformed the weighted k-NN classifier: ICBR 1NN. Using a looser accuracy criterion provides additional context. As expected, the accuracy rates of the prompt types, direct solution, and k-NN classifiers increased with the looser criterion. However, fewer prompt types performed on par with or above direct solution levels. Overall, when ICBR 1NN was evaluated with ChatGPT, it outperformed the direct solution when considering accuracy within one class higher and within one class higher or lower. When evaluated with Llama 2, ICBR 1NN outperformed direct solution only when considering accuracy within one class higher and slightly underperformed when considering accuracy within one class higher or lower. Considering the risk associated with triaging a patient lower than is actually appropriate, ICBR 1NN can still be considered a contender in this domain. The remaining prompt types and formulations with equivalent or better performance in the expanded accuracy categories depended on the LLM used for evaluation. ECBR 2NN outperformed the Direct Solution baseline in both expansion categories when ChatGPT was used for evaluation, but not with Llama 2. With Llama 2, ICBR 2NN outperformed the Direct Solution baseline when the expansion was one class higher, but performed equivalently when the expansion was one class in either direction. We suspect that difference in ECBR vs ICBR may be attributed to adaptation ability, as will be discussed shortly, but the important similarity between these results is the benefit of providing a second similar case, in the 2NN case formulation. This suggests that while providing one case is generally sufficient for improving performance, under certain circumstances providing more cases could be useful.

Another interesting observation is that by the looser performance criteria, providing the LLM with case knowledge leads to equivalent or improved performance over k-NN classifiers. The improved performance was seen with ICBR 1NN and ECBR 2NN prompts evaluated on ChatGPT, whereas the equivalent performance was primarily seen with ICBR 1NN and ICBR 2NN evaluated on Llama 2. This is particularly interesting in light of the different domain knowledge available to the LLMs and the k-NN classifiers. The unweighted k-NN classifier had access to the entire case base (102 cases) and the weighted k-NN classifier had access to optimized weights along with the entire case base. The

LLMs did not have access to the optimized weights and seem to perform similarity assessment poorly (for ECBR prompts), yet they still generally performed at the level of k-NN and sometimes surpassed it. This supports the benefit of harnessing LLMs for this task, and the usefulness of providing cases.

Overall, the accuracy tests demonstrated a clear pattern of cases improving the performance of LLMs over direct solution baselines and established several different prompt and case formulation pairings that consistently led to increased accuracy. A common theme among these results was that the Llama 2 tests tended to show weaker performance patterns than ChatGPT. This may reflect the size difference of the models, as ChatGPT is over twice the size of Llama 2. Regardless, both models generally support the same trends.

Adaptation: We considered adaptation to have occurred if the nearest neighbor case (k-NN-provided for ICBR and LLM-chosen for ECBR) had a different solution from that proposed by the LLM. For each prompt/formulation we noted:

- How many times did adaptation occur?
- If adaptation occurred, was the adapted class correct?
- How many times did adaptation occur when the nearest neighbor had the correct classification (i.e., when adaptation was unnecessary)?

Table 4 displays the results from each question. Note that the second and third columns for each LLM are not out of the 25 test cases but out of the total number of adapted cases. Generally, the rates of adaptation among ChatGPT responses were above 50%, while Llama 2 rarely had adaptation rates that high, which indicates that ChatGPT was more likely to adapt than Llama 2. The data reveal two interesting trends that may help explain the difference in results between ChatGPT and Llama 2. First, Llama 2 tends to adapt much less often than ChatGPT and this may hurt accuracy for the ECBR prompt types. With ChatGPT, ECBR prompts had consistently higher rates of adaptation occurring than ICBR prompts, except for the NUN formulations. The higher rates of adaptation among ECBR prompts may be due to the observed limitations in ChatGPT similarity assessment. Llama 2 and ChatGPT perform

Table 4. This table displays LLM adaptation capabilities, including the total percentage of adapted cases, adapted cases that had a correct solution (strict accuracy), and adapted cases where the Nearest Neighbor (NN) had the correct solution (i.e., no adaptation should have occurred).

Prompt Type and Formulation	ChatGPT			Llama 2		
	Adapted Cases	Adapted Cases That Were Correct	Adapted Cases Where NN was Correct	Adapted Cases	Adapted Cases That Were Correct	Adapted Cases Where NN was Correct
ICBR 1NN	56%	35%	14%	64%	31%	18%
ICBR 2NN	52%	15%	30%	16%	0%	25%
ICBR NUN	72%	27%	33%	48%	0%	50%
ECBR 1NN	68%	35%	29%	12%	33%	0%
ECBR 2NN	84%	38%	14%	32%	25%	38%
ECBR NUN	76%	31%	31%	52%	23%	31%

similarity assessment about equally well. However, ChatGPT seems to perform more adaptation to make up for it, which could account for the higher accuracy rates during ChatGPT evaluation. Second, rates of correct adaptation were only roughly equivalent under 1NN case formulations; all other formulations had decreases of at least 10% in correct adaptation with Llama 2. This may also explain why the ECBR 2NN results were not as strong with Llama 2 as they were with ChatGPT. Despite the very poor ICBR 2NN percentages of correct solutions from adaptation, the low likelihood of adaptation occurring probably reduced the accuracy drop from this prompt type.

These results illustrate that for our tests, adaptation ability was LLM-specific and that it impacts the performance of both ECBR and ICBR prompt types as well as which case formulations work best with these prompts. Adaptation ability will be a rich area for further study for implementing CBR as a process for LLMs.

6   Future Work

This paper considers the potential benefit of providing LLMs with cases and prompting them to perform case-based reasoning. We conducted an experiment exploring whether cases could be used effectively as a source of external knowledge, analogously to other LLM knowledge integration methods. Encouragingly, our study suggests that CBR may be beneficial for reducing LLM errors, but this requires substantiation on tests with additional domains and LLMs, for multiple types of CBR tasks.

In addition, we would like to directly compare the accuracy using prompts containing CBR retrieved information to prompts containing RAG-retrieved snippets of general information, to quantify the impact of CBR in comparison. Finally, considering that a key motivation for improving the responses of LLMs is to ensure their trustworthiness, it would also be beneficial to test whether responses generated with cases are considered to be more intuitive and trustworthy than responses generated with knowledge snippets, and whether presenting users with cases as well as LLM solutions increases trust and the ability for users to assess the quality of LLM responses.

Acknowledgements. This work was funded by the US Department of Defense (Contract W52P1J2093009). This research was supported in part by Lilly Endowment, Inc., through its support for the Indiana University Pervasive Technology Institute.

References

1. Cheetham, W., Watson, I.: Fielded applications of case-based reasoning. Knowl. Eng. Rev. **20**(3), 321–323 (2005)
2. Cunningham, P., Doyle, D., Loughrey, J.: An evaluation of the usefulness of case-based explanation. In: Ashley, K.D., Bridge, D.G. (eds.) ICCBR 2003. LNCS (LNAI), vol. 2689, pp. 122–130. Springer, Heidelberg (2003). https://doi.org/10.1007/3-540-45006-8_12

3. Gao, Y., et al.: Retrieval-augmented generation for large language models: a survey. arXiv preprint arXiv:2312.10997 (2023)
4. Gates, L., Leake, D., Wilkerson, K.: Cases are king: a user study of case presentation to explain CBR decisions. In: Massie, S., Chakraborti, S. (eds.) ICCBR 2023. LNCS, vol. 14141, pp. 153–168. Springer, Cham (2023). https://doi.org/10.1007/978-3-031-40177-0_10
5. Hammond, K., Leake, D.: Large language models need symbolic AI. In: Proceedings of the 17th International Workshop on Neural-Symbolic Learning and Reasoning, La Certosa di Pontignano, Siena, Italy, vol. 3432, pp. 204–209 (2023)
6. Leake, D.: CBR in context: the present and future. In: Leake, D. (ed.) Case-Based Reasoning: Experiences, Lessons, and Future Directions, pp. 3–30. AAAI Press, Menlo Park (1996)
7. Leake, D.: Cognition as case-based reasoning. In: Bechtel, W., Graham, G. (eds.) A Companion to Cognitive Science, pp. 465–476. Blackwell, Oxford (1998)
8. Lewis, P., et al.: Retrieval-augmented generation for knowledge-intensive NLP tasks. In: Advances in Neural Information Processing Systems, vol. 33, pp. 9459–9474 (2020)
9. Liu, J., et al.: Generated knowledge prompting for commonsense reasoning. arXiv preprint arXiv:2110.08387 (2021)
10. Mialon, G., et al.: Augmented language models: a survey (2023)
11. Nievas, M., Basu, A., Wang, Y., Singh, H.: Distilling large language models for matching patients to clinical trials. J. Am. Med. Inform. Assoc. ocae073 (2024)
12. Paranjape, B., Michael, J., Ghazvininejad, M., Zettlemoyer, L., Hajishirzi, H.: Prompting contrastive explanations for commonsense reasoning tasks. arXiv preprint arXiv:2106.06823 (2021)
13. Peng, B., et al.: Check your facts and try again: improving large language models with external knowledge and automated feedback. arXiv preprint arXiv:2302.12813 (2023)
14. Prakash, A.V., Das, S.: Would you trust a bot for healthcare advice? An empirical investigation. In: PACIS, p. 62 (2020)
15. Touvron, H., et al.: Llama 2: open foundation and fine-tuned chat models. arXiv preprint arXiv:2307.09288 (2023)
16. Valmeekam, K., Sreedharan, S., Marquez, M., Olmo, A., Kambhampati, S.: On the planning abilities of large language models (a critical investigation with a proposed benchmark) (2023)
17. Watson, I.: Case-based reasoning is a methodology not a technology. Knowl.-Based Syst. **12**(303–308) (1996)
18. Wiratunga, N., et al.: CBR-RAG: case-based reasoning for retrieval augmented generation in LLMs for legal question answering. arXiv preprint arXiv:2404.04302 (2024)
19. Xu, Z., Jain, S., Kankanhalli, M.: Hallucination is inevitable: an innate limitation of large language models (2024)
20. Yancey, C.C., O'Rourke, M.C.: Emergency department triage. In: StatPearls [Internet]. StatPearls Publishing (2022)

Using Case-Based Causal Reasoning to Provide Explainable Counterfactual Diagnosis in Personalized Sprint Training

Dandan Cui[1,2(✉)], Jianwei Guo[2,3], Ping Liu[2], and Xiangning Zhang[2]

[1] China Institute of Sport Science, Beijing, China
ditto9@gmail.com
[2] Capital University of Physical Education and Sports, Beijing, China
[3] Shanghai University of Sport, Shanghai, China

Abstract. Intelligent sport training (IST) is an urgent need for both professional athletes and ordinary people, but personalized intelligent diagnosing is still lacking. In this paper we proposed a personalized sports training diagnosis framework called CBCR, which combines CBR with causal inference in 2 ways: 1) In the case selection stage, the traditional distance metric is replaced by the weighted distance based on causal effect; 2) In the counterfactual diagnosis stage, the solution is the counterfactual training effects estimated from the individual causal model. We developed a set of sprint diagnosis algorithms on a very small case base, and evaluated it on data from both Olympic candidates and college students, and by an Olympic final case study as well.

Keywords: CBR for health and exercise · Intelligent Sport Training · 100-meter Sprint · Causal Inference · Counterfactual Explanation

1 Introduction

In intelligent sports training (IST), there are basically 3 tasks for an "AI coach": 1) control, i.e. the coach's monitoring on the athlete's training; 2) evaluation, i.e. the coach's diagnosing of the athlete's performance, and 3) planning, i.e. the coach's decision of the athlete's planning for the next training cycle [1]. The good news is that, in the control task, perceptional intelligent technologies like computer vision (CV) [2], and multimedia sensors [3] provide more and more data than ever, which have already become standard equipment for both athletes and hobbyists. While the bad news is that, up to now, most IST systems can only complete the evaluation task and planning task with the help of a remote human coach [4] or rules preset by experts [5], or a combination of both [6]. Although computational intelligence algorithms have played some role in the training load optimization problem of endurance events such as cycling and triathlon [7], and CBR algorithms have been used to recommend training plans for marathon beginners [8–10], the existing methods are still unable to imitate the diagnosis of key training problems like elite human coaches. Thus most sports enthusiasts are still obtaining training knowledge through search engines, and the training plans of low level athletes are generally not personalized enough, which restricts the efficiency of performance enhancement.

© The Author(s), under exclusive license to Springer Nature Switzerland AG 2024
J. A. Recio-Garcia et al. (Eds.): ICCBR 2024, LNAI 14775, pp. 418–429, 2024.
https://doi.org/10.1007/978-3-031-63646-2_27

Inspired by the successful case-based training diagnosis reasoning of elite sprint coaches [11], this paper proposes a personalized sports training diagnosis framework called CBCR, i.e. Case-based Causal Reasoning, which combines CBR with causal inference [12], and develops a set of 100-m sprint diagnosis algorithms on a very small case base, which can provide sprinters with data-driven and highly personalized counterfactual diagnoses of speed rhythm. The main contributions of this paper are: 1) In the case selection stage, the traditional distance metric is replaced by the weighted distance based on causal effect, which is derived from a structural causal model discovered from the case base; 2) In the counterfactual diagnosis stage, the solution is no longer the case itself, but the counterfactual training effects estimated from the individual causal model.

2   Related Work

Unlike self-trained beginners, elite athletes undergo highly personalized training under the guidance of elite coaches. In recent years, a form of training diagnosis based on success cases has been widely adopted among elite coaches, known in Chinese as the "Champion Model" [11], which can also set up a personalized spiritual role model for an athlete [13]. For example, Su Bingtian, who dramatically broke the Asian record with a mark of 9.83 s in the men's 100m semifinals at the Tokyo 2020 Olympics, was coached by Randy Huntington, who used a foreign athlete with a similar body shape as a reference to help Su optimize his technique and break the Chinese record of 9.99 s in 2017. This approach is highly compatible with CBR.

In fact, the CBR method has been successfully used for race performance prediction, training program recommendation for marathon beginners [8,9]. In addition, CBR's counterfactual explanation generation technique has also attracted much attention in explainable AI [14,15], and has been used to improve the explainability of marathon injury predictions [10]. However, the training diagnosis of elite coaches based on the Champion Model is significantly different from the classical CBR method used by marathon beginners: CBR takes the cases in the base as solutions, but elite coaches do not copy all the features in the Champion Model. Good coaches are good at digging into the root causes of problems and focusing on breakthroughs. This AI technique of mining causal mechanisms from observational data is called "causal inference" [12].

From the perspective of causal inference, there are 2 inadequacies in the use of CBR alone in the problem of personalized sports training: 1) In the selection of case, CBR treats all the features independently. But in practice, for a specific athlete, there is an interplay between the height and weight of the body morphology, and a mutual constraint between the intensity and the frequency of the training load [16], and a mutual limitation between acceleration and endurance for speed rhythms [17,18]. Moreover, the influence of different characteristics on performance is not always the same [19]. 2) In the generation of counterfactual, the counterfactual is individual rather than population [20]. Even if referring to the same "champion model", Su's expectation of technical improvement is different from that of other athletes, so it is necessary to calculate the counterfactual based on the current user's individual model. Therefore, in order to solve the problem of personalized training diagnosis and simulate elite coaches' reasoning process, it is necessary to add Causal Inference on the basis of CBR.

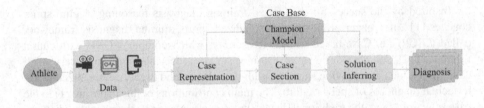

Fig. 1. Overview of our CBCR diagnosis framework to imitate the champion-model-based diagnosing process of elite coaches

There are two main frameworks for causal inference techniques: 1) The Rubin framework [21], which simulates randomized controlled experiments to estimate the potential outcomes, and has been used for personalized treatment selection in medicine [22]. 2) The Pearl framework, which was developed from Bayesian networks and is a graphical causal model based on directed acyclic graphs (DAG) [12]. Bayesian networks are themselves a simulation of the belief updating process of human reasoning [23], and have recently been used to simulate the cognitive structure of CBR [24]. Furthermore, graph-based causal inference made even greater achievements in exploring causal mechanism from observational data [12]: drawing interpretable graphic structures of variables by causal discovery, identifying quantified causal effect, and estimating potential treatment effect as well. So naturally, in recent years, it has been rapidly applied in genetics [25,26], health management [27], epidemiology [28], and has also brought a new opportunity for the development of sports training. Some sport scientists have already noticed this technology and have theoretically presented the necessity and feasibility of its application in resistance training [29] and injury prevention [30]. In this paper, graphical causal inference techniques are used for the first time in practice in combination with CBR to address the problem of personalized sprint training diagnosis.

3 Proposed Method

In the CBCR diagnosis framework, we propose 3 modules: case representation, case selection, and solution inferring. Figure 1 shows the proposed framework.

3.1 Case Representation

Speed Rhythm. Regarding the factors that influence the performance in sprint, the factors can be divided into internal factors and external ones, and internal factors work in several levels as Fig. 2 shows. These levels influence each other from bottom to top, which forms a causal chain. Among these, the closest level to performance is velocity. Similarly, the most direct human perception of sprinting is speed, and the speed of 100-m running shows a certain rhythm (the green blocks in Fig. 2). For example: coaches often say that a certain athlete starts too fast in a certain game, resulting in a too large deceleration at last; or a certain athlete should focus on improving endurance, etc.

Regarding speed, although different sensors or motion capture algorithms outputs data in different modalities and accuracy, both the player and the coach have a consistent cognitive feeling like a 3-phase continuous sprint process: accelerating at first, then maintaining the maximal velocity for a while before an inevitable deceleration at last [17]. A cognitively consistent domain model for the 3 phases as simple as possible is needed to achieve effective causal modeling on our small data sets at the very starting stage for now. Usually, a sprinter's velocity-time curve was fit by using a mono-exponential regression model in function (1). [19]. Thus, the performance of a sprinter is profiled by 2 parameters: the sprinter's maximal horizontal velocity (v_{max}) and the acceleration time constant (τ_1). However, it can only model the acceleration phase. Following up on one of our previous efforts [31], we redesigned the model to profile all 3 phases of the 100 m sprint.

$$v(t) = v_{max}(1 - e^{-\frac{t}{\tau_1}})\qquad(1)$$

The trend of relative loss of velocity can be expressed by (2), where τ_2 is a deceleration time constant: the bigger τ_2, the slower the decline of velocity and the longer the deceleration process:

$$v_{endurance\_ratio}(t) = e^{-\frac{t}{\tau_2}}\qquad(2)$$

Then the prototype of the full-length time-velocity function should be as shown in (3)

$$v(t) = v_{ideal}(1 - e^{-\frac{t}{\tau_1}})e^{-\frac{t}{\tau_2}}\qquad(3)$$

The unit of time variable and constants is second(s), and the unit of velocity variable and constant is meter/second(m/s). v_{max}. More rigorously, "maximal velocity" in the previous literature is expressed by ideal maximal velocity v_{ideal} in our approach. Therefore, the 3 modal-independent cognitive parameters of speed rhythm are extracted.

Champion Model. Champion models are stored as cases in the base. The structure is:

Location: As we can only learn from an athlete who runs faster than us, the champion models are located according to their performance in the memory. In our current 100-m system, it is the mark score M_{ark}.

Key Variables: Unchangeable or physical features are used as keys to select a case in the base. In our current 100-m system, they are gender, age, height and weight. As the variety of gender is not covered in our data, the Key variable set is $\{A_{ge}, H_{eight}, W_{eight}\}$.

Value Variables: Features that aimed to be changed through training are used as values to do counterfactual diagnosing. In our current 100-m system, they are the cognitive parameters extracted in the cognitive representation module, and the value variable set is $\{V_i, T_1, T_2\}$.

To simplify the notation, henceforth in this paper, we use H for height in meter and W for weight in kg and Vi for v_{ideal} in meter/second, T1 for τ_1 in second, T2 for τ_2 in second.

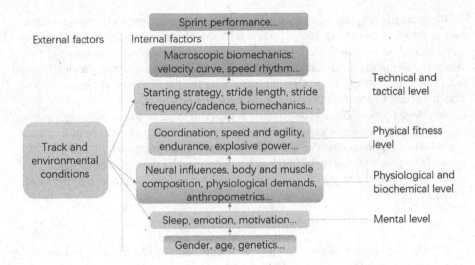

Fig. 2. The factors that influence the performance in sprint.

3.2   Case Selection

First, causal discovery between key variables (including age, height and weight) and performance (mark in 100-m sprint) is carried out via PC algorithm [25].

Then, similarity is measured. The total causal effects (TCE) are calculated based on a structural causal model (SCM) based on the directed acyclic graph (DAG) output by PC algorithm [12] on the champion model dataset. Then TCE are taken as weights, and therefore a causality based selection of champion model is accomplished.

As we have only a very small training set with 102 champion models for now, we build a linear causal model for simplicity in this paper. Nonetheless, the statistically significant linear correlation between mark and the key variables ensures the validity of the linear model in the current training set ($p < 0.01$ for mark-height, mark-weight, mark-age, age-weight and height-weigh) to a certain extent. Based on linear hypothesis, DAG in Fig. 3a can be expressed as the following structural equations, where U is the residual that will be personalized in the counterfactual inferring:

$$\begin{cases} W_{eight} = aA_{ge} + bH_{eight} + U_{weight} \\ M_{ark} = cA_{ge} + dH_{eight} + eW_{eight} + U_{mark} \end{cases} \tag{4}$$

Total causal effect of all key features are therefore calculated. In our current implementation, the similarity measure is cosine similarity, weighted by causal effects between different keys and performance. There is still much room for improvement in the future.

3.3   Solution Inferring

First, DAG of value variables (ideal maximal velocity, acceleration time constant, and deceleration time constant) and performance (mark in 100-m sprint) is discovered via PC algorithm [25] on the champion model dataset, i.e. the case base.

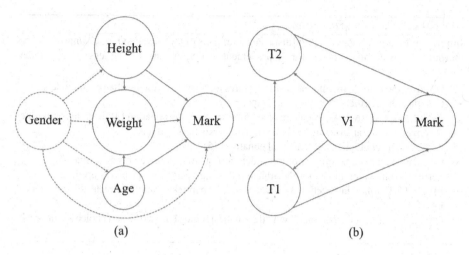

Fig. 3. The DAGs discovered from our case base. Figure a on the left shows the DAG of causal effect estimation for case selection, in which the dotted parts are not covered in current data. Figure b on the right shows the DAG for solution inference.

As we stated above, a linear causal model for diagnosis is trained due to the small size of current dataset. Nonetheless, the statistically significant linear correlation between the cognitive parameters ensures the validity of the linear model in the current training set ($p < 0.01$ for T1-T2, T1-Vi, T2-Vi) to a certain extent. As the causal relationship between performance and values is already regulated by Eq. 3, linear assumption can only be used for the other parts in Fig. 3b:

$$\begin{cases} T_1 = aV_i + U_{T_1} \\ T_2 = bT_1 + cV_i + U_{T_2} \\ M_{ark} = \min(t| \int_0^t V_i(1 - e^{-\frac{t}{T_1}})e^{-\frac{t}{T_2}}\,dt \geq 100) \end{cases} \quad (5)$$

And finally, counterfactual predicting is accomplished according to the effect of treatment on the treated (ETT) [12]. In a linear structural equation model (SEM), there are 3 steps to infer individual counterfactuals. Take T1 as an example:

1. Abduction: current user's Vi, T1, and T2 are brought into Eq5 fitted by the training data, and the U variables are updated to user's personal value, and therefore the population model turns into an individual model.
2. Action: the equation of T1 is modified to the T1 value in the selected champion model, and therefore a counterfactual intervention is imitated.
3. Prediction: The user's Vi is brought into the modified Eq5, and T2 and Mark are calculated to obtain the user's counterfactual performance change if the user follow the accelerating tech of the champion model.

The whole diagnosing algorithm is summarized in Algorithm 1.

Algorithm 1. Training Diagnosing

Input: profiles and the split times in [distance, time] pairs of the player and the champion models
Output: Predicted first choice for improvement which is one of the cognitive parameters

1: Discover the causal structure of profile features and marks given the champion models
2: Calculate the coefficients of structural equations (4)
3: Calculate speed rhythm parameters of each "champion" by equation (3) given his split time
4: Discover the causal structure of speed rhythm parameters and marks
5: Calculate the coefficients of structural equations (5)
6: Calculate cognitive parameters of the athlete by equation (3) given his split time
7: Select one champion model for the athlete following Section 3.2 given his profile
8: Predict ETTs following Section 3.3 given cognitive parameters of the althlete and the selected model
9: Output the name of the parameter with the smallest minus ETT as the first choice for improvement

4   Evaluation

4.1   Datasets

We collect 102 person-times of men's 100-m sprint data covering 17 major competitions from Athens World Championships in 1997 to Doha World Championships in 2019, including Usain Bolt, Christian Coleman, Noah Lyles, and Su Bingtian, with marks ranging from 9.58 s to 10.59 s, heights ranging from 172 cm to 196 cm, weights ranging from 65 kg to 91 kg, and ages ranging from 19 to 37 years old. These are the champion models to build the case base.

To test our system on both Olympic athletes and ordinary people, we collected 2 kinds of testing data: data from the 5 Olympic candidates of China National Team are collected from public events in year 2021, timed by CV algorithm [2] with manual correction, and data from 50 male college students are collected in the track field on our campus, timed by sensors [3] placed at 0 m, 30 m, 60 m, 90 m and 100 m splits.

Table 1 shows 2 examples of testing data in the case representation. Table 2 shows the champion models selected for players in Table 1. Finally a diagnosing is worked out as Table 3 shows. For instance student1, if he changes his acceleration time to the same as the model's, his mark will be 0.21 s longer; if he changes his ideal maximal velocity to the same as the model, ideally his mark will be 2.1 s shorter and so on. Therefore, the diagnosis of plan for him is to improve maximal velocity ability first.

Table 1. Examples of Testing Data

Player	Vi	T1	T2	Mark	Age	H	W
Stu1	10.06	1.19	125	11.64	20	1.68	64.5
Ath1	12.29	1.39	105	9.98	32	1.73	72.0

Table 2. Champion models for the testing players

Player	Age	Height(m)	Weight(kg)	Mark(s)	Name	Event	Vi	T1	T2
Student1	22	1.76	68	10.32	Shuhei TADA	Golden Grand Prix Osaka 2018	12.50	1.50	58.72
Athlete1	30	1.80	73	9.95	Frank FREDER-ICKS	World Athletics Championships Athens 1997	12.49	1.48	99.30

Table 3. ETTs as plan diagnosing

Player	ETT T1	ETT Vi	ETT T2
Student1	0.21	−2.10	0.67
Athlete1	0.06	−0.15	0.02

4.2 Expert Evaluation

Since it takes a long time for the impact of the training plan to improve sport performance, we adopt the expert evaluation method for our experimental result. The most authoritative expert is the national team coach, but it is unrealistic to ask him to evaluate such many college students. In view of this, we design a more practical scheme.

We invite a sport scientist in addition, who has been working with the coach for the national team since 2017. Then both the 2 experts are invited to evaluate the results of the Olympic athletes and the statistical consistency between their opinions is tested. For the results of the college students, only the sport scientist evaluate them. Nonetheless, the consistency between the two experts in the previous step provides a guarantee for the authority of the results.

Case Selection. The two modules are evaluated subjectively by the 2 experts. For the case selection module, we carried out a paired comparison. In this step, case selection by cosine similarity without weighting is taken as baseline. Therefore, we have a pair of champion models for each item of test data. Then experts are asked to choose one or both or neither for each pair. The scoring criteria are: -1 for baseline better, 0 for neither good, and 1 for our system better or both good.

Evaluation on data of the 5 athletes are carried out first. The coach gives total 4 points and the expert gives the same. Based on their high level of consistency, the expert evaluates data of the 50 students alone and gives total 4 points.

Solution Inference. As case selected by our system are no inferior to the baseline in every case, only diagnosis output by our system is evaluated. In this step, we carried out a Mean Score Opinion (MOS) test evaluation, which is often used to evaluate the subjective user experience of a human-computer-interactive system [32]. The scoring criteria are: 1 for wrong; 2 for doubtful; 3 for reasonable; 4 for valuable; 5 for adopted.

Again, evaluation on solution inference for the 5 athletes are carried out first. As Table 4 shows, the coach gives average 3 points and the expert gives average 2.8 points.

Table 4. MOS scores for the 5 athletes

Athlete	No. 1	No. 2	No. 3	No. 4	No. 5
Coach's Score	2	3	4	3	3
Expert's Score	2	3	3	3	3

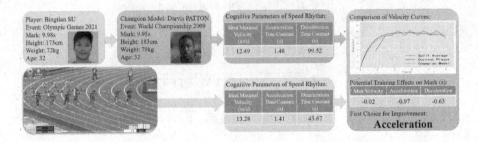

Fig. 4. Intelligent sport training diagnosis of the men's 100m final in Tokyo Olympic Games, using the proposed approach.

Based on their high level of consistence with Pearson's correlation coefficient $r = 0.79$, $p = 0.11$, the expert evaluates data of the 50 students alone and gives average 3.6 points.

The evaluation results show that although our approach is superior to baseline, the coach doesn't highly approve of it, especially in the solution inference step. However, score for students is higher than for athletes in both steps, which suggests that our pilot work could be more helpful for ordinary people with no human coach than for the Olympic athletes. But a case study shows us something new.

4.3   Case Study

Back to Tokyo 2020 Olympics, Su clocked 9.98 s in the final, slightly lower than every-one had expected. Apparently, Su started to fall behind at about 6 s after the start. While in Randy's opinion, the problem was the acceleration phase. Since up to now, it was impossible to obtain more accurate data except the TV broadcast videos, we captured via CV [2] from miguvideo.com the split times only accurate to 0.1 s. As Table 5 shows, the data also shows that Su's ranking is indeed more behind near the finish line.

With such input, we made a challenge to see if our system can output the same diagnosis as Randy. As Fig. 4 shows, the ETT of acceleration time constant (τ_1) is obviously superior to other parameters, so the first choice for Su is to improve the starting acceleration technology according to Darvis Patton's champion model: our AI coach holds the same opinion with Randy which implies:

- In the case representation module, the accuracy of each split-time is almost unquali-fied in sprint data analysis, but our model can output effective speed rhythm param-eters, which most statistical analysis cannot do.
- In the case selection module, our system chose a champion model that is much taller than Su. This is because the causal relationship between height and weight is taken

Table 5. Su's split times and rankings captured from TV broadcast videos

Distance(m)	10	21.5	30	38.5	47	55.5	64	72.5	81	89.5	100
Time(s)	1.8	2.9	3.7	4.4	5.2	5.9	6.7	7.4	8.2	8.9	9.98
Ranking	5	5	4	4	4	5	5	5	5	6	6

into account, rather than as an independent and identically in traditional CBR. Such considerations for a particular athlete has been deeper than the thinking of many human coaches.

- The solution inference module is the most mysterious and valuable part of the entire cognitive chain. Counterfactual predictions accurately simulate the imagination of an Olympic coach about personalized training effects, which is difficult even for most ordinary coaches.

5   Conclusions and Future Work

In this paper, we proposes a personalized sports training diagnosis framework called CBCR, i.e. Case-based Causal Reasoning, which combines CBR with causal inference, and develops a set of sprint diagnosis algorithms on a very small case base, which can provide sprinters with data-driven and highly personalized Counterfactual diagnoses. We conduct experiments on data from both Olympic candidates and college students, then carry out expert evaluations. We also use an Olympic case to illustrate why our framework can still show performance benefits without improving any particular algorithm. Although further evaluation is to be carried out on bigger data sets, experiment results are prospective now.

Our future work forms a really long list. First of all, we are collecting more data and ground truth in 4 ways:

- Collecting more champion models from public events
- Running our system on national team members to get more evaluation from Olympic coaches.
- Tracking performance of college students by testing and diagnosing regularly to get longitudinal ground truth.
- Running our system online by developing a web application to collect public data.

6   Social Impacts and Ethical Concerns

During our experiments, the social impact has already begun to take shape. For example, hence the official data of the Tokyo Olympic Games has not been released yet, Our system output becomes an irreplaceable reference for the coming winter training of the national team. At the same time, our experiment received enthusiastic support from the student participants as they have never received such kind of professional training guidance before. Besides, the champion model can help beyond sports in terms of technique by setting up a spiritual role model for our users [13]. In our under development web application, in order to avoid possible negative effects, especially sports injuries, we are very cautious about system output and avoid putting forward specific training load. Therefore, in the current training, our plans are required to be confirmed by coaches or teachers and realized.

In addition, our unified framework can also inspire domains like medical healthcare which are dominated by the cognitive intelligence of human experts. And we believe that work on the causal and cognitive parts of IST will not only benefit sport training, but eventually artificial intelligence itself, no matter how long the road ahead. As Newell noted on the possibility of unified theories of cognition-"I do not say that they are here. But they are within reach and we should strive to attain them".

Fundings. This work was supported by the Project 24-18 Supported by the Fundamental Research Funds for the China Institute of Sport Science and the National Natural Science Foundation of China (Grant No. 62106159).

References

1. Rajšp, A., Fister, I.: A systematic literature review of intelligent data analysis methods for smart sport training. Appl. Sci. **10**, 3013 (2020)
2. Sun, K., Xiao, B., Liu, D., Wang, J.: Deep high-resolution representation learning for human pose estimation. In: Proceedings of the IEEE/CVF Conference on Computer Vision and Pattern Recognition, pp. 5693–5703 (2019)
3. Yanagimoto, Y.: Device for measuring passing time of runner (2019)
4. Aranki, D., Peh, G.X., Kurillo, G., Bajcsy, R.: The feasibility and usability of runningcoach: a remote coaching system for long-distance runners. Sensors **18**, 175 (2018)
5. Örücü, S., Selek, M.: Design and validation of rule-based expert system by using Kinect V2 for real-time athlete support. Appl. Sci. **10**, 611 (2020)
6. Mata, F., Torres-Ruiz, M., Zagal, R., Guzman, G., Moreno-Ibarra, M., Quintero, R.: A cross-domain framework for designing healthcare mobile applications mining social networks to generate recommendations of training and nutrition planning. Telematics Inform. **35**, 837–853 (2018)
7. Fister, I., Fister, I., Jr., Fister, D.: Computational Intelligence in Sports. Springer, Cham (2019)
8. Feely, C., Caulfield, B., Lawlor, A., Smyth, B.: Using case-based reasoning to predict marathon performance and recommend tailored training plans. In: Watson, I., Weber, R. (eds.) ICCBR 2020. LNCS (LNAI), vol. 12311, pp. 67–81. Springer, Cham (2020). https://doi.org/10.1007/978-3-030-58342-2_5
9. Feely, C., Caulfield, B., Lawlor, A., Smyth, B.: A case-based reasoning approach to predicting and explaining running related injuries. In: Sánchez-Ruiz, A.A., Floyd, M.W. (eds.) ICCBR 2021. LNCS (LNAI), vol. 12877, pp. 79–93. Springer, Cham (2021). https://doi.org/10.1007/978-3-030-86957-1_6
10. Feely, C., Caulfield, B., Lawlor, A., Smyth, B.: An extended case-based approach to race-time prediction for recreational marathon runners. In: Keane, M.T., Wiratunga, N. (eds.) ICCBR 2022. LNCS, vol. 13405, pp. 335–349. Springer, Cham (2022). https://doi.org/10.1007/978-3-031-14923-8_22
11. Su, B., Deng, M., Xu, Z., Liang, W., Jiang, Z., Wang, G.: New era Chinese men's 100 m sprint: review and prospect. China Sport Sci. (Chinese Version) **39**, 22–28 (2019)

12. Pearl, J.: Causality (2009)
13. Morgenroth, T., Ryan, M.K., Peters, K.: The motivational theory of role modeling: how role models influence role aspirants' goals. Rev. Gen. Psychol. **19**, 465–483 (2015)
14. Delaney, E., Greene, D., Keane, M.T.: Instance-based counterfactual explanations for time series classification. In: Sánchez-Ruiz, A.A., Floyd, M.W. (eds.) ICCBR 2021. LNCS (LNAI), vol. 12877, pp. 32–47. Springer, Cham (2021). https://doi.org/10.1007/978-3-030-86957-1_3
15. Warren, G., Smyth, B., Keane, M.T.: "Better" counterfactuals, ones people can understand: psychologically-plausible case-based counterfactuals using categorical features for explainable AI (XAI). In: Keane, M.T., Wiratunga, N. (eds.) ICCBR 2022. LNCS, vol. 13405, pp. 63–78. Springer, Cham (2022). https://doi.org/10.1007/978-3-031-14923-8_5
16. Brodáni, J., Katerinka, M.: Training load determining the sport performance of the woman race walker to 50 Km. Slovak J. Sport Sci. **8** (2022)
17. Locatelli, E., Arsac, L.: The mechanics and energetics of the 100 m sprint. New Stud. Athletics **10**, 81–81 (1995)
18. Mackala, K.: Optimisation of performance through kinematic analysis of the different phases of the 100 m. New Stud. Athletics **22**, 7 (2007)
19. Healy, R., Kenny, I.C., Harrison, A.J.: Profiling elite male 100-m sprint performance: the role of maximum velocity and relative acceleration. J. Sport Health Sci. (2019)
20. Pearl, J., Glymour, M., Jewell, N.P.: Causal inference in statistics: a primer (2016)
21. Imbens, G.W., Rubin, D.B.: Causal Inference in Statistics, Social, and Biomedical Sciences. Cambridge University Press, Cambridge (2015)
22. Tu, Y., et al.: Personalized treatment selection using causal heterogeneity. In: Proceedings of the Web Conference 2021, pp. 1574–1585 (2021)
23. Pearl, J.: Bayesian networks: a model of self-activated memory for evidential reasoning. In: Proceedings of the 7th Conference of the Cognitive Science Society, University of California, Irvine, CA, USA, pp. 15–17 (1985)
24. Ménager, D.H., Choi, D.: Hybrid event memory as a case base for state estimation in cognitive agents. In: Massie, S., Chakraborti, S. (eds.) ICCBR 2023. LNCS, vol. 14141, pp. 134–149. Springer, Cham (2023). https://doi.org/10.1007/978-3-031-40177-0_9
25. Glymour, C., Zhang, K., Spirtes, P.: Review of causal discovery methods based on graphical models. Front. Genet. **10**, 524 (2019)
26. Amar, D., Sinnott-Armstrong, N., Ashley, E.A., Rivas, M.A.: Graphical analysis for phenome-wide causal discovery in genotyped population-scale biobanks. Nat. Commun. **12**, 1–11 (2021)
27. Richens, J.G., Lee, C.M., Johri, S.: Improving the accuracy of medical diagnosis with causal machine learning. Nat. Commun. **11**, 1–9 (2020)
28. von Kügelgen, J., Gresele, L., Schölkopf, B.: Simpson's paradox in Covid-19 case fatality rates: a mediation analysis of age-related causal effects. IEEE Trans. Artif. Intell. **2**, 18–27 (2021)
29. Nuzzo, J.L., Finn, H.T., Herbert, R.D.: Causal mediation analysis could resolve whether training-induced increases in muscle strength are mediated by muscle hypertrophy. Sports Med. **49**, 1309–1315 (2019)
30. Shrier, I., Platt, R.W.: Reducing bias through directed acyclic graphs. BMC Med. Res. Methodol. **8**, 1–15 (2008)
31. Cui, D., Jiang, Z.: A champion model of men's 100 m sprint based on functional data analysis. In: 2021 IEEE 6th International Conference on Big Data Analytics (ICBDA), pp. 103–107. IEEE (2021)
32. Viswanathan, M., Viswanathan, M.: Measuring speech quality for text-to-speech systems: development and assessment of a modified mean opinion score (MOS) scale. Comput. Speech Lang. **19**, 55–83 (2005)

Item-Specific Similarity Assessments for Explainable Depression Screening

Mauricio G. Orozco-del-Castillo[1]($\boxtimes$), Juan A. Recio-Garcia[2] ,
and Esperanza C. Orozco-del-Castillo[3]

[1] Tecnológico Nacional de México/IT de Mérida, Mérida, Yucatán, Mexico
mauricio.orozco@itmerida.edu.mx
[2] Department of Software Engineering and Artificial Intelligence,
Instituto de Tecnologías del Conocimiento, Universidad Complutense de Madrid,
Madrid, Spain
[3] Cinvestav-IPN, Departamento de Matemática Educativa, Mexico City, Mexico

Abstract. Depression, a prevalent mental health issue worldwide, is deeply influenced by the cultural and sociodemographic context, particularly in the Yucatán region in Mexico. Traditional depression screening methods, relying on self-reported questionnaires, often fall short in capturing the patterns of depressive symptoms specific to the area. This study introduces an innovative case-based reasoning (CBR) approach for depression screening, utilizing an item-specific similarity measure optimized through genetic algorithms. The main goal is to demonstrate the benefits of optimized similarity metrics to offer personalized reasoning capabilities that account for individual differences, thereby overcoming some of the limitations of one-size-fits-all retrieval approaches and achieving an accuracy comparable to other state-of-the-art machine learning (ML) alternatives. In contrast to these ML models, the proposed CBR approach has the additional benefit of being inherently explainable. Understanding the similarity between individual response patterns and cases of depression symptomatology allows for a more specific and culturally sensitive screening process. The findings suggest that this method could improve early detection and intervention strategies, offering an alternative to traditional scoring of self-reported depression questionnaires as well as a path toward more timely and effective mental health care in regions with unique cultural and demographic characteristics.

Keywords: case-based reasoning · depression screening · self-reported questionnaires · item-specific similarity · explainable artificial intelligence

1 Introduction

Depression stands as a formidable challenge in global mental health, affecting millions worldwide and presenting a multifaceted burden that spans personal suffering, societal impact, and economic cost [13]. In Mexico, this challenge is compounded by unique cultural and sociodemographic factors that play a pivotal role in shaping mental health outcomes [15]. In Yucatan, particularly, the

J. A. Recio-Garcia et al. (Eds.): ICCBR 2024, LNAI 14775, pp. 430–444, 2024.
https://doi.org/10.1007/978-3-031-63646-2_28

complexity of depression's impact is further intensified by unique regional challenges, demanding innovative approaches to mental health care that are sensitive to the local context [15]. Early and accurate detection is paramount for effective intervention and management; however, due to the complexities that depression presents, detection is a very challenging task [25]. Traditional screening methodologies tend to rely on self-report questionnaires and clinical interviews. Self-report questionnaires provide a very practical way of detecting depression symptoms but lack the reliability of a face-to-face interview and may not accurately reflect the depression model of a given demographic group [23]. On the other hand, clinical interviews may present subjectivity issues and are very time-consuming [7]. This underscores the pressing need for innovative approaches to depression screening that improve precision while remaining sensitive to the diverse manifestations of this condition.

The advent of case-based reasoning (CBR) in the realm of artificial intelligence offers a promising avenue for innovating depression screening. By leveraging historical cases to solve new problems, CBR provides an explainable framework for decision-making that can accommodate the complex and varied presentations of depression. This methodology's potential for psychological assessments is particularly compelling, given the heterogeneity of depression symptoms and the importance of contextual factors in diagnosis [14]. Here, explainability is a crucial factor, and CBR allows an understanding of the relevance of such factors.

By adapting solutions from similar past cases, CBR can offer personalized screening approaches that account for individual differences, thereby overcoming some of the limitations of one-size-fits-all screening tools. However, this paper does not only focus on the evaluation of the benefits of personalized case bases for a target population segment or concrete individuals, but also highlights the relevance of optimized similarity metrics that can enhance the personalization capabilities of CBR. Building upon foundational works [11] who have demonstrated the efficacy of genetic algorithms (GAs) in optimizing feature selection and retrieval processes within CBR systems, our approach addresses the specific cultural and symptomatic aspects of depression screening in Yucatan. The underlying hypothesis is that while most CBR approaches benefit from ad-hoc case bases to personalize and adapt outcomes to specific populations, such personalization is significantly enhanced by optimizing the similarity metric used for case retrieval. Without such optimization, as seen in previous studies, the application of generic similarity metrics for ad-hoc case bases may not fully leverage the personalization benefits of the CBR process, potentially squandering the engineering costs and reasoning potential of such elaborated cases.

Depression screening is one of these scenarios. The efficacy of existing depression screening tools is often hindered by a lack of specificity and the inability to fully capture the multifaceted nature of depression symptoms across diverse populations [28]. Unlike traditional uses of GAs for generic feature weighting, our method adjusts the weighting of depression questionnaire items providing insights about specific cultural and symptomatic aspects observed in the Yucatan population, thereby refining the accuracy and applicability of depression screening in this unique context [19]. We propose an innovative CBR framework that integrates an item-specific similarity measure to enhance the screening process. This approach leverages a weighting vector optimized through a GA, emphasizing the differential relevance of questionnaire items, thereby enabling a more personalized retrieval of the cases used for depression assessment.

The proposed CBR methodology also has a secondary goal: to demonstrate the validity of simple screening tools to surrogate large and expensive psychological artifacts. It is a common problem in depression screening that popular tools have proprietary licenses, or their applicability is hampered by the large number of items that the users must answer. This is the case with several traditional tools such as the Beck Depression Inventory (BDI), the Center for Epidemiologic Studies Depression Scale (CES-D), and the Carroll Rating Scale for Depression (CRSD). Through the application of the CBR methodology, our aim is to demonstrate the validity of alternative tools such as the Patient Health Questionnaire (PHQ-9) or the Generalized Anxiety Disorder 7-item (GAD-7) as simplified and open estimators of depression scores. Although the correlation between the simplified artifacts and the target depression scores could be achieved through other state-of-the-art machine learning (ML) regression techniques, we demonstrate the adequacy of the CBR paradigm to provide comparable performance while offering valuable insights into the differential diagnostic capabilities of the simplified depression screening tools.

The ensuing sections elaborate on the background (Sect. 2), the methodological foundation (Sect. 3), present the results of the optimization process and similarity assessments (Sect. 4), and discuss the implications of our findings in the broader context of depression screening (Sect. 5). Finally, we draw conclusions from our study, reflecting on its contributions to the field and suggesting avenues for future research (Sect. 6).

2   Background

Depression, characterized by pervasive sadness, loss of interest, and diminished ability to experience pleasure, stands as a significant global health concern. The World Health Organization ranks it among the leading causes of disability worldwide, affecting millions and exerting a profound impact not only on individuals but also on families and societies at large [12]. The complexity of depression, with its diverse symptomatology and varying severity, poses substantial challenges in diagnosis and treatment, often leading to underdiagnosis and undertreatment [4]. The social and economic burdens of depression are immense, encompassing healthcare costs, lost productivity, and the intangible suffering of affected individuals and their loved ones [5].

Traditional methods for screening depression tend to focus on self-reported questionnaires, such as the BDI and the PHQ-9, which have been widely utilized in both clinical and non-clinical settings for their simplicity and efficacy in identifying symptoms of depression [18]. However, these screening tools are not without limitations. In primary care, where a significant portion of depression diagnoses occur, the effectiveness of these tools can be hampered by factors such as time constraints, the varied presentation of depression symptoms, and the potential for underreporting due to stigma associated with mental health conditions [17]. Moreover, while these instruments have high sensitivity, their specificity can be compromised in diverse populations, leading to false positives and unnecessary further assessments [10]. Face-to-face interviews, like the Hamilton Depression Rating Scale [16], offer greater diagnostic reliability but are time-consuming and require skilled professionals, often in short supply [20]. This highlights the need for an approach to screening that goes beyond the conventional methodologies, accounting for the complex nature of depression and its presentation in various demographic groups.

CBR stands out as a distinctive approach within the domain of artificial intelligence, characterized by its ability to solve new problems based on the solutions to similar past cases [9]. This methodology operates on the premise that learning from past experiences can inform the resolution of future dilemmas, making it particularly suitable for applications where theoretical knowledge is sparse but a wealth of case data exists [8]. The application of CBR in health sciences, and specifically in mental health, opens new possibilities for personalized and contextually relevant diagnostic processes [27]. By drawing on the rich tapestry of individual case histories, CBR enables a more nuanced approach to diagnosing complex conditions like depression, where symptoms and their significance can vary widely among patients [1].

GAs, an approach within evolutionary computing, have a well-established history in various domains, including AI, where they serve as a robust optimization technique inspired by the principles of genetics and natural selection [22,29]. Within the context of CBR, GAs have been effectively applied to refine feature selection and retrieval mechanisms, significantly enhancing the adaptability and efficacy of CBR systems. Some studies [11] have shown that GAs can optimize the weighting of features and retrieval processes in CBR, thereby improving the system's performance in complex decision-making scenarios such as medical diagnostics. The adaptability and global search capability of GAs make them particularly suited for optimizing item-specific weighting in psychological assessments, where the solution space is vast and the optimal weights are not readily apparent. By iteratively evolving a population of potential solutions, GAs can efficiently navigate the solution space to identify optimal or near-optimal item weights [6].

The concept of item-specific weighting plays a pivotal role in psychological assessments, particularly when evaluating constructs as complex and multifaceted as depression. Each item in an assessment tool can vary in its relevance to the overall construct being measured and, thus, in its contribution to the diagnostic process [30]. Traditional approaches often assume equal weighting of items, potentially obscuring the picture of an individual's psychological state. Incorporating item-specific weighting allows for a more refined analysis, acknowledging that certain symptoms or responses may carry more diagnostic weight than others. This approach aligns with modern psychometric theories, such as

Item Response Theory (IRT), which advocate for the differential weighting of items based on their properties and their contribution to the latent construct being measured [26].

3   Methodology

The present study adopts an innovative approach by integrating CBR with GAs to optimize a component of a similarity measure with the intent of depression screening, particularly among undergraduate students in Yucatan, Mexico. This research was designed to explore the potential of a refined, item-specific similarity assessment in psychological questionnaires, aiming to enhance the accuracy and personalization of depression diagnostics. Leveraging the variability of responses within self-reported questionnaires, the study seeks to identify patterns that correlate with depression scores derived from other, possibly more comprehensive assessments, serving as the ground truth. By employing a methodological framework that combines the adaptability of CBR and the optimization prowess of GAs, this study endeavors to uncover the subtle yet significant indicators of depression, thereby contributing to the development of more effective screening tools.

The study cohort comprised 160 undergraduate students, all residing in the Yucatan region of Mexico, who volunteered to participate in this research. The age range of the participants was 18–23 years, encompassing a diverse representation of the student population within this demographic. This study did not employ any specific exclusion criteria, aiming to ensure a broad and inclusive sample reflective of the general undergraduate community. The recruitment process was conducted through university channels, leveraging digital platforms and university networks to reach potential participants.

The study received approval from the corresponding ethics committee, ensuring that all research activities adhered to the highest standards of ethical conduct. Participants were informed about the study's objectives and their rights as participants, including confidentiality and the voluntary nature of their involvement, through a digital platform where they also provided informed consent. This digital consent process allowed participants to engage with the consent materials at their own pace, ensuring they were fully informed before agreeing to participate.

Participants were asked to complete a series of psychological assessments online, including the GAD-7 scale and the PHQ-9, alongside more extensive scales such as the BDI, CRSD, and the CES-D. The GAD-7 and PHQ-9, comprising only 16 items combined, offer a more streamlined approach compared to the 83 items collectively found in the BDI, CRSD, and CES-D. This reduction significantly eases the assessment process, making these scales particularly suitable for initial screenings in high-volume or resource-limited settings such as primary healthcare. By using these shorter scales, this study aims to establish whether these instruments can efficiently predict depression scores as those derived from the more comprehensive scales, potentially offering a faster, yet equally reliable, screening method that could enhance early diagnosis and treatment interventions.

In this study, a "case" is defined by the individual responses to the GAD-7 and PHQ-9 questionnaires, coupled with the averaged normalized depression score from the BDI, CRSD, and CES-D assessments:

$$c = \langle d, s \rangle,$$
$$d = \langle \overrightarrow{\text{GAD-7}} + \overrightarrow{\text{PHQ-9}} \rangle,$$
$$s = \text{avg}(\text{BDI}, \text{CRSD}, \text{CES-D}).$$

To meet the operational needs of the similarity measure introduced in [21], questionnaire responses were normalized to the $[-0.5, 0.5]$ interval. The chosen similarity metric, optimized through GAs, was specifically selected over more common metrics like cosine or Euclidean distance due to its ability to handle the directional and magnitude variations in the questionnaire responses effectively. This metric considers not only the absolute differences in responses but adjusts for the relative importance of each item, allowing for an analysis that reflects the complex symptomatology of depression. This approach is particularly beneficial in capturing the gradations in depressive symptom severity, which may be often overlooked by common metrics. The similarity between two case descriptions, $\mathbf{d}_i$ and $\mathbf{d}_j$, is evaluated using this measure which accounts for both the magnitude and direction of each feature's influence, with the elements of vector $\mathbf{w}$ ranging from $[-1, 1]$ to denote the relationship of each element with the measure $\mathcal{S}$ [21] (in our case, depression):

$$\mathcal{S}(\mathbf{d}_i, \mathbf{d}_j, \mathbf{w}) = \left\| (1 - |\mathbf{d}_i - (\mathbf{d}_j \odot \text{sign}^*(\mathbf{w}))|) \odot \frac{\mathbf{w}}{\|\mathbf{w}\|} \right\|. \tag{1}$$

The core of the similarity measure lies in its ability to quantitatively evaluate the concordance between two distinct case profiles, $\mathbf{d}_i$ and $\mathbf{d}_j$. The equation is based on the assessment of the absolute difference between the two profiles, $|\mathbf{d}_i - \mathbf{d}_j|$, which quantifies the raw disparity across corresponding elements. This difference is then modulated by an element-wise product of $\mathbf{d}_j$ with $\text{sign}^*(\mathbf{w})$ (which maps positive elements and zero in $\mathbf{w}$ to 1 and negative elements to -1) effectively adjusting the directionality of each feature's impact. The adjusted differences are then diminished from unity, $1 - |\mathbf{d}_i - (\mathbf{d}_j \odot \text{sign}^*(\mathbf{w}))|$, to invert the scale such that higher values correspond to greater similarity. This resultant vector is further modulated by the normalized weight vector $\frac{\mathbf{w}}{\|\mathbf{w}\|}$, ensuring that each feature's contribution is proportionate to its relative importance as dictated by $\mathbf{w}$. In this vector, values range from -1 to 1, where -1 indicates an inverse relationship of the corresponding element (in this case, depression), 1 signifies a direct relationship, and intermediate values represent varying degrees of similarity, with 0 denoting no significant relationship. Finally, norm calculation aggregates these weighted differences into a singular scalar value, $\mathcal{S}$, representing the overall similarity between the two case profiles. This scalar value, bounded between 0 and 1, offers a metric of similarity, with values closer to 1 indicating high concordance and those near 0 suggesting dissimilarity [21].

The optimization of the item-specific weighting vector **w** was achieved through a GA, which aimed to minimize the discrepancies between the similarity assessments of cases and their actual depression score similarities, thus ensuring that cases with comparable depression levels were identified as similar by our measure. The GA used a subset of the data, designated as the training set, comprising 75% of the samples (120 cases), leaving 25% (40) for validation.

The GA aimed to leverage the training data to minimize the cost function $\mathcal{C}$, which quantifies the discrepancy between the calculated similarities by the function $\mathcal{S}(\mathbf{d}_i, \mathbf{d}_j, \mathbf{w})$ and the actual depression score differences from the solutions of the cases and determined by $\Delta(s_i, s_j)$. The cost function is defined as:

$$\mathcal{C} = \frac{1}{N} \sum_{i=1}^{N-1} \sum_{j=i+1}^{N} \left| \mathcal{S}(\mathbf{d}_i, \mathbf{d}_j, \mathbf{w}) - \Delta(s_i, s_j) \right|, \tag{2}$$

where N is the number of cases in the training dataset, and $\mathbf{d}_i$ and $\mathbf{d}_j$ represent the questionnaire response vectors for cases i and j, respectively. The optimization process commenced with 50 "preliminary" GAs, each iterating over 15 generations with a 100-member population, employing a 0.7 crossover fraction and a 0.10 mutation rate. The elite individuals from these runs formed a substantial part of the initial population for a subsequent, larger GA phase. This second phase, with a 2000-strong population over 50 generations and a 0.15 mutation rate, aimed to further refine vector **v**, intensifying selection pressure to identify an optimal vector that effectively reflects the differential importance of symptoms in depression screening. The high mutation rate was empirically determined to prevent the GA from getting trapped in local minima.

After the GA optimization concluded, a further refinement step was applied to the resultant optimal vector using a constrained optimization technique. This additional step aimed to fine-tune the solution by seeking the local minimum nearest to the GA's output. This hybrid optimization approach ensured that the vector was not only globally informed by the GA but also locally optimized for greater accuracy. The final, refined optimal vector then underwent a validation process using a k-nearest neighbor (k-NN) approach, assessing its efficacy in grouping cases with analogous depression scores. The training set was used to establish baseline similarities and the validation set served to test the predictive accuracy of the model. For each case in the validation set, the similarity to all cases in the training set was calculated using the optimized vector **v**, and the k-NN algorithm was employed to identify the nearest cases based on these similarity scores. The mean normalized depression scores of the nearest cases were then compared to the actual scores of the validation cases to assess the error rate, providing a quantitative measure of the model's performance. This iterative process allowed for the fine-tuning of the model and the identification of the optimal k value that minimized the error.

4   Results

The optimization process produced a final weights vector, pinpointing the differential significance of each item within the GAD-7 and PHQ-9 questionnaires for depression assessment. This optimization unfolded in two stages, initiating with the preliminary GAs, which exhibited an initial average fitness value of 0.083175. The initial low fitness scores observed during the preliminary phases of the GA reflect the complexity of accurately modeling depression through questionnaire responses. The marginal improvements in fitness scores, culminating in a final value of 0.0619, indicate the challenging nature of optimizing a similarity metric that must account for a wide variety of depressive symptoms across individuals. These scores suggest the potential need to refine the GA's parameters or explore additional features that might capture the patterns of depression more effectively. This value, indicative of the average mismatch between calculated similarities and actual depression score similarities among cases, diminished to 0.065603, on average, by the conclusion of these preliminary phases. The subsequent GA phase yielded a vector with a refined fitness value of 0.0619. This systematic decrease in the cost function representes a more accurate concordance between the similarity measure and depression scores. The resultant vector, with elements ranging from -5.60×10^{-8} to 0.0126 for the combined 16 items from GAD-7 and PHQ-9, reveals a discerning item-weighting scheme. Notably, item 9 of the PHQ-9 questionnaire exhibited the highest weights (0.0126), suggesting a greater relevance in the depression screening process, whereas several items are deemed less critical, as evidenced by their zero or near-zero weights, particularly items 2, 5, and 7 from GAD-7, and item 3 of PHQ-9. Figure 1 illustrates these weightings, with subfigure (a) depicting the values for GAD-7 items and subfigure (b) for PHQ-9 items.

The validation of the optimized similarity measure systematically varied k from 1 to 10 to assess its impact on the measure's accuracy. For each value of k, the similarity between each case in the validation dataset and all cases in the training dataset was computed using the optimized vector. The average depression scores from the BDI, CRSD, and CES-D for the k most similar training cases were then compared to the actual scores of the validation cases to calculate the error rate. The MAE, representing the mean difference between predicted and actual depression scores, reached its minimum at $k = 3$, with a value of 0.0432. This indicates an optimal balance between similarity precision and generalization. The normalization of scores to a 0–1 range allows for a direct interpretation of MAE values: an MAE of 0.0432 implies that, on average, the predictions deviate from actual scores by 4.32%, providing a context for assessing the clinical significance of the error rates. This trend is depicted in Fig. 2, illustrating the error rate's dependency on k.

In order to compare the proposed approach to other state-of-the-art approaches, Fig. 3 reports the mean average error of several ML regressors. As we can observe, the GA-optimized k-NN method obtains very accurate results, mostly when $k = 3$. These results are also significant due to the black-box nature of the most accurate ML regressors (Gradient Boosting or Support Vector

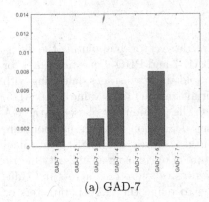
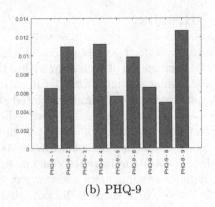

(a) GAD-7   (b) PHQ-9

Fig. 1. Optimized weights of questionnaire items derived from the genetic algorithm. The bar graph in (a) illustrates the weights for each item in the GAD-7 questionnaire, indicating their relative importance in the assessment of depression. The bar graph in (b) displays the weights for items in the PHQ-9 questionnaire. The variation in weights across items reflects the efficacy of the approach, with higher weights suggesting greater relevance in detecting depressive symptoms in the given sample.

Regression), demonstrating the benefits of our approach regarding performance and the explainability of the prediction model.

The final optimized vector reveals a weighting of the GAD-7 and PHQ-9 questionnaire items, explaining the differential importance of specific items in the assessment of depression. The validation process, utilizing a k-nearest neighbor approach, further validates the practical applicability of this measure, demonstrating its potential to accurately group cases with similar depression levels and explain the insights of the screening process. The subsequent section will delve into a comprehensive discussion of these insights, exploring their implications for depression screening methodologies and future research directions.

5   Discussion

The explanation capabilities of the proposed CBR method offer significant insights into the differential diagnostic capabilities of the PHQ-9 and GAD-7 questionnaires, as evidenced by the highest and lowest values of the elements in the optimized weighting vector detailed in Table 1. The optimization process not only reveals a clear prioritization of certain depressive symptoms over others but also underscores the intrinsic value of the GAD-7 and PHQ-9 items in depression screening. Notably, the absence of negatively contributing items, with the minimum value being negligible at -5.60×10^{-8} (as reported in Sect. 4), suggests that all elements within these scales hold potential relevance, with the most critical items reflecting key aspects of depression as assessed by the PHQ-9. Specifically, items related to self-harm thoughts, fatigue, and hopelessness were assigned the highest weights, indicating their paramount importance in the

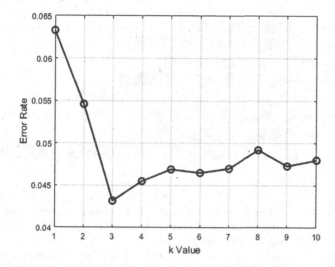

Fig. 2. Mean average error (MAE) rate with respect to the number of neighbors in the k-nearest neighbors algorithm. Each point represents the error rate calculated as the average discrepancy between the predicted and actual depression levels across the validation dataset. The error rate achieves its minimum at $k = 3$

depression screening process. This pattern not only highlights the PHQ-9's targeted effectiveness in capturing core depressive symptoms but also highlights its practical utility in settings requiring quick and effective mental health assessments. The shorter format of the PHQ-9 and GAD-7 is particularly beneficial in primary care and community settings where quick screening is essential to manage high patient volumes effectively. The streamlined nature of these tools facilitates broader accessibility and reduces assessment fatigue, potentially increasing the response accuracy among participants. Moreover, the differential weighting revealed through our optimization process validates the significant emphasis on critical depressive symptoms, ensuring that even with fewer questions, the diagnostic integrity of the screening is maintained.

The analysis not only affirms the PHQ-9's critical role in identifying depression but also evidences the relation between depressive and anxiety symptoms. Achieving the identification of significant items provides us with the opportunity to distinguish the focal points of comorbidity between these disorders. This is exemplified by the first item of the GAD-7 related to feelings and thoughts that indicate the inability to remain calm.

In the context of Yucatan, a region marked by notably high rates of suicide among young adults [2,31], the use of shorter, culturally adapted scales such as the PHQ-9 and GAD-7 becomes even more critical. These scales' ability to quickly assess critical depressive indicators like suicidal ideation (heavily weighted in our study) is essential in a region with high suicide rates among young adults. By employing scales that respondents are more likely to complete due to their brevity, our methodology not only caters to the local healthcare

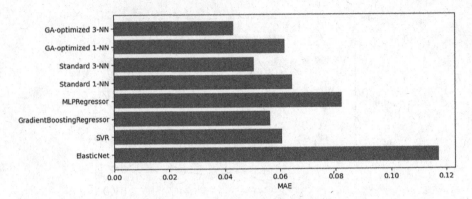

Fig. 3. Mean Average Error (MAE) rate of the proposed GA-optimized k-nearest neighbors algorithm compared to other state-of-the-art ML approaches. GA-optimized 1-NN, 3-NN: Results reported in Fig. 2. Standard 1-NN, 3-NN: k-Neighbors regressor using Euclidean distance. ElasticNet: Linear regression with combined L1 and L2 priors as regularizer. GradientBoostingRegressor: Gradient Boosting for regression. SVR: Epsilon-Support Vector Regression. MLPRegressor: Multi-layer Perceptron regressor.

system's needs but also addresses the urgent need for effective screening tools that can be widely disseminated and easily administered in various community settings. Notably, GAD-7 item 1, "Feeling nervous, anxious, or on edge", also emerged with a substantial weight, ranking as the fourth largest, highlighting the correlation between anxiety and depression symptoms in this setting. This insight points to the importance of including anxiety-related indicators in the assessment of depression, especially in contexts with high suicide rates. Conversely, the relatively minor emphasis on PHQ-9 item 3, "Trouble falling or staying asleep, or sleeping too much," suggests that sleep disturbances may not hold equivalent diagnostic significance for depression within this cultural context, despite its origin from a depression-focused questionnaire. The lower-weighted items, mainly from the GAD-7, further accentuate the questionnaire's focus on anxiety symptoms, which, although critical, may not be as indicative of depression severity in this demographic context [24]. The emergence of these specific symptoms highlights the potential utility of our tailored similarity measure in this unique cultural and demographic setting. It highlights the necessity of a sensitive and customised approach to depression screening that accounts for the local epidemiological trends and the psychosocial aspects influencing mental health. By identifying symptoms most aligned with the regional manifestation of depression, our study offers a framework that could enhance early detection and intervention strategies, potentially mitigating the risk factors associated with the high incidence of suicide among Yucatan's youth, a region where the cultural and sociodemographic backdrop plays a pivotal role in mental health outcomes [3].

Our study introduces a novel approach to screening for depression symptoms that deviates from traditional point-based systems. Rather than assigning points to individual responses on questionnaires, our methodology involves com-

Table 1. Items with the Highest and Lowest Weights in the Optimized Vector from PHQ-9 and GAD-7 Questionnaires

Questionnaire	Item	Description	Weight
PHQ-9	9	Thoughts that you would be better off dead or of hurting yourself in some way	0.0126
PHQ-9	4	Feeling tired or having little energy	0.0112
PHQ-9	2	Feeling down, depressed, or hopeless	0.0109
GAD-7	1	Feeling nervous, anxious, or on edge	0.0100
PHQ-9	6	Feeling bad about yourself - or that you're a failure or have let yourself or your family down	0.0098
GAD-7	2	Not being able to stop or control worrying	0.0000
GAD-7	5	Being so restless that it is hard to sit still	0.0000
GAD-7	7	Feeling afraid as if something awful might happen	0.0000
PHQ-9	3	Trouble falling or staying asleep, or sleeping too much	0.0029
GAD-7	3	Worrying too much about different things	0.0062

paring the entire set of responses to those from previous cases of diagnosed depression (according to a given ground truth). This comparison leverages the optimized weighting vector, which emphasizes the relative importance of specific symptoms. Ideally, this methodology would be calibrated against more reliable diagnostic processes, such as clinical interviews, thereby combining the depth of face-to-face diagnosis with the accessibility and efficiency of self-report questionnaires. The potential of this approach to streamline depression screening is particularly noteworthy. Traditional screening methods often rely on comprehensive questionnaires, which collectively encompass a significant number of items. In contrast, our method effectively allows the utilization of fewer items which could achieve comparable diagnostic insights. This efficiency not only reduces the burden on individuals undergoing screening but also enhances the feasibility of widespread mental health assessments.

Furthermore, our methodology opens the door to identifying multiple vectors corresponding to local optima within the data. Such vectors could represent distinct patterns or models of depression, reflecting the heterogeneity of the disorder. Individuals' responses could then be compared against these various models, offering a sensible understanding of their specific depressive profile. This aspect of our approach holds promise for personalized mental health care, where interventions are tailored to the unique manifestation of depression in each individual, potentially increasing the effectiveness of treatment strategies.

6 Conclusions

The methodology introduced in this study, utilizing GAs to optimize a similarity measure for depression screening, represents a significant contribution to the CBR paradigm applied to mental health research. This approach not only allows for the specific weighting of questionnaire items based on their diagnostic importance but also introduces a dynamic framework that can be adapted to explain different demographic contexts, achieving performance comparable to other state-of-the-art ML approaches. The ability to identify multiple similarity vectors corresponding to local optima offers a flexible model that can capture distinct patterns of depression, accommodating the disorder's heterogeneity. Such methodological innovations pave the way for future studies to explore the application of similar techniques across different mental health conditions and demographic settings.

This study's investigation into the optimization of a similarity measure for depression screening using a CBR approach within the unique demographic context of Yucatan, Mexico, has yielded significant insights. The derived optimized weighting vector underscores the critical importance of specific PHQ-9 items-particularly those concerning self-harm, fatigue, and hopelessness-in identifying depressive symptoms. The prominence of these items aligns with the prevailing model of depression in the region, characterized by high rates of suicide among young adults. Conversely, the relative underemphasis on certain GAD-7 items highlights the measure's capacity to distinguish between symptoms of depression and anxiety, further validating the approach's specificity. The results not only reaffirm the relevance of the PHQ-9 in depression screening but also illuminate the intricate interplay between depressive and anxiety symptoms within the broader spectrum of mental health assessment.

The practical implications of our findings extend significantly beyond the immediate context of Yucatan, suggesting a broader applicability for improving depression screening and mental health interventions globally. By enabling a more personalized and efficient approach to screening, our methodology can facilitate the early detection of depression symptoms, potentially leading to timely and more effective interventions. The capacity to tailor screening tools to the specific characteristics of depression within various populations holds promise for enhancing the accuracy of diagnoses and the efficacy of subsequent treatments. This approach, rooted in the identification of the most salient depressive symptoms within particular demographic groups, could lead to the development of streamlined questionnaires that maintain diagnostic integrity while reducing the burden on respondents, thereby improving engagement and the likelihood of early intervention.

The implications of this study extend into several promising avenues for future research. A critical next step involves validating the optimized similarity measure against clinical diagnoses to ascertain its efficacy in real-world settings. Furthermore, exploring the applicability of this methodology to other mental health conditions could broaden its utility and impact. Given the method's adaptability, extending the research to demographic settings beyond Yucatan, Mexico, could provide invaluable insights into the cultural and regional nuances of depression screening. Such endeavors would not only enhance our understanding of depression's multifaceted nature but also contribute to the development of more universally applicable and culturally sensitive diagnostic tools.

This study contributes a valuable perspective to the field of mental health research, particularly in the screening of depression. By integrating the precision of GAs with the practicality of widely-used questionnaires, we propose a model that emphasizes personalization and cultural sensitivity in diagnostic practices. The potential of this approach to refine and enhance depression screening, especially in regions with unique mental health profiles like Yucatan, Mexico, holds promise for significant advancements in mental health care.

Acknowledgements. Supported by the PERXAI project PID2020-114596RB-C21, funded by the Ministry of Science and Innovation of Spain (MCIN/AEI/ 10.13039/501100011033) and the BOSCH-UCM Honorary Chair on Artificial Intelligence applied to Internet of Things.

References

1. Bergmann, R., Althoff, K., Minor, M., Reichle, M., Bach, K.: Case-based reasoning. Knowl. Eng. Rev. **9**, 61–64 (1994)
2. Cabello-Rangel, H., Márquez-Caraveo, M., Díaz-Castro, L.: Suicide rate, depression and the human development index: an ecological study from Mexico. Front. Public Health **8** (2020)
3. Dávila Cervantes, C.A., del Pilar Ochoa Torres, M., Rodríguez, I.C.: Analysis of the impact of mortality due to suicides in Mexico, 2000–2012. Salud colectiva **11**(4), 471–484 (2015)
4. Gelenberg, A.: The prevalence and impact of depression. J. Clin. Psychiatry **71**(3), e06 (2010)
5. Hidaka, B.H.: Depression as a disease of modernity: explanations for increasing prevalence. J. Affect. Disord. **140**(3), 205–214 (2012)
6. Immanuel, S.D., Chakraborty, U.K.: Genetic algorithm: an approach on optimization. In: 2019 International Conference on Communication and Electronics Systems (ICCES) (2019)
7. Kerr, L., Kerr, L.D.: Screening tools for depression in primary care: the effects of culture, gender, and somatic symptoms on the detection of depression. Western J. Med. **175**(5), 349–352 (2001)
8. Ketler, K.: Case-based reasoning: an introduction. Expert Syst. Appl. **6**, 3–8 (1993)
9. Kolodner, J.: An introduction to case-based reasoning. Artif. Intell. Rev. **6**, 3–34 (1992)
10. Lichtman, J.H., et al.: Depression and coronary heart disease: recommendations for screening, referral, and treatment. Circulation (2008)
11. López, B., Pous, C., Pla, A., Gay, P.: Boosting CBR agents with genetic algorithms. In: McGinty, L., Wilson, D.C. (eds.) ICCBR 2009. LNCS (LNAI), vol. 5650, pp. 195–209. Springer, Heidelberg (2009). https://doi.org/10.1007/978-3-642-02998-1_15
12. Malhi, G., Mann, J.: Depression. Lancet **392**, 2299–2312 (2018)
13. Marcus, M., Yasamy, M.T., van Ommeren, M., Chisholm, D., Saxena, S.: Depression: a global public health concern (2012)
14. Marling, C., Whitehouse, P.: Case-based reasoning in the care of Alzheimer's disease patients. In: Aha, D.W., Watson, I. (eds.) ICCBR 2001. LNCS (LNAI), vol. 2080, pp. 702–715. Springer, Heidelberg (2001). https://doi.org/10.1007/3-540-44593-5_50

15. Martínez-Nicolás, I., et al.: What seems to explain suicidality in Yucatan Mexican young adults? Findings from an app-based mental health screening test using the SMART-SCREEN protocol. Curr. Psychol. **42**(35), 30767–30779 (2023)

16. Miller, I., Bishop, S., Norman, W., Maddever, H.: The modified Hamilton rating scale for depression: reliability and validity. Psychiatry Res. **14**, 131–142 (1985)

17. Mitchell, A.J.: Clinical utility of screening for clinical depression and bipolar disorder. Curr. Opinion Psychiatry (2011)

18. Mitchell, A.J., Coyne, J.C.: Do ultra-short screening instruments accurately detect depression in primary care? A pooled analysis and meta-analysis of 22 studies. Br. J. Gen. Pract. (2007)

19. Mitchell, A.J., Vaze, A., Rao, S.: Clinical diagnosis of depression in primary care: a meta-analysis. Lancet **374**(9690), 609–619 (2010)

20. Morriss, R., Leese, M., Chatwin, J., Baldwin, D.: Inter-rater reliability of the Hamilton depression rating scale as a diagnostic and outcome measure of depression in primary care. J. Affect. Disord. **111**(2–3), 204–213 (2008)

21. Orozco-del Castillo, M.G.: An element-wise contribution-based vector similarity measure for artificial intelligence applications: a brief exploration. J. Artif. Intell. Comput. Appl. **1**(1), 26–28 (2023)

22. Pal, S., Bhandari, D., Kundu, M.: Genetic algorithms for optimal image enhancement. Pattern Recogn. Lett. (1994)

23. Palmer, S.C., Coyne, J.C.: Screening for depression in medical care: pitfalls, alternatives, and revised priorities. J. Psychosom. Res. **54**(4), 279–287 (2003)

24. Reyes-Foster, B.M.: The devil made her do it: understanding suicide, demonic discourse, and the social construction of 'health' in Yucatan, Mexico. J. Relig. Violence **1**, 363–381 (2013)

25. Reynolds, C.F., Patel, V.: Screening for depression: the global mental health context. World Psychiatry **16** (2017)

26. Rodriguez, A., Reise, S., Haviland, M.G.: Applying bifactor statistical indices in the evaluation of psychological measures. J. Pers. Assess. **98**, 223–237 (2016)

27. Sosa-Espadas, C.E., Orozco-del Castillo, M.G., Cuevas-Cuevas, N., Recio-Garcia, J.A.: IREX: iterative refinement and explanation of classification models for tabular datasets. SoftwareX **23**, 101420 (2023)

28. Spitzer, R.L., Kroenke, K., Williams, J.B.W., Löwe, B.: A brief measure for assessing generalized anxiety disorder: the GAD-7. Arch. Int. Med. **166**(10), 1092–1097 (2006)

29. Tang, W., Man, K., Kwong, S., He, Q.: Genetic algorithms and their applications. IEEE Signal Process. Mag. (1996)

30. Thomas, M.: The value of item response theory in clinical assessment: a review. Assessment **18**, 291–307 (2011)

31. Velázquez-Vázquez, D., Rosado-Franco, A., Herrera-Pacheco, D., Aguilar-Vargas, E., Mendez-Dominguez, N.: Epidemiological description of suicide mortality in the state of Yucatan between 2013 and 2016. Salud Mental (2019)

CBR-RAG: Case-Based Reasoning for Retrieval Augmented Generation in LLMs for Legal Question Answering

Nirmalie Wiratunga[1(✉)] [ID], Ramitha Abeyratne[1] [ID], Lasal Jayawardena[1,2] [ID],
Kyle Martin[1] [ID], Stewart Massie[1] [ID], Ikechukwu Nkisi-Orji[1] [ID],
Ruvan Weerasinghe[2] [ID], Anne Liret[3] [ID], and Bruno Fleisch[3]

[1] Robert Gordon University, Aberdeen, UK
{n.wiratunga,r.abeyratne,l.jayawardena,k.martin3,s.massie,
i.nkisi-orji}@rgu.ac.uk
[2] Informatics Institute of Technology, Colombo, Sri Lanka
ruvan.w@iit.lk
[3] BT France, Puteaux, France
{anne.liret,bruno.fleisch}@bt.com

Abstract. Retrieval-Augmented Generation (RAG) enhances Large Language Model (LLM) output by providing prior knowledge as context to input. This is beneficial for knowledge-intensive and expert reliant tasks, including legal question-answering, which require evidence to validate generated text outputs. We highlight that Case-Based Reasoning (CBR) presents key opportunities to structure retrieval as part of the RAG process in an LLM. We introduce CBR-RAG, where CBR cycle's initial retrieval stage, its indexing vocabulary, and similarity knowledge containers are used to enhance LLM queries with contextually relevant cases. This integration augments the original LLM query, providing a richer prompt. We present an evaluation of CBR-RAG, and examine different representations (i.e. general and domain-specific embeddings) and methods of comparison (i.e. inter, intra and hybrid similarity) on the task of legal question-answering. Our results indicate that the context provided by CBR's case reuse enforces similarity between relevant components of the questions and the evidence base leading to significant improvements in the quality of generated answers.

Keywords: CBR · RAG · LLMs · Text Embedding · Indexing · Retrieval

1 Introduction

Retrieval-Augmented Generation (RAG) enhances the performance of large language models (LLMs) on knowledge-intensive NLP tasks by combining the strengths of pre-trained parametric (language models with learned parameters) and non-parametric (external knowledge resources e.g., Wikipedia) memories [15]. This hybrid approach not only sets new benchmarks in open-domain

This research is funded by SFC International Science Partnerships Fund.

J. A. Recio-Garcia et al. (Eds.): ICCBR 2024, LNAI 14775, pp. 445–460, 2024.
https://doi.org/10.1007/978-3-031-63646-2_29

question answering by generating more accurate, specific, and factually correct responses but also addresses critical challenges in the field such as the difficulty in updating stored knowledge and providing provenance for generated outputs. For example, in the context of legal question-answering, RAG-based systems can retrieve publicly available legislation documents from open knowledge bases to provide context for user queries. However, such a system would require output that could be validated, and moderation of content generated by LLMs has been highlighted as a critical concern [11].

Case-Based Reasoning (CBR) presents an excellent opportunity here, as previous solutions form the basis of a knowledge-base which can be evidenced in best practice or regulations [17]. CBR can enhance the retrieval process in RAG models by organising the non-parametric memory in a way that cases (knowledge entries or past experiences) are more effectively matched to queries. Previous work on ensemble CBR-neural systems has also highlighted the benefits of CBR integration, demonstrating improvements in factual correctness over purely neural methods [21]. Accordingly, in this work we present three contributions.

- Firstly, we formalise the role of the CBR methodology to form context for RAG systems.
- Secondly, we provide an empirical comparison of retrieval methods for RAG, using alternative representations (i.e. general and domain-specific embeddings) and similarity metrics (i.e. inter, intra and hybrid similarity).
- Finally, we present these contributions in the context of the legal domain and provide results for a generative legal question-answering (QA) application[1]. Our results highlight the opportunities of CBR-RAG systems for knowledge-reliant generative tasks.

This paper is structured as follows. In Sect. 2 we describe influential work targeting the legal domain from CBR and LLM literature. In Sect. 3, we formalise CBR-RAG and its application to legal QA, while in Sect. 4 we detail the different methods for creating and comparing embeddings to perform case retrieval. In Sect. 5 we describe the different encoders used to create embeddings. Finally, in Sect. 6 we discuss the methodology and results of our evaluation, followed by conclusions in Sect. 7.

2   Related Work

CBR boasts a long-standing history in the legal domain, with initial efforts concentrating on extracting features to index law cases effectively. These features, referred to as 'factors', are pivotal in systems like HYPO [3], which employ fact-oriented representations applied to trade secret law and extended to legal tutoring with the CATO [1] system. More generally with Textual CBR, a key focus has been on extracting features for case comparison, using methods that range from decision trees, as exemplified by the SMILE system in creating indexing vocabularies for legal case retrieval [5], to association rules for case representation [23].

---

[1] Reproducible code is available: https://github.com/rgu-iit-bt/cbr-for-legal-rag.

Much of this has now been advanced by the adoption of neural transformations of input text through transformer-style embeddings with LLMs.

The application of LLMs presents an interesting approach in addressing challenges within the legal domain. LLMs use language understanding capabilities to interact with users, enabling extraction of key elements from legal documents, and present information in an understandable manner to enhance decision-making processes. For this reason, GPT-based [14,18] and BERT-based [7] transformer models are popular for LegalAI. However their black-box nature and tendency to hallucinate and lack of factual faithfulness present significant challenges for deployment [13]. Retrieval-Augmented Generation (RAG) systems address this by presenting the LLM with factual data to generate responses [15,16], employing a variety of sophisticated fact identifying mechanisms [2,19]. However currently such retrieval methods in RAG do not make use of CBR's potential for varying matching strategies across different segments of the content being matched. Here we are reminded of research in CBR involving the integration with IR systems, specifically where CBR has been effectively used to retrieve 'most on-point' cases to guide the search and browse of vast IR collections [17]. Our work draws inspiration from these integrative approaches, applying the principles of CBR to improve contextual understanding within LLMs.

LLMs are typically pre-trained on general text and subsequently fine-tuned on legal texts to learn domain-specific representations. Obtaining sufficiently large data sets for LLM training poses a significant challenge. For example, pre-trained LLMs may be fine-tuned using the LEDGAR dataset [20] for legal text classification downstream tasks or on extensive corpora like the Harvard Law case corpus[2] using masked-language modelling or next-sentence prediction techniques. Thereafter tested on other legal downstream tasks, such as those found in the CaseHOLD dataset [8], which include tasks related to Overruling, Terms of Service, and CaseHOLD itself. We observe that there remains a notable scarcity of LLMs specifically applied to legal question answering tasks. This is likely because existing legal QA datasets are mostly small, manually curated datasets (for example, the rule-qa task in the LegalBench collection [10] is formed from 50 question-answer pairs). However the recent release of the Open Australian Legal Question-Answering (ALQA) dataset[3], comprising over 2,100 question-answer-snippet triplets (synthesised by GPT-4 from the Open Australian Legal Corpus), presents an opportunity for LLMs to expand to legal QA.

3   CBR-RAG: Using CBR to Form Context for LLMs

In CBR-RAG, we integrate the initial retrieve-only stage of the CBR cycle with its indexing vocabulary and similarity knowledge containers to enable the retrieval of cases that serve as context for querying an LLM. Consequently, the original LLM query is augmented with content retrieved via CBR, creating a contextually enriched prompt for the LLM.

---

[2] https://case.law/.

[3] https://huggingface.co/datasets/umarbutler/open-australian-legal-qa.

Figures 1 illustrates a high-level architecture of a generative model for Question-Answering systems, highlighting the integration of CBR within it. Here we denote the generative LLM model as, G, and the prompt, P, used to generate the response as a tuple, $p = (Q, C)$, where Q is the question reflecting the user's query, and, C, is the context text with relevant details to guide the response generation. The response generated by the model for the query, Q, is denoted as the answer, A.

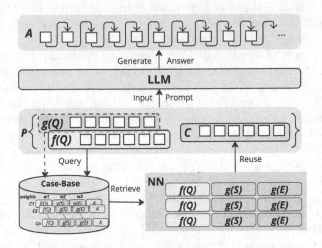

Fig. 1. CBR-RAG

3.1 Casebase

We used the Australian Open Legal QA (ALQA) [6] dataset to create the casebase. The dataset is formed of 2,124 LLM-generated question-answer pairs from the Australian Open Legal Corpus dataset. Each QA pair is corroborated by a supporting textual snippet from a legal document within the corpus for factual validation. An example case about the 'interpretation of reasonable grounds in searches without a warrant' appears in Table 1. Here the support text provides the context in which the question should be answered. The bold text further highlights examples of named entities that might usefully be captured separately for case comparison purposes.

Figure 2 provides a frequency distributions of the legal acts identified in the casebase with the most frequently referenced legal acts in the dataset listed in the table (extracted using the prompt in Table 3). The most frequently mentioned act is the 'Federal Court Rules' out of 785 unique legal acts. Within the dataset, 1,183 (57%) cases were found to have no reference to legal acts, while only 44 acts appeared in more than 1 case. Accordingly, relying solely on legal acts for indexing would not be suitable for this casebase. Instead, it presents an

Table 1. Examples Legal Q&A case

Component	Description
Case Name	Smith v The State of New South Wales (2015)
Question	How did the case of Smith v The State of New South Wales (2015) clarify the interpretation of 'reasonable grounds' for conducting a search without a warrant?
Support	In **[Case Name: Smith v The State of NSW (2015)]**, the plaintiff **[Action: was searched without a warrant]** **[Location: near a known drug trafficking area]** based on the plaintiff's nervous demeanor and presence in the area, but **[Outcome: no drugs were found]**. The legality of the search was contested, focusing on **[Legal Concept: whether 'reasonable grounds' existed]**
Answer	The case ruled 'reasonable grounds' require clear, specific facts of criminal activity, not just location or behavior

Index	Act (Freq)
1	Federal Court Rules (9)
2	Civil Aviation Regulations 1998 (8)
3	Land & Env. Court Act 1979 (8)
4	Corporations Act 2001 (Cth) (7)
5	Migration Act 1958 (Cth) (6)
6	Customs Act 1901, Tariff Act 1995 (6)
7	Industrial Relations Act 1996 (6)
8	Environmental Planning and Assessment Act 1979 (5)
9	Trees (Disputes Between Neighbours) Act 2006 (5)
10	Migration Act 1958 (5)

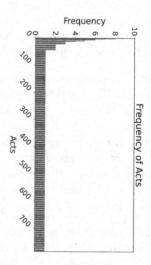

Fig. 2. Ten most frequent legal acts in the casebase are listed on the left, and the legal act frequency distribution appears on the right.

opportunity for experimentation with neural embeddings to form the indexing vocabulary, with weighted similarity contributing to the similarity knowledge.

4 Representation and Similarity

We formalise our retrieval and representation methods. Let's denote the casebase as a collection of cases $C = \{c_1, c_2, \ldots, c_n\}$ containing question and answer legal cases. Each case c, in the context of RAG is formalised as a tuple,

$$c = \; <Q, S, E, A>$$

where Q represents a **question**, A represents the **answer**, S represents the **support** for a given answer from an evidence base, and E represents a set of **entities** extracted from S. This case representation underpins RAG in its use of S. Typical CBR for question answering would be composed mainly of problem-solution components (i.e. question and answer respectively together with any lessons learnt), structuring cases as problem-solution-support enhances answer generation for the LLM by providing factually accurate context. Furthermore, while only the most relevant component of a document is extracted as the support text, the link to the full document is available in the original ALQA corpus.

4.1 Representation

Initially, in textual form, each part is represented by neural embeddings. For diverse retrieval scenarios, we use a dual embedding form for Q to enable matching it with not only other questions but where necessary matching it to the supporting text or the entities as follows:

- **Intra Embeddings**, $f(\cdot)$, optimised for attribute matching. These embeddings facilitate attribute-to-attribute comparisons where local similarities can be computed between the same types of attributes (e.g., questions with questions).
- **Inter Embeddings**, $g(\cdot)$, designed for information retrieval (IR) scenarios. These embeddings allow for matching that is not restricted to like attributes, enabling inter-attribute similarity assessment. This approach is particularly useful in situations where a question may be relevant for comparison to the support text or the entities.

A representation using intra-embedding is useful for tasks like semantic textual similarity that focus on finding sentences with closely related meanings, even if phrased differently. For example, a sentence like 'The judge dismissed the case due to lack of evidence.' would find a semantically similar counterpart in 'The court threw out the lawsuit because there was insufficient proof' Conversely, an inter-embedding representation is suited for tasks aimed at searching for documents relevant to a query. For example, a legal query on 'copyright infringement in digital media' may yield cases with outcomes such as rulings on unauthorised content distribution or streaming without permission. These highlight the distinction between representations needed for ascertaining semantic similarity with intra-embeddings ($f(.)$), and finding relevant content with inter-embeddings ($g(.)$).

The dual-embedding case representation, accommodating both forms of retrieval tasks, is given by:

$$c = <f(Q), g(Q), g(S), g(E), A>$$

Similarly, the prompt can be expressed using the inter embedding as follows[4]:

$$p = <f(\mathcal{Q}), g(\mathcal{Q}), \mathcal{C}>$$

4.2 Case Retrieval

We use case retrieval to augment the context part of a prompt, p, given its query, $\mathcal{Q}$. Accordingly, there are three comparison strategies for case retrieval: intra-, inter-, and hybrid-embedding based retrieval.

Intra-embedding retrieval involves matching on the basis of embeddings obtained from function $f(.)$. Here $f(\mathcal{Q})$ which represents the embeddings from the prompt's query is matched to query parts of the cases in the casebase. The best matching case identified from intra-embedding retrieval is defined by:

$$\beta_k = \underset{c_i \in C, \, k}{\text{top-k}} \, \text{Sim}(f(\mathcal{Q}), f(Q_i)) \tag{1}$$

Here, top-k refers to the selection of indices corresponding to the k highest-scoring cases as determined by the similarity measure. β represents the indices of these retrieved cases, while Sim is a similarity metric (e.g., cosine similarity) that measures the similarity between the intra-embedding of the prompt's question and the intra-embeddings of the question parts of each case in the casebase.

Inter-embedding retrieval uses $g(\mathcal{Q})$ from the prompt to search the casebase, focusing on identifying relevant cases akin to an information retrieval style search, where attribute-to-attribute matching is not strictly followed. The best matching case is identified as follows:

$$\beta_k = \underset{c_i \in C, \, k}{\text{top-k}} \, \text{Sim}(g(\mathcal{Q}), g(X_i)) \tag{2}$$

where X_i can be either S_i (the Snippet part) or E_i (the Entity part) of the case.

Hybrid embedding retrieval is an alternative matching that involves a combination of both intra and inter-embeddings of the prompt's $\mathcal{Q}$ representations being used to match cases in a hybrid weighted retrieval approach:

$$\beta_k = \underset{c_i \in C, \, k}{\text{top-k}} \, (w_1 \cdot \text{Sim}(f(\mathcal{Q}), f(Q_i)) + w_2 \cdot \text{Sim}(g(\mathcal{Q}), g(S_i)) + w_3 \cdot \text{Sim}(g(\mathcal{Q}), g(E_i))) \tag{3}$$

Here attribute importance weights w_1, w_2, and w_3 can be set based on domain knowledge or optimised if needed. Here both representation forms of the prompt's

---

[4] Note: Our notation uses calligraphic font for the prompt components $(f(\mathcal{Q}), g(\mathcal{Q}), \mathcal{C})$ to distinguish them from those of cases. Despite the stylistic difference, both prompts and cases employ similar embedding representations.

query $f(\mathcal{Q})$ and $g(\mathcal{Q})$ are used for retrieval. Given the top k cases $\{c_{\beta_j}\}_{j=1}^k$, we can extract the context for the prompt based on the retrieval option ρ as follows:

$$\text{Context, } \mathcal{C}(\rho) = \begin{cases} \{S_{\beta_j}\}_{j=1}^k & \text{if } \rho = 1, \text{ "support-text-only"} \quad (4a) \\ \{Q_{\beta_j}, S_{\beta_j}, E_{\beta_j}, A_{\beta_j}\}_{j=1}^k & \text{if } \rho = 2, \text{ "full-case"} \qquad (4b) \end{cases}$$

5   Embedding Models

In this work, we explore embeddings generated by BERT, AnglEBERT, and LegalBERT; the latter being pre-trained on diverse English legal documents, with the rest all being general-purpose embeddings. We next provide an overview of these models, as illustrated in Fig. 3, and discuss how they can be used to generate the f and g forms of representations.

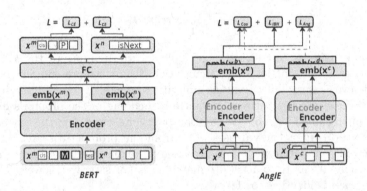

Fig. 3. Architecture and training process for BERT and AnglEBERT. Note that Legal-BERT has the same architecture as BERT, but is pre-trained on legal text.

5.1   BERT

The Bidirectional Encoder Representations from Transformers (BERT) model [9] is a language model for learning generalisable text embeddings. The model is formed of an encoder block (taken from the transformer architecture in [22]), followed by a fully-connected layer. The bidirectional nature of BERT is derived from its pre-training technique, which conditions on both the left and right contexts of input sentences simultaneously. The model uses a self-supervised learning strategy that combines masked-language modeling (MLM) with next sentence prediction (NSP) to acquire contextually rich word embeddings. During training, a pair of sentences is fed into the model, and a random subset of words is replaced with the [MASK] token, establishing a sequence-to-point task. The objective here is to predict the masked words by using the context provided by both previous and subsequent words. Furthermore, a [CLS] token is inserted at the beginning of the input sequence to accumulate contextual information from the entire sequence, facilitating tasks like sentence relationship classification. Pre-training with both MLM and NSP, can be seen as typical text prediction and is controlled by the standard cross-entropy objective function. BERT is pre-trained on a combination of large general purpose text datasets totalling 3.3B words and has demonstrated strong performance across many domains.

5.2   LegalBERT Trained on General Legal Data

Domain-specific knowledge is known to be beneficial for legal tasks [7,20]. For example, the word 'case' may refer to a variety of containers (brief case, suit case, display case, etc.), but also a court case. While semantic relations with the latter are likely to be impactful for legal question answering, the greater frequency of the former in general corpora will result in embeddings more weighted towards that context. The LegalBERT family of models [7] enhance the BERT model by further pre-training on an additional 12 GB of diverse English legal documents from a mix of UK, EU, and US legislation and case law. We expect embeddings learnt with documents from the legal domain will be useful for legal Q&A.

5.3   BERT with AnglE Embeddings

The AnglE embeddings [16] adopts a contrastive learning strategy (similar to Siamese networks [4]) to learn embeddings through matching both positive and negative text pairs, where a positive pair is considered to be similar (above some threshold usually). The process begins with BERT embeddings, input to AnglE for optimisation. Its novelty stems from one of the three loss functions, that are designed to overcome the vanishing gradient issue encountered in cosine similarity-based comparisons, particularly at the extremes of similarity (or dissimilarity). This is achieved by comparing embeddings based on angle and magnitude within complex spaces, effectively bypassing cosine similarity's saturation problem. Once trained the AnglE embedding model can be used to generate text embeddings using a final pooling layer [16].

One of the difficulties when using AnglEBERT for a specific domain is that one must generate a supervised training set (unlike with BERT which can be trained in an unsupervised manner using the MLM and NSP self-supervision methods). This is because the AnglE method adopts a contrastive learning strategy, where the supervised dataset must include paired instances for training. This can be prohibitive in contexts where domain expertise is required for labelling.

5.4   Dual-Embedding Case Representation with AnglE

For the purposes of this work, we leverage dual-embeddings introduced in [16]. In terms of the inter-embedding retrieval, a specific embedding prompt cue $Cue(Q)$

is used to contextualise the relevance of the query embeddings towards matching with attributes other than that of questions, as follows:

$$Cue(Q) = \text{"Represent this sentence for searching relevant passages:"} \{Q\}$$

The idea here is that the cue is used to influence the embedding generation towards inter-retrieval oriented embeddings as follows:

$$g(Cue(Q))$$

For intra-embedding retrieval the prompt text is empty, i.e. input the text without specifying an additional prompt cue. This means the embedding function f processes the query Q directly, as $f(Q)$. Table 2 provides an example of question and support text version that are used as input to each of BERT, AnglEBERT and LegalBERT with relevant prompts to enable the generation of the alternative embeddings that we intend using during case matching with CBR.

Table 2. Comparison of an example question with and without the Cue text (in blue) to create inter and intra embeddings.

Embedding	Question
intra	$f($"What were the court's findings regarding the financial liabilities of Allco Finance Group Ltd to Blairgowrie Trading Ltd?"$)$
inter	$g($"Represent this sentence for searching relevant passages:" + "What were the court's findings regarding the financial liabilities of Allco Finance Group Ltd to Blairgowrie Trading Ltd?"$)$

6   Evaluation

The aim of our evaluation is two-fold: 1) to understand the impact of inter and intra embeddings on weighted retrieval, and 2) to understand the generative quality of RAG systems when coupled with a case-based retrieval-only system. To analyse weighted retrieval we compared several representation combinations of embedding models and similarity weights as follows:

- compare three alternative forms of text embeddings using the encoders presented in Sect. 5 - BERT, LegalBERT and AnglEBERT;
- compare four alternative weighting schemes to assess utility of question, support, and entity components within case representations. These include:
  - Question only, represented by the weights [1,0,0] (see Eq. 1),
  - Support only, with weights [0,1,0],
  - Entities only, using weights [0,0,1] (see Eq. 2),
  - A hybrid approach, combining these components with weights [0.25, 0.40, 0.35] (refer to Eq. 3).

Accordingly BERT[0,1,0] would denote using a Support only version of retrieval with the BERT embedding; and using the same naming convention, AnglE-BERT[0.25,0.4,0.35] indicates a hybrid dual embedding method where AnglE-BERT embeddings are used with the specified weights for case retrieval. Here weights are allocated based on empirical experiments conducted on the test set. Our baseline comparator is an LLM with no case retrieval i.e. No-RAG.

We selected Mistral [12] for answer generation at test time, due to its open-source availability, allowing us to use a model distinct from OpenAI's GPT-4, which was employed for formulating the Q&A casebase. This approach effectively simulates consulting an alternative expert in place of a human specialist.

6.1 Legal QA Dataset Analysis

The ALQA dataset, introduced in Sect. 3 is a synthetic Q&A dataset generated from real legal documents in the Australian Open Legal Corpus. Here sentences extracted from documents, each coupled with a prompt, are used to generate corresponding questions and answers from OpenAI's GPT-4 model. We performed a multi-stage analysis to ensure that this dataset was appropriate for our retrieval and follow-on answer generation tasks.

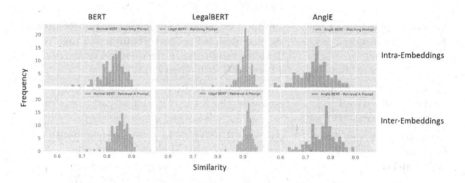

Fig. 4. Cosine similarity distribution for intra- and inter-embeddings.

Dataset Validation involved a randomly sampled manual analysis of the questions and answers performed by the research team to ensure the dataset contained no LLM-based anomalies (i.e. hallucination, factually incorrect statements, etc.). We then converted the question text into intra- and inter-embeddings using BERT, LegalBERT and AnglEBERT and examined the similarity distribution by calculating the cosine similarity between each instance and its nearest neighbour (shown in Fig. 4). We observe that the similarity distributions are mostly Gaussian, with the most frequent values between 0.7 and 0.8 cosine similarity for both embedding types produced by BERT and AnglE-BERT. Embeddings learned by LegalBERT seem to be more densely clustered, as indicated by the higher similarity. This could suggest a reduced ability to discriminate based on similarity compared to BERT and AnglEBERT. The results of this analysis were promising, as they suggest the embeddings circumvent issues associated with vocabulary-based representations (such as sparse similarity distributions).

Case-Base consisted of the ALQA dataset where each case consists of the full Q&A content as discussed in Sect. 3.1. While originally containing 2,124 question-support-answer triplets, 40 were removed due to offensive content, and therefore our case-base contains 2,084 cases. The case representation was also expanded to include entities to form the complete tuple as discussed in Sect. 4.

Table 3. Prompts used in this research.

Scenarios & Generator	Prompt
Extract legal acts to pair cases for test set creation. **Gpt-3.5-turbo-0125**	Extract the legal act(s) in this text. Print 'None' if nothing is found. {TEXT}
Extract entities for case representation. **Gpt-3.5-turbo-0125**	Extract named entities and unique identifiers as a single text (separated with white-space) line from this " + TEXT. Print '' if nothing is found. {TEXT}
Generate Qs from text pairs for test set creation. **Mistral-7B**	Produce a question and answer where the answer requires detailed access to both Text 1 and Text 2. Don't refer texts in the question or answer. {Text1: TEXT1 - Text2: TEXT}
Generate answers from snippets for retrieval analysis. **Mistral-7B**	Answer QUESTION by using the following contexts: {TEXT1 - TEXT2}
Generating answers from cases for retrieval analysis. **Mistral-7B**	Answer QUESTION as a simple string (with no structure) by using the following question, citation, and answer tuples as context: {Question: Q1, Citation: C1, Answer: A1 - Question: Q2, Citation: C2, Answer: A2}

Test Set Creation focused on creating a discrete test set of questions that reference applicable knowledge in the case-base, without directly mapping to a single case in the case-base. To guide the generation of unique questions for test purposes, we first analysed the case-base in terms of unique legal acts mentioned in all cases. We then selected case pairs based on the common acts and, using Mistral-7B [12] generated 35 new question-answer pairs, each answerable using the combined information from both cases in a pair, as detailed in the prompt presented in Table 3. The rationale is that by pairing cases with common legal acts, we can encourage Mistral to create novel test Q&A pairs. These pairs are unique in that they necessitate synthesising information from both cases in the pair to form a coherent question and corresponding answer, ensuring that the resulting pairs differ from the questions and answers of the individual cases in the case-base, thereby creating a set of new test cases that are reasonably disjoint. All test data was manually reviewed by at least two members of the research team to ensure they meaningfully combined information relevant to both parent cases while remaining distinct. After review, we removed 3 cases, which left a total of 32 cases to act as test data[5].

6.2   Retrieval Analysis

We first evaluated the quality of case retrieval, by exploiting the fact that each of our 32 test cases had originated from a pair of parent cases. Accordingly, for each test case, we treated the pair of parent cases from the training set as relevant, and all other cases as irrelevant (allowing calculation of ranked precision and recall). We then performed a similarity-based retrieval using the k-Nearest Neighbors algorithm, exploring a range of k values consisting of prime numbers between 1 and 37 We calculated results using F1-score for retrieval@k to evaluate relevance and visualised using a heat-map (see Fig. 5). Here the best performing algorithm was Hybrid AnglEBERT with [0.25, 0.40, 0.35] weights and $k = 3$. However, the F1 scores generally remain low. Upon examination, we found that 40.63% of the test instances failed to retrieve at least one parent test case. This may stem from lack of fine-tuning in the embeddings, which we shall address in future work. Accordingly, k was selected as 3 for the subsequent generative experiments, with $k = 1$ as a comparative baseline. The context window from Mistral-7B was capped at 4,096 tokens which was sufficient to contain all retrieved tokens.

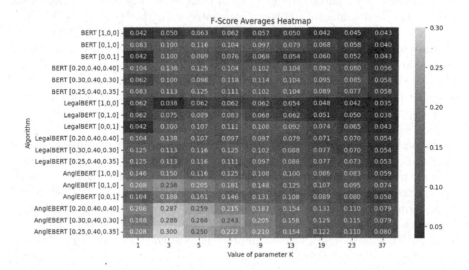

Fig. 5. F1 score for Retrieval@k

---

[5] Test dataset available at open-australian-legal-qa-test.

6.3   Generation Results

We evaluated the quality of generated output using 3 algorithms run with $k = 1$, $k = 3$ and the baseline for No-RAG. Results are shown in Table 4.

Table 4. Cosine scores between generated text and answers

		No Context	Support	Full Case
$k = 0$	No-RAG	0.8967		
$k = 1$	Hybrid BERT	–	0.8986	**0.9068**
	Hybrid LegalBERT	–	0.9020	0.9043
	Hybrid AnglEBERT	–	0.9121	0.9074
$k = 3$	Hybrid BERT		0.9007	0.8998
	Hybrid LegalBERT	–	0.9034	**0.9045**
	Hybrid AnglEBERT	–	0.9092	***0.9141**

The Mistral-7B-open model was utilised as the LLM to generate answers for test case questions within the RAG context, employing CBR-RAG retrieval methods. Generated answers were converted to embeddings using Mistral for cosine-based comparison with the expected answers from the test cases (i.e. reference text). We expect that the similarity between generated and expected answers reflects the effectiveness of the underlying CBR-RAG setup.

Relatively high cosine scores were observed with the No-RAG baseline due to the generator having parametric memory in most of the legal questions asked by default. The best semantic similarity was noted with the Hybrid AnglEBERT variant when 3 nearest neighbours were fed into the generator in the form of full cases forming context for RAG. It provided answers on average with 1.94% increase in performance. All hybrid variants performed better than the No-RAG baseline. We also observed that including the full case in the prompt provided better results compared to including only the Support text in most hybrid algorithms. Overall, Hybrid AnglEBERT outperforms the BERT and LegalBERT variants with higher semantic similarity observed when $k = 3$.

We performed a series of ANOVA tests to evaluate whether results were significant. Following this we carried out paired tests between the best-performing methods from each of the BERT and LegalBERT groups (in bold), as well as the baseline No-RAG. Here we found that hybrid AnglEBERT k=3, significantly outperforms (asterik) both 'No-RAG' and hybrid LegalBERT k=3, at the 95% confidence level, as shown by a one-tailed T-test. Against hybrid BERT k=1, AnglEBERT k=3 shows significant improvement at the 90% confidence level.

7   Conclusions

In this paper we have presented CBR-RAG, improving LLM output by augmenting input with supporting information from a case-base of previous examples.

An empirical evaluation of different retrieval methods with knowledge representation and comparison using BERT, LegalBERT, and AnglEBERT embeddings confirmed that responses generated by CBR-RAG outperform those of baseline models in similarity to ground truth. Our findings confirm that using a case-retrieval approach in RAG systems leads to clear performance benefits, but selecting an appropriate embedding for case representation is key. A qualitative analysis with a domain expert would be an ideal next step to validate these results. The fact that AnglEBERT had the best performance suggests that its contrastive (similarity) approach to optimising for embeddings remains more important than the standard self-supervised masked training strategies used by LegalBERT, even if trained on general legal data.

In this paper none of the embedding methods, including LegalBERT (trained on broader legal collections), were fine-tuned to the ALQA-specific legal corpus. Therefore, in future work, we are keen to explore the impact of fine-tuning using contrastive self-supervision methods and determine the necessary data supervision burdens for this process, which could pose disadvantages in certain domains. Moreover, given the hybrid embeddings' success, which combines multiple representations for fine-grained similarity comparison, we are keen to expand CBR-RAG with more retrieval capabilities, including the learning of weights for retrieval with hybrid representations. Finally, we found that combining multiple neighbours while maintaining a coherent prompt is challenging, so we plan to explore case aggregation strategies in the future.

References

1. Aleven, V., Ashley, K.D.: Teaching case-based argumentation through a model and examples: empirical evaluation of an intelligent learning environment. In: Artificial Intelligence in Education, vol. 39, pp. 87–94. Citeseer (1997)
2. Asai, A., Wu, Z., Wang, Y., Sil, A., Hajishirzi, H.: Self-RAG: learning to retrieve, generate, and critique through self-reflection. In: The Twelfth International Conference on Learning Representations (2024)
3. Ashley, K.D.: Reasoning with cases and hypotheticals in hypo. Int. J. Man-Mach. Stud. **34**(6), 753–796 (1991)
4. Bromley, J., Guyon, I., LeCun, Y., Säckinger, E., Shah, R.: Signature verification using a "Siamese" time delay neural network. In: Advances in Neural Information Processing Systems, vol. 6. Morgan-Kaufmann (1993)
5. Brüninghaus, S., Ashley, K.D.: The role of information extraction for textual CBR. In: Aha, D.W., Watson, I. (eds.) ICCBR 2001. LNCS (LNAI), vol. 2080, pp. 74–89. Springer, Heidelberg (2001). https://doi.org/10.1007/3-540-44593-5_6
6. Butler, U.: Open Australian legal corpus (2024). https://huggingface.co/datasets/umarbutler/open-australian-legal-corpus
7. Chalkidis, I., Fergadiotis, M., Malakasiotis, P., Aletras, N., Androutsopoulos, I.: LEGAL-BERT: the muppets straight out of law school. In: Cohn, T., He, Y., Liu, Y. (eds.) Findings of the Association for Computational Linguistics: EMNLP 2020, pp. 2898–2904. Association for Computational Linguistics, Online (2020)
8. Chalkidis, I., et al.: LexGLUE: a benchmark dataset for legal language understanding in English. In: Muresan, S., Nakov, P., Villavicencio, A. (eds.) Proceedings of

the 60th Annual Meeting of the Association for Computational Linguistics, Dublin, Ireland (Volume 1: Long Papers), pp. 4310–4330 (2022)

9. Devlin, J., Chang, M.W., Lee, K., Toutanova, K.: BERT: pre-training of deep bidirectional transformers for language understanding. In: Proceedings of NAACL-HLT, pp. 4171–4186 (2019)

10. Guha, N., et al.: LegalBench: a collaboratively built benchmark for measuring legal reasoning in large language models. Preprint arXiv:2308.11462 (2023)

11. Hacker, P., Engel, A., Mauer, M.: Regulating chatGPT and other large generative AI models. In: Proceedings of the 2023 ACM Conference on Fairness, Accountability, and Transparency, pp. 1112–1123 (2023)

12. Jiang, A.Q., et al.: Mistral 7b. preprint arXiv:2310.06825 (2023)

13. Lai, J., Gan, W., Wu, J., Qi, Z., Yu, P.S.: Large language models in law: a survey. preprint arXiv:2312.03718 (2023)

14. Lee, J.S.: LexGPT 0.1: pre-trained GPT-J models with pile of law. preprint arXiv:2306.05431 (2023)

15. Lewis, P., et al.: Retrieval-augmented generation for knowledge-intensive NLP tasks. In: Advances in Neural Information Processing Systems, vol. 33, pp. 9459–9474 (2020)

16. Li, X., Li, J.: Angle-optimized text embeddings. Preprint arXiv:2309.12871 (2023)

17. Rissland, E.L., Daniels, J.J.: A hybrid CBR-IR approach to legal information retrieval. In: Proceedings of the 5th International Conference on Artificial Intelligence and Law, pp. 52–61 (1995)

18. Tang, C., et al.: PolicyGPT: automated analysis of privacy policies with large language models. preprint arXiv:2309.10238 (2023)

19. Thulke, D., Daheim, N., Dugast, C., Ney, H.: Efficient retrieval augmented generation from unstructured knowledge for task-oriented dialog. Preprint arXiv:2102.04643 (2021)

20. Tuggener, D., von Däniken, P., Peetz, T., Cieliebak, M.: LEDGAR: a large-scale multi-label corpus for text classification of legal provisions in contracts. In: Calzolari, N., et al. (eds.) Proceedings of the Twelfth Language Resources and Evaluation Conference, Marseille, France, pp. 1235–1241. European Language Resources Association (2020)

21. Upadhyay, A., Massie, S.: A case-based approach for content planning in data-to-text generation. In: Keane, M.T., Wiratunga, N. (eds.) ICCBR 2022. LNCS, vol. 13405, pp. 380–394. Springer, Cham (2022). https://doi.org/10.1007/978-3-031-14923-8_25

22. Vaswani, A., et al.: Attention is all you need. In: Advances in Neural Information Processing Systems, vol. 30 (2017)

23. Wiratunga, N., Koychev, I., Massie, S.: Feature selection and generalisation for retrieval of textual cases. In: Funk, P., González Calero, P.A. (eds.) ECCBR 2004. LNCS (LNAI), vol. 3155, pp. 806–820. Springer, Heidelberg (2004). https://doi.org/10.1007/978-3-540-28631-8_58

Author Index

J. A. Recio-Garcia et al. (Eds.): ICCBR 2024, LNAI 14775, pp. 461–462, 2024.
https://doi.org/10.1007/978-3-031-63646-2

Printed in the United States
by Baker & Taylor Publisher Services